THE
PROFESSIONAL
JOURNALIST:

A Guide to the Practices and Principles of the News Media

SECOND EDITION *THE*
PROFESSIONAL
JOURNALIST:

A Guide to the Practices
and Principles of the News Media

JOHN HOHENBERG

Columbia University

HOLT, RINEHART AND WINSTON, INC. · New York · Chicago
San Francisco · Atlanta · Dallas · Montreal · Toronto · London · Sydney

To
THEODORE M. BERNSTEIN
W. PHILLIPS DAVISON
FRED W. FRIENDLY

PREFACE

This is a new and thoroughly revised edition of *The Professional Journalist*. It is a practical guide to the principles and practices of the news media. Unlike earlier editions, which were centered largely on the metropolitan press and wire services, this one is broadly applicable as well to broadcast journalism in all its phases and to the expanding suburban and small city newspapers of the country.

The preparation of this volume has been a pleasant task, primarily because of the acceptance of the original work by so many schools and colleges as well as professional news organizations with training programs. In these pages, the emphasis remains on the substance and techniques of journalism and the maintenance of high professional standards. Since social criticism is dealt with in a companion work, *The News Media*, it is somewhat less in evidence here, although it is by no means ignored.

In addition to new material on radio and television, there is new or expanded treatment of much press and wire service practice and substance that keenly interests small city and suburban newspapers in addition to the metropolitan press. Particular attention is paid to such subjects as public service journalism, public opinion reporting, investigative reporting, specialized assignments, and Washington and foreign correspondence. New decisions on the law of the press are included, as are relevant materials on such issues as free press and fair trial and the responsibility of the news media in the coverage of civil disorder.

The book is organized into four sections. The first presents a broad view of the work of the journalist and his principal tools—language, methods, and other fundamental procedures. In the second, these tools are put to a wide variety of uses in the print and broadcast media. The third section deals primarily with the reporter—a key figure in all forms of journalism—and discusses his responsibilities, practices, and ethical considerations, as well as the laws affecting journalism. The final section deals with the newest aspects of American journalism—the drive toward public service in the news media, the uses of depth reporting and analysis in the news columns and the documentary, the increasing emphasis on interpretation of the news, and the special requirements of the various media.

I am particularly indebted to Dr. Theodore Peterson, Dean of the College of Journalism and Communications of the University of Illinois, and to the Rev. Dr. John B. Bremner, Professor of Journalism at the University of Iowa, for their wise counsel in putting together this second edition, and also those to whom this volume is dedicated.

My thanks go to Wes Gallagher, general manager of the Associated Press; Roger Tatarian, editor of United Press International; the late William R. McAndrew, president of NBC News, and Richard S. Salant, president of CBS News, for material assistance in the form of texts and background information for the new edition. All of them, of course, are absolved from responsibility for what is written here.

My deepest gratitude goes once more to my wife, Dorothy Lannuier Hohenberg. As for the new generation of journalists, we both wish them good luck, good health, and many happy landings.

John Hohenberg

Columbia University
October 1968

CONTENTS

PART 1

BASIC PRACTICE
IN JOURNALISM

chapter 1

The Journalist

A news revolution without parallel in journalism is developing on a world-wide scale in these declining years of the twentieth century. It is broadening and deepening every aspect of public communication affecting 200 million Americans both at home and abroad.

Never before has so much information been available to so many people within so short a time. And yet, this era of high speed transmission and reproduction has only begun. Much more may be expected from the communications satellite and the multichannel undersea cable, intercontinental facsimile and the banks of computers, the laser with its promise of transmission through light beams, and all the other oncoming developments that foreshadow the twenty-first century.

THE IMPACT OF THE JOURNALIST

Today, as a result, the impact of the journalist on public opinion is one of the strongest motivating forces in our society. He acts and reacts through an information system of unmatched delicacy, complexity, and power. Newspapers and wire services, radio and television, magazines and mass-produced books combine to give him greater influence and responsibility than he has ever had before. All this has happened in less than two centuries of independent journalism in the Western world, and much of it has come about in the first twenty years of television.

The role of the journalist has changed perceptibly since the simpler and far less dangerous latter nineteenth century, when he used pad and pencil, the telephone and the telegraph to serve the press as the exclusive source of all the news. Professionally, he conceived it to be his primary duty to act as a mirror of the world about him; even then, his conscience smote him when he saw the shame of the cities and the scandal bred by a small foreign war.

No journalist of consequence in these darker and more ominous times is content to remain an inanimate object. Once he has attained professional stature, he is no longer a mere observer of events, a transmission belt for facts that may or may not represent the truth. He becomes, by turn, an analyst, an interpreter, and very often even an active participant in the history of our age. Therefore, what he thinks, what he says, and what he does now can exert an enormous influence on a mass audience, including those far beyond the borders of his own land.

The Four Ideals   Regardless of the advances of science and technology, the practice of journalism in the open societies of the Western world is based today, as it has been in the past, on four ideals that often seem utterly unattainable.

The first is the never-ending search for the truth.

The second is to push ahead to meet changing times instead of waiting to be overtaken by them.

The third is to perform services of some consequence and significance to mankind.

The fourth and by all odds the most important is to maintain a steadfast independence.

If these goals seem to be beyond the reach of the journalist in an imperfect world, it is nevertheless in character for him to struggle toward them. For all his faults, and they are many, he is fated to attempt the impossible—to find, gather, organize, explain, and disseminate the news, ideas, and opinions of the day to an ever-increasing audience. The degree of his accomplishment may be measured in the extent to which the public is informed on matters that vitally affect its interests. He may seldom hope for unqualified success. But if he fails, then assuredly the whole basis of self-government—an informed electorate—fails as well.

In this sense, the journalist remains the vital and indispensable cog in any system of democratic government.

The Journalist's Nature   What makes a journalist? Some say moral values; others, a superior education. Some believe it is a flaming competitive spirit; others, a sense of style, a flair for the dramatic, a crusading interest in digging out the truth.

Although no response can be complete in itself, there is an essential element implicit in both the superior journalist and his assessment of his own nature. It is a love of his work and a fierce and uncompromising integrity. And this is as true of the men and women who serve the newer media—television and radio—as it is of those who have brought newspapers, news agencies, and news magazines to a very high level of performance in the United States.

Wes Gallagher, who was for many years a foreign and war correspondent and later the general manager of the Associated Press, once expressed his view of the chief quality needed by a journalist in this manner: "Journalism requires a discipline of mind unique among professions and difficult to attain and maintain, particularly in our emotional times. It requires a sympathetic understanding of mankind, but also a cold objective analysis of how mankind meets the problems of this age."[1]

Walter Cronkite, managing editor of CBS News, rightly stressed vigilance as another prime journalistic quality by pointing to the extraordinary development of pictorial news transmission. In less than a decade, he lived through the era of sound on film, then video tape, and finally a network of communications satellites, always adjusting to new conditions. As he said:

> Television is full of change and ferment. The same human eagerness to exploit the new techniques as they arrive is the weapon with which to beat down the tired and the trite. But, like most everything else worthwhile, it takes constant vigilance, constant guidance, correction, and direction.[2]

James Reston, executive editor of *The New York Times*, came to the conclusion, not unexpectedly, that vitality was the key to successful journalism. In going over the records of the roster of the *Times'* Washington correspondents to search out some identical quality, he made this observation:

> I am struck by the fact that all of them have this one great quality—vitality, drive, aliveness—call it what you will. It occurs to me, therefore, that the most thorough education and the finest training in some specialty are of no avail to make a newspaperman outstanding unless he also has the necessary vitality to get on with the job.[3]

The Requirements For those who wish to make a beginning in journalism, regardless of the media involved, the minimum requirements may be summed up briefly as follows:

—A thorough education, sound training, and discipline.
—Familiarity with the basic skills of the journalist.

---

[1] Wes Gallagher, Sigma Delta Chi Foundation Lecture, published in *The Quill*, December 1966, pp. 24–27.
[2] Walter Cronkite, "Television and the News," an essay in *The Eighth Art*, New York: 1960, p. 235.
[3] In a conversation with me.

—The will to work at tasks that are sometimes frustrating and often unrewarding.

—A deep respect for one's personal and professional integrity.

For reporters, whether they serve the print or broadcast media, it is no longer enough merely to cover the news; they must probe deeply into its background and meaning. They are still, however, only as good as their sources, and they are invariably dependent on the full support of their news organizations. And while it is vital for them to respect confidences and protect informants when necessary, it is even more important for them to know when to hammer on closed doors. There isn't enough reportorial hammering and challenging in these times. A little more toughness of fiber and stiffness of backbone would help.

For writers, it is basic to learn to present the news clearly, accurately, concisely, and interestingly and to know how to interpret it when necessary. True, the familiar word, the short sentence, and the single idea to each sentence whenever possible are the essential tools of the writer. But they are of little moment without style—the priceless ingredient that separates the professional from the amateur.

For the editors and the news directors, even more than for their fellow journalists, there must be curiosity and there must be vision. It is scarcely enough for a newspaper editor to see that his hard news is generally written in the past tense, and for a news director to preserve the immediacy of radio or television by putting much of his report in the present tense. Techniques are not as important as fidelity to the public interest.

"Go With What You've Got"   For all journalists, there are the hard realities of time and space. Each one must live for the minute, for the hour, for the edition deadline. No journalist can wait until he thinks he has attained perfection. There comes a time when he must adhere to the old deadline rule: "Go with what you've got." At that moment, the writing of the story must begin; the newscast must be taped or put on live. And if, when that moment of truth arrives, there is some material that is not sufficiently developed for use, another old newsroom saying still applies: "When in doubt, leave out until you check the facts." For facts reported without understanding can betray the truth, as the excesses of the Joe McCarthy era so painfully demonstrated.

It seems so simple to set these things down in a few paragraphs. Yet, it requires a lifetime of experience to put them into practice as a professional. The journalist, in sum, requires a very special faith in his work and a formidable inner discipline—that stouthearted quality known as staying power, a refusal to be either dissuaded or discouraged.

Herbert Bayard Swope, executive editor of the New York *World*, used to tell his staff in a hoarse and awesome roar: "I don't know of any sure way to success but there is a recipe for certain failure. Just try to please everybody and you'll surely fail."

TRAINING FOR JOURNALISM

In the 1920s, when radio was in its infancy and television just a dream, it was a rarity to find a man or woman with college training in an American newsroom. Those staff members who were graduates of the few journalism schools of quality usually hid this dark secret until they were established professionals. The very term "journalist,"—applied so generally now to the whole field of news communication—then conjured up the image of a dilettante who wore spats, carried a cane, and liked to have a red rose in his buttonhole. Such men were thought of as "trained seals"—special writers akin to columnists—rather than reporters. It was a time when the press was king and members of editorial staffs referred to themselves as "newspapermen" with a special note of pride. Many still do.

In the early part of the century, however, journalism was considered a profession by only a handful. These were the top editors, principal reporters, and featured writers who believed their work to be something more than a mere trade or business. It was their conviction that journalism had a body of established ethics, practices, and procedures that could be transmitted to the next generation in the newsrooms. By and large, that was how newspapermen were trained. But the expression, "the newspaper business," came more naturally to them than "our profession." For veterans of the newsroom, that is still true.

The gathering, preparation, and publication of the news in the lively, far less complicated era of the twenties in the United States was handled competently, and often brilliantly, by skilled newspapermen who had no particular training except in the hard school of the streets. They were professionals in every sense but, on the whole, they did not consider themselves members of a profession even on the most eminent newspapers. As for radio, it was a time when any out-of-work actor could read a newspaper over the air or, if he were particularly enterprising, he might "rip and read" a wire service news report as his contribution to the day's intelligence.

Journalism: Profession, Business, or Trade?   Journalism had glamor in those days, but little or no prestige. There were, of course, outstanding figures in the field. To mention only a few: Carr Van Anda, H. L. Mencken, Damon Runyon and Grantland Rice, Frank Ward O'Malley and Will Irwin, Irvin S. Cobb and Richard Harding Davis. But between them and the less favored figures of the newsrooms, a great gap existed.

First of all, the difference was apparent in personal prestige and public recognition. But more important, salaries for the rank and file were lamentably low—so low that a good reporter as late as the early thirties received only $25 or $35 a week. And before the era of New Deal reforms, many a newspaperman worked a six and seven day week and put in long hours every day without daring to suggest overtime. This was the age when the image of the journalist became fixed as a poorly-paid scrivener of little account and almost no future unless he turned to press agentry or show business. It took journalism many years to eradicate so lamentable a posture in the United States.

Basically, the newspapermen who entered the Great Depression felt they simply had no professional interests. The intellectuals in the newspapers' city rooms could scarcely feel very elevated when they knew that the printers in the back shop earned more than they did, on the average, and often laughed at them as indigent poseurs. As for the publishers, most of them considered the production of newspapers solely as a business and few showed any appreciation of their public or professional responsibilities. It was, of course, as true then as it is now that the paper that cannot show a profit loses not only its independence but its life; what was not so widely recognized was the essential nature of a professional staff in building public confidence in a news organization. Even the government saw nothing professional about the work of the journalist, as was evidenced by the rulings of the Wage-Hour Administration.[4]

A Changing Status   Nothing better illustrates the changing character of journalism, and its evolution toward professional status, than the almost complete turnabout in the training of the younger generation of journalists in the United States.

Whereas college graduates were few in the ranks of journalism in the first thirty years of the century and graduates of journalism schools were even more rare, it is difficult today to begin reporting the news for any organization of standing, print or electronic, without a college degree. Holders of two or more degrees, in fact, are numerous.

Nor are women the rarity they once were in the nation's newsrooms. There might have been one on the staff of the average daily outside the society department in the twenties, but her status was generally uncertain and her pay miserable. During World War II, however, the women began moving into journalism in considerable numbers and proved their compe-

---

[4] Wage-Hour Administrator Elmer E. Andrews, as quoted in *Editor & Publisher*, August 5, 1939, pointed out that professional and executive-type employees were excluded from the Act but ruled that reporters, rewrite men, copy editors and subordinate deskmen were covered by the Act, not being professionals.

tence. They are found today in positions of responsibility in all media, from newspapers and news magazines to television, and some distinguished themselves as combat reporters during the Vietnam War as well.

And so today college-trained men and women are in the majority on the staffs of all but the relatively small newspapers and TV-radio stations. Graduates of journalism schools, in particular, have won a respected place for themselves.[5] Yet, it is only a little more than fifty years since American editors heaped abuse on Joseph Pulitzer for daring to suggest that journalists were educated, not born. He once quipped bitterly: "The only position that occurs to me which a man in our Republic can successfully fill by the simple fact of birth is that of an idiot."

The battle has been fought and won. The newest journalists, as a group, tend to be well-educated, well-trained, fully grounded in the humanities, and knowledgeable in the social sciences and, to a greater extent than ever before, in foreign languages. These are necessary qualifications if they are to be successful in journalism. And that is only the beginning, for the age of specialization is now upon us. The prince of reporters—the general assignment man—is not destined to increase either in number or in all-around activity.

What Is A Professional? You may well ask, therefore, what distinguishes the professional of today from the craftsman of yesterday beyond a change in mental attitude, more thorough preparation, and a somewhat improved public image in the United States. First of all, it is the establishment by slow stages of a community of interest among journalists of all media. The time has long since passed when newspapermen and electronic journalists (the term is Eric Sevareid's) considered each other as deadly rivals with nothing in common. Nor are the hard-driving news magazine staffs on the outside of the group, looking in; they, too, have proved themselves under the most trying conditions. The most ubiquitous of all—the wire service staffs and the photographic journalists—have had perhaps less recognition than they deserve. But together, this hard core of some 60,000 journalists has been primarily responsible for informing the American people—and a very large part of the rest of the world, as well. It is the ethos of the journalist, more than anything else, that has held together so fiercely independent a group of individuals.

---

[5] A study by Eric Odendahl (*Journalism Quarterly*, Summer 1965, pp. 463–464) showed that 76 dailies reported 57 per cent of their staffs were college graduates, 34 per cent with journalism degrees. Another study by Susan Tebbe (*Journalism Quarterly*, Autumn 1967) showed 44 per cent of 117 managing editors of West Coast dailies had journalism degrees, 20 per cent had majored in some other discipline, and 36 per cent did not have a college degree. Of their news staffs, 52 per cent had majored in journalism.

Today, organizations of journalists flourish at all levels and in all media. These groups hold so many year-round meetings that the most prominent editors, correspondents, columnists, and commentators could be away from their offices more often than they are in them, if they chose to attend them all. Indeed, the swing toward professional activities has been so pronounced that much greater selectivity will have to be exercised in the future if such work is to retain its value. From research to prizes and other honors, journalism in all its forms has assumed the outward trappings of a profession.

Much remains to be accomplished, however, in bringing the media and the universities closer together. The arrant anti-intellectualism of the nineteenth-century newspapers is no longer so evident, but the spirit lingers on. And, peculiarly enough, this seems to be more true of the electronic media than it does of the modern newspapers of substance.

Yet, in the face of educational advances, even these remaining hostile attitudes are fading. Among the undergraduate college generation in this era, some 25,000 journalism majors can be counted and 55 Schools of Journalism are accredited.[6] But this is the beginning, not the end. Graduate journalism programs are increasing and some of the leaders in journalism education are moving from the familiar one-year master's degree to a two-year course of graduate study.

Mid-career studies, inaugurated more than two decades ago by the Nieman Fellowships at Harvard, are proliferating, but most of the beneficiaries are newspapermen. Columbia University has advanced fellowships in science writing and international reporting, plus an experimental on-the-job training program in Hong Kong for correspondents with a qualified background in Far Eastern studies and languages. Northwestern has similar advanced studies for journalists in urban affairs, including training in Washington correspondence. Stanford and the Southern Regional Education Board both offer advanced training under generous fellowship programs. The most professional program of all, that of the American Press Institute, is wholly financed by the participating newspapers and provides seminars for experienced newspapermen. In the electronic media, such opportunities are also growing, as the program of CBS Fellowships testifies.

Thus, if the journalist is to keep up with the times, he is likely to be returning to the classroom and the seminar table at frequent intervals during his career. It is a notable advance for a group that celebrated the corner saloon as a major center for professional courtesies and discourtesies barely forty years ago.

---

[6] *Headlines*, 1967, published by The American Newspaper Publishers Association, October 1967, p. 4; see also *Editor & Publisher*, December 2, 1967, p. 26.

THE RECRUITING OF JOURNALISTS

Paul S. Swensson, while director of The Newspaper Fund, estimated that 5,000 new journalists a year were required to fill existing and recurring vacancies in the news media.[7] With journalism schools placing less than 2,000 persons a year into the news media, it is obvious that they alone cannot fill the demand; at the better schools, in fact, high-ranking students are sought after by campus recruiters and generally have a number of offers, in and out of the profession. It is therefore an empty academic exercise to debate whether journalism graduates have more or less acceptance than those from liberal arts colleges. The not unpleasant truth is that both are very much in demand; in most places, journalism graduates quickly establish an early advantage because of their training.

Where do the journalism graduates go? In a recent year, out of 3,694 B.A.s and 793 M.A.s, 17.5 per cent went into daily newspapers and 1.7 per cent to weeklies; 8.3 per cent each to public relations and advertising; 2.4 per cent, magazines; 2 per cent each to radio and television and 1 per cent, wire services. Of the remainder, 30 per cent went into graduate schools, military service, or teaching and the rest into nonjournalism activities. It is possible that both newspaper and electronic media recruitment will show increases when those in graduate schools or the military enter the job market.[8]

"The decade of the Seventies," says Swensson, "promises even more opportunities in journalism. Competition from other professions will not ease. The visible supply of talented young people for the news world falls short of estimates of the profession's needs."

The Press   Newspapers have become the most aggressive recruiters in journalism today. The reason is apparent: their needs are greater than the other news media. As an overview, there are 1,754 daily newspapers in the United States that sell more than 61 million copies every 24 hours and have gross receipts of nearly $7 billion annually—almost $5 billion from advertising and the rest from circulation. They have increased their total employment over two decades by nearly 50 per cent to more than 350,000 in all departments, including editorial.[9]

---

[7] Paul S. Swensson and Patrick W. Kennedy, Journalism's New Era; *The Quill*, November 1966, pp. 20–29, is the source of the estimate of personnel requirements. The placement figure is from their brochure for the Newspaper Fund, *An Employment Report, 1967.*
[8] Swensson & Kennedy, Journalism's New Era, p. 22. See also Headlines for October 1967, p. 1, published by American Newspaper Publishers Assn. and the Newspaper Fund's 1967 employment report on journalism graduates.
[9] Barron's Weekly, July 1, 1968, p. 3 and following, and July 8, 1968, p. 9 and following.

While there has been an inevitable contraction of the press in key metropolitan areas, notably New York City, the suburban and small city dailies have shown surprising growth. The Newhouse, Knight, Gannett, and Thomson chains have expanded their holdings; moreover, Gannett, Cowles Communications and others have gone on to found new newspapers. The leaders in print journalism—the great newspapers, the chains and the news weeklies—have also diversified their interests by acquiring new broadcast properties or expanding old ones. All this has been done at the price of eliminating newspaper competition in all but a handful of cities in the United States. Until the scientific revolution either reduces newspaper costs or makes possible an entirely new newspaper (such as the dream of an electronic paper), the trend is not likely to be reversed.[10]

Broadcast Media   Although the broadcast media do less recruiting than the newspapers, they generally outbid the press for talent but seldom do much to develop their own special brand except at the level of all-day radio news stations. The reasons are not hard to find. Radio is enjoying a revival based on music and news. Television is a $2 billion a year business mainly in sponsors' fees for advertising, and its pretax profits are approaching $500 million annually. Consequently, the network and blue ribbon independent news organizations prefer to engage skilled professionals whenever they can. As Walter Cronkite puts it:

> It seems to me there can be no substitute for newspaper or wire service experience. Broadcasting is a postgraduate business. Anybody with an excess of talent can shortcut, but for the average man in broadcasting, we have no way of training him beyond the first few paragraphs—how to recognize the element that makes a good lead. I think a youngster who wants to be a television reporter will eventually make a better television reporter if he spends some years in the vastly less complicated atmosphere of a newspaper or wire service newsroom where the story—the whole story—is the thing.[11]

News Magazines   This is also very largely true of the highly profitable news and picture magazines. *Time*, with annual gross revenues approaching $90 million, and *Newsweek*, with gross revenues approaching $45 million annually, also bid for the established professionals as a rule.[12] Except for dozens of young women researchers and clerical help, there is not too

---

[10] The first page of the London Express was sent by satellite and cable from London to San Juan, Puerto Rico, in 15 minutes late in 1967.

[11] Cronkite, "Television and the News." See also Cronkite interview in *Editor & Publisher*, October 14, 1967, p. 21. TV profits in *Time*, September 8, 1967, p. 54.

[12] *Wall Street Journal*, July 12, 1967, p. 1.

much chance for beginners in this highly specialized field. The newspapers are still the best bet.[13]

Motivation   Despite all the complexities of the new journalism, the prime motivation for a journalistic career has not really changed. It remains a compelling desire to work with the immediacy of news. There is, after all, an artistic as well as a professional side to journalism, and who can explain the artist?

In its opening phases, the motivation toward a career in journalism is little different than it was forty years ago. It is as true now as it was then that most journalists begin on their high school or college newspapers or radio stations or on the teen page of their local newspapers. Often, these youngsters go on to other things. But for those who stick, journalism frequently becomes a life's work. The late starters, who shift to journalism from other fields, remain in the minority although some invariably rise to eminence.

What, then, is the appeal of journalism?

Surely, it is not great wealth. Although there has been a welcome and too-long deferred advance in the financial rewards of journalism, the average professional is well aware that he is unlikely to become a millionaire unless he makes a success of management. Few journalists can rival the good fortune of S. I. Newhouse, who rose from small beginnings to own a great newspaper chain, or Lord Thomson of Fleet, once a door-to-door salesman in Canada, who built an international newspaper empire on the basis of his humble beginnings.

There is, moreover, no assurance of a life of ease and comfort. The journalist does not live (with the exception of an occasional 10 A.M. managing editor) who enjoys bankers' hours, regardless of union contracts or special considerations. As for security, there have been some improvements in this direction, particularly in the newspaper field, but the journalist scarcely has the assured benefits of the teacher or government employee of comparable status.

---

[13] The Newspaper Fund's 1967 employment report, based on a survey of the earnings of graduates of journalism schools in 1967, gave the following averages for BA's: public relations, $119 a week; wire services, $116; magazines, $113; TV news, $113; daily newspapers, $109; radio news, $106; weekly newspapers, $100. For MS's, the weekly average earnings were considerably higher, but it should be borne in mind that most holders of masters' degrees have some professional experience: radio news, $170; public relations, $152; TV news, $150; magazines, $141; daily newspapers, $136; wire services, $130; weekly newspapers, $120. For experienced newspapermen, *The New York Times* Guild contract sets a $250 a week minimum for reporters and $275 for departmental editors, effective 1970. For television correspondents in the principal metropolitan centers, the minimum is in excess of $350 a week depending on the disposition of special fees.

The talk of glamor in journalism, once so prevalent, has largely disappeared with most of the picturesque newspaper characters who inspired plays, movies, and radio shows out of all proportion to their importance. Not even the war correspondent's reputation as a dashing character has survived, for the day-to-day photographic record of the newsmen in the Vietnam War showed they were as dirty, tired, bedraggled—and as brave— as the troops with whom they moved. Until television's first war, the correspondent had been a dreamlike figure such as Richard Harding Davis, or a mild, friendly, little man like Ernie Pyle. When he came into the American living room on television night after night, the dream vanished; the solid substance of men working under enemy fire remained.

And what of romance—the lure of far places and strange peoples, of travel in sun-tortured India, or watching the behavior of Red China from a post such as Hong Kong, or studying the Soviet Union from Moscow or perhaps Tashkent? Too bad, but it is given to relatively few to become foreign correspondents even for affluent American news organizations. And indeed, once a foreign assignment is awarded, the correspondent finds himself competing day and night with a group of several hundred journalists who are, with few exceptions, the keenest and best-prepared in the profession. Foreign correspondence is no longer a children's game, at which any dolt can play if he happens to turn up in the right place at the right time. It is desperately serious business.

Great wealth and security, glamor and romance—these are not, by and large, the dividends that journalism pays. They are a part of the legend of journalism, a lazy man's Never-Never Land that existed in fancy and never in fact.

These are the realities:

Journalism is a restless profession, as changeable as the news in which it deals. Its appeal is universal, its social value high for those who take it seriously. Its fascination is compounded each day of novelty, surprise, satisfaction, fulfillment, sometimes disappointment, and occasionally even shock over the ceaseless variety in the story of mankind.

When nearly two-score reporters scrambled from a press bus at the Trade Mart in Dallas on November 22, 1963, prepared to cover a speech by President John Fitzgerald Kennedy, they saw a young newspaperwoman hang up a telephone and run toward them. It was Marianne Means of Hearst Headline Service and she said, "The President's been shot. He's at Parkland Hospital.".

Tom Wicker of *The New York Times*, who heard her, wrote afterward: "One thing I learned that day; I suppose I already knew it, but that day made it plain. A reporter must trust his instinct. When Miss Means said those eight words—I never learned who told her—I knew absolutely that they were true."[14] Five years later, when another assassin shot the President's brother, Senator Robert F. Kennedy, that same reportorial instinct forewarned the nation that the wound was mortal.[15]

THE MEDIA—OLD AND NEW

The communication of news has always exerted the appeal noted by Wicker, writing of a moment of supreme crisis. The communicators accordingly have derived influence and abiding satisfaction from it in proportion to their importance in the process.

Norman Cousins, the editor of the *Saturday Review*, once demanded in an outburst against the mounting dangers of the atomic age: "Who speaks for man?"

More precisely than anyone else, it is the journalist. If the nineteenth century was the era of the novelist who dominated mankind's literary horizon and his conscience as well, then surely the twentieth century belongs to the journalist. From the confrontations with the President of the United States at his news conferences to the numerous frank demands for an accounting from the leaders of every other government on earth, the journalist—when he is bold and unafraid—speaks for man.

The Demand for News   The United States is far from the saturation point in newspaper circulation. The United Nations Educational, Scientific and Cultural Organization has shown that Americans buy 326 daily newspapers per 1,000 population, a rate exceeded by ten other countries including the United Kingdom, Japan and Sweden.[16] Such findings have led to estimates that an anticipated population of 220 million in the United States by 1975 will have the capacity to buy 100 million newspapers a day, a 66 per cent increase over the present.[17] The development of great specialized newspapers such as the *Wall Street Journal*, with a circulation of more than 1 million, and of large suburban newspapers such as *Newsday*, in Garden City, N. Y., with 425,000 circulation, are only a part of the newspaper story. New dailies and groups of newspapers are springing up in rapid growth areas all over the nation. The facsimile newspaper, through which identical editions can be reproduced electronically over great distances, is a reality in Japan and the United Kingdom and already figures in The *Wall*

---

14 Tom Wicker: "A Reporter Must Trust His Instinct," in "The Kennedy Years," by the editors of The Viking Press, Inc., and *The New York Times* (New York: 1963).
15 Los Angeles *Times*, June 5 and 6, 1968.
16 UNESCO: World Communications, 4th ed.
17 R. B. Nixon, *Journalism Quarterly*, Winter, 1955, pp. 10–20.

Street Journal's West Coast edition. Nor is it impossible, in the forseeable future, that a little black box in a corner will produce, at stated intervals, a newspaper in the home through electronic impulses from some far distant newsroom.

Including the 26 million copies of weekly newspapers and the 50 million copies of Sunday newspapers that are sold, it is estimated by the Nielsen Media Service that newspapers are read by 87.3 per cent of American families. There is persuasive evidence to show that newspaper readership rises among better educated and higher income groups, reaching 95 per cent in households headed by college-educated persons and 98 per cent in households reporting incomes of $10,000 or more a year.[18] With a rising population and the increasing spread of education at higher levels, it is clear that newspaper readership is nowhere near its ceiling.

In radio and television, the United States has the largest audiences in the world. From its beginnings in 1920, radio enjoyed an enormous development until 228 million receivers and 5,000 transmitters were in use in less than fifty years. These covered 54 million homes in the United States (98 per cent of all households), nearly 60 million in automobiles and 11 million in public places. As the figures indicate, many homes have more than one set. The growth of television has been even more spectacular; twenty years after its beginnings in 1946, 773 stations were transmitting to 67 million television sets covering 94 per cent of all American homes, some with two or more sets. While it is true that entertainment and merchandising substantially exceeded news transmission as the principal function of the electronic media, with education a very poor fourth, the $2.2 billion in television advertising and $890 million in radio advertising have been hard blows for the print media to absorb. Most newspapers, supreme as local advertising media, have long since had to get along without heavy national advertising, but magazines, with less than $2 billion as their share of advertising expenditures, have been seriously affected.[19]

Despite the competition of the newspapers and the electronic media, American magazines have piled up awesome records of circulation—particularly in the news and picture field. *Look* and *Life*, each with nearly 8 million circulation for an issue, testify to the dramatic pull of the picture story on the American public. *Time*, with 3.5 million; *Newsweek*, with 2 million, and *U. S. News and World Report*, with 1.4 million, prove there is a very large public that is dissatisfied with both the kinds of newspaper and electronic news reporting it is offered.[20] For those who are still under

---

[18] *Headlines*, 1966 (October 1966) ANPA publication, p. 6.
[19] Radio-television statistics are from the Television Information Office of the National Association of Broadcasters and the Radio Advertising Bureau.
[20] Magazine statistics are from the Magazine Advertising Bureau of the Magazine Publishers Association.

the delusion that immediacy is a major necessity for print journalism (a myth that was destroyed by radio forty years ago), the 16 million circulation of the *Readers Digest* and 10 million for *TV Guide* should be a corrective. Timeliness will always be a function of journalism, but the newspapers cannot be first with news and pictures except in rare cases. Yet, this does not diminish, but actually enhances, their role as communicators of news.

Two Views of Television   Much the same thing is true of television's limitations. In the coverage of space shots, national conventions, sports events, and other spectacles which the public can view at first hand, television is superb. But can television give all the news, with suitable interpretation and background, during the course of the average network newscast? Of course not.

David Brinkley, who wrestles with the problem five nights a week on NBC's Huntley-Brinkley Report, estimates that television can cover ten per cent, perhaps less, of the news in a good newspaper on any given day. The essentials of governmental budget problems and taxes, of complicated programs like Medicare and other aspects of Social Security, the work of urban renewal, housing, public health, and roadbuilding, the fight against air and water pollution, the daily tabulation of stock and bond markets and similar statistical material—all this can only be touched in a television news program. Some of it, for obvious reasons, cannot be covered at all unless the newspapers do it. As Brinkley says:

> It is impossible—physically and otherwise—to cover news in complete and voluminous detail on television. It just cannot be done. Nor is it possible to effectively deliver any kind of commentary on television . . . Television is a pictorial medium essentially, and if there is no picture, if there is no movement, if there is nothing happening, nobody is going to listen.[21]

It is clear, therefore, that television is unlikely to drive the bulk of newspapers out of business any more than radio or the movies did. And despite all the worrying about the tendency of television to pull people away from the printed word, reading has not exactly gone out of style. In addition to the rise in newspaper and magazine readership, the paperback book has boosted sales and readership in the book publishing industry during the period coinciding with television's greatest growth. With an annual gross income of more than $1.5 billion, American book publishers are printing more than a billion books a year and bringing out some 20,000

---

[21] Problems of Journalism: American Society of Newspaper Editors' Proceedings, 1965. David Brinkley's remarks, pp. 41–44.

new titles a year.[22] Population growth, of course, accounts for some of the heightened activity in the world of print, but by no means all of it. Book publishers, for example, know from experience the surge of sales that accompanies television's exploitation of books. And among newspapers that also own television stations—a scarcely isolated phenomenon—each generally promotes the other with benefit for both.

The evidence is overwhelming that the media complement each other far more than they act as rivals in the dissemination of news. During a newspaper strike in a great city such as New York or Detroit, both radio and television have tried repeatedly to fill the news gap with only partial success. Electronic journalists, in fact, have generally been the first to express both relief and gratification when struck newspapers resumed publication. Imagine trying to cover so familiar a newspaper function as the daily obituaries in a few minutes of air time—or the equally important vital statistics of births, engagements and marriages! As David Brinkley once remarked to a convention of newspaper editors:

> We have two or three advantages that you don't, whereas you have two or three that we don't. The only sensible thing for us to do is to exploit our strengths and live with our weaknesses, and for you to do the same thing. In fact, you cannot compete with us . . . I think the question of our replacing newspapers is perfectly silly. We can't do it; we wouldn't do it if we could.[23]

The upshot of such realistic attitudes has been the opening of an era of cooperative coverage in the public interest. The most dramatic manifestation of such new journalistic endeavors in the United States has been the News Election Service—the joint reporting of national elections by the two great wire services, the Associated Press and United Press International, linked with the three networks, the National Broadcasting Company, Columbia Broadcasting System and American Broadcasting Companies. Moreover, some of the major newspapers have been the first to purchase the various computerized vote projection services developed by the networks. Such joint coverage is bound to be of lasting public benefit.

THE PUBLIC MIND

Despite the undoubted accomplishments of the American information system and the repeated assurances that it is the best the world has to offer, it is obvious that a considerable segment of the American public is not as

---

[22] Statistics on book publishing from *Publishers' Weekly*.
[23] Problems of Journalism: American Society of Newspaper Editors' Proceedings, 1965.

well informed as it should be. Surveys have disclosed deplorable areas of public ignorance. From 20 to 25 per cent of the respondents in a poll on the Vietnam War, for example, were not able to identify properly the Vietcong as the military arm of the Communist National Liberation Front. Almost the same number in another poll did not know that the Communists were in control of the Chinese mainland. And *The New York Times* disclosed that nearly one-third of the Americans surveyed by its reporters did not know that Berlin was located 110 miles behind the Iron Curtain in East Germany.

Social scientists can document such findings at all levels of public intelligence. Allowing for the trick phrasing of questions, the obtuseness of interviewers who conduct some of the polling, and a certain amount of misunderstanding between those who ask the questions and those who answer them, the result still must be taken as a danger signal. The American system of mass communications is far from perfect.

Our news media, without doubt, could be more efficient and their public more alert. However, getting people to read or to listen, and then remember, is a universal problem. Generally, a mass audience is conditioned to accept first what it wants to hear, to see, or to read. The unexpected, the unpleasant, and the unfamiliar often have to be accompanied by a considerable shock—or endless repetition—to make an impression on the mass mind.

In the study of mass communications, the feeble public response to certain kinds of stimulation is appallingly familiar. It is known as "weak feedback." The message goes out with a lot of strength behind it, but the echo is often very faint. Between the sender and receiver of the message there is inevitably a lot of interference. The result is often imperfect and even garbled reception, particularly in the era when brief radio bulletins are first with the news.

The Editors' Problem   Every editor knows that there are severe limits on what a mass audience can absorb. People are far too busy with their own immediate concerns and interests to have itemized knowledge of such complicated matters as the background of major Supreme Court decisions at home or the political upheaval that has created so many new nations in Africa.

If this situation were taken at face value, our news media would prepare their output for an audience with an intelligence quotient capable of coping with a Mother Goose rhyme book. Such an approach has been attempted, both in print and on the air, but not with distinguished success. In a nation with 60 million people in school and almost half the population under 25 years of age, it is a grievous mistake to underrate either the public's intelligence or will to learn new ways. The responsible editorial principle is never to overrate the background knowledge at the public's command and never to underrate its intelligence.

As keen an editor as Herbert Bayard Swope used to spend two hours a day reading newspapers, grumbling all the while that it was too much. But he never contended that he was able to absorb everything. Other editors have estimated that it requires three hours or more to read a paper such as *The New York Times*, the Washington *Post* or Los Angeles *Times* every day with reasonable thoroughness, but very few actually do it. It is an exceptional editor who is able to spare that much time to read his own newspaper.

It cannot be expected, therefore, that the public will devote as much time to newspaper reading as to listening to news reports. Surveys have shown repeatedly that the average citizen spends about 30 minutes a day with his newspaper. If he reads around 250 words a minute, and stays with it for the full half hour despite all the distractions that accompany newspaper reading, the most he can cover is 7,500 words. Chances are that it may be less. Small wonder, then, at the journalistic insistence on using every device of style, organization, and language to capture the reader's attention and keep it. Similarly, the television newscaster with a 30-minute show knows that the moment he lets his audience down, he will lose viewer interest. The statistic that television viewers spend up to six hours a day with their sets, so often quoted by electronic publicists, is totally misleading as far as news is concerned. A glance at any day's broadcast or viewing schedules will show that, with the exception of the all-news radio stations, the electronic media devote a minority of time to news as a general rule. It would take a one-hour newscast to cover the news on page 1 of a paper like the Washington *Post*.

There has been a long, fruitless and rather boring argument over whether the public receives most of its news from newspapers or from the electronic media. The fact is that both are well-nigh universal in the American home. While the mass public relies on television, the better-educated public, without any doubt, tends to depend more on a good newspaper (but not the shoddy examples that pass as newspapers) and appears in recent years to have diminished its television viewing. On the first breaks in the news, radio has been the prime source of public intelligence for two generations; in the last generation or so, television has come along to share the honors. But for complete news, reported in depth and interpreted with honesty and good judgment, there is still no substitute for a good newspaper.

INTERPRETATION

In the competition with the electronic media and the news and picture magazines, newspapers have made numerous changes to build greater reader interest. There has been a substantial swing toward the six-column news-paper, instead of the familiar and narrow eight columns. Some of the oldest and most famous have begun to use larger body type as a concession to the eyesight of their older readers. Stories have been chopped off on Page 1 instead of being continued. Fewer complete texts have been run, first because of lack of space, and second because of fear of dullness. More attractive pictures have been used to dress up the pages, some without a great deal of reason. Gossip and rumor, in too many cases, have been dignified with serious headlines.

With the exception of the leading newspapers, all of them well-entrenched in public esteem and without serious rivals in their field, the American press has overreacted to the challenge of television. Some papers have gone overboard on comics, features, advice to the lovelorn and similar temporary attention-getters. Others have gone in for circulation contests that produce new readers, but generally only until the contest is over. These nostrums on the whole do not seem to have proved anything. Rather, they have tended to debase the end product.

The successful newspaper, more than any other news medium, must specialize in news. That is its principal offering, with its advertising second. It cannot compete with television in entertainment, although this scarcely means that a newspaper can afford to be dull. Nor can it compete with the schools as a source of instruction, although that has always been a by-product of an independent and intelligently conducted press. News—learning—diversion: these are all proper newspaper functions. To them must be added the ingredient of interpretation, which is more important to the press today than ever before.

News—and Opinion   Once it was widely taught and sincerely believed that the news columns of the American newspaper were composed of purely factual material, while the editorial page consisted entirely of opinions, and the two never mixed. This was the supreme concept of journalistic objectivity. Yet, even where this dubious proposition was enforced, it was never really possible to make it work. Such rigid objectivity exists only in the minds of those who like to believe there is such a thing as "pure news" which flows in its pristine state from some mysterious source, uncontaminated by the addition of flavoring or color.

The mere process of deciding whether to print an article or omit it is an exercise of opinion by the editor. Whether an article carries a large head-line or a small one, whether it is put on Page 1 or back with the want ads, similarly, is not the result of any objective process but one of editorial choice. The reporter who covers a speech and the rewrite man who puts his story on paper both exercise their legitimate judgment on what facts to feature, what quotes to use, what material to leave out. The concept of objectivity, as it was defined in the pre-electronic days of the press, is therefore a myth and has been very generally recognized as such.

What was and is valid is the basic premise of honesty and impartiality in the presentation of the news. The American newspaper was founded on that basis. The best ones have always endeavored, within the limits of human frailty, to present the news fairly and honestly in the news columns, leaving persuasion to the realm of the editorial page and the featured columnist. This is a realistic assessment of journalistic objectivity. It presupposes that the writing of the news also involves the necessity of telling what it means, whenever necessary. It does not mean under any circumstances that the newspaper has the right, covertly exercised, to try to persuade the reader to adopt its point of view by allowing editorialization in the news columns. Explaining, backgrounding, and analyzing the news are all proper parts of the interpretive process and belong in the news columns. It is also highly desirable to publish the considered opinions of an expert on a particular subject, whether or not he is a staff member, to make a complicated news development more intelligible to the public. But the line must be drawn at persuasion, recommendation, and exhortation, techniques which belong outside the news columns.

This concept of the right to interpret the news, sharply limited though it may be, still does not please a minority of editors who cling to the old notion of pure objectivity. The "objective" editors, for the most part, decline to trust their own staff writers and reporters to present a fair and unbiased account of sensitive news—particularly sensitive local news—and show why it is significant. Some of this mistrust eventually seeps out to the public, usually because of arguments between staff members and editors over the proper presentation of the news. When it happens, public confidence in the newspaper inevitably declines.

The Meaning of the News   Happily, a majority of American editors believe in interpreting the news today and insist that it is necessary to public understanding. Both the Associated Press and United Press International send interpretive dispatches over their wires almost as quickly as they send the news. The responsible press prides itself on its many specialists and the validity of their interpretive writing in many fields. Interpretation is accepted by such newspapers as necessary. And when the electronic journalist is able to do a documentary in which there is reasonable time for explanation and interpretation, he thinks of it as a high point in his career.

All this is a far cry from the days when Walter Lippmann was the editor of the New York *World* and had to do things in the manner decreed by the concept of objectivity. As he once explained:

> When I first went to work on a newspaper, which was after World War I, the generally accepted theory was that it was the duty of the

news columns to report the 'facts' uncolored by 'opinion' and it was the privilege of the editorial page to express opinions about what was reported in the news columns.

To this simple rule of the division of labor between reporters and editorial writers we all subscribed . . . In practice we all, reporters and editorial writers, broke the rule and this led to many disputes, good-natured and some not so good-natured. The news columns would have opinions with which the editorial writers disagreed. The editorial pages would contain statements of fact that the news editor had not certified.

In the course of time most of us have come to see that the old distinction between fact and opinion does not fit the reality of things . . . the modern world being so very complicated and so hard to understand, it has become necessary not only to report the news but to explain it and interpret it.[24]

This is elaborated on by Dr. George Gallup, a pioneer in the fine art of public opinion analysis:

A strong case can . . . be made for including much more background material, more interpretation of the news. Readers like to be told what is important and what is not important. The theory that newspaper readers want to make up their own minds, that they want only the bare facts, is refuted by all kinds of evidence.

They want help in understanding the news and recognizing its importance. They don't want bias. Too many already think newspapers 'slant' the news to suit the editorial views of the paper. But I insist, interpretation can be free of bias, just as free as the selection of details in the story which purports to be completely free of bias.[25]

Who Writes What? The questions immediately arise: "Who is to decide which news requires interpretation and which does not? How will the writer know when to interpret, and to what degree? And who is to decide on the validity of the interpretation?"

For experienced newspapermen, who have earned the trust of their editors and the public, these questions seldom offer problems that are insuperable. Any interpretation, to be valid, should be so written and so documented that an editor—and the general reader—can readily understand the basis for the writer's judgment. Such interpretations may be discussed later, even challenged; subsequent events may prove them to be wrong. But this scarcely means that a qualified reporter, who knows the news at first hand, should not make an honest attempt to tell the public what it means. The fear of making a mistake in judgment should not be permitted to paralyze the intellect of the journalist, nor the freedom of the editor to

[24] The Bulletin of the American Society of Newspaper Editors, January 1, 1956, p. 7.
[25] Blue Book of the Associated Press Managing Editors, 1957.

publish his work. The newspaper that fears controversy is not likely to last very long anyway.

There are some old-line editors who stubbornly insist that interpretation is opinion, and therefore has no place in the news columns. Of course, it is opinion; it would be nonsense to pretend that it is not. But when a writer decides to pluck a sentence out of the middle of a speech and feature it, that also is a matter of opinion; at the very least, he should be required to explain to the public why that particular sentence was so important. This is proper interpretation.

When Lester Markel was associate editor of *The New York Times*, he once told the International Press Institute that there was a relatively simple formula for determining what was interpretation and what was not. Here is how he phrased it:

> To report that the Kremlin is launching a peace offensive is news. To explain why the Kremlin is setting the doves cooing at this time is interpretation. To state that any Kremlin peace offer should be rejected out of hand is opinion (which) . . . should be confined to the editorial columns.

The analysis is ingenious, but unfortunately it does not always apply. Interpretation of the news isn't quite that simple. Nor can it always be said that the editor must decide. Frequently, the editor is in no position to decide and the reporter on the spot has to tell the meaning of the news to the best of his ability. In any case, the newcomer to a newspaper—even if he has had a lot of experience on other newspapers or wire services—is seldom called upon immediately to do stories that are sensitive and require careful interpretation. Each paper has different methods, different routines, different requirements. It takes time to learn what the paper's policy is. And during the process of learning, the best rule is to proceed with caution and to act responsibly in dealing with the meaning of the news. In an age when publicists both in and out of government make so many exaggerated claims and announcements, it would be an abdication of editorial responsibility merely to print what was said and fail to assess credibility in one way or another. The interpretive method, in such cases, is indispensable in the handling of news.

WHY NEWSPAPER TRAINING?

It is neither a tradition nor an accident that, despite the diversity of mass communications, the newspaper retains its place as the principal spokesman for the news media, especially in the United States. Unlike radio and television, the newspaper is not licensed and need not have any particular regard for the Federal Communications Commission or any other branch of government. Unlike the news and picture magazines, with their weekly or twice-monthly deadlines, the newspaper appears several times daily and can communicate quickly with the public. To a greater extent than media with a very large stake in national advertising, the newspaper with highly diversified local advertising is less subject to advertising pressure where this pressure still exists.

In brief, the newspaper is generally more independent than its competitors. Because this is true, it is still the principal rallying point for public opinion and remains the foremost vehicle for public service journalism. The newspaper is also far more versatile than its competitors; because it is able to go to more places and print more news than other media can provide, it has generally been able to win greater acceptance among leaders of the community in which it is published.

All other news media lean heavily on the nation's principal newspapers, their syndicates and the wire services as primary sources of the news. This does not mean that the electronic media and the news magazines do not have competent national staffs or that they do not originate news of their own. Indeed, the electronic journalists and the staffs of the news weeklies are well able to hold their own in any competition with wire services or newspapermen. But the wire services, in particular, remain the source of most of the national and international news, not only for radio and television but for the newspapers as well. And it is perfectly obvious that the relatively limited staffs of local radio and television stations, with few exceptions, can scarcely expect to compete with the better newspapers in local coverage except on a big breaking story.

The Newspaper's Dilemma   For all these reasons, familiarity with the newspapers and wire services in the United States becomes almost mandatory for most of those working in other journalistic fields. It is true that television has begun training newsmen without previous journalistic experience, a practice inaugurated by radio stations, and that some magazine writers have never worked for any other medium. But for most journalists, newspaper or wire service training is still basic to the profession and nearly all news organizations prefer their staffs to have it.

This, of course, poses many problems. The journalist who wishes to specialize in the electronic media or in magazine writing finds difficulty in accepting the rather exacting routine of newspaper and wire service training. Even worse, the competing media unsystematically raid the smaller newspapers (and occasionally some of the larger ones) as well as the wire services for younger talent. Finally, the newspapers resent being used as a training ground for the other media and do everything they can to prevent their best young staff members from leaving.

There is still another factor in the competition for the best of the young journalists—the flourishing public relations field. Almost without exception, the 5,000 companies and specialized departments operating in public relations advise young prospects to get newspaper or wire service experience first. If they engage television or radio specialists, they are generally professionals who are recognized in their own field.

No newspaper, great or small, will knowingly spend three to five years in the painstaking and often expensive training of a young journalist and then cheerfully lose him to television, radio, public relations, or the news magazines. But despite rising salaries in the newspaper field, few but the leaders can afford to pay the rewards that are offered to seasoned performers in the competing media. At the top of the profession, however, there is now little difference among the media, but the stars in the journalistic firmament never have been very numerous.

The young journalist who devotes the first third of his life to education and training has a right to expect far greater rewards than he now receives. The chances are, primarily because of the competition within journalism, that he will make steady progress toward a better life. In the old harum-scarum days, when the Bohemian spirit was more prevalent in newsrooms than it is today, some could argue that the work was its own reward. That is certainly no longer true. The modern journalist is a family man, for the most part, and he wants the advantages for his family that are at least equal to those of his neighbors. He is entitled to them.

THE DEVELOPING NEWS MEDIA

The duties and responsibilities of the news media are increasing with the demand for better information about our highly complex world. Newspapers of higher quality and greater scope are needed. Improvements of many kinds are overdue in our wire services. Television, after years of improvisation, is developing a first-rate format for news presentation on a day-to-day basis and increasing its time span for the news. Moreover, with the rise of the all-news station, radio is finding that it will have to recruit more newsmen if it is to compete seriously with the press.

Yesterday, many an editor thought that he had done a good job if he merely told the news. Today, the public wants much more. The manifold uses of reporting the news in depth and interpreting it require greater development. And that in turn calls for a very high level of professional training and competence for the younger recruits in journalism. While the age of high speed communicaiton is bound to revolutionize the news media as we know them, it is going to take people to run them in whatever form they develop—dedicated, talented, responsible people. They are, as they always have been, the backbone of journalism.

chapter 2

The News Operation

Most professional news operations are calmly and efficiently managed with few surface signs of tension. The bawling editor, the jittery reporter, and the temperamental writer or commentator have no place on deadline in a well-ordered news organization. Even when a staff is under great pressure, whatever the journalistic medium, the inexperienced eye will detect little sign of stress. Of course, it is there all the same. When you have six minutes to do the lead story of the paper or no preparation at all for an on-the-spot television report, the sensation of having butterflies in one's stomach is no myth.

What follows is a summation of the principal features of the most basic of all news operations, that of the daily newspaper. The wire service, radio, and television routines will be considered in their proper places.

THE OPERATORS

The inside operating personnel of a newspaper's editorial staff, as distinguished from the reporters, photographers, and others who generally work outside, consist of editors and writers. On most newspapers there is a clear distinction between rewrite men, who produce much of the local and regional news stories; the copy editors, who read all news material and write the headlines, and the editors—generally known as deskmen—who direct the various operations. The names, in common with all journalistic nomenclature, err on the side of modesty rather than pretense. They do not truly describe either the duties or the responsibilities of these managers and processors of the news flow.

Actually, this middle group in journalism exercises a unique, and sometimes decisive, influence on the way a newspaper presents the news of the day. In no other profession, business, or industry is the top management so dependent on the intermediate managers and processors for presentation and production. If this were not so, a newspaper simply could not get out.

Delegation of Authority   The publisher is a newspaper's top executive. The five departments—editorial, advertising, mechanical, circulation, and business—are responsible to him. It is he who must make the final decisions.

Because of the pressures of time, space, and people on the shape of the news, many newspaper publishers delegate authority over editorial policy to their editor-in-chief. However, the editor-in-chief, customarily, finds he has all he can do to run the editorial page and the columnists, represent the paper as both its voice and its conscience, and keep in touch with the working news operation. The delegation of power, therefore, usually continues down the line with sole responsibility over the news going to the managing editor.

This individual, whether he is known by the loftier title of executive editor or the more usual one of managing editor, thereby becomes solely responsible for getting out the paper and guiding the news staff. Whether he or his superiors like it or not, the paper is bound in a sense to reflect something of his personality and interests and of those of his associates. That is inevitable. News does not occur in a vacuum, and it cannot be handled by robots.

THE ORGANIZATION

It is apparent that, except on the smallest newspapers, no one man can give detailed direction over all aspects of gathering, writing, processing, editing, and publishing news. The news organization in practice has tended to divide roughly into three parts that are generally known as the news side, the city side, and the various departments such as women's pages, sports, financial, and amusements. The managing editor is responsible for all of them, but in practice they operate more or less under the general directives he gives to the individual editors.

This loose and somewhat confusing organizational pattern is the despair of the newcomer to newspaper journalism. He has probably gathered, through TV, movie, or fictional romances of journalism, that the city editor is all powerful. It always comes as a shock to the romantics to find that the city editor is only one of a number of responsible executives in the news department and that the work of the news editor and his staff takes in a wider area of responsibility. The separation of authority must be clearly understood, or it can lead to inevitable confusion.

The News Side The so-called news desk in a newspaper office, as distinguished from the city desk, has a number of functions that make it the key to the entire news operation. The news side generally consists of the managing editor, his assistants, the news editor, the telegraph and cable editors, the head of the copy desk (slot man) and his copy editors, the makeup editor, and the clerks who assist in their work. On smaller papers, some of these functions are combined.

With the exception of departmental copy—financial, sports, and the like—all news copy flows to the various components of the news side for processing. This includes copy from the city desk, the suburban desk, and the telegraph and cable desks. Generally, the entire copy flow is directed at one top-level executive who is either an assistant managing editor or the news editor (the title matters less than his actual functions). This editor, with perhaps one assistant, has the fantastic responsibility of handling and evaluating all news copy for the paper. He must scan it for length and assign to it an appropriate headline to indicate its importance in the day's news. He marks directions on the copy for others to carry out.

Several methods are used to brief the news editor, for it is clear that he can scarcely be expected to read every word of every story. Sometimes he briefs himself merely by scanning leads. Or he may read a summary of the slugs of stories given to him by the other desks. But whatever his method, his news judgment must be quick and accurate.

From his desk the copy flows to the copy editors (a title not only more dignified than copyreader but easier to distinguish from proofreader, who performs a mechanical function primarily designed to catch typographical errors in the composing room). After being read on the copy desk for errors of fact, style, grammar, and spelling and trimmed to appropriate length, the copy is given its designated headline. It then goes to the composing room to be set in type.

The makeup editor takes over at this point. He has a dummy of Page 1 made by the managing editor or news editor after a brief editorial conference before the edition. There also may be dummies for a split page (first page, second section) or for Pages 2 and 3. But the rest of the paper must be dummied by the makeup editor with whatever news remains. It is his job to direct the assembling of the paper in the composing room by working with the printers. In many shops union rules forbid editorial employees to touch type. It is obvious that there is a need for dummies and specific editorial direction on makeup.

The telegraph and cable editors on the news side are frequently the same person; in fact, the job of makeup editor may be added as a third responsibility. Where there is no special Washington or foreign staff—and usually only the largest papers have their own—the telegraph-cable editor's job consists of keeping up with the wire service file. It is more than a mere scissors-and-paste job, however, since wire services have not yet reached the state of perfection where each paper can receive exactly the kind of story it wants at precisely the right time. Even with a teletypesetter operation, where the copy comes in on a punched tape that is fed directly to a Linotype machine, the resultant column of type has to be scanned for length and meaning.

To sum up the news side process: It is an entity that is closely tied to the mechanical side in the composing room, stereotype department, and press room. The circulation department must maintain liaison with the news side, for it is here that the circulation manager learns of major news breaks that may require the printing of more papers or a change in the distribution scheme. The advertising department, after dummying its ads for the day, gives the layouts of the various pages with the resultant news hole to the news side. If the business office has a complaint about the cost of the editorial operation, it is usually taken up first with the managing editor and the news side.

The City Side On the nation's largest newspapers, the old city desk is no longer recognizable. With the movement of many city dwellers to the suburbs, the coverage of new areas has outgrown the makeshift device of creating suburban editors. In addition, the superior suburban newspapers have demonstrated that they can hold their own in competition with the giants. Thus, a newspaper of the caliber of *The New York Times* has found it necessary to create what it calls a metropolitan editor, with jurisdiction over the coverage of both city and suburban areas.

Yet, whether he is called a metropolitan editor or city editor, the executive in charge of local news by no means exerts the unlimited authority and prestige that once were his. Of course, he still has an influence on local news patterns. Depending on the size of his staff, the number of shifts it works, and the extent of its local coverage, he can mobilize a rather complete production group of his own.

On the big metropolitan and suburban papers, the city editor has at least one assistant and sometimes two or three—an assignment editor, a production editor who works with rewrite men, and a liaison man with the photo desk and swing man who relieves his colleagues on days off. Necessarily, on a small paper, one man may do all these jobs, write headlines, and handle makeup as well.

Departmental Desks   The lines of authority between the city desk and the departmental editors are as rigidly observed as those between the city desk and the news desk. Everything proceeds in channels, almost as if it were a military organization; in view of the time factor, some such discipline is not only desirable but necessary. The sports side, for instance, has its own space assignment and fills its pages, going to the managing editor for general directives. The same is true of business-financial, amusements, and the rest of the departments.

The Individual   What this organization amounts to is a mechanism whose operation is governed by the managing editor, but whose separate parts have such a high degree of individual movement that they revolve at approximately the same pace and in the same direction by a seeming miracle. Without very much individual attention, except possibly during the single brief editorial conference that is usually held daily in most newspaper offices, the deskmen and deskwomen carry on efficiently. The activities of the individual, however, are limited very largely to his own group or department.

A reporter on the city side, for instance, takes an assignment from a deskman on the city desk. The understanding is that he will call back that same deskman, who knows what the story is, instead of bothering the city editor or some other deskman. If the man who has given the assignment goes off duty, the callback is handled by his replacement. Except in an emergency, the reporter stays within this chain of command. Even under extraordinary circumstances he does not go outside the city desk to give his views on the writing of headlines, the "play" of the story in the published edition, or the writing of captions unless he works on a very small paper and is asked to do it. Even if he has been working with a rewrite man, he does not call that rewrite man directly but goes through the city desk channel.

The same restrictions that apply to reporters apply to the other individuals on the newspaper's staff. A copyreader does not have the right to consult directly with a reporter on the meaning of a sentence, unless he receives instructions to do it, or knows him so well that differences can be adjusted smoothly. The copy has to come back through the news desk and city desk to the writer, who then passes it back through the same channel. In no case, without specific permission, is it possible for a writer or reporter to go to the composing room to make changes in one of his stories. A young reporter once did it to slip his byline on one of his stories and was fired for his pains.

This channeling of the individual, in a profession that is seemingly so casual, is always something of a surprise to those who are first being introduced to journalism. There is good reason for it. If a story could be changed without the knowledge of the copy desk, the headline might not be fixed to conform to the new version. If a reporter could fix his own copy after handing it in without telling the city editor, many a city editor would be out of touch with the handling of the news. A news organization is run without the boxes or lines of authority that designate the military chain of command, which is all to the good; but, even if the lines of authority are few and not clearly visible, they are kept tight and must be strictly observed.

THE NEWS STAFF

The size and function of news staffs are changing with the decline in the number of metropolitan dailies, the growth of the suburban and small city newspapers, and the increasing trend toward automation. Once it was the fashion to look to *The New York Times*, with its 160 local reporters, 60 copy editors, 45 foreign correspondents and 1,400 total editorial staff, as the model for the profession. Today, there is more inclination to follow the example of a number of well-managed dailies in communities of medium and moderate size.

How Many Are Needed?   Newspaper staffs vary widely in size, organization, emphasis, and in their ability to cover the news. Sylvan Meyer, a Georgia editor, found a wide variation in staff size and function in a survey of small city dailies of 5,000 to 15,000 circulation. There was, in Meyer's view, no particular pattern and no standard personnel procedure.

A daily of 5,124 circulation reported four full-time and one part-time news personnel while another of 14,000 circulation had 12 permanent and no part-time people. A paper with 8,300 circulation had six full-time and 14 part-time staffers; another, with 8,400 circulation, had just six permanent people, no others.

The number of deskmen on these dailies ranged from one to five, but some of these were also part-time reporters. About the only agreement the papers registered in the survey was that departmental editors processed and laid out their own pages. On many of these small dailies, as might be expected, managing editors also handled their own makeup and telegraph copy, reporters wrote headlines, and women employees were distinguished by their rarity.

For metropolitan dailies, there are similar variations. Some have larger staffs than *The New York Times* in some departments. But there are also metropolitan dailies of consequence that sometimes work with about eight or ten reporters, four or five rewrite men, and six copy editors. In fact, one man has been known on occasion to get out a single edition, with the help of a full mechanical force, and do a passable job. It is not recommended, however, as a steady exercise either for the man or the paper.

Wherever staff services are too skimpy to give a paper adequate coverage, it is obvious that wire service and syndicate copy is being used to plug up the news hole. That means, in turn, that little news is originated by the paper itself.

Such standardized products have little appeal, in consequence, to the individual citizen of a community, since there can be only token coverage of the news of that community. A standard filling, no matter how professionally and competently done by the news side, will not really satisfy readers unless there is some evidence of local and departmental work as well. The image that the paper reflects of the world immediately around it will be distorted. It takes an individual staff, working against time and circumstance and sometimes even against itself, to bring the feel of life to a newspaper.

PM's and AM's   Since there are about 1,450 afternoon papers and about 300 morning papers in the United States, it is apparent that the PM operation is more typical. However, it is also true that morning papers are more influential in some of the larger cities. The 500-odd Sunday papers represent, on the whole, an attenuated morning-paper operation.

As far as staff work is concerned, the main characteristic of an afternoon paper operation is change. Except for news from overseas, where there is a wide time differential, an afternoon paper's editions are put out as the news develops during the day. That means a lot of changes, unless the news operation is conducted with care and good judgment.

A normal morning-paper operation, on the other hand, generally is fairly stable. Barring major news breaks, a morning paper can go in with its first edition fairly complete and subsequent changes can be kept to a minimum except when there is a political campaign or major sports event. As for Saturday and Sunday papers, many are either so thin in news or so stuffed with filler prepared in advance that the news operation is primarily to hold down the amount of fresh news to a minimum.

Scope of News   The scope of the day's news also makes a difference to a staff in the conduct of its operations. During a baseball World Series, for instance, there is a tacit understanding that only the most essential news will be processed while the games are in progress. Teleprinters and composing rooms are tied up when World Series interest is at its height. Other events that keep newspaper staffs busy, such as the death of a President of the United States or a spectacular new outer-space development, also almost automatically curtail the handling of secondary material.

Another consideration is the amount of advertising for a particular day, since on most newspapers advertising determines to a very large extent the size of the paper and the amount of available news space on a given day. Finally, the news operation may be affected by unusual weather conditions—a hurricane that knocks out power and snarls communications, a heat wave that sends the potential readers scurrying from the city, or a blizzard or cold wave that makes newspaper delivery a problem.

The reporters, processors, and managers know all these things and govern themselves accordingly. The date book, a daily list of coming events, and the wire service schedules are their guides. It is seldom that a "downhold" order has to be explained when big news is breaking, and this is as true for the broadcast media as it is for print.

CHANGING NEWS PATTERNS

Because of its proximity to developing events and ideas, the middle group in journalism often is the first to identify what is and what is not news. There is a considerable time lag, as a rule, before the most influential group in journalism, the editors and publishers, can assay the flow of events. And it is even longer before public reaction, the final and ultimate news force, makes itself felt.

Who Says It Is News?   Thus, a young man handling a night desk for a wire service in Washington, D. C., can take over the entire national and world facilities of his organization to put out a major news bulletin if he believes it worthwhile. Another young man on the dogwatch for a morning newspaper and in sole charge of its editorial staff during the last hours of publication can send in Page 1 with a late break if he thinks it justified. An even more youthful executive in charge of news for a television station in the late evening can interrupt a program with big news.

These men have no time to weigh the consequences of a mistake and, indeed, seldom worry about it. Actually, the probability of error in such instances is small. By background, experience, and training people in the middle group are well aware of what is generally considered to be news. They also know the gradations of interest.

There is no formula for this. Nor is there a book of news tables that one can consult, as an engineer whips out his book of logarithms. The things that are and are not news vary from one day to the next, from one country to another, from one city to another, and without doubt from one paper to another.

If the Secretary of State meets the Soviet Ambassador on a quiet day, the story will not amount to much if both remain silent. However, if the meeting takes place after the United States receives a particularly abusive

Soviet threat, it may mean more. It will probably be news in the United States, but not in the Soviet Union, unless Soviet publications are permitted by their government to print the story. Washington and New York may be interested in the meeting, but if there happens to be a big fire on the same day in Butte, Montana, Butte will not be interested in the international story. The difference, then, is not in the news assessment of the middle group of managers and processors, but in the policies, circumstances, and pressures that are brought to bear on them.

Identical News If a news subject is based on a long speech by a political figure of consequence, it is a familiar phenomenon to find that virtually all newsmen pick out the same paragraph on which to base their leads. The reporters and rewrite men doing the advance stories could not have consulted each other, for they picked up the advance text at different times and wrote their stories in widely separated offices. They would have scorned to telephone each other to ask, timidly, "What do you think the lead is?" In fact, had they done such a thing, it would have been a confession of professional incompetence.

On events of all conceivable varieties it happens over and over again that leads are practically identical on competing publications and the electronic media. Those who are unfamiliar with journalistic procedures may conclude quite wrongly that this is the result of some secret method of comparing notes and deciding on a standard presentation. Actually, this rarely happens, unless everybody uses the same wire service account, and that certainly is not a matter for consultation.

The fact is that the middle group in journalism is so cohesive by reason of its training, and even its general educational and cultural background, that its news approach tends to vary only through circumstances. An evening paper reporter does not have to be told what lead a morning paper will use to follow up an account he has just written for his own sheet. Therefore, he can go to work confidently on the next expected development in the story to get up a piece for his own first edition on the following day. A rewrite man on one newspaper can almost call the lead that will be used on a given story by the opposition (especially if he knows who is writing it), and therefore may try to match it—or use some other angle. An editor is likely to know what stories will interest the opposition and will proceed accordingly. That is just as true of broadcast journalism as it is of print.

This very familiarity of the middle group with its own news symbols leads to some amusing situations. In the few cities where there are still competing dailies in the same time cycle, it has happened that each has outguessed the other. One has featured Story A over Story B, and the other has done just the opposite. In the next editions each paper may reverse the position of the two stories and again fail to agree.

The same kind of thing is often repeated, with troublesome consequences, by editors who want rewrite men to use the kind of lead that is most likely to be featured by the opposition. Any writer of character would prefer to do exactly the opposite. To them, the worst blow of all comes when they try not to employ a standardized reaction, and then are told to start over again to conform to a story just in on a wire service teletype.

The test of a newspaper's individuality is whether its editors try for a fresh approach, rather than a standardized one, to show the public that one newspaper is not just like every other—and does not want to be.

Newsmen Are Made   Because a journalist works for a particular newspaper or station in Chicago, Kansas City, or St. Louis, he does not take on the customs, habits, and various other peculiarities of that news organization forever after; nor does he necessarily subscribe to its editorial beliefs, unless he is a policy man, editorial writer, or top management official. The body of knowledge and experience common to good journalists makes a professional of him and gives him his capabilities. In radio and television, as in newspapers, newsmen are made, not born.

It is seldom that a working professional finds that he has difficulty in fairly reporting the news, even in a hot political campaign in which he may have deep personal beliefs that tend to turn him against one candidate or another. The journalist is trained to do an honest job, regardless of his personal convictions as a citizen. Where he is in a position to mold or execute policy, however, the only decent thing for him to do if he differs substantially from his management is to resign, or at the very least, to abstain from writing political editorials as several distinguished editors have done when their personal beliefs ran counter to that of their publishers. With the increase in electronic editorials, the electronic journalist is now coming face to face with such hard realities as well. The journalist who permits his personal integrity to be breached is no journalist at all.

A Sense of Morals   It is judgment, finally, that determines how, why, and in what manner the news of the day must be handled; either the judgment of the editor, or in the absence of his instructions, the members of the middle group of journalism.

It is, therefore, a tribute to their sense of responsibility that so much good stuff does appear in the columns of the American press in spite of the daily temptations to grab for circulation in every sex case and cheesecake picture. Drivel is written, it is true; and some newspaper accounts are still told in the florid and unrestrained spirit of the Gay Nineties. Newspapers are by no means the sole offenders here; the custodians of television, literature, and the stage have much to account for, too.

Oxie Reichler, a former president of the New York State Society of

Newspaper Editors, is one of a number of responsible newspaper executives who believe in the uses of restraint in news handling. He asks:

> Are we sissies on my paper because we eliminate the details about how a burglary was contrived or how a deranged person worked out a tricky suicide? (I know that television conducts what amounts to training courses in murder and mayhem, burglary and rape, but we don't—we comb it all out.)
>
> Are we namby-pamby because we eliminate from our divorce reports the detailed testimony of the witness who actually was at the bedroom keyhole and spilled it all? Are we wrong when we do this even in a local situation, and when our metropolitan neighbors aren't bothered about such qualms in connection with the same story?
>
> Are we misguided do-gooders because we rebel at printing pictures of dead bodies and gory scenes that tear at the sensibilities of many readers?
>
> Should I be ashamed that, on the Yonkers *Herald Statesman*, we go to great pains not to print words or pictures that might make a reader sick to the stomach if she happens to be reading our paper at dinner?
>
> I don't think so—and I want to suggest that it is a direct and important form of public service to edit our papers so that they are clean and refreshing, informing and morale-building, with no do-it-yourself columns for committing crimes, defeating justice, or circumventing the orderly processes of our society and our economy.
>
> I feel sure that—somewhere inside each of our newspaper plants— there is found that banner of responsibility which is the first boast of the American press. If it isn't fluttering over our city room, if it isn't shining visibly out of our Page 1 logotype, we had better haul it out in a hurry and unfurl it.

ETHICS AND BUSINESS

Journalists still exist who maintain that almost anything short of outright breaches of law is justifiable in order to permit a newspaper to stay in business. It is not.

If it were true, the old New York *Graphic* of disreputable memory with its faked pictures and daily ladlings of the scum of the news would have survived as a power in journalism. Although it attained a 700,000 circulation at one time, it died of malnutrition because people of substance and responsibility would have nothing to do with it and advertisers knew it. The codes of ethics that have been adopted by editors and broadcasters represent something more than statements of pious intent. They are the ideal toward which every journalist should aspire.

While too many good newspapers have died because they could not keep up with the times and face up to the more rigorous intermedia competition of today, it is worth noting that, in the main, the better newspapers are the ones that have grown the fastest since the beginning of the television era, among them are *Wall Street Journal, The New York Times* and Los Angeles *Times.* And sex does not happen to be outstandingly popular in their columns unless it happens to be defined as sociology. However, the New York *Mirror,* a tabloid that based itself on sex stories and rolled up 1,000,000 circulation, vanished without a trace.

This is not to argue that racy, or even gamey, news should not be published and that certain types of pictures should be virtuously suppressed. This kind of material should be measured by the same editorial standard as any other kind of news: if it is in the public interest, it should be published. Nobody pretends that such judgments come easily. *The New York Times,* for example, refused to publish a picture of the first Buddhist priest to burn himself to death in Vietnam, sitting at a street intersection with his saffron robes aflame; more than a year later, another such suicide picture was used in the *Times'* columns. At the risk of a great deal of criticism, CBS News gave time on a national telecast to Morley Safer's sensational pictures of a Marine setting fire to the thatched roof of a Vietnamese village suspected of harboring the enemy. A newsphoto of Jacqueline Kennedy in a miniskirt was widely used during the argument between her lawyers and William Manchester over the publication of his book, *The Death of a President.* Naturally, she would have been more presentable in a ballroom gown, but the miniskirt picture was the latest at the time and the least arty.

There are still newspapers that are so afraid of giving offense to someone that they distort or even falsify the news out of the very loftiest of motives. It is, unfortunately, not a legend that a timid suburban weekly reported a distinguished citizen had died suddenly, but neglected to report that he did so by diving out a sixth-story window. And there are still radio and television programs that neglect to mention hard facts that are displeasing to the Federal government or major advertisers, or if they are used, tone them down.

But these things are not typical of the best in American journalism. Its leaders today believe as much in vigorous use of freedom of the press as did their more violent predecessors. But they have a livelier sense of responsibility as well, and that is all to the good. Without it, any news operation must inevitably fail.

chapter 3

The "Why" of News Style

The uses of restraint and discipline are of great importance in journalism today, when so much news is of an inflammatory nature at home and abroad. The newscaster, the wire service reporter, the newspaperman, and the writer for news magazines all must be on their guard. The old careless flamboyance that was the trademark of colorful American news writing earlier in this century now is as dated as the Charleston. Regardless of the medium served by the journalist, he must emphasize accuracy, clarity, good judgment, and responsibility in whatever he writes.

Now, as never before, editors must beware of news that is overwritten either in meaning or in length. The unskilled writer, of course, is bound to make such discipline an excuse for reporting the news in a kind of drab monotone. Yet, as every professional knows, there is an enormous difference between a dull story and the sensitive understatement of the news that carries its own impact. That difference often may be expressed in the proper use of news style in both the print and broadcast media.

THE EDITORIAL MIND

The journalist has always feared the deadly accusations that he is dull or, at the other extreme, guilty of the equally serious journalistic crime known as "fine writing."

A Struggle Against Routine   In the daily battle against dullness the writer of news must resist habit and mental torpor, the panic that sometimes follows the irascible demands of the man on the desk, and the frightening lack of time. Yet he must be equally on his guard against the literary atrocities he has come to know as "fine writing"—the vague generalities, pretensions, absurdly high flown phrases, wandering sentences, and the mincing niceties of the would-be litterateur.

Between these extremities lie the sensible disciplines listed in the style book, the guide to that sometimes complicated but always helpful set of common-sense rules known as news style. These are standards set by each news organization for the guidance of its own people and by wire services for their members or clients. Newspapers take such things far more seriously than the broadcast media.

Hemingway's Lesson   Years after he left the Kansas City *Star*, Ernest Hemingway recalled the first principles of news writing as laid down in the *Star*'s style book. The first paragraph, then as now, was as follows:

> Use short sentences. Use short first paragraphs. Use vigorous English, not forgetting to strive for smoothness. Be positive, not negative.

As quoted by Charles A. Fenton in *The Apprenticeship of Ernest Hemingway*, the writer who won both the Nobel and Pulitzer prizes had this to say about the influence of the style book:

> Those were the best rules I ever learned for the business of writing. I've never forgotten them. No man with any talent, who feels and writes truly about the thing he is trying to say, can fail to write well if he abides by them.

A Lack of Standards   There is, unfortunately, no single standard by which to measure news style. It is a mistake to try to develop assumptions in this field that will apply generally to all news organizations because each is its own arbiter of what should be said and how it should be said. Not many for instance, go to the lengths of the Kansas City *Star* in prescribing a manner of writing.

Nor is there any accounting for editors. The more learned are likely to be lenient, on the whole, regarding the finer points of grammar but those with a skimpy education may bear down wrathfully on every split infinitive. Charles Chapin, the toughest city editor who ever worked in New York, expected his reporters to break all the rules to get the news but he was as prissy as a schoolmarm in reading copy.

Roy H. Copperud, director of the Editorial Workshop in *Editor & Publisher* magazine, has advanced the argument that the feeling of newspaper editors for English usage often seems about two generations in arrears, and this is probably true.

One illustration is the classical newspaper insistence on defining individuals as "persons" and large, indefinite groups as "people." This distinction is made in nearly all handbooks on newspaper style. Few newspapers use "people" as the plural of "person" even though it is sanctioned by the Bergen Evans *Dictionary of Contemporary American English* and *Webster's New International Dictionary*.

Thus, a typical newspaper story of an automobile accident may begin, "Two persons were killed today in an auto accident. . . ." Or, in reporting attendance at a political meeting, the approved style in most papers is, "More than 1,000 persons heard the governor's speech." In referring to racial or religious groups, however, it is correct newspaper usage to write of "the American people" or "the Catholic people."

Copperud took exception. He wrote:

> This ukase appeared in the AP Log: "Ten persons may be killed in a fire, but not ten people." And that was all. Ah, the splendid isolation of it—isolation from usage, from books on language, from common sense, from observation, from everything but hand-me-down newsroom "grammar."[1]

Theodore M. Bernstein, assistant managing editor of *The New York Times*, stated the traditional view as follows: ·

> PERSON. "Old drawings found in an attic here are adding laurels to a deceased artist whose prime job had been to make persons laugh." That usage would make several persons laugh, but the artist's job was to make people laugh. Use "people" for large masses; use "persons" for an exact or small number.[2]

The point illustrates the insistence of the leaders of American journalistic opinion on precision in style, regardless of popular usage. The public will always say, "Three people were hurt," but it has an offensive sound to a generation of journalists that was trained to shun the expression and cannot quickly overcome it. Habit is more powerful than usage in determining what style should be.

The newcomer to journalism should not be surprised because the use of a word is taken with the utmost seriousness. It is one of the facets of the profession that is little publicized. Yet such matters daily occupy the atten-

---

[1] "Persons Are Funny," by Roy H. Copperud, *Editor & Publisher*, June 28, 1958, p. 50.
[2] Theodore M. Bernstein, *Watch Your Language* (Channel Press, Inc., Great Neck, N. Y., 1958), p. 53.

tion of writers, reporters, editors, and commentators throughout the land. It is fitting that this should be so.

A Matter of Principle   The reason for this preoccupation with form, as well as content, is not hard to find. Primarily it is a matter of principle. And the principle, inadequately stated, is:

"Why change?"

The argument goes something like this. Newspaper editors like to think that their publications are both accurate and authoritative and therefore entitled to the respect of the communities they serve. They seek to make them acceptable in every sense to a wide range of readers both young and old.

As long as a newspaper enjoys public confidence, an editor is inclined to be slow to make changes. The smallest alteration in dress, as the outward appearance of a newspaper is known, often requires long and careful deliberation on a successful newspaper. Similarly, such newspapers are unlikely to vary the familiar and accepted patterns of English usage for readers of their news columns. Advertisers on the same pages may proclaim, "Winstons taste good like a cigarette should," and similar abominations, but the style of the news story remains above the grammatical battle.

To broadcast journalism, where there is greater informality, change is far more welcome.

The Need for Standards   Although editors are understandably reluctant to distract their audience with radical swings of style, that is not the entire case against change. As has already been pointed out, the newspaper deadline is a strict disciplinarian. If newspapers were to accept piecemeal all the modern variations of English usage, some editors argue that there would be constant turmoil between those who write and those who edit.

Conformity to arbitrary standards in the preparation and handling of copy therefore becomes mandatory on leading newspapers. When changes in these standards are decided upon, each one is carefully explained in printed announcements sent to the entire staff. This is done to make certain there will be no interference in the normal functioning of the complicated news machine. If such explanations were not made, the result would be endless arguments between reporters, writers, copy editors, and deskmen. Bernstein says:

> If writing must be a precise form of communication, it should be treated like a precision instrument. It should be sharpened and it should not be used carelessly. A book of instructions for the use of this device would suggest to the writer that he choose the exact word, the one that flies straight to the target, rather than the diffuse word that hits other

things beside the target; that he place each word where it will do its job best; that he construct his sentences so that they are tidy and logical. . . .[3]

The most radical changes in journalistic style nearly always accompany the success of a new medium of mass communication. Thus, Briton Hadden's carefully devised "Timelanguage" kicked up a public fuss when Henry Luce began publishing *Time* magazine. Its stress on inverted sentences caused Wolcott Gibbs to complain in *The New Yorker*:

> Backward ran sentences until reeled the mind.
> Where it all will end, knows God.

With success, *Time*'s language moderated. It is not now—for all its color and peppery editorial comment—the Timelanguage that Hadden so carefully planned. Conservatism often comes with success and age, even in the handling of structure and style.

There are some who believe the informality of the electronic media is, in effect, a license to write a newscast in a sloppy manner. Not so. The *AP Radio News Style Book* begins with this admonition:

> The first essential to being a good radio news writer is being a good news writer. You must know news and you must know how to handle it. It is a mistake to assume (and it has been assumed by some) that writing news for radio is a much easier task than writing it for other mediums. Radio news writing demands greater compression, which call for greater skill.[4]

USES OF THE STYLE BOOK

The style book, thus, becomes a primary tool of the journalist as a catalogue of procedures. If a newspaper does not have one of its own, then it must abide by the standards of the wire service it uses in these days of teletypesetter copy.

Differing Styles It would be almost hopeless to seek agreement even among leading papers on the finer points of newspaper style. Appended to this text is a style book based on practices that seem to have majority acceptance.

Editors write style books. They are often genuinely enthusiastic about them and never seem to tire of discussing obscure points in them. Reporters

---

[3] Bernstein, *Watch Your Language*, pp. 6–7.
[4] Andrew C. Lang, *The AP Radio News Style Book*, p. 5.

and rewrite men, whose copy is polished against the unyielding whetstone of the style book, are less demonstrative for understandable reasons. They are seldom consulted on what goes into the style book, on most papers, and obviously have less interest in it. Thus, style book rules can and do become points of contention between writers and copy editors. But the copy editor, having the last look at the copy, is usually the ultimate winner.

What a Style Book Can Do   Most style books, at the very beginning, dutifully enter a disclaimer that they cramp a writer's style of composition. The Kansas City *Star*'s book says:

> The stylebook is not intended to set up a narrow pattern of writing or to discourage freshness and originality. Its purpose is to develop more readable stories by standardizing capitalization, abbreviation, punctuation, spelling, syntax and certain geographical usage.
>
> Although the copy desks are responsible for proper marking of copy, reporters should familiarize themselves with the rules and write accordingly. Co-operative effort will result in a finer newspaper.

The most influential style book, from the standpoint of acceptance among editors, is the combined *Associated Press-United Press International Style Book*. It covers common usage in such basics as capitalization, abbreviations, punctuation, numerals, spelling, and copy markings, and specifics in the handling of financial markets, religious news, sports, and miscellaneous matters. With the coming of the typewriter-style teleprinter, and the abandonment of the all-cap style, nothing can be left to chance. As the AP itself once stated the case for style book usage:

> Presentation of the printed word should be accurate, consistent, pleasing to the eye and should conform to grammatical rules. The English language is fluid and changes incessantly. . . Because of the constantly changing usage, no compilation can be called permanent. Nor can any one volume be infallible or contain all the wisdom and information of the ages. When there is doubt, consult an authoritative source and stay with it.

What a Style Book Cannot Do   No style book can substitute for the hard work, acquired skills, and natural artistry that are the mark of the professional writer of news.

It cannot be used to decide what points are most important in a story, nor can it develop hints on how news should be presented or organized. No rules have yet been devised to substitute for thinking.

These are the limitations of style books. But to a certain extent, many of them do not attempt to fulfill some of the functions for which they are designed. Their authors seldom bother to explain basic newspaper procedures that are too often taken for granted, beginning with the mechanics of copy preparation and including the complications of slugging, markups, and other technical operations. The style books that deal with such things usually brush them off with a few primer-like sentences. Consequently they remain mysteries to some reporters to the end of their days.

PREPARATION OF COPY

When an editor broaches the subject of copy preparation, the average reporter feels insulted. He thinks he knows all about it. And anyway, he believes it to be such an elementary matter that he should not be bothered with it.

Yet copy is not very well prepared in most newsrooms. It is often dirty, sometimes unreadable in spots. While the writer's name must be on it, the source of the writer's news may be carelessly given or omitted altogether. Such simple matters as paragraphing, runover, and even marks to show whether the story has ended or is to be continued are handled indifferently, leading to needless confusion.

There is no deskman who has not, at some time in his career, asked an inexperienced writer, "Did you end that weather story?"

Invariably the writer will answer, with a superior air, "Why yes, I sent over the last take ten minutes ago."

And the deskman will murmur wearily, "Did you? I didn't see an end mark on it. I'm not a mind reader."

When such mistakes are avoided and copy is clean, the writer often has more work piled on him than he can conveniently handle. It is perhaps a sad commentary that sometimes a pedestrian news writer, who can turn out clean and mechanically perfect copy quickly, gets a great deal more attention from editors than a gifted writer whose pages must be decoded.

The only instruction the average reporter receives in copy preparation generally comes on his first day in a newsroom. A harassed deskman or a bored colleague may tell him to write on one side of the paper, put his name in the upper left-hand corner and use double or triple space, depending on the desk's editing requirements. After that, he is on his own.

The subject deserves more serious and extensive treatment. Imperfect or downright sloppy copy preparation accounts for considerable delay in editing. It is also the cause of a certain amount of inaccuracy, particularly when copy is so dirty that it can be read only with difficulty.

Most newspapers require news material to be written on sheets of 8½" × 11" newsprint, each having two to five second-sheets and carbons attached. This cumbersome sandwich of paper is known as a book, and writers who spoil too many of them quickly become unpopular in a news-

HOW TO PREPARE COPY

This is how newspaper copy should be prepared. It is the first page of an unedited news story, written by the reporter whose name appears in the upper left-hand corner. The word "assigned" indicates that he was assigned to the story and wrote it himself. If he had rewritten the story from another reporter's notes, or a wire service, he would have credited these sources instead.

Note that the slug of the story, "POLICE," is emphasized and appears by itself halfway between the reporter's name and the beginning of the story. All paragraphs are indented one-third of the way across the page and there are generous margins on the side and bottom.

It is standard practice to begin the first sheet of a newspaper story one-third to one-quarter of the distance from the top of the page, to end a paragraph on a page, and to indicate that the piece is not finished by writing "MORE" in the lower right-hand corner. If the story is complete on one page, it is marked with a symbol (# # # or XXX) or the word, "End."

room. A few organizations make up these books out of half-sheets, 8½″ x 5½″, in the mistaken notion that the smaller space somehow will result in shorter stories.

Whether the sheet, or "take" of copy, is full-size or half-size, too many news writers insist on crowding it with material. This is the principal error in much newsroom copy preparation. When sentences in news writing average 20 words, more or less, and paragraphs run to no more than four or five lines each, it scarcely pays to try to put more than about four or five paragraphs on a full-sized take. This material then can be edited with ease.

The first take of a story ought to contain no more than two or three paragraphs at the most. Copy begins one-third of the way down the page so that editing directions may be written clearly. Generous margins of an inch or more are left on both sides and at the bottom. No word should be split at the end of a line because this increases the possibilities of typographical errors when the copy is set on a Linotype machine. Sentences and paragraphs should always be ended on a page, and not run over, because each take, and often parts of a take, may be set on different machines.

Standard Procedure   In addition to the name of the writer in the upper left-hand corner, a few words should be listed after his name to indicate the origin and source of the story. If he covers and writes the news himself on assignment, it is sufficient to write the word "assigned" after his name. If he rewrites wire service copy, clips, or does the work of a reporter, he shows this by typing after his name, "Re AP, UPI, *Times* clip, Johnson." If he does a story based on the advance text of a speech, he so indicates with, "Re speech advance." Or, to use the pithy newsroom expression, "Re hand-

Harrington - assigned

POLICE

Police Chief Warren G. Westervelt asked Mayor Caruthers

yesterday to add 500 men to the city's police force before Jan. 1.

"I can't prevent crime in the streets unless I have the

men to do it," Chief Westervelt said. "We simply don't have enough

police to make this city safe."

Asked at a news conference how much the enlarged police

force would cost and where he would get the money to pay the additional

men, he replied:

"I don't know. That's the Mayor's problem. Go ask him.

All I can tell him is what's needed."

At City Hall, it was learned that the Mayor was angered by

Chief Westervelt's outburst. "I want to talk to him before I say

anything about his proposal," the Mayor said.

The two officials will meet at City Hall in the Mayor's

office at 10 a.m. today.

MORE

HOW TO EDIT COPY

Here is how edited copy looks after it leaves a reporter's desk in a newspaper city room. The credit line at the top shows that Harrington, on rewrite, has taken information from two other reporters and the Associated Press. His slug, NL (abbreviation for New Lead) POLICE, shows that he is topping a story already in the paper. In the lower right-hand corner, the writer leaves no doubt about the end of his story and also shows where it joins the previous account.

The editing shows that the deskman had his own ideas about how the story should be handled. This is universally true in journalism. Nobody's copy is sacred. The regulations on copy preparation, of course, have been followed. The editor's notation, HTK, means that the copy is to be set by the printers and the headline is, as the expression goes, "to kum." The editor has made various changes in the text that are self-explanatory.

out." If he takes dictation from a reporter, he writes after his own name, "Dic Johnson," to indicate who did the dictating.

When a story ends on one page, it should be clearly shown with an end mark such as xxx or # or even the old telegrapher's signal for the end of a message (30), now rarely used. Some papers, and all wire services require writers to indicate the time a story was completed as well.

If a story runs more than a take, the word (*more*) is written in the lower right-hand corner or a diagonal arrow is drawn pointing in that direction to show that the piece is still open. After the first take, all succeeding sheets begin with copy about an inch and a half from the top.

All paragraphs should be sharply indented, from one-quarter to one-third of the way across the sheet. This is to permit greater ease of editing and, in addition, to provide a simple way of counting down the required number of paragraphs to show where a new lead joins with an old story, or where an insert is to be placed.

Finally, if writers take care to have black, well-inked ribbons on their typewriters and keys that are not clogged, their work will be at least mechanically acceptable. Their accuracy can be increased by thorough reading of each page, plus neat editing with a soft black pencil, before it is handed in. There is nothing in this recital that requires more than normal care, yet laxity in copy preparation still plagues many a city desk. Haste is not an excuse for poor work.

IDENTIFYING A STORY

Next to poor copy preparation, the slugging—or identification—of newspaper copy is the source of most deadline difficulties.

Every piece prepared for a newspaper, from the lead story to the

Harrington rew Sessions, Mainwaring and AP

NL POLICE

Mayor Caruthers ~~has demanded~~ *asked* Police Chief Warren G. Westervelt's resign~~ation, it was learned last night.~~ *To* *last night×*

Furious over ~~Chief Westervelt's demand that~~ *the* *is request for* 500 more ~~men be added to the city's~~ police ~~force~~ before Jan. 1, the Mayor ~~bluntly~~ told him by telephone that he was through.

~~It was learned at~~ Police Headquarters, ~~that~~ the 65-year-old chief ~~intended to~~ *indicated that he would* apply this week for retirement after 41 years of service on the force. Neither he nor the Mayor would comment publicly.

The break between the two officials came ~~with dramatic~~ *soon* ~~and unexpected suddenness~~ after Chief Westervelt *had* demanded an increase in the size of the city's 8,000-man police force. ~~He had been under increasing pressure in recent weeks to check the rising crime rate, the worst in the city's history.~~

end NL POLICE

~~pikup 2nd graf "I ... prevent"~~

smallest filler item, must have a name so that it can be identified. These names are known as slugs and they usually consist of the key word that describes a story. A story about the President might be slugged "President," and one about the United Nations could be simply "UN." Other familiar and self-identifying slugs are "storm," "fire," and "slay."

Purpose   These slugs have many purposes. They are placed on each piece of copy in a story. As a rule the slug goes on the first take about an inch or two below the writer's name, then is repeated on each successive take in the upper left-hand corner directly after the number of the take. The same slug also is written on the headline designated for the story so that story and headline can be matched up in the composing room. If the story is large enough to be scheduled by the makeup editor, the slug with its headline size is placed on a dummy with the space allowance for them to indicate their position in the paper. When changes are made in the story, such as new leads, inserts, ads or corrections, the slug quickly identifies the piece that is affected. (New Lead Mayor, Insert A Yanks, Add Moscow, etc.)

Slugs are for the use of reporters, editors, and compositors and are supposed to be tossed away before the type to be printed is placed in page form. Unhappily, a slug sometimes is overlooked and gets in the paper. For that reason writers are invariably warned never to use a gag as a slug, or a profane, insulting, silly, or meaningless slug. The word "kill," which to a printer means that a story is not to be used, cannot be made a slug and neither can the word "must," which is an editor's designation for a piece that must go into the paper.

Keeping Stories Separate   Slugs must not be so general that they are likely to be duplicated by another reporter, or confused with a similar story. On this basis, "Auto" would be a bad slug for an automobile accident because there are so many of them. And "Obit," too, would not be meaningful unless the name of the subject was included because most newspapers carry several columns of them every day.

Consequently, it is sometimes necessary on a big story with many angles to use one general slug, and then a second word to differentiate one story from another. In this manner "Storm–Greenwich" would indicate the story was about the Greenwich angle of a general storm account. "Series–Yanks" would show that a sidebar, or side story, about the Yankees was so designated in general World Series baseball coverage. And "Smith–Obit" would be sufficient information for any deskman that the item was an obituary of a man named Smith.

If a story continues from day to day, it is standard newspaper practice to give it the same slug. Thus, when a local reporter slugs his story "budget," no editor needs an explanation of what to expect.

Wire Service Practice   While the same general rules for copy preparation apply to wire services, wire copy slugging has to be more precise. Because some time may elapse between the sending of all takes of a story on a teleprinter, each take must be carefully identified and keyed to the preceding piece. Therefore, wire services generally do not number their takes in sequence but put them together in a series of adds, as additional material is known. Some newspapers also do this, particularly when they have a lot of wire copy being filed by staff members.

In substance, this is the way it is done: After the first take of a wire service story, which is slugged in accordance with the detailed instructions in Chapter 13, succeeding takes are called adds. Each is identified by a pickup line at the top of the sheet of copy. For example, this would be the pickup line for the second page of a UPI Washington story slugged "Strike":

1st add Strike (Washington) . . . the Commission said.

By matching up all takes by pickup lines and checking the "time off" punched in the lower right-hand corner, an editor can put a wire service story together quickly. (For those who are mystified by the time symbols, PED means P.M., Eastern Daylight Time, and ACS means A.M., Central Standard Time.)

Radio–TV Copy Preparation   There is no substitute for precision in the preparation of copy for radio and television. Where items have to be measured in terms of two or three seconds, and sound and video tapes have to be inserted at exactly the right moment, the writer's script has to be precisely cued and timed from beginning to end.

Basically, a script for radio is prepared on the assumption that the newsman or commentator will speak at the rate of 180 words a minute. Thus, an aggregate of four pages of 15 lines each, averaging ten words to a line, is the equivalent of the news in a five-minute cast (fixed items and commercials take the rest). These 700 words are broken down into individual items, usually about two or three items per minute, with each item bearing an appropriate slug in large letters. After the lead item is selected, the rest of the newscast is assembled easily by slugs and the exact time allocated to each. For a 15-minute newscast (covering approximately 12 minutes and 2,000 words), the items may be a little longer but the theory of copy preparation is the same.

For television, there is the added complication of describing and measuring each bit of film, sound on film, or videotape that is used. The script thus has to be prepared in two separate columns on the page, one marked Video at the left, with the slug and time of each pictorial segment, and the other marked Audio at right, with the text of the newscaster's remarks synchronized to coincide with what is being shown to the viewer, if it is not accompanied by a correspondent's own report. The slugging, instructions, and exact timing make a 30-minute network television news show script an awesomely detailed preparation. (For specifics, see Chapter 15.) Beside it, the simple business of preparing a sheet of newspaper copy is child's play, although the writing takes equal precision and skill.

STYLE AS A MANNER OF WRITING

Style is a two-faced word in journalism. In the sense of the foregoing discussion, it refers to uniform rules of spelling, syntax, abbreviations, and similar matters. In its most important sense, however, style refers to an individualistic manner of writing. Editors or news directors who fail to separate the two are likely to have trouble getting the best out of their writers.

The ambivalence of the editorial mind with regard to style is at once the delight of the critics of journalism and the despair of the well-educated newcomer. While writers are always encouraged to try to develop a more readable style, they are also limited by the dictates of the style book.

Little can be done about this. Both are vital in journalism, particularly in newspaper work. The best advice that can be given to a newcomer is to memorize the style book, work to develop a highly personal style of writing, and then hope for the best.

chapter 4

The Uses of Language

The news media cannot be casual about the uses of language. They must transmit news, opinions and ideas to mass audiences as efficiently as possible. They cannot afford to discount the value of grammar. Their standards must be at least as high as those of the best-educated elements among their readers, listeners, or viewers, or they will forfeit public respect.

Slovenly language may not prevent 50,000 people from buying a book or seeing a play, but it would be well-nigh fatal, if continued very long, to the reputation of a newspaper, a news magazine, or a news program.

A GRAMMATICAL CHECK LIST

There are no exceptions to the rule that correct grammatical usage is essential to good journalism. The preciseness of language sharpens the meaning of fact. That is why the two go hand in hand.

Here, in condensed form, is a grammatical check list. It includes some of the principal shortcomings of professional journalists and suggests procedures that are generally acceptable in American newsrooms:

Adjectives It is customary in every professional work on writing to caution against the use of adjectives, certainly sound advice. Most writers, even inexperienced ones, quickly learn that adejectives are treacherous and select the few they use with care. When Georges Clemenceau was editor of the newspaper, *La Justice*, he told a new reporter, "Young man, when you write a sentence you are to use a noun, a verb, and a complement. If you use an adjective, you must ask my permission."

The pile-up of adjectives is obvious in a phrase such as "the bright, sunny, beautiful, blue sky." Even amateur writers would hesitate to use it. Yet, on the spurious excuse that space may be saved, adjectives are awkwardly piled up in constructions such as "sleek, slim, golf champion John Hamilton."

The normal use of English will avert such errors.

Adverbs   The flat adverb sometimes is mistaken for an adjective. "Go *slow*," is correct usage, *slow* being a flat adverb. But, "He drove careful," is obviously wrong, *careful* being an adjective that modifies a verb. The rule is that adverbs, flat or not, modify verbs whereas adjectives modify nouns.

Therefore, if the modifier specifically refers to the subject, it must be an adjective; if it refers to the verb, it must be an adverb. Thus, "He drove carefully," would be a correct use of the adverb.

In the use of copulative (linking) verbs (appear, feel, look, seem, smell) the writer must choose carefully between the use of a predicate adjective and an adverb modifier. "He feels bad," connotes illness. To write, "He feels badly," would mean that something was wrong with his sense of touch.

Antecedent   The pronoun, *it*, is a danger signal in copy. Always check the antecedent.

Articles   There is a notion among some editors that an article can be dispensed with in many sentences. The result has been to encourage the growth of a kind of telegraphic writing in which "the," "a" and "an" are bowled over like ninepins. Some samples:

> Sense of the meeting was against zoning.
> Rash of activity broke out in City Council last night.
> Dedication of bridge is set for Tuesday.

There is inconsistency, as well, in the dropping of articles. Many writers omit "the" in referring to Congress or police. But they would not thinking of dropping it before the various armed forces, the Supreme Court, the Legislature, or the City Council. The indiscriminate omission of articles saves little space, leads to confusion, and annoys readers.

Collective Nouns   Congress, the cabinet, and the government are among the collective nouns that are singular in American usage and plural in

Britain. We write, "Congress was in session," but the British form is, "The government were called to account." Plural nouns such as police and fish should not be mistaken for collective nouns. Nor is it ever advisable to be inconsistent in the agreement of subject and predicate by writing: "Sears is having their big sale today."

Ellipsis   The omission of words necessary to complete a sentence involves the use of ellipsis. There is a rule, modified by exceptions, that a word may be omitted if its meaning can be supplied or understood from a corresponding part of a compound sentence. The word to be supplied must be in the same grammatical form as the one to which it corresponds. This is correct: "One person was killed and another injured." This is incorrect: "One person was killed and 12 injured." To be correct, the word "were" would go after 12.

Not Only   In using the term *not only* the writer must watch parallel construction or the meaning of his sentence may be twisted. The rule for correlative conjunctions is that one must parallel the other; that is, it must follow the same part of speech. Thus, the expression, *not only*, is usually paired with the expression, *but also*. It would be incorrect to write, "The defendant was not only found guilty of grand larceny, but also of assault." To make sense, the "not only" must be moved after the word "guilty." Then, each of the phrases directly precedes the preposition "of" and is parallel in construction. Other correlative conjunctions that are used in pairs and that follow the same rule include such expressions as *either—or*, *neither—nor*, and *both—and*.

Number   Disagreement in number between subject and verb is an unwelcome feature of much news copy. Singular verbs crop up with dismaying frequency after plural subjects, particularly when a qualifying clause intervenes that confuses the writer. It is incorrect to write, "Part of their silver and linen were stolen." The subject is the noun *part* and it takes a singular verb. The same error may be detected in this sentence: "A box of rifles and hand grenades, discovered on the ship, were seized by the Federal agents." The singular form of the verb should have been used. However, in the following sentence, a plural verb should have been used: "Much flame and smoke, while obscuring the building, was seen for miles around." In a compound subject joined by *or, nor, either—or*, or *neither—nor* the verb agrees with the subject nearest to it. This sentence, therefore, would be correct: "Neither the captain nor his men were seen." But when a simple subject is modified by an expression such as *in addition to* or *together with*, the verb still must agree with the subject and therefore it remains singular: "The sergeant, together with his companions, was injured."

Preposition at End of Sentence   At one time ending a sentence with a preposition was a grammatical crime in the first degree. The only recourse for a culprit, when detected, was to throw himself on the mercy of the court. The rule against prepositional endings has been relaxed here and there—but when one is used in news copy a good excuse had better be thought of.

Sequence of Tenses   The rule of good sense should be applied to a determination of the proper sequence of tenses. It has become so complicated that the average writer is bewildered by rules. The first thing to remember is that the alignment of tenses in a sentence should follow the rules of parallelism and normal time sequence. Thus, it is normal to write: "The President says he feels fine." Also, transposing to the past tense, it is correct to write: "The President said he felt fine." But, in an exceptional case, the parallel construction must be broken to take account of circumstances. For instance, it would be silly to write: "Columbus said the world was round." It still is. (Well, anyway, it's pear-shaped.) Therefore, the correct method of writing current truths expressed in the past is: "Columbus said the world is round." There is further variation when reference is made to an event preceding the simple past. Then, the past perfect tense must be used as follows: "The President said that he had been ill." However, when the sentence itself indicates the priority in time of various events, it is not necessary to do so by juggling tenses. Thus, it would be correct to say: "The President recalled that this was the anniversary of his illness a year ago." But it is not correct to report: "The President said he will go to Chicago." What actually happened was that he "said he would go to Chicago." When in doubt, the writer should examine his sequence of tenses and ask himself whether they make sense. Then, he ought to think of the suffering reader.

Split Infinitive   Infinitives are split at will in some universities, but copy desks still worry about slipping an adverb between "to be," or "to have," or "to split." The general rule is that a writer must have good reason for splitting an infinitive. The best reason is clarity. For instance: "Air Force scientists at Cape Kennedy said they intended to use the installation to better develop intercontinental ballistic missiles." Here, the deed is done. The infinitive is split. If the copy editor makes it "better to develop," he is guilty of a strained effect. If he changes the clause to read that the scientists want "to develop better intercontinental ballistic missiles," he twists the sense of the story. Therefore, the split infinitive in all probability will be allowed unless some superpurist decides to change the sentence altogether.

Subjunctive   The subjunctive mood is honored primarily by newspapers and wire services. In certain simple conditional clauses some editors with more self-assurance than others will permit the indicative mood to be used. Such a clause is given in the following sentence: "If the mayor was involved, he did not say so." In the case of a purely hypothetical clause, the subjunctive is used as follows: "It's as if the moon were made of green cheese." When a conditional clause is contrary to fact, then the use of the subjunctive is mandatory, as in the following: "If Justice Smith were no longer a member of the Supreme Court, he would probably take up mountain climbing."

That and Which   The easiest way to separate this old puzzler is to use "Bernstein's Law," as follows: "If the clause could be omitted without leaving the noun it modifies incomplete, or without materially altering the sense of what is being said—or if it could be reasonably enclosed in parentheses—it should be introduced by 'which'; otherwise, by 'that.' For example: 'The Hudson River, which flows west of Manhattan, is muddy.' (A nondefining clause; it could be omitted or parenthesized.) But: 'The river that flows west of Manhattan is the Hudson.' " To repeat the rule: "That" introduces a limiting or defining clause; "which," a nondefining clause.

Verbs   The historical journalistic insistence on the use of verbs in the active voice, where possible, is perfectly sound, but the device may become banal with over use. In many summary weather stories even newspapers of quality have reported events such as these:

> A torrential rainfall pelted the city last night. It snarled traffic, delayed trains, and flooded cellars.
> High winds lashed residential areas. Pedestrians struggled toward temporary shelter. In low-lying parts of the city, sheets of blinding rain caused sewers to overflow. . . .

The astonished reader cannot be blamed if, upon reading such hopped-up language, he hurries home and tells the wife and kids to head for the hills. Of course, this is merely routine handling of a heavy rainfall with emphasis on verbs in the active voice. When a hurricane strikes, the writer's language may be a little stronger.

The intransitive verb is not to be despised. Some of the world's most moving and dramatic events can be told best with the use of an intransitive verb. For instance:

Rome—The Pope died today.

What could be more effective than this simple statement of fact?

There are times, too, when a verb in the passive voice is most effective, as in the following:

SUPREME HEADQUARTERS ALLIED EXPEDITIONARY FORCES, June 6— The invasion of Europe has been launched by a mighty American-British force.

Not all the smashing, lashing, dashing, crashing pile-up of verbals can create the effect of a simple, unaffected statement of big news. Where verbs in the active voice contribute to the clarity and mood of a story, of course, they are to be preferred, but some of the excesses of indiscriminate use can only be deplored.

Here are a few instances in which the active voice is effectively used:

Passive: The election was won by a 74-year-old man.
Active: A 74-year-old man won the election.

Passive: The governor was cheered by the delegates to the convention.
Active: The convention delegates cheered the governor.

Passive: The bank was robbed by three men.
Active: Three men robbed the bank.

Writers are well advised not to switch from active to passive voice, and vice versa, in the same sentence.

Verbals   This is the grammatical chamber of horrors.

Exhibit A is the dangling participle. A participle is a verb used as an adjective. When it dangles, it is an erratic modifier. For example: "Walking from the dark room, his eyes blinked." He did the walking, not his eyes. Dangling participles may be avoided by putting the participle in direct contact with the noun or pronoun it modifies. For example: "Walking from the dark room, he blinked."

Exhibit B is the misused gerund. A gerund is a verb used as a noun. It may take a modifier, but if so, the noun or pronoun must be in the possessive case. It is incorrect to write: "He did not approve the candidate speaking first." What was not approved was *the candidate's speaking*, and that is the way it should have been written. The intent of the sentence is the basis for determining whether the gerund takes a possessive. Try the words, *act of*, in the above sentence as a test. In the sentence, insert these words before the gerund *speaking*: "He did not approve the candidate (act of) speaking first." It is awkward. Therefore, the use of the possessive, the *candidate's speaking*, is indicated.

Will and Shall   The grammatical rule governing *will* and *shall* is too generally disregarded in most newsrooms. The language, "I shall go," or "I should like," seems too precious for journalistic use. Actually, the distinction is a good one and should be maintained. *Shall* is used with the first person and *will* with the second and third persons when simple future or mere expectation is to be expressed. In expressing determination, command, promise, or obligation, the order is reversed. The first condition is met by this sentence, "I shall try if you will help me." The second condition is illustrated as follows: "I will be heard," or, "You shall obey me."

Actually, in newsrooms it sounds intolerably prissy to use *shall* in any sense but interrogation. "Shall we go?" or, "Should he be answered?" are forms that are still used. Otherwise the distinction between shall and will seems to have been as conveniently forgotten as that between can and may. An occasional editor may still insist that there is a distinction. He is, of course, right.

Who and Whom There is no nonsense about the correct use of *who* and *whom*. The simple rules are still in effect on every copy desk in the land, and writers are held strictly to account. The error in usage here is one of the most common in journalism, and one of the easiest to detect.

A sentence properly using *who* as the subject of a clause follows: "The Mayor was the only candidate who, in the committee's opinion, would be acceptable to the voters." Another sentence in which *whom* is properly used as the object of a verb is: "The Mayor was the candidate whom the committee preferred." A simple test may be made by recasting the sentence and substituting the pronouns he or him for who or whom. The first sentence would then read: "In the committee's opinion, he would be acceptable." Thus, *who* is the correct pronoun.

USAGE

Some words and expressions are frequently misused by news writers. Below are some that have achieved notoriety:

All-America. Often misused as All-American, referring to members of All-America football teams.

All right. Often incorrectly spelled alright. The expression is two words, like under way and per cent.

All-round. Misused as all-around. The correct expression is all-round athlete.

Allude. Should not be confused with *refer*.

Anyone. It is one word.

As a result of. Usually misused as "the result of. . . ." Often, something happens as *a* result of . . . . In other words, more than one result is usually possible.

Banquet. Usually it is a dinner. "There has not been a dinner in New York worth calling a banquet in years."

Boat.   A small craft, propelled by oars. It is often misused for a ship, which is larger and is a seagoing craft.

Bride.   A woman about to be married, as well as a newly-married woman. Her husband is not a groom, but a bridegroom.

Broadcast.   Present and past tense of the verb are identical.

Burglar.   Usually misused. There must be breaking and entering before a larceny can be called a burglary. The act of stealing is more often a theft or a robbery.

By.   A preposition expressing relations of place or direction and commonly referring to persons. "With" generally refers to things, and "through" may refer to either persons or things.

Capital.   Washington, D. C., is the capital. The building is called the capitol.

Casualties.   In war these refer to both dead and injured. The term means losses from any cause.

Chair.   Misused as a verb. To say that Jones chaired a meeting is incorrect. He presided.

Citizen.   A man may be a citizen of the United States, but not a citizen of Britain. He is a British subject.

Claim.   Often incorrectly used. It is not right to say that a district attorney claims a defendant is guilty. This is a charge, an accusation.

Collision.   Some prissy writers, thinking they are avoiding libel per se, write that two automobiles were in collision. It is just as safe, and better English, to write that they collided.

Compare.   Two like objects are compared to each other. Two unlike objects are compared with each other.

Comprise.   Do not confuse with compose. Comprise means to include.

Counsel.   Used as a noun, this refers to a person who gives advice. He may be a part of a council, which is a deliberative body.

Critical.   A person may be in a critical condition, but this does not necessarily mean that he is dying.

Data.   This is plural. The singular, datum, is seldom used.

Different than.   Use different from.

Don't.   It means do not and must never be used for doesn't, meaning does not.

Due to.   Must refer to a noun, if used. It is wrong to write, "She agreed to go, due to her husband's insistence." This is correct: "Her agreement to go was due to her husband's insistence."

Engine.   An airplane has engines, not motors.

Etc.   Should not be used in news stories.

False titles.   Expressions such as movie queen Elizabeth Taylor, television comic Jackie Gleason, and concert pianist Van Cliburn, are false titles. They should not be used as such. Instead, use them after the names of persons, as modifiers.

Farther.   Refers to physical distance. Further is used for time and all else.

Figuratively.   Do not confuse with literally.

Finalize.   Do not use.

Forecast.   Present and past tense of the verb are identical.

From.   A man does not die from heart failure. He dies of heart disease.

Good.   Use as an adjective, not an adverb. It is wrong to write, "She danced good." This is correct: "She danced well."

Hanged. A man is hanged. A picture is hung.

Healthful. Means to give health. Healthy means having health.

Hike. Pure headlinese when used in conjunction with wages. A man receives a raise, not a hike or boost.

It's. Means it is. *Its* is a pronoun.

Judge. The Federal bench is occupied by judges, except in the United States Supreme Court where there are justices. The highest of these is the Chief Justice of the United States.

Kind of. Do not follow with the article, a.

Lawyer. A member of the bar is a lawyer, not an attorney. However, a lawyer may be an attorney (adviser) to an accused person.

Less. A reference to quantity: "Less than one-third remains." Fewer refers to numbers: "Fewer than ten attended."

Lie, lay. Lay is the past tense of lie. "He lay down." Lie is present tense. "It lies there."

Like. A preposition that expresses comparison. "He pitched like Bob Gibson." It cannot be substituted for the conjunction *as*. "The prisoner did as he was told." Not "like he was told."

Majority, plurality. If only two candidates are running for office, the winning margin is a majority. If more than two are in the contest, the margin of the votes of the first candidate over the second is a plurality but the first candidate also may have a majority of all votes cast.

Narcotics. Do not use the expressions, dope and drugs, when narcotics or habit-forming drugs are meant.

None. Singular, except when the usage is awkward.

Numbers. Do not start a sentence with numbers. Spell them out instead.

Over. Not to be used for the expression, more than. Over means above. The expression, more than, means in excess of.

Pass away. The short word, die, is better.

Plenty. A noun. Not to be used as an adjective or adverb.

Practically. Means the opposite of theoretically. "The crop was practically worthless." Virtually means in essence, or in effect, but not in fact. "He rules virtually as a dictator."

Principal. An adjective meaning chief or main. Principle, a noun, means a general truth.

Proven. The correct word is proved.

Providing. Provided is better. "The ship was due at Cherbourg at 8 A.M., provided its speed was maintained.

Raise. Children are reared, not raised.

Reason is because. Do not use. Because means "For the reason that."

Render. Fat is rendered, but not music.

Rise. It is prissy to write that a man has received a pay rise. Call it a raise. Everybody understands that.

St. James's. The United States has an ambassador at the Court of St. James's, not St. James.

Scot. The people of Scotland are Scots. They drink Scotch and soda sometimes.

Sustain. Injuries are received or suffered, not sustained.

Toward. The final "s" has been dropped in toward, afterward, forward.

Transpire. Means to become known gradually, and should not be used in the sense of to happen or to occur.

Try. The old college try has made this verb into a noun.

Very. When used with a past participle, it should be accompanied by the word much. "I am very much pleased," not "very pleased."

Whether. Do not use as whether or not, unless an alternative must be given the same weight.

Widow. A man who dies is survived by his widow.

SPELLING

One of the principal complaints of editors is that most newcomers to journalism are deficient in spelling. Editors are not alone in making this chronic complaint. Young lawyers, doctors, and engineers also have been criticized for the same failing. However, any generalization is dangerous. Without presuming to draw conclusions from evidence that may be both biased and based on insufficient evidence, I would venture the observation that no generation of modern writers has approached perfection in spelling, including my own.

The following list includes words that have been chronically misspelled for many years by both older and younger generations of journalists:

accessible	council	hygiene
accommodate	counsel	hyperbole
affect	curlicue	immolate
aggression	defense	impeccable
all right	deity	incalculable
analogous	demurrer	incompatible
anyone	dependent	incorruptible
appall	dietitian	indispensable
appendicitis	diphtheria	indomitable
arraignment	discernible	inevitable
assault	dissension	ingenious
atoll	drunkenness	ingenuous
ballistic	ecstasy	innocuous
battalion	effect	inoculate
bettor	embarrass	inseparable
buses	endorse	insistence
canoeist	eying	judgment
carrot	frivolous	likable
capital	fulfill	kidnaped
capitol	furor	kimono
changeable	gaiety	liaison
claque	gauge	mangy
commitment	glamor	Manhattan
consensus	guerrilla	marshal
contemptible	hemorrhage	naphtha

nickel	phony	sanitarium
niece	Philippine	sacrilegious
ninety	plaque	seized
observer	Portuguese	supersede
occult	propeller	vacillate
occurred	queue	vilify
oculist	recommend	weird
offense	regrettable	whisky
passenger	renege	xylophone
peaceable	saxophone	zephyr
permissible		

The pitfalls in this list are not entirely of a writer's own making. Some of these words have several accepted spellings, but only one is used generally in American journalism. (Observer is accepted by most newspapers, but observor is equally correct.) Others are correct by American standards, incorrect by those of Britain and other Commonwealth countries. (We spell it glamor, offense; the British, glamour, offence.) There are also homonyms —words that sound alike but are spelled differently and have different meanings (council, counsel). Of course, there are also many words that are exceptions to the normal rules of spelling.

Good spelling requires a good memory. It means, too, that dictionaries must be consulted frequently. Except for pathological cases, those who spell poorly either were never trained correctly in school or are too careless now to change their ways.

Bad spelling cannot be attributed to the speed and facility that are required of many writers of news. The fastest writers, somehow, often turn out to be the strongest in spelling and grammar. But many a young writer is blamed for poor spelling when his real fault is that he has not had a sufficient opportunity to curl up with a style book and find out which of several acceptable spellings is preferred by his particular news organization.

Of course there *are* some unfortunates who cannot spell. They are the problem children of journalism.

CONCISENESS

Sometimes news phrases are wordy. They may be tautological. Or, worst of all, they may be incorrect.

Every editor has a list that violates the journalistic virtue of conciseness in one way or another. Below in bold type are some of the most frequent offenders, with suggestions for improvement and comments in regular type face:

At the present time.   At present, now.
Big in size.   Big *is* size.

Biography of his life.   That is what a biography is.

Checked out.   As used by TV detectives, who check out clues, this is a redundant expression. Drop the "out."

Combined together.   Drop the "together."

Consensus of opinion.   A consensus means opinion.

Dead body.   A body is presumed to be dead.

Early pioneer.   How late is a pioneer?

Entire monopoly.   Either it is a monopoly or it is not. Drop "entire."

Hallowe'en evening.   E'en is a contraction of evening.

Head up.   As coined by the Togetherness Boys, the expression means to head a committee. The "up" is superfluous.

High-powered rifle.   Rifles are. If it is only a pop-gun, say so.

Knots per hour.   Knots measure speed per hour.

Most unique.   It cannot be. Drop "most." It is like saying somebody is very dead.

Present incumbent.   Drop the "present."

Repeat again.   That is what repeating is—again.

Ten P.M. tonight.   This is guaranteed to drive deskmen out of their minds. It is no better when it is written, "Five A.M. this morning."

True facts.   When are facts false?

Two alternatives.   An alternative refers to a choice between two things.

Unknown man.   Correct expression is unidentified man.

Well-known.   Do not use. If a man is well known, the readers will realize it without being told. The same is true of the use of "prominent citizen."

There are other pet hates among journalists, such as Sahara Desert and Sierra Nevada Mountains. (Sahara means desert, and Sierra means mountains.) The list could grow to unreasonable length. It is intended primarily as a compilation of the most common offenses.

PUNCTUATION

The unskilled writer frequently uses too much punctuation.

There are too many quotation marks around single words and partial quotations. There are too many dashes and hyphens, too many commas, semicolons, and colons, and not enough periods. This is a broad complaint, to which there are, of course, numerous exceptions. But in an effective writing style punctuation should be distinguished by its sparseness and utility. Here is some good advice from the *Associated Press Style Book*:

Punctuation is the visual inflection. The marks should clarify meaning and, like shouting, should be employed sparingly. Skillful phrasing avoids ambiguity, insures correct interpretation and lessens need for punctuation. When punctuation is used, it should be employed solely to bring out what is intended. If punctuation does not clarify, it should be omitted.

Some of the principal errors in the use of punctuation are discussed below.

Periods The period is the most useful of all forms of punctuation. The main error made by news writers, in general, is that they do not use enough periods. Nor do they use them at sufficiently frequent intervals. A period should be used more often than it is.

Quotations The failure to place commas and periods inside quotes is frequently noted in news copy. Another error is the placement of quotation marks in several paragraphs of quoted material that follow one another. All that is required is to place a quotation mark at the beginning of each paragraph in the series and to omit it from the end of all paragraphs except the last quoted one. Often quotes are placed about single words or phrases when they are not needed. In general, writers should avoid quoting a word or a phrase unless there is a specific justification for it. To quote a word or phrase because it is unusual or slangy or cute is an error, unless it can be directly attributed to someone in the story and has a special meaning that requires quotation marks. As for double attribution, it should be used sparingly and with great care.

Hyphens and Dashes Hyphens pull language together. Dashes perform the opposite function. Both are used far more than is necessary. The rules for hyphenating compound words are given at length under *compound* in *Webster's New International Dictionary*, a standard guide. A dash should be used only when there is an abrupt change of thought.

CAPITALIZATION

Many newspapers in the United States are embracing lower-case style. The so-called down style is more convenient, easier to handle, and probably faster to work with than the more formal and more correct full capitalization that is characteristic of the most carefully edited publications.

When a newspaper uses lower case or down style, it often goes further in this direction than it may wish. The reason is that copy editors are generally so rushed, and so few in number, that they do not indicate carefully what is to be capitalized. Therefore, by default, the actual decision on what to capitalize and what to set in lower case is left to the printers in too many cases.

The result is that, in many a newspaper of excellent reputation, there will be uncapitalized words on Page 1 (and elsewhere) such as Congress, the United States Supreme Court, the Federal Bureau of Investigation, the United States Air Force, and sometimes the United States itself. In all except the most fanatically down-style papers, these excesses are accidents.

In checking the style books of newspapers the inexperienced journalist will find quickly that a certain basic minimum of proper nouns must be capitalized. A newspaper is not intended to be a copy book, but it also should not be a typographical nightmare.

Such are the basic uses of language that must be known to every journalist. They must be practiced faithfully. Without them journalism would be chaotic and undisciplined. Wisely used, these techniques emphasize the expressiveness and versatility of the English language. They frame the manner in which a writer expresses himself and give his work depth and meaning.

chapter 5

News Writing Is Clear Writing

Every news organization must observe three basic principles in its operations, if it is to be successful. First, it must always present something new. Second, it must address itself to a particular audience. And third, above all, it not only must make itself understood, but also must be certain it is never misunderstood. These principles, in their essentials, apply to all the news media and those who serve them.

ON UNDERSTANDING NEWS

Like all abstractions, the concept of news means different things to different people. To a morning newspaperman, it is what happened yesterday. To an afternoon newspaperman, it is what happened today. To a wire service, radio, or television newsman, it is what happened a moment ago.

What Is News?   There are almost as many definitions of news as there are journalists. Here is an academic definition, the basis for which was given fifty years ago by Dean M. Lyle Spencer at the University of Washington: "News is any event, idea or opinion that is timely, that interests or affects a large number of people in a community, and that is capable of being understood by them."

Turner Catledge, while he was executive editor of *The New York Times*, once gave a simple, professional definition: "News is anything you didn't know yesterday."

This is a cynic's definition, adapted broadly from the celebrated definition of law: "News is what editors say it is."

And finally, a statement of fact: "News is what is broadcast or printed in newspapers."

All these can be picked at, in particular the last. There is no guarantee that all news media provide news.

Characteristics of News   The ancient verities of the news are accuracy, interest, and timeliness. To these must now be added a fourth verity, explanation. Of what use is an accurate, interesting, and timely news account if people cannot understand it?

Even on the basis of these four pillars, however, no journalist could devise an infallible formula for news although all except dullards know quickly enough when they have missed a story. It is not something that can be done by slide rule, examined under a microscope, or counted up on an adding machine.

There are too many variables. In addition to accuracy, interest, timeliness, and explanation, others are persons and places, sources and techniques, and even the media themselves. Actually, there is news in everything if you know where to look for it. Sometimes a statement becomes news because it is not true. This was the case with President Eisenhower's celebrated denial, after a U-2 spy plane had been shot down at Sverdlovsk, that the United States had been overflying Soviet territory. The Kennedy administration was similarly embarrassed by its initial denials that the CIA had master-minded the "Bay of Pigs" disaster, as was the Johnson administration with its frequent and premature proclamations of victory in Vietnam.

From time to time, there may be earthshaking news in announcements that are not of immediate interest to the average man. Consider the following, which was modestly played in *The New York Times* of January 31, 1939:

> The splitting of a uranium atom into two parts, each consisting of a gigantic "cannon ball" of the tremendous energy of 100,000,000 electron volts, the greatest amount of atomic energy so far liberated on earth, was announced here yesterday by the Physics Department of Columbia University. . . .

It was the first news of the splitting of the atom, forerunner of work on the atomic bomb. But until Albert Einstein pointed it out to him, not even President Franklin Delano Roosevelt understood it.

As for timeliness, even the Lord's Prayer can be updated. Joe Alex Morris, in "Deadline Every Minute," tells of Hugh Baillie's story of General Douglas MacArthur leading his troops in the Lord's Prayer after recapturing Seoul in the Korean War. After filing, Baillie received this message from his home office:

THIS IS FIRST TIME ANY CORRESPONDENT EVER SCORED
FIRST PAGE PLAY WITH LORDS PRAYER

There is also no guarantee that the public in general understands big news when it breaks. When hard-pressed Britain devalued the pound from $2.80 to $2.40 late in 1967, both newscasts and newspapers in the United States made much of panicky gold buying as an attack on the dollar. But even among the correspondents, few were able to explain clearly what was going on because they weren't sure themselves.

Is News Always Bad? Critics invariably point out that crisis, disaster, and catastrophe are the stock in trade of journalism. They argue that the news media are primarily a catalogue of horrors involving individuals and society as a whole.

There is, of course, some truth to this. But it is not the whole truth. Pulitzer prizes have been awarded to a campaign for blood donations, to a city editor who tried to save the life of a little girl, to an editor who tried to help both sides in a strike, to an editorial writer who invited the Russians to see how Iowa grows corn and hogs, to a photographer for a picture of a policeman talking with a little boy at a Chinese New Year's Day parade.

It is sheer nonsense to imply that the news media must have bad news to stay in business. Newspapers for years have led civic campaigns for urban renewal and fought for the passage of bond issues to rebuild the shattered inner cores of American cities. Television documentaries have been based on such varied subjects as expositions of American foreign policy, discussions with Walter Lippmann and explanations of complicated developments in Asia, Africa, and Latin America. At the height of the urban rioting that so distressed the nation, the Gannett newspapers patiently sought to publish examples of progress in American race relations. These, surely, are not the mark of a ghoulish profession.

True, any editor or news director who wants to feature civil strife, knife-wielding delinquents, phony Hollywood romances, and similar fare can do so with little effort. But it takes work to find news in happy children, contented families, and peaceful nations. These, too, are a part of journalism although they are not as prominent in the news as the events that scare the public.

Any sensible newspaper, news magazine, or news program tries to give the public a balanced view of the world. To do it requires an enormous amount of patience and understanding. The less-exploited categories of news cannot be handled with the simplicity of old-fashioned cops-and-robbers journalism. When the bad, the good, the not-so-bad, and the not-so-good can be brought into balance, the journalist may be satisfied that he has done a day's work.

TOWARD A BETTER UNDERSTANDING

The field for news has broadened immeasurably since the turn of the century. Once the police blotters, court, and government offices provided most of the news. Today no self-respecting editor can ignore science, health, and education; housing and urban redevelopment; automotive, and airspace news, and a score of other areas that were scarcely touched in years gone by. Business news has crowded its way off the financial page and landed on Page 1, along with news of inflation, and labor news is devoted to something more than strikes and picket lines. News of civil rights is of the first importance.

It is no longer a novelty to see thoughtful, critical work on serious music, books, the drama, ballet, and art on the amusement pages along with the usual movie reviews or to hear competent critics on television. Women's pages have become more interesting, generally, instead of being repositories for old publicity handouts from the grocery chains and flour companies.

Even the sports reports have felt the change. They are no longer confined largely to spectator sports such as baseball, football, horseracing, and boxing. Such participation sports as golf, boating, fishing, hunting, and bowling are crowding the pros for attention.

More People, More Subjects   What has happened, in brief, is that Americans have a larger average income than ever before, considerably more leisure time, and a widening sphere of activities. Their measurement of news is closely related to self-interest.

Most editors have a lively appreciation of this. Once the public was genuinely interested in the vicarious thrills of learning about the wealthy, the notorious, the fashionable, the beautiful, the mighty and the wicked; about sex, crime, disaster, babies, and animals. It is not enough any more.

Having had a broad introduction to the better life, the average American wants more news about good living. He is vitally interested in his health and the education of his children. Having something in his pocketbook, he is touched by anything that affects it—beginning with taxes. He does not pretend to understand science, but he is concerned about it and plods through news about it.

Nor is that all. Since he spends more for national defense than anything else and sees so much evidence of it around him, he snaps up information about it. He is not yet a political sophisticate in a class with the average European, but he is voting in greater numbers than ever before. Social problems that touch his life deeply affect him, whether it is racial integration or juvenile delinquency.

He still wants his sports, comics, pictures, and all the old familiar features to which he's become accustomed in his newspaper. To lose Blondie or Steve Canyon would be a national calamity. Moreover, he has boundless curiosity about people of all kinds and about human interest situations as well when he sees them on television.

While he can take his heroes or leave them alone, he simply adores his heroines. The Dream Girl is always in style. If an American has any more universal interest, it is probably the weather and his historic devotion to local news.

What Do They Want to Know? It is seldom today that the public is able to obtain its news from any one source. Newspapers, radio, television, magazines, and word of mouth all share in the news dissemination process to a varying degree, depending on the event, the time of day, and the location and occupation of the individual.

The man who drives to and from work in his own car is likely to depend on radio during that period of the day, having no other readily available source. The housewife, going about her chores with the television set turned on, naturally will rely on televised news. Those who use public transportation to and from work generally make painful efforts to read their favorite newspapers and magazines on a dimly lit bus, a jammed commuting train, or a suffocating metropolitan subway. In offices and most factories, the news is passed along by word of mouth. It is only during leisure hours, therefore, that people can deliberately choose their news medium and stick with it. Even then, however, there are the inevitable interruptions at home.

Under the circumstances, it is remarkable that so much news does get through and a lot of it is reasonably well understood. To anybody who has lived with the news disseminating process for any length of time, the public's patience and doggedness in seeking out the news despite all difficulties represent a heartening faith in the democratic process. True, as all surveys agree, there is a healthy public skepticism toward the news media, particularly in the reporting of controversial events. But that is something the journalist has learned to live with. It is the reason for his constant effort to turn up more facts, to check his sources, to document events as completely as possible, and to develop meaningful interpretation.

While it is possible for a newspaper to be entertaining, and some are, television is the prime entertainment medium. But television, too, has realized that entertainment is not enough; the network news periods have lengthened and the news content on responsible local stations has increased.

The all-news radio stations—dull and repetitious though most of their programs are—serve a useful function, as does radio news in general. And the alert news magazines are a constant prod to the faster media to do a better job. Because, as every journalist knows, the public demand for news is insatiable.

In a nation with well-nigh half its population under 25 years of age, the news media must change with the times and they recognize it. A responsible editor, J. Edward Murray, put it this way:

> We've wasted space on trivia, on cliché crime, and on catastrophe, on reams of meaningless political infighting. And we've neglected the bread-and-butter economics, education, religion, the arts, and the sciences of man: anthropology, sociology and psychology. We have also missed or under-exploited some of the great news stories through shallow reporting . . . the water story, the pollution story, the conservation and beautification story, the story of conflicting research goals. . . .
> The changing reader, with his rising educational, cultural and intellectual interests, will be satisfied only by the excellence of truly good reporting on stories such as these. Newspapers are not going to give up spot news to television and radio. Nor are we going to analyze and interpret to death every big, breaking story that comes along. But we are going to get in our best competitive licks, and give our best service to the reader, through serious and complete reporting of a very high order.[1]

How People Read   Since television has become a major source of news for the nation, it follows that the newspaper must develop into a more efficient medium of communication if it is to maintain its standing and prestige. This means that a greater account will have to be taken of the public's reading habits.

How do we read? Certainly not a word at a time. Only children who are beginning to read do that as a rule. The average adult recognizes words in groups—sometimes two or three words at a time. He takes about a third of a second for each group. Then, he pauses for about a quarter of a second between one group of words and another in order to assign provisional meanings to what he has read. As he goes on, his provisional understanding may change. He then will go back to look at a key word group. Once satisfied that he has the proper understanding of the sentence, he goes on. This stop-go-backward-forward movement is characteristic of the average reader.

Improved Reading   Eye cameras at the Armed Forces Information School, have developed a pattern in repeated examinations of military personnel. A beam of light focuses on the eyes of a reader, thus permitting pictures to

---

[1] J. Edward Murray, "The Changing Newspaper Reader," *The APME Red Book*, 1965, pp. 34–35.

be taken of reading habits. The restless, jumping movements of the eyes show the pattern: one word group, a pause; another word group, a pause; then a shift back to a previous word group, a pause; then, on to the next unfamiliar word group. At 250 words a minute, an average of a little more than four words a second, this process explains why a ponderous writer has trouble in communicating with the average reader. He simply cannot always make himself understood.

The Armed Forces Information School, however, has also shown that even the average slow reader can be trained to speed up and also increase his comprehension because, fundamentally, slow reading is not necessarily an indication of a sluggish mentality.

Military instructors, in six-week periods, have widened the eye span of readers of all types by training them to recognize in succession groups of five, seven, and nine numbers within the light flash of one one-hundredth of a second. By widening the eye span, more words in a group have been recognized. Readers, therefore, have not been obliged to glance back and forth in their texts to check on meanings. They have become more efficient, moving along steadily and taking in large word groups and meanings in smooth progression.

We have not yet reached the era, however, in which the publics that seek the news are willing at all times to train themselves in comprehension, as do those who go in for an appreciation of fiction, drama, classical music, and art. Newspapers, of course, can and do try to educate their readers as well as inform them, but mass training for improved reading and comprehension is a distant ideal.

Therefore, the editor and publisher, as well as the reporter and writer, have no present choice but to try to tie in with the current habits of the readers of their newspaper. The large metropolitan dailies, the suburban dailies, and the small city dailies and weeklies have such widely varying reader audiences that no generalization on these habits is possible. Each newspaper, in its presentation and writing of the news, reflects what editors believe their readers will understand.

Clarity in Writing   It is self-evident that the writer whose work is clear, simply organized, and easy to understand is more likely to find an audience in today's complicated world than a ponderous genius. The writer who is opaque in his presentation, whether he deals in science, semantics, news, or love letters, is only storing up trouble for himself. It takes more effort to be clear, simple, and direct. Sometimes it also takes more courage. Journalists must use the language that people understand.

The 5 W's and H   Even in the mid 1930s, the long opening sentence or lead was a fixture. It ran 60, 70, and sometimes more than 100 words and often was difficult to understand. The reason for the excessive length of many of these opening sentences was that it had become a tradition to jam the sense of the whole story into it.

It was also a rather ingenious form of self-preservation for the news writers of the day; for, if the whole story could be summed up in the first sentence, no grumpy deskman could complain that one point or another had been missed. When the opposition newspaper came up with a different banner headline, the news writer could point smugly to his own atrocity of a lead and remark to his desk: "Well, I had that point in the lead. We could have featured it, too, if it hadn't been for our dumb copy desk." This was the real reason for the traditional leads that featured the 5 W's—*who, when, where, what, why*—with *how* as an added starter.

Today lead sentences rarely exceed 20 or 25 words, and some are shorter. This is not merely a matter of word-counting; after all, a short sentence can mix up a reader faster than a long one. The disposition of editors today is to insist, wherever possible, on one idea to a lead sentence —and to the rest of the story as it applies. Sometimes the important factor may be the *who*, or the *why*, but it is seldom if ever that modern writers cram all the 5 W's into the first sentence. If the story is short, they do not even try to cover all the 5 W's in their space limit.

Consequently, deskmen and writers now must decide which idea is worth featuring. They can no longer run clauses together like beads on a string. They must make up their minds and exercise a decent amount of news judgment. That has been a welcome development. It has marked the beginning of a change in old habits of news writing that flouted the first principles of seeking and keeping public attention.

PROBLEMS OF MASS COMMUNICATION

Language is as old as man. "Nothing," says the *Columbia Encyclopedia*, "is known of its origin but its existence reaches back so far into the dawn of human life that the estimated 6,500 years that writing has been in use are trifling by comparison. Next to North Chinese, English is the most widely used language of the 1,000 or more speech communities that exist in the world."

Yet, the first of the recognized line of English dictionaries was Nathan Bailey's in 1721.

Much of the pioneering work in language study to advance the efficiency of communication was done by Professor Edward Lee Thorndike, the educational psychologist, at Teachers College, Columbia University. From Thorndike and his associates, who counted nearly 20 million words in a wide range of English literature, have come accurate determinations of the frequency of use of thousands of words. This demonstration gave a firm basis to the notion that effective written language should contain a high proportion of words that are familiar to the average reader.

The English Language Consider the size of the English language, which most authorities now estimate at more than 600,000 words. Out of these, as has been demonstrated by Professor Edgar Dale and Mrs. Jeanne S. Chall, at Ohio State University, some 3,000 words are familiar to fourth-graders and presumably to the average reader as well. In fact, a quarter of written English is generally believed to be composed of ten words—*the, a, and, to, of, in, I, it, is,* and *that.*

There are about 850 words that form what we know as basic English —basic because they are four out of every five words we use. Thorndike's research showed that 10,000 words make up some 98 per cent of written English. Teachers often require a vocabulary of 30,000 words.

Between the 10,000–30,000-word range, therefore, lies the bulk of any writer's vocabulary. At the lower range is the average man's understanding of English words. It is obvious that above this point reader recognition tends to shrink rapidly.

Dr. Rudolph Flesch, in *The AP Writing Handbook*, gave this advice to the wire service's writers:

> Don't use words that are not generally used in everyday conversation, if you can help it. Remember, the AP isn't in the business of increasing people's vocabulary. If you *have* to use a word that *may be* unfamiliar to an ordinary reader, explain it. Follow the example of the reporter who explained that tularemia is rabbit fever. In particular, be sure to explain geographical terms for readers who live at a distance.

What Do They Understand? It is easy to conclude that a writer can avoid trouble with an audience by using short words and shunning the polysyllabic words. It is not quite that simple, however.

The word *peace* is on the Dale-Chall list of words intelligible to fourth-graders. But what is peace? Try to define it. The author belongs to a seminar of professors of various graduate schools at Columbia University. For four years, on and off, the seminar members tried to arrive at a definition of peace that would please all. Finally, with a great deal of reluctance, the following was agreed on: "Peace is the absence of war."

Many simple words have widely varying meanings. By *democracy*, most Americans think of a state in which government protects individual freedoms; but Russians, who also lay claim to democracy, consider it to be a system that places the state's interest above all individual rights.

The word, *table* has many meanings. To cite only one source of conflict, it conveys a diametrically opposite meaning when used as a verb in the United States and at the United Nations. In the United States, to table a resolution means to drop it, shelve it, pigeonhole it, prevent action on it. But at the United Nations, when a diplomat introduces a resolution, he speaks of tabling it—presenting it, asking for a vote on it, putting it on the table.

Just as these relatively simple words like *peace, democracy*, and *table* can cause confusion, even proper nouns can arouse a wide variety of meanings. Take New York City. To most citizens who live in it, New York is the greatest city in the world. To many out-of-towners who feel they are pushed around in New York, it is a terrifying experience. To use a historic out-of-town phrase about New York, "I wouldn't live in that place if you gave it to me."

Nor do words have fixed meanings. Yesterday, "creep" was a description of movement and "square" was a geometrical form. Today "creep" means an objectionable person and "square" is a name for the hopelessly conventional.

It is not sufficient, therefore, to use words that are on somebody's list for reading comprehension. Whether they are short or long, they must be easily understood within the context of the experience of their readers.

The right words, used in the wrong place, can often lead ot strange results. When Warren Austin was the United States Ambassador to the United Nations, he astounded the Security Council during a debate over Palestine by pleading with Jewish and Moslem spokesmen: "Let us approach this in the Christian spirit."

Word images can also change with incredible swiftness. Not so long ago, *school* summoned up a familiar image of students and teachers. But with the coming of the integration crisis in the South, the word image summoned up by *school* became a symbol of a southern way of life in Mississippi, a symbol of law and order in Washington, D. C., and a symbol of utter confusion to observers of American life from overseas.

It is not enough, therefore, to communicate in patterns of familiar words. They must be words that also convey the same understanding to both readers and writers.

Tired Words   It has been fashionable, for as long as there has been instruction in writing, to warn against the use of tired words. The cliché, the word or expression that has been used so often that it is hackneyed, has been made as obnoxious as a snake at a picnic.

These are some of the trite expressions that have been rightly condemned:

Along these lines	A goodly number
Meets the eye	Budding genius
A long-felt want	At one fell swoop
Sadder but wiser	Method in his madness
Launched into eternity	Busy as a bee
Last but not least	Cool as a cucumber
Green with envy	Blushing bride
With bated breath	Wild and woolly
Fair maidens	Dull thud
The great beyond	White as a sheet

Dr. Bergen Evans, writing in *The New York Times*,[2] once presented the following as an example of cliché-stuffed writing. It was a description of an audience reacting to a political orator.

> They know they are in the presence of a man who gets down to brass tacks, hits the nail on the head, and doesn't beat around the bush; a man who means business, who is fully aware that although we have entered the atomic age, we have not relinquished the faith of our fathers, and who believes that although we cannot rest upon our laurels we must not rush in where angels fear to tread. Such a speaker is a man after our own hearts. He has his feet on the ground. He knows the score.

To encourage the timid writer, who freezes at the typewriter for fear of writing something trite or awkward, Dr. Evans also added this necessary clarification:

> If the phrase is sincerely meant, spoken deliberately with a full awareness of its exact meaning and its shopworn state, or gaily borrowed in ridicule, it is not a cliché, no matter how often it has been spoken. It is a cliché only when it comes without meaning, though often with a most pompous pretense of meaning, from an unmeaning mind.

The point is worth stressing. Nobody advocates piling one tired word on another or stringing out dreary, shopworn phrases in a news story. But where a word or phrase transmits the exact meaning that a writer wants to convey, it is no longer a hackneyed expression but a useful symbol of understanding.

Gobbledygook   The sonorous, long-winded, and sometimes meaningless phrases so often found in government reports are another threat to clear

---

[2] "Fell Swoop on a Fine Cliché Kettle," by Bergen Evans, *The New York Times Magazine*, July 27, 1958, pp. 13–16.

writing in the presentation of news. Such language deserves the coined name of *gobbledygook*. A horrible example occurred in New York City during World War II when the city was plastered with signs to encourage conserving electricity:

"It is required to extinguish the illumination."

The meaning was: "Turn out the lights."

George Orwell, the author of *1984*, produced another amusing example of gobbledygook:

"Success or failure in competitive activities exhibits no tendency to be commensurate with innate capacity."

Translated, this meant:

"The race is not always to the swift, nor the battle to the strong."

Professor Willard Thorp, writing in the Princeton *University*, called this type of writing "No English." He attributed it primarily to the influence of officialese, of "hot-rod" advertising language, and of second-rate newspaper style. This was an example he gave of "No English":

> A teen-ager dropped into my office today, much worried about his inferiority complex and anxious to adjust. He seemed to think I was a sincere-type professor and had some know-how in inter-personal relations. He said there was a campus-inspired rumor that I am good at human engineering and so thought he'd contact me and get a few constructive angles. First I tried to fit him into some frame of reference and then I processed him by screening him with some questions, and so got the over-all picture. (I discovered, by the way, that his mother is a low-grade homemaker.) I then briefed him on the need for grasping our most unique set-up here and seeing how we are geared for modern living. Next I made him the proposition that he be less negative, more relaxed, and mix with a few of the outstanding youth at the top-flight level of our student body. He would be sure, I said, to find them like-minded percentagewise. When we finished off, he thanked me for our little stream-lined get-together.[3]

Professor Thorp commented on his parable:

> Some of the offensive expressions are hand-me-downs from pseudo-scientific writings; some derive from the writing of sociologists and psychologists; some emanate from the sales-conference and the business convention. Several reveal the codified anxieties of modern life, while others are the slogans of "positive thinking" which are supposed to cure these anxieties.

In any case, it is an example of gobbledygook. It should not defile the clarity of news writing.

---

[3] "The Well of English, Now Defiled, or Why Johnny Can't Write," by Williard Thorp. *University*, Princeton University Quarterly, Spring, 1959.

The Jargon of Journalism   For the millions of Americans who are interested in the news, the writer is bound to make a special effort to guard against the jargon of journalism. It can wither the freshest news. It can make certain types of stories sound alike regardless of how or when they occur.

Thus, during the Christmas holidays, crowds in growing America invariably set new records as they flock from the city to their family hearths. Heat waves almost automatically begin July 1 and cold waves December 1 in the more temperate parts of the country. On summer weekends, along both coasts, thousands rush to the seashore.

When opposing politicians meet, it is often a showdown. In the United Nations, of course, this is either a crisis or a deadlock. When representatives of the United States and the Soviet Union meet at a conference table, they usually clash. On election day the voters invariably troop to the polls under (check one: cloudy, rainy, snowy, fair) skies. Investigations are either quizzes or probes. When someone is criticized, he is flayed. If he is merely questioned, he is grilled. If he says nothing, he is likely to be termed defiant. If the police seek a suspect in connection with a crime, they throw out a dragnet. When they arrest him, he is seized—or jailed. If they do not have a clue or are too lazy to find one, mystery surrounds the case.

A ship that has a mishap too often limps into port, which would be quite a performance if it ever happened. When there is a collision of automobiles, trains, planes, or ships, it is a crash. And, of course, if more deaths occur, the death toll mounts as the probe begins. When royalty visit an American community, they never fail to reign over the city today.

Perhaps the worst offender in this department is the sports page. Walter Wellesley (Red) Smith, the sports columnist, once presented the following mythical interview between a sports editor and an applicant for a baseball writer's job:

> *Q*. What is a baseball? *A*. The national pastime.
> *Q*. Good, very good. Now what is the game played with? *A*. The horsehide and ash.
> *Q*. Excellent. And what else? *A*. The sphere, hassocks . . .
> *Q*. Yes, yes. I see you have the idea. And what is the game played on? *A*. It is played on the velvety sward.
> *Q*. What does the rookie run like? *A*. A deer.
> *Q*. What has he for an arm? *A*. A rifle.
> *Q*. Describe the man who has played baseball for five years. *A*. An old pro with know-how.

There was a lot more of this, but it amounted to the same thing. It was the sports equivalent of the amateur writer who uses Jupe Pluvius, Old Sol, and John Q. Public in a weather story, Dame Rumor in political speculation, Dame Fashion on the women's page, and Grand Dame in the society news.

Gustave Flaubert stated the case well when he wrote in *Madame Bovary*: "Human language is like a cracked kettle on which we beat out tunes for bears to dance to, when all the time we are longing to move the stars to pity."

Few writers can be original as often as they would like.

On a deadline, it sometimes happens that leads are written in journalese just as architects resort to blueprints. The long-used word symbols convey meaning to writers, editors, and readers alike.

When there is time and less pressure, however, no news medium is justified in permitting a cluster of tired words and phrases and journalistic jargon to convey its meaning. It is often just as easy to give the reader a simple, clear story of what happened. It is also refreshing.

READABILITY

There are four principal reasons why communication by newspaper is more difficult than other methods of transmitting information, opinions, and ideas. These are, briefly:

1. The newspaper reader is seldom able to give his undivided attention to his paper. At home, there are likely to be constant interruptions in the course of normal family life. On the various forms of transportation, the reader may be physically cramped and uncomfortable. At the office, newspaper reading is done in snatches if at all.

2. Unless makeup is intelligently handled, the newspaper format with its narrow columns and relatively small type is scarcely ideal for reading. Except for tabloids, the turning of pages is likely to be a problem for the traveler; at home, the split sections are always causing a wrangle in families.

3. Hasty and poorly organized newspaper writing also complicates the communication process. Long, wandering sentences; unfamiliar words, irritating gaps in background and explanatory matter all place a strain on the reader's attentiveness.

4. The vast range of newspaper material in itself brings about a scattering of attention, unless the editing and makeup processes are designed to focus reader attention on the principal news articles or pictures on a page. Even so, unless the beginnings of stories are crisp, clear, and interesting, readers will skim the headlines at the average rate of about a minute to a page, the front page excepted.

These factors have led to a considerable study of newspaper format, presentation, and writing. Nothing, of course, can be done about the conditions under which newspapers are read. Experts in printing, photography, and typography as a rule carry out the many experiments in manufacturing a better product. It remains for editorial men, sociologists, psychologists, and others to work on the task of making newspaper copy more readable.

Is the Medium the Message? "In a culture like ours, long accustomed to splitting and dividing all things as a means of control," writes Marshall McLuhan, "it is sometimes a bit of a shock to be reminded that, in operational and practical fact, the medium is the message. This is merely to say that the personal and social consequences of any medium—that is, of any extension of ourselves—result from the new scale that is introduced into our affairs by each extension of ourselves, or by any new technology."

McLuhan proceeds, on this basis, to describe television as the all-embracing medium of the electronic age, a powerful visual attraction that totally engages the senses with an instant appeal. He sees the press as a far slower medium of communication, dependent on a linear use of the printed word, entirely divorced from the variety of pitch and tone of the spoken, or even the handwritten, word.[4] Without arguing the basis of McLuhanism, which postulates that the form of the medium is more important than its content, it is evident that he has posed the contrast between print and electronic communication in a dramatic way.

Certainly, the gap between the appeal of television and the appeal of the newspaper is not going to be closed by a readability formula. If readers choose to turn themselves into viewers, no formula is going to persuade them to go back to the printed page. Consequently, the answer to the newspaper's attention-getting problem does not lie in word-counting, syllable-counting and sentence-counting. If the medium by some chance turns out to be even half of the message, then it is obvious that the art and the skill of the writer become all-important to the newspaper and the news magazine.

What it all comes down to is the same first rule that Ernest Hemingway learned on the Kansas City *Star*—short sentences, short paragraphs, be positive, not negative. This is in no sense any discredit to the work that has been done for the Associated Press by Dr. Rudolph Flesch, for United Press International by Robert Gunning, and for a number of other news organizations and newspapers by similarly qualified persons. On the contrary, the work has been valuable because it has emphasized, as never before, the first principles of journalism.

For those who have followed the Flesch, Gunning, and other readability formulas as recipes for success in writing, there has, of course, been disappointment. As Dr. Flesch pointed out long ago to the AP's staff:

> Readability doesn't mean blindly following a formula. It means trying to write every story so that the average newspaper reader will read, understand and remember it.

---

[4] Marshall McLuhan, *Understanding Media: The Extensions of Man.* New York: 1966, pp. 7, 206.

Learn to Write There is no easy way to learn to write, as readability students will be the first to agree. A writer must keep everlastingly at it. He has to make mistakes, correct them, redo his work. He has to read, to see how other writers obtain their effects.

Unless he does this, he will never do very well as a writer and will wonder why. Writing never gets done unless it is made an essential part of the day's work. No matter how much Eugene O'Neill drank at certain periods of his life, he was always setting words on paper regularly. The same is true of every writer, including those of newspapers, who develop professional competence.

There are very few like Douglas Southall Freeman, the Virginia editor, who worked on a minute-to-minute schedule as editor, lecturer, teacher, and writer.

Writing habits are important. Talent is important. Knowledge of the reader is important. Knowledge of language is important. But nothing is quite as important as everlastingly sticking at it. This is the only writing formula that really works.

A Message The principal criticism of the readability studies has been that there is no conceivable way of measuring the thought content of a word, sentence, article, book, or newspaper. And this is the crucial problem in writing—to create understanding through the communication of thought.

The difference between *The Ladies' Home Journal* and Thoreau, for example, is not in the length of their sentences or the number of syllables in their words, but in what they have to say and how well they say it.

Walt Whitman wrote:

> I celebrate myself, and sing myself,
> And what I assume you shall assume,
> For every atom belonging to me as good belongs to you. . . .

Highly personal, nothing to worry about in the "Reading Ease" departments, but "Song of Myself" requires something more than a casual glancing through.

Or consider the "Reading Ease" of Lewis Carroll:

> 'Twas brillig and the slithy toves
> Did gyre and gimble in the wabe
> All mimsy were the borogroves,
> And the mome raths outgrabe. . . .

All things considered, the King of Hearts in *Alice in Wonderland* was something of a readability expert, too. He said this was the way to tell a story:

"Begin at the beginning, and go on until you come to the end, then stop."

Try to improve on that.

Watch These Things!

The urge to tell a good story is a familiar human trait. Every writer likes to make his material inviting for the reader, the listener, or the viewer.

Sometimes, unhappily, a story is too good. The pressure for a sharp lead, a bright phrase, or a good quote is too great. The writer cracks. He strains for effect, falls into distortions and worse.

The following discussion lists some of the ways in which a writer can safeguard his work from such perils and at the same time produce an interesting story.

ATTITUDES

The writer in all forms of journalism must be cool, detached, even skeptical as he approaches his material. He has a set of facts, which he either has gathered himself or received from other sources. Depending on the importance of the facts, he may have some instructions on how to handle them. In a straight news story, his job is to select the single most important fact and work it into a lead, which may be one sentence or several sentences— or even several paragraphs. Next, in the body of the story he must document that lead. Throughout he must remember to use relatively short, simple sentences arranged in brief paragraphs; familiar words, precisely used; and a colorful variety of effective language. And, the whole piece must be short.

Such a task as this, assuming it is to be completed within a few minutes, calls for a high degree of skill in organization, use of language, and dexterity on the typewriter. There is no time or place for histrionics, displays of temperament, excitement, or loud talk. Everything depends on the ability of a writer to concentrate and to do his work efficiently.

It takes a certain amount of enthusiasm, of course, even to attempt to do a job like this. If enthusiasm is not carefully controlled, even repressed, disaster can result, for enthusiasm is a heady brew that often overwhelms native caution and even ordinary good sense. The Chicago *Tribune* came out with an extra on election night, 1948, that proclaimed Thomas E. Dewey to be President of the United States. *The New York Times* published an early edition report on election night, 1954, that Averell Harriman had been elected Governor of New York by an overwhelming plurality when it later developed that his winning margin was only 11,000 votes. And the wrong man has sometimes been elected on TV.

This can happen to anybody who writes for the news media. There is nothing devious or sinister about it. Even at the highest levels of journalism miscalculations occur because of overconfidence or misplaced enthusiasm, sometimes both. It is obvious that there are many more such chances for that kind of thing at lower levels—which is one reason why enthusiasm for anything is a quality that is likely to be suspect in the average newsroom. If uncontrolled, it has a tendency to warp the soundest judgment. A calm, questioning attitude is safer.

ATTRIBUTION

Every news story, whether large or small, should have a source. Preferably the source should be identified fully. Whether it can be identified or not, the public must be given some indication of the origin of the information and the relative worth of the source.

The best attribution is to name the source. The next best is the name of the organization, office, or group represented by the source as spokesman. The least satisfactory, but sometimes the most necessary, is some variation of the phrase, "informed source," if the origin of the news must be held in confidence. Only columnists, commentators, and similarly privileged characters are entitled to use themselves as the authority for the correctness of their news, and withhold all mention of sources. Such a privilege does not extend to the ordinary news writer.

The insistence on sources causes inexperienced writers to clutter up their leads for newspaper and wire services. Titles or names of news sources, locations of news conferences, and other necessary but not consequential details need not always go into leads. Such subsidiary information may be tucked into succeeding paragraphs. This is an illustration of cluttered source material in a lead:

> Dr. John D. Kelleher, a top-ranking Defense Department scientist, said today at a City Hall news conference that a multimillion-dollar launching site for a Titan intercontinental ballistics missile would be constructed at Alta Park, twenty miles south of the city limits.

The only essential material for the first sentence is:

> A multimillion-dollar launching site for intercontinental ballistics missiles will be built twenty miles south of this city, a Defense Department spokesman said today.

All the other facts in the over-long first sentence listed above can be reported elsewhere in the story to the full satisfaction of the reader. The caution against the use of excessively long titles, names of persons who cannot easily be identified in a community, and other details should be observed in beginning most news stories. When a President, governor, mayor, or some other widely known personality makes news, however, it is essential to begin with name and title.

For radio and TV, the source is usually indicated at the beginning of the sentence but the anticluttering rule still holds despite that.

CHECKING COPY

Several safeguards are generally used in copy that passes between various editions. They are eliminated before the story is set in type, taped, or put in a script for a news program.

Names When there is a new and strange name in the news, several methods are used to call attention to it in handling stories. The name may be repeated and placed in brackets. The bracketed letters (CQ) or (OK) may be inserted after the name to show that the reporter or rewrite man has checked it for accuracy. A simple pencil check mark may be made above the name, or a rectangle may be drawn around it to assure the desk that it is correct. All these attention-calling devices must be eliminated before the story is used.

When a name is difficult but well known, such as Indira Gandhi, it should be assumed that the deskmen will catch an error in it. But when U Thant became secretary-general of the United Nations, or when Gamal Abdel Nasser emerged as an Egyptian leader, their names were new to editors and precautions had to be taken to be certain that they were spelled correctly.

Figures   The use of figures in the news always entails risks and much checking, but that is no excuse for not using them. For reasons of style, figures are never used to begin a sentence but are spelled out instead. This is one way of being certain that a figure is correctly used.

Another is to repeat a key figure in brackets, if it is being sent by telegraph, cable, or radio rather than written in the office. Still another familiar safeguard is to use the letter (M) after a figure in the millions and the letter (B) after a figure in the billions. The surest way of all to be certain that figures are correct is to go over the story with great care before it is handed in.

CLAIMING CREDIT

With reduced competition among newspapers, the somewhat repulsive practice of claiming credit for every small news development has abated in the press but it is growing in broadcast journalism.

The phrase, "It was learned today," when connected to a newspaper lead, was a modest way of claiming credit for an exclusive break in the news. As long as the breaks were big enough to justify the use of the claim, nobody really objected. Many competing newspapers, however, used the refrain so often, and on so many nonessential angles of the news, that it became discredited to a large extent within the profession. TV, however, will even credit a correspondent with asking a question at a news conference.

Actually there are not too many real exclusives today. A lot of the competitive heat has gone out of newspaper work. The sources of the news also make things difficult by controlling the breaks with more care than they did two or three decades ago. Therefore, when a story is really big and really exclusive, it advertises itself and there is no actual need for the extensive claiming of credit. Now and then one still sees a lead advertising that "The *Evening Gazette* learned exclusively today" of some news development, but many editors think the practice is too flamboyant. TV has yet to learn the lesson.

The writing of news suffers also from overstatement through the use of such credit-claiming verbs as "disclosed" or "revealed." If there is a real disclosure or a real revelation, the use of such verbs is, of course, justified. But it arouses merriment even among less sophisticated readers for a reporter to write, with ponderous solemnity, that the United States Weather Bureau "revealed" tomorrow's weather would be fair and warm.

The lead that points out "revelations" and "disclosures" which are the product of routine reporting belongs with the rest of the trappings of gaslight journalism. It should remain in the files of newspaper morgues.

TIMING

The timing of important meetings creates special problems for newspaper reporters and rewrite men. Unlike broadcast news, the news written for a newspaper may not be read for hours later by the public.

News as It Happens   No newspaper editor wants his paper announcing a parade will begin during the afternoon when he knows that precise edition will be sold along the line of march. But he also cannot authorize a story saying that the parade is under way until he is certain of his facts.

Editors and writers face similar dilemmas in handling political rallies, sessions of Congress, legislatures, or city councils, political speeches, court hearings, and other events that may be in progress during the paper's hours of publication. For those who insist on merely past-tensing the story and running it without waiting for confirmation, a reminder should be given of the many events that have been cancelled at the last minute and of instances in which leading characters in the news failed to perform as scheduled. It is no answer at all to "date the paper" by using the future tense to describe an event that already has happened by the time the edition arrives on the scene.

In order to be accurate and still not make the paper seem too old, writers generally get around the problem by omitting the actual time of a current event (except on wire services) and using such leads as follows:

> The Legislature was summoned today to act on Governor Moore's budget proposals.

> The Republican State Convention was set to open today with Marvin McAllister as the leading contender for the gubernatorial nomination.

> United Nations delegates assembled today for a vote in the Political Committee on United States plans for limiting atomic armaments.

> A 21-year-old clerk was held for arraignment today as a suspect in the murder of his 23-year-old sweetheart.

> The sidewalks of New York blossomed with green today as 50,000 marchers lined up for their St. Patrick's Day parade along beflagged Fifth Ave.

Starting the Action   This technique is known as getting the action under way. It is used so that, even if the paper is picked up hours after the event is over, the reader will not be so painfully aware that he is perusing very old news. What the writer has done is to use something that actually did happen, but preceded the action on which his story is based. Thus, the legislature was summoned before it actually met, the delegates were ready for their convention, the UN diplomats assembled preceding the opening of their meeting, the clerk was held preceding his arraignment, and the marchers lined up before the parade began.

In no case, it may be observed, does the lead say that the event in question actually began. The technique is to anticipate what is about to happen by writing a "squinting" lead. To accompany such anticipatory leads the body of the story should make it clear that the main event is just developing. In the case of the United Nations story, or any other having to do with a deliberative body, this could be written as follows:

> Before the delegates went into session, the U. S. Mission appeared hopeful that its resolution would be approved. The Americans counted on the assistance of the British to help lead the fight against Soviet opposition.

A less skilled writer can always say in a lead, in such cases, that something is "scheduled" or "expected" to happen, but only an amateur writes that something "was to" happen. The "was to" lead has few defenders in professional journalism.

The Present Tense   Most broadcast news is written in the present tense. Newspapers also resort to the present and future tenses to try to bridge the gap between events at the hour of publication and the necessary time lapse in getting out the edition. These are samples of a useful if awkward device for the harried reporter or rewrite man:

> A Congressional committee convenes today to investigate the nation's $70,000,000,000 defense program.

> The United Naitons meets today on the crisis in the Middle East, with the United States demanding a cease fire.

> The New York Yankees and the Washington Senators open the baseball season today.

When Did It Happen?   For a quite different reason, newspapers generally dislike stories that specify something happened "this morning" or "this afternoon" for afternoon publications, and "yesterday morning" or "yesterday afternoon" for morning publications in undated leads. The terms are imprecise. Editors prefer the simple use of "today" or "yesterday" with the exact time specified in the body of the story if it is needed.

Afternoon papers usually describe anything that happened in the early hours of the morning, from 12:01 A.M. on, as "early today" or "before dawn today." They refer to the late afternoon or early evening in leads as "late today." There are no such niceties in morning paper practice because AM reporters and rewrite men are not pressed to bridge the gap very often.

DATELINES

Newspapers generally do not dateline news of the community in which they are published. They also drop datelines from a given area surrounding the community, the radius being anywhere from 25 to 50 miles, depending on the city and the paper. In addition, datelines are omitted from such general stories as storms, holidays, elections, and similar material. When datelines are used, they should be written as a part of the lead, beginning exactly where news accounts normally would start on the page, with the text of the lead following them without a break. The wire services and many newspapers use only the place name and not the date in the dateline, since the paper itself carries the date.

DISTORTION

In an effort to attain a striking effect, inexperienced writers sometimes resort to allusions of a literary nature, epigrams, parodies of popular songs or sayings, and similar bits of chicanery to brighten up a story. This kind of thing is not for amateurs. It is difficult enough for a professional to do well.

Now and then, a piece of this kind will come off, but it is seldom worth the trouble it causes a writer to dream up such a synthetic approach to the news. If the story is good enough, it does not need this type of tinsel. If it is not, perhaps it should not be used.

An Artificial Effect   In any case, the risk of distorting a story by such devices is the best argument against wasting time and news space to seek an artificial effect. Even feature material and other types of soft news generally are not improved by freaks and tricks unless they are witty and original. These are qualities that are hard to come by in journalism.

The twisting of substance is not the only source of possible distortion. Sometimes writers begin stories with top-heavy clauses because they are tired of writing simple declarative sentences. Even editors fall prey to the lure of change for change's sake. There was once a city editor in New York who refused to let his writers begin any story with an article or a noun, common or proper. Naturally, the unhappy writers began spraying the journalistic landscape with participial phrases and clauses which inevitably tended to overdramatize the news. The epidemic did not last long, but while it raged, it damaged the self-esteem of several score reporters and writers and probably caused a certain amount of head-shaking among several hundred thousand readers.

Unnatural Prose   The warning to avoid unnatural prose may be illustrated by the following type of nuisance lead:

Quit.
That's what Housing Commissioner Ringwood did today.

It is a ridiculous way of writing news or anything else. A simple statement that Commissioner Ringwood resigned is shorter and more pointed. It takes more than a trick approach in a lead to startle today's reader of news.

James Thurber is credited with having written the ultimate in ridiculous leads when he turned out the following as a young reporter in somewhat mild protest against unnatural news writing:

Dead.
That's what Joe Schmaltz was today after he fell down a manhole.

EDITORIALIZING

Despite the new-found freedom to background and interpret certain types of news, no writer deliberately injects his own point of view in a story unless he is authorized to do so. The principle of separating the news from editorial opinion is fully supported in every responsible area of American journalism, even though there is no general agreement on where one ends and the other begins. The intent, at least, is clear. Putting it into practice becomes a matter for empirical treatment.

Personal Pronouns   In an era when TV creates news personalities, there is a tendency to revive personal journalism. Although the pronouns "I" and "we" are beginning to creep back into the copy of reporters who write eyewitness accounts of big news, they still are forbidden to most writers for newspapers. For that matter, the editorial "we" is still taboo except on the least sophisticated small-town papers.

Inadvertent Comment   Sometimes editorial comment is inadvertent, particularly in stories by inexperienced writers. Few journalists of experience would attempt to thrust their own point of view into a story. For one thing, they know it will be taken out. For another, it is the worst sin that can be committed in the writing of straight news next to inaccuracy.

Inadvertent editorial comment takes different forms. A New York city editor likes to tell how he picked up a piece of copy by a beginner who was writing about an "elderly" man. He called the neophyte to his desk.

"Young man, how old is elderly? Let's get it in the story."

"Why, the man in the story is fifty years old."

"I am fifty years old," the city editor said sternly, "and I do not consider that I am elderly. Merely give the man's age and do not characterize him as old. Let's have no more editorialization in copy."

Loaded Words   The news writer who uses superlatives is likely to be caught in the vice of editorializing by picking up a loaded word.

Most of these phrases are developed by public relations specialists who like to try to influence people subtly through the news columns. Thus, such concepts as "socialized medicine" should be quoted and attributed to a source if they are used to describe government-sponsored health insurance. The same is true of a campaign slogan such as the "right-to-work" proposals, which generally oppose both labor's closed and union shops. Editors may even be disturbed by a seemingly innocent phrase such as "honoring a picket line." It would be less partial to report that a picket line either was crossed or not crossed.

There are many loaded words, the use of which tends to prejudice the public in one way or another. It is the responsibility of the writer to avoid using them.

ELEGANT VARIATION

H. W. Fowler's stricture against the literary crime known as elegant variation has been used, in some instances, to justify monotonous writing.

For instance, in wire service copy it is often observable that the expression, "He said," is used in almost every sentence in some stories. The justification is that "said" is the perfect word and, given the stricture against elegant variation, there is no reason why "said" should not be used over and over again. The practice has now spread. Few reporters will bother to strain for the exact shade of meaning to describe how a man spoke as long as he knows in advance that the desk will eliminate it.

The result has been unfortunate, on the whole. It takes a Hemingway to handle the beauty and rhythm of English in such a way that the use of such expressions as "he said" or "she said" in every sentence makes good reading. Nobody, and certainly not I, would call a banana an "elongated yellow fruit" or describe a brunette as a "maiden with raven tresses." That constitutes prima facie evidence of elegant variation. The protest here is against lazy reporting.

Stories of speeches and press conferences are often lifeless. Some of them are mere stenographic records of what happened. If reporters were encouraged to try to define exactly the manner and circumstances of an oral statement, a little of the dullness of speech reporting might be dissipated. In place of a too rigid observance of the elegant variation precaution, there is perhaps some need for a common sense variation to try to find the exact word. "He said," after all, is only one form of statement and is bound to be used more than others. A man also may have insisted, recalled, protested, admitted, conceded, declared, murmured, rasped, shouted, or even thundered. Those who write "said-said-said" are safe from ridicule. They do not, however, contribute to the fine art of making the news interesting.

GOOD TASTE

No decent journalist intentionally harms persons in the news. Nor do responsible news organizations attempt to profit through morbid public interest in disgusting news involving sexual matters.

Not all copy intended for the columns of the *American Medical Journal* and similar publications finds its place in the news media. The media also are not, and by their very nature cannot be, prudish where the public health or the public interest is at stake. It is one thing to publicize necessary information on venereal disease, for instance, and quite another to use material on abnormal sexual practices. Between the guidelines of the public interest and good taste the news media try to maintain a decent and helpful course of conduct toward the community.

The rule of good taste also must be followed in making reports based on strong language in public affairs. Usually it is unnecessary to use profanity or blasphemy merely as a matter of straight reporting. The fact that someone said it is not sufficient excuse to repeat it. But if the President of the United States uses profanity, of course, the particular word is at least indicated to the public. Then profanity becomes news, and there is a sound excuse for violating the canons of good taste.

There are, of course, laws in many states that protect juvenile offenders and relief clients from undue publicity, but the news media have their own unwritten rules of conduct as well. They vary widely. Underlying them all is the assumption that a news organization which is to win and hold the respect of the community must observe the ordinary courtesies and practices that show good taste.

For many years dialect stories have not been used in responsible newspapers, and dialect itself has been edited out of reports of conversations where there was no real need for it. The dialect story no longer is particularly funny.

Persons who figure in the news, in most parts of the country, are no longer identified by race, color, or nationality unless there is some point to it. Stories that poke fun at crippled persons or embarrass women, stories that make difficult reading or listening in the home in front of children, and sexy pictures of an extreme nature are used only by the most frivolous of the news media.

However, it should not be assumed that efforts to maintain a high standard of journalism in the matter of taste constitute a kind of blue-nosed self-censorship. That is very far from being the case. A good news program or newspaper can be just as lively as a bad one.

HARD WORDS

Every writer knows that some words automatically characterize a news story.

First   One of the most overused is the word *first*. If something is done for the first time, supposedly that is news. Too often, routine events are overly dramatized by the use of such a headline word, often with threadbare justification. The first man on the moon is news, but the first in line at the opening of a new grocery store can scarcely be in the same category.

The same is true of the headline word *last*. It is used too often and with too little reason.

Largest   The largest crowd in some place's history, the lowest temperature on record in another place, the smallest person in a third, the largest in a fourth, the oldest settler, the closest football game, the prettiest girl, the cutest baby—all these superlatives are supposed to be the automatic signal for a story. And by and large, they are for some news organizations although the public is satiated by such mummery by now.

The trouble is that the theory of unique occurrence has been used so often and for so many years that the public is likely to be bored with it unless the claims made are amply justified.

In the reporting of speeches, the public has been cudgeled with appeals, demands, assurances, and proposals until it seems as if no fresh approach is possible on stories of this kind. The old, frayed headline words ought to be examined with care before being worn again to dress up a very tired old story. They are just about worn out.

"MISTER"

Many newspapers refuse to "mister" anybody except the President of the United States. That goes for the wire services and broadcast media as well. In this manner they escape the problem of whom to address as Mister and whom to call just plain Jones or Smith. Some newspapers use Mr. with the names of all men in the news columns (but not sports) except for criminals. In some cases the Mr. is used until men have been convicted of a crime.

The style for the use of Mr. always creates problems. Generally stated, most American newspapers do not use Mr. with the full name of a man except on the society page. But after introducing him in the news columns by his full name (Thomas J. Hamilton), he is referred to as Mr. (Mr. Hamilton) whenever further mention is made of him.

NEGATIVE NEWS

Editors, as a rule, dislike stories that denote lack of action in a developing situation. This is the source of the frequent admonition to news writers to be "positive, not negative." There is a lot more to this than merely refraining from using the word "not" in a lead. That is often an entirely academic matter in all the news media.

What Is Negative News? The substance of the prejudice against so-called negative news is not in the wording, but in the assertion in a lead that nothing is happening. When a bride halts outside the church and says she is not going to be married, that is the most positive kind of news—particularly for the bridegroom. When a President of the United States announces he will not run for re-election, the only thing negative about such news is his intention. But when a writer notes that strike talks "marked time today," or diplomatic reactions "were awaited today," or a political convention "continued today," he is merely saying that nothing has happened.

For better or worse, the editorial feeling against negative substance in leads has been translated into certain basic procedures as well. Some of these are merely a play on words and mean very little, except that they gratify an editorial whim. Others convey a positive meaning by dropping negative terms.

Changing Negative Leads Here are examples of news stories that have been given drama and force by changing from a negative to a positive approach:

> Negative. Police Commissioner Hamilton said today that he would not adopt Mayor Riddle's plan of shaking up the police force.
> Positive. Police Commissioner Hamilton today rejected Mayor Riddle's demand for a police shakeup.

The negative approach in the following example deadens the essential conflict in the story. The positive translation makes the news vital by placing it in proper perspective. The positive lead also is shorter.

Negative.   There was no chance left today that the Warrington Woolen Mills would remain in this city instead of moving to the South.
Positive.   The Warrington Woolen Mills, a major source of local income, moved South today.

Here, the news is actually concealed in the negative lead which casts a positive action in negative, second-day form. The positive approach makes the news mean something, as the added clarifying phrase indicates. Again, tightening the lead makes it crisper and shorter.

Negative.   Not much of a crowd assembled in Times Square last night to welcome the New Year, due to television.
Positive.   New Yorkers abandoned their traditional New Year's Eve celebration in Times Square last night. They watched TV instead.

The point is made in these contrasting leads that the failure of crowds to appear in Times Square meant an interruption in a famous custom. In the negative lead no one strange to the ways of New Yorkers would have realized the significance of the news. The positive lead set the account straight.

Emphasizing Negatives   There is another reason why editors shudder over negative leads. In criminal cases, where the news is that someone has been found not guilty, journalists sometimes contract severe cases of nerves over using the story in precisely that form. If a verdict has been sent overhead (by telegraph) or put on the teletype, the strain increases. There is always a fear that the "not" might be dropped out of the lead by a careless operator or printer—or even a careless rewrite man. It has happened.

To safeguard the handling of such news, many news organizations have adopted the practice of describing a verdict of "not guilty" as a verdict of "innocent." In some cases they have gone beyond this defensible practice to say that someone pleaded "innocent" instead of "not guilty," although there is, of course, no such plea as "innocent" in law.

No one who has ever been the victim of a dropped-out "not" can fail to be sympathetic to the effort to replace "not guilty" with "innocent" where it applies. When it does become necessary to use the words "not guilty," then an additional safeguard in transmission (but not in actual publication) is to adopt the old cable practice of repeating the negative as follows:

NOT RPT[1] NOT GUILTY

Other ways of emphasizing a negative in copy include spacing between letters (n o t), underlining them (<u>not</u>), or capitalizing the word

---

[1] *Rpt* is the abbreviation for the word repeat.

(NOT guilty). In any case, the risk is evident because no such device can be used in the paper or on the air. As long as everybody concerned is aware of the risk, there is less chance of a dropped negative. Few editors, though, are happy about taking such risks if they can legitimately avoid them.

OMISSION OF NECESSARY DETAIL

One of the sources of murky writing is the constant effort to shorten sentences at the expense of clarity. The dropping of articles is one symptom. An even more annoying trend is the use of inference to identify leading actors in a news story.

This situation frequently occurs in the writing of news that involves persons who are not generally known to the public and who therefore must be introduced in some way other than by using their names in the lead. For instance:

> A messenger boy saved 30 fellow-employees from a fire that razed McMichael's Supermarket today.
> Sammy James, 17, gave the alarm. . . .

It is only inference that leads the public to identify Sammy James as the messenger boy referred to in the lead as the hero of the fire. If the words, "The messenger," were placed before Sammy's name, there would be no doubt. There is no reason for such omissions.

ONE IDEA TO A SENTENCE

The principle of one idea to a sentence, which has been stressed throughout this text, is not new, but it has gained wide acceptance as a means of clarifying news writing. An example of limiting a sentence to a single idea, taken from the file of early Pulitzer prizes, follows:

> The biggest shadow in the world—235,000 miles high, 105 miles wide and 75 miles thick in its densest part—fell across San Diego today, the shadow of the moon as it crossed the face of the sun.

Such was the beginning of Magner White's classic description of the eclipse of the sun, published in the San Diego *Sun* on September 10, 1923. It is possibly to do the same with any story in the news. Catchall sentences, either in the lead or the body of a news account, are seldom necessary.

It is the misuse of Rudyard Kipling's six faithful serving men—the who, the what, the why, the where, the when and the how—that contributes to catchall sentences. Ideally, news stories should attempt to answer these questions whenever they are pertinent, but never in one sentence. Certainly there is no rule, written or unwritten, that obliges a news writer to lump everything in a lead. The most effective leads, in fact, are the ones that direct the public's interest into the body of the story.

Double-barreled Leads   During the twenties, when news writing was marred by bulging sentences, writers fell into the habit of describing action to the accompaniment of cheering crowds. The cliché style of writing, one of the symbols of tabloid journalism, aroused so much amusement that a musical comedy was entitled, "As Thousands Cheer." That disposed of the double-barreled lead for some time. It still crops up, here and there, principally in the sports pages where the cliché will always find a home.

A Better Method   Careful news writers make every effort to limit themselves to one idea to a sentence. This is particularly necessary in handling complicated, swiftly developing news stories where clarity is mandatory.

The rule does not cover every sentence in a news story, of course; nor is it desirable that it should. Graceful writers who know how to use the English language can be trusted to construct both stories and sentences as they believe best. There is no doubt whatever that the process of one idea to a sentence, where it applies, increases comprehension. It is particularly applicable to broadcast journalism.

Nobody advocates going back to kindergarten style and writing, "Oh, see the cat. It is a grey cat. Its eyes are green." The average man is well able to absorb a complicated idea, but it is too much to ask him to grapple with a complicated sentence at the same time. Experienced writers of the past generation, by and large, have tried to practice the concept of one idea to a sentence even if they have not always succeeded.

PARAGRAPHING

The brevity of the news paragraph is often a puzzle to the inexperienced news writer. He is used to the traditional paragraph of the English theme, which may run a full page or so but never just one sentence. The petty tyranny of the schoolmarm and the assistant professor of English has paralyzed his senses, so that he understands only with difficulty that the paragraph in journalism is often a mere typographical device for maintaining attention.

Beginning Paragraphs Differently   Once the newcomer to journalism grasps that thought, he is suddenly assailed with a lot of well-meant advice to begin each paragraph differently. The stated purpose of this widely held journalistic practice is to fascinate the public by variety. Some overzealous advisers even urge news writers to try not to begin many sentences with an article. In theory, an article is supposed to slow up a story.

Some of this is journalistic mythology. The rest is nonsense. Where variety can be achieved without strain or unnatural language it is, of course, desirable. All too frequently inexperienced journalists who try to vary the beginnings of their paragraphs find that they have made a literary hash out of their stories.

Sentences should flow naturally from one to another. If several begin the same way with good reason, nobody is going to worry about it as long as the story is interesting.

Block Paragraph   When a story is written in block paragraph style, each paragraph except the first one theoretically can be separated from the rest, shaken up in a hat, and then reassembled without making much difference to the story. It is a beautiful, but impractical, theory. Few stories can be written in such a way, even for wire services. One paragraph in a news story usually does depend in some way on the preceding paragraph as a matter of coherence, if nothing else.

Just about the only time that the block paragraph device really works is when a big story breaks and the object is to get as much type on Page 1 as possible in a hurry. Then, the impact of the news itself acts as a kind of unifying force for the story even though the paragraphs do not mesh.

Block paragraphing supposedly is a device that permits a story to be cut easily from the bottom. If the makeup editor is not watchful, it can create a minor crisis. For when block paragraphs are used, indiscriminate trims can result in this kind of a paragraph at the end of a story:

> Mrs. Peterson wiped the tears from her eyes, embraced her new daughter in-law, and said:

End of story.

PAST TENSE

It is traditional that straight news is written in the past tense for newspapers and the headlines that top it are cast in the present tense for the most part. Experienced newspapermen are seldom bothered by this familiar journalistic dichotomy but newcomers to the profession usually have their troubles. They also are bothered by the present and present-perfect tenses in broadcast journalism and use them for newspaper stories.

A Difference in Tenses   Why, they ask, should there be one tense for text and another for headlines in newspapers? Why can't it all be done simply, as in radio? The answer is that the two standard practices developed separately but for many years have been joined to create the effect of immediacy on newspaper pages.

When an atomic submarine stays under water for months, when jet air travel creates new records for transoceanic travel, when a President is elected, or when a Pope dies, the newspaper story is written in the past tense. The event is thus recorded. It is part of the history of the day. Thereby the newspaper derives an air of permanence and authority that cannot be captured by any other medium of quick information for a mass audience. But the headline, being written in the present tense, tops this substantial and permanent account with an urgency that supposedly communicates the immediacy of the event to the reader.

The Future, Past-Tensed   The uses of the past tense are sometimes strained. In order not to "date" an afternoon paper, which must print while the news is happening, future events often are introduced through the use of the past tense. For instance:

> WASHINGTON—The White House announced today that the president would meet congressional leaders at 5 p.m.

It would be much simpler to write:

> WASHINGTON—Congressional leaders will meet the president at the White House at 5 p.m.

Yet, wherever possible, the future tense is avoided by newspapers when they are dealing with events scheduled to occur during their hours of publication for that day.

Past-Tensing an Advance   Here is an example of the use of the past tense in an advance story of a parade or similar event:

> WASHINGTON—In warming weather, six miles of marchers, musicians and multicolored floats assembled today for the Presidential inaugural parade.
> The President himself, riding with his official family, was No. 10 in the line of march down Pennsylvania Ave., past stands built to seat 61,000. There was room also for some 700,000 standees to view the parade. . . .

A close reading of the account shows that the parade had not begun. Even from the lead, it is apparent that the piece purports to do nothing more than to give the arrangements for the inaugural parade which is to begin later in the day.

When Not to Past Tense The trouble with past-tense news writing begins when an effort is made to stretch it to cover categories other than hard news. For instance, it sometimes happens that an article which has only a tenuous connection with the breaking news is cast in the guise of hard news. This could be a feature, an interpretive article, almost any soft news with a "hopped-up" lead.

Any reader, journalist or not, will sense at once in skimming such an account that there is no recording of history, no real necessity for the terse, swift-moving, informative cadences of hard news. Soft news, or no news at all, is being handled as if it were hard news. But, of course, nobody is fooled.

In such matters it is far better to adopt the standard present-tense characteristics of radio and TV news handling. Often a mild little news event, which may seem unnecessarily pompous when written in the booming hard news style, becomes quite acceptable if it is present-tensed. Here is an example:

> Residents of one apartment in the Washington Houses project of the New York City Housing Authority have found a solution to one of their major problems. An exposed pipe in the bathroom of their apartment leaks water every time the tenants in the apartment above use the facilities. So the tenants below take an umbrella to the bathroom with them.

If in doubt, when handling news, however, it is always safe to write in the past tense.

QUALIFYING A STORY

The urge to oversimplify is powerful. It assumes everything in the news to be black and white, which is seldom the case. That is why the careful news writer will always qualify whatever he writes in the interest of accuracy. Few stories can be written without qualification of some kind.

Two-faced Qualifiers Because of the complexity of much of the news today, ingenious writers have invented words and expressions that can only be described as two-faced qualifiers. For instance:

> Mayor Joseph Westfall indicated today he might run for re-election. . . .

Obviously the Mayor said nothing bearing directly on the subject; otherwise, the word "indicated" would not have been used in the lead. Hence, "indicated" may be a trick word. The reader is entitled to ask how the Mayor did his indicating. Was it by a wink, a shrug, a broad grin, a brisk rubbing of his hands when he was asked the question? Surely, it would be more accurate to report exactly what happened instead of using "indicated," a two-faced qualifier.

What Is "Possible"?   Another two-faced qualifier—"possible"—is used with painful frequency in news writing:

> District Attorney Frank Garbutt showed a possible inclination to recommend acceptance of the defendant's plea of guilty to second-degree murder.

What makes the prosecutor's attitude possible? Or impossible? Either he will or will not recommend acceptance of the plea. To use his exact words would be the fairest way of reporting the facts. Interpreting their meaning by using the word "possible" can only confuse the public.

Nor is "possible" used only in this context. It has been general practice for police reporters to say that accident victims have a "possible skull fracture." There is no such medical term, of course. It should not be used until the diagnosis shows whether there is a skull fracture.

Qualifying "Qualified"   Perhaps the worst of all the two-faced qualifiers is the word "qualified" itself. It is used in this context when writers do not want to do an "iffy" lead:

> UNITED NATIONS, N. Y.—Russia gave qualified acceptance today to U.S. plans for inspection and control of arms limitation planning.

In other words, what Russia did was to say that the United States plan was acceptable provided certain conditions desired by the Kremlin were met. Often, such conditions in themselves are completely unacceptable to the United States. It would be just as fair to write that Russia "in effect" rejected, or gave a qualified rejection, to the United States plans. The words "in effect" are frequently used to try to show the real meaning of a set of proposals.

This use of the word "qualified" has spread to negotiations of all kinds —in domestic politics, labor contracts, and even the signing of TV stars or baseball players to contracts. Where editors have insisted on eliminating such news double talk, writers have attempted to use such terms as "conditional" or "implied" acceptance. These are just as objectionable. In describing negotiations of any kind, there is no easy way to sum up the positions of contending sides. News writers are ill-advised to try.

"In Effect"   Writers may safely use the key phrase, "in effect," as has already been shown, to illuminate an ill-defined situation. Admittedly, it is an editorial expression rather than an interpretive device. The reporter is saying quite plainly what he believes the effect of certain proposals is to be. Yet, if carefully and accurately used, the words "in effect" can be helpful. For instance:

> Governor Harrold in effect today blocked a move by the city to extend municipal bus service. The Governor vetoed a bill that would have made a state loan available to the city for this purpose.

In this context the use of "in effect" is certainly justified. If the writer reports merely that Governor Harrold vetoed a loan for the city, he misses the point of the story. The "in effect" lead, however, must be used with great reserve and care.

RUMORS AND REPORTS

The use of rumors in news stories causes endless trouble, even when the rumors turn out to have some substance. A wise writer, supported by an experienced editor, rarely resorts to the practice of dropping a rumor high up in a story on the theory that it is "just for luck" and nobody will notice if it is not substantiated. Such practices discredit journalism as a profession and undermine its structure of responsibility to a discerning public.

What Is a Report? There is an enormous difference between the use of unverified material, such as rumors, and news that is unquestionably correct but cannot be given immediate official confirmation. Such "soft" news is called a report—a journalistic use of the word that has a special meaning when it is applied to pending events. The journalistic type of report differs from the conventional report, which usually describes a document of some kind.

To illustrate, there were many authentic reports from Peking of the turmoil that broke over the succession to Mao Tse-tung but it was a long time before they could be confirmed. And there were many other reports of peace feelers from North Vietnam at the peak of the American bombing offensive during the war there, all of which were denied by the Communist side at that stage of the conflict.

Another familiar use of the term is in the circulation of perfectly valid reports of who will win Nobel Prizes, usually put out by semiofficial sources 24 hours in advance. Such reports invariably have preceded the official announcement of the prize awards.

Rumors Journalistic semantics, however, have no arbiter and are loosely and sometimes irresponsibly used. A rumor will be given a respectable disguise as a report, at times, in order to make a story look a little more solid than it actually is.

A careful reading of the documentation for the so-called report will disclose its fundamental weakness, in many cases, so that nothing is really gained by dressing up a rumor and using it.

No responsible news organization will use a story reporting that a murder jury stands 7–5 for acquittal, when it is obvious that the only basis can be corridor rumors or betting odds. Nor are wild guesses as to the outcome of a nominating convention or election to be dignified as reports. A journalistic report should be limited to material that the journalist has good reason to believe is true, but currently unverifiable. Used in that sense, the technique is extremely useful.

SPECIFIC NEWS WRITING

News writing must be specific. It is often a waste of time to string generalities together.

Give Meaning to the News   Generalities too often blur the news picture. Instead of writing that a man is tall, it is better to describe him as six feet four. Instead of calling a girl pretty, she should be described briefly. Instead of reporting that a speaker was nervous and upset, it would be more effective to write that he shouted and banged on the table.

If statistics are to be used, they must be given some meaning. To say that New York City's subways have only one candle-power illumination confuses the public. It is more informative to write that the average New York subway rider sometimes reads his paper by less light than Abe Lincoln had when he studied by firelight.

Certain other types of news must be related to specific audiences if they are to have meaning. Five dead in a San Francisco fire is of little interest in New York, except if it is stressed that the persons involved were from New York.

Color, Quotes, and Names   Colorful details often can create news where none could previously be found. When a builder announced that he was putting up a 40-story building in mid-Manhattan, he received no special notice because there are taller structures in the area. When he said he intended to paint his skyscraper bright red, he made Page 1.

Direct quotation frequently can increase interest in the news. Most readers like conversation and novelists dote on it because it makes for a lively, colloquial style. There is no law against it. Editors want all the good quotes they can get.

It should never be forgotten that names make news. Also, that people like to know about other people. Even buildings and bridges have names, and they should be used. Some of the most fascinating places in America have wonderful names—Death Valley, California; Ten Sleep, Wyoming; Paradise Valley, Washington.

To tell the news effectively, all these devices of journalism should be used where they are applicable. It is a formidable armory of weapons for any writer—action, color, topical material, unusual facts, special appeal, personal references, brief descriptions, and meaningful quotes.

TIME ELEMENT

There is so much confusion over the use of the words "today" and "yesterday" in leads that many newspapers now substitute the day of the week for them. Commonly, the use of "today" in leads is stressed in afternoon papers and datelined stories for morning papers. The word "yesterday" is generally used for undated (nondateline) leads in morning newspapers. For radio and television, there is no problem. "Today," "tonight," and "yesterday"—and all other elements of time—are used when they apply.

Placing the Time Element   For all news media, the time element ought to be included in the story where it naturally belongs. Usually, it is placed close to the verb in the opening sentence. It is straining for effect to write the following:

> A jet plane today smashed the New York–London flight record.
> A jet plane was today hailed for smashing the New York–London flight record.

It is smoother and simpler to write:

> A jet plane flew today from New York to London in record time.

When Tomorrow Is Today   The problem of the time element is not limited to its placement in the lead sentence. In a morning newspaper bearing the date of July 1, for instance, all dispatches using a date except those filed after midnight will necessarily bear June 30. Therefore, a datelined story about events on July 1 must be written as follows:

> CAPE KENNEDY, Fla., June 30—A new type of ballistic missile was placed on its firing platform today for a countdown that may last until 7 A.M. tomorrow before it is fired.

The reader will have to do a double take to realize that the story of the missile countdown that may end "tomorrow" is under yesterday's date-line, so that it actually may already have been fired today. It is less confusing to substitute the day of the week as a time element and drop the date from the dateline. Thus, if July 1 happened to be a Wednesday, the story would read:

> CAPE KENNEDY, Fla.—A new type of ballistic missile was placed on its firing platform Tuesday for a countdown that may last until 7 A.M. Wednesday before it is fired.

The reader thereupon is asked to remember that July 1 is Wednesday, or today. There seems to be little to choose between the respective formulas. Both are widely used.

Where Yesterday Is Taboo   Just as there are two schools of thought regarding the use of the day of the week and the date of the month to show when a news event occurred, so do editors differ in the stress that they place on the use of any kind of time element.

There are some, mostly on the laissez-faire morning newspapers, who do not really care if today or yesterday is in the lead, as long as the story somewhere specifies when the event occurred.

On afternoon papers, in particular, however, a breed of editor still exists who will not tolerate the use of the word "yesterday" in any lead when it can be avoided. Such editors want the reader to know his news is fresh, that it happened today, and they want the word "today" in the lead. Apparently they do not recognize the existence of radio or television, where the newscast of an hour ago is old stuff.

"WRITE LIKE YOU TALK"

Writing for wire services, newspapers, and news magazines has become far less formal in this generation and is likely to be even more relaxed in the next. The stiff, formidable phrasing of the thirties is no longer good form, even in the most conservative of the print media.

Yet, many newspaper editors in particular still shy away from the conversational approach to the news, although the electronic media encourage it. Except for an occasional feature story, newspapermen try to preserve the precision and tight organization of the written word. For example, Theodore M. Bernstein remarks in *Watch Your Language* that he is suspicious of the "Write Like You Talk" school of editor and observes: "Whatever the people say is okay by me; the people speak real good."

As Bernstein explains, "Writing is and must be a more precise form of expression than extemporaneous speaking."

For radio and television, however, it is necessary to give the illusion of informality even though the news is often more tightly written. The Associated Press, in its rules for broadcast journalism, observes: "Generally speaking, it is best to employ a conversational, informal style in writing for the air."[2] But that does not mean the electronic news writer can afford to sink into tortured, unnatural, or excitable prose any more than his colleagues of the press.

Nobody can justify a "Write Like You Talk" news report, regardless of the medium for which it is written. But the skillful, informal news account that bridges the gap between the public and the news media can often be extremely effective, particularly when it gives the illusion of conversation. It is a wise journalist, however, who knows when to try it and when to revert to safer and more traditional methods.

---

[2] *AP Radio-Television News Style Book*, p. 6.

PART 2

THE WRITER AS
JOURNALIST

chapter 7

Basic News Structure

The structure of a news story is heavily influenced by five factors. These are the shape of the news itself, the time and the space that are available to record it, the skill of the writer, and the nature of his medium of communication. With so many variables, it is clear that there can be no single structure for a news story any more than there can be one approved way of telling it. In expert hands it should be as flexible and graceful in its structure as any other art form based on fact, thought, feeling, and language. If this is not always as true as it should be, the rigidity of the editorial mind is more to blame than the precepts of journalism itself. News is life. The patterns of news should reflect it.

THE INVERTED PYRAMID

The oldest, most convenient, most useful, and most abused news structure is the inverted pyramid. It is a mold that separates facts in diminishing order of importance. The most important is on top, so that it can take the headline and attract maximum attention. The lesser ones are at the end where they can be chopped off at will to fit the demands of space, time, and editorial operation.

The factual (or straight) news story usually fits conveniently into the inverted pyramid pattern. This is particularly true when a news story is written for wire service use, since some editors may want long accounts and others the barest minimum. The following story of the arrival of the Mayflower II in the United States illustrates the inverted pyramid principle:

> PROVINCETOWN, Mass. (UPI)—The Mayflower II arrived in the new world today after crossing the Atlantic in 53 days, 14 days faster than the original Pilgrim ship.
> "We thank God for no accidents, good weather and a good crew," said the Mayflower's skipper, Capt. Alan Villiers, after the 92-foot replica of the original vessel tied up at a buoy in Provincetown Harbor.
> The ship was towed by the Coast Guard cutter Yankton as it entered the harbor after arriving from England.
> Villiers said tonight the Mayflower will leave at 5.30 a.m. tomorrow for Plymouth, 24 miles across Cape Cod Bay. He plans to get there at 1 p.m. and will take a tow if he can't sail, he said.

The complete account of the Mayflower's arrival was considerably longer. Moreover, it will be seen that the story could have been shortened still more by cutting it from the bottom.

Is the inverted pyramid the only structure for this story? Obviously not. It could have been told in a number of different ways, and certainly was; but for a wire service that was carrying a factual news report, the inverted pyramid was the most convenient form.

Criticism of the Inverted Pyramid   Newcomers to journalism, particularly those who seek to improve it, invariably leap on the inverted pyramid construction as an anachronism.

They argue that it forces a newspaper to tell a story three times—in the headline, the lead, and the body of a news account. They call the structure grotesque because they believe it to be a handicap to storytelling since the climax comes at the beginning instead of near the end. Another prevalent criticism is that the inverted pyramid form is outdated, an illogical holdover from the days when a newspaper was always first with the news. When the broadcast media tell the news in capsule form, surely it is necessary to question the traditional news style.

The Virtues of Straight News   There is nothing new, of course, in the idea of telling a story so that the main development comes first. The effectiveness of the Book of Genesis is not noticeably handicapped because of its opening, "In the beginning God created the heaven and the earth." When the messenger ran from the Plains of Marathon in 490 B.C. and gasped the news of the great Greek victory to the exultant Athenians before he died, it did not make his story any less arresting.

The inverted pyramid was not invented by the press in America, although that is the source of its popularity as a news-recording device. Its use by newspaper correspondents in the field is generally tied to the invention of the telegraph, which placed a premium on getting the news first, fast, and right. In the United States, the Civil War period marked the introduction of the inverted pyramid construction to newsworthy dispatches.

This, for instance, was the way the first telegraphic bulletin about the assault on Fort Sumter was sent to New York on Friday, April 12, 1861:

> CHARLESTON, April 12—The ball is opened. War is inaugurated. The batteries of Sullivan's Island, Morris Island and other points were opened on Fort Sumter at 4 o'clock this morning. Fort Sumter has returned the fire and a brisk cannonading has been kept up.

The inverted pyramid format, both then and now, has been most effective in the handling of major news. Yet, in talented hands, its usefulness has been adapted to news that did not depend for its interest on the immediacy of dramatic events. The nation had known for days of the burial of the Unknown Soldier that Kirke L. Simpson finally recorded for the Associated Press night report on November 11, 1921. Yet, his Pulitzer Prize-winning story opened on this climactic idea:

> WASHINGTON, Nov. 11 (AP)—Under the wide and starry skies of his own home-land America's unknown dead from France sleeps tonight, a soldier home from the wars.
> Alone, he lies in the narrow cell of stone that guards his body; but his soul has entered into the spirit that is America.

It has been argued with great conviction that the newspaper ought not to tell the news in the first paragraph because it is only duplicating or echoing the faster radio and television bulletin coverage. Yet, when the AP "A" wire carried its climactic story on the six-day Suez War under this lead, the banner headlines flared across the nation:

> TEL AVIV (AP)—Israel proclaimed victory tonight in the Sinai Peninsula campaign against the United Arab Republic. On the eastern front, both the Old City of Jerusalem and Bethlehem were captured from the Jordanians.[1]

The evidence is overwhelming that the newspaper is not about to abdicate the news presentation function to the broadcast media.

New Methods   Yet, new ways of telling the news are being used with striking effectiveness in the news magazines as well as the broadcast media. The anecdote, the chronological approach, the recollection of some previous or similar happening, the impact of a forceful personality, the interesting remark, and many other devices of the news feature are being im-

---

[1] AP File, June 7, 1967.

posed on the telling of the news. Necessarily, the newspaper cannot stand or fall on the inverted pyramid and obviously has no intention of doing so.

Many newspapers have adapted broadcast techniques of news presentation. The personal, present-tense style of the broadcasters and commentators has had an enormous influence on newspaper material to which it may be adapted. Some newspapers have attempted to become daily news magazines, but with somewhat appalling results. Even the short story and the essay have been tried here and there as news forms, but with little favorable public response.

The experimentation will continue in all the media, for both style and format are in the process of change. It is far more likely that the broadcast media will increase the time they allow for news, analysis, opinions, and ideas than that they will cut their news content. Faced with a growing challenge, the newspapers will have to develop better in-depth coverage of the news and much more effective ways of writing it and presenting it.

Certainly, it is no longer necessary to begin every story with what is known as the "Bang-Bang-You're Dead" type of lead. The news magazines and the writers for the electronic media have proved with ease that it is possible to capture public attention and hold it without merely repeating the headline news. The inverted pyramid lead is not the only answer to the effective presentation of the news. Except for bulletin-type material, originality in the beginning of most news stories is highly desirable.

BUILDING BLOCKS OF NEWS

Whether a news story opens with a single sentence or several paragraphs, the function of the lead is to focus the attention of the reader. This is true whether the article is long or short, so-called straight news or a feature, a summation of a rather ordinary happening, or a complicated investigatory story.

Two-part Organization   The two-part makeup of the news story—the lead and body—is its dominant point of style. Necessarily, the lead and its phrasing are decisive in this structure; in effect, it does much to determine how the article as a whole is to be organized. Here is a sampling of various types of opening statements:

Straight news:
> A berserk laborer yesterday shot to death a pawnshop manager, then shot it out with 65 police officers for almost four hours before he was critically wounded and captured.
> —San Diego *Union*

A feature:

A vast army of antipoverty workers is prowling the nation's slums, invading schoolrooms and hospitals, and providing in the process both a service and a challenge to the professionals who guard the nation's traditional health, education, and welfare institutions.

—National Observer

An investigatory story:

The LBJ success story comes in two volumes: Public Service and Private Enterprise. Lyndon Baines Johnson produced Volume I, from poor boy to Presidency, as everyone knows. Lady Bird Johnson is credited with putting together Volume II, the business saga, and in many respects it is equally astonishing.

Its title could be: How to Put $17,500 into Broadcasting and Come Out With Multi-Millions.

—Wall Street Journal

A report in depth:

A rust-spotted old taxi held together mostly by hope came winging around the curve of the Prado in Havana and swung into the straightaway along the Malecon. A cardboard sign stuck in the window read: "Sin Frenos (no brakes)."

When a pedestrian tried to hail him, the driver leaned out the window, gestured wildly as he rushed by shouting, and pointed down the street where he calculated he might coast to a stop. Cuba is like that today—a crippled machine moving along in a state of controlled disorder, running on hope. . .

—Miami Herald

A crusade:

In proud Chicago, the Midwest's colossal business city, the most profitable business today may well be organized crime. The bomb-and-bullet cartel grosses a fantastic $2 billion a year—$64 every time the clock clicks off a second—from the Chicago rackets, authorities believe.

—Chicago Daily News

War correspondence:

VAN TUONG, Vietnam (AP)—The mission of U. S. Marine Supply Column 21 yesterday was simple: Get to the beachhead, resupply a line company and return to the 7th Fleet mother ship anchored a mile out in the bay.

It never found the line company. And it never returned . . . Survivors said the Vietcong rose out of hedge rows and swamps . . .

Documenting Leads   Whether the lead is one sentence, several sentences, one paragraph, or several paragraphs, the body consists almost entirely of documentation. While the public may not be quite so captious, editors uniformly insist that any statement made in the lead of a major news story should be adequately documented in the body of the story.

In effect, that determines the structure of the story. To illustrate with a simple example, if the lead of a story about an automobile accident says that two persons were killed, the body of the story must contain their names, ages, and addresses or explain why these cannot be provided. In the case of a speech, interview, or news conference, a lead based on what was said must be supported by pertinent quotations to show the source of the paraphrase.

In a political election the result announced in the lead must be supported by the actual voting summaries plus whatever statements there are that bear on the outcome. In trials or hearings the verdict as reported in the lead requires detailed narration in the body of the story to show exactly what was said and how the announcement was made. In police news if a person is reported arrested in a lead, the exact charge against him and the basis of the accusation must be in the body of the story. In obituaries the lead that reports the death of a person must be backed up by documentation that elaborates on when and where it happened and, if possible, the cause. In sports contests such as a baseball or football game, the documentation usually consists of the main points of the game that contributed to the final score as reported in the lead.

There are so many ways of documenting a straight news story that the structure, instead of being rigid, can be adapted readily to fit the circumstances of the story. News agency stories usually are well documented because they are read by thousands of editors and news directors with a very critical eye. On newspapers that are not carefully edited, however, the lack of proper documentation for leads often gives the impression that stories either are overwritten or inaccurate. As for television, the documentation is usually a well-photographed and well-organized film story or interview, much of it ad-lib. But that doesn't make it any easier to do.

A WELL-ORGANIZED STORY

The formal—and often forbidding—manner of telling the news, inverted pyramid style, has been in fashion in the United States for more than fifty years. There is nothing wrong with it except that it is generally predictable and invariably old-fashioned. Thus, when a governor is inaugurated, it is customary to write as follows in crumbly but well-measured phrases:

> Governor J. Blanton Mendenhall took the oath of office today and pledged, in a 27-minute inaugural address, to fight for economy in government.

The pattern is being broken with regularity by journalists with an original turn of mind, who are encouraged by a new breed of editor to try to get away from routine. Consequently, when a movie actor was inaugurated as Governor of California in the presence of a United States Senator who had been a former song-and-dance man, Lawrence E. Davies wrote as follows in *The New York Times*:

Anecdotal Lead

SACRAMENTO, Calif., Jan. 2—With 32 television cameras focused on him, Ronald Reagan, grinning broadly, remarked to Senator George Murphy of California early this morning:

"Well, George, here we are on the late show again."

Mr. Reagan, the 55-year-old hero of one of the most unusual political dramas of the era, took the oath of office as Governor of the largest state in the union at the unlikely hour of 12:16 A.M.

Documentation. Note the continuity of the story

Then, turning to Senator Murphy, his fellow Republican and a fellow former actor who had once preceded him as president of the Screen Actors Guild, the new Governor made his observation about their old movies that had kept them before the public on "late" and "late late" television shows during successful campaigns.

Mr. Reagan defeated Gov. Edmund G. Brown by 3,476,554 to 2,543,116 last November to end Mr. Brown's eight-year Democratic administration. Mr. Murphy entered the Senate in 1964, also replacing a Democrat, Pierre Salinger.

Other Facts Elaborate on Theme, Introducing Second Main Point

Now, before about 150 invited guests, including legislative leaders and friends and supporters of Mr. Reagan, along with perhaps 150 representatives of the press, radio and television, the Republican Governor was making a debut that was seen by many millions on TV before the day ended.

Hardly more than 12 hours after his oath-taking, Governor Reagan briefly addressed a joint session of the Assembly and Senate, where striking Republican gains in November left reduced Democratic majorities in both houses. The 33d Governor called for legislative cooperation in a plan to reorganize the executive department of the state government.

Documentation of Second Main Point

"Our executive branch," he said, "cannot operate in this useful, effective, and economical way unless the many agencies, bureaus, and departments are grouped together in a logical manner and their day-to-day activities are coordinated by executives operating out of the Governor's office."

Among his specific proposals was one for a director of the budget working from the Governor's office, "performing overall review of programs, budgets, and expenditures."

Back to Detail on First Point

California has never seen a parallel to the post-midnight swearing in of Mr. Reagan. It took place in the Capitol Rotunda in front of a statue of Queen Isabella of Spain and Christopher Columbus, a statue that emphasizes the Spanish influence on early California.

The seven-member gubernatorial party took its place on a small wooden platform at midnight before the tiers of cameras. A minute later the University of Southern California chamber singers, in an arc on the rotunda balcony, sang, "America the Beautiful" to open a ceremony of music, prayer, oath-taking, and speech-making that lasted about 25 minutes.

Associate Justice Marshall F. McComb of the State Supreme Court, a repeated dissenter to the court's liberal decisions, administered the oath to Mr. Reagan after Senator Murphy had sworn in Robert H. Finch, a 40-year-old Los Angeles lawyer, as Lieutenant Governor. . .

Amusing Touch to End Story

Through a misunderstanding, Mr. Reagan already was, in effect, California's Governor when he placed his left hand on a 400-year-old Bible, raised his right hand and solemnly replied, "I do," to a series of questions put by Justice McComb in the official oath.

He swore to and signed the oath last week before a deputy secretary of state, but he was under the impression then, it was explained later, that he was taking a simple loyalty oath apart from the inaugural oath itself.

The effectiveness of the piece depends almost entirely on the manner in which it is organized, once the anecdotal lead catches the reader's attention. But even tight and logical organization would not suffice, were it not for the neat manner in which each section of the story is joined to the next without strain or artifice. The writer's reportorial eye for color and detail thus turned what might have been a routine story into an interesting and even amusing narrative. The very limitations of time and space were turned to advantage.

This is the kind of thing experienced news writers put together without even thinking about detailed organization plans. They do what comes naturally, having had to learn how through years of practice.

DRAMA IN THE NEWS

In expert hands, even a straight news account, told in inverted pyramid style, need never be dull. Nor should it be assumed that only tabloids and sensational papers play such stories. Here is an example of how such pieces can be done with restraint and good taste, taken from the *Wall Street Journal*:

> NEW YORK—A Brooklyn surgical team failed yesterday in an attempt to transplant a heart to a dying two-and-a-half-week-old baby boy.
>
> The infant received the heart of a two-day-old male infant who had died of a fatal birth defect of the brain. The heart functioned for about six and a half hours and then suddenly, unexpectedly stopped. Prior to that the infant had seemed to be doing reasonably well. Neither child was identified.
>
> "It should be made clear that we consider this, unequivocally, an unsuccessful operation," said Dr. Adrian Kantrowitz, head of the 22-man team that performed the operation at Maimonides Medical Center.
>
> The operation took place early yesterday morning. The attempt to transplant a human heart underscores surgeons' increasing confidence in their ability to transplant organs. However, the failure in Brooklyn emphasizes the many problems that are involved.
>
> The key unanswered question is whether doctors can overcome the rejection phenomenon in the case of the heart as well as they have conquered it in cases of kidney and liver transplants. The body regards the transplanted organ as "foreign" in the same way it regards bacteria, viruses, and allergy-causing substances as foreign. Thus, it tries to get rid of the invader.
>
> The heart transplant attempt in Brooklyn had been planned for the last two and one-half weeks, Dr. Kantrowitz said. The infant was born at Maimonides with a severed defective heart valve that would have been fatal. The Brooklyn doctors then began searching for a possible donor of a heart, an infant born with anencephalia, the absence of vital parts of the brain. Such infants die within two or three days after birth.
>
> More than 500 patients were contacted, Dr. Kantrowitz said. A hospital in Philadelphia notified Maimonides Monday that such an infant had been born there. "We spoke to the parents and they were very intelligent and understanding," he said. The infant was flown to New York and preparations were made for the operation. After several hours, the Philadelphia infant died and the operation began at 4:15 A.M., within minutes after his heart had stopped. The transplant was completed at 6:30 A.M.

The infant receiving the heart seemed to be doing fairly well. About one o'clock yesterday afternoon, however, the heart suddenly stopped. "We tried what we considered a life-saving procedure and we failed," Dr. Kantrowitz said.

This story was effective because, once the summary lead was written, it developed into an entirely natural narrative without a trace of artificial tension or hopped-up language. Necessary explanations were inserted as needed, so that the reader was never left in any doubt about the facts in the case.

chapter 8

Biography for the Millions

The body of journalism is fact, but people are its very heart. They give it life, warmth, and meaning. They also shape its direction and its destiny.

The first responsibility of the news media in a democratic society is to serve the people. No newspaper can afford to ignore that responsibility. Nor can any radio or television station shrug off the requirements of public service. The penalty of public disapproval sometimes can come very quickly.

Whether people live behind a lace curtain, an iron curtain, or no curtain at all, they are primarily interested in news that directly affects them and their neighbors. The job of the news media is to translate this intense personal interest into news values that merit the attention of tens of thousands—and sometimes of millions—of people.

PEOPLE IN THE NEWS

The history of many cities and towns can be traced in the reporting of its births and engagements, its birthdays and anniversaries, its marriages, its celebrations, its illnesses, its deaths and memorials. Whether such news is of ordinary persons or the leaders of a community, it is bound to be eagerly welcomed by their families, friends, and even casual acquaintances. Where such news can be used in considerable volume and detail, it becomes an asset to a newspaper, radio, or television station.

When Names Are News   The biographical item, however, should not be regarded as a kind of lowest common denominator in the news. Names by themselves do not make news; otherwise newspapers would resemble telephone books and city directories. Something has to happen to make news of a name, and the importance of the news varies in direct proportion to the meaning that the event has for the community.

Necessarily, many biographical items may be worth only a paragraph or two. Because of their brevity and because they record the basic facts of a life or a death, such short pieces may seem stylized and almost standard in their preparation. On the women's page, in the social notes, or in the obituary columns, they often are. In the general news section they are more likely to deviate. Regardless of where they are published, the most important element in the preparation of items about people is to get the names right and correctly report all facts essential to these stories.

The newcomer to journalism too often smiles with a superior air when he is informed of such precautions, and a few minutes later promptly misspells a name. He is usually under the misapprehension that he must do even an item about a birthday or a Rotary Club meeting in words that sing. An accurate story, done in unadorned but clear language, is preferred for such assignments. The two-paragraph masterpiece is a rarity.

Naming Names   The most disturbing thing about any news report is an error of fact. The first thing an editor will check, therefore, is the use of proper names and titles, or other designations.

The differences in form between the print and electronic media may never be used as an excuse for slipshod work on names. If the name is incorrect, an editor—and the public—may well question the information in the story as well. Many editors, as a result, advise their writers to put a small check mark over each proper name to indicate that it has been checked and found to be correct.

Newspaper practice in handling names is based on completeness, including middle initial if any and title or additional designation. For both newspapers and wire services, it is advisable to use the names of personalities in the news (except for sports and amusements) exactly as their owners sign them, plus title if there is one.

In the news columns of newspapers, it is not customary to use Gene McCarthy, Teddy Kennedy or Nelson Rockefeller, but Senator Eugene J. McCarthy of Minnesota, Senator Edward M. Kennedy of Massachusetts, and Governor Nelson A. Rockefeller of New York. If there is a nickname such as "Punch" Sulzberger or "Spike" Canham and some reason exists to use it, the usual news style is to write it Arthur O. (Punch) Sulzberger, publisher of *The New York Times*, and Erwin D. (Spike) Canham, editor-in-chief of the *Christian Science Monitor*. But generally, newspapers and wire services are grimly formal, whether their readers like it or not.

Sometimes this kind of thing can be overdone by the overzealous and inexperienced. It is ludicrous and inaccurate to write about William Mays or Robert Hope, Richard Skelton or Harry Crosby. These are household names in the United States—Willie Mays, the San Francisco outfielder; Bob Hope and Red Skelton, the comedians, and Bing Crosby, the singer, and should be so used. Nor should Abe Fortas, the jurist's full name, be incorrectly changed to Abraham.

Parodies of news writing can result when the rules of the news columns are applied to sports pages. When Hank Bauer was an outfielder for the New York Yankees, *The New York Times* solemnly reported the aftermath of a night club escapade as follows: "Mr. Bauer, a long-ball hitter, was dropped to eighth in the Yankee batting order. Mr. Berra was withdrawn from the lineup altogether, while Mr. Mantle trotted out to his regular place in center field." *The New Yorker* just as solemnly picked up the sentence and reproduced it intact.

There is considerably more flexibility in usage for radio and television, but just as firm an insistence on getting names right. There is much more liberal omission of first names of prominent personages if their title precedes the name. Middle initials are generally omitted in the interest of brevity or simplicity, and middle names as well, except where confusion would result, as in changing a name such as John Paul Jones. Titles invariably precede the name to make it easier for the listener to identify the subject. As for nicknames, they are generally put in parentheses in the script to give the announcer the option of using them or dropping them.

Despite the growth of a less formal spirit in the news media, even more so in the news magazines than anywhere else, most newspapers still bear down on names as a test of the accuracy of reporters. It is one of the reasons that editors still put most newcomers on vital statistics to give them a sense of responsibility.

Gossip The gossip column has had a marked effect on the reporting of news about people who place themselves on public exhibition. Syndicated writers of these columns and their heavy-handed local imitators have dealt principally with those who thrive on publicity and are willing to take the risks of synthetic fame—including some of the leading personalities of politics, sports, amusements, and cafe society. Love affairs, unsavory marital rows, pregnancies, and other highly personal matters have become part of the daily grist in such columns.

The solemn debates about the invasion of privacy that have resulted seldom take account of the fact that those who bid for public attention can expect to retain only a scanty private life. The gossip writers, on their part, have sanctimoniously quoted Charles A. Dana: "I have always felt that whatever the Divine Providence permitted to occur I was not too proud to print." For those victims who felt their reputations were strong enough to stand the strain, excesses by gossip writers have been balanced by appeals for punitive damages under the laws of libel. Some have collected handsome sums.

Responsible newspapers, controlled by serious-minded editors, have ignored the gossip column. There is little evidence to show that they have been hurt by it, and a considerable belief that they have actually gained. The gossip column, after years of notoriety, has entered into a serious period of decline.

The situation, then, is basically one of control. For the staff writer and reporter, gossip is the cheap news that drives out the good—and therefore is to be handled with care if at all. The staff member tries not to write gossip or to use the banalities of the gossip columnist. When he writes personals, they must be done in such a way that they reflect dignity, fairness, and good taste. The average person, reading about his marriage or anniversary in his newspaper, or hearing of it on the air, should not have to blush, cringe, and feel apologetic in front of his friends.

Fact and Fancy   This clear separation of gossip and fact also applies to the language that is used in the writing of personal items. No reporter should try to do a simple personal item in the cliché-ridden style of an unsophisticated country weekly. People do not have blessed events, unions in holy wedlock, or tragic departures. They are born. They are married. They die. The simple verbs and the basic expressions should be used, not disguised under threadbare phrases that were not original in the journalism of a century ago. Familiarities in the news columns are not permitted, and feeble good humor is best eliminated, something the local broadcast media might take to heart.

If this makes the personal item seem stark and bleak to the unpracticed eye of the inexperienced journalist, he should remind himself that he is a reporter, not a gossip, and that his mission is not to entertain but to inform. He can vary the monotony of the biographical item, not by lazily slinging banal phrases, but by getting a few more facts into the story.

SOCIAL ITEMS—AND NEWS

There was a time when news of society was based on an avid public interest in the activities of socially prominent persons in New York City, Newport, Bar Harbor, Southampton, and a few other Eastern centers. Pages devoted to society and women's news either were very exclusive, or crammed with gossip about the so-called 400 of society.

Those days have gone. Even in metropolitan centers, editors are given wide latitude in the processing of the social item. Of the thousands of persons who submit information on personal items for publication, newspapers are accustomed to use as many as they can after suitable checking. Availability, rather than social standing, is one of the indices that determines whether an item is to be used or not.

Although similar in subject matter, a social item about a birth or an engagement cannot be given the same treatment as a news story. The social item, having no general news appeal, usually makes no particular point of identifying the persons involved in the opening sentences. It is also written in a restrained, rather formal style.

Births Social items about births are usually one-paragraph accounts giving the names of the parents, date of birth, name and sex of the child and sometimes its weight and the number of other children in the family. The following is standard:

> Mr. and Mrs. R. Bruce Louchheim, of Redding Road, Fairfield, Conn., announce the birth of their second son and fourth child, Arthur David Louchheim, on Jan. 4. Mrs. Louchheim is the former Miss Sara Jean Mainwaring of Greenwich, Conn.

The restrained, fact-studded style of this social item contrasts oddly with news stories about births. For instance, there is little resemblance between this announcement and the following, done in news agency style:

> BROOKLYN—The wife of an $80-a-week department store clerk gave birth here today to quadruplets—two boys and two girls. The four babies and their mother, who already had six daughters, were reported "doing fine" at Kings County Hospital.
> The four babies, ranging in weight from three pounds one ounce to four pounds, were born within a 30-minute period to Jeanne May Sammons, 36, who had twins four years ago. The children were placed in separate incubators, the boys in one and the girls in another.
> The father, Crawford Sammons, 38, sells men's hats in a downtown department store. He said he planned to look for a larger apartment soon.

Engagements and Marriages The processing of social items dealing with engagements and marriages also follows a formal and well-established pattern. There are differences only in degree, based on the prominence of the persons or families involved. These are emphasized, not particularly in the manner in which the item is written, but in the additional facts that are presented and the play which the announcement is given on the page.

In engagements the items feature the names, educational and professional backgrounds of the principals, their home addresses, the identities of their parents, and their marriage plans. It is rare to give the ages of engaged persons on the society page, or delve into their previous marriages, if any. This is an example:

> Mr. and Mrs. William Mellon Dudley, of East Moriches, L.I., announce the engagement of their daughter, Helen Gray, to Mr. Samuel James Delafield, son of Mr. and Mrs. Pendleton Delafield, of 1140 Fifth Avenue, New York, and Westhampton Beach, L. I.

Engagement news stories are handled without such formality. Due regard is given for the ages and previous marriages of the subjects, and any other details that may seem pertinent. The following is an example of a story about an engagement:

> LAS VEGAS, Nev.—What happens when a brother act meets a sister act? You guessed it.
> Lonnie and Bill Ringwood, 25-year-old twin singers at a local hotel, announced their engagements today to the Pettison Sisters, whose act immediately preceded theirs. Lonnie said he had made arrangements to be married to June Pettison, 23, at the same time that his brother and June's sister, Annette, 21, took their vows. The double ceremony will be some time next week.
> "It just shows what can happen when you keep watching the same girls every night in the week," Lonnie said.

When marriages are processed as social items, they are reported with just as much reserve as engagements but, where appropriate, colorful details are added. The bare announcement of a marriage includes the names, parents, and backgrounds of the principals, but not their ages, and the church and clergyman. When there is room, and interest in the bride and bridegroom warrant it, the bride's dress, flowers and attendants are described and the names of the groom's best man and the ushers are also given.

The following is a typical society-page account of a marriage:

> Miss Gail Demarest, daughter of former Senator and Mrs. Arthur J. Demarest, was married yesterday to John David Sandeson of Spokane at the First Presbyterian Church.
> A cousin of the bride, the Rev. Dr. Henry Hallam Knight of the Community Church, officiated. Mr. Sandeson is the son of Professor William Finch Sandeson, of the State University, and Mrs. Sandeson.
> The bride wore a gown of white silk taffeta and Chantilly lace and carried white orchids and stephanotis. Her attendants wore yellow silk, with bouquets of yellow and white flowers.
> Mrs. Winfred G. Paynter, sister of the bride, was matron of honor, Mr. Sandeson's brother, Kenneth Sandeson of Pullman, was best man.
> After the ceremony, there was a reception at the Metropolitan Hotel attended by Mayor George W. Worthy, Comptroller J. Cornell Simpson, and other officials in both the city and state administrations.

Miss Demarest, an alumna of the State University, is now an instructor in English there. Mr. Sandeson is completing work at the University on his Ph.D. in history.

When the couple return from a wedding trip to Canada, they intend to make their home in the University district.

When a marriage attracts sufficient attention to merit more general treatment in the news columns and on television, the social item form is, of course, discarded. Here is the way the nation's largest newspaper, the *New York Sunday News*, began an account of that rarest and sweetest of social events, the White House wedding:

By Judith Axler and Paul Healy

WASHINGTON—A broadly smiling Lynda Bird Johnson, tall and regal in a simple silk A-line gown, and her dashing Marine Captain, Charles S. Robb, exchanged a whispered "I love you" and were married today before 500 standing VIPs in the historic White House East Room.

President Johnson, watching proudly and somewhat sadly, added his own twist to the emotion-packed double-ring Episcopal ceremony before an improvised three-step altar. When asked, "Who giveth this woman in marriage?" Johnson deviated from the standard reply and answered, "Her mother and I."

A few minutes later, his "Princess" Lynda, 23, and Chuck, 28, tall and dark in his Marine dress blues, kissed and then strode through a traditional arch of swords formed by six uniformed Marine officers.

The military touch was fitting, for Robb is scheduled to go to Vietnam in three months. His best man, Marine Captain William Douglas Davidson, also was in dress uniform. The ceremonial music, including Mendelssohn's "Wedding March," was played by the scarlet-coated Marine band.

Lynda and Chuck made a handsome couple, equal to the story-book atmosphere that had transformed the White House for the wedding of the year. Fir branches and boughs of the red berries and green holly adorned the simple altar. A White House-made gold-painted cross was in the center of the holly.

Yuletide decorations were everywhere in the mansion, but what delighted the guests most was the festooned pink tent that had been pitched on the roof of the colonnade connecting the residence with the West Office wing. Just off the State Dining Room, where the reception was held, the tent area offered food and drinks amid huge Mexican paper flowers in blending shades of red and Christmas trimmings.

The only participant who shed tears on Lynda's happy day was her matron of honor and younger sister, Luci, who also wept for joy when she was married in a Catholic church ceremony 16 months ago. Lynda's maid of honor was her best friend, Warrie Lynn Smith. She had five bridesmaids. Chuck had six groomsmen, all in cutaways, plus his best man.

The Rev. Canon Gerald McAllister of San Antonio officiated at the traditional Episcopal ring ceremony. Lynda, an American history buff, chose to stand where three other presidential daughters took their marriage vows—Eleanor Wilson, Nellie Grant, and Alice Roosevelt. . .[1]

Announcements   All newspapers and local broadcast media receive many requests for the use of announcements of meetings, dances, benefits, luncheons, and dinners by social, civic, fraternal, and charitable organizations. Because of the volume of such news, all items must be written briefly and simply. Nothing makes a newspaper or a newscaster more ridiculous than to try to inject a personal slant or heavy humor in what is essentially a news note. The following are examples of how such material is handled:

> The Riverhead Lions Club will meet Wednesday noon at the Perkins Inn to hear Seth Hubbard, the lawyer, describe his recent trip to Australia and New Zealand.
> Mrs. Jean Jacques L'Hommedieu will lecture at the Maison Francaise Thursday night at 8 on the French poet, Gerard DeNeval.
> The annual dinner and meeting of the State Fine Arts Academy will be held Sunday night at the Sheraton Hotel. Dr. Samuel Linsley Hofstadter, the president, will describe the Academy's newest acquisitions.

Birthdays   The birthdays of the famous, the honored and respected, the eccentric, and the patriarchs always provide material for writers of news. Some are amusing, some sad; many are philosophical, looking back over life and picking out its lessons. The feature is a hardy perennial but it always has been popular, when it is written without affectation, and probably it always will be. This is an example of how such stories are done:

> HUNTINGTON—Mrs. Carrie D. Spear is celebrating her 100th birthday today in hale and hearty condition—and to what does she attribute all this? Year after year of beer.
> The cheerful, alert lady, whose doctors describe her as "nothing short of amazing," doesn't smoke but she likes her beer. At every lunch and dinner, when the 15 other elderly guests of the Hilaire Farm Nursing Home have their tea or milk, Mrs. Spear has a glass of beer. Asked last night to what she attributed her long, healthy life, she giggled and said, "I reckon I'm a museum piece today because I drink so much beer. That keeps me going."
>
> —*Newsday.*

OBITS

The difference between a seasoned journalist and a beginner can be quite marked when they handle an obituary. The beginner, with an insulted air, is likely to hasten through the job as a bit of distasteful routine. The veteran

---

[1] *New York Sunday News*, December 10, 1967.

will do careful and even painstaking work because he knows how tricky obits can be.

Principal Points in Obits Since every obit must announce at the outset that someone has died (not succumbed, or passed away, but *died*) the beginner assumes quite mistakenly that all obits are alike. The veteran realizes, however, that this is the very thing that makes an obit difficult to do on occasion.

Each life is different. Each obit, therefore, should be different, but getting at the facts is not always a simple matter. Bereaved families, eager relatives, helpful friends and undertakers are not always the most reliable sources, and old clips are seldom complete. Nor can physicians always be reached and persuaded to give the cause of death if the certificate is not available. For that reason the cause of death sometimes has to be omitted.

If obits were written only for the scrutiny of families, they would be wooden and mealy-mouthed affairs. They are not.

They depend on detail, and more detail, for effectiveness. In a few hundred words they should convey exactly why a particular death was news. No mere dry-as-dust summation of routine career facts will satisfy the inveterate reader of obits, and there are many of them.

All the devices of journalism—the colorful incident, the well-remembered saying or quip, the personal traits, anecdotes, and observations of friends and associates—should be used whenever possible to show what manner of person it was who died.

For obits that have no additional news angle, and therefore go either on the obit page or on Page 1 for big news names, the first few paragraphs sum up the circumstances of death. These are the name, age, identification by position, business, trade, or profession, and time and place of death. The age, being of special importance, sometimes is given a short sentence by itself after the opening sentence.

Then follow, in whatever order is pertinent, the cause of death, home address if it is different from the place where death occurred, those who were at the deathbed, other survivors, and funeral arrangements.

If a reporter learns somehow of any last words or final incidents that are pertinent to the story, they are given prominence. After these few paragraphs comes the obituary proper, the record of the person's life. This generally includes, as a minimum, the date and place of birth, names of parents, education, business and professional affiliations, and career highlights. Whenever there is more than one marriage to be recorded, and children by more than one marriage, the greatest caution is required with a check on any dates that are used. Obituary style requires a writer to record that a widow survives a married man, and a husband survives a married woman.

When a death is announced in the morning papers, the afternoon papers in the same city generally do not repeat the lead but switch to the second-day angle—the announcement of the funeral services. Of course, where there is no competition, the same obit can be carried throughout the day, but it seldom is. The second-day procedure, stressing the funeral, is almost as stylized as the announcement of a death. Even if the funeral arrangements are carried in the original obit, they are made the basis of the second-day lead for the paper in the succeeding cycle. This is an example:

> A funeral service for James R. MacDuff, who crusaded for tight law enforcement while he was State Motor Vehicle Commissioner, will be held tomorrow in Schenevus, N. Y., a village in Otsego County where he was born. He died yesterday at the Albany Medical Center at the age of 71 following a brief illness.

When death occurs in unusual circumstances, the story is handled in an appropriate manner. Sometimes there is a brief feature angle to the story, as was the case in this short piece:

> HOUSTON, Tex. (AP)—Mrs. Eva Deschner, who rallied from serious illnesses many times in the last two years and told her family she would not die before her 97th birthday, died Wednesday on her 97th birthday.
> "Mother always was a strong-minded woman," said a daughter, Mrs. Julia Gabler.

An unexpected death, in public surroundings, also is written with some appreciation for the circumstances. It may be followed by a brief obit, but the story should detail exactly what happened. This story is done in a variation of straight news style:

> CHICAGO—David Topuridze, a concert pianist, finished playing Beethoven's "Moonlight Sonata" at his recital here last night and toppled from the piano bench. He had suffered a heart attack.
> While the hushed audience looked on, two physicians hurried from their seats in the auditorium and attempted to revive the musician by massaging his heart. One of them, Dr. Hilary DeForest Beckwith, Mr. Topuridze's personal physician, was heard by those near the stage to murmur, "Hurry. There's just a bare chance."
> The other physician, Dr. Amory Ledbetter, made an incision in the musician's chest with a penknife. The doctors then took turns massaging the heart. While Dr. Beckwith said that Mr. Topuridze had responded briefly to the emergency treatment, he died before an ambulance reached the auditorium in the Loop.

Except for the deaths of a Churchill or a Kennedy, obits are generally summarized in a few crisp sentences for the broadcast media. During the various newspaper strikes of the sixties, both local radio and television stations made efforts to supply the kind of detailed obituary notices that are common in good newspapers but there simply wasn't enough time—or enough interest—in the material.

There are, of course, many newspapers on which the obit is so stylized that the details could be filled in on a blank form without making a great deal of difference. The stories read like it, too. But the better newspapers really care about making obits mean more than just a lot of printed matter to run beside the paid ads.

For the famous, it is the general practice on both newspapers and wire services to run the news of the death in relatively brief form, then carry an obit, often prepared long in advance, under a dash. This was the manner in which the death of T. S. Eliot was recorded:

> LONDON—T. S. Eliot, the American-born British poet whose words seared a new image of man into the modern consciousness, died at his home here last night. He was 76.
>
> Eliot had suffered a mild heart attack in 1958 and at one time two years ago had been a patient in a London hospital that specializes in respiratory diseases. He was one of the best known and most honored poets of the century—a Nobel Prize winner, an officer of the French Legion of Honor, and the recipient of the U. S. Medal of Freedom.
>
> ———
>
> With his bowler and tightly furled umbrella, Thomas Stearns Eliot seemed in appearance more the bank clerk he had once been than the revolutionary poet whose vision of man's despair is indelible in contemporary thought.
>
> In person, he was tall, stooping, with hooded eyes, and an ascetic face whose austerity grew more acute with age. "How unpleasant to meet Mr. Eliot!" he once wrote. But this most influential of modern poets was anything but unpleasant: shy, detached, meticulously polite, amusing.
>
> Eliot is now so securely enthroned that histories of literature declaim of an "Age of T. S. Eliot." Yet, the publication of "The Love Song of J. Alfred Prufrock" in 1915 and "The Wasteland' in 1922 aroused furor, fury—and cheering. And when he received the Nobel Prize for literature in 1948, it was for his "work as a trail-blazing pioneer of modern poetry."
>
> The poet was born in St. Louis in 1888, the son of a brick manufacturer and the descendant of a long line of New England Puritans. After his graduation from Harvard in 1909, he studied at the Sorbonne in Paris. With the outbreak of World War I, he went to London, which was to become his home, and worked as a teacher and later a bank clerk before joining the London publishing house of Faber and Faber. At his death, he was a director of the firm.
>
> Much of Eliot's poetry has been so often quoted that certain lines have taken on the limpness of clichés. Most familiar is "This is the way the world ends . . . not with a bang but a whimper." In an interview in

his 70s, he disavowed the prophecy. "I'm not so sure the world will end with either," he said . . .

—*Newsday*

The wire services and most large newspapers maintain current hold-for-release obituaries on file of as many big news names as possible. Often newspapers put some of these in type and, in the case of national and international leaders, make up a whole page or more of news and pictures in advance to be used when the subject dies. The broadcast media are able to call on their film libraries, as well as the wire service advance obits, for quick reports when someone of the stature of Sir Winston Churchill dies. Similar material was kept available for years on the former Presidents, Herbert Hoover, Harry S Truman, Dwight David Eisenhower, and many other famous Americans.

The chore of examining such obituaries and bringing them up to date often is given to reporters and rewrite men in newspaper offices when there is nothing else for them to do. As a rule, inexperienced journalists are not trusted with work of this kind even if it is routine. It is also of major importance. One mistake in the obituary of a famous man, even if years pass before it is published, can bring a stack of letters of protest from indignant subscribers. Such errors, once made, cannot easily be detected and corrected in a hold-for-release story if they get past the copy desk and are congealed in cold type.

FUNERALS

Most funeral reports are restrained, dignified, and brief. Nearly everything that could be said about the dead person has been said in the obituary. In the funeral little is left except to tell when and where it was held, estimate the number of persons who were present, identify members of the family and close friends if such names are pertinent, give the name of the clergyman involved and the place of burial or cremation. In describing the funeral of a famous person, the routine is more or less the same but the facts may be more colorful.

Whether the funeral is recorded on film for television, with an accompanying commentary by a newsman, or published on Page 1 of a newspaper under the byline of an established writer, the key to successful reporting is restraint. Even in great tragedies, such as the funeral of an assassinated President or the last rites for an astronaut killed under dramatic circumstances, it is the fashion to avoid a show of emotion as much as possible except when there is extraordinary justification for it. The event itself should be permitted to convey its own emotional quality to the reader or viewer.

Therein lies the artistry of the journalist, whether he works with a typewriter, a microphone, or a camera.

Here is such a story:

By Bill Rives

TIOGA, Texas—Royce Scoggins, Marine private first class, was buried here Friday. He was this area's first fatality of the war in Vietnam.

He had been shot in the head. He had not yet reached the midway mark of his 18th year.

It was one of the largest funerals ever held in Tioga. Virtually the entire town of approximately 500 residents closed down during the services—which were conducted by three ministers at the Tioga Baptist Church—and during the burial rites that followed.

The church overflowed long before the services began. Hymnal music, sadly soft, came from a piano. Other than that, inside and outside, there was almost total silence. The church is just off Highway 99 and the only noise came from an occasional automobile passing through this farming community.

Flowers were heavily banked all the way across the church in front of the first row of pews and directly behind the casket. A United States flag draped the coffin.

The Rev. Hugh Newsom, pastor of the First Baptist Church in nearby Collinsville, where Royce Scoggins went to school and to church, quoted a Biblical passage:

"He cometh forth like a flower and is cut down."

Royce Scoggins, you might say, was nobody special. Except to those who knew him and held him dear. After all, he hadn't had much time to achieve anything of note.

But while he was nobody special, he did have a special quality.

He fit the pattern of the American boy, the one you see on billboards, in newspapers and magazines, and on the TV screen. He was a blond-haired youngster with clear blue eyes. Freckles ran over the bridge of his slightly pug nose. In the summertime when it was hot, and he was running or jumping or playing baseball, the freckles seemed to grow and multiply, nurtured by the beads of perspiration that popped out and trickled or ran—depending upon how fast he was moving—to the broad smile of his mouth.

He was shy, except when he was with his own kind. Around adults, and around girls, he was awkward and uncomfortable. But around other boys his own age, he was exuberant and vibrant, and, without knowing it, a genuine contender for the human equivalent of perpetual motion.

The pallbearers, sitting solemn-faced in the first pew on the left side, were former classmates of Royce at Collinsville High School. One of them, Jerry Hestand, had broken his right ankle playing basketball a few weeks before and still wore a walking cast, covered now with black fabric. . .

At the burial grounds, when the ministers had paid their last tribute to Royce Scoggins, an honor guard of seven Marines raised rifles and fired three times. Out of sight, behind the canvas tent that shielded the family and the casket from the sun, stood a fourth minister, the Rev.

Artie Alexander, pastor of the Calvary Baptist Church of Pilot Point. He was pressed into service as a bugler He had been a professional musician 15 years before entering the ministry.

He put the instrument to his lips and the sound of "Taps," beautiful but cruel, rolled over the gently undulating land that Royce Scoggins had loved.

—Denton (Texas) Record-Chronicle

chapter 9

How News Fits Time and Space

There are finite limits to the shape of the news. It must fit certain factors of time and space in even the greatest of news organizations. Editors, therefore, cram their spikes with overwritten, overstuffed copy. What they use is carefully calculated for size. The newspaper's treatment of this eternal problem is discussed in this chapter and the adaptation of it to broadcast journalism follows in a subsequent chapter.

THE WRITER'S PROBLEM

It is one of the commonplaces of writing that a writer must know his audience, what he has to say to them, and, finally, he must know himself. When a writer is under editorial direction, whether strict or lenient, he must also know the editorial mind and this is perhaps the greatest puzzle of all.

Editorial Instruction   Editors vary widely in the degree of instruction and guidance they give to writers.

The laissez-faire editor merely says, "Take so-and-so on the telephone and let's have a piece on what he's got." Or he may drop a bundle of clips, notes, or wire copy on a desk and tell the writer, "Let's have a few paragraphs." He may not have time to elaborate. Or he may not think it necessary.

The trained professional, however, generally knows what to do. He has plumbed the editorial mind. He can pretty well guess, through experience, what is desired. But the newcomer can only struggle with his puzzle and adhere to the one rule that will never make trouble for any journalist: "Keep it short!"

There are no calipers for the measurement of news values so that an editor and a writer can communicate as scientists do. If they know each other well and have worked together for some time, the communication is taken for granted. A word, a look, a gesture of the fingers, or an abrupt, "Let it run," and the writer knows what is expected of him. In any case, the end product usually fits the space allotted to it. If it does not, it will be bitten off—and probably on a deadline—much to the writer's anguish.

Writing to Space   On more methodical papers—and the pressures of economy are forcing an increase in their number—several devices are used to achieve greater precision in the news. This process is called "writing to space," a problem that has haunted writers since the Ten Commandments were handed down from Mount Sinai.

Some editors, determined that everything shall be "written to space," are almost painfully explicit. They describe exactly what is wanted, how the account is to begin, and its precise length in words. They even have writers set the stops on their typewriters to the exact length of a line cast by a Linotype machine. They will prescribe shorts that must be written in no more than 22 words, or maybe 33.

Others link the length of news accounts to the varieties of headlines that are suggested for them, except for the lead stories on Page 1. A single-line one-column head in small type, for example, may carry an automatic space limit of 60 words. A slightly larger one-column headline will be for a story that is held to 150 words. A short spread head may be pegged to 400-word stories. Beyond that point a space limit may be estimated for each story that is assigned.

Whatever the system, its successful operation depends on teamwork and mutual understanding because its measurements cannot be completely accurate. For example, when an editor asks for 100 words, he expects to get ten typewritten lines because the usual city room estimate is based on ten words to a typewritten line. If he limits a short to a stick of type, a stick being a printer's measurement equal to two inches, he expects about 80 words because body type runs about 40 words to the inch. If he asks for a paragraph, he wants no more than 40 or 50 words, that being the average size of the "short short" on a normal eight column page.

Checking Results   The writer knows quickly enough if he has solved his editorial problem. When he is writing for an edition deadline, he hands in his copy take by take. If the lead is all wrong, back comes the first take with perhaps a smudged pencil mark next to the second or third paragraph. That may mean the editor prefers this for the beginning of the story. Or maybe he was just careless. In any case, the writer who is thoroughly professional accepts this uncertainty as part of his work and tries a different lead.

As for his space limit, he is reminded quickly enough when he approaches it, just in case he has forgotten. The editor may say, "That's about enough," or, "Better wind it." Or he may say nothing but simply write an end mark on the story.

Periodically newspapers and wire services go through a frenzied period that is known as "tightening up." During such a time normal news values are almost impossible to maintain because the editorial mind has gone on a rampage. For some obscure reason it has been decided that all stories are too long. Consequently, all stories must be reduced in length. No organization is immune from this kind of seizure, and there is no known cure for it. It must run its course.

SHORTS

The writing of good shorts is an art. It may also be a precise art. Where a story can be told briefly and well, it is the best example of "writing to space." It is not often that such shorts can be told best in the style of the inverted pyramid. Sometimes, chronological order is effective. Frequently the punch of a short-short story can be compressed into a few lines of type. A delayed beginning, a tag line, a quote, a keen observation—all these devices may be used to make shorts come alive.

There is no name for this kind of organization, except possibly a box because that is how such shorts often are published. In structure they resemble a square because there is usually an almost equal division of space between the lead and the body.

These are shorts that are used to brighten the news routine:

LONDON—Some of London's music critics were upset today because they had praised Piotr Zak's Third Symphony when it was given its first performance last night. Belatedly, the British Broadcasting Corporation announced that the broadcast attributed to Mr. Zak, identified as a young Polish composer, in reality had been a taped potpourri of noise made by two of its employees.

And was Mr. Zak upset, too? No, the BBC said, because there is no Mr. Zak.

A golfer lost $2,000 today because he missed a putt on a golf course last summer. Maxwell J. Hardison, 53, the golfer, was accused of throwing his putter away when the ball failed to drop into the cup. His partner,

G. Wilfred Mannersley, 62, charged the putter struck him on the head, causing a concussion, and sued in County Court here. As a result, Mr. Mannersley won a $2,000 verdict.

SINGLE-INCIDENT LEADS

The simplest form of organization for a story is one that is based on a single-incident lead. The account may have more than one news idea in it, but these are not of such importance that they must be clustered right after the first paragraph, as is true for an inverted pyramid. Therefore, the organization takes the form of a ladder:

Lead incident
    Documentation
    _____

        Second incident
        Documentation
        _____

            Third incident
            Documentation
            _____

The length of such a story may be calculated easily by limiting the number of news ideas that are selected for development and using only the most essential documentation for each. It can be written precisely to space.

Writing About Speeches   The average speech, which is not necessarily Page 1 material but still is worth publishing, usually can be handled in the ladder form of organization.

It should be noted, in the following account, that the rule of one-idea-to-a-sentence is reasonably well observed. Only the central news idea is in the lead. The speaker's name, the time and place of the meeting, the reason for the speaker's remarks, and similar details are scattered through the story where they logically belong. Formerly, all such material was rounded up into a block-buster of a lead. The device of scattering speech detail through the story is almost a regulation pattern for news writers today. It is also used, more or less, for the handling of political meetings, legislative proceedings, hearings of various kinds, and similar events that must be written in a given space, and without superfluous detail.

This is the format, but writers should not assume it is an inflexible device:

Lead Incident   The new director of the city's Museum of Modern

Art promised today that he would broaden its benefits to the community.

Documentation for Lead

Dr. Frederick V. R. Langsam, the director, who succeeded the late Albert Arnold Bunker, made public his plans in a "White Paper on Art."

The "White Paper" was summarized in a speech by Dr. Langsam before his Board of Trustees at the Museum's auditorium.

"We are going to send some of our best pictures, including some Picassos, into the deprived parts of this community," he said.

At the Museum itself, he added, such modern devices as indoctrination films and pocket-size tape-recorded guides would be used to explain the collection to the public.

Second Incident

Dr. Langsam also said he might find some surprises in the Museum's treasure-trove of art, now stored in various warehouses.

Documentation for 2d Incident

"As a good museum man," he explained, "I know that fashions in art change and some works of modern artists that have been stored now will find an appreciative public. This city is likely to have some surprises."

Third Incident

The Museum's director conceded frankly that the Museum's public image needed improvement.

Documentation for 3d Incident

"People have thought of us as a stuffy old barn run by a lot of fuddy-duddies," he said, "and maybe they have been right. We're going to open up from now on, I can tell you."

Among the measures Dr. Langsam proposed in his "White Paper" were improved relations between the Museum and the city's public schools. "Let's bring art to the children instead of leading the children into the Museum by the hand," he urged. He also wants to close the gap between the Museum and the State University to strengthen the Museum's reputation among art scholars.

Added Detail

Dr. Langsam was a professor of art history at the State University before he assumed his present post.

During his academic career, he won a reputation for springing surprises, known as "Langsam's Happenings," to attract the public to academic surroundings. He said there would be no "Happenings" at the Museum.

The following single-incident lead further illustrates the pattern and emphasizes the method through which detail is scattered in the story instead of being plastered into the first paragraph:

> A leader in California's war on auto smog estimated here yesterday that at least 50 per cent of Houston's air pollution comes from auto exhausts.
>
> Donald A. Jensen said the relentless surge in auto population could create an annoying auto smog problem in Houston in years to come unless controls are clamped on.
>
> Jensen is executive director of the California Motor Vehicle Pollution Control Board. He assayed Houston's auto smog outlook in a speech in the Hotel America before a regional meeting of the National Petroleum Refiners Association.
>
> "About 80 to 85 per cent of Los Angeles' smog is now traceable to the invisible exhaust gases from the area's 4 million cars," he said.
>
> He based the "at least 50 per cent" figure for Houston on the city's sprawl, extensive use of cars, and constricted public transport system— all factors shared by Los Angeles.
>
> —Houston *Post*

One of the difficulties about writing reports of speeches is the need for attributing all statements, in quotes or paraphrase, to the speaker. On some city desks it is the fashion to use a monotonous "he said—he said— he said" on the theory that this is exactly what he did and it is the best word to use. At the other extreme is the writer who uses such nonsensical variations as "he opined" or "he averred."

Surely there is room between these two extremes for an exact determination of what actually happened. If reporters did not take the care to make such observations, they would overlook good headline verbs in their leads. A speaker may have demanded, charged, challenged, accused, warned, shouted, insisted, explained, asserted, pointed out, or any number of other variations thereof. However, except when a speaker has taken a formal position, it should never be reported that he has stated or declared his views. These are formal words—statements and declarations. They should be reserved for such situations.

The single-incident lead, as applied to speeches, lends itself readily to other news accounts in which all main points need not be jammed into the first two or three paragraphs. This is an example:

Doctors at City Hospital have used an artificial tube and valve fashioned from the patient's skin to replace a shattered larynx and restore the voice of a State University freshman.

The student, Campbell B. Stinchfield, 18, of Chicago, greeted reporters with, "Hello, everybody. Come right in." They were his first spoken words since he was injured in an automobile accident on Route 162 near the city's southern limit.

In two operations, the new larynx, made from skin taken from Stinchfield's thigh, was installed.

The operation was performed by Drs. Wilford J. W. Carstairs and Helge O. Halvorsen.

Dr. Halvorsen said the procedure was the first of its kind and "rather simple, although it will take a year or two to get the kinks out."

MULTIPLE-INCIDENT LEADS

The story with several angles that must be featured high in the lead, and documented in turn, becomes a fairly complicated matter to organize. Once again, the selection of the news ideas that are to be featured is the key to the amount of space that will be required. This type of organization is somewhat more akin to the inverted pyramid, but it cannot be bitten from the bottom as recklessly as that old sponge for printer's ink.

This is generally the organization scheme for a multiple-incident lead, when reporters have the time to figure out exactly how they want to construct it. Assuming three major news ideas must be included near the top of the story, the ladder would assume a somewhat different shape:

Lead Incident

_____

  Second Lead Incident

  _____

    Third Lead Incident

    _____

      Connecting Paragraph

      _____

        Documentation for Lead Incident

        _____

          Documentation for Second Lead Incident

          _____

            Documentation for Third Lead Incident

            _____

              Other details

If each major news idea is easy to express, the three top incidents may be summarized in one paragraph each. Often this is not possible, and two or more paragraphs may be required to give the highlights of each news idea. It is likely that a key quotation, a textual paragraph of importance, or some other part of the documentation, may have to be thrust high in the story to call it immediately to the readers' attention. This is why no estimate can ever be made on the length of leads for all news stories. In some cases they may be a sentence, in others 400 or 500 words.

A multiple-incident lead, of course, can be butchered by a writer who ignores connectives. The separate parts of a story, where possible, should be made to hang together. When they do not, the result is scarcely a story but a series of bulletins strung together in what is known as block-paragraph style. Cut them up, toss them in a hat, draw them out, and rearrange them, and they will still read as block paragraphs. The temptation of an amateur writer, trying to glue his paragraphs together, is to write involved sentences. It is disastrous to yield to it. Following are some of the simplest connective words and phrases that help make a story coherent:

Also	With
But	Without
Soon	Later
Before	However
After	Nevertheless
Meanwhile	As to
In spite of	About
Next	For instance
Finally	Nearby
Better	Farther off
Worse	Whatever

Redoing a Story   The easiest way to illustrate the difference between the handling of a single- and multiple-incident lead is to redo the Museum of Modern Art story by crowding the main points into the lead. It follows:

Lead Incident	Some of the city's prized Picassos are going to be sent from the Museum of Modern Art into slum areas.
Documented Lead Incident	The Museum's new director, Dr. Frederick V. R. Langsam, promised its trustees today in a "White Paper on Art" that he would send the Picassos and other art treasures into parts of the city that had had little previous exposure to culture.
Summary of Other Points	In a speech at the Museum's auditorium, he also pledged he would change the institution's "stuffy old barn" image by exhibiting art in the schools, resorting to explanatory movies and recorded guides for visitors and taking some of its art works out of storage.

Transition Graph, to be followed by Detail.

Dr. Langsam, who succeeded the late Albert Arnold Bunker, said, "We're going to open up from now on, I can tell you."

The remainder of the documentation would be picked up, each section in turn, with the paraphrase in each case illustrated with quotes. Naturally, the virtue of such organization is to jam the principal news at the top. The main fault is that the reader is likely to lose the thread of the story and forget all about the documentation. However, in major speeches during political campaigns or those outlining local, national, or state policy, a reporter has no alternative but to get the news at the top.

Tabular Leads   The multiple lead may be better fixed in the public mind by using a tabular system of organization. In the new beginning for the Museum of Modern Art story, for example, the first paragraph may stand and then be followed with this:

> The Museum's new director, in a "White Paper on Art," also pledged:
> 1. To exhibit art in the schools.
> 2. To use explanatory movies and recorded guides for Museum visitors.
> 3. To change the Museum's "stuffy old barn" image.

The documentation of the lead and the two following points then would proceed as has already been indicated. Sometimes the figures for the succeeding points are omitted and bullets or paragraph marks are used instead. It adds up to the same thing. Another device for summary purposes is to use key words or phrases, followed by the gist of remarks about them, such as:

> Dr. Frederick V. R. Langsam, the director, laid down these other main points in his "White Paper on Art":
> Schools—Art exhibits would also be sent there.
> Communications—Explanatory movies and tape-recorded guides will be used in the Museum itself to aid visitors.
> Image—The Museum's "stuffy old barn" image is going to be changed.
> "We're going to open up from now on, I can tell you," Dr. Langsam told the Museum's trustees in a speech in its auditorium.

Generally it is awkward to use the key word or phrase system for summary purposes high in a story, but it fits in very well at the end of stories that must be written tightly in order to touch on a few additional points made in a speech.

This is an additional form of tabular lead on a story other than the relatively easy speech form:

The River City Police Department is riddled by lax discipline, old-fashioned administration and inefficient procedures.

While the city's police force is as large and well-paid as those in municipalities of comparable size, standards for performance, promotions, and job applications are sagging.

These were the salient conclusions made public at City Hall today of a year-long survey by a panel of experts into the work of the Police Department. Mayor Harold V. Dawkins, who pledged that such a study would be made during his successful campaign for election, stressed these major points in the report:

1. The Police Department's record-keeping is inaccurate and open to serious question on other counts.

2. Less than 20 per cent of the force is assigned to patrol work on weekends, when crime usually reaches a peak.

3. Patrol post boundaries are outmoded and patrolmen are assigned arbitrarily to three shifts in equal numbers, although high crime hours are at night.

4. Many patrolmen frequent bars while on duty, despite efforts of supervisory officers to halt the practice.

"This survey," Mayor Dawkins said, "indicates that a thorough-going reform is needed in the organization of our Police Department and I'm going to see that a beginning is made, regardless of who is hurt. River City is entitled to better police protection . . ."

Necessarily each of the tabular points must be documented in both these leads in order to provide the reader with a decent explanation of them. As may also be seen, there is always the possibility that a pencil-happy deskman will let the lead stand, if it is so ably summarized, and carve off the documentation, thus leaving the reader in dazed ignorance of why these striking statements are so.

THE STORY ASSEMBLED

In the multiple-incident lead that follows, the general form of story organization is clearly outlined by the manner in which the main points are assembled. The various angles are blended into the opening paragraphs without numbers, dots, or other tabular devices:

CAPE CHARLES—Virginia's link with its Eastern Shore is severed and probably will remain so for at least a week.

A spokesman for the commission that operates the Chesapeake Bay Bridge-Tunnel said today that it will take at least that long to repair damage caused late last night when an unmanned coal barge slammed bow-on against the 17-mile-long crossing.

Sent adrift by 30-mile-an-hour winds from her anchorage three miles west of the bridge-tunnel, the vessel rammed the bridge and knocked at least one 75-foot section about four feet out of line.

Power cables and telephone lines were snapped, metal railings were twisted and chunks of concrete were gouged from the trestle as the barge, driven southward, bumped along the bridge for three miles until it ran aground on Chesapeake Beach on the mainland side.

Today, the Coast Guard flooded the hold of the barge, stabilizing the vessel and preventing further damage to the bridge.

Leon Johnson, bridge-tunnel chief engineer, said, "We know damage is extensive." However, he would make no estimate pending the completion of surveys. Another official said that preliminary studies indicated damage in the neighborhood of $1,000,000.

Divers will begin examination of underwater damage tomorrow to the long concrete pilings that support the trestle. . . .

—Richmond *Times-Dispatch*

Despite the demands of space and time, not all such organization schemes can be carefully contrived. There is a type of narrative that falls into a natural story pattern and in effect tells itself if the writer has the wit to see it. For such pieces, old hands at telling the news say, "Get out of the way of the story." It makes its own pattern, as the following illustrates:

ATLANTIC BEACH—The former Miss Judy John became the bride of Mr. Pete John at Lou's Restaurant yesterday and all hell broke loose.

A whirling, stomping, jumping, shouting gypsy party exploded in the big dining room after a go-between led dark-haired, 21-year-old Judy from her mother to the groom's mother. That was the ceremony. Miss John was now Mrs. John, the bride of her second cousin.

There were no wild Romany violins to set the blood racing. Instead there was the bump-thump of a non-gypsy rock 'n roll quintet—youngsters with sheep-dog haircuts who called themselves the Initial Phase. They played mechanically, their eyes darting from side to side.

Lou's is a short walk from the beach, but it was a dismal day and the only cars parked outside were dozens of pickup trucks with out-of-state license plates. The gypsies had been in town for three weeks. Somebody said they'd elected a king but nobody seemed to know his name or where he was.

There was only one answer to a non-gypsy's question about gypsies: "Give me $5 and I'll read your palm. You don't have five? . . . Make it two." The gypsy women sparkled in gold and vivid reds, greens, and blues. They wore sashes and scarves and headbands and pounds of gaudy jewelry.

Judy John came out to the bar and sat down at an empty table. Out on the dance floor, her 22-year-old groom was hopping around with one of the rainbow girls. "I'm tired. I've danced with everybody here, I think," Judy said. She was wearing a white wedding dress but around her neck was a huge necklace of gold coins. "It doesn't mean anything. It's just pretty," she said. The marriage had been arranged by her mother and the groom's, but she was happy, she said.

The restaurant's proprietor, Lou Calabrio, wore a strained smile. The gypsies had come at noon, carrying their own hams and chickens, he said.

They had cooked and served their own food, and the restaurant had provided the booze. There were supposed to be 75 guests, but 250 showed up.

—Newsday

THE CHRONOLOGICAL STORY

The chronological story often may be useful, lively, and economical of space for news that can be handled with a feature twist. The trick is to begin in such a manner that the reader's curiosity will be piqued so that he follows the story. There are many effective devices through which this can be done.

The Unexpected Event   Sometimes, there is a happening that can be turned to good advantage in the news columns—an event so unexpected that it makes news. This is one way of handling such an occurrence:

> When Thomas Dunn raised his baton at Philharmonic Hall yesterday to rehearse the Festival Orchestra of New York, 22 beagles came loping on stage.
> Mr. Dunn seemed not to be as surprised as the beagles. They sniffed the stage, the musicians, and appraised the bass violin as a possible substitute for a hydrant. The sound of recorded barking off-stage didn't upset them; like well-behaved visitors, not a beagle barked back.
> Mr. Dunn gestured and the French horns piped hunting calls, but the beagles paid no attention whatever. They were well aware that there were no rabbits at Philharmonic Hall. So the orchestra played on and the beagles were left pretty much to their own devices.
> It was all according to plan, except for the beagles' unnatural silence. For the work being rehearsed was the Hunting Symphony by Leopold Mozart, father of Wolfgang Amadeus, who wrote instructions in the score for dogs to bark in response to the opening notes of hunting horns.
> Mr. Dunn brought in the Buckram Beagles, a Long Island hunting pack, from Brookville, complete with the Master of Beagles and three uniformed whippers-in. But there wasn't a bark in the pack during the afternoon, which would have pained the composer no end.

The straight chronological news story, which begins mildly and works up to a stirring climax, also has made a place for itself in journalism. One of the best is Don Whitehead's Pulitzer Prize-winning story of General Dwight D. Eisenhower's secret visit to the Korean War front lines as President-elect in 1952. Its opening paragraphs are quoted to show how it differs from the pell-mell opening of the average straight news story:

> By Don Whitehead
> WITH EISENHOWER IN KOREA, Dec. 5 (AP)—It was 5:30 a.m. (EST) on Saturday, Nov. 29, when two men stepped quickly through the door-

way of the residence at 60 Morningside Drive in New York City into the cold starlit night.

Their overcoat collars were turned up as though against a chill. They strode swiftly to the limousine that had pulled up at the curb a few feet from the doorway, ducked into the car, and it drove away. The street was bare and silent once again.

One of the men was United States Secret Service Agent Edward Green and the other was President-elect Eisenhower. This was the beginning of the Eisenhower mission to Korea where he hoped—as millions of Americans did—that a way could be found to bring an honorable end to the bloody fighting which in two and one-half years had claimed 126,000 American dead, wounded, and missing . . .

Throughout the carefully related story, the quiet tone of the writer never rose. The patient, considered mood of understatement remained the same. Yet, the piece was so precisely written that editors all over the nation published it without significant cuts. Such was the quality of permanence conveyed in the simple, but meaningful, narration of a great event.

Contrast this with the even more dramatic chronological narrative of the assassination of President John Fitzgerald Kennedy, as told by Merriman Smith of United Press International. Only a few hours after the first bulletins from Dallas that shocked the nation on November 22, 1963, Smith hurried to the typewriter and wrote his famous story that won the Pulitzer Prize. The piece next day began quietly and simply:

By Merriman Smith

DALLAS, Nov. 23 (UPI)—It was a balmy, sunny noon as we motored through downtown Dallas behind President Kennedy. The procession cleared the center of the business district and turned into a handsome highway that wound through what appeared to be a park.

I was riding in the so-called White House press "pool" car, a telephone company vehicle equipped with a mobile radio-telephone. I was in the front seat between a driver from the telephone company and Malcolm Kilduff, acting White House Press Secretary for the President's Texas tour. Three other pool reporters were wedged in the back seat.

Suddenly we heard three loud, almost painfully loud, cracks. The first sounded as if it might have been a large firecracker. But the second and third were unmistakable. Gunfire.

The President's car, possibly as much as 150 or 200 yards ahead, seemed to falter briefly. We saw a flurry of activity in the Secret Service follow-up car behind the Chief Executive's bubble-top limousine. Next in line was the car bearing Vice President Lyndon B. Johnson. Behind that, another follow-up car bearing agents assigned to the Vice President's protection. We were behind that car.

Our car stood still for probably only a few seconds, but it seemed like a lifetime. One sees history explode before one's eyes and for even the most trained observer there is a limit to what one can comprehend.

Everybody in our car began shouting at the driver to pull up closer

to the President's car. But at this moment we saw the big bubble-top and a
motorcycle escort roar away at high speed.

We screamed at our driver, "Get going! Get going!"

We careened around the Johnson car and its escort and set out down
the highway . . .

In this manner, the account continued, telling an extremely complicated story in simple and easily understandable terms. It takes masterful
reporting to do such work.

THE MECHANICAL SIDE

Few journalists have a thorough understanding of the processes of newspaper production, and that is a pity. A basic acquaintance with the work of
the mechanical departments is vital to everyone who writes by the clock. It
is almost impossible to function on a deadline without being able to write
instructions to printers, make markups for makeup editors, and have at
least a nodding recognition with the requirements of the stereotype and
photoengraving departments and the press room. A journalist cannot write
in a vacuum.

Measuring Type   The principal newspaper linear measurement is not calculated in inches or centimeters but in points, a point being one seventy-
second of an inch, and in ems or picas, which are 12 points each or one
sixth of an inch. Technically, an em, being a measurement of area, equals
a pica only when it refers to 12-point type; but, actually, the two terms are
interchangeable in both editorial and composing room. An en, half an em
or six points, is generally referred to as a nut to avoid confusion with an em.

Thus, if a writer wishes to separate items under different datelines in
the same story, he merely writes "3-em dash" and the printer inserts a dash
one-half inch long at the designated spot. Or, if an editor wishes to indent
a paragraph on both sides for emphasis, he writes in the margin, "Indent
one nut," or perhaps an even smaller measure, and he will accomplish his
purpose.

Turn Rules   The initials, T.R., which stand for the printing instruction,
"Turn Rule," are often used in various ways in the process of assembling
a story in type. The most familiar use of the rule, of course, is the column
rule which is a hair line right side up but a broad black stroke when it is
turned upside down. The black borders seen around a picture, article or
page, as a mark of respect to someone of prominence who has died, are
formed by turning the rules. Any piece of dead type, however, may be used
to carry out the printing instruction, "Turn Rule."

When a newspaper story is being assembled in a series of adds, as in the text of a speech, it is common practice for the deskman handling the story to write at the end of the first add, "T.R. for 2nd add Jones text," if Jones happens to be the slug. This is notice to both the composing room and the makeup editor that more of the text is still to come. The last section, accordingly, would be marked, "T.R. for 8th and last add Jones text." A makeup editor, merely by watching the slug lines, therefore can tell how the production process is coming along.

In making a markup it is customary, although not absolutely necessary, to write, "T.R. for Insert Jones," at the point where the insert is to go. Even without the words "T.R. for . . ." the Linotype operator will set it anyway, put it between two column-width pieces of rule and send it to the correction bank where another printer will prop it up in the original type to show that a change is coming. For a pick up after a new lead, the instruction on the markup would read, "T.R. for N.L. Jones," or, to be more specific, "T.R. and pick up after N.L. Jones."

The turn rule instructions, when carried out, clearly call to the attention both of the composing room and makeup editor that changes are expected in a particular story. The slug lines, standing up like flags, prevent the page from being closed until the corrections or other changes have been made.

A Better Background   There are literally hundreds of applications of small, but important, procedures such as type measurements and turn rules for the knowledgeable newspaper writer. There is no great mystery about them. Any competent deskman or copy editor, if he is in a good mood, will take the novice on a tour of the mechanical departments that will serve as an introduction, at least, to the production process. Standard texts on the subject, plus practical experience, will do a great deal to show the inexperienced newspaper writer what he can and cannot do when he is writing by the clock. Particularly in these days, when automatic composition through the teletypesetter is widely used and photocomposition is developing rapidly, no journalist can afford any longer to ignore the ways in which his work is reproduced for a mass public. Larger type, wider columns, shorter stories, and quicker production are bound to leave their mark on the writer in the years directly ahead. He will need a better mechanical background than he has ever had before.

chapter **10**

News Nobody Likes

A journalist needs no instructions when disaster strikes his community. Whether it is a fire, flood or hurricane, an earthquake, wreck or explosion, his duty is to cover the story and help get out the news regardless of personal risk, effort or cost.

This is the journalistic tradition. It is lived up to in the United States, boldly and proudly, by all the news media. Radio, the most immediate source of the news, has served as the good watchman on many an occasion. Television has brought the community and the nation face to face with disaster in its most striking form. But it has remained for the news agencies and the newspapers to publish, in intricate detail, the casualty lists, the extent of damage, the myriad facts that cannot be made available to the public by any other medium.

Nobody profits from a disaster, least of all a newspaper cut off from its advertisers and sometimes even its own plant, or a television station that gives all its time to the public service in an emergency. Nor can it fairly be said that the more common stories of fire losses, auto, train and airplane accidents, ship collisions, and the like are of particular benefit to the news media. They don't "sell newspapers" because the regular circulation procedures of the press are disrupted by a community emergency. And on television, a dim-witted part of the public that lusts for entertainment often resents looking at public service footage.

No one who has ever walked wearily through mud, rain, and darkness to the scene of a wreck will contend that it is exciting or glamorous. Like the news of a defeat in war, such material simply docs not bcncfit thc ncws media as a general rule. It is the news nobody likes. It is also the news everybody must have.

STORMS

What is a storm? The news media must be precise in announcing that a tornado, hurricane, or blizzard has struck the area. The United States Weather Bureau designations are offered as standard here, but it should be noted that they differ slightly from the standard of the familiar Beaufort's Scale. These are the Weather Bureau's definitions:

DESIGNATION	MILES PER HOUR
Calm	Less than 1
Light air	1–3
Light breeze	4–7
Gentle breeze	8–12
Moderate breeze	13–18
Fresh breeze	19–24
Strong breeze	25–31
Near gale	32–38
Gale	39–46
Strong gale	47–54
Storm	55–63
Violent storm	64–73
Hurricane	Above 74

Beaufort's Scale, devised by Sir Francis Beaufort, R. N., in 1805, describes a whole gale as one that uproots trees and defines a hurricane as a wind of more than 75 miles an hour velocity. Actually, hurricanes, tornadoes, cyclones, and typhoons are all members of the cyclonic family. A cyclone is a system of winds that may be several hundred miles wide and circulates about a center of low barometric pressure. It travels at 20 miles an hour or more, and usually from west to east in the United States.

Commonly, a tornado—the most destructive and violent of all local storms—consists of winds rotating at 200 miles an hour or more. It may last from a few minutes to hours, cut a path of destruction from a few feet to a mile wide, and move forward anywhere up to about 300 miles at a speed of up to 68 miles an hour. The hurricane, a severe cyclone that originates in tropical waters, is a huge wind system as much as 500 miles in diameter. It is slower than a local twister, moving at 10 to 15 miles an hour. In the western Pacific, it is called a typhoon.

The severity of rain and snowstorms is measured by the number of inches of precipitation over a given period. By custom, the public has come to accept any snowstorm of prolonged intensity as a blizzard; actually, the Weather Bureau defines a blizzard as fine, dry snow driven by a wind of 35 miles an hour or more, reducing visibility to less than 500 feet, during a period of low temperature.

Casualty Lists Reporters reaching the scene of any disaster will find as many estimates of dead and injured as there are survivors while the rescue work is being organized. However, no experienced reporter will accept an estimate from a hysterical or unqualified person. Figures from authoritative sources should be checked carefully, one against the other, and the sources identified as far as possible so that in first reports from a disaster scene the initial estimates are likely to be within a certain range of the lowest to the highest numbers specified by the various authorities.

As soon as possible, reporters should begin working on their own to gather their figures, documented by the names of the dead and injured. If a count shows that twenty bodies have been recovered (and it is one of the most distasteful parts of a reporter's job to make such a tally), then the reporter eventually must have twenty names in his list of dead. Until the list is complete, partial identifications are acceptable if they are so specified. The list of the injured, and their identities, is compiled from the various hospitals and emergency shelters at which persons are treated.

The efficiency and judgment of reporters invariably are tested by the manner in which casualty figures see-saw from the time a disaster occurs. When the first estimate is 50 or 60 dead and it eventually narrows down to 14, that is simply bad reporting and bad judgment. No such wide swing in casualty figures is ever justified. There may be a variation of five or ten, in a major disaster, or the figures may mount hour by hour as more bodies are discovered and the missing are accounted as dead, but in no case should wild guesses be made at a final total.

The same precautions should be taken in characterizing the extent of the tragedy, the estimates of property loss, and the explanation for the size of the death toll. While eyewitness stories frequently are dramatic, and bear on the reasons for the extent of casualty lists, no account that seems to a reporter to be fanciful should be turned in until it has been checked.

The main story, whether in print or broadcast media, should be handled conservatively with the emphasis on understatement if there is doubt about the extent of the disaster. Nothing is gained by flinging adjectives about, when a whole town has been shaken to its foundations. People do not want to be thrilled by magnificent prose. They just want to know what happened.

Here are examples of storm leads:

TOPEKA—A line of tornadoes tore through eastern Kansas last night, cutting a 15-mile path of destruction through Topeka about 7 o'clock. Eleven persons were killed and more than 200 injured in Topeka.

The line of storms moved eastward and funnels touched down at many points, including Jarbalo, Valley Falls, and near Olathe. A man was killed when one struck his trailer house seven miles west of Tonganoxie, Kansas. Several homes were destroyed at Wakefield, Kansas.

Topeka police were digging through rubble last night to rescue trapped and injured residents. Hundreds of persons were homeless.

Every major building on the Washburn University campus was destroyed or heavily damaged. A ten-story building in downtown Topeka was roped off and was in danger of toppling.

Units of the National Guard were called out, and about 100 airmen were summoned from the Forbes Air Force Base. . .

—Kansas City *Times.*

BELMOND, IOWA—At least six persons were killed and an estimated 200 were injured Friday afternoon when a tornado dropped out of pitch-black clouds and flattened this Wright County town of 2,506 persons.

Scores of business buildings and homes were destroyed or damaged. The storm loss runs into hundreds of thousands of dollars.

It was one of the worst days in Iowa's long tornado history. Storm clouds literally covered the state and, in addition to the disaster at Belmond, damage was felt near Lenox in Taylor County and near Colfax in Jasper County.

The funnel clouds also were sighted near Newton, Monroe, and Cedar Rapids. The storms also spawned lightning, which was blamed for two other deaths in southern Iowa near Mount Ayr.

The Belmond dead were identified as . . .

—Des Moines *Register*

COCOA, FLA.—Tornadoes—the violent whirling winds usually most feared in landlocked midwestern states—twisted across central Florida from the Gulf coast to the Atlantic Monday, leaving death and destruction in their erratic, devastating path.

Spinning suddenly but fiercely out of a dark, fast-moving squall line, the tornadoes first roared down in the Tampa area, then skipped to near Lakeland and finally dipped down in central Brevard County.

At least nine persons were known dead, three in the Tampa area and six in Lakeland. Five more Tampans were missing.

More than 350 persons were injured, including 133 in the Cocoa area. Brevard was spared any death toll, but the property damage here will soar past $3 million. People's life savings were wiped out in minutes.

Spawned by a sea storm over the Gulf, the tornadoes ripped into the Tampa-St. Petersburg area about 8:30 a.m. For nearly two hours, the funnel-shaped clouds and twisting winds swept a 40-mile path across the state before roaring into the Atlantic off Cape Kennedy.

In Tampa, a housewife said it sounded "like a thousand freight trains" bearing down on her house. At Cape Kennedy, a veteran missile worker likened the noise to "a dozen rockets lifting off simultaneously."

Sections of six cities including Cocoa were left looking like battlefields. Four other towns and rural areas suffered severe destruction. Property damage across the state was in the millions . . .

—*Today*, Brevard County, Fla.

Radio newswriting generally follows the same basic themes in storm copy, except that it is present-tensed for the most part. As for television, the bulk of the reporting is very often ad-libbed on the spot to accompany film. Necessarily, the enormous amount of detail—casualty lists, eyewitness accounts, tales of individual heroism or tragedy—can only be carried fully in a newspaper, and not just any old newspaper either. It takes a good one to inspire a staff to get together the lead stories, sidebars, eyewitness pieces, and lists of dead, injured and missing, all under deadline pressure.

GENERAL WEATHER NEWS

A reporter was once assigned by his newspaper to write a story about a perfect day and gave up in despair. A photographer that same day came back to the office with more good pictures than the paper could use—young people dreamily strolling hand in hand, old people sunning themselves in the park, laughing children at play, animals frolicking at the zoo. The ever-present television camera has an even more dramatic facility for bringing such pleasant scenes to the viewers across the nation, but it seldom does. There is too much pressure for drama to keep millions interested in some small facet of the news, too little for the common virtues of life itself.

There are many ways of telling weather news and the journalist uses all of them, whether the weather is good or bad. Even if there is no story in the newspaper, the United States Weather Bureau forecast is always published in one of the ears on Page 1—the boxes on either side of the nameplate. Either the government forecast or the paper's own prediction, obtained from private forecasters, is printed in a prominent position inside the paper. As for the electronic media, weather is one of their most prominent features on almost all broadcasts.

Most daily newspapers also run the government weather table from various major cities, the regional weather forecast, the long-range weather forecast, and the weather map with appropriate explanations. Radio and television, unable to provide such detailed factual data, will run radar maps and have an announcer give appropriate explanations. At airports and Coast Guard stations, meteorologists also are called upon frequently for interviews by all the news media.

The enormous amount of statistical weather data given to the public in great detail means that the average newsman should make it his business to be reasonably familiar with the principles of weather forecasting. No journalist can for very long escape writing or talking about the weather. When a weekend or a holiday is near, when there is a big sports event or an outdoor convention of consequence, the weather is an important part of the story. It cannot be ignored.

The basic facts that must be included in any weather summation include the latest forecast, mean and hourly temperatures when pertinent, humidity, barometric pressure, wind strength and direction, and a comparison with the record highs and lows for that particular date and season. In hot weather, Americans torture themselves with a measurement called the temperature-humidity index (THI), which tries to estimate human discomfort (as if that were possible). To determine THI, wet and dry bulb temperature readings are added, then multiplied by 0.4 and 15 is added to the product. In theory, when the THI passes 75, half the people will be uncomfortable; when it reaches 80 or more, everybody feels awful.

It is an amiable and harmless journalistic custom to salute a "record" high or low for a particular date, which is slightly synthetic, since most government and other weather records are less than 100 years old. When all highs and lows for a single date such as May 12 or December 13 are compared in the record, it is obviously possible to have a "record" day every so often. The ancient journalistic weakness for "firsts" can also be satisfied by checking on the weather for the first day of the season, the first storm of the winter, the first heat wave of the summer, and the hottest and coldest days of the month, season, or year. To those who play the game of highs and lows, a reminder should be given that the "record" is not always established on the hour but may come between hourly readings. Like everything else, the reporter must ask the Weather Bureau for it because the information is not always volunteered; nor is it a good policy to depend on such supplementary services as the weather information supplied in some cities by telephone companies.

There is one other precaution that is recommended to everyone who writes about the weather, whether the story deals with disaster or is just a routine short. A glance out the window, just before writing, will sometimes save everybody trouble. Weather forecasting is far from perfect, and even the most efficient government meteorologists have been known to change their predictions within an hour or less.

In resort cities and localities weather news sometimes is used for its promotional value. Thus, Florida media are likely to play the news of cold weather in northern states, from which so many tourists come, or rain in a rival tourist paradise such as California. Local weather, too, is more likely to be newsworthy in such areas.

Heat Waves, Cold Waves, and Storms   When the hot spells of summer and the cold spells of winter set in, they are news. The classic patterns of weather reporting then are spread over several days, with hourly temperatures featured and enlarged upon by appropriate comparisons with previous days or years. It is comparatively simple to document a heat wave or a cold wave with statistics from the usual government sources. They are plentiful and available for the asking. The accompanying events also are familiar and generally easy to cover. Crowds take to the parks, lakes, mountains, and seashore in the summer heat, with a certain amount of official and business activity being curtailed at extreme periods. During the winter a sub-zero cold spell can seriously disrupt both business and transportation but much of this material can be obtained from official sources, chambers of commerce, and transportation information. Gathering such data takes time, but usually it is plentiful.

The troublesome part of handling extremes in the weather for use in the news media is to determine which deaths, injuries, and losses are directly attributable to them. Such casualties seldom are officially proclaimed. Reporters have to exercise their best judgment—and a considerable amount of restraint—and deskmen are presumed to check on them. Nevertheless, broadcasts and banner headlines announcing that ten persons have died of the cold summon up images of frozen bodies found in remote places. In reality, most of them are likely to be victims of heart attacks that may or may not have been induced by overexertion. The same is often true of deaths attributed to the heat. It would be a nice exercise in general reporting to determine, in any given heat or cold wave, how many persons actually died because of extreme weather conditions. There is, as a rule, too much poetic license in such reportage; it taxes the public's credibility in its news media.

Twenty or thirty years ago it was the custom to give more prominence to weather casualties, but many editors have long since become skeptical of such practices. There have been instances, fortunately few, in which the demise of a man kicked by a horse on a hot day has been offered as a heat casualty. It is standard practice now, when several deaths are attributed to the weather in a given area, to identify the victims and document the manner of death somewhere in the story. Unless there is something unusual about such a casualty list, it is not always made the feature of the story. Moreover, automobile accidents sometimes are listed separately if the cause is not clearly linked to the weather.

Writing the Story The most difficult thing for a newcomer to journalism to understand is that a heat wave, cold wave, or storm, which is known to have occurred in the area, must be announced in the media and explained from beginning to end. There is nothing unusual about this. A hundred thousand people may have seen the Army-Navy football game and millions of others may have watched it on television, but the newspapers and subsequent regular broadcasts still record the fact that there was a game, which side won, what the score was, and the pertinent details. The evidence is impressive that the public is often particularly interested in getting more detail, background information, and color on news of which it has some advance knowledge.

Since the weather is a universal topic of discussion, the first rule in any weather report is to begin at the beginning by telling what is right or wrong with the day, what the results are and why, and whether improvement can be expected. The following are typical leads used by wire services or newspapers. Some may be edited for electronic use merely by changing the past tense of the verbs into present perfect and eliminating the time element if desired:

> A cold wave from northern Canada rolled over the northeastern part of the nation today, forcing the temperature in the city to two degrees above zero. No relief was in sight. . . .
>
> The mercury shot into the 90s today on the fifth day of the August hot spell, but thundershowers forecast for tonight promised temporary relief. . . .
>
> Whipped by a 30-mile-an-hour wind, a snowstorm pelted the city today and reached a depth of four inches in the first five hours. The Weather Bureau forecast an all-night fall, with a probable depth of 12 inches before morning.
>
> Thousands of commuters, facing delays in getting home tonight and uncertain of being able to reach their offices tomorrow, besieged hotels for reservations. Most trains were reported behind schedule in mid-afternoon. Bus traffic was slowed. Flights at Municipal Airport were on schedule for the time being. . . .

One of the characteristics of weather stories is the use of vigorous verbs and sweeping general statements of conditions, which conceivably can lead to an impression that things are worse than they really are. It is one of the risks of writing colorfully about facts that are more or less generally known. Between the dry-as-dust official phrases of the weather report and the hopped-up writing of an overenthusiastic wire service man doing an undated lead, there is a sound middle ground which reporters should seek. That is to tell the story colorfully and accurately, with emphasis on the information that interests the public.

Here are typical weather stories, prepared for newspaper publication:

> B-b-b-baby, it's cold outside. C-c-c-coldest day of the winter so far. And more of the s-s-s-same is on the w-w-w-way.
>
> At 6:45 a.m., the U. S. Weather Bureau said the thermometer had dropped to four degrees above zero. That was exactly six degrees lower than the previous season's record of 10 degrees last Dec. 5. It was also the coldest Jan. 20 in the Weather Bureau's records here.
>
> The forecast for today was for little change in temperature with a high of about 15 degrees. For tonight, you can expect zero.

OSWEGO, N.Y.—This beleaguered community of 22,000 was snow-bound today, virtually cut off by road, rail, and air from the rest of the state.

Mayor Vincent A. Corsall declared an emergency and appealed to Albany for aid. Deliveries of milk and food could not get through snow-choked roads. Mail deliveries were suspended. All schools were closed. Most businesses could not function.

This was the consequence of a driving 22-hour snowstorm that piled up four feet of snow in Oswego, which is 38 miles from Syracuse on the shore of Lake Ontario. With the temperature at 20 degrees, an army of emergency snow-shovelers began digging the city out but it was expected that several days would elapse before traffic could begin moving freely again.

All such accounts invariably are followed by cleanups, detailing the number of machines and persons mobilized to do the job of snow clearance and the measures for emergency relief. But on the day of the storm, the most essential information that any news medium can give is the forecast. It is the best illustration of how the commonplace makes news.

Electronic Forecasting Weather forecasts emanate primarily from the United States Weather Bureau, although some news organizations do maintain their own forecasting service. Nevertheless, the taxpayer is entitled to weather news as a public service and it has been considered to be a public service for many years.

With the coming of radio, it became the practice of most stations to sell their weather news period to advertisers if they could. Consequently, the public must suffer through a lot of nonessential weather information as a "come-on" and then a commercial before getting the few words of the United States Weather Bureau forecast at the end. The television stations further developed this commercialism of what should be a public service by using "weather queens"—buxom young ladies who were supposed to put sex into the weather news—in order to attract viewers to the commercial message. The public was not overwhelmed with this concept; consequently, the better television stations fell back on individuals who were billed as scientific authorities to give the weather message after an appropriate buildup and commercial message.

Radio led the way back to good sense by restoring the simple, unadorned weather forecast, attributed to the United States Weather Bureau without frills. It is the least the public can expect.

EARTHQUAKES

Four out of five earthquakes occur around the borders of the Pacific Ocean. They also may be experienced with some degree of frequency from the

West Indies across the Atlantic and Mediterranean and on to the Himalayas and East Indies. All in all, 1,200 seismograph stations detect about a half million temblors a year. But of these only about 1,000 cause specific damage although up to 100,000 or more may be felt in some slight degree.

The measurement of earthquakes is done on the Richter Scale, designed by the geologist, C. F. Richter. Under it, the magnitude of the quake is made proportional under certain conditions to the logarithm of maximum recorded amplitude. These are typical Richter Scale figures of earthquake magnitude:

2 —Smallest shocks to be reported.
4.5—Smallest shocks causing slight damage.
6 —Shocks that cause moderate destruction.
8.5—Largest known earth shocks.

FIRES

Like the news of storms and other natural disasters, news of fires must be handled with the greatest care in accounting for casualties. The same procedures recommended for the compiling of lists of storm dead and injured are advisable. The top police and fire officials at the scene and hospital authorities all can be helpful in insuring the accuracy of fire casualty lists, but often final identifications must wait on the appearance of relatives at a morgue or funeral home. These are heart-rending scenes, which are difficult for even an experienced reporter to witness.

There are other hazards in the reporting and writing of fire stories. In a report on the cause of a fire, it should be borne in mind that anything said by a fire chief or fire marshal is not privileged. Therefore, if the authorities suggest the blaze was set, it is not the job of the reporter to accuse anyone of arson unless a suspect is arrested and booked on such a charge. It is also dangerous, in reporting the cause of a fire, to attribute negligence to the owners of a house or other building although such risks frequently must be taken if fire authorities choose to make a public statement to that effect. The only course a reporter can take, in such an event, is to seek a reply promptly from the person or persons accused.

Certain information is mandatory in any fire story, in addition to the casualties and the probable cause. The exact address of the structure involved is not enough. It must be described as a residence, office, loft, or factory building. The number of stories should be given and the type of construction, whether it is frame, brick, concrete, or fabricated steel. If it is a building of a particular type, such as a tenement or a substandard dwelling, that should be reported. The time the blaze was discovered, how many fire alarms were turned in, the number of firemen and vehicles that responded, the time when the flames were brought under control or put out, and the effect on nearby buildings and traffic are generally included in the average fire story.

If it is possible to give a fair and accurate estimate of damage, that is obviously one of the features of such a story. The size of damage estimates, however, frequently depends on who gives them—whether it is the owner of a building or a fire official or an insurance adjuster. When there is doubt, the news media should give the legitimate damage estimates that are made and such explanations as are available.

Stories of heroism or narrow escapes from death, eyewitness accounts, and other material generally associated with disaster coverage are often the principal part of a fire report, if there have been no casualties. Otherwise they are mentioned fairly high in the lead, and then documented in the body of the story at an appropriate point.

A Fire Lead   Here is a lead on a fire story that illustrates the variety of material that may be featured:

Eighty-seven children, eight to fourteen years old, and three nuns were killed Monday afternoon in a fire which turned the upper floor of Our Lady of the Angels Catholic School at 909 N. Avers Avenue into a trap of flaming horror. Of the dead pupils, 53 were girls and 34 boys.

An estimated 90 others, including three nuns of the Sisters of Charity, which operated the school, and a janitor were severely burned or otherwise injured. They were treated in seven hospitals.

The worst school tragedy in Chicago's history resulted in scenes of undescribable grief at the school, which is around the corner from the church of the same name at 3808 Iowa Street; at nearby hospitals, and at the morgue where the victims were laid out for identification by parents.

There was anguish and heartbreak as parents screamed and struggled with policemen outside the burning building in mid-afternoon; as they searched for missing youngsters while firemen were probing the smoldering building; and as they identified the victims at the morgue.

The horror of the blaze itself, which began at 2:40 P.M., only 20 minutes before the 1,200 pupils in the building would have left classes, was equally overwhelming. Witnesses saw children leaping from windows of the two-story building; saw them appear at windows and then fall back. What could not be seen—the trap apparently closed by billowing and blinding black smoke and flame—was worse.

There was heroism by firemen who battled their way into the flames to bring out victims, some alive; by priests and nuns who led out pupils while the building was turning into an inferno; by a nun who appeared at a window and then died with her charges.

City and county officials and representatives of the Roman Catholic Church began investigations of the blaze, seeking to learn how it started and how the children were trapped.

By Monday night, the following story of the fire had been pieced together:

The fire started with an oil-type blaze in a stairwell in the northeast corner of the building—although the school was heated by coal. It roared up the stairwell. Dense, black smoke suddenly poured into the corridors as it spread to the ceiling. This occurred extremely rapidly. The stairwell must have been filled with flames by the time the fire alarm sounded. . . .

—Chicago *Tribune*

TRANSPORTATION ACCIDENTS

All forms of transportation accidents—automobiles, buses, trains, ships, aircraft, and now space ships—are reported as they occur. It is unhappily true that the individual automobile crash, because it is the most common, receives comparatively less attention than the others although it is responsible for more than 50,000 deaths a year—approaching the American death toll in both the Korean and Vietnam Wars. There is an obvious difference in the treatment given by the news media to two deaths in an air crash as compared with two deaths in an auto crash. Two deaths of astronauts in a space ship, preparing for launching at Cape Kennedy, is, of course, far more spectacular than anything else and receives the full treatment in television film and headlines.

It is, without doubt, patently unfair to air travel to feature every air crash and play down the average automobile wreck, particularly in view of the excellent safety records of the commercial airlines. Moreover, it is scarcely responsible journalism to underplay the role of the automobile as the great killer of our society. But, good or bad, these are the news values that exist today and only public pressure can change them. When rocket travel comes of age, presumably the treatment of aircraft accidents will be somewhat more fair than it is today. Both the press and the electronic media act as if the airplane were invented only yesterday—and probably some old-time editors still think of air travel as a novelty.

Automobile Accidents   Many attempts have been made by the news media to dramatize the slaughter on the nation's highways. For a time, it was considered a public service to give a blood-curdling tinge to accounts of auto crashes, but the technique had about the same effect as the publicity that has been given to cancer research in connection with cigarette smoking. With the exception of crusading newspapers, news stories generally have returned to a straight news treatment of automobile accidents.

Over holidays and summer weekends, it has been the custom to feature the auto death forecast of the National Safety Council and moodily comment on whether or not it was exceeded—an editorial chore that seems to have had little more effect than a shock treatment. The fact is that the day-by-day totals of automobile accidents are shocking enough, to those who are impressed by such things, and the holiday death forecasts serve only to pile horror on horror.

There seems to be no point in tinkering with automobile accident news. In place of the awesome national roundup of hundreds of deaths during a holiday period, the names, ages, and addresses of the victims and the time and circumstances of their deaths are more meaningful news in their own communities. Contrast the following two stories for human interest:

> The nation's highway death toll soared to 575 last night for the four-day Christmas holiday. Of the traffic fatalities, 36 were in New York State.
> The death total was below the 620 predicted by the National Safety Council for the four-day period. It also was unlikely to exceed the record of 706 for a four-day holiday in the United States.

> A 14-year-old girl plunged into the flaming wreckage of a truck yesterday near Bridgeport and dragged its unconscious driver to safety. Then she put out the fire on his clothes with her new, red Christmas jacket.
> The heroine, Mathilda Johnstone, of New Haven, was riding in the family car with her mother, Mrs. David Willis Johnstone, when the truck sped past them on U. S. Highway 1. A few moments later, it went out of control, plummeted from the road into a ditch and overturned.
> As soon as Mrs. Johnstone stopped the car, Mathilda rushed to the truck and rescued the driver, Sam Don Persson, 28, of Silver Lake. He was reported in fair condition last night at Bridgeport Hospital.

The difference between these two accounts is that a reporter tried to make an individual incident come alive in the second instance, while the first was just a tabular summary of a weekend of accidents. It illustrates one of the axioms of journalism—there is more human interest in one person than in a crowd of 10,000.

Ship Accidents   The news of ship collisions, fires at sea, and other nautical disasters usually breaks first by radio. Very often, it is followed by intensive radio coverage either through communication with rescue vessels or aircraft, messages from such agencies as the Coast Guard or RCA Communications, assistance from amateur radio operators, or announcements from owners of the ships involved. Until the rescue vessels reach port, if mishaps occur at sea, reporters must be communications experts and the one with the best resources usually gets the most complete story.

In the case of a ship accident offshore that is worth the trouble, newsmen may be authorized to hire planes or tugs to go to the scene. This is always done by television cameramen and the picture syndicates when there is a major disaster at sea, unless the scene is too far from shore. When survivors are being brought to shore in lifeboats, newsmen have to spend many long hours on the beaches, sometimes in storms, waiting to get the first-person accounts of the disaster.

The first time radio was used in a sea rescue on January 23, 1909, Operator Jack Binns on the "Republic" sent the first distress call (it was then CQD, not SOS). He told of a collision involving his ship and the "Florida" off Nantucket Light and appealed for help. As a result, all but six of the "Republic's" passengers were saved.

Many years later, in the following account based on an Associated Press report, it may be seen that radio still gives the news of disasters at sea:

A German freighter burst into flames on the Atlantic Ocean today, but all save one of the 23 men aboard were rescued.

The body of the dead crewman, who could not be identified immediately, was left aboard the 259-foot freighter, Caldas, 40 miles off the fishing village of Chincoteague, Va.

The Coast Guard reported the ship's last distress call at 12:53 P.M., which read: "Fire on board. Smoke coming into wireless room."

The Coast Guard reported that 17 crewmen had abandoned ship and had been picked up by the American freighter, Somerset Trader. The captain and four others who stayed aboard the Caldas in an attempt to save her had to take to lifeboats themselves soon afterward. They were picked up by the Coast Guard cutter Kiwana.

All were later transferred to the freighter Atlantic Heritage, bound for Philadelphia.

A Coast Guard C-130 rescue plane and the Coast Guard cutter Cherokee from Norfolk also aided in the effort to save the stricken freighter. The Coast Guard said the 14-year-old vessel had a gaping hole in its starboard side and a 10-degree starboard list, but was still afloat tonight.

Often, in ship disasters, it is necessary to "write around" the number of casualties when it is difficult to determine exactly what happened. Sometimes, it is specified in the lead that 130 persons were on board, but the body of the story says there is no immediate word on what happened to them; or, as the radio messages pile up, some indication is given that part of the passengers were rescued and the fate of the rest is not known. In any event, whenever there is a disaster on land or at sea, it is a familiar precaution to hold out hope for the missing until a body count indicates that they are dead.

Train Accidents   In many ways, the coverage of an accident on a crowded train is the most difficult of all except the natural disaster. Here, no one has a passenger list such as is generally available after ship and aircraft disasters. The problem of identifying survivors is one that tries the patience of even the most painstaking of veteran reporters. Radio and television, having given the first news, quickly lose interest and turn to some other event but the newspapers must stick with the unrewarding task of compiling the casualty lists and checking them. With the police and the hospitals, the newspapers are the only organizations that are willing and able to perform this kind of public service.

The first news of a train accident usually comes from someone living near the scene. Often, the railroad people themselves do not know what happened until they conduct an inquiry. A good newsman, who is on the job quickly and moves around, often finds out more than anybody else at the scene of such a disaster.

If the train has not gone off a bridge or been destroyed by fire, an accurate count of the dead and injured can be made fairly quickly. Where there is uncertainty over what passengers survived, a reporter faces a long and difficult job of checking. At that point, the news is likely to develop everywhere at once—hospitals, police stations, funeral establishments, railroad waiting rooms, even over the switchboards of the news media that receive appeals from anxious relatives or friends for information about possible survivors.

Here is the first break on a railroad accident that illustrates the problems of initial coverage:

> A five-car Jersey Central commuter train, carrying about 100 passengers, plunged through an open drawbridge into Newark Bay today.
>
> At least forty persons died and 21 others were injured, a railroad spokesman estimated. The accident occurred shortly after 10 A.M. near Elizabeth, N.J.
>
> By early afternoon, skin divers had recovered 13 bodies.
>
> The train had started from Bay Head, a North Jersey shore resort, and was bound for its Jersey City terminal. Passengers at the terminal take the Hudson Tubes for New York City.
>
> Two Diesel locomotives and the first two passenger cars crashed through the open span and were quickly submerged in 40 feet of water. The bridge is 50 feet above Newark Bay.
>
> A third car remained dizzily suspended, half in the water and half out, for almost three hours. Then it, too, plunged to the bottom of the bay.
>
> No reason was given immediately for the failure of the engineer to stop the train before roaring across the drawbridge. . .

Except where the final death toll has been determined, it is standard practice to base the lead on the accident itself. The extent of the casualties, with suitable qualifications, can be given in the second paragraph and easily changed. This procedure holds good for the electronic media as well as print. The reason for not engaging in necessarily unfounded speculation is evident in the above story. With the exact number of passengers uncertain, and only 13 bodies recovered, it is fairly obvious that the estimate of 40 dead and 21 injured can be little more than an educated guess by the railroad spokesman on whom it was pinned.

Aircraft Accidents There are two general types of coverage for aircraft accidents.

When commercial planes alone are involved, a combination of methods used in ship and train accidents is usually advisable. The Federal, state, and local authorities responsible for regulating air traffic may have part of the story. The local airport may prove to be a valuable source for obtaining the last messages from the aircraft involved and their locations.

It is true that the companies have passenger lists of a sort, but they can never be taken at face value. That is because of the substantial percentage of "no shows" (persons with reservations who do not use them) and the standbys who go aboard at the last minute to fill vacancies. Stewardesses are supposed to take the names of all passengers aboard, and their seat locations, but these lists seldom are available after an accident; moreover, on occasion, they aren't even compiled because the stewardesses are too busy serving drinks and food.

In any case, it takes time to check through the ticket stubs and find out who actually did go aboard a plane that is later involved in an accident. If the disaster scene can be reached, it tells much of the story and survivors fill in many of the details. But often the wreckage is inaccessible and organizations such as the State Police must be relied upon for first reports. If the United States Air Force has a base in the vicinity, the commander or his information officer may prove helpful, too. But much of the work must be done by the newsmen for the mass media without much guidance—and often a lot of interference as well.

When an Air Force, Navy, or Coast Guard aircraft is involved in an accident, the rules change sharply. The Defense Department's procedures for issuing information on aircraft accidents often curb independent reporting by newsmen. The news media, in such cases, must depend on the military for initial reports of casualties. The restrictions on publication become even tighter when a military aircraft carrying a nuclear weapon is involved. The laws concerning disclosure of atomic information provide stiff penalties for the unauthorized issuance of information in such cases. When H-bombs were lost off Palomares, Spain, following an Air Force accident there, the Spanish authorities leaked the news long before the Pentagon confirmed it.

Here is the essential part of a report of an accident involving a commercial aircraft, which illustrates many of the general problems of coverage:

> STOCKPORT, England (Reuters)—An airliner loaded with British vacationers plummeted into the center of this northern industrial town

today, killing 72 persons aboard the plane. Twelve persons survived. No one on the ground was reported injured.

It was the second air disaster involving British tourists in 24 hours. Last night, 88 persons were killed when a chartered British DC-4 crashed in the French Pyrenees.

The plane that crashed today was a four-engine Argonaut returning from Palma, Majorca, laden with sun-tanned Britons. It swooped low as it approached Stockport and hit an electric power substation before crashing in flames into the city center.

The plane fell on the side of a small, wooded gully called Hopes Carr. A police spokesman said it was a miracle that it had hit the only spot in the center of town where there are no houses.

The impact of the plane, which belonged to British Midland Airways, flung several of the 12 survivors free while scattering luggage, snapshots, and souvenirs of Majorca amid the wreckage.

Hayden Holden, a teenager who was watching through binoculars, said he saw the plane swoop low over a row of warehouses, and then crash. "It seemed to swerve and then dive and then part of it burst into flames," he said.

Some time will elapse before the cause of the crash can be established.

SOARING INTO SPACE

With the coming of the space age, journalism has begun to grope for a new dimension. The enormous achievements of the spacemen have been marred by tragedies. As time goes on, the moon flights and the expeditions into outer space are bound to create martyrs as well as heroes. These accounts should not be told in the same way as those of the mishaps that befall the earthbound. And yet, the limitations of journalism are such that the reader does not have the same opportunity as the viewer to appreciate the tremendous impact that astronauts have on the public. The telecasts of the aftermath of tragedies at Cape Kennedy or in the Soviet Union, with their close-ups of sorrowing people and their magnificent long shots of vast State funerals, simply cannot be matched in print. If the newspaper retains an advantage in the United States, it is only because the printed page is nearly always readily available whereas the masters of commercial television present the news when they choose.

Here is an account of the deaths of three Apollo astronauts at the outset of the American race to the moon:[1]

CAPE KENNEDY, Fla. (AP)—The three-man crew of astronauts for the Apollo 1 mission were killed tonight in a flash fire aboard the huge spacecraft designed to take man to the moon.

Those killed in the blaze on a launching pad were:

---

[1] From the Associated Press file, January 27, 1967.

Virgil I. Grissom, 40 years old, an Air Force lieutenant colonel, one of the seven original Mercury astronauts.

Edward H. White 2d, 36 years old, a lieutenant colonel in the Air Force, the first American to "walk" in space.

Roger B. Chaffee, 31 years old, a Navy lieutenant commander, who had been awaiting his first space flight.

The three astronauts apparently died instantly. They were the first American spacemen to be killed on the job and, ironically, died while on the ground.

Three other astronauts died in airplane crashes in the line of duty, but today's tragedy involved the first "on premises" deaths in the American space program—the first time anyone was killed while in space hardware.

The fire broke out at 6:31 p.m. while the three men were taking part in a full-scale simulation of the scheduled Feb. 21 launching that was to take them into the heavens for 14 days of orbiting the earth.

They were trapped behind closed hatches, according to the National Aeronautics and Space Administration.

(Officials said an electronic spark must have ignited the pure oxygen that pressured the cabin, UPI reported.)

Paul Haney, spokesman for America's astronauts, said he understood there had been a fire in the cockpit. He said monitors had received no word from the astronauts during the fire . . .

The grim, sparse account of the American tragedy was matched within a few months by an accident that cost the life of a Soviet spaceman. This was *The New York Times* report of the event:[2]

By Raymond H. Anderson

MOSCOW, April 24—Col. Vladimir M. Komarov, pilot of the Soviet Union's first manned space flight in more than two years, was killed today when his craft's main re-entry parachute snarled and the ship plummeted 4.3 miles to earth.

He had been in orbit around the earth a little more than 24 hours before attempting to land. No details were given on where or exactly when the spacecraft crashed or on how many orbits had been completed.

The Soviet astronaut is the first man known to have died on a space flight.

Col. Komarov, the only man aboard, was testing the Soyuz 1, a heavy new craft intended for a series of manned Soviet space flights this summer.

Tass, the Soviet press agency, said the ship had performed normally in orbit and had been successfully braked with retro-rockets for re-entry into the earth's atmosphere.

"However, when the main parachute was opened at an altitude of seven kilometers (about 23,000 feet), the lines of the parachute, according to preliminary information, got snarled and the spaceship descended at great speed, which resulted in Komarov's death," the press agency stated. . .

---

[2] From *The New York Times,* April 25, 1967.

chapter 11

Handling the Story on Rewrite

When a President dies or a war begins, when a new Pope is chosen, or when a rocket is shot off toward the moon, the story must be written quickly. The lead should be out of the typewriter within a matter of seconds after the event if the account is for a wire service, a newspaper deadline, or immediate broadcast.

Nor do great events alone receive such spectacular treatment. In the ordinary run of local news it may be necessary to give quick handling to a fire, a robbery, a baseball game, the death of a prominent citizen, or even an interview with a sweepstakes winner.

Often on such occasions, both wire services and newspapers call on a skilled writing specialist to do the job quickly, accurately, and interestingly. There is no time to spin theories or philosophize over the news. There is no place for amateurs. It is the spot for a rewrite man. Generally, he takes over.

THE FINE ART OF REWRITE

To the uninitiated, who have no reason to give any thought to newspaper techniques, it may seem sometimes as if a man sits at a typewriter and does a story and pretty soon the paper comes out. If he is a rewrite man, it helps. To those outside the profession, the words "rewrite man" sound as if they should apply to a tired hack.

Consider only one circumstance that is familiar to anybody who has ever worked for even a short time in a newsroom:

Several reporters are out on a story, covering various angles at widely separated points. Two or three editors are giving them directions as they phone in, and at least one deskman is checking wire service copy as well. Copy boys are fluttering all over the place. Page 1 is being held in the composing room for a quick replate.

At such a time the whole burden of the operation rests on the man at the typewriter—the rewrite man. He is geared to it. He really lives for such moments. His notes are piled around the desk, seemingly in disarray, and wire copy is thrust here and there. With a glance at the clock, he rolls a book of copy paper and carbons into his typewriter and begins writing without apparent effort. A few lines—a paragraph or two—and he gives his first take to a boy or a waiting deskman. Then, smoothly and easily, take after take reams through his typewriter until he reaches the deadline and his story is done.

No mere hack would ever be trusted to handle the major stories of a great newspaper or wire service under such circumstances, week after week and month after month. Even if he were, he would not last very long. He would not have the know-how.

What Makes a Rewrite Man? The first quality of a superior rewrite man or woman is the ability to turn out accurate, clear, and interesting copy without hesitation under all conceivable circumstances. The copy should be as clean as an expert stenographer's. It should be more readable than that of less practiced writers.

Facility and adaptability are other qualities that are mandatory on rewrite. A rewrite man may handle in the same working day a dramatic straight news story, a light feature, a thoughtful interpretive piece, or even a street tragedy tinged with human interest.

His news judgment must be sharp and accurate. No deskman can be forever telling him what his lead should be. He must know from his background of newspaper reading and his specialized knowledge. However, if it happens that the editor in charge wants a lead other than the one that has been written, the rewrite man should be able to change the slant without fuss. He is supposed to turn out a story, not an argument.

It is obvious from this that a rewrite man must be a responsible person, well-read and well-mannered. In his dealings with editors and reporters he is always in the middle and likely to be blamed by all sides in any failure that befalls a complicated newspaper operation. The mark of a superior rewrite man is that editors trust his judgment, reporters have faith in his ability to write their stories well, and copyreaders do not have to correct his grammar and spelling but can concentrate on the substance of editing his work.

The Rewrite Habit There is nothing particularly new about the practice of rewrite, most of which is not rewrite at all but the specialized job of writing news under pressure. When Alexander Graham Bell invented the telephone, he also created the journalistic situation that made the rewrite man necessary. Charles E. Chapin, who terrorized the staff of the New York *Evening World* while he was its city editor, is generally believed to have been the first in New York journalism to have reporters telephone their facts to a writing specialist in the office instead of returning to do their own stories.

As afternoon newspapers in metropolitan centers began issuing more editions per day—at one time some of the biggest papers put out as many as eight editions regularly—it became necessary to use reporters principally to gather the news. The term "legman" came into being, and many a metropolitan reporter simply became a fact-gatherer for the rewrite man.

From the afternoon papers the practice of rewrite spread to the morning field whenever reporters were too far from the office to come in, too close to a deadline, or too inept to do their own pieces. There was a time immediately before World War II when rewrite was even more general than it is now, and editors began to realize that something valuable was slipping away from journalism—the firsthand account of a news event.

During the World War II period and immediately afterward, however, the number of newspaper daily editions drastically declined. Editors saw that the proliferation of editions was both unnecessary and undesirable. With added time the morning newspapers tried to get more reporters' copy into the paper and, to some extent, began balancing the heavy emphasis on rewrite. But because of the demands of time and space, rewrite has maintained and even expanded its importance in the PM field.

From an experiment, rewrite became a habit. It is now a necessity.

What a Rewrite Man Can Do A competent rewrite man, who knows the background of his story and has a good idea of the scene and the principal characters, can illuminate the bare details of a reporter's work with considerable newsworthy detail. Being detached from the event itself and under no compulsion to leap to the telephone with every new detail, the writer has a broader view that should make his story more meaningful. Frequently it does.

The reporter at the scene cannot consult the morgue, or library, for the fill-in material that is often so necessary to make a story both authentic and interesting. Nor can he divine what is happening at other points that may have an important bearing on the development of the story. The rewrite man, anchored to his desk, actually has more mobility than the reporter, therefore, as far as the writing of the story is concerned.

The rewrite man has the inestimable advantage of being in the office.

He knows what space is available for the story, what kind of play it is getting, what angle to use for his lead. He can govern himself accordingly. A reporter who is out of touch might be quite excited about some detail that would not be used by the rewrite man for fear that it could crowd out another more vital aspect of the story.

Finally, the rewrite man has direct and immediate contact with his superiors and can discuss his operations with them, if the story is big enough. Except when he makes a mistake, the average reporter often has to operate on the basis of a few words of direction by telephone, when somebody on the desk thinks of it.

Yet, for all his advantages, not even the most clever rewrite man can make his story seem as real as that of a reporter who knows how to describe the sights, sounds, and smells associated with the news. A good rewrite man, in fact, is too wise to try to counterfeit reality by imagining a news scene in too great detail. That way, he can fall into error and destroy the effect of his work. The reporter will always be the legs, eyes, and ears of the newspaper. There is no possible substitute for him.

A Rewrite Man's Duties What a rewrite man does varies from paper to paper and from bureau to bureau of a wire service. The scope of his job depends largely upon how good he is and how much work he can handle well. Some rewrite men do nothing but obits and shorts. Others handle the main stories in the paper day after day. Still others, with a gifted telephone manner, are used to backstop reporters by making calls on breaking news.

In general, any good rewrite man can expect to turn out between 1,500 and 3,500 words a day on the average. Experts, on a big news day, do 5,000 and 6,000 words. Not all of this will be in the paper at the end of the day, of course. News changes. As it does, earlier developments are dropped. This is true both of newspaper and wire copy.

There is always something for a rewrite man to do, even if others on the staff are kept sitting around. He may be rewriting and checking clips from other newspapers or pulling together wire copy from various points. He may be assigned to handle a campaign, weaving the work of a dozen reporters into a coherent whole. If he has the time and ability, he may be asked to turn out a feature on the basis of reporters' notes or, perhaps, indifferent reporters' copy. Late in his shift, if the news pressures slacken, he may be given some publicity or other material to work up into a story for the next day. Or, he may be asked to bring up to date obits that have been set in type against the time that famous persons die, do advance stories on parades, speeches, conventions, trials, and similar set events, or develop comment by telephone on some pertinent break in the news.

These are all side issues to his main job, which is to write a very large proportion of the hard news. Throughout the nation there are papers with competent staffs of reporters on which the rewrite man is not so dominant a figure. But there are many more, particularly in metropolitan areas, where he is depended upon to handle the principal local stories and sometimes others in the state and nation as well.

Rewrite men have performed seemingly incredible feats ever since the practice of writing from someone else's notes began. One of the first, Will Irwin, wrote the magnificent story of the San Francisco earthquake of 1906, "The City That Was," from wire service and other fragmentary reports that came to him in the city room of the New York *Sun*. Trials, conventions, elections, murders, international conferences—every aspect of the news in fact—all have been handled through similar techniques.

Some rewrite men have had the stamina to organize the most complicated kind of news and write a story of 3,000 or 4,000 words in a relatively short time, using no more than a few hours. In extraordinary cases the fastest and most competent rewrite men have been known to do stories of 800 to 1,000 words in about 10 or 12 minutes after taking suitable notes from a reporter. Nor is such a typewriter virtuoso merely a stenographer, spinning words out of a notebook. Even under trying conditions he is expected to do a thoroughly readable job, and usually he is able to deliver.

REWRITE PROCEDURES

There are no blueprints for working on a rewrite desk. No accepted body of procedure has ever been drawn up for this difficult and demanding job. Yet, there are certain things that good rewrite men do to reduce the hazards of processing the news. These are some of them:

Listening to Reporters   When a rewrite man is told by his desk to "take" a reporter, he puts on headphones, slips a sheet of paper in his typewriter, plugs in on the call, and courteously gives his name. The next thing he does is to get the reporter's telephone number in case the reporter is cut off or runs out of change if he is in a pay booth.

The reporter generally begins by summarizing his story in a sentence, very much like a lead, but he will then "give in" the facts in his own manner, usually chronologically. No competent rewrite man will ever interrupt a reporter except for good cause or direct him in telling the story. While the facts are being reported, the rewrite man's job is to listen and take notes.

In the movies and on television this serious process is often burlesqued and made the source of some rather painful comedy dialogue between reporter and rewrite man. The rewrite man is depicted as a character, sometimes with a hat on, who keeps snapping "Yah—yah—yah" into the telephone out of the corner of his mouth, presumably to let the reporter know somebody is on the line. Or he may make nasty remarks about the reporter's professional and personal life.

If this were done on a major story, it would hopelessly jam the delicate machinery of news gathering and news transmission. The rewrite and reporting processes must be handled smoothly, and with a minimum of friction, or they break down. The reporter, consequently, tries to tell his story completely but quickly, spelling all difficult or unusual names and repeating figures. When he has finished, he asks, "Any questions?" The rewrite man then concludes the process by filling in the blanks.

A wise and considerate rewrite man will always ask the reporter, if there is time, what he thinks is the principal part of the story. No rewrite man of experience will ever try to tell a reporter his business or suggest improved methods of covering a story. Nor will he keep the reporter on the telephone any longer than is necessary. Few phone booths are light, airy, or comfortable.

Writing Methods   Each rewrite man develops his own writing habits, and no two are exactly alike. All good ones know, as soon as they finish taking notes or reading clips and wire copy, how they would like to start the story. Often, the lead "feels" right the first time it is tried, and the rewrite man then knows the story will pretty well tell itself. If the lead seems awkward, or not quite apposite, most rewrite men will take another try at it if they have the time. However, no rewrite man can do what Lauren (Deak) Lyman did when he wrote the Pulitzer Prize story of the secret departure of the Lindbergh family for England in 1935—13 leads before he hit the "right" one for *The New York Times*.

The first principle of writing on a rewrite desk is to keep copy moving. Under no circumstances can a rewrite man delay starting a story, merely because the edition deadline is an hour off, unless he is directed to do so. When he has a story, he writes it. The closer he gets to a deadline, and the more important his story, the shorter he should try to make his takes of copy. It is easier to handle them that way, both on city and copy desks and in the composing room.

He must be careful of his slugs, his page numbers, his editing directions, and, above all, his end marks on stories. One way he can help keep himself out of trouble is to keep a carbon of everything he writes on a spike beside him. At the end of the day these carbons and the notes from which they were written should be wrapped in a small bundle, dated, and put away for at least three months in case a question is raised about the story.

It is easy, of course, to tell an inexperienced young newspaperman to put a piece of paper into the typewriter and begin writing. However, few can do it without practice because they do not really have the power of decision that comes with assurance, practice, and knowledge. What happens to most beginners is a severe attack of "buck fever" on their first days on rewrite. This is a journalistic ailment that renders its victims helpless and pitiful. The symptoms are a patchwork of false starts, a frantic burst of typing followed by a glazed stare, and a depressed feeling of utter frustration.

The only cure is to keep eternally at it until the day comes when the lead magically begins forming on paper an instant after the first sheet goes into the typewriter. Nobody can say what alchemy of the mind brings this about, but it does happen to those who are destined to write the nation's newspapers and its wire service reports. It is given to some to be expert rewrite men after only a few years of all-round experience. Others never learn, although they have deservedly good reputations as journalists, because they are not comfortable when they must write under pressure. It takes a writer with a clear mind, few inhibitions, good technical ability, and much self-confidence to do the rewrite job.

Rewriting Clips Most editors maintain that they always have clips from other papers checked before they are rewritten, and some actually manage to do so. It is, of course, known that the rewriting of clips to get short spreads, routine departmental items, fillers, and similar material has been done for a long time and is quite likely to continue. There is at least one major news organization that runs a clip desk, illustrating its reliance on the material developed by others.

There is no question here of news piracy. The line between picking up news that is public property and news that belongs exclusively to one publication, syndicate, or wire service is easily recognized. If the morning paper has a story of a speech by the mayor at the opening of a fair, it is obviously much easier for an evening paper to rewrite the story rather than detach a reporter (at time and one-half cash) to cover a routine event that will be old by the time its first edition goes to press. But if the morning paper has a story that the mayor did not appear at the fair because he is about to undergo an operation for cancer, nobody will dare pick up the story until it has been checked and confirmed. If the story is unconfirmable, the only way it can be used is to credit it to the source that first published it—something a competing newspaper hates to do.

Newspapers generally copyright the contents of each edition and therefore contend that all material in the edition, not otherwise accounted for, belongs to them. Of course it does, in the form in which it appears. No paper, though, can copyright the body of human knowledge. Nor can it copyright facts that are issued as common property. Some papers print such facts sooner than others, either through differences of edition time, superior reporting, or sheer accident. But all papers are entitled to use facts that are generally known.

UPDATING

When it becomes necessary to rewrite a clip from another paper or combine such old news with fresh material developed by a reporter or wire service, that is the job of a rewrite man.

His first effort should be to try to get something fresh on the story by making a telephone call. There is nothing deader than rewriting an old clip that was originally based on an older handout. If the rewrite man can get nothing new, he should at least update the news by featuring a different slant and using a lot less of the whole story. The rewrite man who merely repeats a previously published story, or picks up words and phrases at random, does not last very long.

The practice of updating old news is called using a "second-day angle." In the case of the first edition of an afternoon newspaper, which is in the position of using facts already in a morning paper with no new development in sight, the technique is usually to base a lead on the next anticipated turn in the story.

If a person's death is announced in a morning paper, for instance, the afternoon paper rewrite could feature the arrangements for the funeral. In the event of a fire or accident the next succeeding angle would be the inevitable investigation. The story of a speech would be followed by the reaction to it, if any, and the announcement of an arrest would be continued with the expected arraignment of the prisoner. The verbs that are dear to the hearts of rewrite men searching for second-day angles in old stories include such work horses as emerged, confronted, faced, awaited, expected, held, seemed, appeared, and others in the general area denoting continuing action. For instance:

> George J. Dockweiler emerged today as a narrow victor in the election for City Council president. Final results from yesterday's election showed he had defeated Ernest Quentin, his Democratic rival, by 22,652 votes. . . .

> Maxim Carpescu, owner of the Hotel Mabuhay, was confronted today with a $50,000 damage suit from a guest who charged she slipped and broke her leg in one of his bathtubs. The complainant, Mrs. Ernestine Garrabrandt, filed suit yesterday. . . .

> Three teen-age robbery suspects faced arraignment today in the theft of $15.22 from a South Side grocery store. They were captured last night. . . .

> The toll in the Southeast Railway wreck stood at ten dead today and appeared likely to go higher. Rescuers searched in the debris all night. . . .

Rewrite men often have to use such methods to update material previously published on which there is nothing new. On many an afternoon paper or wire service overnight cycle the rewritten "today" leads are so smoothly past-tensed that they have to be looked at twice to determine if they are based on breaking news or second-day angles.

Morning papers having the whole day's news for their field are not so dependent on updating the previous story while waiting for a fresh break. The Associated Press, too, in recent years, has leaned toward the practice of doing away with second-day angles unless they are necessary. Instead, the AP simply uses the present perfect tense for its second-day leads on overnight files, if there are no new or anticipated developments, and drops the time element (yesterday or last night) into the body of the story.

For instance, if the mayor of a city spoke last night at the opening of the Salvation Army's drive for funds and the speech was reported in the morning newspaper, the afternoon lead could begin:

> Mayor Jones has appealed for funds to help the Salvation Army. Opening the organization's drive for funds last night at the Hotel Astor, the Mayor said, etc. . . .

Or, if the mayor made an appointment several days ago but delayed its announcement until today, the present perfect tense could be used to get around the cumbersome time element as follows:

> Mayor Jones has appointed Walter D. Smith, 52-year-old lawyer, as deputy housing commissioner. The appointment was made Monday and announced today at City Hall. . . .

An improper use of the present perfect tense, however, can confuse and even mislead the reader. If a story is new, it should be indicated by using the word *today* or *yesterday* in the lead instead of resorting to the "something-has-happened" approach, which could have occurred any time.

It should also be noted that while the present perfect construction is eminently sensible, and is used by both wire services and major newspapers at times, many editors stubbornly insist that the time element must go in the lead of any straight news story.

To illustrate, the two "something-has-happened" leads about Mayor Jones could also be written as follows for an afternoon newspaper to satisfy a captious editor:

> The annual Salvation Army drive for funds was under way today following an appeal from Mayor Jones. Under the Mayor's leadership, the drive began last night at the Hotel Astor with a dinner. . . .
> Mayor Jones made public today the appointment of Walter D. Smith as deputy housing commissioner. The 52-year-old lawyer was appointed Monday, but the announcement was held up until today at City Hall. . . .

Mistakes in Second-Day Leads   The best rule to follow in "freshening up" an old story is to dig up a few new facts of some significance, or drop the whole business. Old news does not sell either newspapers or news magazines; as for the electronic media, there simply is no time for a news rehash. The continual process of probing and reporting is the best guarantee that a few old-line rewrite tricks will not be used in an effort to disguise the bankruptcy of editorial direction.

True, second-day leads are always useful in anticipating the next development in a breaking story; but if that next development does not come very soon, then an artificial story should not continue to take up space or time in the day's report. Probably the grand-daddy of all second-day leads is the following, which is still sometimes seen in an afternoon paper's obit page that carries death notices published in the morning paper or heard over radio or TV:

> J. Samuel Methfessel, a philanthropist who gave away $20 million, is dead today.

It may be observed, in all truth, that Julius Caesar also is dead today. The stretched second-day lead is, in this case, both an eyesore and an embarrassment to a decent newspaper. It would be much better—if it is absolutely necessary to repeat the obit—to report that Mr. Methfessel died yesterday, to lead with the funeral plans as is usually the case, or to begin with a colorful incident from the philanthropist's life. Almost anything is better than a nonlead, also known in pure New Yorkese as a "nothing lead."

In recent years, a number of editors have tried to do away altogether with the artificial second-day lead and some have made great progress. One of the innovators, Roger Tatarian, editor of United Press International, offered the heretical notion that—in instances where it applied—a reporter's personal story of an event would be well worth publishing. The outstanding instance in the sixties was the celebrated "Murder of the Young President," which won a Pulitzer Prize for Merriman Smith and gave the world a vivid firsthand account of what it meant to witness the assassination of President Kennedy in Dallas on November 22, 1963. Other devices to do away with the rehash included the use of chronological stories to reconstruct some major news event, the engagement of experts to criticize a cultural event or explain a new development in economics, and the increasing trend toward lavishly illustrated stories.

REWRITING WIRE COPY

Since 1918 when the Associated Press obtained an injunction against International News Service to prevent the lifting of AP news, the wire services have been understandably nervous about picking up news from each other. There is nothing in any law, moral code, or sensible procedure that obliges any of the news media to submit tamely to being beaten on a story. If that happens, a recovery must be made by every legitimate means and the rewrite man is often the man for the job. There is, however, little reason for extensive rewriting of wire copy for newspaper use. The wire services have good rewrite men of their own. They usually do a first-class job because it is their business to give their members or clients what they want.

However, some city editors are nervous about permitting AP or UPI copy of local origin to get into their papers, with credit. The same is true of wire copy that originates in any other area that should have been covered by a staff reporter. The question could be asked of the city editor, "Why wire copy? Where was your staff man?"

It is standard practice, of course, to backstop any local story with wire copy even if it is covered by a staff reporter. The rewrite man combines facts, where necessary. Some papers rewrite wire copy on the doubtful premise that "our men do it better." What the editor probably wants to do is to make certain that his paper differs from the opposition, where it exists. The criticism is widespread that American papers are too standardized because of the overly generous use of wire copy in some instances.

In any case, it is the rewrite man who has to redo the wire copy. He has these standard practices to guide him:

1. Wire Copy of Local Origin. In general, such wire copy may be rewritten without credit to the agency unless some special arrangements apply. Except in Washington, it is rare to see a local story credited completely to a wire service.

2. Regional Wire Rewrite. In most metropolitan areas it is standard practice for papers to use a dateline on news coming from outside a 50-mile limit from the city of publication. The result is that stories within that area are usually rewritten by the papers.

When wire copy goes into the paper under a dateline, and is not substantially changed, naturally credit must be given to the agency. If the paper adds material of its own and gives the story a different slant, then the wire service logotype is dropped.

The rule is that when the form and meaning of a wire story are substantially changed so that it is no longer truly the story of the originating agency, the wire service credit must be removed. Naturally, this does not apply to the normal processes of editing, or even transposing paragraphs to use a different lead.

3. National Wire Copy Rewrite. Wire service copy from Washington and abroad is cut so sharply by many small papers (and some big ones) that the result sometimes is practically meaningless. For this reason the European practice of combining competing wire service accounts is becoming popular. It is to be regretted. The line, "From Our Wire Services," is usually a tip-off that a paper has decided to give only bulletin service on events that do not directly help circulation.

4. Undated Leads. There is, however, a real need often for combining agency accounts with whatever news a paper's own staff is able to get. This applies to stories that break over a wide area, such as a storm, a major accident, or other disaster and similar news that comes in from many points.

The rewrite man performs a unique service by doing what is known as an undated lead (that is, without a dateline). In effect, this is a story of a national event written locally. The following is an example:

Tornadoes ripped savagely across the Carolinas and Virginia today, killing at least six persons and injuring more than 150 others.

The deadly black funnels blasted factories, offices, and homes along a 150-mile strip. Trees were uprooted. Billboards were ripped up. Rivers flooded their banks. Power and telephone lines sagged in tangles that paralyzed communications.

The undated lead would run for no more than 300 or 400 words, in this type of account, and then break into news stories from various spots that were severely affected. Necessarily, papers in the area might well have more material than wire services so the device of an undated lead would give a broad view of the damage.

Wire services use such undated leads with even greater frequency than newspapers in handling national or international events that cover a number of major news centers.

5. Weaving Wire Copy Together. When AP, UPI, and local copy must be combined without substantial rewrite, it becomes a job for the telegraph, cable, or copy desks rather than the rewrite man. Yet, sometimes he also is called in to operate.

In such a situation the news desk itself must make the decision on which story to use as the basic account. If AP is to be the main account, then material from UPI and local sources may be bracketed into AP if it is done clearly. For instance, in a general AP story about the Middle East, UPI might have an essential fact which a paper taking both services would want to use. It could be done like this:

(According to UPI, Arab diplomats were meeting secretly at Cairo to try to determine a course of joint action.)

The same kind of treatment might be accorded a fact developed locally that would fit into a basic wire service account. The principle, in any case, is to set off and clearly identify one wire service from another. AP and UPI cannot be woven together unless they are rewritten with the logotypes of both being removed.

When there are two wire service stories on the same subject and under the same datelines, naturally they may be worked in together if they are from the same agency. If they are from different agencies, one may be bracketed into the other or one may follow the other, separated by a dash. When a brief elaboration follows a basic story and originates from a different source, as would be the case with a short AP piece from Washington being tacked on a major UPI story from the same city, the additional material is called a "shirttail."

A REWRITE MAN'S OBLIGATION

A rewrite man is only as good as the reporter who turns in the facts to him. He sees through the reporter's eyes, hears through the reporter's ears, goes to the scene on the reporter's legs. He is the reporter's closest collaborator. His obligation is to support the reporter.

When there is doubt about the angle of the story, and the reporter himself is not too clear on what is happening, the rewrite man should omit it until it has been checked. When the wire services say one thing and the reporter says another, it is customary for the rewrite man and the desk to rely on the paper's own man until he is proved unreliable. When the reporter has no time to develop background, it is the rewrite man who should always send for clips from the library to see if he can save the reporter time and effort.

These are some of the things that any rewrite man can do to make the relationship between the reporter and himself smooth, sensible, and valuable to the organization.

chapter 12

Sharpening the Lead

There is nothing like a good beginning for a story. Journalism stresses it. Writers strive for it. Editors demand it. Yet, among every generation of journalists, there are relatively few who are able to produce meaningful, and sometimes, original leads.

Too often the writer of news becomes a mere word technician, his art impaled on an editorial spike. He buries ideas under a mound of stale and stilted language. He becomes bemused by the tradition that things must sound official rather than interesting—a professional weakness that is not necessarily limited to journalism. He loads his leads with official sources, official titles, official phrases—even official quotes—and wonders why they are called long, cumbersome, and dull.

The doleful truth is that all the devices of "officialese," which are supposed to impress the public with the importance of the news, seldom do so. The measured cadences of the government report, the sonorous public relations man, and the advertising specialist actually dam the flow of the news when they clutter up a lead. The superior journalist has always known this and acted accordingly. He has never been afraid to use the writers' art to communicate, clarify, and even illuminate the news. That art, and the professional ability and courage to use it, are among the greatest needs of journalism today.

GOOD LEADS—AND BAD

In writing a lead, the first instinct of the news technician is to "play it safe," to "hang it on somebody," as the journalistic saying goes. The first instinct of the artist is to tell the story.

Patterns for Leads   Suppose a crowd has collected about a wrecked automobile at a street corner outside a park. A passerby stops and taps a truck driver on the arm.

"Hey, Mac. What happened?"

"Two kids got killed. Car jumped the curb."

In effect, the truck driver has performed the same function as a writer summarizing a news event. He has answered the essential question posed for anyone dealing with hard news:

"What happened?"

If a writer had nothing else to think about, he could write the lead without worrying. In the ancient news formula so dear to the news technician, the lead must contain both the facts and the source of the facts, whether or not it is necessary to give the source the same prominence as the facts. Under this procedure, assuming the facts in the street incident just referred to came from the police, the traditional news writer would produce something like this:

> Police Chief J. W. Carmichael announced today that two children were killed outside Prospect Park, at Jackson Ave. and 16th St., N.W., when a "recklessly driven" automobile jumped the curb near where they were playing at 2 p.m. and ran them down.

This forty-word horror contains all the bad habits of the traditional news writer. A tragedy such as this need not have its lead embellished with the name of a police chief or a partial quotation from his words of wisdom to make the story sound formal, official, and important. The principal reason why these things are put in is that the reporter, writer, or editor—as the case may be—feels the news must be "hung on" some official to make it safe, particularly when there is an allegation of reckless driving.

There are two arguments against such writing. First, it is dull. It makes a monotonous official sing-song out of an event that should arouse a community. Even more important, a question of accuracy is involved. Either the reporter knows the facts are accurately reported, or he does not. If they are accurate, he does not need the police chief to guarantee them in the lead but can refer to him elsewhere. If the story is inaccurate, whatever the police chief says will not excuse the publication of such an account.

The name of the police chief, therefore, should be used only in the context in which it has some meaning. The event, not the source, should be stressed. The source is a secondary consideration. Yet, without some thought and effort, a lead that is shorter but even more prosaic may emerge:

> Two children were killed and 12 others injured today when an automobile hit them outside Prospect Park.

This is the good old news story blueprint lead for accidents of all types. It has been used for fifty years by lazy or inexpert news writers and could be kept standing, with blanks for the figures of dead and injured, the place, and the type of vehicle.

The story does not really attempt to answer the question: "What happened?" It grinds out statistics and records in prosaic language. Yet, in an event of this kind, the news writer should try to take the reader to the scene—to let him see it, hear it, smell it. That is only possible by describing the action as is done below:

> A speeding yellow sports car jumped the curb outside Prospect Park today, plowed into a group of children at play, and killed two of them. Twelve others were injured.
> Police Chief J. W. Carmichael attributed the tragedy to reckless driving. The driver, slightly injured, was. . . .

Thus, in three sentences totaling 40 words, the facts are packed into the beginning of the story in such a way that the public has a vivid image of what happened and how it happened. Facts—action—color—these are the ingredients of a fast-moving lead on a spot news story.

In place of the humdrum "two killed, twelve hurt" approach, the reader is shown how this automobile accident differs from all other automobile accidents. It is a specific, rather than a general, lead. It uses vigorous verbs in the active voice rather than the less appropriate passive voice. It eliminates needless attribution and locations, since it may be assumed that they will be written into the story as it develops. The awkward phrases and needless quotes of the official type of writing in the first lead are also dropped.

In essence this is the difference between sharp leads and dull leads. The dull leads are the product of habit, lazy writing, and carelessness. They become weighted down with needless attribution, needless quotes, hackneyed phrases. To make a lead sharp requires a good news sense and a decent command of the English language. Above all, it must make an honest attempt to answer the primary question: "What happened?"

WHAT A LEAD REQUIRES

The happy inspiration that produces a quotable lead seldom strikes the news writer as he struggles with his story. Particularly on a deadline. He has to make do. But every lead, quotable or not, can be accurate, clear, and precise.

The Deadly Way   There is no more deadly way to begin a story than to use the "so-and-so said" lead when it does not really apply. For instance:

> WASHINGTON (AP)—The White House announced today the submarine Nautilus has completed. . . .

It was the announcement that the Nautilus, an atom-powered submarine, had cruised under the ice across the North Pole. The APME Blue Book commented wrathfully:

> Would the man who wrote that lead call up his wife and tell her, "The White House announced today . . ."? Darn right he wouldn't. But here was rugged old habit. Senator Claghorn said . . . Deputy Sheriff Glubb said. . . .
> Why, in Gutenberg's name, deaden the announcement of a thrilling achievement with those wooden words . . . somebody said? What was so important about the source that it had to get in front of the news?

Two more wire service leads, of which the AP itself heartily disapproves, are:

> JERUSALEM (AP)—A dispute between Israel and Syria brought another round of claims and counter-claims today.

> RIO DE JANEIRO (AP)—Diplomatic sources today said African and Asian coffee producing nations will have equal say with Latin American countries in formulating policies of the proposed international coffee organization.

The first lead is so determined to be impartial that it squeezes all the action out of what could have been a significant Middle East story. If a specific case had been described the curse of dullness might have been lifted.

In the second lead the most frayed of all attributive devices is needlessly thrust into a story of interest to all Americans because it concerns their cup of coffee. Sometimes, diplomatic sources must be used to explain that individuals and organizations cannot be named, but it seems ludicrous to use the device in a lead about a cup of coffee.

The wire service leads that follow provide a welcome contrast. Lightness, humor, imagination, and originality make these openings sparkle— and if wire services can do it, newspapers most certainly have no excuse not to try:

> WASHINGTON (AP)—The Supreme Court yesterday knocked out the International Boxing Club. By a 5–3 vote the court upheld the decree of a

U. S. District Judge ordering the IBC in New York and Chicago to break up its giant prize-fighting empire.

BRIGHTON, England (UPI)—Mrs. Pamela Bransden slowly counted five, snapped into a hypnotic trance, and gave birth to an eight-pound baby. It was as easy as that.

Today she relaxed at her home here, delighted that she had become Britain's first self-hypnosis mother.

LONDON (AP)—Buckingham Palace bounced to the beat until 2 a.m. today and Queen Elizabeth II joined the hired help. It was the annual party for the palace household staff. . . .

LEADS FOR ALL OCCASIONS

The sharp news lead crops up in every conceivable situation. It may be produced by a great name of journalism or by a relative unknown. It may set the stage for the telling of a momentous news story. Or it may describe the weather.

These are some of the classics that are recalled whenever American newspapermen discuss the fine art of sharpening a lead:

(By Lindesay Parrott in the New York Evening Post on a St. Patrick's Day parade)
Fifty thousand Irishmen—by birth, by adoption and by profession—marched up Fifth Avenue today.

(By H. Allen Smith in the New York World-Telegram on a one-sentence routine weather forecast)
Snow, followed by small boys on sleds.

(By Harry Ferguson, UPI executive editor, on the execution of Bruno Richard Hauptmann)
The State of New Jersey, which spent $1,200,000 to capture and convict Bruno Richard Hauptmann, executed him tonight with a penny's worth of electricity.

Before his body ever hung loose and heavy against the straps of the electric chair, officials collected from witnesses a dozen affidavits, swearing that Hauptmann had died in the place, time, and manner prescribed by law. Then they closed their four-year file on the murder of Charles A. Lindbergh, Jr.

(By Shirley Povich in the Washington Post on Don Larsen's perfect World Series game)
The million-to-one shot came in. Hell froze over. A month of Sundays hit the calendar. Don Larsen today pitched a no-hit, no-run, no-man-reach-first game in a World Series.

(By Robert J. Casey in the Chicago Daily News describing what happened after a Texas explosion wiped out a public school)
They're burying a generation today.

(By Charley Williamson in the Yonkers (N.Y.) Herald Statesman on events in Elmsford, N.Y.)

Tranquility ran rampant in Elmsford last night. No accidents, no fires, no traffic violations, no wife-beatings and no dog bites.

SOME PRECAUTIONS

In the urge to be bright, clever, or profound an inexperienced writer frequently overlooks the basic reason for a lead—to tell the news. No matter how fine the lead may be, it is not worth using if it fails in this test.

It may not be necessary to use the attribution of the news in the opening sentence, or even in the first two or three paragraphs, but it must be in the story somewhere. The public always has the right to know the source of his news, if it can be divulged. It also should be told why a news source cannot be identified, if that happens to be the case.

When the news source is of major importance, naturally, it must be featured. No one would consider beginning a Presidential news conference by eliminating the name of the President of the United States. The story would have no meaning. For example, when Japanese bombs began dropping on Pearl Harbor, it was imperative to inform the nation that the announcement came from the White House, that it was genuine, and that it meant we were at war.

Similarly, the effort to sharpen leads by dropping unessential quotes or partial quotes should not be made a pretext for eliminating quotes from the whole story. Quotes frequently are the essential documentation for a lead and should be used immediately after a paraphrase that summarizes them.

The reason why full quotes are seldom used as a lead sentence is that they do not often tell the story as well as a writer's paraphrase. When they do, however, they should be used. The brief statements in which Presidents Coolidge and Eisenhower announced their availability as Republican Presidential nominees in 1924 and 1956, respectively, were widely used by newspapers as leads. The public had anticipated these statements so they were self-explanatory.

Here, however, is a quote lead that takes a lot of explaining:

> "I was furious when that disreputable young man had the audacity to sit in my antique rosewood chair."
> That's how tiny, 82-year-old Louise Freeland today described her brush with a gun-toting escaped convict whom she talked into surrendering to Sheriff's officers.

It might have been better to tell what happened, even if the story is an obvious sidebar to a main account, rather than let the quotes stand as the lead.

As for partial quotes in a lead, the tendency has been to dispense with them unless they are the key to the story. It is usually more helpful to use such material as a complete quote to document a paraphrased lead. Too many writers have quoted words and phrases that did not have to be quoted, thus casting doubt on the sense in which they were used. In a story about a Nebraska mass killer who was caught, one AP account said, "Her stepfather had urged Starkweather to 'stay away' from the Bartlett home." As the APME Blue Book pointed out, the "stay away" quote was meaningless.

These are details—the string around the news package. They must be watched, but they should not be made more important than what is inside the package.

EFFECTIVE NEWS LEADS

It is a familiar, and harmless, practice to set up a lot of different categories for various types of news leads and call them by an easily recognizable name. Actually, such categories do not exist. They vary from one paper to the next, and even from one wire service bureau to the next. Editors and writers make up their own names for the various ways in which stories can be begun.

Merely for the sake of convenience, therefore, rather than to try to establish categories by fiat, some effective types of leads are given with a brief discussion of how and why they are used by American newspapers and wire services, which serve both print and electronic media.

Straight News Leads   The three so-called straight news leads (also called leads on hard news) presented below began major stories that were widely played in the American news media at the time they broke. They serve as an effective means of summarizing the news for the hurried reader:

> An Air Force jet fighter plane, veering sharply from the runway on takeoff, spewed death, fire, and destruction through a half-dozen eight-family housing units at Eielson Air Force Base yesterday. At least 14 persons, including the pilot of the plane, were killed and eight were seriously injured.
> —Fairbanks (Alaska) *Daily News-Miner*

> BUDAPEST, Hungary—What began here Tuesday as a demonstration turned that same night into a revolt and yesterday became a war that was still raging today. It is a war by Soviet troops and Hungarian political policemen against the mass of the Hungarian people.
> —*The New York Times*

> A wild outburst of gunfire from a corner of the House gallery hit five Representatives today, injuring one critically. In the turmoil of flashing guns and Congressmen falling to the floor, three persons were arrested.

They had shouted "Free Puerto Rico" as they suddenly turned an orderly session into pandemonium.

—Washington *Star*

All these leads stress the action that led to disaster, emphasizing the differing news situations. It would have been easier and briefer, perhaps, to have begun with a "deadpan" total of casualties and pinned the news on a source. But the writers in each case were conscious of the unique character of the story and tried to set the stage in the opening sentences.

Such leads may be a phrase, a sentence, several sentences, a paragraph, or several paragraphs, but they must delineate the action, the locale, and the meaning of the story or they fail in their effect. The following four-sentence lead meets all these conditions and gives a moving account of a minor tragedy in a big city:

A 17-year-old high school senior was shot dead in a lower East Side housing development yesterday by a Housing Authority policeman who was chasing the youth as a suspected purse snatcher.

Patrolman Charles Leonard fired six shots, four of them as a warning, before a bullet from his revolver hit Robert Chura in the back as Chura sprinted along Cherry St., about 65 feet from the East River Drive.

The slug pierced Chura's heart.

"If only the kid had stopped running," Leonard said, disconsolately, on learning his shot was fatal.

—New York *Daily News*

The Personal Lead   While the first person singular is still discouraged as a reportorial device, except in eyewitness stories, there is almost a fad for "you" leads. Some are good, but too many of them give the impression that a slight story is being blown up out of all proportion to its importance.

A few examples of the personal touch in the news and the kind of stories to which they apply are:

WASHINGTON—You know that decorative female who sits just inside the entrance of every administration building of every big corporation in the land?

The National Labor Relations Board (NLRB) has just wound up a year and a half of agonizing judicial scrutiny to determine whether this doll is a plant guard or a receptionist.

Their answer: She's a receptionist and should not be included with the plant guards for collective bargaining purposes.

—Chicago *Daily News*

Here is a method of putting the personal touch into a dull highway construction story:

COLUMBUS—You may soon be riding on super, multi-lane highways you dreamed about but never expected to see in Ohio.

—Akron *Beacon Journal*

And here is a personal lead. Had the story been written routinely, it would have been a paragraph about the inevitably dull Indian land claims.

Give Ohio back to the Indians? Absolutely, the Indians say.

Testimony before a House appropriations subcommittee showed today that Indian tribes have filed Ohio land claims that total 117,000,000 acres. That is roughly four times the area of the state.

The lead that asks a question and the lead that begins with a quote were far from favorites among old-line deskmen, but both are cropping up with greater frequency today. The urge to vary the beginnings of news stories is great and these are ways of doing it. To be effective, they have to be bright. And a writer cannot always be bright in handling routine news items of the kind cited.

The Contrast Lead One of the stand bys of feature-type news leads is the contrast lead. In its most familiar form it reports the election of a company president who began as a $4-a-week office boy. Sometimes, to vary the monotony, this saga may be split into two sentences, the first of which refers to the humble beginning and the second to the hero's latest triumph.

This stencil has grown faded with use. Infrequently, a writer with an original turn of mind can adapt the same theme to a new subject with wit and effectiveness. When Van Cliburn came home from his musical triumph in Moscow, one reporter wrote:

Harvey Lavan (Van) Cliburn Jr. of Kilgore, Tex., came home from the Soviet Union yesterday with seventeen pieces of luggage. They bespoke his triumph as a pianist in Moscow. He had three when he went over.

The Delayed Lead Sometimes a situation can be exploited in an interesting way so that an ordinary item stands out. This technique usually results in a delayed lead, inducing the reader to delve several paragraphs into the text to find out what has happened. In the profession, it is called "backing into a story." While it has its advantages, it can also be a headache if it is improperly handled.

The birds and the bees again are getting their pollen mixed in Richmond County so it's time for the potato with the tomato top.

But, said J. W. Chambers, Richmond County farm agent, the tomatoes on top of the potato vines aren't really tomatoes. . . .

—Augusta (Ga.) *Chronicle*

The marriage ceremony was the same as dozens the court house chaplain, the Rev. Della Saxon, has performed in her tiny chapel off the lobby of the court house. But the circumstances were different.

The bride was 78.

The bridegroom was 89.

The best man was 73.

But it was a fine wedding for Mrs. Julia Mae Barnhart, of 207 Stull Ave., and John Adam Marton, of Eaton, O.

—Akron *Beacon Journal*

The Anecdotal Lead   Magazines used to begin many articles with anecdotal leads, provided the anecdotes were bright and applicable and not too wasteful of space. The practice seems to have dwindled in recent years in favor of a more direct news approach. However, newspapers have been so eager to pick up pointers from magazines to interest mass audiences that the anecdotal lead has had a rebirth in the news columns. Below is one from the *Wall Street Journal*, a pioneer in trying to find better ways to tell the news:

CHICAGO—Mrs. Joyce K., a 69-year-old Boston grandmother, had her gall bladder removed by an experienced surgeon in a Boston hospital a few months ago. The operation saved her life.

With her history of heart disease, use of anesthetics would have been dangerous. So. Mrs. K. was hypnotized just before being wheeled into the operating room.

Mrs. K. is just one of the many case histories that were discussed here over the weekend at the first annual meeting of the American Society of Clinical Hypnosis.

When the anecdote is short and pointed, as this one is, it can be used to bring the reader quickly into a news situation that might not attract his attention if it were routinely written. The trouble with anecdotal leads, as some magazine editors concede, is that they do not really attract as many readers as unusual statements—the basis of good straight news leads.

Besides, few anecdotes are good enough to occupy the amount of Page 1 space that could otherwise be used for a news lead.

Gag Leads   There is no sadder face in a newsroom than that of the writer who has just been told by a deskman to write a funny story. When a situation is funny, the practiced news writer lets it tell itself and modestly disclaims credit for a humorous effect. But when a deskman gets a fixed idea that he has a lot of inhibited comedians on the rewrite bank, who are just waiting to send the readers into stitches, it means trouble for everybody.

Journalistic humor requires a skilled, practiced hand. In the past generations there were such writers as Ring Lardner, Frank Sullivan, and Irvin S. Cobb, who were thought of in their times as newspaper humorists. Today, Art Buchwald and a few others carry on this tradition.

Knowing his limitations, the experienced journalist seldom trifles with humor. Yet, now and then, a gag lead happens to come off. The following is an example:

An athletic but self-effacing postman digressed from his appointed rounds shortly after six o'clock last night to duck into the Chambers St. Station of the IRT subway and make a special delivery—a haymaker that knocked a fleeing stickup man cold.

—New York *Daily News*

chapter 13

"Go With What You've Got!"

When I was a young reporter, struggling for just one more fact by making a telephone call a few minutes before the edition deadline, a long-forgotten deskman pointed at the clock and snapped inelegantly, "Go with what you've got!" Without doubt, the additional fact might have helped my story; equally without doubt, it would not have made the paper because my lead would have been too late. I have never forgotten the rough and ungrammatical advice; nor, for that matter, have I let others around me forget it. For whether they write for a newspaper or wire service, radio or television, a news magazine, or perhaps even a book publisher, there comes a time when the story must be told as it stands. Otherwise, it may not be told at all.

WRITING BY THE CLOCK

Except for wire service men, those who write for deadlines can gauge their efforts by the clock. If they have an hour to do a developing news story, they are in luck. Usually they have about twenty or thirty minutes, enough for an adequate story. Sometimes there are only five or ten minutes to do the job.

Necessarily, except for an unexpected news break, few writers can wait until five minutes before a deadline to begin a lead. Not every story can be held right to the last second before deadline; for, if it ever happened, the avalanche of copy could not be processed in time. The flow of copy must be smooth and well regulated.

From these observations it follows that the first rule of deadline writing is not to crowd the deadline except with the lead story. It should also be fairly obvious that the literary manner of a deadline story is by no means as important as its organization. If a developing story is not written in such a way as to permit easy expansion, quick handling on a deadline becomes difficult if not impossible.

Many a story on a rapidly changing event is made up of a succession of new leads, inserts, and adds. The wonder is not that such assembly-line writing jobs read as well as they do, but that they are even put together. The process is intricate. It requires experience, patience, great skill at organizing detail, and a maximum of cooperation between reporters, writers, and editors.

PARTS OF THE STORY

Such stories can be no better than their parts because each part is often written separately and out of sequence. To add to the confusion, there is no standard nomenclature for the separate parts. It varies between the news media. The following summary attempts to rationalize these differences and match up the various names of the parts of stories written under deadline pressure.

New Lead   The term *new lead* is used by newspapers to denote a new start on a story that is in type. It is often referred to as a new top in the broadcast media.

Wire services top their stories with a *first lead*, then a *second lead*, and so forth. The reason for the difference in names is that newspapers, having editions, do not need as many fresh tops as wire services and broadcast media.

In topping an existing storm story for a newspaper, for instance, a writer would begin with the term *New Lead Storm* as his slug. This would be followed by *New Lead Storm—2* and *New Lead Storm—3*. The copy, if written in the office, would conclude as follows: *"End New Lead Storm, Pick Up Type."*

A *markup* then would be made to show where the new lead fits into the old story. On a copy of the old story (a proof or carbon or a clip from the paper) the paragraphs that are to be killed would be indicated. At the paragraph where the new lead is to join the old story, these instructions should be written: *"Pick Up After New Lead Storm."*

Here is an example of how a new lead is written down into an existing story so that the two join smoothly at a designated paragraph. The technique is known as "making a clean pick up."

THE NEW LEAD THE OLD STORY

Slug: New Lead Storm

Slug: Storm

An all-day snow storm tied up Centerville today and threatened to reach a depth of 15 inches before tomorrow.

At least five persons died in auto accidents that were attributed to the storm. In the first four hours, up to 2 p.m., the snow reached a depth of four inches.

It snarled traffic, played havoc with bus schedules and made walking dangerous.

The snow crossed up the Weather Bureau. It predicted at first that the snow would change to rain. A later forecast warned of an all-night snow fall that would pile at least 15 inches on the city.

End New Lead Storm
Pick Up Type

The first snow storm of the winter swirled over Centerville today, but the Weather Bureau said it would not last long.

With the first flurry of white flakes at 10 a.m., Forecaster F. L. Maynes announced that the snow was expected to melt rapidly. The 10 a.m. temperature was 31 degrees and Maynes said "it's likely to go up above the freezing point."

But, he went on, "There is just a chance that the temperature will stay just where it is, and if that happens we'll be in for a real storm."

The Street Superintendent, A. R. Ward, took no chances. He put his entire force on a standby basis, tested his snow plows and arranged to hire snow removal trucks if they were needed.

xxx

HOW TO MARK UP A STORY

This is a markup. On the left is a story of a subway delay, clipped from newspaper and pasted on a sheet of copy paper. The crossed-out portions show what is to be eliminated. The directions to the printer, which are to be set and inserted in the standing type as a reminder that additions are to be made, show exactly what material is yet to come for the next edition. Note that the top direction varies from the ones below. (The T.R. means Turn Rule, a direction to the printer to reverse the rule, making the black line seen on the bottom and top of Insert A.) Actually, the direction for the New Lead could just as correctly read, "T. R. for N. L. Delay," but the direction as given is clearer. The new lead and inserts, set and reproduced at the right, are in galley proof. Once the printer puts the additional material into the old story, picks up a new headline and sets the reassembled story into a designated space in the type form, the job of changing from one edition to another for this particular account is done.

IND Train
Delayed

Thousands of Queens subway riders were delayed up to 25 minutes today after a breakdown of service during the rush hour on the IND line.

The Transit Authority said the trouble began at 6:54 a.m. when a Manhattan-bound express developed flat wheels at the Continental Av. station in Forest Hills.

It was taken out of service, and passengers were transferred to following trains with a delay of about six minutes.

The damaged train was then headed for a siding at Court Square in Long Island City. However, difficulty in moving the train soon backed up traffic on the express line.

2 Trains Stalled

Two trainloads of passengers were stalled behind the damaged train for 20 and 25 minutes respectively.

At 8:05 a.m. other Manhattan-bound expresses were rerouted to the local tracks between Continental Av. and Queens Plaza, slowing both express and local service. All trains ran about 15 minutes behind schedule.

The damaged train finally got as far as Roosevelt Av., where efforts to get it to Court Square were abandoned. It was shunted to the Jamaica-bound tracks, which carry only light traffic in the morning, was to be moved to 179th St.

At 8:41 express traffic was switched from the local tracks between Continental Av. and Roosevelt Av., but service remained behind schedule for the remainder of the rush hours.

Cause Not Determined

A Transit Authority spokesman said the cause of the flat wheels was not determined immediately. He added that the most common cause is a hard stop which causes skidding on the rails.

Earlier, there was a 17 minute delay beginning at 12:22 a.m. affecting five trains on the southbound Lexington Av. IRT at Fulton St. The authority said workmen who were stringing new cable accidentally hit the third rail with it, causing a short circuit which blew signal fuse.

When a fuse blows, all signals automatically go to red, halting all trains in the area covered.

P.K.up after N.L. Delay

N L DELAY

Thousands of subway riders were delayed today in Queens, Manhattan and Brooklyn by transit system breakdowns.

The most serious occurred in Queens, where the IND's Manhattan-bound trains ran up to 25 minutes late and service was disrupted during the morning rush.

T.R. For Ins A Delay

INSERT A DELAY

At 8:41, express traffic was shunted from the local tracks between Continental Av. and Roosevelt Av., and at 9 a.m. full service was restored on the rest of the line between Roosevelt Av. and Queens Plaza.

The crippled train was taken out of service at Continental Av. at 9:15 a.m.

In addition to affecting E and F expresses, the breakdown also slowed service on the GG locals and the BMT Brighton Line, which uses the IND local tracks for part of the way.

T.R. For Ins B Delay

INSERT B——DELAY

In Brooklyn, signal trouble at the Bergen St. station of the Seventh Av. IRT held up four Manhattan-bound train beginning at 8:02 a.m. In addition, a Brooklyn-bound train was turned around at Wall St. to relieve some of the congestion in Manhattan.

Mechanical trouble snarled the northbound Lexington Av. IRT local line from 9:29 to 9:50 a.m. when a train stalled in the 23d St. station.

Three trains behind it were unable to proceed, but others were routed to the express tracks. Until the mechanical trouble was repaired, there was no northbound local service between 23d and 42d Sts.

In the markup that indicates where the new lead would join the old story, it is clear that the pick-up point in the storm piece is the second paragraph of the old story. The new lead has been written with this in mind. Necessarily, the details of the storm would be added to the part of the story that remains in the paper.

Lead All   A *lead all*, as its name implies, tops a new lead. It is seldom used. On newspapers, when a lead all is necessary, it is kept very short.

The spot for a lead all is when a new lead has cleared the city room and a fresh break in the story occurs before the edition deadline. In such cases a lead all can be written quite easily by framing the latest break into a terse first paragraph and turning the new material smoothly into the previous story. This is an example:

> *Lead All Storm*
>   Mayor Wallis closed nearly all city offices today as an all-day snow storm tied up traffic and threatened to reach a 15-inch depth before tomorrow.
>
> *End Lead All Storm*
Pick Up Type

The markup would indicate the second paragraph of the previous new lead as the pick-up point. If there was time, the Mayor's statement would also be inserted into the story at an appropriate point in order to document the lead all.

Insert   An *insert* should be written in such a way that it will fit smoothly into an old story or a new lead. A lazy way of doing this is to begin an insert with the words, "meanwhile," "earlier," or "at the same time." These threadbare devices do not make for a smoothly joined story and should not be used, except on a deadline.

If an insert corrects material previously sent, it merely replaces the old paragraphs. If it adds to or elaborates on detail already in the story, it may be necessary to condense some of the type that is in the paper to make room for the new material. If that is done, it should all be a part of the same insert.

As is the case with a new lead or lead all, an insert must be accompanied by a markup or it is useless. This applies to wire service and special copy, too; telegraphic directions have to be put into a markup. The mayor's statement, if inserted in the storm lead above, could easily be done as a substitute for the third paragraph of the new lead as follows:

Insert A Storm
The Mayor took his emergency step as the snow snarled traffic, played havoc with bus schedules and made walking dangerous.

"I am asking all city department heads to close their offices by 2.30 p.m.," he said, "with the exception of those that are directly concerned with clearing the streets. This is an emergency."

End Insert A Storm

It is a good practice to name succeeding inserts with letters of the alphabet. In this way the sequence of inserts can be maintained, and there is also an automatic check on how many have been written. This is standard newspaper procedure but is not usually followed by wire services.

Add   The *add* in a newspaper story is written to go at the end. Some stories are made up of many adds tacked to a lead. In others, the add is almost an afterthought. For example, unless there is something remarkable about the five persons whose deaths were attributed to the storm, they could be listed by name, age, address, and occupation as an *Add Storm*. If greater prominence were desired, the names could be inserted higher in the story. Usually a markup is not necessary to place an add.

Bulletin   A *bulletin* for newspaper use is written in no more than forty or fifty words so that it is completely self-contained. When there is no time to make a new lead or a lead all so that the story will read coherently, a bulletin containing the fresh news is written. It is placed on top of the previous news account and separated from it by a dash.

The bulletin is a device that is used to get the latest possible news into the paper on a deadline, and, therefore, it should be used only on material that warrants it. This would be a deadline bulletin for the storm story:

Bulletin Precede Storm
Two autos collided on snowswept Route 82 north of Centerville at 2.40 p.m. today, killing at least six persons.
3 em dash
End Bulletin Precede Storm

Flash   A *flash* is reserved for the biggest kind of news, outside the sports pages. Typically, it consists of a dateline, three or four words, the name of the sender, and the time. It cannot be used in print because it is so curtailed; it always must be followed by either a bulletin or some type of lead. This is a flash:

WASHINGTON MAN LANDS ON MOON

It saves time, in the long run, to send a bulletin rather than a flash because the bulletin eliminates one step in the information process. The flash, being shorter, however, is likely to be faster by a few seconds. If it has any utility, it is to support advertising claims of a news beat.

Kill   Another journalistic word that must be used with great care is *kill*. It means that material to which it refers should be destroyed.

On routine corrections it is advisable to use a different term, *eliminate*. For example, in doing a note on the previous storm insert, the correction would be: *"Eliminate Third Graph New Lead Storm."*

The word kill should be saved for extraordinary situations. The mandatory instructions, *Must Kill*, can never be used on a newspaper without the permission of the editor in charge unless the reporter is filing from a distant point and is on his own.

Sub   As its name indicates, a *sub* substitutes for a previous news account. *Sub Weather*, when it is written, would automatically dispose of the weather story that is in the paper. It is a newspaper term and is seldom used in wire service practice.

Of course, a sub is usually impractical except when it is short and eliminates a short previous account. In the weather story that has been built up over several hours, it would be foolish to do the news a second time for some purely esthetic reason.

PIECING THE STORY TOGETHER

When the lead to a long news story is expected shortly before the deadline, much of the story must be written in anticipation of the lead. It must also be done in such a way that, regardless of what happens to shape the lead, the earlier part of the story will fit it.

This technique of writing a story backward is known in newspaper work as doing *B copy* or *B matter*. Some newspapers call it *A copy* or *A matter*. Still others slug it *running* or *lead to come*. For purposes of discussion, B copy will be used here as the term for the earlier part of the story that is written in anticipation of a lead to be done a few minutes before the deadline.

Running stories of this type often have to be written in several pieces, one stacked atop the other. The way they are assembled, in the order in which they appear in the paper, is *lead* (not *new lead*), *A copy*, and *B copy*. Often the A copy is eliminated as a needless and complicating step so that the two pieces that remain are merely lead and B copy.

B Copy   This is a process that wastes space. It should be used only on major stories, or on sports events calling for detail that is written before the lead is begun.

It is wasteful because, by its very nature, B copy includes material that could easily be chopped from the end of a story. Except when it is done in chronological order, B copy contributes little to the art of good news writing.

Its sole justification is that no paper can go with just a paragraph or two on the outcome of an election, convention, trial, contest, sports event, or similar account. Thus, when a writer anticipates the passage of a new law, or a verdict, or an election of a mayor or governor, or the end of a football game, he does B copy.

The trick is to write it in such a way that it will easily join to any lead that is written, regardless of how the lead may begin or end. In effect, the documentation for the lead is bound to be in the B copy somewhere.

Therefore, the way the B copy begins is important. In doing an election story, the B copy could start:

> *B Copy Vote*
> The polls closed at 7 P.M.
> During the day there was a heavy turnout of voters because of the interest in the election and the sunny Fall weather. Much of the vote was in by 2 P.M., but lines still curled away from many a polling place at the closing hour.
> The issues. . . .

Similarly, in a news account of a trial, the B copy could begin with the hour at which the judge delivered his charge and gave the case to the jury. An account of a convention fight, leading up to the nomination of a particular candidate, could open with a summary of the remarks of the first speaker and continue chronologically. A baseball game, or other sports account, could fit snugly into the B copy pattern by beginning with the action and describing it tersely as it develops, inning by inning or quarter by quarter.

Necessarily, the writer must have a fair idea of which names or titles are to appear in the lead of the story. In order to avoid repeating full names and titles, he would leave them out of the B copy, using only the last names of the principal actors. Such considerations would help to make the B copy and lead fit smoothly together.

WRITING BACKWARD

To illustrate the process of writing a story backward, here is a curtailed version of a murder trial verdict as done for a newspaper:

> *B Copy Getty*
> The verdict climaxed a long, tense day of courtroom drama. Supreme Court Justice Holmes gave the case to the jurors at 11.03 a.m. He charged

them to acquit Marilou if they believed her to have been insane at the time of the slaying of her father.

"But," said Justice Holmes sternly, "if you find Miss Getty knew the nature and quality of her act, and knew in fact that it was wrong, then you must find her guilty of murder in the first degree."

Marilou was pale but calm as the judge gave his charge. Her mother, a large woman in a crumpled black dress, sobbed audibly.

For much of the afternoon, the courtroom was deserted except for a few attaches and newspaper reporters. Then, toward 4 p.m., word sped about the quiet marble corridors of the Court House that the jury was coming in.

Thus, the stage was set for the last act of the drama that has fascinated much of the nation for the past two weeks.

The State had tried to prove that Marilou committed a "mercy murder" when she shot and killed her father with his revolver. District Attorney Lindsey hammered away at the theme that no one has a right to take a human life.

Defense Attorney Streator insisted, throughout, that Marilou was insane at the moment she pulled the trigger. He did not contend, however, that she was out of her mind before or afterward.

Marilou was her own best witness. Testifying in her own defense, a tall, plain-looking girl with curly black hair, she kept a small Bible clutched in her hands. She told jurors quite simply that she could remember nothing of the events on the night her father was fatally shot from the moment she entered his room until she came to in her own room.

The State was never able to shake her story.

End B Copy Getty
A Copy Upcoming

A Copy Getty

Marilou, summoned from the hotel where she had been staying, entered the low-ceilinged, oak-paneled courtroom at 4.16 p.m. to hear the verdict. Her mother and her attorney, Arthur P. Streator, were with her. District Attorney Mead Lindsey followed them.

Marilou still wore the simple black dress, with a small gold pin at the throat, in which she had appeared throughout the trial. A small black hat was pulled down over her black curls. Her shoes were low, black, and flat-heeled.

Her mother was weeping as Justice Holmes entered, short, red-faced, but grave. A few moments later the jury filed in to take its place and the courtroom waited tensely for the words that determined Marilou's fate.

End A Copy Getty
Pick Up B Copy

FLASH   MARILOU GETTY ACQUITTED   GRIMMEL 4.32 PM

Lead Getty

Marilou Getty was acquitted today of the "mercy murder" of her father.

A jury of four men and eight women, most of them in tears, set the tall, 19-year-old choir singer free at 4.31 p.m. They had deliberated five hours and 28 minutes.

Marilou embraced her weeping mother, Mrs. Catherine Getty, and said:

"I was sure they would not find me guilty."

Supreme Court Justice Davis J. Holmes dismissed the jurors but did not thank them for their services. To Marilou he said gruffly,

"You are free to go home with your mother. Try to take care of her."

By its verdict the jury showed that it had believed Marilou's story that she was temporarily insane when she fatally shot her father, Morgan R. Getty, a builder whose doctors had said he would die in a month of cancer. The slaying occurred last October at the Getty home, 365 Baldur Place.

End Lead Getty

Pick Up A Copy Getty, Then B Copy

Dummy Leads In the story of the Getty verdict alternate one-paragraph leads would have been prepared to cover several possibilities if the paper had been closer to its deadline and unable to wait for a "live" lead from the courtroom. On receipt of the flash the correct *dummy lead* would have been slipped atop the A copy in the Page 1 form and sent to press with previously prepared headlines to match. Here is how some of the dummy leads would have looked:

Lead Getty—Acquit—Hold for Release

A Supreme Court jury today acquitted Marilou Getty, 19, of the "mercy murder" of her cancer-stricken father, Morgan R. Getty, last October 24.

End Lead Getty—Acquit—Hold for release

Lead Getty—1st Degree Murder—Hold for Release

Marilou Getty, 19, was found guilty of first degree murder in Supreme Court today for the "mercy slaying" of her cancer-stricken father, Morgan R. Getty, last October 24.

End Lead Getty—1st Degree Murder—Hold for Release

Other dummy leads would be prepared, of course, to follow the various additional contingencies.

The dummy lead procedure is frequently used in sports events to catch an edition with a final result. Only two alternate leads have to be prepared for most contests, win or lose, so that the handling of the story in the composing room is comparatively simple. While the dummy lead is being slipped into place and the page justified, a single line of type is set giving the final score. That follows the lead and makes the flat announcement of the winner a little less drab.

The Fudge Box Such late news is also handled on some newspapers in a separate two-column box on Page 1, known as the *fudge box*. The fudge box is printed directly from type inserted in a small two-column cylinder that is synchronized with the main presses. The cylinder is composed of six curved segments that are bolted into place.

While the main presses go on running, the fudge box cylinder can be stopped, a segment containing late news substituted for an earlier one and then started again. While the fudge box cylinder is halted, the fudge box contains only white space in copies of the paper that are run off the main presses. The rise of TV and the decline of newspaper competition have robbed the fudge box of much of its value.

Cold Plating   Still another device, which is not very practical any more because of the slackening of competition, is to have entire dummy stories written and headlined to take care of various possibilities on a major news break that is anticipated. This process is known as *cold plating*, since plates are cast in advance and held in the press room. When the flash comes in, the right plate is slipped on the press and a few thousand copies are run off until the "live" edition can be locked up.

These "dummy" editions, however, defeat their own purpose in these days of electronic journalism. They tell the reader a great deal less than he already knows from listening to the radio and TV. Cold plates were all right in 1904. They are an anachronism today. A "dummy" edition can only undermine public faith in newspapers. It is useless to pretend that such extreme measures have any validity in view of the superior speed and flexibility of the broadcast media.

chapter 14

Human Interest in the News

Two generations or more ago when the deadpan news story was considered ideal by many American journalists, editors generally divided news content into three parts—straight news, features, and policy material. Today these categories are blurred. Under the pressures of broadcast journalism on the one side, and the news magazines on the other, no newspaper can afford to depend any longer on the deadpan news account. Nor can any news medium adopt a lofty, impersonal tone.

A DIFFERENT PATTERN

The old editorial division separated stories of special human appeal, but without any particular time element, from the reporting of current events and opinion-molding.

Straight news, as the term implies, was the undiluted record of immediate events written in an impersonal style by all except reporters of special eminence. Features, the generic name for any department, illustration, or news account outside the breaking news, could be written almost as fancy dictated. This, it should be remembered, was the age of the sob story and almost unrestrained journalistic expression.

The success of a less stylized and more personal form of news story, as practiced on the weekly news magazines and by TV-radio news writers, has changed newspaper patterns. It is no accident that the old straight news-feature division has given way to the somewhat broader concept of hard news, which describes anything that has actually happened, and soft news, which covers both features and interpretive news material.

The Rainbow of Human Interest   In today's journalism the rainbow of human interest arches over the entire field. The weekly and monthly picture and general circulation magazines, in particular, have developed the old newspaper feature into an effective, colorful, and well-documented job that puts its skimpy, slatternly ancestor to shame. The public has taken to the slick magazine performance. The newspapers have had to scramble to try to keep up and still lag far behind their slower, but keener, competitors.

One of the principal changes that has emerged from this developing situation is in the form and content of newspaper writing. The straight news story still persists, and will always be useful on a deadline. With it has come a mingling of the old straight news and feature patterns—the things that have a special interest for people.

Long ago, hard-boiled editors roughly defined human interest as "blood, money, and broads." Tabloid editors proceeded on the general theory that people were interested in reading about pretty girls, babies, and animals. As a result, the human interest feature of thirty or thirty-five years ago was likely to be a sensational blood-and-thunder yarn, a Sunday "gee-whiz" story about the electric eel, or some mild little piece of time copy (stories that can be run any old time, or AOT). Of course, good features were done then, too, but it generally took somebody of the stature of Frank Ward O'Malley of the New York *Sun* to put them over. The sob stories dripped all over Page 1.

As a result of the mingling of straight news and human interest, it is becoming increasingly difficult on many papers to tell where one ends and the other begins. Even a major spot news break taking a big headline is likely to begin with a feature-type lead, if the writer happens to think of a good one. In the Chicago school fire that killed 87 children, the lead on one Chicago paper was simply: "87 children." The story developed from there.

What has happened is that the human interest element in the news is being included more and more in situations that used to call for the simple declarative sentences of straight news handling. This is basically a matter of broadened reporting, of doing something more than merely recording events.

The Technique   The technique is to fit the event into an understandable context. The reporter now takes a hard look at the people who are the actors in the news. He reports the things that they do as well as the things that they say. He includes such personal touches in his copy, and the copy desk passes them if it is wise. He weaves in colorful background, explanatory matter, reactions—anything that will give his account more meaning and therefore more interest.

There is, of course, no guarantee that weighty formal news of great importance will be made clearer by telling it in terms of heroes or villains, or even pretty ladies. The human interest twist, while it invariably adds to public attentiveness, also entails the inevitable risk of distortion. Little is to be gained in attempting to report a complicated negotiation with the Russians in terms of a Rotary Club meeting or to try to picture an Intercontinental Ballistic Missile on the basis of Junior's Fourth of July rocket.

The greatest criticism of journalism is not that it overcomplicates, but that it oversimplifies. One is as great a journalistic fault as the other. Simple things have to be simply told, it is true. But there is no substitute for the explanations that must be made of complicated things to give them depth and meaning.

The human interest touch, therefore, has its uses and its limits.

It can illuminate the news at many levels if it is applied with taste and discrimination in appropriate situations, but nothing is likely to be more embarrassing to a reporter than a mawkish personal story where the news calls for clear writing and a detached position. Such pieces usually are spiked. That is why American editors, as a rule, proceed cautiously with the personal story and keep a careful watch on the human interest content of the news.

The Problem of Space   The choice of a journalistic method can only be dictated by knowledge of and experience in the field, based on good judgment. Today's personal journalism is not the rampant crusading of other times. Nor can it be defined, on the whole, as the domination of a newspaper by a single powerful individual—a Horace Greeley, James Gordon Bennett, Joseph Pulitzer, or the like. The modern American news organization is largely a team operation. On the staff level, therefore, the human interest element is introduced as a technique of news gathering and news writing, and in television, superior film work.

Barry Bingham, editor-in-chief of the Louisville *Courier-Journal and Times*, one of the most perceptive of American journalists, puts it this way:

> Too many papers still depend on "hot flashes and late bulletins." Some otherwise healthy editors suffer from headlineitis, a hangover from the past days of hectic street-sale competition.
>
> I'm convinced that readers are showing a failure of appetite, brought on by too much hard, tough, indigestible news. But I want to make the main course—the news—more palatable instead of switching to double portions of cream puffs for dessert.
>
> More comics? No. More features? No, unless [it] means a feature treatment of solid news. That I go for.

The sources of human interest, therefore, may now be found built into the news. That is the basis for the revival of personal journalism in the United States. It is developing side by side with the old straight news story, which will not be supplanted.

THE NEWS MAGAZINES

In less than fifty years, the weekly news magazines have made themselves an indispensable part of the American system of news communication. Although they can and do exploit the "back of the book" or departmental news to a far greater extent than most newspapers, and break their fair share of exclusives, the newsbook writers have won a strong hold on public attention because of their style and flair. Where the average newspapers have failed, the news magazines have succeeded and they are likely to continue to make gains at the expense of the weaker dailies.

The old *Time* formula popularized by Briton Hadden was to "start anywhere, go somewhere, then stop." Essentially, this is what newsbook writers still do today. Despite all the complaints of slanting and editorializing in the news columns, and dressing up nonessential items to titillate the public, the news magazines thrive on what the journalists of another day called simply "feature writing." Only, the newsbook writers on the whole perform better than the old-timers ever could.

THE NEWS FEATURE

As the beginnings of the following newspaper and wire service pieces amply demonstrate, almost anything can be turned into an interesting news feature —if the writer knows how:

> The best figures in the U. S. are developed in two ugly, three-story warehouse buildings on flat, desolate lawns in Suitland, Md.
> They are the kind of figures businessmen pant for, sociologists long for, and bureaucrats passionately desire to possess. They are the kind of figures some congressmen condemn as revealing too much. In short, they are the lush, countless statistics compiled by the U. S. Census Bureau, which draws profiles of America by asking more questions of more people than all newsmen and private pollsters combined.
> The census bureau can say with authority that Americans in a single year imported 4,543,000 pounds of anchovies in oil, a full 1,000,000 pounds less than a decade ago, but at nearly $1,000,000 additional cost. The bureau knows that 26,169,000 pounds of aspirin were bought in a single year, that 12,900,000 pounds of apple sauce were canned, and that in the same year there were 1,853,000 Boy Scouts between the ages of 11 and 18.

As expenses of gathering local news rise, it is likely that still more combinations will be effected where competing news organizations can afford to get their news from the same sources.

SPECIALS AND SYNDICATES

The mounting cost of maintaining correspondents overseas, in Washington, and even in state capitals has brought about a reduction in the number of "specials"—as newspaper correspondents are known—who are permanently assigned outside their offices. This is a loss to the profession. A talented special can do a better job for his own paper on many assignments than an agency that has to service thousands of papers.

News Syndicates   The wire services are encountering stiff competition from the newspapers that can afford to maintain large and competent staffs of reporters in the national and international field. *The New York Times*, operating one of the oldest news syndicates in the field, services more than 200 newspapers in the United States and abroad. The Los Angeles *Times*, one of the newest news syndicates, has surged ahead rapidly in a few years, partly because of its loose partnership arrangement with the service offered by the Washington *Post*. The Chicago *Daily News*, and the Copley News Service are among the others that have established reputations in the syndicate field.

On big news, whether it is in the next county, in Washington, or abroad, the American press still gives saturation coverage and will try, in many cases, to rush specials to the scene, but the fire-house principle of reporting is not really thorough. The special literally dashes from his plane to the scene of an international conference, gets out pencil and paper, jots down notes, and files his first story before he can catch his breath. He picks up background as he goes and hopes for the breaks. Such reporting, even by experts, is not calculated to give wire service executives sleepless nights.

The habit of depending on the wire services is insidious. Because they are capable and dependable, it is easy for an editor to fall back on them for his national and foreign coverage and salve his conscience by telling himself he does not have a man to spare. Almost insensibly the same reasoning can take possession of some editors when it comes time to assign a man to report on the state legislature and the governor. The general reporting of important state and national news has, therefore, tended to drift more and more into the domain of the wire service bureaus although newspapers of consequence still do the job that readers expect of them at this level.

The decline of the special has also had its effect on local news reporting and writing. Where there is a good wire service bureau or local wire service in a city, the temptation is great to assign reporters only on the major news of the day and let the agency men handle all the rest. That tendency has led, over the years, to a practice on some newspapers of running locally originated wire service copy without credit or of rewriting it to make it appear of staff origin. Understandably this has led to a demand for more news writers of ability, originality, and—most of all—speed. No matter how flossy the writing, it has not made up for the slackening use of reporters on local, state, national, or international news. Good news writing still takes good reporting.

Feature Syndicates   Although the wire services also distribute feature material, this function is shared with the big feature syndicates. In their modern form such syndicates are business organizations that contract with artists, writers, and photographers for a host of popular features that are sold to hundreds, and often thousands, of newspapers. One of the main characteristics of a feature syndicate is its large sales staff, which is constantly circulating among newspapers both here and abroad with offers of a dazzling variety of circulation-building materials. The wire services and newspaper syndicates sell, too, but very few are able to rival an organization such as the Hearst-owned King Features Syndicate, largest in the field. Feature journalism is the business of such syndicates, and a very big business, too.

Several hundred feature syndicates offer their sales lists to editors. Among the biggest sellers are the comic strips. The political columnists have a healthy newspaper following as do some of the newer women's features, but interest in gossip columns is declining. Sports columns, being so heavily dependent on local interest, usually do not have a wide syndicated audience.

Syndicates offer everything that can occur to the brain of an editor and be translated into popular journalistic merchandise. Both fiction and nonfiction best-sellers are offered in serial form by syndicates. They market cooking columns, children's care columns, bridge columns, fashion news, health columns, editorial cartoons, canned editorials, various kinds of advice not overlooking family counseling, finance, and advice to the lovelorn, literary and drama criticism, bedtime stories, and other staples.

Newspapers are charged by the feature in accordance with their circulation and their ability to pay. Whereas large newspapers pay a high price for a popular comic, small ones can get a popular columnist for a few dollars a week. Editors often come to New York, headquarters of some of the big syndicates, with long shopping lists.

Contributing to the feature syndicate is scarcely in the same class with the professional work of the journalist who deals primarily in news. If anything, feature syndicate work is a kind of amalgamation of the worlds of art, light literature, and journalism. The writers of news seldom know what goes on in it because they have little contact with it until they make a name for themselves.

WIRE SERVICES AT WORK

By the most knowledgeable estimates wire services provide 90 per cent of the foreign news that is published in the American press and 75 per cent or more of the national news. Many newspapers accept at least half their state-wide news from wire services as well. Therefore, except on leading newspapers, it would seem that only local news seems to call for individual exertion. The same is very largely true of the broadcast media.

Standards   If the reliance on the wire service for news results in a more or less standardized pattern of foreign, national, and state-wide news coverage, it is not primarily the fault of the agencies. In laying heavy demands upon them, the individual newspapers would appear to be somewhat more to blame. Certainly, considering the handicaps of time and diverse other pressures that are put upon them, the agencies perform minor miracles every day to get the news—and occasionally they perform a big miracle.

It would be a grievous error to assume that the agencies, having inherited so much responsibility by default, perform their duties by whim and by chance. Far from it. They are under the most rigorous scrutiny of any organization in the land, for not even a Senate select committee can bore in with more angry vigor than a posse of outraged editors who do not believe that they are getting what they are paying for.

A wire service must meet the standards of thousands of editors of all shades of political and religious beliefs, all nationalities and sympathies. What may be of interest to one news organization may be of no consequence to a wire service, except if an editor requests special coverage, but what may seem interesting to a wire service does not always please its members or clients. Editors being what they are, it is difficult enough to satisfy one of them, let alone hundreds or thousands at a time.

The wire service, therefore, ordinarily takes great care to present all sides of a story that is controversial. It may not be the best way to handle a wire service report, but it is usually the fairest way.

Wire service people are not paid to take sides. They are the impartial sources of information for all sides. The wire service reporter or writer, consequently, is closely watched for any shade of editorializing in his copy. For those of experience and proved judgment, permission is given to background and interpret the news on stories requiring it. But to tell why something happened, the interpretive process, is quite different from arguing over what should be done about it, the editorial prerogative. This is the first thing that novice wire service reporters must learn, sometimes by being discharged.

Criticisms   Every conceivable criticism of wire service work has been made by editors. They have complained on occasion that wire services send too many bulletins, too many versions of a developing story, too much copy on the average political story, sometimes too little on a good feature. In the rush of putting a report together, hapless agency men are frequently accused of featuring the last thing that happened when it may not be the most important. Or, they may be charged with the particularly heinous crime of glorifying the trivial.

The APME Blue Book records the complaints of editors who called attention to "the vast amount of trivia" in an Associated Press report and asks solemnly, "What are trivia? Suppose we could agree on trivia, what would we substitute?"

Trivia, like the outpouring of new leads on major stories, are a part of wire service work. The wholesalers present a full line of merchandise. The retailers buy. The principle is still *caveat emptor.*

The wire services have their faults and they are many, but they also have virtues. Often, the agencies have been ahead of well-informed diplomats on the great events of world affairs. In the military it is not an earth-shaking secret that many an intelligence officer would be lost in a maze of slow-moving and murky official communications if he did not have a wire service teleprinter in his office.

When a politician has something to say, whether it is of consequence or not, one of the first questions he asks his press secretary is whether the wire services have been informed. Whether the news is big-time or small-town, headline or feature material, sex or science, business or crime, the wire services can be depended on to get it out. They are the basic reporters for the whole top-heavy edifice of modern mass communications.

American journalism could not exist without them. They have made themselves indispensable.

WIRE SERVICE PROCEDURE

The techniques of wire service handling of developing news differ from newspaper procedure in several respects.

Schedules   Preceding the opening of each cycle, a schedule is sent to all editors on a given circuit to let them know what material is available for transmission to them. This schedule, or budget message, tells editors each story that they will get by slug, description, and often by word count. It does not, of course, tell the precise time that each specific piece will go on the wire because that is bound to vary. The breaking news, which is handled as it happens, can knock out the most carefully prepared news budget.

There are slight differences between UPI and AP procedure but in the main they follow the same principles because they are always working on some paper's deadline. The various takes of their stories are moved in order, but not necessarily consecutively. They may be put between bulletins of other material that is given precedence.

Wire Service Slugging For all these reasons it is not practical for a wire service story to be written in newspaper fashion with the page slugs numbered 1-2-3-4. Instead, wire copy consists of a first take and a series of adds for most stories. Each add is easily identifiable because it bears the slug and dateline of the original and a time sequence of transmission.

Slugs in wire service work also are devised as a code to indicate urgency of transmission. Those generally used by the American wire services are Flash, Bulletin and Urgent in descending order of importance. Although the all-cap printer has gradually given way to the faster typewriter-style printer, the familiar routine of transmitting the news to newspapers, news magazines, and radio and television stations has remained pretty much the same.

Wire Copy Transmission The two wire service pieces that follow illustrate what an editor sees when he is an AP member and also subscribes to UPI. The particular examples were selected at random from the file of an ordinary day and are given here in their essentials. Both are about the same announcement. It isn't the kind of story that matters very much as far as time differential is concerned, as long as it is moved promptly on the wire. There also is no particular superiority in presentation between one service and the other. But the editor is given a choice of services, which is the main consideration.

Here is the essential file of both services on the story, with the necessary explanations:

110A
Rover 2/28 WA
Bulletin
WASHINGTON (UPI)—Congress was asked today for $91 million to begin development of a nuclear-powered rocket engine for deep space probes to be known as the "Rover."
(More) BA1127AES

The first number in the bulletin (110A) indicates the dispatch is filed on the "A" wire and that it is the 110th take of that particular cycle. In the next line, Rover is the slug, 2/28 is the day of the file and WA is the abbreviation for Washington, from which the bulletin is filed. The final number is unscrambled as follows: BA is the signature of the teletype operator or puncher, and the time is 11:27 A.M., Eastern Standard Time (1127AES).

In the next take, 111A, note that the pickup line is composed of several elements—the number of the add, the slug, the dateline, the number of the first take, three Xs merely to set off the last word of the previous take, and that word, which happens to be "Rover." The whole thing then is put together as follows, with an unintentional garble in the first line of the text:

>111A
>1st Add Rover Washn 110A X X X "Rover"
>Explaining that a nuclear engine, with a potential of 200,000 to 250,000 pounds of thrust, the White House said "Rover" could almost double the present Saturn V payload.
>It could "be used in future manned landings and explorations of far distant planets," a spokesman said.
>Congress was asked to add the $91 million to the budget for the Fiscal Year which begins July 1. Money for "Rover" was part of a $149.8 million proposal which also would provide two significant new nuclear research facilities at a total cost of $58.8 million.
>(More)   BA1130AES

Two takes of the story now are off the machine in three minutes, which is moving copy along at a pretty fair rate. But before the next take is off the machines, seven more minutes elapse. Note that the pickup line specifies it is the 2nd add and again repeats the slug, the dateline, the number of the first take, and the last word of the previous take.

>112A
>2nd Add Rover Washn 110A X X X million
>One would be a laboratory for "basic physical and biomedical research" involving the meson, which the White House described as "one of the fragments of the atom that scientists are interested in studying."
>The other new facility would be a center for advanced research into "controlled thermonuclear fusion as a potential source of electricity."
>Both research projects would be built at the Atomic Energy Commission's Los Alamos Scientific Laboratory in New Mexico.
>BA1137AES

Now, with the end of the story, an observant editor has noted the garble in the first line of the 1st Add and the following correction is filed in the standard UPI manner. Note how instructions are given before and after the correction to show editors where it fits:

113A
Corrn Rover Washn 110A 2nd Pgh: Fixing garble.

The White House explained that Rover, a nuclear engine with a potential of 200,000 to 250,000 pounds of thrust, could almost double the present Saturn V payload.

Pickup 3rd Pgh: It could

BA1138AES

After 40 minutes elapse, UPI puts out a first lead which is a bit more dramatic and, in its second take, includes somewhat more information. This time, instead of a bulletin, the story is given the next lower order of priority on the wire, urgent, but both takes move with reasonable promptness. Note the wording of the pickup line on 125A, 1st Add 1st Ld Rover, and the instructions to editors at the end of the take to show where it joins with the original story.

124A
Rover 2/28   WA
Urgent
1st Ld Rover 110A

WASHINGTON (UPI)—The White House today asked Congress for $91 million to start development of nuclear-powered space rockets powerful enough for "future manned landings and explorations of far-distant planets."

The supplemental funds would go into the Rover engine program, which is shooting for nuclear propulsion of the sort needed if Americans are to explore neighboring planets.

A White House announcement said that a nuclear engine with 200,000 to 250,000 pounds of thrust could almost double the payload of the Saturn V rocket being developed for the Apollo moon program.

(More)   TM1218PES

125A
1st Add 1st Ld Rover Washington 124A X X X program.

Chairman Clinton P. Anderson, D.-N.M., of the Senate Space Committee, praised the action as one of "tremendous impact."

Anderson said the development of a still more powerful rocket called Nerva is expected to cost about $1 billion over a ten-year period. But he said he understood this could be paid off in only a few space missions "because of the high performance achievable with nuclear propulsion."

The $91 million required for Rover was part of a $149.8 million proposal which would also provide two important nuclear research facilities at a total cost of $58.8 million.

Pickup 5th Pgh 110A: One would

TM 1231PES

The differences between AP and UPI filing methods are apparent in the following dispatch. While the designation of the "A" wire and the numbering of the take are the same, there is no slug on the bulletin. Instead, the slug appears for the first time on the pickup line which is simpler than the kind used by UPI. The abbreviation WX in the pickup line is the AP code for Washington. Except where it is absolutely necessary, AP no longer designates the number of the add but leaves it to editors to match up the takes in proper sequence. Note, too, there is no pickup line between A159 and A160 because they follow each other on the wire. Here is the way the AP ran the bulletin, three succeeding takes, and a correction on the Rover story.

A158
Bulletin
WASHINGTON (AP)—The White House asked Congress today for money to begin the development of a nuclear-powered rocket engine, "The Rover."
LT1122AES Feb. 28

A159
Washington—Johnson Rover A158WX Add: Rover
For this and other scientific projects, Congress was asked for a total of $149.8 million for use in the Fiscal Year beginning July 1.
In addition to the nuclear-powered rocket engine, the White House asked for funds for a physics laboratory for basic physical and biochemical research and a specialized facility for further exploration into controlled thermonuclear fission as a potential source of electricity.

A160WX
"The projects will advance America's ability to harness atomic energy for the peaceful exploration of space," a spokesman said. "They will also help us chart new courses in nuclear science."
He said development of a nuclear-powered rocket engine will take time, and that present plans call for delivery of the first test model in the 1970s.
LT1126AES Feb. 28

A165WX
U R G E N T
WASHINGTON—Rover A158WX Add: The 1970s.
A number of flight and ground tests will precede full use of the engine in space programs, the White House announcement added.
A total of $91 million is sought in the next fiscal year for the rocket development and the remaining $58.8 million to develop the new research facilities.
Both new research facilities will be built by the Atomic Energy Commission at its Los Alamos, N.M., scientific laboratory.
PE1156AES Feb. 28

A179WX
Rover Correction
Washington—Rover A158WX Third Graf make read X X X thermonuclear fusion etc., (sted fission)
JC1247PES Feb. 28

It will be seen that there is little to choose between the two accounts presented here. Both moved bulletins promptly, the AP a few minutes ahead of UPI. But UPI had more detail in a shorter space of time. Both decided the story should go on the wire at once and therefore marked the first paragraph as a bulletin. The AP used an "urgent" designation on A165WX to make certain it was given the next order of priority on the wires. Note the method of identifying the location of corrections because the same procedure is used for placing inserts in moving stories.

Both services use numbered leads in progression. However, after the original story is filed, UPI will come up with first lead, second lead, third lead, and so on, while AP will use lead, second lead, third lead, and so on. If a "write-through" is ordered, something newspapers generally call a sub story, wire services often merely use the next numbered lead in the progression and at the end carry the notation "eliminates previous" and give no pickup line.

There is another peculiarity in wire service procedure that is not generally in accord with newspaper practice. Because of the confusion in morning papers which carry undated leads with the notation that something happened yesterday, and dated leads of yesterday that something happened today, the wire services use the day of the week and drop all dates for morning papers. However, for afternoon papers, today—and not Monday or Tuesday—is still the rule for leads, dated or undated.

The Unexpected Event   During the long and bitter confrontation between Israel and the United Arab Republic in the Middle East, many hostile incidents erupted with dramatic suddenness. It was, of course, difficult to determine what had happened and to assess the importance of the event. This is an illustration of such an event, as it came off the AP "A" wire from the first bulletin to the night leads:

> A076
> Bulletin
> By the Associated Press
> Egyptian forces opened fire at the southern end of the Suez Canal near Port Tawfiq today and Israeli troops fired back, an Israeli army spokesman announced in Tel Aviv.
>   P&LS934AED Oct 24
>
> A077
> Undated Israel-Egypt A076 Add: Tel Aviv.
> He said Israel informed U.N. observers of the shooting but fighting continued.
> The spokesman gave no further details and there was no report on any fighting from Egypt.
> The announcement came amid a clamor in Israel for vengeance against Egypt after its sinking of the Israeli destroyer Elath. But informed

sources said the Israeli government planned no hasty reprisals and would "let the Arabs sweat it out for awhile."

P&LS936AED Oct 24

A095
Israel-Egypt lead
By the Associated Press
Egyptians and Israeli forces bombarded each other with artillery and mortars today across the Suez Canal near Port Tawfiq at the southern end.

An Israeli army spokesman said artillery fire hit and set aflame the oil refineries at Port Ibrahim, across the canal from Port Taufiq. He said the refineries were going up in smoke, cutting off part of Egypt's oil supply.

The spokesman asserted the Egyptians opened up with small arms and then loosed artillery fire, whereupon the Israelis on the east bank of the canal replied. One light Israeli casualty was reported.

The announcement: 3rd graf A076

Eds: Taufiq is correct.

r 1114 AED Oct 24

A102
Undated Israel-Egypt lead A095 add: reported.

An Egyptian artillery communiqué accused the Israeli forces of opening up with machine guns. It admitted that oil refineries were burning.

Israel said U. N. truce observers were informed but both sides reported the firing was still going on.

The announcement: 3rd graf A076

DF1139AED Oct 24

A113
Israel-Egypt correction
Undated Israel-Egypt lead A095 sub 2nd graf to correct site oil refineries

An Israeli army spokesman said artillery fire hit and set aflame the oil refineries of Port Suez, across the canal from Port Taufiq. He said the refineries were going up in smoke, cutting off part of Egypt's oil supply.

The spokesman: 3rd graf

DF1221PED Oct 24

A116
Urgent
Israel-Egypt 2nd lead
By the Associated Press
Egyptian and Israel forces engaged in a blazing artillery duel today at the southern end of the Suez Canal and Egypt claimed it shot down one of Israel's Mirage jet fighters.

An Egyptian communiqué also asserted four Israeli tanks were shot up in the fighting near Port Taufiq, which erupted only four days after Egyptian missiles sank the Israeli destroyer Elath in the most serious incident since the cease fire last June.

An Israeli: 2nd graf lead A095

DF&P1231PED Oct 24

The next piece was the night lead (NL) which summarized the fighting along the Suez Canal and tried to evaluate it. It had been scheduled in the budget (bjt) previously moved on the "A" wire for morning newspapers and the summary line at the top gave the total number of takes in the story, the wordage in the first take, and the total length. Enough of the story is given here to show how it developed: Note that the "A" wire numbering has begun afresh with the opening of the AM cycle and that the day of the week is used in the lead:

A018
Israel-Egypt bjt NL   280 2 takes total 570
By the Associated Press
Egypt and Israel engaged in a furious artillery and mortar duel across the southern end of the Suez Canal Tuesday. An Egyptian refinery complex was left blazing and a Cairo communiqué claimed an Israeli Mirage jet was shot down.

The withering Israeli bombardment of the refineries in Port Suez was seen in Tel Aviv as a reply to the sinking of the destroyer Elath by Egyptian missiles Saturday with the loss of 47 lives.

Informants in Tel Aviv said towering tongues of flames leaped up from the refineries, which produce about 80 percent of Egypt's petroleum needs, when the U. N. truce observers in the area arranged a cease fire late in the day.

A Cairo communiqué said several fires were raging in the refinery complex.

Egypt and Israel accused each other of opening fire.
MORE
WW244PED Oct 24

Changing Datelines   Frequently, in a breaking story, it will be necessary to change the locale from which the news is being reported. In the following account of Henry R. Luce's death, the first break came from New York but the event occurred in Phoenix, Arizona, and was handled as follows:

A115
Bulletin
NEW YORK (AP)—Henry R. Luce, editorial chairman of *Time* magazine, died early this morning in Phoenix, Ariz., a spokesman for the magazine said here today. Luce was 68.
RP931AES Feb 28

A 116
New York Luce Add A115: 68.
The spokesman said there were no details on the cause of death except that it occurred at about 3 a.m. at the Luce family home in Phoenix.
RP932AES Feb 28

A 117
URGENT
Telegraph editors: In connection with Henry R. Luce death (A115) biographical sketch 3489 is hereby released.

The AP Feb 28
RP933AES

A118
Urgent
New York Luce AddA116: Phoenix.
Luce resigned in April, 1964, as editor-in-chief of *Time*, Inc., the magazine firm he cofounded some 43 years ago.
"I'm 66 years old," he said at the time. "I'm in good health and I'm eager to keep active."

RP944AES Feb 28

A142
Urgent
Luce Precede Lead
PHOENIX, ARIZ. (AP)—Henry R. Luce, editorial chairman of *Time* Inc., one of the most influential magazine publishing companies in the world, died today in St. Joseph's Hospital of a massive coronary attack. He was 68.
Luce, who maintained a winter home here, had appeared in robust health last Tuesday night when he attended a Phoenix dinner honoring Vice President and Mrs. Hubert Humphrey. But he entered the hospital yesterday and died at 3 A.M. today.
Luce resigned: 1st graf A118 New York dateline

BN1044AES Feb 28

Inserting copy   Any copy may be inserted in a story already on the wire if it is carefully tailored to fit in a precise spot, with suitable directions to all editors. The insert cannot be sent out whimsically without directions, any more than it is possible to send a new top without a suitable pickup line.

There are slight variations in practice between AP and UPI in handling inserts. The following was the way in which AP sent an insert for the above story, marking the beginnings of paragraphs to identify the spot where the copy should go. This was the way the piece read:

Phoenix Ariz Luce Precede Lead A142 Insert after 2nd graf: Luce who.

In Washington, President Johnson described Luce as a "pioneer of American journalism" and praised his "enlightened judgments."
Luce resigned: 1st graf A118 New York dateline

ED1045AES Feb 28

UPI marks its inserts by using the last word of the paragraph after which the new copy is to go, and picking up with the first words of the succeeding paragraph. Here is a brief story of a Vietnam War incident and an insert that came along after it:

040A
Hochmuth 11/14 NX
DANANG (UPI)—Maj. Gen. Bruno A. Hochmuth, commander of 20,000 U. S. Marines battling invaders along the demilitarized zone (DMZ), was killed today when his helicopter blew apart in flight and crashed into a shallow lake.

Military spokesmen said four others perished in the crash with Hochmuth, a 56-year-old Texan known to his men as "Bah." He commanded the 3rd Marine Division.

The pilot of a protective "chase" helicopter reported seeing an explosion before the General's helicopter broke into two pieces and fell into the lake near Hue, 400 miles north of Saigon.

PT/RW609AES

048A
Hochmuth 11/14 NX
Insert Hochmuth Danang 040A after 2nd Pgh XXX Division
But for a quirk of fate his aide, Capt. Robert B. Starke of Denver, Colo., would have been aboard the helicopter. Starke was recovering from a centipede bite and did not take the trip.

Pickup 3rd Pgh: The pilot

RW650AES

COMPARISON WITH NEWSPAPERS

No newspaper correspondent has to write as many leads, inserts, and adds as the wire service writer. The correspondent must make only specified editions and can afford to wait.

Wire services cannot. They know very well that too many leads and inserts make for difficult handling. They try to hold down on them. They also know, on a major story, that they must not be beaten on any essential fact. The heat of competition is still on in wire service journalism. Therefore, when in doubt, they file. The directions for inserts, leads, and pickups are supposed to conform to previous material with the same precision demanded of newspaper correspondents and editors. But wire service men have a different problem. The total of all their leads may be more than any one paper can use, but each individual lead must be done so that any paper can publish it if necessary.

A correspondent, however, may combine several paragraphs in his old story with a few new facts and send the whole thing along as an insert to save space. When a correspondent ends a lead, he always tries to make certain that the part of the old story he picks up reads as if it were done to fit his new top. If it does not, he makes corrections or inserts until it conforms. A correspondent in any case should try to be more precise than his wire service rivals in everything he does.

Because of the necessity of having beginnings for all stories, wire services rarely resort to the "B" copy routine. What they do is to start any-where with a lead, even on relatively slight material, and proceed with the running story until they come up with a development that will make a better top. Then they send it. Such fact-by-fact accounts are developed under a slug such as RUNNING (for conventions, trials, and so forth) and the periodic summations are slugged 1ST LEAD, 2ND LEAD, 3RD LEAD, with appropriate pickup points in the running copy. The running story, of course, develops chronologically and continues in that order with ADDS. In wire service practice, therefore, development of news forces the growth of a story in both directions—on top and at the bottom.

Since newspaper space is at a premium, however, that means telegraph and copy editors are bound to keep trimming wire service accounts. It is one reason why, when a newspaper can afford to do so, it sends its own correspondent to cover a major story.

How a Special Handles Copy   The newspaper special generally uses wire service slugging and directions (except for the excessive use of such words as "bulletin" and "urgent") to indicate how his copy should be handled. By keeping his own carbons, or blacksheets as they are known, he can transmit directions on where a new lead should pick up a previous account or after what paragraph an insert should be put. A deskman or copy editor then translates the special's wire, radioed, or cabled instructions into a markup so that the type can be handled properly in the composing room.

The wire service's influence on American journalism is so great that a number of newspapers find it simpler to have their out-of-town reporters file in wire service style and terminology. Therefore, it is just as likely that a special will use FIRST LEAD ROCKET as NEW LEAD ROCKET. It depends on the paper, the correspondent, and the desires of the editor. Whether a reporter writes for a wire service, does his story in a newspaper city room, or files for a newspaper from the ends of the earth, he still must slug his story, watch his leads in numerical order, take care of pickup directions for his leads, inserts, and adds, and handle his own corrections.

Some specials, especially young ones, fondly believe that a deskman has the time to handle his material exclusively with loving care and tender-ness.

Editors, whether they work on wire service or newspaper desks, must take care of not one but many stories in the course of their working day. Unless a writer knows that his desk will handle his pickups for leads and inserts and clean up the latter part of his stories, he had better do it himself by sending appropriate directions. Then he will be sure.

SOME HISTORIC STORIES

The wire services cannot wait to polish leads and make sure that every comma is in place when big news is breaking. And yet, despite all the pressures on the men at the typewriter, at the desk, and at the teletypes, the news is conveyed with dramatic force on many historic occasions.

When the first American orbited the earth in 1962, before Cape Kennedy was so named, this was the bulletin AP coverage that preceded the final wrap-up:

> BULLETIN
> CAPE CANAVERAL, FLA., FEB. 20 (AP) ASTRONAUT JOHN H. GLENN JR. PARACHUTED TO A SAFE ATLANTIC OCEAN LANDING TODAY WITHIN SIX MILES OF THE RECOVERY DESTROYER USS NOA. OBSERVERS ON THE NOA WATCHED HIS SPACE SHIP FLOAT DOWNWARD AT 2:43 P.M. THE DETROYER SPED TO PICK HIM UP.
> THE LANDING WAS FOUR HOURS, 56 MINUTES AFTER BLASTOFF.
>
> JN245 PES

This was the way UPI told the nation of the "eyeball to eyeball" confrontation between the United States and the Soviet Union during the great atomic missile crisis later that year:

> UPI A177 WA
> 1ST GENERAL LEAD CRISIS (A156N)
> WASHINGTON, TUESDAY, OCT. 23 (UPI)—U. S. PLANES AND SHIPS MOVED INTO POSITION IN THE CARIBBEAN TODAY TO CLAMP AN ARMS BLOCKADE ON CUBA.
> PRESIDENT KENNEDY SAID THE ACTION WAS NECESSARY BECAUSE SOVIET MISSILES CAPABLE OF CARRYING NUCLEAR WARHEADS ARE NOW ON CUBAN SOIL.
> THE NAVAL FLEET HAD ORDERS TO SHOOT IF NECESSARY TO ENFORCE THE QUARANTINE OF CUBA ORDERED BY KENNEDY AND ANNOUNCED TO THE NATION IN A TELEVISION SPEECH LAST NIGHT.
> PICKUP 2ND PGH A 156N: THE ACTION . . .
> WO1235AED

Here are the bulletins from Merriman Smith of UPI that gave the first news to the nation of President Kennedy's assassination in Dallas in 1963:

> UPI A7N DA
> PRECEDE KENNEDY
> DALLAS, NOV. 22 (UPI)—THREE SHOTS WERE FIRED AT

PRESIDENT KENNEDY'S MOTORCADE TODAY IN DOWNTOWN DALLAS.

JT1234PCS

UPI A8N DA
URGENT
1ST ADD SHOTS DALLAS (A7N) X X X DOWNTOWN DALLAS.
NO CASUALTIES WERE REPORTED.
THE INCIDENT OCCURRED NEAR THE COUNTY SHERIFF'S OFFICE ON MAIN STREET, JUST EAST OF AN UNDERPASS LEADING TOWARD THE TRADE MART WHERE THE PRESIDENT WAS TO MA

FLASH

FLASH
KENNEDY SERIOUSLY WOUNDED PERHAPS SERIOUSLY PERHAPS FATALLY BY ASSASSINS BULLET
JT1239 PCS

UPI 9N
BULLETIN
1ST LEAD SHOOTING
DALLAS, NOV. 22 (UPI)—PRESIDENT KENNEDY AND GOV. JOHN B. CONNALLY OF TEXAS WERE CUT DOWN BY AN ASSASSIN'S BULLETS AS THEY TOURED DOWNTOWN DALLAS IN AN OPEN AUTOMOBILE TODAY.
MORE JT1241PCS

UPI A10N DA
1ST ADD 1ST LEAD SHOOTING DALLAS (9N DALLAS) X X TODAY
THE PRESIDENT, HIS LIMP BODY CRADLED IN THE ARMS OF HIS WIFE, WAS RUSHED TO PARKLAND HOSPITAL. THE GOVERNOR ALSO WAS TAKEN TO PARKLAND.
CLINT HILL, A SECRET SERVICE AGENT ASSIGNED TO MRS. KENNEDY, SAID, "HE'S DEAD," AS THE PRESIDENT WAS LIFTED FROM THE REAR OF A WHITE HOUSE TOURING CAR, THE FAMOUS "BUBBLETOP" FROM WASHINGTON. HE WAS RUSHED TO AN EMERGENCY ROOM IN THE HOSPITAL.
MORE144PES

These historic fragments, the frantic first draft of history, vividly illustrate the basic mission of the wire service—to get the news quickly, report it accurately and remain poised for developments. There is no time here for fine writing—only the short, sharp words and phrases that alert millions of people all over the world to the news as it clatters from the pounding teletypes. They serve radio, television, the newspapers, and the news magazines alike, for their mission is universal.

chapter **16**

Broadcast Journalism

When Edward Bellamy imagined something akin to modern television in his Utopian romance, *Looking Backward, 2000–1887* A.D., few in the United States believed such things could be. Bellamy was regarded as just another impractical Socialist visionary who had had the good luck to write a best seller that made him wealthy.

Nor were there many more converts on a blustery day in November, 1901, when Guglielmo Marconi proved that long distance wireless was not a dream. It didn't seem to make much difference to the hard-headed realists of the era that the inventor, flying a kite with copper wire in Newfoundland, had heard the three dots of the letter S in Morse code flashed across the Atlantic with his crude apparatus.

Yet, within three years, the *Times* of London was covering naval actions in the Russo-Japanese War with a wireless-equipped vessel. Within eight years, a wireless operator was credited with bringing rescue ships to the scene of a maritime disaster in time to save all but six of the 1,600 passengers of the White Star liner "Republic" after a collision.

A generation after Marconi, radio was outstripping the press in the swift presentation of the news. In a little more than two generations, television was bringing distant scenes into millions of homes with routine daily network news programs. Today, broadcast journalism has come of age. It depicts the set event—from space shot to Presidential news conference—with faithfulness and fidelity on the small screen. It reports demonstrations, riots and wars—sometimes with almost unbearably painful detail. And as a cachet of its reliability, it has gained the right—and the prestige—to share equally with the older media the responsibility of gathering and presenting all major election returns in the United States.

With broadcast journalism in a continuing state of development and the wire services and print media breaking out of decades of frozen technology, more surprises are ahead. Any system of communications that can go from a kite to globe-girdling satellites in less than man's allotted life span of three-score and ten years, has the capacity to create a revolution in the presentation of the news. There is no doubt that such a revolution is now under way. How far it will go depends almost entirely on the extent to which television is able to liberate itself from the domination of show business. It has the voice and the vision. It needs the will.

THE RADIO WIRE

Outside the United States and a few other advanced nations, radio is the prime reliance of most of the world's peoples for their daily news. Where there are no newspapers, or where newspapers are few and under government control, radio is the only source of news for millions in Asia, Africa, and parts of Latin America.

Inevitably, at the governmental level in these areas, radio has become the principal medium through which a ceaseless struggle is carried on for influence over public opinion. Most of the powerful transmitters owned and operated by governments therefore specialize in news—or what passes for it. In the West, such establishments as the Voice of America and BBC seek credibility by trying on the whole to present news honestly, despite some understandable lapses, over a long period. In the Communist world, and in other forms of closed or partly-closed societies, prime sources such as Radio Moscow, Radio Peking, and various affiliates seldom put out material that either is critical of their respective governments, or otherwise embarrasses them.[1] The uncommitted nations, in large part, follow variations of these widely conflicting policies, depending on their dominant political philosophies.

Where independent domestic radio systems exist, as in the United States, news broadcasts should be an hourly testimonial to a station's determination to serve the public and no other master. In responsible hands, this is usually the case. But too often, a small local station—like a small local newspaper—is likely to lose sight of the essential condition of its existence in the daily struggle for survival against competition. Unhappily,

---

[1] When the Czech news media tried feebly to assert their independence in the summer of 1968, backed by a liberal minded government, Russian troops took over the country.

backsliders can also be found among the larger and more affluent organizations in both broadcast and print media.

Yet, one of the most remarkable parts of the whole system of independent radio news presentation is the continuing integrity and growth of the source for much of its material—the so-called radio wire. In the United States, separate radio wires are operated by both the Associated Press and United Press International on the same principle as the general news system typified by the "A" wire. For a large percentage of the more than 5,000 radio stations and more than 700 television stations in the United States, the radio wires are the main reliance for much of the news they broadcast. Moreover, the radio wires of the agencies frequently plug up holes in the generally good network coverage, the separate service of the large independent stations, and even the Voice of America, BBC, and many another governmental outlet. It is not unheard of for Communist transmitters to quote American radio wires on conditions in the United States, usually adverse.

For many years, radio stations using the AP and UPI radio wires have far outnumbered newspapers that use the general news wires. For the small stations, the radio wire is surprisingly cheap; even more important, it supplies them with a never-ending flow of news summaries. In the underprivileged area of broadcast journalism which is somewhat larger than similar areas of newspaper journalism, the "rip and read" technique still is the rule rather than the exception because many a station functions with a one or two-man news staff and sometimes none at all.

Necessarily, the lordly correspondents of the networks and the blue-ribbon independents among both radio and television have complained for years about the inadequacies of the radio wires. The hard-working rewritemen who grind out the copy for the agencies have been accused of every journalistic high crime and misdemeanor, from inaccuracy to chronic dullness and inability to use the English language with grace and clarity. When the gentlemen of the networks and the independent station staffs have been in a thoroughly insulting mood, they have usually remarked in a hurt manner, "Why, we always use the 'A' wire and do our own rewrite instead of paying any attention to the radio wire." Historically, the newspaper special has always said much the same thing about the supposed unreliability of *his* principal competitor, the "A" wire, only in his case the special insult is, "You know what I told my desk? I told them to spike the 'A' wire copy."

Whether the competition is in the electronic or newspaper field, or both, few specials can ever bring themselves to admit that the news agencies have special virtues of their own. Yet, by glancing over a radio wire file and then turning the dial to current newscasts at random, it is easily demonstrable that the agencies are the sources for much broadcast news. The radio wires, therefore, are basic to most news programs, even if they are rewritten. This is almost as true of television as it is of radio, although the pictorial requirements of television make it impossible to proceed on the substance of the radio wire alone. Despite their lofty attitudes toward agency copy, the networks would no more give up the radio wire than the Washington staffs of *The New York Times* and Washington *Post* would give up the "A" wire.

RADIO WIRE OPERATIONS

In major bureaus such as New York City, the agencies' radio services generally work on a three-cycle basis. These are the "early," from 11 P.M. to 7 A.M., corresponding to the "A" wire overnight file; the "day," from 7 A.M. to 3 P.M., and the "night," from 3 to 11 P.M., both equivalent to the "A" wire day and night cycles. In smaller bureaus and overseas, the early and day files are combined into a single PM cycle and the night file is expanded into a longer AM cycle. But regardless of the system, the agencies' radio wires keep turning out the spot news summaries of one-minute headlines, 5-, 10-, and 15-minute roundups of news, and such added broadcast news material as sports, financial, and weather summaries.

There is a news budget for each cycle of the radio wire, just as there is for the "A" wire. New tops, the radio equivalent of the new lead, are frequently filed to update pending material. Where there is an important new development, the radio wire carries bulletins for immediate use. In general, material is prepared and slugged in much the same basic manner as copy for any other agency wire.

The radio writer, however, must be brief. For developing news, he must write in the present tense. His work must be clear and to the point to cut down the risk of misunderstanding, always a radio bugaboo. Consequently, the short sentence and the one and two-syllable words are features of the radio wire.

The following spot summary of five items illustrates the manner in which a radio wire one-minute headline roundup is prepared:

Here is the latest news from the Associated Press:
NEW YORK . . . A Liberian freighter has signaled it is taking on water and is in danger of sinking 470 miles East-Southeast of New York.

NEW YORK . . . A British freighter has taken aboard three women and two men from the stricken yawl Petrel—also at the mercy of the Atlantic storm.

WASHINGTON . . . The Food and Drug Administration has asked a New York importer to recall all retail stocks of foreign dolls which have been found to be highly inflammable.

BURLINGTON, IOWA . . . A mysterious but apparently minor illness has affected workers at the Army ammunition plant near here and the Federal government is investigating it.

CHICAGO . . . A new snowstorm is moving south across the central Rockies.

This is expanded, in simple and obvious fashion, into the popular ten-minute news summary that is more in evidence on the radio wire than anything else:

A Liberian freighter has signaled it is taking on water and is in danger of sinking in an Atlantic gale. The New York Coast Guard says the ship "S S Georgia" gave her position as about 470 miles East-Southeast of New York. A spokesman said the cutter Vigilante out of Provincetown, Massachusetts, has been diverted to help the Georgia. The cutter had been en route to the 70-foot yawl Petrel—also being pounded by the storm.

A British freighter is standing by the stricken Petrel after taking aboard five of its ten passengers 360 miles Southeast of New York. Three women and two men were transferred to the freighter Cotswold. The five other passengers—all men—have elected to remain aboard the Petrel until a Coast Guard cutter arrives to take it in tow.

The Food and Drug Administration has asked a New York City importer to recall all retail stocks of some imported dolls which have been found to be highly inflammable. The dolls, ranging in size from seven to sixteen inches, have been distributed nationally. Thus far, the administration adds, it has received no reports of any injuries involving the dolls.

A U. S. government report is expected within the next ten days on a mysterious, but apparently minor, illness that has afflicted workers on a project at the Army ammunition plant near Burlington, Iowa. Some 50 to 100 employees have been hit by the ailment in the past six months.

A snowstorm in the Southern Rockies and the intermountain region has prompted heavy snow or hazardous driving warnings for Northern Arizona and Western New Mexico. Several inches of snow fell on Kingman, Arizona, and one to three inches covered the ground today in southern Wyoming, Utah, and Nevada.

With a change in the status of an item in the summary, the new top is sent without fuss and directions are included for the information of station news directors. One way of doing it is as follows:

News Dirs: Following is new top for Ships section above:
(Ships)
The Coast Guard says 29 Greek crewmen aboard a Liberian freighter 470 miles Southeast of New York report they may have to abandon ship. A Coast Guard spokesman says a rescue plane is flying over the stricken vessel—S S Georgia—and a rescue ship is only about

20 minutes away. The freighter's position is about 120 miles East of the disabled pleasure yacht Petrel which appears to be holding its own. A British freighter has taken aboard five of the Petrel's ten passengers and is standing by the 70-foot yawl.
—Dash—
The Food and Drug etc. x x x picking up third graf original item.

In the same manner, the radio wire can and frequently does carry additional material to expand a five-minute summary to ten minutes, if desired. For the 15-minute summaries, which are elaborate for radio, separate treatment is required but the same general methods and rules are observed.

Regardless of the time span of a newscast, all copy for radio is intended for the ear and not the eye. It makes a difference in the informality with which radio news is treated. Also, words and phrases that are difficult to pronounce must be dropped. Very often, dependent clauses used in a newspaper story are made into a separate sentence for a radio story.

A major difference with newspaper procedure is the use of attribution. In a newspaper, it is considered dull to begin with a routine bit of attribution, such as "Police say . . . " or "The State Department has announced. . . ." But in radio, there is so much concern over misunderstanding that the attribution often comes first. Thus, a proper newspaper lead may be: "A fire at Gamm's Department Store that killed four persons may be the work of a firebug, police reported today." But on radio the dangling attribution is eliminated as follows: "Police say a firebug may have caused the fire at Gamm's Department Store that killed four persons."

The factual precision of newspapers also comes in for relaxed treatment on the radio wire. Middle initials are often dropped and titles curtailed if they are too long. Figures are rounded out wherever practical. Moreover, too many figures in a short newscast are bound to be confusing and some are eliminated. If ages are used, there generally has to be a good reason. And not all precise addresses are considered important in radio wire copy. With these exceptions, the tenets of journalistic accuracy must be observed as rigidly for radio as they are for any other news medium.

In the constant pressure to update the news, so that the listener will hear a "different" newscast on the hour, the radio wire has the same basic weakness as much other agency copy. While the news in essence has not changed, the phrasing is turned and twisted in an effort to infer that something else is about to happen in the brief time between broadcasts. From experience, the listener usually knows he is being conned, sighs, "same old stuff," and turns off his radio. Thus, all the updating—even though the agencies insist on it—actually does very little good. Sometimes, it even does harm, for there is so much updating on a piece of spot news, such as a train wreck, that the listener who has just tuned in cannot tell what has happened, or when.

Nevertheless, the content of the radio wires day in and day out provides solid evidence that a great deal of work is thoroughly if not elegantly done. Improvements are always possible in so detailed a service; from time to time, they are made with good effect. But despite their weak points, the agencies' radio wires remain the first essential for the news programs of the electronic media.

RADIO NEWS PROGRAMMING

There is an enormous range in radio news programming. Nothing very elaborate can be expected from a local station of 1,000 watts or less, with a minimal staff, beyond the use of radio wire material. The all-news stations are growing but few have the personnel, the drive, and the imagination to vary the dullness of much of their presentation. Therefore, with not many exceptions, the development of significant radio news programming is left almost by default to the big independents and the networks with their showcase owned and operated stations. These are the places where news staffs of some importance are being developed, and where originality in dealing with the news is being shown.

Inevitably, the first question any editor asks of his news staff at the outset of a brief conference over programming is, "Who's got a lead?" This is, of course, not at all the same as a newspaper lead. It refers to the opening item of the news program—the equivalent of the leading headline in the newspaper. In the mystique of radio news programming, an inordinate amount of importance is attached to the lead item. It is, in its own way, almost as much of a symbol to radio as a good colorful cover is to a news magazine. For television, it is even more meaningful because the competition is stiffer.

Once the lead item is decided upon, the business of radio programming proceeds in fits and starts. As the deadline approaches and the news begins to change, rapid switches are made. And very often, while a program is on the air, bulletins come in that make newscasters edit their script as they read it. The only thing certain about radio news programming is that it is always subject to change.

While the anchor man of a radio news program is a kind of talisman, he cannot be expected to perform miracles. He needs good reporters, interesting taped interviews, detail from the scenes of breaking stories, and the skill of good writers if he is to make his program come alive. His voice, his sense of timing, and his ability to ad lib when necessary all contribute to the quality and appeal of the program. But unless his news director and producer can provide the necessary teamwork, he cannot really function at peak efficiency.

A good program carries with it a kind of controlled excitement, particularly in the most popular listening periods for news in the morning and early evening. Here is the headline-and-lead format for one of the oldest network programs of radio news:

> Massive fire in New York. . . German chancellor arrives in Paris . . . Another battlefield error in Vietnam as troops move into the Mekong Delta . . . Nationalist China reports air battle over the Formosa Strait . . .
> Good morning. This is Dallas Townsend in New York with the CBS World News Roundup.
> Before dawn today in the City of New York, brilliant flames lit up the sky over the Borough of Queens. Fire had broken out in a large residential area, heavily populated . . . and it raced out of control for several hours . . .

The program quickly switched to a reporter at the scene of the fire in Queens with a vivid taped account of what was going on. This is an example of the flexibility of radio news programming; in a world news program, the director did not hesitate to come in strong with a lead of both local and national significance—a fire in the country's largest city.

Sometimes, this kind of material is inserted in a program at an appropriate spot, usually after a break for a commercial. Thus, NBC's News of the World shows how it can be done after a commercial: "Now, news by direct report—a big fire in Chicago. Here is Ray James . . ." After James' report, this vivid bit of writing about a Midwestern storm attracts the listener:

> Blizzard winds on the northern plains. . . They are carrying temperatures as low as 25 below zero. Light snow is flying in the wind. North Dakota, South Dakota, Minnesota, northern Iowa are seriously affected. Gusts up to 100 miles an hour are gouging out old snow cover and piling it up in mountainous drifts. Bus and air travel are being halted. Power and communications lines have been ripped out. Hundreds of schools have been closed. Trucks have been blown off the highways in southeastern South Dakota . . .

This illustrates the essentially informal manner of radio news writing. Phrases, partial sentences, vigorous verbs, and crisp writing all combine to create a sharp image. That is the essence of the art.

Radio Techniques   When news is written for radio, it is often cast in a different context so that the listener can identify his interest with the latest developments. To newspapers, this is the "feature approach," sometimes called "featurizing the news." The news magazines have always done it better than most newspapers and radio and television, in effect, have tried to rival the news magazines. The trick is effective when it can be done with logic and reason; however, there is an inevitable risk of distortion when the feature angle is overstressed. This is how CBS reported one of the most difficult news stories of recent years—an imaginative account of a big step toward the eventual world trade agreements:

> After all these years, mankind's basic food still is what it almost always has been—grain. And this morning a far-reaching agreement seems in the works on the sharing of grain. The United States and the European Common Market countries are making progress in that direction . . . and there may be more of it today in Geneva—at a meeting of cabinet ministers from the six Common Market countries—France, West Germany, Italy, Belgium, Netherlands and Luxembourg. If an agreement is worked out, it will cover the entire non-Communist world, and become an essential element of the Kennedy Round agreements on trade. And the agreement, again assuming that it will be worked out—is intended to cover not only the grains that humans eat—wheat and rye, for example—but the feed grains needed to raise poultry, cattle, and hogs. The aim of the agreement is to stabilize prices, production, and markets. And the United States hopes it will become a main channel for supplying aid to underdeveloped countries, especially India. . .

A straight news lead on the above, by contrast, would have gone something like this:

> GENEVA—Cabinet ministers from six Common Market nations gathered here today to put the finishing touches to a far-reaching agreement on sharing grain. If agreement can finally be reached, it will be regarded here as a step toward reaching an accord with the U. S. on the Kennedy Round proposals to cut levies on trade. . .

The technique of attracting the attention of the listener before actually telling him what is happening can be extremely helpful in news of a surprising nature. It comes under the old formula usually stated as follows: "Tell 'em what you're going to tell 'em, then tell 'em what you have to tell 'em, and finally tell 'em that you've told 'em." For example, in an announcement that Sister Jacqueline Grennan would leave the Sisters of Loretto and remain as president of their school, Webster College, under a secular Board of Trustees, CBS led the listener to the story in this way: "A remarkable thing in both the educational and religious world is happening at Webster Groves, Missouri. A Roman Catholic college and the nun who leads it are joining the secular world . . . "

It is by no means an inviolate rule that radio and television news should be told in the present tense. Roundups, which summarize the day's events, are often handled very much like summaries in newspapers; more-over, there are newscasters who insist on the use of the word "today" in every past-tensed item just to be sure that the listener understands when the event took place. At its best, this radio news writing technique approxi-mates superior newspaper or news magazine journalism. But when it is misapplied, the effect is similar to that of reading yesterday's newspaper aloud. Mainly, much depends on who is doing the reading and what sense can be made out of the news.

This is an item from an NBC newscast that differs in no way from standard news presentation and dispenses with all of radio's familiar gim-micks:

> The Supreme Court ruled today that a person holding a valid pass-port cannot be prosecuted for going to Cuba in violation of a State De-partment travel ban. The unanimous ruling said the government *did* have the right to require special validation of passports for travel to various areas but that it could not be used as a basis for a criminal charge. In addition to Cuba, the State Department restricts travel to a number of other Communist controlled countries. The restrictions have been repeat-edly challenged by the American Civil Liberties Union and others. The Supreme Court noted in its judgment today that 600 people have violated the restrictions since 1952.

Such stark straight news items may also be heard on some of the most popular radio and television news programs. The advantage is, of course, a perceptible saving of time by doing away with the excess wordage re-quired by leading a listener in and out of an item. The disadvantage is that the listener will not be able to absorb everything that is thrown at him so quickly in such a compressed format. As a general rule, it takes the prestige of a Cronkite to violate all the accepted formulas of electronic news pres-entation. He does it whenever he thinks it is necessary.

Another time-honored bit of radio news programming is the final humorous item—a throwaway anecdote that is intended to conform to the most ancient rule of show business: "Leave 'em laughing." When it is used, it follows the weather at the conclusion of the news script. But like newspaper humor, radio humor has always been in devilishly short supply. It is also a sobering truth that most broadcast journalists cannot read light material without creating a funereal mood—the curse of much radio news. Consequently, items that seem perfectly harmless and even draw a slight smile in the reading turn out to be little horrors at the end of a radio news-cast. The following is an example of a gag that laid an electronic egg for CBS:

> "Here it is Friday the 13th again . . . and time for another spot of good old Triska-decka-phobia. It's a two-dollar word meaning, as if you

didn't know, Fear of 13 . . . a primitive bugaboo that dates from the dim mists of antiquity. A chap named Nick Matsouakas is head of the National Committee of 13 against Triska etcetera . . . and he's been trying to dispel the myth for a generation. This morning, his committee signs a lease in Brooklyn for a 13-foot strip of pavement it hopes to make the smallest park in the world. It will pay 13 cents a month rent and plant 13 trees in 13 pounds of soil. Nick says it will prove the fear of 13 is silly."

It is no wonder that the humorous concluding item is going into a justifiable decline.

MECHANICS

It isn't necessary to be a member in good standing of the Institute of Radio Engineers to be a radio newsman or writer. Nor is a producer or news director required to be expert in the theory and practice of launching communications satellites or constructing efficient microwave circuits. It does help to know that radio has progressed beyond the era of the rotary spark gap, that there is a certain amount of difference between a Galena crystal and a transistor, and that the image Orthicon tube does represent an advance over the DeForest Audiotron and the Western Electric VT-2. While it is undoubtedly possible to do a professional radio news program without being initiated into the mysteries of such old and new radio devices, a basic understanding of radio techniques can avert a great deal of woe. For one thing, it enables newsmen to communicate with the technicians who operate a station's intricate and expensive equipment. For another, it gives newsmen a good idea of what can and cannot be done in gathering, presenting, and distributing the news of the day.

Some of the simplest mechanical precautions in any radio news program are merely the products of good sense. Thus, difficult or unusual names or words are spelled phonetically in scripts to help the newscaster. For example, Ronald Reagan becomes "Ray-gan," Mekong becomes "May-kong," and Mao Tse-tung becomes "Mah-ow See Dung." For scripts that require it, any number of well-worn transitional phrases are used to bridge separate sections—"Now for news at home," "Elsewhere in the country," "Turning now to news from abroad," "Among other events today," and the many variations thereof relating to time, place, and substance. Nor is it considered demeaning in radio to pick up a telephone or check through an envelope of clips to verify a name or a fact.

Aside from such considerations, the dominant mechanical factor in the preparation of any radio or television news program is time. Most newscasters read from 170 to 180 words a minute and calculate a 16 to 17-line page of typing (with one-inch margins) as requiring about a minute to read. For the average station, only the last few items are timed, with the elapsed time of the script marked in big numerals in the upper right hand side of the page so that the newscaster knows when he must conclude. However, the more important the station, the more rigid are the time controls applied to the radio news programs. And on the networks, there is usually very little room for maneuvering. A five-minute newscast actually includes only three and one-half minutes of news, allowing for commercial and sign-off, and a 15-minute newscast runs somewhere between 12½ and 13½ minutes, depending on commercials.

Consequently, if a newscaster has a 15-minute program beginning at 11 A.M., almost the first thing he does is to "back-time" his closing items. He knows the sign-off and station public service announcement take 30 seconds; therefore, he marks the time, 11:14^{30} boldly in the right-hand corner of his closing page. He times the weather, usually inserted before the sign-off, and finds it is 20 seconds. At the start of the weather page, he again marks the time, 11:14^{10}. The item directly preceding weather is a brief sports roundup of 45 seconds, the time on the page being 11:13^{25}. And before sports is a one-minute commercial, which brings the "back-timing" process to 11:12^{25}. With these pages laid out on the table beside him, the newscaster has a ready check on when he must begin the final commercial and be assured of concluding in time. If necessary, he may use or discard filler items or otherwise pace himself in a prearranged manner. But he has no choice other than to conclude on schedule.

To illustrate how little time there really is for very many items in the average five-minute newscast, most stations try to include about eight assorted pieces in the three and one-half minutes actually assigned to the news. This comes down to less than 30 seconds per item, slightly less than eight typewritten lines each. What it means is that all complications will have to be dropped; the best that can be offered, under the circumstances, is bulletin-type coverage. And if there is a taped interview with a news personage or a correspondent, as is usual in most such spots, even fewer items may be included.

In the longer radio news programs, particularly those of 15 minutes, the script is generally broken into three sections of about five minutes each (including commercials). Thus, tapes may be distributed fairly evenly without crowding out other essential news. In order to insure that the program runs smoothly, a cue sheet is prepared with the beginning and closing words of each tape, plus the elapsed time. In a CBS World News Roundup, a part of the cue sheet looks like the reproduction opposite.

There is nothing in journalism that quite equals the painstaking second-by-second scheduling of the electronic media, the programming jitters, the heightened anticipation as the program goes on the air, and the sense of relief when it is over. By contrast, the unscheduled intervention of a reporter

WORLD NEWS ROUNDUP

FIRST SECTION

Tape 1. Oganesoff--Tokyo   In cue: Latest events on the mainland.

        Time:1:12 sec.   Out cue: ... in Tokyo.

Tape 2. Kalb--Washington.   In cue: The principal schools of thought.

        Time:1:16 sec.   Out cue: ... CBS News, Washington.

In a time summary of the NBC News of the World, every change from the anchor man to the program announcer in Studio 5C of the RCA Building in New York and further switches to tape carries a cue as follows:

NEWS OF THE WORLD

Beatty	7:30:00-7:30:40	sw	5C Ann.	In a moment the news.
5C Ann.	7:30:40-7:31:45	sw	Beatty	Now here is Morgan Beatty
Beatty	7:31:45-7:34:45	sw	5C tape	To Welles Hangen in Hong Kong
5C Tape	7:34:45-7:35:30	sw	Beatty	Welles Hangen, NBC News, Hong Kong
Beatty	7:35:30-7:35:40	sw	5C Ann.	And more news of the world
5C Ann.	7:35:40-7:36:40	sw	Beatty	Again Morgan Beatty
Beatty	7:36:45-7:37:30	sw	5C tape	To Ray James in Chicago
5C tape	7:37:30-7:38:30	sw	Beatty	Ray James NBC News, Chicago
Beatty	7:38:30-7:38:40	sw	5C tape	To Charles Quinn, Montgomery
5C tape	7:38:40-7:39:40	sw	Beatty	Charles Quinn, NBC News, Montgomery
Beatty	7:39:40-7:42:50	sw	Ann	And that story when I return in a moment
5C Ann	7:42:50-7:42:55	sw	Beatty	Now with the closing story, Morgan Beatty.
Beatty	7:42:55-7:43:05	sw	5C tape	Here is Joseph Michaels
5C tape	7:43:05-7:44:15	sw	Beatty	Joseph Michaels, NBC News
Beatty	7:44:15-7:44:20	sw	5C Ann	NBC News, New York

with a bulletin is handled with efficiency and smoothness once the basic decision is made to interrupt the usual network or local station routine. Even though the words "News Show" are now regarded with extreme disfavor in broadcast journalism, striving as it does for an image of solidity and prestige, the atmosphere of the theatre cannot be exorcised merely by saying it does not exist. It is an intrinsic part of electronic news presentation and accounts in part for the very large audiences it attracts throughout the nation. For radio, news at length and in depth has been a tonic in many parts of the country.[2]

TELEVISION

Television is the most complicated form of journalism and the most dynamic. It is weighted down with equipment, snarled by various types of regulations, boxed in by elaborate techniques, confused by its own frequent lack of direction, and victimized by an often excessive timidity in the face of controversy. Its corporate personality is split between the glitter of show business, the commercial requirements of advertising, and the professional demands of good journalism. It is an amalgam of some of the best—and some of the worst—elements of the stage, the movies, the newspapers, wire services, and radio. It is the most researched, the most criticized, the most investigated, and the recipient of the most free advice of any of the news media. It is also the most rapid in adapting and developing new ideas, spends fantastic amounts of money to cover the top news of the day, and patiently keeps trying to invent better ways of informing the public.

Television has many advantages—the immediacy of radio news, the quick projection of the sights and sounds of daily events into millions of homes, the involvement of people in the news, the flashing brilliance of color film, and the dramatic projection of the most personal form of journalism in the shape of eyewitness reporting. Its limitations, however, are also great. The most severe handicap, of course, is the inability to cover the news in depth in its regularly scheduled news programs, which amount to bulletin coverage plus brief snatches of illustrative material. But when big news breaks—the assassination of a President, the death of a Pope, a space shot to the moon, the sudden eruption of war in Asia, Africa, or the Middle East—then television is unsurpassed. Despite that, television's own corps of devoted journalists are the severest and most effective critics of their medium. Whatever improvements they make today, they realize full well that tomorrow's technological progress will create still more problems for them to solve.

In essence, television illustrates in exaggerated form almost every major difficulty the journalist is likely to encounter. The newspaper reporter, for example, needs only his pencil, a folded wad of copy paper, a typewriter, a telephone, and a good pair of legs to do his work. The television newsman moves with a small mountain of equipment—cameras, sound, film, tape, lights, testing instruments, and the personnel to operate them. Once the

---

2 William H. Honan, "The New Sound of Radio." *New York Times Magazine*, December 3, 1967, p. 56.

story is covered, the newspaper reporter goes to the telephone and dictates or he types for quick transmission a complete account of what has happened. Not the television newsman. Having moved all his gear and his people into place with the precision of an officer in the field, he then knows he will have all of two or three minutes to tell a big story—400 or 500 words—against a background of action on color film that will overshadow anything he can say.

Inside the studio, the news director does not have the luxury of planning to spread his account over two full newspaper pages with illustrations, or perhaps a half-dozen pages of a news magazine. He must cram all his expensive film and sound and expert narration—obtained at such great effort—into the context of a 30-minute news program minus time for commercials and other announcements. And if by chance the event is big enough, he must worry about how to meet the complaints of the television fanatics who reject all special news programs, no matter how excellent, if they are denied the pleasures of television comedy or soap opera. Finally, television is not its own master in the sense of printed publications or the independent wire services in the United States. Let one side of a political issue be covered in the news on television and all the others inevitably clamor for a hearing on prime time, invoking the rules of the Federal Communications Commission. Generally speaking, television has no defense for this and must yield.

TECHNIQUES OF TV NEWS

It is impossible to work in television journalism without an understanding of the uses of newsfilm, video tape, the various methods for recording sound, and the systems for transmitting pictures and messages. In the studio, anybody who has anything to do with the organization of a news program must know what is involved in the processing of newsfilm from the laboratory to the room where it is cut and spliced. Even if the journalist has nothing to do with these complicated techniques, he must appreciate the problems that are involved; otherwise, the best-conceived program can end in utter disaster.

Newsfilm   The pictorial side of television is an art in itself which is best left to the expert photographers and film editors who dominate the field. However, the newsman, the correspondent, the producer, and the news director all are involved to a degree in the assignment, the operation, and the use of various kinds of newsfilm—black and white, color, silent (SIL) and sound on film (SOF), the footage, and the size. It is an intrinsic part of the planning of every television news program to keep a running record of the receipt of newsfilm, together with a description of each segment.

The daily record of CBS News Film, for example, includes items such as the following on an oblong sheet divided into spaces for various categories of information: First comes a number, in this case 972. Next, story title: "Pilots survive jet crash." Then, the reporter, Pappas; location, Vietnam; source, a photographer, Bellanger; footage, 400; type, SOF, and stock, 16 mm. color. Information such as this goes to the film editor, news director, and their associates and is kept current throughout the day. In addition to the film crews of a network or an independent station, television editors also purchase newsfilm from such agencies as Viznews, Telenews and United Press International and, on occasion, from smaller outfits or free lancers.

Video tape   Video tape, that most flexible and remarkable process for handling sight and sound, has made possible many of the seeming miracles of television news presentation. Since the tape can be played back immediately, it has many advantages over film. Moreover, it eliminates film processing and can be kept indefinitely. Whole programs are recorded on it for reuse. In the studio, it is catalogued and categorized like newsfilm upon receipt and held for eventual use.

Editing film and tape, particularly when sound is involved, becomes an exceedingly complicated process for writer and editor. Yet, it is done every day. In general, what it amounts to is selecting the most meaningful part of a film or tape segment for use in a predetermined part of the program. Sometimes a film simply cannot be compressed into 45 seconds or a minute—the normal allowance for the illustration of a routine item. Different arrangements are then made. But far more frequently, the editor or writer assigned to do the cutting takes out a stop watch, makes a list of the various individual parts of the film, decides which parts to eliminate, and then tries to tie the whole thing together.

The Writing   If some studio narration is needed, the writing has to be adapted to what is shown, calculating from 24 to 28 frames of film per second, depending on certain technical factors, and 36 feet of 16 mm. film to the minute. If the correspondent in the field has attached his own narration to the film, there are likely to be additional complications for the editor to solve. Should there be a major news event for which only library background footage is available, it has to be tied in by the writer; or, if the available film is of the news of yesterday or the day before, its use must be joined with the narration of the latest events.

Regardless of how much is written about these things, they are actually best learned by doing. Like the intricate process of putting type, cuts, headlines, and advertising together in a newspaper or magazine, no amount of description or exhortation can be quite as enlightening as meeting the problem head-on. And this is where experience, background, and knowledge of the medium count a great deal.

THE COMPLETED PROGRAM

When a completed program is shown on a national network for 30 minutes, it is so smoothly and beautifully put together that the viewing public is not conscious of all the effort that has gone into it. The cameras move, seemingly in the most natural and agreeable manner, from the principal newscaster in the studio to live, film, or taped segments of other portions of the program. On occasion, there is a pleasant variation of medium and close-up shots of the anchor man of the newscast, who is nearly always portrayed as calm, decisive, authoritative, and solemn almost to the bursting point. Behind him, the device of rear screen projection may be used to show still pictures, maps, charts, sketches, even headlines on occasion through the use of flipcards on an easel. Or, this may be varied by slide devices taking up the whole screen, known as balops or telops. Almost everything is done to maintain the viewers' interest, from cutting down the anchor man's un-illustrated remarks to working in feature film when there isn't enough newsfilm to give the program a lift. Except for recognized stars like Eric Sevareid, the interpreter of the news is not permitted to sit and talk and stare at the home audience for very long; even Sevareid must give his views in two to three minutes as a rule.

When the program is over, the public necessarily must judge it by the substance it has just heard and seen. The techniques are applied in such slick fashion that they are generally not even detected by the inexperienced eye. Were it not for technical mastery, editors, writers, and newsmen could not even put a program together, for there is no end to television's development as a news medium and to the devices that are put into practice to make it more efficient. For example, in order to ease the difficulty of editing sound on film, an ingenious double-projection method has been devised so that two cameras are put into use to give the best possible result. It is only when there is an awkward break in the routine—sometimes the failure to start the lead-in of a taped segment the requisite three seconds before it is needed—that the public realizes there is such a thing as television techniques. This is at once the strength and the weakness of television, for its devices are often so well managed that a very large section of the public has come to believe that it can get along on a steady diet of television news alone. Few of television's professional newsmen would dare to give up reading newspapers and magazines, however, and trust themselves to the vagaries of their own medium. The hard facts of communications today do not justify that kind of exclusivity. For in truth, the news media are, to a very large degree, interdependent and other-directed in their motivation.

WRITING FOR TELEVISION

If the television correspondent must act as reporter, film director, and editor, those who write for television must combine the skills and insights of the playwright, the script writer for motion pictures, and the practicing journalist. It is not enough to say that television writers must consider both the eye and the ear. In a real sense, they must unify in word and mood a jumble of sights and sounds and give them meaning. This represents creativeness of the highest degree. Good television reportage, like good drama, is most effective when it appeals to reason rather than emotion, when it strives to make its point through artistry instead of crude histrionics, when it bases itself on the uses of restraint and understatement and lets humankind see at firsthand the stuff of which it is made. To do this with an economy of words and a few carefully selected scenes each day in no more than 30 minutes—the span of a television network news program—is no mean feat. It is not recommended for amateurs.

For some notion of the complications facing a team of writers on a daily network news presentation, it is worth analyzing briefly a typical Huntley-Brinkley program for NBC. In this instance, Chet Huntley is in New York at Studio 8G in the RCA Building while David Brinkley is at his usual post in the NBC Studios in Washington, with the camera switching back and forth between them. The program is divided into five segments with a total of 33 items, each of which is both separately and cumulatively timed. Commercials are, of course, included. At the outset, the news is peace talks in the Vietnam War with interviews involving such figures as North Vietnam's Mai Van Bo in Paris, South Vietnam's Nguyen Cao Ky in Saigon, an NBC correspondent at the State Department in Washington, and commentary by both Huntley and Brinkley. Then follows a segment devoted to national politics, with assorted other national and international news in the remaining segments, and a group of brief concluding items that may be used as time permits. Two opening segments on a schedule are shown herewith.

The remaining three segments of the program follow such a scheme. Thus devised, the schedule routine goes to a number of persons including the director, technical director, assistant director, production assistants, film studio, television control, communications, and those responsible for video tape, audio, and other technical parts of the program.

In a roundup program such as Huntley-Brinkley, the writing is so sharply and crisply done that it cannot be viewed as a television script, a radio script, a piece for a wire service or a newspaper. It is put together on a split page, the narration (AUDIO) on one side done in half-lines that

THE HUNTLEY-BRINKLEY REPORT

Time	Subject	Audio	Video
SEGMENT I			
1. 6:30:00 (:10)	H & B opening A) Huntley B) Brinkley	8G Wash.	8G Wash.
2. 6:30:10 (:45)	Huntley & VIZ (Mai Van Bo, Paris)	8G	8G. VIZ "Bo"
3. 6:30:55 (:45)	Wash #1 (Washington reactions-Bo)	Wash	Wash
4. 6:31:40 (:20)	Anncr & program opener	8G-Anncr	8G Color title
5. 6:32:00 (1:00)	Commercial (pretaped)	Sound on tape	Videotape
SEGMENT II			
6. 6:33:00 (:30)	Huntley (Intro to Ky, Saigon)	8G	8G
7. 6:33:30 (4:20)	Videotape (pretaped) (Ky & David Burrington)	Sound on tape	Videotape
8. 6:37:50 (:15)	Huntley (Intro to State Dept)	8G	8G
9. 6:38:05 (1:15)	Wash #2 (Jas. Robinson at State)	Wash	Wash
10. 6:39:20 (:30)	Huntley & VIZ (Viet casualties)	8G	8G Viz-Casualties
11. 6:39:50 (1:00)	Commercial (Intro & comml)	Sound on film	35mm color

take two seconds each to read, and the visual effects (VIDEO) on the other side with appropriate directions. The dramatic opening of a major Huntley-Brinkley news program is reproduced on the following pages.

It may easily be seen from the script, with its many precise directions and careful timing, that teamwork between the director, producer, writer, and large staff of technicians is indispensable if the whole complicated business is to come off properly. Yet, as far as the public is concerned, the focus of attention is a serious-faced Chet Huntley, reporting in measured tones the spectacular death of a racing man with on-the-spot films of exactly what happened. All the interior work, with directions and various bits of business, never shows any more than it does in a film or a play; yet, it is no less essential that it should be done with fidelity to detail and great consideration. The basic script is, of course, not the only document that

AUDIO	VIDEO
(H & B opening :10)	
<u>Huntley:</u> Chet Huntley, NBC News, New York	VIZ: H & B
Brinkley: And David Brinkley, NBC News,	
Washington	
(To Huntley :30)	
<u>Huntley:</u> British racing driver Donald	VIZMO: Campbell
Campbell, who had driven more than 400	
miles per hour on land, was killed	
today while attempting to establish	
a new water speed record in a hydro	
plane powered by a 5,000 horsepower	
jet aircraft engine.	
Campbell died on Lake Coniston in	VIZMO: Map
England trying to break his own	
record of 276 miles per hour.	
He completed an initial run of	
297 miles per hour. On his second	
required pass, his boat exceeded 300	
miles per hour. By radio, Campbell	
reported that the boat, Bluebird, was	
tramping or bouncing.	
"I can't see much," radioed	
Campbell. "It's going."	ROLL TAPE
	CAMPBELL VTR #1
Then, at about 310 miles per hour	
the boat lifted from the water,	
somersaulted and crashed.	TAPE SHOWS CRASH
	SENT VIA SATELLITE
(SOUND ON TAPE :35)	
HUNTLEY: (Resumes :10) The Bluebird	
sank immediately in 120 feet of water.	
Campbell was strapped in the cockpit. The	
British Broadcasting Corporation, which	

supplied these films, projected the crash

(ROLL TAPE, CAMPBELL #2) in slow motion;

but Campbell's assistants could not

determine why the hydroplane crashed.   TAPE SHOWS SLOW
                                                         MOTION OF CRASH:
                                                         CAMPBELL VTR #2

(SOUND ON TAPE   :30)

Huntley: (Resumes :30) Donald   Huntley: 8G Studio

Campbell died at the age of 45. He was

the son of the late Sir Malcolm Campbell

who established speed records on land

and water in the years between the two

World Wars.

Sir Malcolm tried to discourage his

son from following in his footsteps.

Donald Campbell stuck it out in business

until his father died in 1949 and then

began an assault on his father's speed

records.

On American television, some years ago,

he talked about racing (ROLL TAPE,

CAMPBELL #3 INTERVIEW), somewhat

technically. Privately, he said: "I do it   16 MM Color Reel A
                                                   CAMPBELL #3 INTERVIEW
because I must."   (1:15)

INTERLOCK NARRATION & SOUND

EFFECTS, 1:15, OUTCUE:

"IT WOULD BE A FUNNY MAN THAT WASN'T."

(LAUGHTER)

(Switch to Announcer opening   :20)   BILLBOARD   :20

ANNOUNCER: The Huntley-Brinkley   VIZ: H & B

Report is produced by NBC News and

brought to you in color by _____,   ROLL FILM ON
                                                MOUTHWASH COMMERCIAL
the new mouthwash...

emerges from the hours of work. In addition to the time schedule, there are cue sheets and various other technical guides for those who work with sound, film, and camera.

The brevity of television writing is nowhere more in evidence than on a major network news program. Although three or four minutes may be given to a lead item, or a group of items that constitute a lead with appropriate illustrations, the news is packed in with dispatch in the latter segments of the program. Few do it as thoroughly as Walter Cronkite. Some 15-second items in his script are reproduced on this page.

Thus, it appears that the best rule to observe in writing for television is the rule of flexibility. From the examples provided by Cronkite, Huntley-

16. CRONKITE

The Welfare Department tonight recommended that cigarette makers be required to report the amount of tar and nicotine on packages and in advertising. And Democratic Senator Warren W. Magnuson said he will sponsor such legislation in the new Congress.

16A. CRONKITE

The. Welfare Department warned Alabama today that it will lose federal money for public assistance and child welfare programs after next month unless the programs are administered without racial discrimination. The Welfare Department estimated the amount involved at about 95 million dollars a year.

FOLO 16A CRONKITE

Major aluminum producers today raised prices by a half-cent to a cent and a half a pound. A spokesman said the move was discussed in advance with Gardner Ackley chairman of the President's Council of Economic Advisors, but there was no indication of the White House reaction.

Brinkley, and other roundup news programs, it is perfectly obvious that all writing for the electronic media cannot be tossed off informally and put into present tense any more than all writing for newspapers can be stiffly formal and jammed into the past tense. These are stencils, and stencils that are used too often must be abandoned.

The style of a writer depends on his training, his mood, his skill and, above all, the circumstances of his task. And in television, circumstances change with greater rapidity than in any other news medium. The writer, therefore, cannot afford to freeze into any particular mold. What he writes is judged by today's standards; tomorrow, the standards may change. If this means writing for television is likely to be confusing from time to time, that is the penalty for working in a swiftly developing news medium. Yet, for those who have the knack, there are boundless satisfactions and, very often, rich rewards.

CRITICISM OF TV NEWS

The better television news programs have outgrown some of the glaring faults of radio, particularly on the networks, but local television sometimes is not so scrupulous. The urge to "billboard disaster" in order to attract and retain viewers is not being resisted by news directors and writers who should know better. It is unfortunately still the fashion in too many cases to bracket commercials in a news program by saying at the conclusion of one item: "I'll be back with news of a Kansas tornado that killed ten people," then taking up after the commercial with: "Now for that Kansas tornado . . . . here's Bill Smith . . . " This shows a peculiar insensitivity to the feelings of those who have friends or relatives in Kansas, and are justifiably anxious about them, but must wait for the news until after a sales pitch for a deodorant or mouth wash is forced upon them.

This same callousness is shown in isolated incidents when cameramen or correspondents who use the powerful instruments of television knowingly or unknowingly provoke a street crowd into demonstrations. During one of the riots that burst in the ghettos of some of the largest cities in the nation during the latter part of the 1960s, a cameraman was heard urging a youngster: "Go ahead, kid, throw a rock. I haven't seen you throw a rock." Although most television cameramen and correspondents are not guilty of these senseless provocations, and perform their duty as skillfully and as courageously as the newsmen for the other media, the sins of a few have caused television to be blamed even more than newspapers for the spread of the riots.

Richard S. Salant, president of CBS News, put the situation this way: "The real problem is responsible reporting—making yourself inconspicuous when it is apparent your camera is encouraging performance and not 'shooting bloody'—gore for gore's sake."

The great need of the times for all journalists, regardless of their media, is self-restraint. It is no solution to keep newspapermen, still cameramen, and radio and television personnel out of crisis areas, thus letting irresponsible rumor sway desperate and frightened people. The turmoil of the cities will not be lessened if somehow newsmen will stay away until a riot is over, or leave their cameras home, or even delay and censor their own accounts of what little they are able to see. The truth is that even when there has been partial or total local self-censorship (and it has happened here and there), the news of the rioting has been circulated promptly outside the affected areas and as promptly played back to them.

Self-regulation is the essential ingredient in the coverage of civil disturbances, for the journalist must recognize that he no longer can be a mere objective bystander in the coverage of the news. The electronic media have made him a participant in the news, whether he likes it or not, and he must recognize the responsibility of his role and live up to it if he is to continue to merit the freedom he enjoys in the United States.

Documentaries   Some of television's finest hours have been produced in the field of the documentary. In skillful hands, this type of illustrated commentary has illuminated the news for millions of people and given them a deeper understanding of some of the outstanding problems of our time. The tradition of CBS's "See It Now" series, pioneered by Edward R. Murrow and Fred W. Friendly, has been perpetuated by such filmed depth reports as ABC's study of Africa and NBC's detailed examination of American foreign policy. If the networks have erred, it is in not producing as many documentaries as are necessary and in failing to provide the prime time that they so richly deserve. In the field of public service journalism, which is discussed at length elsewhere in this volume, the documentary could make television pre-eminent if it were properly and extensively used by talented and imaginative professionals.

TELEVISION'S FUTURE

The glamor of television's past is exceeded only by its promise for the future. It has become a power in journalism in barely a generation. With the expansion of the communications satellite system and the perfection of techniques now in the experimental stage, television's reach for the news will be limited only by its willingness to increase its capacity for public service. What the medium now requires is not a greater capability for commercial use but a period of industrial and professional statesmanship. For television as entertainment has reached the saturation point, while television as a public service medium is barely on the threshhold of its greatest development.

There is rising criticism of television's role in the reporting of street disorders and riots in the cities, particularly in black communities. It is widely recognized that both black and white militants may be "turned on" when they see a TV camera and do things that their less adventurous colleagues find untypical and even shocking. This accounts in part for such criticism as that of a clergyman, the Rev. C. B. Marshall of Brooklyn, who protested during a city-wide teachers' strike in New York City in late 1968: "It's getting to seem like you [newsmen] are always looking for riots and blood and to hell with the real issues." Of course, TV has itself to blame when it focuses on only one aspect of the news.[3]

Without doubt, the growth of public television—with or without government sponsorship—will be a crucial factor in the expansion of the medium in news and public affairs. The creation of commercial television in Great Britain did much to shake the British model of public television, the BBC, out of the doldrums. Just what direction public television eventually will take in the United States remains to be determined, but certainly its competitive drive will put the commercial television sector on notice that there is no status quo. A better and far more vital kind of television news programming is likely to emerge from this kind of spirited rivalry, and will most probably be in the public interest.

---

[3] *The New York Times,* Oct. 26, 1968, p. 24.

PART 3

PRINCIPLES
OF REPORTING

chapter 17

The Lives of a Reporter

Gene Miller was worried. He had just learned of some suspicious circumstances in the case of a man convicted of murder in Florida. To the average reporter, the vague feeling that something was wrong would have been brushed aside. The fellow had been convicted, hadn't he? He was in jail. Why worry?

But Miller began to worry. As a sensitive man with a deep commitment to principle, he decided to investigate the puzzling case. No one on his paper, the Miami *Herald*, drove him to do it. He worked on his own. Nor did he sit down in righteous wrath and write a Florida version of "J'accuse!" Without evidence, it would have made little impression.

Patiently, carefully, the reporter went over the routine in the murder case. He examined the arresting officers, the witnesses, the background of the convicted man, the evidence surrounding the confession he had made.

At length, Miller proved that an innocent man had been imprisoned for six years for a murder he had not committed. At a second trial, the man was acquitted; eventually, the Florida Legislature granted him compensation of $45 thousand.

But that wasn't all. In another case, entirely separate from the first, Miller again succeeded through patient and detailed inquiry in freeing an innocent woman in Louisiana who had been imprisoned for two murders she had not committed.

A HARD ROUTINE

Such feats are rare in the annals of American journalism. Yet, although Gene Miller won a Pulitzer Prize, neither he nor his editors credited his success to anything more than the ability to make routine pay off.[1] For, in all truth, so much excellent reporting is based on routine. As Morton Mintz of the Washington *Post* once said after breaking the expose of Thalidomide, the drug blamed for malformed babies: "Many truly important items are actually very dull. Most members of the Washington press corps want the glamor jobs. In so doing, they forgo much that makes significant news."

When Oscar Griffin of the Pecos (Texas) *Independent* broke the story that led to the conviction and imprisonment of Billie Sol Estes, the Texas farm tycoon, it was basically an investigation that began with routine. Similarly, when George Thiem of the Chicago *Daily News* traced checks that sent an Illinois State auditor to jail for fraud, it was also "just routine." Routine, too, helped John Frasca of the Tampa *Tribune* to clear a suspect in a Florida robbery and produce the evidence that led to a confession by the real culprit. And when Norman C. Miller of the *Wall Street Journal* broke a salad oil scandal that cost investors millions of dollars, he was far more the patient examiner of records than a James Bond type.

The point cannot be overstressed. The basis of nearly all good reporting is hard work. The reporter whose results are based on sheer luck is a rare bird, found mainly in the paperbacks with lurid covers and television soap operas.

HOW REPORTERS WORK

It is easy to tell a good reporter from a poor one. The good one knows that much of his working time will be spent in routine, and he is fully prepared to do it well. The poor one brushes off such mundane details as reading newspapers, checking names and addresses, asking questions about seemingly unimportant details, and taking careful notes when he can.

The difference between the two is that the good reporter knows he must cover all kinds of stories, and most of them will be small; the poor one lives only for the big news break that may never come his way.

Beginners have to learn these facts the hard way.

During a critical vote at the United Nations General Assembly a young reporter noticed that a delegate of Oriental appearance at the other side of

---

[1] Gene Miller, "Blindfolded Journalism," *ASNE Bulletin*, November 1967, p. 1.

the rather dark chamber was raising his hand regularly to vote with the Soviet bloc. The young reporter duly noted and wrote that Nationalist China's delegate had been supporting the Soviet Union, which would have been a shock to Formosa.

Paul Ward, the Pulitzer Prize-winning reporter for the Baltimore *Sun*, was sitting behind the young reporter but took the trouble to walk 100 yards to the Asian delegate's desk and check. The delegate was from Burma, which made an entirely different story. Ward abided by one of the first rules of reporting—never take anything for granted; always check. The young reporter thought it was all right to guess.

The Assignment Sheet   An editor, quickly going over an assignment sheet, can tell at a glance how a news organization's reporters are deployed. He is able to note which ones are trusted with assignments that require care and effort and which others receive tasks calling for less skilled professionals.

The assignment sheet is the journalist's "order of battle" in his daily campaign to cover all news fronts. Noted are the assignments each reporter has received and a few words about developments.

An assignment sheet should be so concisely and neatly kept that even an uninformed editor, picking it up without advance briefing, can tell in general what the news of the day is and how the desk is using its resources to cover. He should then be able to listen to reporters calling in, or coming to the desk to describe what news they have, without wasted motion.

Few reporters ever see the assignment sheets. Some of them call in and get their assignments. Others are summoned to the desk, briefly told what to do, and dispatched on their jobs. Except for a complicated series or some special assignment, no reporter gets detailed guidance from the desk on what he is to do, where he is to go, and exactly what transportation to use.

Going on an Assignment   When a reporter receives a spot news assignment, the first thing for him to do is to go to the source of the news at once. It is only on a feature assignment or interview that he may have time to consult the library and make a leisurely departure. He used to rely only on pad and pencil but today, if he is wise, he takes a tape recorder as well.[2]

Reporters learn from experience when and where to go for certain types of stories. For fires, accidents, and disasters of other kinds the scene of action is often the best source of news. For police news, however, it is not always certain that a visit to the scene of the crime will be the most direct way of picking up the threads of the story unless the principal news

---

[2] See *Newsweek*, December 25, 1967, p. 74.

sources are there. At political and diplomatic conferences the biggest news is usually made far away from the speakers' platform. In labor negotiations, with both sides sealed up in a conference room, the news can break from any number of places.

The important fact for any reporter to remember is to keep moving. Too often, reporters find that most of their time is spent waiting for people to condescend to see them. When that happens, it is the reporter's business to cut down on the waiting time either by using the telephone, writing a note, or using some other method of reaching his source. In any case, regardless of whether anything or nothing happens while he is on the assignment, a reporter must call his desk at regular intervals of from 30 minutes to an hour. Otherwise the whole news-gathering system is paralyzed through lack of communication.

Every reporter quickly learns that the best approach to a news source largely depends upon circumstances and opportunity. The leisurely business of calling an important man and asking for an appointment at his convenience is a fine way of doing business—for columnists and editorial writers. A reporter too often has to depend upon a telephone call, a curbstone interview, or a scribbled note submitting a question.

No professional journalist should adopt tricks, disguises, or other shenanigans without the knowledge and consent of his superiors. It is perfectly true that reporters have made praiseworthy contributions by doing firsthand stories of their work as hospital orderlies, school teachers, policemen, firemen, and even detectives, on occasion, but no newspaper wants its reporters doing that kind of thing regularly without some very real and basic need.

It is only when direct methods fail on an assignment that a reporter should even consider a stratagem. Many a news source has been located quickly, not by skulking through supposedly haunted houses at midnight, but by merely looking up his name in a telephone book or city directory. Many a reporter has gained access to a hard-to-see news source by going in the front door and announcing himself. Before any reporter acts on a stratagem, he should consider whether it will be to his advantage if he succeeds, and also whether it will embarrass him and his news organization if he fails.

Reporters can make their own breaks by doggedly doing their routine work well. Often, by checking both sides of a story, they will find an aggrieved person who will provide good leads for further inquiry. Through firmness, courtesy, and persistence they sometimes can persuade an aloof news source to discuss his position with them. Many a reporter, determined to be fair, has found that his patience and his efforts have been rewarded with unexpected disclosures.

Wherever it is possible, a thorough inquiry should be made into the backgrounds of the principal actors in the news. In a murder trial, during which the defense contended death was due to an accident, a girl reporter discovered that the judge some years before had shot and killed a hunting companion by accident. During the investigation of a large corporation which was in financial difficulty, it developed that one of its principal officers had been a notorious exconvict who had changed his name. The author of a best-selling book of humor and philosophy was disclosed to have served a prison sentence in connection with a stock fraud, and to have succeeded in rehabilitating himself.

Ask—Ask—Ask! How does a reporter accomplish such feats? Usually this is done by asking questions, often politely but always persistently—not just any question, but one that is so phrased as to produce a newsworthy answer.

The reporter who breezes into the county clerk's office and asks gaily, "What's new?" is likely to be told, "Nothing." But if he asks for permission to look through the latest actions seeking damages, he is likely to come up with a small but interesting story. It is to the advantage of the reporter to have some idea of the story he is after and the probable area of knowledge of his news source. It makes the probing so much easier.

Few reporters can be play-actors and get away with it. The loud voice, the accusing finger, the dramatic manner are not becoming to a responsible journalist. Nor does it ever help a reporter to quarrel with his source, threaten him, or anger him. Such histrionics may jar loose one story, but they are likely to cost a reporter the confidence of the man who gives it to him. To those who can maintain a smooth even temper and a moderate manner go most of the rewards of the professional news gatherer.

The loud and brassy reporter is his own worst enemy. He seldom proves to be an ornament either to his organization or his profession.

Sometimes it is the news source who is arrogant, overbearing, and even threatening. The most even-tempered reporter may be excused, under such pressures, if he becomes angry. However, as most reporters know, anger is not particularly helpful in gathering news although it is on occasion becoming to an editorial writer. The experienced reporter, regardless of provocation, maintains his poise by staying off the defensive and asking questions.

Young reporters, going on their first assignments, invariably ask themselves before approaching their first awesome news source, "Why should he talk to me?" It is true that few reporters today command a personal following. Young reporters, however, need not feel abashed by lack of experience. They will be received, not because of what they are, but because of what they represent. From such beginnings they will learn quickly enough to make their own way by asking the right questions of the right persons at the right time.

Taking Notes   Some good reporters take a few notes now and then, scribbled on the back of an old envelope or a shred of copy paper. Others have taken notes about the weather even while crossing Times Square on a beautiful spring day. These are the established professionals whose methods vary in accordance with their temperament, their habits, and their needs.

Today's reporters, especially the younger ones, are likely to find that considerable note-taking will be more useful to them than the casual attitude of veteran reporters. The reason is that modern reporting must be more careful, more thorough, and if possible more accurate than the news gathering of thirty-five or forty years ago. There are many methods, both electronic and documentary, of checking the accuracy of newspaper reports today that did not exist in the last generation. It is virtually imperative for a reporter to have a handy record of where he went, what he did, and what was said to him. Not every reporter can cover every assignment with a tape recorder.

Many old-time newspapermen merely grabbed a handful of copy paper, folded it three times sidewise, and scribbled notes whenever it occurred to them. A more regular system of note-taking is advisable in these more complicated days. The pocket-size stenographer's notebook is now standard equipment for the careful reporter, who develops his own system of speedwriting if he does not command adequate shorthand. All entries are dated, and nothing is thrown away, even after the notes are used. Customarily, reporters keep copies of their stories with the original notes in some convenient place so that they may be checked if there is ever any question about the story.

Necessarily, there are many occasions on which a reporter cannot take notes. It makes politicians and diplomats nervous to have a notebook thrust under their noses during a casual conversation. That is generally true about others who, for one reason or another, dislike talking for the record. As a rule, whenever a reporter finds it impossible or inconvenient to take notes during a conversation, he makes a record of the event as soon as he can, drawing on his best recollection. Few reporters have anything even approaching total recall, but any well-trained reporter can remember quite accurately the highlights of a conversation or action if he makes notes about it immediately after it happens.

When a reporter becomes an actor in a news story, such as a hurricane about which he is doing an eyewitness account, the importance of recording facts and impressions becomes apparent. No reporter, fighting his way through a storm, can be expected to stop and scribble a few words in a notebook about his heroic conduct. Once he reaches safety, however, and has a little time to pull himself together before writing his story, it helps to jot down the highlights of his experiences.

Similarly, when a reporter is involved in a prolonged experience from which a story eventually will be written, it is always helpful if he makes very complete notes each day and files them against the time when he must begin his articles. This was the method used by George N. Allen, a New York reporter who acquired a teacher's license and taught for two months in a Brooklyn junior high school to obtain material for a firsthand series of articles on school conditions. He had more than 300 pages of notes when he concluded his experience.

Note-taking cannot be done at random. There must be some method to it, otherwise the reporter becomes a mere stenographer. The shorthand expert who takes down every word of a complicated court hearing quickly finds, if he tries to do a rapid report at the end of the day, that he is buried under his material. For that reason trained reporters leave a margin at the left of the page on which they take their notes. Beside every block of material, they write a few words in the margin to indicate the subject matter. Even at the end of a day-long court hearing, if this system is adhered to, it is possible to skim quickly over the marginal notes, decide which are the most important, arrange them in the order that will be most fitting for a news story, and begin talking to a rewrite man, dictating, or writing.

Checking Copy   Inexperienced reporters sometimes are placed on the defensive when officials, public or in private industry, demand the right to examine notes or approve copy before it is submitted to the newspaper. It is a fixed rule on all newspapers and wire services that their editors, alone, have the right to determine what a reporter should do with his facts and how a story should be written. Overly aggressive news sources should, of course, be told this in a polite manner. Whenever there is insistence on the right to see a story before it goes in the paper, a reporter can only refer his source to his editor and await the outcome. He should never yield his copy for examination, except under conditions of acknowledged censorship, or for military clearance when necessary.

In certain types of assignments, such as science writing, a few of the established journalistic experts have voluntarily sent their news stories to the authors of scientific abstracts on which the stories were based. The purpose was to insure accuracy. In no case was the scientist given the right to change or omit facts that were included by the journalist. However, the scientist was asked to point out errors and make any appropriate comments, and editors were consulted on whatever changes were to be made.

Such procedures are almost inevitable on complicated technical stories, but the reporter must always be careful to preserve his copy and prevent substantive changes for any reason other than to insure accuracy.

THE REPORTER AND HIS OFFICE

No reporter can be any better than the direction and support he receives from his office. On general assignment, or on some specialized subject such as science or military affairs, the problem of reportorial morale is generally not serious. However, on the beats—police headquarters, city hall, the district attorney's office, courts, and others—the reporter is often left to his own devices because he has a fixed assignment.

Pool Reporting   There are two kinds of pool reporting—admitted and unadmitted. The first, which has been forced on the news media since the disgraceful mob scenes of journalists that followed President Kennedy's assassination, is of great importance as a matter of public policy. In the coverage of a President, a foreign potentate, a great religious leader, or in a matter involving national security, it has become more and more essential. The pool reporters, generally selected by the correspondents themselves, have an enormous responsibility to both the public in general and the mass media in particular.

It is the unadmitted pool reporting that presents far greater hazards. Even though editors have always declaimed against the pool, it is a matter of common knowledge that reporters on beats in most large cities—where there is still competition—have practiced pool reporting for many years. Such pools have been formed as a matter of self-protection by the reporters themselves. And editors, instead of breaking up the pool, have accepted pool-developed news because it would cost a good deal more to put on extra reporters to get the same results. Although most good reporters dislike pool reporting, not one of them can now be sure that he will not have to work with a pool at one time or another. Therefore, it is necessary, in any discussion of reporting, to set down the general principles on which a combination like this operates independently of editorial control.

1. If a reporter works with a pool, he guarantees that all news he receives *under the agreement* will be given to the pool and sometimes he will not even attempt to turn in any part of a story until every member of the pool is ready to do so. Those who have seen reporters running for phone booths at an agreed signal, or dropping a coin in a phone box at a word from one of their number, know what pool coverage is like. It means that the weakest and the strongest share alike. (In photographic pools, photographers in some cities even make certain, in extreme cases, that they snap the same picture from exactly the same angle.)

2. If a reporter receives a special assignment from his office while he is working with a pool, he must at once disengage himself. He does this by informing members of the pool that he is now responsible to his office directly and can no longer give and receive his information through the pool. Accordingly, he is cut off from the pool and goes out on his own until further notice. When his special assignment is over, and he again declares himself in on the pool, he may resume his normal status provided he has done nothing to embarrass the pool members in their relations with their city or assignment desks.

These informal regulations have grown up over the years from the beats in the big cities and still persist wherever the reporters and photographers, and their electronic associates, enter into agreements independent of their own editors and managers. They antedate any union of journalists, print or electronic, and are not to be found in any union contract. While some reporters may inform their offices that a pool arrangement is operating, if the story is big enough, editors frequently have to find out for themselves.

It is only when there is admitted pool reporting that the editors, and sometimes the publishers, enter into the decision-making on what shall be covered. But even here, the editor is far less important than the source— usually a high government official or a judge at a controversial trial—that forces the news media into a pool arrangement. Then, special rules must be adopted to fit each particular case; the routine practiced by the beat reporters who pool their stuff is not precise enough to be used at higher levels. For such things as White House weddings and Presidential trips under tight security, the pool is here to stay. But it is not the best method for covering a story.

Call Backs   The most frustrating experience a reporter can have in his relations with his office is to call in with a major news story and talk with a deskman who knows nothing about it. The delays involved in explaining who gave the assignment and why and what has happened since are likely to curdle the spirit of the most enthusiastic reporter. Yet, this kind of faulty liaison is all too common in both print and broadcast media.

It is recommended professional practice for call backs by reporters to be handled by the person who originally assigned them or by someone on a later shift who has been briefed on what reporters are doing. Poor liaison between editors and reporters can quickly lead to the demoralization of the best of news organizations.

Overnight—or Second-Day Angle?   When a reporter is handling a continuing story on an afternoon newspaper or wire service, and giving his notes to a rewrite man, wise editors usually insist that the overnight—the story for the first edition of the next day—should be written by the man on the scene.

There are two good reasons for this. The first is that the reporter is likely to have a fresher approach than a night rewrite man, who must hash together a second-day angle out of the morning paper clips. The other reason is that the writing of the overnight can give the reporter a closer sense of identity with the story that he is covering. Many times the overnight is the only story an afternoon newspaper reporter can write. He phones in the rest to a rewrite man.

The difference between a second-day angle on old news, as rewritten in the office, and an overnight, as done by a reporter on the scene, is not too clearly understood. Some newspapermen mistakenly assume they are the same.

That is not really true. A reporter who is in direct touch with a news source can get new material to freshen up an old story. A rewrite man, working in the early morning hours, must make the best of what has been printed already by updating it. Therefore, the reporter's overnight is always to be preferred to a rehashed second-day angle dredged by a rewrite man from the last few paragraphs of a morning paper clip.

For example, in covering a political campaign most newspapers of stature assign a reporter to travel with each of the major candidates. The candidates, of course, make most of their important speeches at night. That gives the morning newspaper reporter a fresh story, but it places the afternoon newspaperman at a considerable disadvantage. Often, there is nothing for the first edition of an afternoon newspaper except a rehash of a speech that has already been covered in the morning papers.

If no reporter were traveling with the candidate, many an afternoon newspaper would have to print a first edition story such as the following:

> Marvin J. Zugsmith, Republican nominee for U. S. Senator, has accused Democrats in Congress of going on a "spending spree."
> In a speech at Merion City last night, Mr. Zugsmith warned. . . .

This is the way some wire service stories are handled for the overnight wire when there are no new developments. A rewrite man in the office might dress up the same story by past-tensing the lead and working up a forced second-day angle as follows:

> Democrats in Congress were confronted today with a charge by Marvin J. Zugsmith, Republican nominee for U. S. Senator, that they were spending Federal funds needlessly.
> Mr. Zugsmith's accusation was made at Merion City. . . .

A reporter, traveling with Mr. Zugsmith, would leave the speech to the morning newspapers and concentrate on a new angle if he could. At the very least, his story would lead with the candidate's next move in the campaign, discuss it, and deal with the last night's speech on the basis of the reactions it aroused. The overnight, therefore, would be a fresher story.

Editors always prefer a "live" overnight by a reporter to a rewritten "dead" second-day angle by a rewrite man.

These are not problems that particularly bother the electronic media, where newsmen and camera crews are sent out with instructions to find something new and fresh and vital in a static but important news story. But in print, too much rewriting of the wires and the morning paper (or papers) frequently makes for a dead first edition. A reporter with spark and imagination, who is willing to make an effort for a different kind of story, can make an old story come alive for a newspaper just as an inquisitive camera can for television.

DEAD OR ALIVE?

In a static news situation, such as a New York City tugboat strike that has just ended its fourth day, the traditional way to handle the story for an afternoon paper's first edition is to rewrite the clips and the wires. Often, the result will read something like this:

> New York's 3,500 striking tugboatmen entered the fifth day of their strike today without a settlement in sight.
> Both union and management negotiators prepared to meet again for talks, with the help of federal and state mediators. The principal issue was the union's demand for more time off for its members . . .

The reader can see at a glance that the "freshened angle" isn't really an angle at all. It is merely a numerical lead which, instead of recounting the events of the fourth day of the strike, triumphantly announces that the fifth day is about to begin. In a word, the story is dead. How can it be brought back to life?

An enterprising reporter produced the following:

By Michael Berlin

> Ray Harrison says he's "one of the lucky ones."
> "I've been 24 years on tugs, mostly in New York and up and down the coast."
> Harrison, a 54-year-old deckhand, has taken his seniority and invested it in one of the better shifts—four days on, two days off—and one of the newer boats, the Dalzell Eagle (launched in 1960).
> "In the old ones," he says, "you sleep in the forepeak below the

water line. Tough quarters. Damp small bunks, so a tall man can't fit in 'em."

Most of the city's 3,500 striking tugboatmen work longer shifts, on the boat 24 hours a day, working a full 12.

"You don't sit down, except cruising between jobs, and even then you got the maintenance of the boat—chipping the paint, swabbing the decks. You *want* to keep busy to pass the time."

Harrison, a solid man with thick, calloused fingers from a lifetime of hauling on towlines, says, "That's the big thing we want. More time with our families."

And the strange thing in this strange strike—where there are no pickets, where union and management have the same building, 17 Battery Pl.,—is that management wants more time off for the men, too.

"They're beginning to agree that we need more time off," Harrison grudgingly admits.

The issue, as the strike enters its fifth day today, is the cost of the free time. The tug companies have agreed to add a fourth crewman to each tug, which would give the men a day off for each day on.

But to cut the cost, the tug firms want cutbacks in other benefits.

Life on a tug is no bed of roses, but it is cozy.

"Most crews work together pretty much," says Harrison. "On the Eagle, we generally have 11 men on at a time, and the two crews work six hour shifts.

"When there's a ship rush on, we do a lot of ship work, towing ships four–five hours a day. Then we tow barges—oil, cement, trap, rock. They keep the boats on the go—there's never a slack time in the 24 hours. You never know where you'll be going from hour to hour. We go up to Albany, over to Jersey, sometimes New Haven . . . "

Thus, the life of a tugboatman emerges in colorful detail from what might have been just a dead rewrite with a conventional second-day angle. A reporter *can* make a difference.

chapter 18

Ground Rules for Reporters

The four principal duties of a reporter are to tell the news accurately, explain what it means, protcct his sources when necessary, and respect such confidences as he is willing to accept. To help him do his job, he has developed a body of practice that applies in varying degree to every assignment from the smallest school board to the White House.

If these methods are used with courage and good judgment, they can be effective in penetrating the twin defenses of public relations barriers and needless official secrecy that have hedged in many private and public news sources. Like all procedures, they can be abused by complacent reporters or sources given to perverting or withholding the truth.

That does not make them any less necessary. The reporter soon finds that he is judged by his colleagues, his editors, and his sources by how well he knows the ground rules, how effectivcly he uses them, and how faithfully he observes them.

THE ATTRIBUTION OF NEWS

Next to accuracy, the most important principle in the handling of news is the manner in which it is attributed to a source, or sources. News conferences, interviews, and written public statements vary in news value with the degree of attribution that is permitted, or agreed upon in advance. Sometimes, of course, an overly cautious reporter uses too much attribution or uses attribution when it is not necessary. These are the main gradations:

On the Record The basic premise on which most American reporters operate is that, within certain broad limitations, everything told to them or learned by them is for publication, or "on the record."

One limitation is any specific agreement or understanding made by a reporter and his source to withhold some or all of the news, or keep it "off the record." Such agreements should have the approval of a reporter's superiors, if it is a matter of principle.

Another limitation, even more important, is the body of law affecting the news media. This includes the law of libel, the law against an invasion of privacy, and certain broad statutes forbidding the use of certain kinds of news such as atomic secrets and, in many states, the names of juvenile offenders and relief clients.

Responsible reporters and the news media that employ them are equally insistent on observing the accepted standards of good taste as well.

Finally, reporters like all citizens are bound by the precepts of the Constitution of the United States and the various Federal, state, and local laws that regulate individual and corporate behavior. These, too, are likely to have an effect on what may or may not be printed, particularly in cases involving such matters as contempt of court or contempt of Congress.

Forty years ago reporters were not conscious of their limitations to any great degree. They made it a practice to go to a meeting or interview, take notes on what they heard, and write the story with a liberal mixture of direct quotations whether or not they were exactly what the speaker had said. The same kind of coverage was given lawmaking bodies, the courts, and the various offices of executives either in government or private industry.

Those who made news were named. The things they said were attributed directly to them. If a public official timidly suggested that it might be well to hold up a voluminous document for a few days to give reporters a chance to study and understand it before writing about it, he was accused of betraying the freedom of the press. If he tried to give counsel to reporters on the meaning of the news, but asked not to be quoted as the source, he was hooted down as a propagandist.

In these more complicated and dangerous days the old rule of "everything on the record" has undergone some rather violent changes that old-time reporters and editors would never have accepted. Public figures have now learned the risks of talking "off the cuff" and usually prepare their statements in advance if they intend to speak for publication. The inventions of the tape recorder and video tape have done more than anything else to force reporters to be scrupulously honest about direct quotations.

It is good practice for a reporter to consider the material that is made known to him to be on the record, within the limits as defined here. He had best check it carefully with his source and go over any doubtful quotes for accuracy before dashing to the telephone or news wire. News today is far more complicated than it used to be, and it requires a great deal more care and explanation.

For Attribution, But Not for Direct Quotation   The initial variant in the rule of putting as much news as possible on the record is to specify that there may be paraphrase, but no direct quotation. No reporter likes to accept this kind of limitation because direct quotations give authenticity to the news. Yet, there are times when he must.

Since American reporters as a whole do not take shorthand and they do "fix up" quotes where necessary to make them a fair approximation of what the speaker said, nobody with an important statement of policy is willing to take chances with the system. If he does not have time to issue the statement in advance, and if it cannot be held until an agreed release time, then he invokes the rule against direct quotation.

Necessarily, the source must be a dominant one in the news to call upon this rule. No mere actress or night club playboy could specify grandly, "You may use what I say, but not in direct quotation." Such a privilege is reserved on occasion for the President of the United States, the Secretary of State, an occasional military briefing of importance, and now and then, major pronouncements on state, local, and private industry levels.

However, judges, politicians, and diplomats still avail themselves of the "no direct quotations" rule when they can. If reporters are able to overcome the reluctance of sources to be quoted, then the press is doubly responsible to see that the material used is completely accurate and not merely "fixed up." The electronic media here act as good policemen.

Attribution to a Spokesman   Before World War II the presence of a spokesman in a news story was not as common as it is today in domestic American journalism. Editors generally insisted that the sources of the news must be identified by name, whether or not they could be quoted directly. The presence of an anonymous figure, who could not be described in any way except in relation to what he represented, was almost an affront to many reporters and editors.

Yet, after World War II spokesmen blossomed in the Federal government and at the United Nations. They cropped up in stories from Congress and the legislatures. When it became evident that the editorial bars were down, and the news media were so eager for news that they would accept even anonymous sources, spokesmen appeared as authorities for news about city halls, boards of education, police headquarters, and even street cleaning departments.

It is common now for spokesmen to make news for even small companies in local papers. They are found in sports pages and in women's news. Soon, if the practice is not checked, they may find their way to church notes—but it is certain they never will be used in advertising.

It is difficult to trace the origin of the practice. On the European continent and in Britain, reporters for many years respected the desire of working-level government officials to remain anonymous. It is still a rule, for instance, in the British Foreign Office that briefing officers are not named because the British civil servant must remain anonymous, leaving credit and blame to elected officials. When Americans picked up the habit, they put the British to shame.

The difference is that in Britain and on the European continent it is usually not difficult to find out who has done the talking if the news is attributed to an anonymous spokesman. In the United States there are so many more sources of the news that the public may not always be certain of the rank and authority of the anonymous spokesman, but must depend on the "play" of the story for some idea of his importance. It is just one more degree of shrinkage in the practice of full attribution of the news.

When government or private sources say, "You may attribute the following to a spokesman for the such-and-such department," a reporter has only two choices. He either uses the story, in accordance with the conditions laid down, or he omits it and so informs his desk. Usually, owing to the pressure of competition, he has to use the story if it is of any consequence. A great deal of diplomatic and military news is now issued only through unidentified spokesmen, and there is not a great deal that one reporter can do about it.

The practice has been accepted. The news media have limited themselves.

Background   Anonymous attribution is the most difficult and confusing practice in American journalism, but at the same time it is one of the most important, for it is the key to the use of a lot of news for which nobody will be the authority. The reporter and the news media must take risks, for the only attribution of so-called background news is "well-informed sources," "official sources," "diplomatic sources," "officials," or no source at all but the reporter's name and the name of his organization.

The word "background" is in itself a semantic puzzle. In one sense, when it is used in connection with the writing of a story, background means the historical detail that helps explain some current event. In a reporting sense background means the use of material in a story without any attribution to the source by name or to any nation, state, or organization he may represent. The origin of the term in connection with reporting doubtless may be traced to the introduction of such material by a news source,

"Now, I can't be named as the authority for what I'm about to tell you but I'll give it to you for your background."

A variation on this is for a source to remark to a reporter, "This is just background material for your personal use."

It is important for reporters to remember that background material is given to them to be used, but they need not print it if they see no real reason to do so. Not all background material, after all, is newsworthy. A lot of it is of trial-balloon character, to be withdrawn if it arouses opposition. Some of it is issued by sources who do not really know what they are talking about. And occasionally, somebody tries to put over background material as out-and-out publicity for some cause, idea, or person. It is a human peculiarity that editors who will not print a story when it put on the record will sometimes fall for the same material when it is put out mysteriously for background by a conniving official (and, in a rare case, maybe a conniving reporter).

Background, as a journalistic practice, is as old as print. European foreign offices have used it as long as there have been favored correspondents and favored newspapers. It was adapted for American use during World War II by Washington reporters who generally credit Ernest K. Lindley, of *Newsweek* magazine, with being the first to employ it. Finding that high officials could not talk to him on the record, and being unwilling to talk to them off the record, Lindley persuaded them to give him needed explanations of current and coming events under a pledge that he would not identify them as his sources. Thus, background came to be a half-way house between on the record and off the record.

Officials and Background The reporting device spread all over Washington, and from there radiated into every state in the union. Few news organizations in the United States today are able to identify all sources of all news because of the growing number of restrictions on use. Therefore, the "informed source" and the "official circle" have moved in as not particularly welcome guests in journalism at all levels. No young or inexperienced reporter is advised to trifle with background reporting unless he has the firmest kind of instructions from his editors. The reason for this is that there are relatively few news sources experienced enough to be able to handle background material without costly errors in judgment.

Reporters and Background Writing in *The New York Times*, James Reston had this to say about background reporting:

> This is a remarkable rule, for it imposes upon the writer what can only be described as a compulsory form of plagiarism. That is to say, the

official explains what he has been doing or is about to do or is thinking about doing, on the specific understanding that the writers may publish what he says on their own authority without any attribution to him or his department, or even to "an official source."

The reporters are permitted under these ground rules to say that the Government is planning to do these things or thinking about doing them, or if they are inordinately cautious, they can dream up such phrases as "there is one view in the Government." But they cannot give any authority for what they are told.

This has many advantages for both the official and the reporters. The official, if he is thinking about introducing a new policy but isn't quite sure how it will be received (officials are almost always in this state), can thus discover the public reaction to his proposal without being identified with it. More important, he can explain some of the intricacies of his problems (including his difficulties with other officials) and thus help win understanding and approval for what he proposes to do.

Similarly the reporters stand to gain, for in such meetings they acquire an understanding of what is going on and are therefore better able to inform their readers. But the trouble is that, if there is a misunderstanding of what is said, or if what is said causes embarrassment to the Government, the White House can always repudiate the published stories, and the reporters, who cannot disclose their source, are left without any plausible defense.

Little sympathy should be wasted on the reporter without a "plausible defense" in a background story. Human nature and human conduct being what they are, it is inevitable that the source of a background story of importance eventually will be disclosed if there is controversy about it.

Reporters are protected by no law that gives them authority to refuse to disclose sources, although in practice they faithfully protect such sources. The difficulty is that those reporters who are left out of a cozy Washington background dinner, which is given by an official to a favored few, invariably disclose what happened because they are under no pledge or confidence. On the contrary, having been beaten, they are entitled to some slight revenge, and disclosure is one of the best ways they can fight back.

Edwin A. Lahey, of the Washington Bureau of the Knight Newspapers, has seriously questioned the backgrounding procedure. In an *Editor & Publisher* interview, he called it a "news leak" and thought it had been seriously abused, both in Washington and elsewhere. He said:

> The abuse of the news leak and the background dinner routine has caused no little soul searching in the newspaper business. One of these days reporters and editors may have a "background dinner" with no outsiders present, for an honest discussion to determine whether it's worth it.

Like the official and unofficial spokesman, however, the background source has become firmly lodged in American journalism. It will be difficult if not impossible to dislodge him in an era when more and more official sources are being closed to the news media and reporters must take their news where they can find it.

With developing concern over our national security, both government sources and the news media have expanded the backgrounder into a way of journalistic life, although some have rebelled against it. Instead of the single designation, background, there are now degrees of backgrounding. During Dean Rusk's long tenure as Secretary of State, for example, he was accustomed to talk privately with a few selected reporters in what he called a "deep background" session. This meant that the material was primarily for the guidance (a word that may be variously translated) of the correspondents, who pledged themselves under no circumstances to disclose that there had even been such a meeting. In the Defense Department, there also were a few "deep background" sessions but very few correspondents had access to them.

"Deep background" is the closest approach to the British "D Notice" system, under which the press cooperates with the government to suppress mention of material damaging to national security. The British notices, sent to the news media, warn that articles on certain subjects may violate the Official Secrets Act. The "D Notices" (D for Defense) are issued by a committee, formed in 1912, that includes 11 members from the news media and five from government. There have been few violations of the unofficial code—but each one has become a *cause célèbre*.[1]

Off the Record   There is only one rule that applies to information that is given to reporters off the record and accepted by them as off the record. It should not and must not be used. This is a confidence that must not be violated.

Young reporters and others unfamiliar with the ways of journalism, invariably ask why anybody would want to tell reporters a secret that should not be published. There are many circumstances under which such disclosures become necessary, as a matter of public policy. During World War II correspondents attached to General Eisenhower's headquarters had to be alerted and generally briefed on their assignments for D-Day. The wartime journeys of President Roosevelt and the trip of President-elect Eisenhower to Korea were well-kept secrets on which the press had to be briefed. In Vietnam, such war-time briefings continued. The Federal Bureau of Investigation, in at least one instance, fully informed the news media of a kidnaping but requested no publicity on the chance that the victim could be saved—an exploit that was carried out with credit to all concerned. In

[1] Anthony Lewis, "British Given a Glimpse of Press Security System," *The New York Times*, February 26, 1967, p. 29.

politics, diplomacy, science, and crime—to mention only a few fields of major news—no reporter is ever privileged to write all he knows.

The faith with which such confidences are generally kept is a symbol of the reporter's dedication to his profession. He does not work merely for the next news break or the next day; he must be certain that the source who trusts him today with some small confidence will be protected. In five or ten years, a humble source may be a mayor, a governor, a prime minister, and even a President. No reporter can gain such exalted sources in a few minutes.

Each infraction of an off-the-record confidence, therefore, is a matter of the utmost seriousness to the news media as a whole. When one newspaper refused to abide by a request to soft-pedal the news of a kidnaping, and the victim was slain, the incident reflected on all the media. When a district attorney pleaded with newspapers not to publish a story about an eight-year-old boy's "confession" to the murder of his parents until psychiatrists could analyze the case, and one newspaper published it anyway, again everybody was hurt. The eagerness of an Associated Press correspondent to flash the end of World War II, in violation of his agreement with his colleagues and General Eisenhower, certainly did nobody any good. It is not an exploit that is remembered with admiration, any more than is the United Press "false armistice" of World War I which was based not on a violation of confidence but on bad information.

It is quite true that some off-the-record confidences should not be given or, if offered, they should not be accepted. Sometimes a reporter cannot help himself. There is an old saying among journalists that "anything known to more than two persons eventually will be known to everybody."

There have been instances, each involving a major news break, in which a reporter was "sealed up" but the off-the-record confidence was broken by someone else in the same news organization. It has also happened, regrettably, that a reporter receiving a confidence in one city connives with a colleague elsewhere to get the material before the public. In most cases, this is sheer, unprincipled opportunism; rarely is a claim made that such action is in the public interest. The general effect of every such violation of confidence is to reduce the public's credibility in the good faith of its news media.

The Battle Against Secrecy   The attribution of news is a complicated and sometimes confusing business, but a reporter must train himself to be patient and understanding in order to handle it. He should make no agreements he cannot keep and should clear with his desk on all doubtful matters if he is able to do so.

In general, where there are gradations of attribution, it is always a sound policy to try to lift the type of attribution by one notch. That is, if material is given for background, a reporter should try to persuade the source that it would receive more attention if it came from a spokesman. The reportorial effort should be unceasing to try to persuade spokesmen and their principals, where it is at all possible, to disclose their identities. Too much secrecy about the sources of the news is likely to undermine public confidence in the gatherers of the news.

The reporter must never forget that his purposes in a free society are not necessarily identical with those of his sources. Dean Acheson, while Secretary of State, put it this way in a letter to a reporter: "If I am about to go abroad to persuade another foreign secretary to agree to something which I wish to discuss with him first in complete confidence, your job would be served by discovering and reporting my plan. But this would frustrate my purpose. So it is fair, and should be understood, that your job requires you to pry; and mine requires me to keep secret."[2]

NEWS BEFORE IT HAPPENS

So much news is issued and processed before it actually happens that the reporter is under a great disadvantage to give life to his copy. It is, after all, impossible to report the colorful details of a political speech or a rocket launching or a parade before they actually occur. Yet, innumerable advance stories have to be written so that the newspaper will not be "dated" and far behind the course of events as reported by TV and radio. Nobody in newspaper or news magazine work likes to do this, but there is no choice. To delay a story until after a speech has been actually delivered, for instance, may mean not running the news at all.

The Advance   For these reasons the "advance" has become an integral part of American journalism. In essence the handling of an advance is based on complete cooperation and trust between the source and the news media, with the reporters acting as middle men. If the source specifies that his material shall be released at a particular time, the news media either comply with this request or do not use the advance. The practice of holding a story for release is known as an "embargo."

The handling of an important speech, particularly during a political campaign, illustrates this principle in its simplest form. It is axiomatic that a candidate running for election seeks the widest publicity for his speeches and therefore is willing to have them published even before they are delivered. Assume a speech is to be delivered at 10 P.M.; it is common practice

---

[2] John Hohenberg, *Between Two Worlds: Policy, Press and Public Opinion in Asian-American Relations.* New York: 1967, p. 4.

for the embargo to end at 6 P.M. so that the material can appear in all editions of morning newspapers as well as radio and TV newscasts. The embargo directions are always clearly given on the first sheet of the text of advance material.

If the first edition of a morning newspaper hits the street at 8 P.M., it is clear that the text of a speech to be delivered two hours later, or at least a news story about it, will appear under a prominent display. It will also be used by the broadcast media. The manner in which this is justified, both by the source and the editors, is as follows:

The lead will be based on whatever news there is in the speech and it will be written without qualification. But no lower than the second paragraph, it will be noted that the story is based on the release of an advance text with a phrase attributing the news to "a speech prepared for delivery." This qualification usually does not go in the first sentence because the lead then becomes too cumbersome. Here is an example of such an advance lead:

> Governor Williston charged last night that his Republican rival, J. Horton Denfield, intended to increase income taxes in the State if elected.
>
> In a speech prepared for delivery before the Tonawanda Democratic Club's annual dinner at the Hotel Biltmore, the Democratic Governor warned:
>
> "My opponent says our State must match income with outgo. He has pledged a balanced budget, but he refuses to specify what economies he will make to achieve it. I submit there is only one way in which he can accomplish his aim, and that is to raise the State income tax."

There would, of course, be a lot more of this based on the advance text. The same material would be used in the radio and TV newscasts so that it would be thoroughly familiar to any reader or listener by the time the speech actually was delivered. It would be the duty of the reporter, after writing the advance or giving in the essential facts to a rewrite man, to check the actual delivery against the advance text. If no substantial changes were made, the reporter would merely call in or dictate an insert to replace the second paragraph and eliminate all reference to the advance text.

To show that the speech was actually delivered, the sub second paragraph might read:

> The Democratic Governor was interrupted eight times by applause as he spoke at 10 P.M. before the Tonawanda Democratic Club's annual dinner at the Hotel Biltmore. He said:

The third paragraph and all the rest of the material culled from the advance then would be picked up and used as is. There would be no need for change. Occasionally, if there are interpolations in a speech that make some difference in the text, an additional insert will be used. It takes a major shift in emphasis to top an advance that has been used. Changes have to be kept to a minimum.

The growth of television campaigning in Presidential and major Gubernatorial and local elections has greatly reduced the value of advance texts for newspapers. There is little point in using an advance text when it differs materially from what actually is said on the air, as has been the case in recent political campaigns. This and the growth of what is known as the "basic speech," which candidates use over and over again in "whistle-stop" campaigning, have led many newspapers to drop advance texts altogether. Some candidates have been known to order their staffs to prepare any number of advance texts, merely to gain newspaper space, with no actual intention of ever delivering them.

Thus, the old reliance on advance texts must be re-examined. In the future, it is likely that the tape recorder—with machinery for rapid reproduction of the record in type—will be far more useful to newspapers than any canned advance that may or may not be delivered. As for television, it is safe to say that—given responsible management—its usefulness as a news medium during political campaigns will be intensified many times over in years to come.

THE EMBARGO

There are numerous types of embargoes. The most familiar one, and the easiest to work with, is the automatic release which specifies that material may be used in all editions that appear on the street after a specified time, and all newscasts as well.

Often, however, an embargo may specify that a release is "expected at about" a particular hour for all media. In such cases, the story cannot be scheduled definitely but must be held until it is certain that the speech is about to begin. Customarily, such material is used as soon as notification has been received that the delivery of the speech has begun. This kind of embargo applies to major advances such as the President's State of the Union message, the various governors' messages to their state legislatures, and similar material.

Use of Embargoes On complicated data, such as Federal, state, or local budgets or legislative, or private programs to which extraordinary news significance is attached, several days and sometimes as much as a week may be given to the preparation of the story. On budgets, it is not unusual for public officials to hold a "budget school" for reporters to give them special instruction in details and permit them to question experts. All material, whether it is printed or given out in the form of interviews or replies to questions, is then embargoed for a particular hour and issue for use by all media.

Nor are these long embargoes confined to governmental material. Universities and foundations generally have tried to provide reporters with sufficient time, in the form of an embargo, to enable them to familiarize themselves and their editors with complex material. One such report, dealing with the United States' interest in the United Nations, was embargoed for several days by the Carnegie Endowment for International Peace so that reporters could interview the leaders of the study. At the United Nations one of the most famous embargoes was a four-day period during which reporters frantically tried to inform themselves on the principles of the Baruch Plan for Atomic Control.

Conditional Embargoes   The practice of embargoing news in order to avoid an uninformed deadline scramble among newspapers and even worse on radio and television has spread to all major sources of information. However, it is not an unmixed blessing to reporters, writers, and commentators for the broadcast media. The news media give far more than they receive, as a general rule, when they submit to special conditions for an embargo in order to receive certain types of news.

For example, after the original failures in the United States missile program, the Defense Department provided advance information on unclassified missile or satellite shots for the news media only on condition that no use would be made of it before the actual firing. The object was to reduce public anticipation, and thereby take the edge off any continued failures of American space shots in the face of Russia's early successes. However, as the American space program grew and provided many brilliant achievements, this kind of precaution was dropped. Classified space shots still take place at both Cape Kennedy, Florida, and Vandenberg AFB, California, without notice to the news media.

Conditional embargoes were used a great deal during the Vietnam War to prevent the news media from giving inadvertent word to the enemy that a particular troop movement was under way. The practice was to permit use of the news when security measures no longer were necessary; however, more than one reporter held guilty of violating such conditional embargoes was denied the right of coverage for limited periods.

When an Embargo Is Broken   The universal rule on the breaking of an embargo, either by design or inadvertently, is: "A release that is broken for one is broken for all." The cases of deliberate violations of embargoes on major stories are so rare that each one becomes a *cause célèbre*.

When the first color film of the first hydrogen bomb blast was about to be released by the United States Atomic Energy Commission, it was decided to permit advance viewing of the awesome record so that descriptive material could be written. The embargo was to last for one week after the advance showing. However, a syndicated columnist published a review of the H-bomb film almost immediately after he saw it. The Columbia Broadcasting Company then showed the film and the newspapers broke the story.

The breaking of advance releases of *Look* magazine's publication of parts of William Manchester's *The Death of a President* provided an even greater source of controversy. *Look* contended that some of the most prominent newspapers in the nation had broken release dates and used far greater portions of the magazine articles than they were legally entitled to print. Despite threats of court action, most of these arguments were settled amicably. After all, *Look* was not insensitive to the value of nation-wide publicity in the press, as well as the electronic media, for material on the Kennedy assassination for which it had paid more than $600,000.

In addition, there have been instances in which newspapers have deliberately broken releases given to them in advance on the dubious ground that the public interest demanded it. One such case involved a report on the incidence of cancer among habitual cigarette smokers. There have been others, but generally most embargoes have been respected.

In a few cases, even when embargoes have been broken, the stories have not been generally released by the source and the original embargo time has been observed. Such was the case with a notable report by Trygve Lie when he was Secretary General of the United Nations. In it, he proposed a plan for a 20-year peace pact between the West and the Soviet Union. In its anxiety to get a world-wide hearing for the Lie proposal the United Nations information service distributed the story under a three-day embargo. Several small Norwegian papers ran the story at once, but all agencies and major newspapers agreed despite that to uphold the original embargo.

At the local and state levels powerful news sources have also succeeded in holding the mass media to an agreed embargo time, but it is somewhat more difficult to contain the aggressively independent Washington press corps. It seems to be a sound rule, however, to notify a news source that an embargo has been broken and that, in consequence, rival reporters no longer feel themselves bound. Sources and reporters must work together.

False Embargoes The embargo system can be made so complicated that it becomes a burden, rather than a help, to the news media. A case in point was the practice of a distinguished governor of one of the states of the Union who signed many bills passed to him by the legislature but permitted his press secretary to announce them on a quota basis, one for the afternoon papers, another for the morning papers, and so on for a period of 30 or more days after the legislative session concluded. Necessarily the reporters protested that this was managing the news in such a way as to keep the governor's name constantly in the papers. They asked to have the bills made public within a reasonable time after signing. While the governor moderated his practice, he continued it in principle until he retired from office.

Such false embargoes can be contested by reporters, but they cannot be violated. To do so would only be to create chaos. Once a reporter accepts a document bearing an embargo, he is bound not to reveal its contents until the agreed time. He is able to reveal news of such advance material if, by good luck or good management, he can secure details before the embargoed story is actually handed to him.

CHANGES IN ADVANCES

Sometimes, even when an embargo is observed in good faith, circumstances beyond anyone's control create such changes in the text that the advance lead is a false statement. There have been instances when speakers dropped dead between the time of the issuance of an advance and the delivery of the text, causing the news media to use an address by a dead man. In other cases, mercurial speakers have discarded an advance text and talked at random.

One such was the late Mayor Fiorello H. LaGuardia of New York City, who could never be depended on to stick to an advance. Once, at the United Nations, he issued an advance text bitterly criticizing the United States for not fully supporting the international relief program. But in his speech, as delivered, he omitted the attack and blandly told reporters he was not accountable to them for what he did, or did not do.

An Omission   A famous instance of an inadvertent omission that made an advance unusable occurred during one of President Eisenhower's campaign speeches. As is usual with political speeches, this one had been distributed hours before delivery and already had appeared in many newspapers in the country. The big news of this particular address was in its last paragraph, and W. H. Lawrence, then of *The New York Times*, like many other reporters, had based his lead on it. In the actual delivery, the President exceeded his TV time and, quite by accident, omitted the last paragraph. The quick-witted Lawrence jumped on the speakers' platform.

"Mr. President, your TV time ran out and you didn't use your last paragraph," he said. "May we use it in the form of an interview with you?"

The President grinned and nodded. The crisis was averted. No news leads had to be changed to explain that the President had not made the major announcement contained in his advance.

Under President Kennedy, the tape recorder began to be a far more reliable instrument for the press than the advance text. The young President was such a consummate master of television that he never feared to ad-lib in front of the cameras; moreover, his news conferences had so theatrical a flavor that it became a status symbol to those outside the correspondents' corps to be admitted to the State Department auditorium for the show. The only use there was for advances in the Kennedy administration was in such set documents as the State of the Union message, the budget and other key government papers. The President seldom followed an advance text in any of his speeches.

President Johnson, seldom comfortable before television and never at home before large groups of reporters, created even greater difficulties for all the news media. It was the President's habit through much of his administration to call reporters in with little or no advance notice, which was hard on the television people. Newspaper correspondents who did not cover the White House on a day-to-day basis also protested vehemently, but without much result. In addition to disregarding advances, President Johnson also put much of what he did and said on a spot news basis; often, he had to be covered like a police beat, not the best way of insuring full coverage of the nation's highest office.

Thus, the advance has been subject to many changes over the years. While it is still useful in many respects, it must be accepted with considerable reserve by the news media regardless of the source—governmental or private. Advances do not always mean what they say.

In general, when circumstances change an advance and nullify a lead, it is standard practice to use another point to begin the story. Then, an explanation must be made of what was in the advance, how and why it had to be changed, and what actually was said when the speech was delivered. Because of the spread of the writing of news before it happens, such explanations have become fairly common—and reporters usually have to make them. It is also accepted practice to let a source change an advance before the release time, if he has good reason to do so. But the changes should be reported.

"SEALING UP" A REPORTER

A reporter's principal assets are his ability, his integrity, and his freedom. If one is compromised, all are compromised. As soon as a reporter attains some degree of stature in his profession, he will find that constant attempts are made to sway his judgment, to win him over to one side or another, to persuade him to slant his news just a little. Few reporters are affected by such blandishments. Those who are seldom last very long in active, day-to-day journalism.

In rare cases where a reporter is obliged to favor one side or another, because of the policy of his organization, he usually finds that the very people with whom he is allied begin leaking tips and news to his opposition. The unfortunate reporter is "sealed up" while his opposition reaps the benefits of being free of any ties that bind him to a source. This is the price a news organization pays for extreme partisanship in any matter, and eventually it is bound to suffer loss of public respect through lack of confidence in the impartiality of its news.

Once or twice in a reporter's lifetime he will be confronted by a situation in which he is offered vitally important off-the-record news which, if accepted, will seal him up. Sometimes such offers are not the product of any trick by a news source, but are quite legitimate.

While General George C. Marshall was Secretary of State, he once called three American reporters to his temporary offices in Paris during a United Nations meeting and told them he wanted their reactions to an important proposal he was considering. Naturally, all were quite honored and readily agreed to help the Secretary of State and keep his confidence. When General Marshall disclosed that he was thinking of a plan through which the United States would help arm its European allies, which eventually developed into the North Atlantic Treaty Organization, one of the reporters suddenly realized that he was being given an off-the-record story which he already had learned from an entirely different source. The reporter, after much debate with his superiors, used the material he had gained from his on-the-record source, satisfied General Marshall that no confidence had been violated, and thereafter became extremely careful about accepting off-the-record news on any conditions.

It is always a good rule for reporters to stay away from situations in which they may find themselves "sealed up."

chapter **19**

The News Media and Public Relations

A powerful and ever-growing public relations apparatus filters much of today's news flow before it ever reaches the reporter. Sometimes, in sophisticated and expert hands, this process speeds up the flow of the news and increases its volume. When propagandists, amateurs, and bunglers take over the public relations machinery, however, it can be a handicap to the gathering of news and a menace to democratic government.

The growth of what was called a "credibility gap" between the pronouncements and actions of the United States government in the latter 1960s was one of the products of an overdose of public relations at the White House, the State Department, and the Defense Department. The worst feature of the spread of public disbelief in some of the announced objectives of the government, particularly in the Johnson administration, was that a certain amount of doubt also became attached to the news media as well.

Since the strength of a democratic government depends in large part on the trust of the people in their elected representatives and their free press, it is obvious that the misuse of public relations techniques could in time become an overwhelming burden to an open society. And this is as true inside government as it is in the private sector of the nation.

THE REPORTERS' PROBLEM

Whenever a reporter deals with public relations people, and it is almost impossible for him to avoid them except in small towns and modest organizations, his problem is to determine whether the news has been tampered with. Wherever he finds distortion, half-truths, and no truth at all, it is his job to get the story right before passing it on to the public.

This is one of the most difficult aspects of a reporter's work. His historic method of approach, within the bounds of law and good journalistic practice, is to seek unhampered access to the sources of the news—persons, places, records—wherever possible.

Such access serves in effect as a mutual guarantee of good faith between the news media and the agency or person who is publicized. An outstanding example of that kind of cooperation in the public interest is the news conference conducted by the President of the United States. The actions of some public agencies that habitually conduct all business behind closed doors represent the worst kind of public relations.

The Publicity Specialists   Most successful public relations work in the United States is conducted by former newspapermen. They act either as civil servants, as individuals, as corporate officers or employees.

The instances of home-grown public relations specialists are rare. Some have come from advertising or TV-radio. A few have made progress without any previous training of any kind. That is almost impossible today although it was done a half-century ago. While sociologists are useful in public relations, few social scientists leave their field for the hurly-burly of the news, semi-news, and pseudo-news field. The pseudo-event is almost entirely a public relations creation.

General Public Relations   Public relations goes under many names and an assortment of guises. That is because the practice, for all its usefulness, lacks prestige except in institutional fields. Its own publicity is not very good on the whole. On some levels, in fact, there is a kind of stigma attached to the work—a hangover from the days when press agents grabbed news space by sitting actresses in milk baths.

Press agents exist today, admitted and unadmitted. Among the most useful press agents are the small group of experts who handle the principal Broadway shows. Their job is to get the name of their show, and its principals, before the public. They do it in an engaging, and often informative, way.

Corporate and institutional public relations shy away from press agentry. They say they seek goodwill, not mere publicity. Business and industry, foundations and universities, civic, fraternal, and charitable groups prefer to be represented by dignified public relations people on a number of levels.

There is the policy consultant, who does not even have a mimeograph machine in his office but makes his way by giving sound, shrewd advice on public attitudes. Then there are companies, either separate public relations firms or branches of advertising agencies, that deal with the organization to be publicized. On the working level of the organization itself, if it is large enough, there is a staff of publicity men. They not only serve the external news media but also direct house organs (sometimes called house magazines) for employees. Companies like General Motors, General Electric, Standard Oil of New Jersey, North American Aviation, and others are outstanding in their efforts to handle public relations on a professional level.

Government Information   The largest of all public relations groupings is in the government at all levels—Federal, state, and local. Here, because the taxpayers are footing the bill, there is a rather wary reluctance to use even corporate and institutional public relations terms. The policy consultant is a very rare figure in government and is used sparingly on assignments in which his advice is likely to cut costs or increase efficiency. The somewhat humorous distinctions of industry between public relations men as the elite, and publicity men at the working level, are missing in government.

Here, publicity is called by a different name, and it is conscientiously practiced in a different way when directed by responsible officials. Most such efforts in government are termed information work. Those who handle the job are usually called Public Information Officers or Press Officers, the inference being that they deal only in information and do not seek to publicize their respective agencies. If only it were true!

From the working level in government, the progression of titles becomes a dizzy affair. The State Department not only has information personnel, but also Public Affairs Officers. The armed forces have their directors of information, or information services, and briefing officers and information officers as well. So have most of the other major departments of the Federal government. In addition, at the policy level, every official of importance has a press secretary who may be called by some such title as special assistant or executive secretary or, to cite only one, Assistant Secretary of State for Public Affairs.

Such personnel are also found at the state and local levels of government wherever there is sufficient pressure for news from the mass media and enough money to pay for the extra service.

The Operation   It is one of the phenomena of our times that the newspapers, which are the principal beneficiaries of the public relations network, are also its severest critics. No newspaper editor who has ever worked as a reporter would contend seriously that one man could cover the Pentagon or the State Department these days without a lot of help. Yet, when President Eisenhower told the American Society of Newspaper Editors that he would cut military service information staffs to curb service rivalry, he drew prolonged applause. Government information staffs have been consolidated, and sometimes eliminated altogether, without protest by the press. Even the most successful information directors in the service of the United States government could not escape bitter criticism from the news media at times. James C. Hagerty, who served as President Eisenhower's press secretary, was accused of "managing the news" at frequent intervals, as were his successors, Pierre Salinger in the Kennedy administration and Bill D. Moyers in the Johnson administration. It is scarcely a coincidence that none of the three remained in the government service; indeed, both Salinger and Moyers took leave at a time of their own choosing—scarcely a vote of confidence in the Presidential news disseminating function.

The role of the public relations man in business and industry, or in institutional work, is relatively stable by contrast. He is removed from the area of public responsibility, in which he is under constant pressure to account for public officials, their departmental actions, and their expenditures. Nor does he have to rush out the news on a split-second deadline basis. Unless the news is very bad, and therefore likely to leak, he can take his time about making it public. His relations with the news media are often of his own making, and the funds at his disposal tend to be more ample than in government. In corporate public relations the rewards are more likely to be commensurate with the responsibility of the individual. The risks are also greater.

Yet, whether the public relations specialist works in government or in corporate or institutional public relations, his essential worth to the news media is measured by two standards. The first is whether he has access to his principal at all times and can influence decisions bearing on the news. The second is whether he has the confidence and good will of the reporters with whom he deals. The public relations specialist must have both, or he cannot successfully operate, no matter how much news space he gets.

What P. R. Specialists Believe   There are some well-intentioned persons in public relations who think of themselves as a part of the staffs of the news media they seek to influence. They believe this so intensely that they fall into the error of thinking of reporters as essentially lazy people, willing to be spoon-fed with information. As the belief of indispensability takes hold in earnest, they begin arguing that the news media could not function if it were not for public relations people.

All this, of course, is nonsense. The aim of the average public relations man is to represent his client or principal before the public in the best possible manner. Whatever service he gives to the news media in performing his major duty is incidental. He is no more a part of an editorial function than the advertising man who prepares the layouts. It is regretfully true of a minority of poorly trained reporters that they will accept almost anything that is handed to them.

As for newspapers being so dependent on public relations that they could not publish without such material, the truth is that the end product would benefit by printing fewer speeches and official pronouncements and encouraging more competition for news.

This is just as true of television, radio, and the news magazines. While they are not as inviting a target for press agents as the newspapers on a day-to-day basis, a public relations coup in a national medium pays enormous dividends. As a result, the electronic media and the magazines are under constant pressure by the persuaders, both hidden and revealed. Some public relations people contend they are serving the public by putting their "message" over in a national, rather than a local, setting.

The "Honest Broker"   The realistic professional public relations specialist who goes into public relations from newspaper work does not share such beliefs. He looks on himself as a kind of middle man, an "honest broker" who tries to do a decent job of representing his client or his agency and of informing the public as well. He is as scornful as any reporter of propaganda masquerading as news and refuses to deal in such shoddy merchandise because it undermines his standing with the press. He works hard to persuade his principal to let out bona fide news as quickly as possible. If it is good news, it will benefit all who are concerned. If it is bad news, it is best told quickly, directly, and honestly by the originating agency.

The best professional public relations specialist proceeds on the basis that truthful reporting is the soundest policy. He does not try to complain about reporters to their editors when they do something that offends his own superiors. Nor does he try to mislead or give unwanted "guidance" to reporters, knowing such tricks always fail. He understands what reporters want and tries to help them whenever he can. If he cannot, he says so and keeps hands off. Above all, he knows that he cannot do a reporter's job for him and never tries to do so.

It is this kind of public relations man, information specialist, or press officer who provides the basis for a valuable cooperative effort between public relations and the press. If he deals in news of importance to the public, he runs risks almost daily of offending either his principals in the originating agency or the reporters with whom he works. It is through his efforts, just as much as those of the reporters sometimes, that the public is fully and correctly informed. Where the reporter can win praise and prizes there is no glory for the hard-bitten public relations man who tries to do an honest job.

What Reporters Seek   An experienced reporter who deals with a public relations agency expects no favors and asks for none. If he is sent by his office on an assignment involving such a relationship, he expects to be told what the story is and when the break on it can be expected. He will resent traveling for miles merely to pick up a press release, which could have been sent to his office just as easily. If there is a person who is the central actor in the story, the reporter expects a chance to interview him and get the news directly. If claims are to be made, the reporter will be impressed only if proof is also offered. If some papers or other records are involved, the reporter will, of course, want to see them.

No public relations agency or person can expect to trifle with the press or waste a reporter's time and get away with it. A story with a public relations origin may wash out once, but the originating agency will find itself ignored if the same thing happens very often. Reporters have learned over the years that professional public relations people can be extremely helpful with access to news sources, background material, tips, and pictures. Since they have also found that the best public relations men have the highest news standards, they have come to expect that kind of efficiency and know-how from all originating public relations sources.

It may seem like heresy to the old-time newspaper editor, but the newer media do not hesitate to cooperate fully with public relations services in and out of government if the end product promises to be interesting and newsworthy. This is particularly true of television, which is always in search of novel newsfilm. Moreover, the national picture magazines often go out of their way to feature an attractive actress or model on their covers as a come-on for the cash customers. It may not be good journalism, but it is practical.

PRINCIPLES AND METHODS

A reporter working with a responsible and experienced public relations agency or person is guided by a commonly accepted set of standards, principles, and methods that have been developed over the years. Since this informal code is not recorded, and only exists because of its usefulness to the participants, it changes from time to time. Therefore, it is always prudent to review the ground rules with the public relations personnel who are directly involved before embarking on any major assignment.

Equal Treatment   A reporter who deals with public relations sources assumes that all representatives of the news media will be given equal treatment. Certainly he has a right to expect that no one will be given favored treatment. This assurance of equality, however, presupposes that the reporter will be on the job and available on call whenever the publicist has a news break of some kind. If the reporter strays off, he does so on his own responsibility. If he is covered at all under such circumstances, it is because of the kindness either of his colleagues, the publicist, or both. Should he return to his office, without making some prior arrangement, he has no special call on the publicist for protection.

The public relations agency or person also assumes other obligations in dealing with groups of reporters on a continuing assignment, such as city hall coverage, or military, industrial, or scientific news. If a reporter has an exclusive story which he must confide in part to his public relations contact in order to check one angle, the contact man is bound to keep his confidence.

Any attempt to leak the story to the reporter's competition, or to make it generally available for all media, will not gain the public relations man the gratitude of the press corps. Instead, when his violation of confidence is discovered, he will forfeit the trust of every reporter who deals with him. The pledge of confidence that binds the publicist is no different than the one that seals up the reporter who accepts off-the-record information.

The reporter is bound to resent any attempt by a public relations agent to plant a story as a kind of trial balloon. If the story is not news, the reporter is always advised to stay away from it unless his office orders him to follow up the assignment. He is trained not to accept praise for an agency, person, or thing, but to let the facts speak for themselves. For that reason he is suspicious of any special pleading, which he is inclined to regard as propaganda, and he usually stays away from public relations people who indulge in it at the expense of factual news.

News by Telephone   Once a reporter becomes familiar with public relations personnel, particularly in government, he is likely to confine his routine coverage to telephone inquiries. These routine telephone calls from the news media take much of the office time of any busy press officer, or other public relations specialists, and even pursue him at home at all hours. Therefore, a reporter may find that he cannot always reach the person he wants in a public relations office at once. In that case he leaves his number and asks to be called back, which is nearly always done within a reasonable time.

Some reporters are businesslike on the telephone. They have a specific query and seek a newsworthy answer. If it can be given to them, they carefully note the details and ask what kind of attribution is permitted. If such a reporter draws a blank or a "no comment," he cheerfully goes on about his business and tries other sources. By contrast, there are reporters who waste time by drawing some harassed and probably uninformed public relations man into a long, theoretical discussion about a pending news development. Because of his position, the public relations man cannot very well hang up, which he has every reason to do. When a news break does come, the time-wasting reporter is not likely to be among the first to be called.

Occasionally reporters encounter new, timid, or even stupid public relations people who do not know how to handle queries by telephone. Such people invite the reporter to try to guess what news they have by prompting him to ask all kinds of questions. These incredible guessing games are based on the regulation, current in any civilian or military organization where security is involved, that certain information cannot be disclosed unless an inquiry about it is made. Of course, the veteran public relations man merely tells the inquiring reporter the news and lets it go at that.

Handouts The "handout" is the contemptuous name bestowed by newspapers long ago on the public relations news release. Even public relations people now use it without being particularly conscious of its original meaning. Handouts that are used to publicize extravagant claims for various organizations seldom impress reporters from the news side, although they may occasionally end up as short rewrites on the women's page or some other appropriate department.

In the hands of a trained public relations specialist, however, the handout may be extremely useful to a reporter. For instance, the text of an important speech is a necessity. An abstract of it, prepared by a knowledgeable writer, can be helpful to the hurried journalist.

Another type of handout generally sought by reporters is the fact sheet, which sums up briefly the essential facts about any news subject, current or anticipated. Such fact sheets are particularly useful in writing about arrivals or departures, new buildings, and unfamiliar things such as supersonic airplanes, ballistic missiles, and atomic submarines. Chronologies, biographies, and brief descriptions of background events are also generally welcome handouts.

No reporter should adopt the attitude that a handout is an insult to his intelligence. If it is important enough to take the time of a respected public relations man, a reporter ought at least take the time to read it before discarding it.

JUNKETS, GIFTS, AND PARTIES

It may seem incredible to the young and inexperienced, but junkets and cocktail parties have few attractions for serious journalists. Such affairs are part of the job for seasoned political and diplomatic correspondents and must be endured, along with rubber chicken and marble peas on the banquet circuit.

Trick or Treat? News is generally scarce along the commercial party trail and the company is often less than brilliant. As for banquets, the meals are often cold, the drinks watery and the speeches seemingly interminable. After a few years of such public relations largesse, the average journalist would be just as happy if he were let alone to stay home one evening with his family.

Nor are gifts much of a problem to the experienced journalist who deals in the important news of the day. It is perfectly obvious to him, as it is to his editor, that a substantial gift from any news source, actual or potential, may be prejudicial to his work. Some journalists are so careful that they will even send back boxes of gift cigars or bottles of liquor at Christmas-time. Gifts of any kind from public relations sources must be regarded as suspect.

The best rule, and it is insisted upon by all responsible news media, is to permit no staff member to accept any gratuity and to pay for all necessary services including travel costs, hotels, and tickets to shows that are being reviewed. At the level of the working press, there is seldom an opportunity for a reporter to take two weeks off for an expense-paid airplane junket or something equally glamorous. He is too busy with his daily chores. But in the amusement, women's, and society departments, both the opportunities and the excuses to attend publicity parties are far greater and it sometimes becomes difficult to tell when some of these specialized journalists are working or playing.

The automobile, airplane, and motion picture industries, to name a few of the main problem areas, are adept at mixing their legitimate news announcements with friendly diversions. The same is true of the commercial side of television. But, as sometimes happens, the persuaders may have a full house for a junket and then find that they are drawing more criticism than praise for their clients. It is a touchy business, both for the journalist and those who try to win his good opinion. Certainly, on the side of the journalist, there is stricter supervision than ever before of alleged news events that coincide with junketing, gift-giving and partying.

NEWS FROM PUBLIC RELATIONS SOURCES

The news that originates from public relations sources is usually handled in conformity with general journalistic practice. The experienced public relations executive or operative knows this. Only bemused company executives really think that the material put out in their names will be used by the news media in the desired form.

Checking the Facts A reporter should first check the facts of a public relations source. It is worth a telephone call, for instance, to check the release time of a handout and to be sure that the announcement did in fact originate with the stated source. The day of the journalistic hoax is not over. Beyond that, the business of public relations being what it is, any announcement should be tested for what it does not say as well as for such news as is given. No reporter should be content with a handout if he is given the time to do a better job.

Writing from P. R. Sources   A public relations announcement generally serves the interests of the issuing agency. There is nothing wrong with this, as long as the reporter clearly understands that the interests of his organization and of the public relations agency do not necessarily coincide. For instance, it is a threadbare device to put a propaganda message in quotes, attributed to a prominent person, in the body of a press release. Some of the less imaginative publicity men also persist in needlessly attributing an announcement to two or three persons or agencies they want to publicize.

The reporter, therefore, should take stock of whatever facts he has from his public relations sources, before writing, and ask himself the simplest of all news questions: "What happened?" The lead and its documentation then may be separated from all the embroidery and put on paper. The result may not precisely please the issuing agency, but that cannot be helped. The reporter's first responsibility is to the public. It should not be assumed that a public relations announcement must always be discounted. Quite the contrary is true if it is issued from a responsible source and contains news of very real importance to the community.

Here are some examples of how a sharp-shooting public relations office and a newspaper would handle the same set of facts:

1. *A Shift In Executive Personnel*

> J. Cadwalader Winnefall, president of the J. C. Winnefall Manufacturing Company, announced today that Evans B. Arctander, its general manager, had been designated head of the company's London office.
> "We are very proud of Mr. Arctander's record with our company, built up over twenty years of brilliant service, and we are very sorry to lose him," Mr. Winnefall said. "But for some time he has expressed a desire to be relieved of some of his heavy responsibilities and given duties in which his flair for imaginative and constructive business statesmanship could be put to use. I know of no one who could better fill the important office our company has operated in London as an integral part of our corporate setup."
> In accepting the new post, Mr. Arctander wrote in a letter to Mr. Winnefall, "I am most grateful to you and to our executive board for having made the London office my next important post with our company and can assure you that I will do my utmost to serve the company there just as I have in the home office. I have looked forward for some years to a lightening of the heavy load I have been carrying."
> The new general manager will be J. Cadwalader Winnefall Jr., who has been promoted from assistant general manager. Mr. Winnefall was graduated from Princeton four years ago . . .
>
> *
>
> The J. C. Winnefall Mfg. Co. today named J. Cadwalader Winnefall Jr. as its new general manager. He replaces Evans B. Arctander, who has been shifted to the London office.

2. A Fund-raising Report

Follett Hargreaves, chairman of the trustees of Graditton College, appealed today to its 30,000 living alumni to support its $3,000,000 drive for a new athletic field house.

"Graditton deserves your loyalty and your support," he said at a report luncheon in the Graditton Faculty Club, which was attended by the chairmen of alumni committees. "I am sure that all alumni cherish Graditton traditions and want to see us flourish. To this end, the new athletic field house is a most necessary addition to our plant."

The chairman reported funds in hand and pledges of $62,000, an increase of $24,000 over last month. This brings the total contributions to date to $184,456 for the Graditton Athletic Field House Fund. Checks should be made payable to the fund. All contributions are tax deductible.

*

Graditton College announced today that $62,000 had been contributed to a fund for a new athletic field house, bringing the total to $184,456. The goal of the campaign, which began last year, is $3,000,000.

3. A Plea for Economy

Mayor Simpson Gravier called upon all department heads in his administration today to "cut to the bone" all budgetary requests for the next fiscal year.

The Mayor acted in line with his campaign pledge, during his successful election drive last year, to introduce new economies in government. "We're going to hold the line," he said. "If my department heads won't cut their requests, then I'll have to do it for them."

The Mayor has received departmental budget requests to date totalling more than $80,000,000 and has referred them to his budget director for examination. The expense budget for the current fiscal year, adopted by the outgoing administration, is $74,340,000.

*

Mayor Gravier's economy drive ran into trouble today.

The Mayor announced that his department heads already had submitted requests for more than $80,000,000 appropriations for the city budget for the next fiscal year. This is $5,700,000 more than the $74,340,000 expense budget of the previous administration, which the Mayor denounced during his campaign as "shocking" and "wasteful."

Furthermore, all requests are not in.

The Mayor, in announcing the record demands, called on his department heads to "cut to the bone" and also pledged to "hold the line." He warned that he would make some cuts if his department heads did not do so, but did not specify where the reductions would be made.

The Reporter's Duty   These contrasting examples of what message goes out from public relations sources and what the news media send back indicate the nature of the reporter's duty. He sees "managed news" every day, but he must extract from it the kernels of truth and present them to the public. Very often this is difficult, and sometimes it is impossible. With good reason, the correspondents in Saigon during the Vietnam War named their daily press briefing at the American embassy the "Five O'Clock Follies." Certainly, for a very large part of the war, the government saw it one way and the correspondents another. It therefore became the public's task to judge the result.

chapter 20

Reporting on Public Affairs

The journalist is a public figure. Whether he serves newspapers or wire services, news magazines or the electronic media, he plays an influential and sometimes decisive role in determining the shape of the news. The medium, in and of itself, cannot determine the message but the people who operate it can and often do. At news conferences, interviews, briefings, meetings, indoor conventions, and outdoor spectacles of all kinds, the mere presence of the journalist—and particularly the television cameras—can change the character of what is said and done.

Thus, whether the journalist likes it or not, he is a public servant. The forces that he represents generate influences that are, in turn, brought to bear upon him in the arena of public affairs. Among these are the manifold pressures of government, industry, labor, the arts and sciences, and sports, the persuasion of public relations operators, the alternate rivalry and camaraderie within his own profession, the sometimes unspoken but powerful directives of his own employers, and finally, his own intellectual background, his habits, and his training. Out of all this, somehow, he must be able to determine the truth and present it to the public.

These are some of the ways in which it is done.

NEWS CONFERENCES

The news conference, as it has been developed under electronic and public relations auspices, no longer resembles the free, untrammeled exchange of views between reporters and news sources that was characteristic of the old press conference. The conscious acting before the television cameras has taken the spontaneity out of major news conferences. At smaller ones, tape recorders have insensibly influenced all participants to do more talking for the record.

With the coming of electronic journalism, many politicians, conscious of the unseen audience, have shown a lamentable tendency to talk over the heads of reporters to the listening nation, or fraction thereof. As for the reporters, some of them have become mere props on the TV stage. They are now a mild, clean-faced lot in their neat shirts, freshly pressed suits, shined shoes, and fresh haircuts. But their approach is a lot less aggressive than it used to be.

The difference is readily apparent whenever reporters confront a scientist, educator, public official, or politician in an old-fashioned press conference, minus gadgets and electronic aids. Their questions are pointed, their language blunt. If the news source can answer them in the same terms, he does; if not, he sometimes talks off the record and tries to explain his position.

Such easy, personal relationships are impossible when millions are watching over TV, or a tape recorder is whirring in a corner. A good reporter becomes a good actor and elocutionist by accident, rather than by design.

News Conference Rules   Whenever a news conference is called, a few simple rules are followed by the participants. On the part of the news source, or his public relations representative, there is a tacit understanding that there is news to impart and explain that will be worth the time of the reporters who are assigned. On the part of the reporters, they agree to listen and report accurately but they make no guarantees of use in any form.

It is the responsibility of the news source to pick a time and place convenient to all, and provide a tape recorder or stenotype record. If TV and still photographers also are expected, the source must make appropriate arrangements. Where the news conference is one of a regular series—as at city hall or a state capitol—it is understood that everything is on the record and may be quoted. For other conferences, the source's public relations representative announces the ground rules and type of attribution, subject to acceptance by the reporters.

At most news conferences reporters understand that no one is to leave until the last question has been answered and that the door to the conference room will be closed. If there is to be any variation from this practice, it is generally announced before the beginning of the news conference, again subject to agreement.

For the average news conference, reporters expect that about twenty or thirty minutes will be sufficient. If it lasts much more than that, and it is apparent that either the news source or the laggard questioners are wasting time, the senior reporter will usually glance around. If he sees signs of impatience and hears whispers of, "Break it up," he will end the affair abruptly by saying, "Thank you, Mr. So-and-So." Without further ado, everybody will leave the room. To avoid such an embarrassing situation, even the most eminent news sources have learned to compress their remarks. If they have a great deal to say, they hand out a prepared statement in advance and invite questions on it.

No news source in the world, except for the President of the United States, is supposed to be able to answer without hesitation every question thrust at him. Therefore, at most news conferences, the principal source will have subordinates with him and will direct one of them or the public relations representative to answer some of the questions that are put to him. Only at the White House does a President face the press of the world and the nation with only a hasty warm-up to guide him.

The White House Influence So great is the influence of the White House on journalistic methods that the Presidential news conference procedures have been adopted as standard, not only in government but in institutional and industrial public relations as well. Here and there, a particularly influential news source may be able to insist on having questions written in advance and submitted to him. Various Secretaries General have done this at the United Nations from time to time. For the most part, whether the news source is a captain of industry or a ward heeler, the news conference operates on an ad-lib basis.

Reporters with questions ask them, first standing up or raising their hands to be recognized if there is a large crowd. The news source, or the public relations officer in charge of the conference, picks the questioners at random from all parts of the room. Some are known to the source, some are not; but whether they represent media that are friendly or hostile, he tries to answer their questions courteously if he can.

Even in the presence of TV and tape recorders, the atmosphere at a news conference is relaxed and informal. Reporters do not applaud good answers or groan at bad ones. They do not make jokes, and they refrain from making speeches in the form of questions. The questions, as a rule, are framed so as to produce newsworthy answers, not to satisfy the personal, political, or moral prejudices of the reporter or his news organization. That, by reportorial standards, is professional conduct at a news conference.

Sometimes, reporters arrange in advance to concentrate on one or two news points with which their source is familiar, and which may produce a news story. This may or may not be known to the source, but if his public relations advisers are skillful, he will be briefed before the news conference on what questions he may expect and what answers may logically be given.

The News Conference Abroad   The news conference device has become such a staple in American journalism that it has been freely exported, often with strange results. Sometimes the reporters have been used as mere dummies to give a reigning dictator an excuse to answer questions under the most favorable auspices. At other times, only one reporter—usually the senior man—has been permitted to ask questions. Frequently, the American rule against applause, seldom violated in the United States, has been dropped in favor of a cheering section of reporters for the controlled news media of a dictatorial state.

The experiences of foreign correspondents in the Soviet Union have been instructive. While Andrei Y. Vishinsky was the Soviet Foreign Minister, he seemed amused by the news conference device as he observed it at the United Nations and held one or two himself. After reading a speech to his captive audience of reporters, he would invite questions on his remarks; before answering, however, he would demand the name and organization of his questioner and liberally denounce both. Usually, the question was conveniently forgotten.

The news conference within the Soviet Union itself was even stranger. Nikita S. Khrushchev's first session with the press as Soviet Premier was in the form of answers to eight prepared questions that had been presented to him in advance in written form, plus six questions from the floor that were not materially different in substance. During the tension between the Soviet Union and Communist China in the 1960s, foreign correspondents in Moscow were informed of some Soviet moves at news conferences; moreover, the Chinese in Peking made liberal use of the format for their own purposes.

In France during the long regime of President Charles deGaulle, the news conference typically reflected the personality of *le Grand Charles*. It was not unusual to attend such a meeting and find it jammed with 500 reporters, many of them loyal Gaullists, who would frantically cheer and applaud deGaulle's every utterance. It was more like a political rally than a news conference, but it served the vanity as well as the political purposes of the aging French ruler.

Much the same kind of atmosphere enveloped the news conferences of successive Secretaries General of the United Nations—Trygve Lie, Dag Hammarskjold and U Thant. But here the rationale was different. There is, in the United Nations, an almost fanatical idealism that permeates much of the international civil servants' corps and even embraces some of the more impressionable correspondents. Consequently, sharp or hostile questioning of the Secretary General at news conferences is not considered good form by the loyalists. To show their feelings, they often burst into applause when the Secretary General or his aides get off a good answer to a probing question.

The Weakness of the News Conference   It is clear that any determined and aggressive source can dominate a news conference. This is because of the self-imposed restrictions placed on the reporters. If they get news out of the performance, that is usually because the source and the subject under discussion happen to be newsworthy. Actually very little happens at a news conference that is not anticipated in some way.

At top level, of course, it is in the public interest for public officials to make simultaneous disclosure to the nation of news that affects the American people. Thereby, the news conference fulfills a public need. But the pattern set by the Presidency, and followed so faithfully by news sources throughout the land, has resulted in a standardized format for issuance of news. Everybody is treated alike. Everybody gets the same news. Nobody gets a chance for a beat. Competition is thereby restrained.

Sometimes, the urge to make a good showing in the news media is so compelling that a newsmaker of top rank, such as a President or a leading Governor, will hold separate news conferences for television and the press. Nobody likes this, except, of course, the man in charge of the news conference and his public relations people. It is true that there is always a hard core of newspaper reporters who insist that they could get more news all by themselves if it were possible somehow to exclude television and the radio tape recorders; however, when the premise has been tested, it hasn't worked too well except for small, exclusive backgrounders. The television newsman and his all-seeing eye are not going to vanish into the woodwork merely because they are inconvenient to the print media and often are cumbersome in public places.

Yet, to any close observer of the news conference, it is all too clear that the proliferation of the news media has reduced its effectiveness and made it more of a spectacle than an exchange of news and views. The public sees the same newsfilm of a major news conference on television and hears the same words, regardless of station. The same is true of radio. As for the press, one paper tends more and more to resemble most of the others in the play, publication, and writing of the news of an important conference for reporters. While it may be argued that this demonstrates the growth of accuracy and responsibility of the news media, the net effect is the same standardized kind of performance that may be observed in a controlled press. It is only the commentator and the editorialist who generally show that the spirit of the free press is still very much alive. These, together with the investigative reporter, are the antidote to the standardized news conference.

THE INTERVIEW

The principal source of news of a highly individual nature is the interview. It may be somewhat less true now, with watchful public relations people pouring cautions into the ear of the news source, but the controls have not yet been clamped on human nature. Reporters may have to go through public relations sources to see a newsworthy individual, but the effort is often worthwhile. No rules for a standard interview have yet been made. No script for a standard story has yet been written. The interview still offers the reporter his best chance at a story all his own, just as it did in the time of Jonathan Swift.

Types of Interviews   Interviews can take unexpected turns that often yield surprising results. They are as varied and as colorful as the people who grant them, and they depend for their effect on the journalistic ability of those who conduct them. Interviews may be described as follows:

Man in the Street.   This may be anything from a political poll to a talk with neighbors about the character of a murdered woman. It is the most common, and in some ways, the most difficult type of interview for a reporter to conduct. It is also the least accurate reflection of public sentiment. Here there are no public relations barriers, as a rule—just a lot of suspicious and often uncommunicative people. The reporter's job is to win their confidence and persuade them to talk with him. Once they do, he will discover that there are no shortcuts to the process of interviewing, if one wants information. It takes time, patience, dogged persistence, and the ability to listen sympathetically to all kinds of stories.

This was the type of encounter that caused a reporter to be curious about a Polish exile who fanatically wanted the world to outlaw mass murder for racial and religious reasons. It resulted in the first of many news stories that eventually led to the adoption by the United Nations of the now-famous Convention Against Genocide and made a world figure out of its author, Dr. Raphael Lemkin.

The Casual Interview.   Such encounters often are accidental, almost purposeless. A news source and a reporter happen to meet on the street, or at a luncheon or cocktail party, or they have a casual exchange over a drink in the late afternoon. Something that is said, often without design, arouses the curiosity of the reporter. In the digging that follows a major news story may emerge.

Once it was the goal of every journalist to obtain an exclusive interview with the President of the United States because so few had been lucky enough to obtain such a story. A celebrated example was an exclusive interview with President Truman by Arthur Krock of *The New York Times,* which was arranged at a party by Fred Vinson, then the Chief Justice of the United States. However, in the Kennedy and Johnson administrations, it became the practice to welcome influential newsmen and commentators to the White House singly and in groups for whatever good it would do the President and his policies. Consequently, the Presidential interview lost some of its glamor—though none of its importance.

The Personality Interview. This type of procedure is often adopted for lengthy profiles or feature stories about people. Few newspapers are willing to give reporters the time for such efforts that are almost standard operating procedure for magazines. As a result the newspaper personality story often lacks the depth, perspective, and sheer human appeal that is characteristic of many magazine profiles.

Television rarely offers extended exposure to an individual who merely sits and talks, but when it happens the effect is often extraordinary. The Columbia Broadcasting System's annual visits with Walter Lippmann, while they lasted, were memorable because they presented the commentator without adornment and made him a wise companion to the audience for an hour. There have been other successes of this kind on TV, notably with Presidents, Cabinet officers, and leading Governors, but for the most part the personality interview has been left to the magazines, the newspapers, and the wire services.

News Interview. Such talks between reporters and their sources generally take place on short notice. They may be arranged by a reporter directly or through the source's public relations representative. Such meetings are not fishing expeditions. In nearly all cases the reporter has some important, well-defined questions that he and his news organization want the source to answer. Therefore he has not only the right but the duty to seek an interview.

Such an interview was sought by George Thiem, reporter for the Chicago *Daily News*, with Orville Hodge, the State Auditor of Illinois, after the *Daily News* had found convincing evidence that the official had defrauded the state of millions of dollars. Hodge made an unconvincing explanation. He later pleaded guilty to grand larceny and went to jail. The *Daily News* won a Pulitzer Prize.

Telephone Interview. This is an abbreviated version of the news interview. Because it is conducted by telephone by either a reporter or rewrite man, the questions must be clear and well defined. Journalists handle hundreds of such calls in a month and learn by experience how to get a corner cigar store man to tell them about a fire next door, how to persuade a reluctant district attorney to come to the telephone and answer a question about an indictment, how to get enough information for an obit out of a bereaved husband or wife, mother or father. A sympathetic telephone voice helps.

Sometimes a telephone call made from a considerable distance produces gratifying results. A New York reporter, trying to get more information on a Texas school explosion that killed many children, got the town sheriff on the phone and heard him say: "Now, you reporters got to wait. There's a man on the telephone here calling all the way from New York. . . ."

The Prepared Question.   When all else fails, reporters sometimes make up lists of questions and submit them to news sources with a polite but urgent request for a reply. Sometimes they get answers, but more often they do not. At least, the method is worth trying in a tight spot.

During the Soviet's blockade of Berlin in 1948, J. Kingsbury Smith of International News Service wrote out a list of questions in Paris and wired them to Stalin in Moscow. In his reply Stalin gave the tip that indicated the Russians knew that they had been licked by the American airlift. Negotiations began between East and West, ending with the lifting of the blockade.

Methods of Interviewing   The gentle art of interviewing is based on the principle of persuading the other fellow to do the talking. Just how to get him started is the reporter's problem.

Everyone has a different method, depending on people and circumstances. If it is at all possible, a reporter should know as much as the records and clips will tell him about his subject before the interview begins. The opening gambit, after the reporter states his business, may be a bit of light conversation, or some commonplaces about a topic of joint interest, or a casual compliment—almost anything that will establish an easy rapport. Within a very few minutes, though, the interviewer must take charge in an unobtrusive way by asking a question that is likely to touch on the principal subject of the talk.

Once the subject has been sufficiently primed with questions to keep the talk flowing at a satisfactory rate, the reporter enters the most difficult phase of the interviewing process. He must listen. He must be patient, attentive, courteous. Even if the interview has taken a turn not precisely to his liking, he must show no displeasure. If the talk is veering from the subject, he can try to change the channel with a discreet question or two. Under no circumstances can the interviewer so forget himself as to be drawn into a lively discussion in which he does most of the talking, and the subject turns into a somewhat bored listener.

People do not grant interviews to listen to reporters' opinions. For one reason or another they are willing to get themselves into print or on the air and they recognize that submission to an interview is one way of accomplishing their purpose. Yet, it is astonishing to find reporters continually trying to get interviews by declaiming for minutes at a time and giving their subjects no chance to do the talking. The observation may be elementary, but it is important. No talking reporter ever held a decent interview.

Of course, when a subject is hostile and does not want to be interviewed, there is no reason to indulge in polite persiflage. The direct approach is the only method open to the interviewer. If he is wise, he will ask a question that is calculated to give even the most hostile subject a chance to express his position in a favorable manner. Once the subject begins talking, the interviewer should relax and remember to save his toughest question for the last.

VERACITY

Dr. Alfred C. Kinsey, who interviewed thousands of men and women in connection with his sex studies, once was asked how he could tell if his subjects were lying.

"Very simple," he said with calm scientific assurance. "I look them right in the eye. I lean forward. I ask questions rapidly, one right after the other. I keep staring them in the eye. Naturally, if they falter, I can tell they are lying."

The reporter who was interviewing Dr. Kinsey nodded sympathetically over this expression of the master's views. A few minutes later, the distinguished scientist was somewhat startled to find the interviewer leaning forward, staring him in the eye, and asking questions rapidly.

The expert protested, "Now look here, that isn't fair. I just don't like what you're doing."

Most experienced reporters have learned that it does not pay to stare their subjects out of countenance. They become just as annoyed as Dr. Kinsey did, when his own methods were turned on him.

The point is that there is no easy way of testing a subject's veracity. If a reporter thinks he is being lied to, his only recourse is to check the statements that have been made to him in the interview. Subjects who are willing to lie in an interview are usually pretty accomplished, and cannot be upset by stares, grimaces, or even outright challenges.

Thirty or forty years ago, when psychology was just a word in the average newsroom, sensation-minded city editors were addicted to notions that liars could not look a reporter in the eye, people with secrets could not keep their fingers from their mouths, and criminal types had facial features that betrayed their terrible inner natures. These beliefs die hard, particularly among amateur reporters. Just as the Lombroso theory about criminal types has long ago been disproved, the act of watching subjects' eyes and fingers really proves very little. Nervous people never are easy to interview and should be put at ease, instead of being stared at. Quick, perceptive glances by a reporter, especially when the subject is off guard, are often much more revealing.

Notes in Interviews   Any seasoned interviewer must try to cultivate his memory. Except for the "puff" interview, in which a subject knows that something favorable is to be written about him, extensive note-taking makes the average person nervous and inhibits talk. The general caution against note-taking, except where it is both necessary and desirable, should be observed in most interviews. When a figure or a date or the spelling of a name must be noted, it should be done by the reporter without ostentation and with a word of explanation. But as soon as the interview is over and the reporter is by himself, the most extensive notes should be made as the basis for anything that is written.

Precautions   Inexperienced reporters are likely to assume that they are privileged characters merely because they represent a news organization. Acting on this unsound assumption, they sometimes appear unannounced for interviews with persons who do not know them. Occasionally, they also take chances with legal restrictions that are imposed on all citizens, including reporters. Such conduct can only lead to disaster.

When an eager young reporter for a great newspaper violated both health and immigration restrictions by charging out on a New York airport to interview a European diplomat who had just arrived there after a trip to Russia, Federal officials intervened. The reporter protested in vain that his newspaper had assigned him to interview the great man, that he was missing a deadline, and that this was a blow to the free press. The officials led him off and questioned him until they were satisfied his story was true, inoculated him, and let him go. The interview did him no good.

Another overanxious young reporter once rushed up to Ambassador Henry Cabot Lodge at the United Nations with hand outstretched, hoping to bluff his way into an interview. Although it was not generally known at the time, Lodge, as the American representative, was under a protective 24-hour guard because of threats that had been made against his life by Puerto Rican nationalists. Two Secret Service agents closed in on the young reporter before he could touch the surprised Lodge, roughed him up a bit, and hustled him off for questioning. He was released later with official apologies, but no interview.

Regardless of what method a reporter chooses to use to conduct an interview, the first step should always be to identify himself, and his news organization and state his business briefly. Surprises, insults, and arrogance on the part of a reporter usually lead him to grief. Thoughtlessness can be excused in the young, but there can be no excuse for an experienced reporter who tells a respected citizen after an interview, "You have been wasting my time."

CONVENTIONS AND CROWDS

When a reporter is assigned to cover a meeting or a convention, he usually begins by visiting the official, publicist, or agency handling the arrangements. If the public relations people are experienced and knowledgeable, the reporter is in luck. He merely picks up all available mimeographed material, including the program, schedules, advance copies of speeches, biographies, and historical notes and retires to a corner to do his homework. If nothing has been done in advance, and the official in charge is a harassed woman secretary, the reporter may find in effect that he is doing the publicity work as well as his own job unless he is careful.

Procedure Whether or not he has the benefit of sound public relations preparation, the reporter's first writing job is bound to be an advance if the meeting or convention is of sufficient consequence. A brief conversation with the official in charge, plus the reading of advance publicity material, usually is enough for the initial story. If the reporter has to scratch for his own details, he will find the going hard. He will have to locate each speaker and ask for an advance text, or at least an abstract, if there is one.

In the case of a night meeting, or a luncheon, where there is only one featured speaker, the coverage is fairly easy. Following the technique already outlined for the writing of advances, the reporter produces a story based on advance textual material. He then checks on delivery, telephones whatever changes are necessary, and gets his good-night from the desk.

Where a convention lasts several days, a series of advances must be prepared to cover the speech making. In addition, delegates of prominence must be interviewed, others must be checked as feature story possibilities, principals must be lined up for photographs, and off-the-floor private meetings must be watched for surprise news breaks.

Television has introduced an entirely new set of techniques to the coverage of important meetings, both indoors and outdoors. The television newsman, like the newspaper reporter, can do far better work if he is given sufficient time in advance to make suitable arrangements for his coverage. The business of arranging to have key events and key people visible to the camera, with proper lighting and under favorable circumstances, often requires both persuasion and ingenuity. It cannot be done in ten seconds, like a newspaper reporter's curbstone interview. With the introduction of better film and smaller cameras, television is far more mobile than it used to be but the electronic newsman still cannot get into places as quickly as a man with a notebook and pencil.

Perhaps the most dramatic change in coverage has come at the national political conventions where Presidential candidates are nominated. The urge for exposure to national television made a shambles out of the

1960 and 1964 conventions, and threw the 1968 Democratic National Convention into turmoil. Both political and journalistic leaders agree that the domination of so important a national function by the red eye of the television camera is neither desirable nor healthy.

Elsewhere, television has given the public access to events that once were almost ignored by the casual reader, and that is all to the good. But it has placed a heavy burden on the television newsman who has to make the arrangements for coverage. He has all the responsibilities of the reporter—and then some.

Coverage   The reporter for a newspaper, wire service, or magazine, who goes to one meeting, can make arrangements with the publicity people for coverage of other sessions. Or, if the convention is a big one attracting out-of-town coverage, he usually can get a noncompeting reporter from another city to help him check on the delivery of speeches. Generally, such options aren't open to a single television crew covering a major meeting; either they guess right on the big event of the day and are present at it, or they have little to show for their work except frustration.

Reporters who handle conventions learn quickly that there are special advantages in working with competent public relations staffs. The press room set up by the public relations people, for instance, generally includes free typewriters, telephone service, and free food. It was not always so. Before the development of public relations press services, reporters had to beg a typewriter from Western Union or bring their own. They also paid for their own phone calls and food and occasionally had to debate their expense accounts with skeptical editorial auditors.

Life at meetings and conventions is generally much easier today.

The P. R. Side   What do public relations people expect in return? Usually, only fair treatment. Obviously they cannot hope to influence the kind of stories that go out, and no wise publicist ever tries to do so directly. However, it is only natural that a newsworthy convention should attract a certain amount of favorable public notice to the sponsoring organization. If there are some unfavorable stories also, and occasionally they crop up, reporters are not obliged to give their hosts special consideration. The normal practice of using both sides of the story applies, and the public relations people are bound to be asked to state their organization's position.

Conventions are popular in America. In this latter half of the twentieth century, most citizens belong to at least one organization, and many are members of several. Committee meetings, luncheons, dinners, and discussion groups are part of a way of life. Much of this material must be covered by general assignment reporters who have no specialized backgrounds. On such matters as education, science, religion, and military affairs, to name only a few, the specialized reporters are coming into their own.

The general complaint against conventions is that they are dull and repetitious. They need not be. A little drive by reporters, a spark of imagination, a bit of encouragement by an editor rather than the usual air of resignation can do wonders to revive interest in convention news. Not every reporter can cover the annual "Miss America" competition at Atlantic City. Nor can he look forward to coping with the tremendous surge of news from committee room and platform at the quadrennial Republican and Democratic National Conventions. If he is diligent and watchful of detail, he can help his news organization and himself by snapping the deadly routine that binds so much news of local conventions today.

CROWDS AND CROWD FIGURES

At conventions and parades, political meetings and athletic events, street demonstrations and outdoor displays, attendance figures often are bothersome to reporters. It used to be sufficient to get a figure from the police officer in charge, check it with the official or publicist handling arrangements and include it prominently in the story. The public today is a great deal more critical than it used to be, and modern reporters are not as easily satisfied.

The Old Way   On a steaming hot Sunday morning in mid-summer years ago, solemn young reporters would follow an elderly official of the Coney Island Chamber of Commerce to the roof of the Half-Moon Hotel in Brooklyn. He would gaze at the crowded beaches for a few minutes and then announce with great deliberation, "Gentlemen, there are 1,000,000 people at Coney Island today." The reporters dutifully noted the figure, used it in their stories, and the headlines on Monday morning recorded the event: "Million Bathe At Coney Island."

It was taken for granted that a million New Yorkers could crowd Times Square, that 4 or 5 million would witness a St. Patrick's Day Parade up Fifth Avenue and that as many or more could crowd lower Broadway to shower ticker tape on such heroes and heroines as Charles A. Lindbergh, Gertrude Ederle, and Admiral Richard Evelyn Byrd. In other cities and towns, the same casual treatment for crowd figures was often observed and nobody bothered to count. The police said so. That was enough.

The high point of this somewhat poetic way of handling the news came when General Douglas MacArthur paraded through New York City in 1951 after being recalled from his Korean command by President Truman. In answer to the demands of reporters for an official crowd figure, a bemused Police Commissioner announced that 8,000,000 people had seen MacArthur. An enthusiastic New York newspaper promptly bannered the figure across eight columns, overlooking the slight detail that this was larger than the population of the city.

When there was a dispute between the Rev. Dr. Billy Graham and New York police over the number of people who filled the Times Square area to hear him, reporters made their own calculations and used their figures with those of Dr. Graham and the police. The same procedure is generally followed at events that are not covered by television, where the viewer usually can see for himself how big the crowds are. Yet, even here, there are limitations. As late as the latter 1960s, at least one major network with an exclusive contract to televise professional baseball games would refuse to show scanty crowds in a New York stadium—the height of absurdity.

The New Way   Even with television, therefore, it becomes necessary to arrive at some reasonable crowd figure when the statistic is an important part of the story. Any newsman can make his own calculation with little trouble.

In arenas or stadia, such totals are easy to obtain. For instance, for meetings in places like New York's newest Madison Square Garden or the Coliseum, or San Francisco's Cow Palace, the total capacity is known. The number of people in each section also is known, so that each empty section can be subtracted from the capacity figure for a reasonably accurate total attendance. There is no need to rush up to an uninformed police official and take his uninformed guess, merely because he is a policeman. Usually, he knows less than the reporter.

For a parade, the calculation is somewhat more complicated. The number of blocks along the line of march is known, and the average block length can be calculated. By taking samplings of the number of people per 100 feet along the line of march, an average density figure may be obtained. Simple multiplication will then produce a reasonably accurate crowd figure. Similarly, the dimensions of any large and well-known area in a city may be obtained (Times Square in New York, Trafalgar Square in London, Red Square in Moscow) and the crowd density may be observed, thus providing the main figures for a simple calculation. In important cases, a tabulating machine may be used. There is no reason for guesswork in arriving at crowd totals in an age in which so many electronic tabulating devices are available.

The mythology of crowd reporting has been dispelled. It has been found that Times Square, at best, can hold about 250,000 people. About the same number can line lower Broadway for a ticker-tape parade. As for the millions who supposedly jam the great squares and plazas of foreign cities, that myth also has been shattered, as has the old reliance on police as the all-knowing arbiter of attendance at public events. And a good thing, too.

chapter 21

The Press and the Law

A war veteran captured a purse snatcher in a street chase. In writing the story a reporter confused the two and mistakenly identified the war veteran as the thief. The veteran complained he had been libeled, and the newspaper, rather than go to trial, settled the case for $10,000 out of court.

A businessman, accused by a newspaper of "robber baron" tactics, filed suit for libel but later agreed to a settlement out of court. The newspaper contributed $25,000 to his favorite charity.

A writer, after a series of bitter attacks on his personal life by a newspaper columnist, sued for libel and was awarded $75,000 damages by court action.

An auto repairman, accused in a TV program of being part of an illegal car-towing operation, collected $40,000 from the station through a jury verdict after he was exonerated from connection with the racket.

These are illustrations, chosen at random, of the manner in which the law of libel operates. No newspaper, magazine, or wire service can avoid suit by claiming that an honest error was made, or that it merely reported what somebody else had said, if these or other actions make it liable. Moreover, even if the framers of the Constitution did not dream of broadcast journalism, it would be foolhardy for the electronic media to assume that the courts are likely to give them gentler treatment than the press. Because of the vast numbers of people within reach of radio and television, and because a record is available of almost anything that is broadcast whether it is read from a script or ad-libbed, the electronic media generally proceed on the basis that they are governed by the same considerations under the libel law as print journalism.

It is therefore of basic importance for the professional journalist in all media to know the principles of the libel law and act in good faith under its tenets.

FREEDOM—AND RESPONSIBILITY

The freedom of the press in the United States is based on the First Amendment to the Constitution:

> Congress shall make no law respecting an establishment of religion, or prohibiting the free exercise thereof; or abridging the freedom of speech, or of the press; or the right of the people peaceably to assemble, and to petition the Government for a redress of grievances.

However, as Justice Oliver Wendell Holmes pointed out, this guarantee of free speech does not permit a citizen to raise a false cry of "Fire!" in a crowded meeting hall and escape punishment. Nor may a political leader incite to riot because there is a constitutional guarantee of free assembly. No newspaper, similarly, may abuse its guarantee of freedom by sending its delivery trucks through street stop lights or refusing to pay its employees.

All news organizations, like citizens, are governed by all the applicable laws of the locality, state, and nation.

LIBEL DEFINED

There are so many variations in the libel laws of the various states, and differing court decisions within those states, that it is not easy at all times to define exactly what constitutes libel. Although many definitions exist, no definition is commonly agreed upon in the United States. In addition, circumstances, time, and geography all cause changes. It was not libelous a quarter-century ago to call a person a Communist in the United States, but it is today. In most Northern states, it may not be libelous to call a white man a Negro, but such an error is still actionable in some of the Southern states. As a further complication, so many libel suits are settled out of court and so little is published or broadcast about them that it becomes a chore to compile precedents in this area of the law.

General Definitions   The following definition has been used in the Columbia Graduate School of Journalism (and its undergraduate predecessor) for more than 50 years as a statement of general purpose by which a libelous publication may be recognized:[1]

> Libel is defamation expressed in writing, printing or other visible form. . . .
> "Any printed or written words are defamatory which impute to the plaintiff that he has been guilty of any crime, fraud, dishonesty, immorality, vice or dishonorable conduct, or has been accused or suspected of any such misconduct; or which suggest that the plaintiff is suffering from any infectious disorder; or which have a tendency to injure him in his office, profession, calling or trade. And so, too, are all words which hold the plaintiff up to contempt, hatred, scorn or ridicule, and which, by thus engendering an evil opinion of him in the minds of right-thinking men, tend to deprive him of friendly intercourse and society."—Odgers on Libel and Slander.

Thus, there is a clear distinction between libel—defamation expressed in visible form—and slander—oral defamation—which by its nature is more difficult to prove and to punish. The New York State definition of libel (Section 1340 of the New York Penal Code) is one of the broadest and most useful in the United States:

> A malicious publication by writing, printing, picture, effigy, sign or otherwise than by mere speech, which exposes any living person, or the memory of any person deceased, to hatred, contempt, ridicule or obloquy, or which causes, or tends to cause any person to be shunned or avoided, or which has a tendency to injure any person, corporation or association of persons, in his or their business or occupation, is a libel.

Gradations of Libel   In general, it should be assumed that defamation in the news media, published or broadcast, constitutes libel *per se* (libel on the face of it), although this does not necessarily mean that successful action may be brought. There are a number of complete and partial defenses against libel and many additional circumstances under which mitigation of damages may be sought.

Most suits for libel are brought as civil actions, since civil libel is an infraction against an individual, and may be punished by the award of substantial damages. Criminal libel, on the other hand, is a crime against the state and it is prosecuted by the state with punishment including both fines and prison terms in the case of individuals. In substance, there is comparatively little difference between the two by definition, except that crim-

---

[1] Colonel Henry Woodward Sackett, Harold L. Cross and E. Douglas Hamilton, *What You Should Know About the Law of Libel*, distributed by the Graduate School of Journalism, Columbia University, p. 4.

inal libel is broad enough to sustain actions that libel entire groups of people. However, these suits, like others that come under the criminal libel statutes, are comparatively rare.

In a civil suit, if a case of libel *per se* has been established and the various defenses struck down, then general or compensatory damages may be granted at the direction of the court and in accordance with the verdict. In such a case, it is not necessary for the plaintiff to prove monetary loss. If he establishes that he has been libeled without justification, that is sufficient; however, in a few celebrated cases, damages have been confined to an insulting sum, six cents. Cases in which monetary loss has been established are subject to an additional award of special damages, but judgments of this kind are not particularly common because financial losses due to libel are difficult to prove.

Much more common are punitive damages, which must be based on a finding of actual malice in connection with the libel. Actual malice may be predicated on a finding of gross negligence, or ill will, or many other errors of lesser degree. Thus, such a finding constitutes the principal danger in many types of libel suits; it is one reason for the continual insistence by editors and broadcasters on efforts by their reporters to get both sides of a story and use them with a recognizable effort to be fair. Prejudice may be deadly.

The news organization that assumes that it can disregard the laws of libel in dealing with corporations, merely because business concerns do not sue for libel as often as individuals, is also riding for a fall. Obviously, corporations can be damaged by untrue and unprivileged statements that they are violating the law or evading government regulations or cheating their customers. The frequent observation that criminal elements are investing money in legitimate business may be troublesome if a particular corporation is identified without sufficient documentation to support the charge, unless the inquiry is part of a public record.

This question of identity is paramount in examining a statement for purported libel. For, if no one is identified, then clearly no libel has been committed. Moreover, the libel must be published (or made known) to a third party in accordance with the general definitions already given before it is actionable. Finally, the publication must have occurred within the statute of limitations in that particular jurisdiction.

Danger Signals   It is safe to assume that every derogatory term at one time or another has been made the subject either of a complaint or law suit involving libel. Of all the charges that have been the subject of actions, however, the following are the least defensible:

An allegation of unchastity in a woman.

the defendant in the above instance is actually a thief and the politician a bribe-taker, if such charges are not part of an official record.

The general acceptance of truth as a complete defense has disposed of the old English common law plea in criminal libel cases, "The greater the truth, the greater the libel."

The Defense of Privilege   A fair and true report of official proceedings is termed privileged. This includes legislative, judicial, and other public or official proceedings. However, the exact type of hearing that is covered varies from state to state; consequently, no reporter should automatically assume that everything he believes to be a public proceeding is covered.

The defense of privilege in reporting is based on public policy—the right of the public to receive fair and accurate reports of the acts of its courts, legislatures, and other official bodies and governing officials.

Section 337 of the Civil Practice Act in New York contains one of the standard definitions of a privileged document:

> A civil action cannot be maintained against any person, firm or corporation, for the publication of a fair and true report of any judicial proceeding, or for any heading of the report which is a fair and true headnote of the statement published.
>
> This section does not apply to a libel contained in any other matter added by any person concerned in the publication; or in the report of anything said or done at the time and place of such a proceeding which was not a part thereof.

Thus, while New York law makes it clear that a reporter cannot report derogatory matter given to him by a legislator or prosecutor except when it is an actual part of the official record, this is not the rule in every state. In Texas and California the protection of privilege is extended to public meetings. In New Jersey, a police chief or a prosecutor or coroner may make official statements that are privileged even though they are not a part of an actual proceeding. In general, however, it is a safe rule for reporters to consider as privileged only material that is part of a trial or legislative record and not random comments of a derogatory nature that are made outside. Even here, there may be exceptions. A legislative reporter once discovered he could not get a record of a speech delivered on the floor of the legislature, so that a libel suit could not be turned aside on that ground. It required an enabling act to make available the record in question.

This points up the primary difficulty of invoking the defense of privilege in all except the clearest cases—the public hearings of Congress, the various legislatures and city and town councils, the records of public trials, and the like. In many of the states of the Union and in some areas of the

Federal government as well, the growth of the cult of secrecy has cast the greatest doubt on what constitutes a public record that is covered by the defense of privilege.

Harold L. Cross, in his book, *The People's Right to Know*, wrote:

> Subject to varying statutory phraseology and common law rules, a newspaper has the privilege (or right), absolute in some states and in others conditioned upon the absence of "actual malice," to publish a fair and true report of certain "proceedings." . . . "Legislative proceedings" and "judicial proceedings" are almost invariably the subject of such privileged reports. Many states go further and include other "proceedings."
>
> New York, for example, adds "other public and official proceedings." Oklahoma adds "any other proceeding authorized by law." Many other states adopt one or another of these statements or a substantial equivalent thereof.
>
> In ruling upon the availability of the defense of privilege based on reports of "police records," courts in the following states have recognized to varying degrees, and expressly or by necessary or reasonable implication, that "police records" are "public and official," "public official," or the substantial equivalent: Colorado, Louisiana, Missouri, New York, Oregon and Washington. Texas seems to have marched off in the opposite direction. Michigan has several decisions, the cumulative impact of which is not clear but appears to squint at the view that written records of police action are "public and official" whereas mere oral statements by peace officers to the press will not support the privilege. . . .[2]

Nor are the police blotter and other police records the only ones open to doubt. Secret proceedings of public bodies, where no records are kept, certainly are dubious supports for the defense of privilege. There is also a very large body of public record that remains secret for reasons of public policy. These include grand jury proceedings, records of juvenile and domestic relations courts in a number of states, the identities of relief clients in many states, and in Wisconsin the identity of the female in any rape case. The defense of privilege, therefore, is by no means as sweeping as that of truth although it is just as complete when it can be invoked.

The right of a Congressman to speak his mind while on the floor of the Senate or House, regardless of the truth or falsity of his attacks on a person, came to public attention forcibly during the anti-Communist attacks of the late Senator Joseph R. McCarthy. The defense of privilege in the reporting of all such material is based directly on the Constitution, Section 6, Clause 1:

> The Senators and Representatives shall receive a Compensation for

---

2 Harold L. Cross, *The People's Right to Know* (New York, Columbia University Press, 1953), pp. 115–116.

their Services, to be ascertained by Law, and paid out of the Treasury of the United States. They shall in all Cases, except Treason, Felony and Breach of the Peace, be privileged from Arrest during their Attendance at the Session of their respective Houses, and in going to and returning from the same; and for any Speech or Debate in either House, they shall not be questioned in any other Place.

As Professor Edward S. Corwin pointed out in his constitutional analysis: "The protection of this clause is not limited to words spoken in debate but is applicable to written reports, to resolutions offered, to the act of voting and to all things generally done in a session of the House by one of its members in relation to the business before it."[3]

Not even the claim of an unworthy purpose can destroy this defense. Justice Felix Frankfurter ruled in Tenney v. Brandhove in 1951: "Legislators are immune from deterrents to the uninhibited discharge of their legislative duty, not for their private indulgence but for the public good. One must not expect uncommon courage even in legislators."

This, however, does not interfere with the historic right of all citizens in any medium, whether it be a soapbox or television, to criticize their government fairly or unfairly, and regardless of the purity or impurity of their motives. The privilege won by John Peter Zenger at his criminal libel trial in 1735 remains inviolate, as long as the criticism is impersonal. The United States Supreme Court in 1964 reaffirmed that "an otherwise impersonal attack on government operations" is not a libel "of an official responsible for those operations."[4]

The point at which a public proceeding begins, particularly in a judicial matter, is of crucial importance to the defense of privilege. For instance, the swearing out of an affidavit before a justice of the peace is not usually covered by privilege, nor can a summons be accorded such protective covering except where usage is a matter of practice rather than law, as in minor traffic violations. Papers containing affidavits and complaints must be formally served, or filed, and sometimes both, before they may be quoted under the protection of privilege.

On some newspapers, particularly those of a sensational nature, it is the custom to write in a jocular and pseudo-sophisticated manner about certain types of legal actions such as matrimonials (suits for separation, divorce, or annulment). Except in New York and one or two other states, this type of writing is unlikely to be covered by the defense of privilege unless it is proved a "fair and true" report not actuated by malice. The

[3] *The Constitution of the United States, Analysis and Interpretation*, prepared by the Legislative Reference Service, Library of Congress: Edward S. Corwin, ed. (Washington, 1953), pp. 99–100.
[4] *The New York Times* vs. Sullivan (376 U. S. 254).

best assurance in all matters affecting the defense of privilege is to give both sides of the story, if it is at all possible.

The Right of Fair Comment Expressions of opinion contained in editorials, critical articles, letters to the editor, and news items of an analytical nature are covered chiefly by the defense of the right of fair comment, as applied to a libelous publication. The defense is based on public policy—the right of all persons, and publications, to comment and criticize without malicious intent the work of those who court public attention. Among those who invite such criticism, by the nature of their activities, are holders and seekers of public office, authors and playwrights, public performers—such as actors, actresses, and sports participants—and critics as well as others whose careers similarly are based on public attention.

The right of fair comment does not extend to the private life of any person but must be confined to matters of public interest or concern. These include everything from affairs of government to the endeavors of public and semipublic institutions such as colleges and hospitals as well as public entertainment and even advertisements.

While the right of fair comment is confined to expressions of opinion, it is generally true that these opinions must have some basis in fact. It would be manifestly unfair, for instance, to criticize an author for something he had not written or a public official for an ill-considered action he had never taken. Criticism that is founded on fact, therefore, is generally defensible under the right of fair comment even though it may seem poorly based, silly, and illogical, provided there is no malicious intent.

THE NEW YORK TIMES RULE

In a landmark decision in 1964, the United States Supreme Court for the first time invoked the First Amendment to provide a defense against libeling a public official. The high court held that if the criticism of the official's public conduct is not a knowing lie or a reckless disregard of the truth, he has no ground for legal complaint.

The case was that of L. B. Sullivan, commissioner of public affairs for Montgomery, Alabama, who sued *The New York Times* after an advertisement by a civil rights group in the newspaper had criticized the police. Because he headed the police force, he contended that he had been libeled even though he had not been named in the advertisement and the Alabama Supreme Court upheld a jury verdict granting him $500,000 in damages.

Although Commissioner Sullivan presented a record in which he argued that the *Times* had been guilty of malice by reason of unretracted falsehoods in the advertisement, the United States Supreme Court reversed the verdict saying:

"The constitutional guarantees require, we think, a Federal rule that prohibits a public official from recovering damages for a defamatory falsehood relating to his official conduct unless he proves that the statement was made with 'actual malice'—that is, with knowledge that it was false or with reckless disregard of whether it was false or not."[5]

Thus, it would appear that a journalist can make errors of fact in his criticism of public officials as long as he does not knowingly lie or recklessly disregard the truth. However, *The New York Times* Rule should be applied with some sense of caution as to exactly who may be considered a "public official" and what constitutes a "reckless disregard of the truth." Justice William J. Brennan Jr., in the majority opinion in the *Times* case, made no determination of either but in a subsequent case wrote that the official's position "must be one which would invite public scrutiny and discussion . . . entirely apart from the scrutiny and discussion occasioned by the particular charge in the controversy." In an authoritative commentary, Professor E. Douglas Hamilton and Robert H. Phelps have pointed out: "Since this liberal rule gives the press the power to destroy a man, it requires that newsmen exert a degree of responsibility that some have not risen to in the past."[6]

Other Defenses Other defenses against libel, less frequently used, include the publication of defamatory material in self-defense or as a reply, publication resulting from the consent of the person complaining of being libeled, the privilege of a participant in an official proceeding, and the shield of the statute of limitations (usually two years or less in the United States).

PARTIAL DEFENSES AGAINST LIBEL

There may on occasion be no complete defense against a defamatory publication. In such cases efforts are made to reduce the amount that may be returned in favor of a plaintiff by submitting partial defenses that tend to mitigate the damages. One of the principal acts available to any defendant, actual or potential, is to publish a retraction, correction, or apology in approximately the same relative position and of the same length as the libelous article. This, plus such expressions as "the alleged crime," "the suspect," "according to police," and others, serve to emphasize that an effort

---

[5] *The New York Times* vs. Sullivan (376 U. S. 254).
[6] Hamilton, E. Douglas, and Robert H. Phelps, *Libel: Risks, Rights, Responsibilities*, New York: 1966, p. 188.

was made to publish a fair and true report, without malicious intent. These expressions will not avert a finding against a defendant but they often help convince a jury that the ends of justice will be served by a finding for general damages, rather than punitive damages.

Recommendations   These nine partial defenses are recommended as among the most important:

1. That the general conduct of the plaintiff gave the defendant "probable cause" for believing the charges to be true.
2. That rumors to the same effect as the libelous publication had long been prevalent and generally believed in the community and never contradicted by the accused or his friends.
3. That the libelous article came from a press association, or was copied from another newspaper and believed to be true.
4. That the plaintiff's general character is bad.
5. That the publication was made in heat and passion, provoked by the acts of the plaintiff.
6. That the charge published had been made orally in the presence of the plaintiff before publication, and he had not denied it.
7. That the publication was made of a political antagonist in the heat of a political campaign.
8. That as soon as the defendant discovered that he was in error he published a retraction, correction or apology.
9. That the defamatory publication had reference not to the plaintiff, but to another person of a similar name, concerning whom the charges were true, and that most readers understood this other individual to be meant.[7]

Practical Defenses   Every professional journalist can safeguard his news organization and himself against libel suits by being accurate, reasonable, fair, and impartial in his coverage of the news, and careful to avoid any show of malice as construed by the courts.

It cannot be said too often that nothing must be taken for granted in the profession of journalism. It is a safe rule to leave out questionable material until it can be checked and to insist on the letter as well as the spirit of accuracy in everything that is published. The temptation is great, under the pressures of daily journalism, to leap to conclusions, to act as an advocate, to make assumptions based on previous experience, to approach a story with preconceived notions of what is likely to happen. To give way to such tendencies is to invite error, slanted copy, and libelous publications for which there is little or no defense. An open mind is the mark of the journalist; the propagandist has made up his mind in advance.

---

[7] Sackett, Cross, and Hamilton, "What You Should Know About the Law of Libel," p. 21.

The seeds of libel are sown broadcast in the news and sprout in the most unexpected places and at the least convenient times. But to anyone who has practiced journalism for many years, it is a familiar observation that successful libel suits are seldom waged over large issues where a newspaper has taken a position after long and careful study and full knowledge of the facts. Rather, it is the two-paragraph story about a street incident, a switched caption on the picture desk or in the composing room, a wrong address, a misspelled name, or any one of a thousand other commonplaces of daily journalism that give rise to the most damaging and least defensible libel suits. The journalist must be on his guard constantly to state the facts accurately, to differentiate between a person who has been arrested and one who has been held for questioning, to specify that the placing of a charge against a defendant is not an implication of guilt.

There is something more important than being first with the news. That is to get it right. Nor is safeguarding the paper against a libel suit the most compelling reason for emphasizing the care that must be taken with facts. The ultimate stake is public confidence, without which no newspaper can long exist in a democratic country.

THE RIGHT OF PRIVACY

For nearly seventy years efforts have been made by individuals unable or unwilling to sue for libel to seek relief under the doctrine of the "right of privacy." This right has developed as a common law along with an early New York statute on the subject. While legislative and judicial support therefore has developed in support of this doctrine, there is as yet no definitive body of law on the right of privacy. Nor is there uniformity of practice in the various states.

The principle of the right of privacy has been invoked for individuals mentioned in textual news, as well as for those whose pictures have been used without their permission in still photographs, movies, or TV. However, the extent of the statute remains to be tested.

The Brandeis-Warren Thesis   The first authoritative legal statement on the right of privacy was made by Louis D. Brandeis, later to become an Associate Justice of the United States Supreme Court, and S. D. Warren. Many years ago they wrote as follows:

> Instantaneous photographs and newspaper enterprise have invaded the sacred precincts of private and domestic life; and numerous mechanical devices threaten to make good the prediction that "what is whispered in the closet shall be proclaimed from the housetops." For years there has

been a feeling that the law must afford some remedy for the unauthorized circulation of portraits of private persons.

The question whether our law will recognize and protect the "right of privacy" in the circulation of portraits and in other respects must soon come before our courts for consideration. . . .

The principle which protects personal writings and other productions of the intellect or of the emotions is the right of privacy, and the law has no new principle to formulate when it extends this protection to personal appearances, sayings, acts and to personal relations, domestic and otherwise. . . .[8]

Brandeis and Warren held, however, that the right of privacy does not extend to privileged communications under the law of libel and slander, nor to publication of matter of public or general interest. They made these sweeping statements:

The right of privacy ceases with the publication of the facts by the individual, or with his consent.

The truth of the matter published does not afford a defense.

The absence of "malice" in the publisher does not afford a defense.

"The Right to Be Let Alone"   Since the Brandeis-Warren thesis first defined what has come to be known as "the right to be let alone," 35 states have recognized the right of privacy in one form or another and only four states (Nebraska, Texas, Rhode Island, and Wisconsin) have rejected it. More than 300 cases involving this issue have been reported.

As enunciated by a distinguished legal authority, Wilson W. Wyatt, these are four general situations in which damages have been granted under the law:[9]

1.   Appropriation to one's own advantage of the benefit of the name or likeness of another.

2.   Unreasonable intrusion upon the privacy or private affairs of another.

3.   Unreasonable publicity given to the private life of another, even though the facts are true.

4.   Unreasonable publicity which places another in a false light before the public.

The growth of electronic devices that may unreasonably invade the privacy of individuals, and their use by various persons, organizations, and

---

[8] S. D. Warren and L. D. Brandeis, "The Right to Privacy," 4 *Harvard Law Review* (1890), p. 193.

[9] Wilson W. Wyatt, "The Right of Privacy Doctrine," *ASNE Bulletin*, November 1967, p. 3.

public and private agencies, make the law of the right of privacy increasingly important. Just how it may be applied in the future is uncertain, but there is no doubt whatever that it poses major difficulties for all the news media.

Some Precedents   The major point of *The New York Times* Rule, making "actual malice" rather than unknowing falsehood the test for libel of a public official, has been extended into the law dealing with the right of privacy. In an important decision in 1967 (*Time* Inc. v. Hill), the United States Supreme Court held that a "newsworthy person's" right to privacy does not entitle him to collect damages for reports containing false information unless there is proof that the errors were knowingly and recklessly published. In a case that set aside a $30,000 judgment against *Life* magazine, awarded by a New York court to a family that was identified as the original of a Broadway drama about the prisoners of three escaped convicts, the high court by 5-4 ruled that rigid insistence on the right of privacy would abridge freedom of the press. Justice William J. Brennan, Jr., for the majority, wrote:

"Freedom of discussion, if it would fulfill its historic function in this nation, must embrace all issues about which information is needed or appropriate to enable the members of society to cope with the exigencies of their period."[10]

Nevertheless, so many law suits have been brought under the alleged invasion of the right to privacy that the precedents constitute a serious hazard for the practicing journalist. Just where the public interest ends and invasion of privacy begins is something that the courts must determine over a substantial period of time. Today, the prevailing sentiment in the legal profession is that legitimate public interest in a particular individual may nullify action under the laws protecting the right of privacy. Moreover, the test most commonly applied is whether a supposed invasion of privacy would be highly offensive to a reasonable man.[11] Surely, these are variables that pose many more questions for the news media than they answer.

The news media, and particularly television, have good ground to be wary of infringement on individual rights. The traditional press procedure of obtaining both sides of the story is scarcely enough; in the future, the broadcast media are well advised to obtain prior consent for the use of filmed material in sensitive areas when possible.

---

[10] *The New York Times*, January 11, 1967, pp. 14, 24. *Editor & Publisher*, January 14, 1967, p. 11.
[11] Wyatt, "The Right of Privacy Doctrine," *ASNE Bulletin*, November 1967, p. 4.

FREEDOM OF INFORMATION LAWS

There is very little about the Federal Freedom of Information law that merits rejoicing among journalists.[12] A month before it went into effect on July 4, 1967, its usefulness as a weapon for prying news out of government was considerably scaled down by the enactment of changes to make it conform to the Administrative Procedure Act.

The best thing about the FoI law, as it is known to journalism societies, is that some limited decisions by the Federal government to withhold records are reviewable by the courts. However, the burden of applying for judicial remedy is placed entirely on the news media. Thus, a newspaper or television station theoretically may go to court and try to prove that a Federal agency is violating the law by withholding information—a difficult and time-consuming process. While not many newspapers are likely to take on such a court battle, the chances for an electronic rebellion against the FCC are even more remote.

Although a few news organizations have been able to start a trickle of news running from Federal sources that formerly provided little or nothing, the FoI law generally has not turned out to be the panacea for all the ills of suppression. It has too many limitations. Nine sensitive areas of information are specifically exempted from disclosure. These include national security, foreign policy data of a security nature, secret government trade data, personnel files, and medical findings on government employees. It would seem that the State laws protecting the public "right to know" may be of more use than the Federal statute. A total of 29 States have "open meeting" laws, requiring governmental units to operate in the open with some specific exceptions, and 37 States have "open records" laws that give greater access to government data.

The Contempt Issue   More often than not, the issue—in the event of conflict—narrows down to the willingness of the journalist to risk being jailed for contempt of court in order to uphold his right to the news. From the time of John Peter Zenger, this has been the ultimate position of the journalist and more than two centuries have made little difference in it.

One famous case was that of Martin Mooney of the New York *American*, who in 1935 refused to reveal his sources to a New York County Grand Jury during a gambling inquiry and served 30 days in jail for con-

---

12 Robert O. Blanchard, "The Freedom of Information Act—Disappointment and Hope"; *Columbia Journalism Review,* Fall 1967, p. 16; see also *Editor & Publisher,* November 18, 1967, p. 9, in which Rep. Donald Rumsfeld, R.-Ill., reproached the press for an initial failure to use the Act to dig "deeper for government records."

tempt of court. In 1957, Marie Torre, a New York *Herald Tribune* columnist, served 10 days in jail rather than reveal her sources in a controversy over Judy Garland, the singer. In 1966, a 20-year-old college editor, Miss Annette Buchanan of the University of Oregon *Daily Emerald*, was fined $300 for refusing to reveal the source of her article about marijuana smoking on the campus.

The comparatively mild sentences that were handed out for contempt of court in these cases testify to the reluctance of the bench to embark on a punitive campaign against the press. For every case in which a reporter has been dragged into court and punished, there are many more who get off without even a reprimand by facing up to a difficult issue of publication, or use of material in the electronic media, with the determined support of their news organizations. It is this kind of tension that helps to guarantee respect for the rights of the free press.

chapter 22

Crime Reporting

The basic policy in the reporting of crime in the American news media should be to safeguard both the rights of free press and fair trial. One cannot exist without the other. Both are vital to the growth of a democratic society.

There have been excesses in the coverage of crime in the past; without doubt, such things will also occur in the future due to overzealousness and bad judgment on the part of journalists or law enforcement officials, sometimes both. This is a part of the price that must be paid to insure the existence of a free press.

Happily, the leaders of the news media themselves have come to see that self-restraint in the handling of crime news can be a virtue. In many cases, it helps rather than hinders the administration of justice and advances the work of the journalist. Thus, a broadly-based movement for voluntary cooperation between the press on the one hand and the bench and bar on the other has been growing in the United States in recent years. While there is always danger of news suppression in such arrangements, the voluntary agreements have not produced such a result. Instead, the areas of conflict between the news media and the processes of law enforcement have been reduced although they have, by no means, been eliminated.

While such cooperative policies must be formulated at the level of editor and publisher, they do affect the reporter and the newscaster in their day-to-day work. Consequently, today's journalist requires a nice sense of balance and a considerable amount of courage in dealing with crime news. For if he is so timid that he does not make every effort to get at the news, he is of no use to either his news organization or the public at large. But if he is so rambunctious that he rides roughshod over the basic rights of the accused, he is a burden to his newspaper, station, or network.

THE JOURNALIST'S RESPONSIBILITY

The broad coverage of law enforcement is something more than routine news gathering. Properly done, it is a public service and perhaps even a deterrent for certain types of crime in an era when the incidence of crime in general is soaring.

Purpose and Practice   This work cannot be permitted to sink into a deadening routine. Nor can the sources of the news be bottled up by a few timid, self-serving officials who fear to deal with the press. For what happens at police headquarters and in the courts is the key to much of the success or failure of the democratic system.

Because of the limitations of time and staff that impede the electronic media, forcing radio and television to concentrate in the main on headline crime, the newspaper by default remains the primary public reliance for the detailed examination of the work of police, prosecutors, and the courts. Regardless of size or standing, most American newspapers regularly cover police headquarters, the offices of the various prosecutors, and at least some of the major courts.

These communal nerve centers, together with the mayor's office, are usually the first to record spot news that will undoubtedly have an impact on the community—crime or not. A disaster, storm, floods, fires, acts of violence, robberies, captures of crime suspects, investigations in the public interest, verdicts in important criminal or civil trials—all these are a part of the proper concern of officials responsible for public safety.

The objective of the press is to report this news, not to philosophize over it. However, it is also true that more publishable local news is obtained from police, prosecutors, and courts per reporter-hour than in any other category. Since local news remains the bread and butter of the average American newspaper, thoughtful critics of the press frequently ask whether the excessive publication of crime news benefits the public or the publisher.

Because of varying circumstances, there can be no categorical answer to the question. But it can and should be examined with care by every journalist who is at all interested in the future of his profession and its position in the community.

What Price Crime News?   A few active reporters, through intensive coverage of law enforcement agencies and the courts, can develop a high percentage of crime news.

For the average newspaper, the only comparable sources of news in such volume are the wire services and the public relations material from federal and state government agencies. Not even news of local government or the schools, which may frequently be of more importance than day-to-day law enforcement, can be obtained in such volume.

It should not be assumed, however, that crime news is always easy to obtain. Many times, because of a proper concern for the results of an investigation, police secrecy is not only justifiable but mandatory. On other occasions, of course, secrecy is just a cover up to ward off too inquisitive reporters. It is obvious, therefore, that a reporter on a crime story sometimes is placed in a difficult and unfair position because he cannot properly evaluate official motives. He must be guided in such cases by his own sense of responsibility and the judgment of his superiors, if he can reach them.

In the earlier years of this century, when the metropolitan press engaged in almost fanatical headline competition for street sales, sensational newspapers fought for crime news to bolster circulation. If a reporter was assigned to cover a "classy murder" or a "big-time trial," he was the envy of most of his colleagues. "Anything goes," was, unfortunately, the rule of the day, but for the bulk of the American press that era has long since passed.

At a time when the press is very largely home-delivered and newspaper competition has ended in all but a few of the nation's major cities, ordinary crime news can scarcely be considered a prime circulation builder. Moreover, the nature of public interest in crime itself has changed. Consequently, when looters and arsonists take advantage of a riot to wreck a community, no news organization can sit idly by. When marijuana and LSD are sold to children and peddlers of heroin operate openly at times, no editor can remain silent. When the very streets of a city are unsafe because of muggers and other petty criminals, the public outcry of a newspaper becomes a hard-pressed community's reliance for help. It would, indeed, be shocking if any news organization neglected its duty to publicize such matters, regardless of the growth of critical attitudes toward the news media.

SOME LEGAL TRENDS

A powerful movement to curb the news media in the coverage of crime was set in motion by the assassination of President Kennedy in Dallas on November 22, 1963, and the subsequent murder of Lee Harvey Oswald, who was arrested for killing him. The Warren Commission pointed out that it was the clamor of newsmen to see Oswald that made it possible for Jack Ruby to murder him in full view of 50,000,000 television witnesses. Subsequently, the drive of the legal profession to restrict both crime and court coverage was bolstered by two major United States Supreme Court decisions that set sharp limits on what the police could do in interrogating prisoners.

The Escobedo Case   In a landmark decision in 1964, the Supreme Court reversed the murder conviction of Danny Escobedo, a 28-year-old Chicago laborer, because he had not been permitted to consult a lawyer before making a murder confession in 1960. The high court held that his rights had been violated because police barred him from legal counsel prior to his admission that he had been implicated in the slaying of his brother-in-law. He had served four years of a 20-year prison term.

Delivering the decision of the court's 5-4 majority, Justice Arthur J. Goldberg wrote: "A system of law enforcement which comes to depend on the confession will, in the long run, be less reliable than a system which depends on extrinsic evidence independently secured through skillful investigation. If the exercise of constitutional rights will thwart the effectiveness of a system of law enforcement, then there is something very wrong with the system.

"We hold only that when the process shifts from investigatory to accusatory—when its focus is on the accused and its purpose is to elicit a confession—our adversary system begins to operate and, under the circumstances here, the accused man must be permitted to consult his lawyer."[1]

The Miranda Case   The Escobedo Rule was extended in 1966 when the United States Supreme Court reversed the conviction of Ernesto A. Miranda, a 25-year-old mentally retarded Arizona truck driver, because he had not been warned of his right to counsel or that his statements might be used against him before he confessed to raping an 18-year-old girl. Miranda had been serving concurrent sentences of 20 to 30 years.

Holding that the Miranda case involved a violation of the self-incrimination clause of the fifth amendment to the U. S. Constitution, Chief Justice Warren wrote for the 5-4 majority: "We hold that when an individual is taken into custody or otherwise deprived of his freedom by the authorities and is subjected to questioning, the privilege against self-incrimination is jeopardized. Procedural safeguards must be employed to protect the privilege."

The decision also held that a policeman may not question a suspect when he is alone and "indicates in any way that he does not wish to be

---

[1] *The New York Times*, June 23, 1964.

interrogated." He may waive his right to remain silent and have an attorney with him, the court declared, provided the waiver is made "voluntarily, knowingly, and intelligently." But, the court continued, if he indicates in any manner "that he wishes to consult with an attorney before speaking, there can be no questioning."[2]

This, in effect, constituted a set of guidelines for the law enforcement authorities in the States similar to the 1957 Mallory Rule under which the Supreme Court barred prolonged Federal interrogation. Under Mallory, a Federal defendant upon arrest must be taken "without unnecessary delay" before the nearest U. S. Commissioner who then is charged with reminding him of his rights and providing a lawyer if the prisoner cannot afford one. The Mallory Rule also bars any admissions obtained from a Federal defendant during excessive delays in arraignment.

The Consequences   A virtual revolution in police procedures has occurred as a result of these two decisions, along with the Estes and Sheppard cases which are dealt with in a subsequent chapter. The Department of Justice, fortified by the individual actions of various State bar associations, issued a set of press-bar guidelines that counseled police, press, and officers of the court to omit references before and during trials to a defendant's prior police record, statements that a case was "open and shut," and "alleged confessions or inculpatory omissions" by an accused person.

Some of the highest State courts, notably in New Jersey, have given such orders on the backing of judicial authority. However, it is clear that while the courts can and will use their contempt power to enforce decisions against recalcitrant prosecutors and defense lawyers, their authority over police and press is on less firm ground. Thus, the thrust of the legal profession has been toward putting its own house in order and, in effect, trying to withhold news and comment from the news media in the interest of protecting the right of fair trial.

THE REARDON RULES

In this spirit, Justice Paul C. Reardon of the Supreme Judicial Court of Massachusetts and a distinguished committee of lawyers placed the authority of the American Bar Association behind a movement to insure punitive action by courts against lawyers or police who issue unauthorized information. For a time, Justice Reardon also sought to impose sanctions against the press on the same ground but was persuaded to drop the notion on constitutional grounds.

---

[2] *The New York Times*, June 14, 1966; *Time*, April 29, 1966, p. 57.

The Reardon Rules, as originally formulated, give police the authority to issue only the fact and circumstances of an arrest, the text of the charge, the identity of the arresting officers, the length of the inquiry, and the seizure of evidence, if any. The regulations also call on all parties to withhold the following from the time of the arrest of a suspect until the conclusion of his trial:

1. Any discussion of the strength of the evidence, pro or con, and the possibility of a plea of guilty by the defendant.
2. A defendant's admissions or confession.
3. His previous record, if any.
4. Identities of prospective witnesses.
5. The refusal of a defendant to take various tests, including lie detector tests, or the outcome of tests that he did take.

Necessarily, this has placed a heavy burden on the news media, and the press in particular because its reports are more detailed than others. Some newspapers have challenged the courts' authority to invoke the Reardon Rules. In any case, it is evident that no court or bar association agreement can prevent a newspaper from using material about a defendant from its own library of clippings, its morgue, including his prior criminal record if it is obtained from such a source. Nor can publication of this and other material be forbidden on pain of punishment. Not every responsible newspaper is convinced that the public interest will be served best by withholding the background of a notorious hoodlum who is arrested for his alleged part in a murder. The upshot has been that some judges have declared mistrials where they believe the news media in their area have published prejudicial material that either could or actually did reach jurors or prospective jurors.

The police, caught between the argument of the press against bench and bar, have become a great deal more circumspect in their conduct. The old alliance between the law enforcement authorities and the crime reporters has been cracked. In many cases, reporters now find that the police simply will not talk and that, very often, they may even refuse to question a suspect until he is brought into open court.

Of course, such extreme methods sometimes are resorted to for a purpose. A high police official may have the mistaken notion that he can stimulate a public protest in the press against the libertarian principles of the Supreme Court. While a few of the more conservative newspapers have set off on this type of campaign, it has not accomplished much. The more practical-minded newspapers, with the cooperation of the other news media, have generally sought to draft voluntary guidelines for the conduct of police and court publicity in important cases.

A Model Agreement   The Washington State agreement on guidelines between press and bar is widely regarded as a practical model.[3] What it does, in effect, is to warn that precautions should be taken against publication before trial of certain categories of prejudicial information. Among the most important of these are opinions as to the defendant's guilt or innocence, his character, his admissions, alibis or confessions, the credibility of anticipated witnesses, argument over the evidence, or a defendant's prior criminal record.

This represents a concession by the bar in its hitherto inflexible stand against the publication of such data. A request to use reasonable precaution is quite a step down from a legal ban that could lead to punitive sanctions. As for the press, the Washington plan specifies that information may be published on the identity of a defendant and his biographical background with no restraints except to conform to standards of good taste, accuracy, and good judgment, on the text of the charge, the identity of the complainant, the investigating agency, the length of the inquiry, and the immediate circumstances of the arrest.

It is conceivable that the legal pendulum, having gone so far toward the libertarian concept of law enforcement, may in time swing back. A series of 5–4 Supreme Court decisions do not mean that the course of the law has been irrevocably set. Widespread civil disorder could bring about a change toward a more conservative philosophy of government and greater power for law enforcement authorities. But whether or not such changes occur, there is no likelihood that the conduct of the press will revert to the low standards of the early part of this century, when a crime reporter could do just about what he wished. The yield of cooperative action between press and bar has been impressive enough to encourage both professions to continue their voluntary consultations.

Certainly, in such cases as those involving the assassinations of the Rev. Martin Luther King, Jr. and Senator Robert F. Kennedy, the cause of justice would not have been served if either investigations or court procedures had been turned into a circus. The restraint of the news media, at least initially, in no way interfered with coverage and it served the public interest.

CRIME REPORTERS

Crime reporters are men of action. Yet most of them spend their days—or nights—covering the patient and unspectacular routine of police work. Heroics are not for them. Nor are they singled out for special attention.

---

[3] The full text is given in Appendix IV, 4.

They do the job to which they are assigned—asking questions, checking facts, refusing to be rebuffed by dogmatic officials.

The Young Reporter   Of all reporters assigned to particular beats, those covering the police news and the courts are most likely to stick together. The solid front they present to the outsider gives way when a young reporter is assigned to their beat. Unlike the lordly political and diplomatic reporters on the national and international levels, the local crime reporter often tries to make life easier for the beginner.

When John Steinbeck began work as a reporter for the New York *American*, he was assigned to the Federal Court in the old Park Row Post Office building. He has described the kindness he received from the veterans as follows:[4]

> It was a specialist's job. Some of the men there had been on that beat for many years and I knew nothing about courts and didn't learn easily. I wonder if I could ever be as kind to a young punk as those men in the reporters' room at the Park Row Post Office were to me.
>
> They pretended that I knew what I was doing, and they did their best to teach me in a roundabout way. I learned to play bridge and where to look for suits and scandals. They informed me which judges were pushovers for publicity and several times they covered for me when I didn't show up. You can't repay that kind of thing.

Although some police and court reporters of today are better educated than the ones Steinbeck knew, it is a mistake to think of them as a particular type. They are all ages and come from every walk of life. In a single police reporters' room there may be a clever veteran reporter of thirty years' experience but only a grammar school education, a specialist in criminology from Harvard, a French count with a craving for journalistic action, and a graduate of Columbia with a master's degree in journalism. It is not altogether strange, for that matter, to find young women covering police news or the courts, and doing a fine job of it.

The Status of Crime Reporters   To those who have little knowledge or appreciation of journalism, crime reporters are often looked upon as representatives of the lower orders.

Nothing could be more ridiculous, in view of the outstanding records of crime reporters for some of the nation's leading newspapers, which do not ordinarily feature crime news. For example, it was a reporter for the Kansas City *Star*, A. B. Macdonald, who solved the murder of a Texas

---

[4] John Steinbeck, *"Making of a New Yorker,"* The New York Times Magazine, February 1, 1953.

woman and her son by forcing a confession from her lawyer husband. It was a reporter for *The New York Times*, Meyer Berger, who won a Pulitzer Prize for his eight-column account of the mass murders by Howard B. Unruh in East Camden, N. J. Another graduate of this tough school is Joseph Alsop, a columnist, who got his start doing little character sketches of witnesses at the trial of Bruno Richard Hauptmann for the murder of the Lindbergh baby.

Crime reporters have achieved prison reform in New Jersey, the impeachment of a Federal judge in Illinois, the imprisonment of a Federal judge in New York, the exposure of tax frauds in the Bureau of Internal Revenue, of a veterans' land grant scandal in Texas, and of many other instances of wrongdoing.

These are the results of hard work on extraordinary assignments, not the usual police-reporting routine. That still must be done, day by day, and crime reporters must handle the assignment.

SOURCES OF CRIME NEWS

It is always a shock to a young reporter when he discovers that he has no inherent right to examine police records at will, or go swaggering through a police station to talk with prisoners. These images, fostered by script writers who never covered a one-alarm fire, are shattered by a single day's experience on a police beat.

Availability of Records   When Stephen J. Roth was Attorney General of Michigan, he told editors of the state[5] during a discussion of the availability of police records:

> I think that the less concern you have with what you're entitled to under the law, the better off you're going to be. . . . I think your reporters particularly get a lot more cooperation than the law requires the public officials to give them in the matters of automobile accidents, arrests, criminal prosecutions, etc.

Dean Harold L. Cross agreed with this position as a broad principle, while pointing out that sufficient access to records was obtainable in many communities either by law or by custom. His advice to reporters was as follows:[6]

---

[5] Michigan Press Association, Inc. *Editorial Bulletin* No. 9, June 22, 1950, reporting talk by Attorney General Stephen J. Roth at conference May 2–3, 1950.
[6] Harold L. Cross, *The People's Right to Know* (New York, Columbia University Press, 1953), pp. 95–96.

. . . Newspapers get more and better access to, and information concerning, "police records" by voluntary processes, personal contacts, reportorial resourcefulness, desire of police officials for favorable publicity, recognition of the public interest by police officials and their dislike for unfavorable publicity than they could possibly get by compulsory processes under the present state of the law.

To illustrate the crazy-quilt of regulations, the New York City Charter expressly exempts records of the Police Department from examination as public records without the consent of the Police Commissioner; but elsewhere within the same state contrary practices are the rule. At the other extreme, Louisiana requires police records to be open for inspection by law.

The reporter, therefore, must conduct himself in accordance with the situation. To any veteran covering police stations or the courts, this is done through the judicious cultivation of various police officials. It is only a rank amateur who barges into a station house and demands access to the police blotter, which is the surest way of being thrown out of the place. The only recourse for the beginner on the police beat is to work with the veterans, if they will permit it, until he is sufficiently well known to have his own sources; or, if his newspaper is sufficiently prominent, to trade on its reputation.

Police Slips   Most police departments have a routine method for informing the press of incidents that are telephoned or telegraphed to headquarters from outlying precincts. These are usually called "police slips"—written by hand in small organizations and distributed by teletype in metropolitan or interstate organizations.

Police slips are made available to reporters in a central spot, but nobody informs them that something newsworthy is contained in them. Often, because of the exigencies of policework, the slip only suggests the possibility of a major story.

When a B-25 Army bomber crashed into the 79th floor of the Empire State Building in New York City on July 28, 1945, killing 14 persons, the police slip read, "Smoke observed on upper floor of Empire State Building." When Puerto Rican Nationalists shot up the House of Representatives on March 1, 1954, the first word from the police was that shots were heard in or near the Capitol. After shots were fired at President Kennedy's automobile in Dallas on Nov. 22, 1963, some time before it was learned that he had been assassinated, the police radio in the Texas city carried a warning that something was wrong in the Kennedy motorcade. The finding of bodies, reporting of fires and auto accidents, and even the planting of bombs may be covered similarly in a few words that would not be at all suggestive to the untrained person.

A reporter handling a police slip, therefore, is always in the position of checking, verifying, notifying his office, and often going to the scene of a story that promptly washes out. He has many more false alarms than the average fire department, but he cannot afford to disregard even the most routine police slip.

Radio and Teletype   The police radio system, the fire department's alarms, and the interstate police teletypes are all valuable to the crime reporter who is constantly on the alert for the off-beat story, the "different" story, the big story. Few police departments officially welcome reporters to their communications or operations rooms, but as a practical matter they do have access in most places. A good reporter can be of inestimable assistance to the police, but he can also be mighty troublesome if he wants to be. It is through the communications and operations bureaus or branches that the reporter gets his best initial results.

If he has friends in the police department, he can often persuade them to get information from outlying precincts over the telephone. If no official sources are available, he can always call himself and hope that the precinct will be cooperative. Sometimes they are, but frequently on an investigation the reporter must get his news at the scene, no matter how long it may take him to arrive there. Naturally, he can leave his beat uncovered only with his desk's consent.

Dealing with the Police   The first things any reporter must know about the police department are its organization, its regulations, its relationship to other city departments, and its point of contact with allied peace-keeping organizations in the state and federal government.

Whether the department is large or small, one official is usually designated to handle the news media. Sometimes it is the chief or commissioner himself, but more often it is a former newspaperman who is known as a secretary, an executive assistant, or some other title covering his public relations role. Such an official can be helpful, if he is permitted to be, but he also is likely by the nature of his office to withhold more news than he issues.

It is necessary for a reporter to protect himself by maintaining good relationships with other officials who will, for a variety of motives, give him information or check facts. The more a reporter knows about a police organization, the easier it will be for him to acquire such valuable sources.

Mere procedural knowledge of police routine is never enough. A reporter must also know the substance of criminal law, which varies by terminology and statute in most states, so that he can properly describe police activity. For instance, what constitutes a crime in one state may not be construed as law-breaking in another. A felony, which is a serious offense, may cover certain types of crimes in one state but the same crimes may be called misdemeanors, relatively minor offenses, in another state.

Most professional police and court reporters have an excellent practical knowledge of the law, and some even have law degrees. It is virtually impossible to cover police and court news intelligently without acquiring a basic legal background.

THE CRIME STORY

The crime story with universal appeal is likely to attract wide attention, regardless of the prominence of persons involved and their situation in life. The marital tragedy, the family feud, the kidnaping of children, the search for missing girls, and so many other familiar situations therefore receive daily coverage in large or small degree.

Like all other news, there are rough measurements for the importance of crime material. A crime involving persons of prominence, social position, or notoriety is bound to receive attention. Events in better sections of the city are likely to draw reporters to the scene. Spectacular murders, shootings, stabbings, fist fights, or suicides, large monetary losses in robberies or swindles involving property of value all fit into the Page 1 news patterns. So do the tricky crimes and their clever solutions, the eternal build up of mystery and suspense, the drama of unusual arrests, the questioning of prisoners, confrontations, and confessions.

The search for the unusual and the unexpected, which is not often rewarded, has in effect created its own type of cliché news situations. These are the familiar stories of the unexpected in crime.

It is an unusual boy slayer who does not turn out to have attended Sunday school at some time in his life, or sung in a choir, or been a member of a youth organization for model children. The girl who becomes involved in a crime, too, has her defenders among those reporters who discover that she liked home life, was a good cook, and sang hymns until she took up with bad companions. The bandit who snatches $100 in bills from a grocery store but overlooks $1,000 hidden under the cash register is another old acquaintance in the news columns, as is the taxi driver who returns $5,000 in bills to a bemused passenger and receives a ten-cent tip. Thieves who are polite to their victims, instead of rude safe crackers who are still called by the names of "Raffles" or "Jimmy Valentine" in a society that has forgotten both, elderly men who teach children to steal, and thereupon are known as "Fagins"—all these and many others no longer convey any feeling of shock or surprise.

In fact, the very frequency with which the "familiar unexpected" is exploited dulls the attention of the public for the significant case of a well-trained boy who somehow went wrong or the girl who merits greater attention than a cursory headline in one edition as a gangster's choir-singer bride.

Many of the symbol clusters around the crime story deserve to be given painstaking review by the American press.

The Drama of the Usual   If the custom of featuring the supposedly unusual in crime news is worth re-examination, then surely it is also worthwhile to examine the drama of the usual for its newsworthy aspects.

The looting of small homes, the snatching of women's pocketbooks, the rumbles (street fights) between gangs of juvenile delinquents, and the small-time offenses of prostitution and gambling and the petty racketeering that flows from them are the commonplaces of crime in American life. Taken individually, they merit but a few lines, if anything at all, in the average paper. It is the usual run of crime material—routine—uninteresting by old-fashioned editorial standards.

Yet these seemingly small events touch the lives of more people than headline crimes. In many communities, home robberies have outstripped the ability of the police to cope with them and have caused a steep rise in insurance rates. In the nation's largest cities the purse-snatcher and sneak thief are so common that women fear to walk alone in certain neighborhoods. The "rumble" that is ignored by today's news media as the outburst of ill-trained and irresponsible street children becomes tomorrow's gang war. As for the street walker and the policy slip salesman, the narcotic addict and the neighborhood strong-arm man, they make little news by themselves, but in the mass they constitute a major social problem for the nation.

Except for an occasional public service campaign, the issues of better protection for the home, juvenile delinquency, and all the broad problems rooted in crime prevention receive less attention than the stories of the commission, detection, and punishment of crime. Except when there is a spectacular crime in these areas, and editorials demand to know why it occurred, crime prevention is treated as a rather dull but necessary aspect of the news. There is no doubt that it is more difficult to gather such news and that it takes more ingenuity and imagination to develop such stories. It is not in the pattern of the crime story as we know it. Hamlet never consulted a psychiatrist. Sherlock Holmes was not a probation officer.

Crime reporting is likely to be broadened considerably in its scope and influence as the public accepts some of the more fundamental developments of modern criminology.

GUIDE TO CRIME REPORTING

There is no glamor to crime reporting today. It goes far beyond the old-time gangland killings and murders of passion, which were the stock in trade of the sensational press in the Jazz Age. The purse snatcher and the narcotics peddler are not calculated to attract much attention in the news as individuals. But when organized crime is strong enough to challenge the business community in some cities and reckless hoodlums are able to touch off rioting in the ghettos of northern cities, then the news media can scarcely serve the public by merely printing the news. Today's crime reporter often has to go behind the news to investigate, to explain, and sometimes even to recommend.

The following safeguards often are helpful to both reporters and editors concerned with the news of the administration of justice:

Arrests It is a serious matter to report that a person has been placed under arrest. When such a report is made, the exact charge against the arrested person should be given and it should be documented by either a record or attribution to a responsible official. If such documentation cannot be obtained, the reporter had better check his facts. The person in question may not have been under arrest at all. There are euphemisms in police work such as holding someone for questioning, asking witnesses to appear voluntarily to cooperate with an investigation, and similar statements which indicate the person is being detained, but may or may not be subject to arrest. In many states an arrest is not formally accomplished until a prisoner is booked. The news, in any case, must be handled with care.

Accusations It is commonly written that someone is being sought for robbery, suspected of arson, or tried for murder. This is journalistic shorthand, which has gained acceptance through usage, but it is neither precise nor correct.

Persons are sought in connection with a robbery, unless a charge has actually been made, in which case they are charged with robbery. When a person is under suspicion, he is not necessarily going to be charged with a crime, and it is generally not privileged matter to indicate that suspicion is attached to any individual by name. Where the police suspect someone, but lack proof, that person may be held as a material witness—which is far different from being accused of a crime. Therefore, cases of suspicion are not usually given too extensive and detailed news treatment if no privileged material is available for use. The practice of reporting that a defendant is being *tried for murder*, while widely used, is obviously prejudicial and could be more accurately, if less dramatically, stated, as "being tried on a charge of murder," or "on a murder indictment."

Confessions The use of the word *confession* to describe statements made by a person to the police or to prosecuting authorities is dangerous when it is not a matter of public record. The fact that a police chief or a prosecutor has claimed to have a confession, except in open court, may be used only at the risk of the reporter and his organization. The records are full of supposed confessions that backfired later for a variety of reasons and of persons who admitted crimes they could not possibly have committed. Unless and until it is established in fact that a person has confessed, approved procedure for reporters is to use such terms as "statement," "admission," "description," or "explanation." They convey the shade of meaning that is warranted by circumstances and do not subject the reporter or his organization to unnecessary risk.

The reporter must always remember that under the law a person is presumed to be innocent until he has been found guilty.

Investigations   Certain stages of police investigations require secrecy in the public interest. This also pertains to some of the aspects of prosecutions and trials. The secrecy of the grand jury room and of a trial jury's deliberations are soundly based on public policy. Except under the most extraordinary circumstances, no reporter and no news organization have any right to interfere and few have ever attempted to do so.

Often, during the course of investigations, reporters are confined to listing the identities of witnesses who have entered or left a police station or grand jury room, if the names can be obtained. They have every right to try to interview such witnesses, if the circumstances are favorable, before and after appearances of this kind. But it is the business of the prosecution, defense lawyers, and the witnesses themselves to decide whether or not they should talk.

For this reason investigations, in their earliest stages, are likely to produce a crop of speculative reports without much basis in fact unless editors insist on sounder reporting. A clever, publicity-conscious investigator can often hopelessly prejudice the position of hostile witnesses and others who oppose him if the news media do not hold rigidly to their code of presenting both sides of the story. That is why no claim by any investigator, regardless of his position and personal prestige, should be accepted and published at face value without some effort by a reporter to determine the soundness of the statements that have been issued.

Cases of Violent Death   Nowhere is there a greater tendency to jump to conclusions in the field of crime reporting than in the initial reporting of a violent death. The amateur reporter is invariably in a hurry to characterize the event as a suicide or murder when it may be an accidental death. It is advisable, therefore, to report only what is known and avoid speculation in the absence of an official verdict by a coroner, medical examiner, or some other competent authority.

An apparent suicide is one of the most difficult crime stories to handle.

If the police report that a man was found shot to death with a bullet in his right temple and a revolver in or near his right hand, the story should be written in exactly that way. In the case of a police finding that someone "jumped or fell" to his death, the reporter should not go beyond the facts but use that phrase in his copy. If a woman is found dead in bed with an empty bottle labeled sleeping tablets beside her, no conclusions should be drawn.

In all such cases, it is proper to note any other circumstances that have a bearing on the story, particularly as to whether notes were left. It may not always be proper to publish such notes, even if the text is made available by the police, unless the material is privileged. Moreover, unless there is a formal announcement of suicide by a responsible authority, the news account can do no more than to note that an investigation is being made to determine whether the death was a suicide.

When violent deaths occur without any indication as to whether they may be accidents, suicides, murders, or combinations of all three, the story should report the identities of the victims and the manner of their deaths. It is usually fruitless to try to unravel such a mystery in a newsroom. That is the job of the police and the prosecuting authorities. In the absence of any word from them a factual account of the event must suffice.

A murder investigation often tempts reporters to venture into realms for which their profession has not really equipped them. Because a few reporters have achieved fame through phenomenal exploits, all reporters are scarcely justified in trying to play detective when a newsworthy personage has been "done in." Not many even attempt to do so because there is simply not enough time for the routines of both journalism and police work on a fast-breaking story.

There are a few fundamentals of which every reporter must take account.

The first is that police and prosecutors rarely will give him information on a silver platter. That means a tremendous amount of interviewing and research must be done in a very short time so that a coherent story may be written.

The second is that there can be no guarantee of police accuracy; in fact, an impressive body of evidence can be amassed to the contrary. That means police versions of names, addresses, and other facts must be checked.

The third is that police and journalistic terminology are not necessarily identical. The legal term for a slaying is a homicide, but many newspapers loosely and incorrectly refer to such crimes automatically as murder. In a grand jury indictment the homicide eventually may be defined as first- or second-degree murder, depending on whether there was premeditation; or first- or second-degree manslaughter, depending on whether there was provocation or negligence. Manslaughter is not murder so that care must be used in defining a homicide. Indictments charging murder have been found to be deficient in the past, so that a writer should be precise in his statements whenever he refers to the legal basis of any charge.

Assessment of Blame   Whenever there is a fist fight, shooting, or collision involving police action, it is only human to wonder what happened and who was at fault. Often only a trial can determine this; therefore, most reporters use as many versions of the incident as there are witnesses if such extensive treatment is warranted.

Such accounts begin with a statement that two men had a fist fight in a night club, or that there was a shooting match, or that two automobiles collided. The body of the story then documents the noncommittal lead, giving such versions of the event as are necessary. The attribution of documentation of this type always presents a problem for writers who want to avoid using "he said," or "she said," or "the police said" in every sentence.

There are several ways of doing this. One is to quote the various versions, if they are brief enough. Another is to write, "The police version of the incident follows," and then report it without further attribution. In any case, unless there is some official assessment of blame, it is usually not necessary for the reporter to try to act in such matters.

Identification   The identification of persons in crime stories sometimes leads to trouble, no matter how carefully they are checked. Confusion of persons with identical last names, mistakes in middle initials, mixups in addresses, misspellings of names, and police errors all conspire against the reporter. There is no real safety in the familiar formula, "The suspect gave his name as . . . ," or, "The prisoner was identified as. . . ." If the identification is incorrect, the reporter and his organization are in trouble.

It is usually a good rule, in stories that warrant it, to include material showing how the identification was made—by papers in the person's possession, by friends or relatives, or by other means. If there is any doubt, the reporter will find it does no harm to add a clause or even a sentence indicating that the identification was partial and remained to be checked. No news organization need regard itself as an oracle, whose word is final, when the public knows that many things are possible between the commission of a crime and the conviction of a defendant.

CIVIL DISORDER

The coverage of civil disorder imposes enormous responsibilities on the journalist. On the one hand, he must exercise the greatest care not to spread rumors. On the other, he must expose himself to danger if necessary to determine the magnitude of any street incident. But whatever he does, he must always be conscious that careless reporting or the provocative appearance of still or television cameras can cause untold harm in a tense situation, particularly in the crowded inner cores of many American cities.

The conduct of the journalist at the scene of action must be circumspect. A hard-hatted, swaggering white reporter in the center of an angry Negro community can provoke trouble. A television cameraman, training his instrument on a floodlighted crowd, is likely to get more action than he bargains for when fighting has broken out all around him. Nor is there any great sense in sending an armored truck bearing the name of a news organization into a trouble area. These are the things that cause the news media to be blamed for spreading disorder. Complete coverage is desirable at all times, but no one is thereby justified to put on a circuslike performance.

In both written and oral reports of any incident, every effort should be made to arrive at accurate evaluations. An isolated act of vandalism, or a street fight between two boys in the midst of a crowd, must not be called a race riot. And if shooting is heard in a crowded neighborhood at night, it is not automatically "sniper fire" until an investigation determines that snipers are at work. Nor are all fires the work of arsonists. Looting, too, should be carefully defined. Great damage can be done if radio, television, and published wire service and newspaper reports exaggerate a few small incidents. Consequently, in the early stages of any civil disorder, the basic rule is to work and report with the greatest restraint.

Necessarily, once a news organization's editors have evidence to show that they are dealing with a riot of major proportions, there is no justification for not making a complete report available to the community at large. When reporters see arsonists setting fires and looters carrying merchandise from wrecked stores, these things must be communicated. Yet, the need for restraint and patient inquiry cannot be abandoned even in such circumstances. For when shooting breaks out, the reporter is never justified to leap to conclusions that all the damage is being done by demonstrators or that race is aligned against race. Jittery police and National Guardsmen have been known to fire away at almost anything that moves, sometimes with unfortunate results.

These precautions, which are the product of experience in the coverage of civil disorders, have been incorporated into a number of informal arrangements between the press and the authorities. The oldest is the Chicago plan, which seeks to keep a lid on news of a disorder until it is under control, something that is not always practical. Another procedure, followed in St. Louis, makes a police information center responsible for the clearance of all factual information before it is used by the news media. In Omaha, an attempt has been made to wait at least 30 minutes before broadcasting or publishing news of a disturbance. In addition, a number of individual news organizations have set up their own special instructions of a precautionary nature.

But regardless of how careful the journalist may be, it is inevitable that he will be criticized for covering a riot and he may as well make up his mind to it. One of the most pervasive of all prehistoric tribal customs was to kill the messenger who brought bad news, a feeling that still persists in the advanced civilization of today. The journalist, in consequence, must do the best he can. If there is any balm for him in his difficult and even precarious situation, it is the judgment of an Indian journalist who said after the assassination of President Kennedy: "There is one thing of which we can be sure about the United States. Whatever happens there, good or bad, everybody is going to know it and nobody is going to be able to keep it a secret."

WRITING CRIME NEWS

Variations in the handling of crime news in the American news media are illustrated in the following leads, some of them done routinely and others with a flair for the human interest aspects of the story. Even news organizations that do not make a specialty of handling crime news use spirited accounts of the material they select from the accumulation of the day.

The Developing Story   In the following two accounts of the ravages of the Texas sniper, a comparison of the work of the two local papers in the case shows how the story developed. The afternoon paper, the Austin *Statesman,* had to report events as they occurred; the only more difficult assignment was the one handled by newsmen from the local electronic media. The morning paper, the Austin *American,* was able to compile a fairly complete account once the shooting was over. If both stories include more than their share of gore, it should be remembered that local reporters do not have to work under fire as a rule and they don't ordinarily see mass murders occurring before their eyes.

The following is the Austin *Statesman*'s story:[7]

A sniper firing from the observation deck of the University of Texas tower Monday killed at least nine persons and injured at least 24 more before being shot to death by police.

The entire campus area was under siege as the sniper fired on unprotected victims on every side of the tower for 90 minutes, from noon until 1:30 p.m.

Blood literally ran in the hallways of the tower and on the sidewalks

---

[7] These accounts are from the Austin *Statesman,* August 1, 1966 and the Austin *American,* August 2, 1966.

throughout the sprawling campus as the sniper picked off victim after victim with an arsenal of weapons.

The sniper was shot to death by five police officers who went onto the 27th floor observation deck after the man quit firing. Police said the papers on the body of the man they gunned down carried the name "Charles Whitman."

Police who shot the gunman said they found a .22 caliber rifle, a .38 pistol, a 7 mm. rifle, and a 30-06 rifle at different points on the observation deck.

They said the man, about 25, clad in blue jeans under a set of coveralls, had a shoulder-type field pack of ammunition, a trench knife and a pair of binoculars with him.

Bodies of the dead and injured, mostly those felled by the sniper's opening fire, were strewn about the main mall south in front of the tower. They could not be rescued for more than an hour as the sniper's high volume of fire covered the area. They were finally saved by rescuers in an armored car . . .

The Austin *American* was able to go beyond the fragmentary identification of "Charles Whitman" in its story, some hours later, and also had the final casualty figures. This was the way the *American*'s story began:

A blood bath gushed over Austin and the University of Texas Monday, leaving 15 persons dead and 31 others wounded at the hands of a lone gunman who made an arsenal fortress of the University tower.

The 90-minute mass slaughter that brought this city to its knees ended only when city police officers shot down Charles Joseph Whitman, a 25-year-old student.

Besides himself, Whitman's carnage left dead his wife, his mother, and 13 persons on the campus—students, tourists, a policeman, an unborn baby, laborers, Peace Corpsmen, and University staff employees.

Whitman turned the campus into a nightmare of death—as he had planned to do—shortly before noon when he began pouring deadly accurate sniper bullets from the tower's 28th floor observation deck.

Within minutes an area two blocks on every side of the tower was strewn with bodies of the dead and wounded, their would-be rescuers pinned down by Whitman's fire.

More than 50 law officers, maneuvering for aim at the lethal weapons on the tower, returned Whitman's fire until two officers and a civilian made a daring breakthrough at 1:25 P.M. to kill the gunman.

When the battlefield was stilled with mournful silence, this was known about Whitman: native of Lake Worth, Fla., third year architectural engineering student, ex-Scoutmaster, one-time Scout wonder boy, former Marine, and a psychiatric patient.

Before mounting to his executioner's post in the tower, Whitman had fatally stabbed his wife at their South Austin home and had mortally shot his mother, who moved here from Florida to be near her son, at her downtown apartment.

Whitman left behind a series of eerie notes detailing a gruesome 12-hour trail of murder and mental anguish aimed at the climax in the

University of Texas tower. Here is how police recounted the history of the last hours of Whitman's life—and the lives of those who innocently crossed his path . . .

A Break in a Manhunt   When a suspect is sought after a spectacular crime, the police are anxious to use the mass media to circulate accurate descriptions and pictures, where available, to bring the manhunt to a successful conclusion. But once an arrest is made, it is often extremely difficult to obtain a positive identification of the suspect from the authorities; at this stage, the police are naturally worried about preserving the defendant's civil rights to avoid prejudicing his trial. The news media thus have to balance their responsibility to the public with their obligation to preserve the right of fair trial. This is how the Chicago *Sun-Times* handled a touchy but extremely important case:[8]

> A man identified as Richard F. Speck, accused slayer of eight student nurses, was seized by FBI agents and police early Sunday at County Hospital.
> Investigators said that Speck had slashed his wrist in an apparent suicide attempt in a W. Madison St. flophouse where he had holed up while detectives and federal agents were seeking him across the nation.
> At the hospital, police were in doubt about the true identity of the suspect until Federal Bureau of Investigation agents identified him as Speck.
> The tattooed, 24-year-old Speck, an exconvict, has been charged with murdering the nurses in the space of four hours in Chicago's biggest mass slaying.
> Police said he apparently attempted to kill himself because several obvious tattoos made it virtually impossible for him to escape the massive manhunt for long.
> Among the tattoos on Speck's left arm was one that read: "Born to raise hell."
> According to the only nurse to survive the massacre Thursday, Corazon Pieza Amurao, the killer told the women before he murdered them that he intended to loot their purses to obtain money to travel to New Orleans . . .

A Reporter Plays Detective   When the magnificent DeLong star ruby was stolen from the American Museum of Natural History in the fall of 1965, the New York *Daily News* soon came across the trail of the thieves and arranged for the gem's recovery.

Subsequently, the gang was caught, tried and convicted of the crime. William Federici, a reporter for the *News*, could not have guessed at the eventual outcome of the case, however, when he was dickering for the

---

[8] Chicago *Sun-Times*, July 17, 1966.

return of the ruby. Here is the essential part of the story of the recovery of the gem:[9]

> After 10 months in the hands of thieves, the 100-carat DeLong star ruby was ransomed for $25,000 cash in Florida yesterday.
>
> It was recovered by multimillionaire John D. MacArthur, in the company of *News* reporter William Federici and *News* photographer Dan Farrell, in a public telephone booth in a service plaza off the Sunshine State Parkway near Palm Beach.
>
> Shortly after recovery, the ruby was identified as the DeLong, stolen from the American Museum of Natural History here last October. Identification was made by Joseph Segal, 45, owner of one of Palm Beach's most exclusive jewel houses.
>
> Segal knew nothing in advance except that MacArthur wanted a stone appraised, but after weighing it in at 103 carats and examining it, he told MacArthur and the *News* men:
>
> "What is this all about? This has to be the DeLong ruby."
>
> The trio had gone to the Palm Beach Service Plaza four miles from Palm Beach, on the east side of the parkway, after they received instructions from Francis P. Antel, a free-lance writer who delivered the ransom money.
>
> The $25,000, in $100 and $50 bills, was given to Antel by MacArthur earlier in the day to give the holder of the precious stone. As MacArthur and the *News* men drove up to the booth, in accordance with instructions, the phone was ringing.
>
> Federici answered and it was Antel. "Turn around and face the door, reach up, and you'll feel the ruby," Antel said.
>
> Federici found nothing. Antel said, "Keep looking, it's up there."
>
> The men tore the top of the booth apart. Then, reaching over to the left, where the door closes, Federici's fingers touched something that felt like a pebble.
>
> He pulled it down and in the brilliant sunshine the men saw he was holding a colored gem. The sun struck it and the six rays of the star shone clearly, "as beautiful as anything we've ever seen in our lives," they said later . . .

SEX CASES AND OBSCENITY

Although the American theatre and the American novel have dropped all the bars, and almost anything can be published in book form with the thinnest justification, the American newspaper is still relatively restrained. Even the most commercially minded rag cannot approach the excesses of the "theatre of shock," which has run out of shocking items. As for television, despite the familiar complaints of sex and sadism on the home screen, the most lurid shows are mild when compared with the scenes

---

[9] New York *Daily News*, September 3, 1965, p. 3.

presented in modern novels by writers who have a way with four-letter words. It is true that one publisher was sent to jail for obscenity, despite enraged outcries before the United States Supreme Court that the freedom of the press was being violated. But such cases are relatively rare.

This is not to say that the American news media are puritanical. Far from it. Most newspapers and news magazines have a relatively liberal attitude in the handling of sex cases up to a point. Editors can scarcely forget that the government, while generally lenient, can clamp down suddenly on borderline material that is sent through the mails. Consequently, there is a certain amount of discretion on the publication of salacious material in the print media. The rules of good taste generally are the guideline—and that, of course, depends on the responsible editor.

Aside from this, a number of publications still convey faintly the atmosphere of the Mauve Decade. Some newspapers, for example, still prefer the euphemism, "criminal assault," to the term, "rape," although it would be difficult to shock a newspaper reader today. Others call "rape" a "statutory offense." Here and there, publications still can be found referring to a prostitute as anything from a "call girl" or a "B girl" to a "lady of the evening." Of late, the expressions from London, such as "Mods" and "swingers," are put to somewhat different use than the British intended. As for houses of prostitution, they may become "bordellos" or "bagnios" or "houses of ill repute," depending on the type of paper and the age of the editor. Mothers with children born out of wedlock are sometimes referred to for headline purposes as "unwed mothers." Homosexuals, if referred to at all, are sometimes described as "abnormal persons" in the proper press.

In matters of health, the news media are completely frank. For many years, editors and newscasters have come to know that only timid old ladies are shocked by a reference to syphilis or gonorrhea by name, rather than by such a euphemism as "social diseases." The more progressive news media have done valiant work in discussing "the pill" and other birth control measures. Some of the best work in American journalism has been done in this area.

That makes it all the more difficult to understand the insistence of a fairly influential section of the press in trying to "pretty up" the sordid sex case with fancy writing. As for obscene language, most newspapers generally shy away from it and the news magazines are almost as circumspect. And television, in this respect, is edited for the "Old Lady from Dubuque."

chapter 23

The News Media and the Courts

The President's Crime Commission has summarized the function of the news media in reporting on the administration of justice as follows:

> Reporting maintains the public knowledge . . . so necessary for the functioning of the courts. Critical inquiry and reports by the media on the operation of the courts can prevent abuse and promote improvement in the administration of justice.[1]

FREE PRESS AND FAIR TRIAL

Even the greatest of newspapers cannot muster the manpower to cover all the courts within its jurisdiction. There are simply too many of them. Nor can a television station, with a far more limited local staff and time for broadcast, pretend to do the job. The court system in the United States is so far-reaching and so complex that the news media have neither the space nor the time to report on everything that happens in the courts. It has been calculated, for example, that a representative New York newspaper is able to publish only a small percentage of available reports on pending cases.

Why, then, is there such continual conflict over the rights of free press and fair trial? Why, too, does the issue of picture-taking in the courts—

---

[1] Report of The President's Commission on Law Enforcement and Administration of Justice, *The New York Times*, February 19, 1967, pp. 1 and 68.

either by television or still cameras—engender such passionate debate and even bitterness? Basically, it is because the news media can have a profoundly adverse effect on the administration of justice if the Constitutional freedom granted to the press is exercised without restraint or responsibility. This is the lesson implicit in the United States Supreme Court's reversal of convictions in the Estes and Sheppard cases on the ground of prejudicial publicity.

The Estes Case   Billie Sol Estes, a Texas financier, won a reversal of his swindling conviction from the Supreme Court in 1965 because his trial in a Texas State court had been televised over his objection. Estes' 15-year term in a Federal prison based on a Federal mail fraud conviction was not affected.

Justice Tom C. Clark, in a 5-4 decision, wrote that Estes' 1962 trial in Tyler, Texas, had prejudiced his rights because of the presence of live television in the courtroom. Thus, the defendant's eight-year State sentence was nullified and his conviction was set aside in a case that involved the sale of mortgages on nonexistent anhydrous ammonia fertilizer tanks in Texas.

"A defendant on trial for a specific crime is entitled to his day in court, not in a stadium, or a city, or a nation-wide arena," Justice Clark wrote. "The heightened public clamor resulting from radio and television coverage will inevitably result in prejudice. Trial by television is therefore foreign to our system . . . The necessity of sponsorship weighs heavily in favor of televising only notorious cases, such as this one."[2]

The Sheppard Case   The Sheppard reversal was even more spectacular. After Dr. Samuel Sheppard of Cleveland had served nearly ten years in prison on his 1954 conviction of a charge that he had murdered his wife, the Supreme Court in 1966 reversed the verdict. The high court held that "virulent publicity" and a "carnival atmosphere" had made a fair trial impossible. Again writing for the majority, Justice Clark warned the news media that "trials are not like elections, to be won through the use of meeting halls, radio, and the newspaper."

"From the cases coming here," Justice Clark continued, "we note that unfair and prejudicial news comment on pending trials has become increasingly prevalent. Due process requires that the accused receive a trial by an impartial jury free from outside influence . . . Where there is a reasonable likelihood that prejudicial news prior to trial will prevent a fair trial, the

2 *The New York Times*, June 8, 1965.

judge should continue the case until the threat abates or transfer it to another county not so permeated by publicity."[3]

Dr. Sheppard was acquitted at his second trial later in 1966.

Voluntary Agreements   Thus, the President's Crime Commission did not exaggerate the influence of the news media when it warned against the dangers of "unrestrained news gathering" that prejudice the Constitutional rights of defendants to a fair trial. The growth of the spirit of voluntary cooperation between press and bar groups at the State level is a reflection of the determination of both sides to guard against such prejudicial incidents in the future. Some individual newspapers and broadcasters as well, have announced that they will voluntarily withhold prejudicial material from publication—prior criminal records, admissions or confessions, refusal to take a lie detector test, and the like.

Whatever may be withheld from the public during a trial, however, is generally published after the verdict is given. When this was done by some metropolitan and suburban New York newspapers in connection with the trial of an alleged member of Cosa Nostra, following his conviction of conspiracy to commit bank robberies, the trial judge, Federal Judge Jacob Mishler, appeared to be satisfied. He called the voluntarily muted coverage "the most forceful argument against imposing restrictions on the press." However, in the trial of Richard Speck on a charge of murdering eight nurses in Chicago, the Chicago *Tribune* had to go to court to force modification of stringent curbs on coverage by a trial judge. The Illinois Supreme Court, in this instance, acted to relax the restrictions while the trial was on.

It is obvious that the differences between the rights of free press and fair trial are not going to be resolved very quickly. Out of the purest of motives, the courts will have further differences with the press on the degree of coverage of certain cases and the press will insist on its right to publish whatever it believes to be necessary in the public interest. These continuing tensions provide the public with the best guarantee that both fair trial and free press will be safeguarded.

True, there will be more instances in which journalists overstep the limits of rational conduct, just as there will be more cases in which prejudiced judges try to halt fair coverage of proceedings in their courts. But because of the voluntary cooperation between press and bar at the working level, these extremes are far less dangerous to our democratic society on the whole today than they were in the twenties, when justice was administered too often in the manner of a three-ringed circus.

---

[3] *The New York Times,* June 7, 1966.

THE JUDICIAL PYRAMID

The first thing a newly assigned court reporter must do to discharge his responsibilities is to acquire some understanding of the organization of the American court system. At the apex is the United States Supreme Court. To it come appeals from the Federal and State appellate court systems. Within each State is a top appellate court that bears various names, such as the Court of Appeals or, again, the Supreme Court (although the name is no indication of the specific powers of the court). Depending on the size of the State's legal network, such a court may have branches.

Under these come the workhorse courts—those of original jurisdiction which may be known as Superior, Common Pleas, Circuit, or other courts. (Strangely enough, in New York this is the court known as the Supreme Court.) Their functions are generally the same although their jurisdictions may differ. They are the courts of first instance and, in one form or another, are responsible for both civil and criminal matters. Probate courts handle wills.

If the case load is very great, separate criminal courts may be formed. They may be called by such names as General Sessions, Oyer and Terminer, or simply County Courts. Other specialized courts may hear divorce actions. But regardless of how they are organized, courts of original jurisdiction are courts of record, and cases brought before them are privileged as to publication.

On the lowest rung of the judicial ladder are the inferior courts of limited jurisdiction, which may or may not be courts of record. In a county subdivision a justice of the peace may preside over them. In cities the inferior criminal courts are often Police Courts or Magistrates' Courts. The inferior civil courts, sometimes known as "Poor Men's Courts" because they are supposedly less expensive for litigation, are called City or Municipal Courts and handle cases with judgments limited to a fixed sum, anywhere from $3,000 to $6,000.

There is one new development in the continued proliferation of this court system. Where police judges or magistrates once sat without a jury to handle all minor offenses and bind over prisoners in major cases for possible grand jury action, various cities have created many new types of such inferior courts. Among them are Family Courts for domestic arguments, Adolescents' or Children's Courts for a variety of cases including juvenile delinquency, Traffic Courts where defendants line up by the hundreds to pay fines meekly without any practical chance of saying more than "guilty" or "not guilty."

This crowded judicial ladder of localities and states is roughly paralleled by the less numerous but even more powerful system of Federal courts which handle everything from income tax cases to violations of the Mann Act. From the arraignment proceedings presided over by a United States Commissioner, the judicial authority extends upward through the District Courts and the various appellate courts to the highest court in the land.

A nation governed by laws, not men, has need of many courts, each with a different jurisdiction, each with a line of appeal to a higher court.

What Is Covered The sheer numbers of the courts in the land, their differing functions, and the intricate pattern of local, state, and Federal jurisdictions provide the best reason for the spot coverage of court news by a large section of the press. In New York City alone, for instance, there are about 300 judges and official referees, who assist them, plus about 3,500 clerks, attendants, and other staff workers. By contrast, the entire Federal judiciary consists of about 350 judges and some 4,000 other court officers and employees.

The national average for court delays in bringing a case to trial is 30 months, with the worst showing in Chicago where it takes 69 months on the average.[4] Moreover, with new cases coming in at the rate of 8.000 a year in a populous area like New York County, there is little hope that anything will be done to ease the heavy burden of the courts. With two-thirds of all civil cases classified as liability actions, the cause of the tie-up is clear. It can take years, in some jurisdictions, to obtain justice.

Such delays in themselves are bound to detract from public interest in all but the most significant and dramatic cases. The pressure of events is very great, and the public memory is lamentably short. It follows that very large areas of civil court procedures and others of minimal public interest are normally left uncovered, despite their importance. Few newspapers can afford to tie up reporters on long trials which yield little of interest for the news columns.

The emphasis of the news media, therefore, is on criminal courts, matrimonial cases in the civil courts, and occasional other ventures such as the coverage of important wills or contests in the probate or surrogate's courts, or the criminal proceedings in the Federal courts. Of all the courts in the land, the United States Supreme Court is given the broadest and most comprehensive coverage because of its tremendous impact on the states, especially in such matters as integration and other issues affecting civil liberties.

Court Reporting With the growth of the general assignment system of reporting (the so-called fire-house principle of assigning by the story in-

---

[4] *Life*, November 17, 1967, p. 4.

stead of the beat) the numbers of veteran court reporters have been dropping steadily. On many papers there are only one or two men at most who spend their days in the courts, and on a growing number of other papers court assignments are given to general assignment men as stories warrant it.

When a reporter was assigned to the courts and told to develop his contacts with lawyers, judges, and prosecutors, he entered a fruitful field for the gathering of news. Those who still practice it, to the exclusion of all other assignments, are relatively few in number. Over the years most of them have acquired such a wide knowledge of legal backgrounds and precedents that they are sometimes consulted unofficially by the judges whom they cover day by day. Without a continuity of coverage such individuals are bound to be rarities except where they happen to have law degrees.

For those who are assigned on occasion to cover the courts, a basic knowledge of some of the most frequently used legal terms is a must.

TERMINOLOGY

Some of the definitions of legal terms used in court reports follows:

Accessory.   Person who assists in the commission of a crime, either before or after the fact.

Action at law.   Proceedings instituted to enforce a legal right.

Adjournment.   Request for more time to find witnesses or important evidence, or other reasons.

Administrator.   Appointee of a court to administer the estate of a person who has died intestate (without a will).

Affirm.   Used by appellate courts to uphold a lower court decision. Failure to affirm is called a reversal.

Arraignment.   Process through which the prisoner hears the charges against him and pleads to them.

Attachment.   Authorization by the court in written form to take and hold a person or property.

Bail bond.   Security, usually furnished by a professional bondsman, to guarantee the appearance of an accused person in court. When a person is ordered held without bail, the seriousness of the charge is such that the court refuses to turn him loose. When a bond of $5,000 is posted, if that is the amount of bail set by the court, the usual phrasing is that the prisoner was liberated in lieu of $5,000 bail, or simply, freed in $5,000 bail.

Bench warrant.   Court process authorizing an official to apprehend an individual and bring him before the court.

Bill of particulars.   A statement setting forth the specifications in an indictment, information, or complaint.

Change of venue.   Changing the place of trial.

Codicil.   Addition to a will.

Commutation.   Reduction of sentence.

Concurrent sentence. Court decision that a convicted defendant serves only the longest of several terms imposed on him. Consecutive sentence means he serves the sum of all terms.

Contempt of court. An offense against the court, punishable by a fine, jail term, or both.

Consent decree. Court order to which the defendant has consented.

Corpus delicti. Essence of the crime.

Decree nisi. Final judgment to take effect some time in the future.

Defendant. Party against whom an action has begun.

Demurrer. Defense plea that the charge does not constitute a crime, or cause of action.

Deposition. Taking of testimony from a witness before trial.

Directed verdict. Instruction by the court to the jury to bring in a particular verdict.

Double jeopardy. Plea that the defendant has already been tried for the same offense.

Executor. Person named in a will to administer the estate.

Extradition. Process of returning a prisoner from one state to another.

Habeas corpus. Writ requiring production of a detained person in court to inquire into the legality of the proceedings.

Indeterminate sentence. Sentence of "not more than" a certain term, and "not less than" another term of years.

Indictment. Document brought by the grand jury on evidence submitted to it by the prosecutor. A bill of indictment is also known as a true bill.

Information. Document filed by the prosecutor under oath instead of by the grand jury.

Injunction. Court order requiring those named to act or to forbear in certain actions.

Interlocutory decree. Preliminary mandate of the court.

John Doe inquiry. Inquiry by a prosecutor to obtain evidence in connection with an alleged crime.

Letters rogatory. Document under which a witness in a foreign jurisdiction is examined.

Letters testamentary. Authority issued to the executor of a will after he has qualified to permit him to perform his functions.

Mandamus. Court direction requiring someone to perform an act.

Mandate. A judicial direction.

Misdemeanor. Minor crime, as distinguished from a *felony*, which is a serious crime such as a homicide.

Mistrial. End of a trial because of an irregularity.

Motion to dismiss. Motion attacking the basis of the action.

Nolle prosequi. Also, simply *nolle pros*; determination not to proceed with a case.

Nolo contendere. Plea indicating that defendant will not contest the charge.

Pardon. Action by executive relieving criminal from sentence.

Parole. Release on pledge of reappearance at regular intervals, or on call.

Plaintiff. Party who initiates litigation.

Pleading. Document in which the plaintiff's claim or defendant's defense is set forth.

Presentment.   Document brought by a grand jury on its own initiative or upon allegations of private citizens.

Quash.   Motion contending an indictment is defective in form.

Quo Warranto.   Writ by which government seeks to recover an office from a public official or a franchise from a corporation.

Referee.   Appointee of court.

Replevin.   Writ requiring production of property.

Reprieve.   Delay in execution of a sentence.

Respondent.   Party against whom an appeal has been taken.

Sealed verdict.   It is rendered in the absence of a judge, but opened by him when court reconvenes.

Subpoena.   Court order requiring witness to appear and testify.

Subpoena duces tecum.   Court order requiring witness to produce certain documents bearing on the case for which he must appear.

Suits in equity.   A proceeding originally brought before a Chancellor to compel a defendant to refrain from doing something or to compel him to do something.

Summons.   Process of the court instituting an action.

Veniremen.   Members of a panel (venire) of potential jurors, called to be examined for jury duty.

Writ of certiorari.   Writ from superior to inferior court requiring the record to be sent to the former for review.

Writ of supersedeas.   Writ by which proceedings are stayed.

The reporter cannot, of course, use all such terms and others even more complicated in a news story. He would hopelessly confuse the public. Professional practice requires each term to be briefly explained if it is used. For instance: "The defendant pleaded *nolo contendere* (no contest)." Better still, instead of using a term such as *nolle prosequi*, it may be stated as follows: "The prosecution announced it would drop the case." Except in a law journal, there is no reason to clutter up a news story with a lot of legal terminology unless the news cannot be told any other way. This procedure applies particularly to wire service correspondents and specials who cover important legal proceedings in other states for their newspaper. Pleas and other terminology that are familiar to the public in one state are not necessarily known, or even used, in adjacent states.

HOW COURTS ARE COVERED

In the coverage of courts, as in every other aspect of journalism, a reporter is only as good as his sources and his knowledge of how to gain access quickly to records. The many reporters who are assigned to courts by the story, rather than as a regular beat, quickly discover this to be true. No matter how clever they are and regardless of how hard they work, the veterans on the beat are bound to have many more resources.

Court Sources   The key official in any court, as far as reporters are concerned, is the clerk of the court. He is the keeper of the records. With the cooperation of the judge, he prepares the trial calendar which sets dates for hearings and trials of all cases. He also prepares the court docket, which amounts to an abstract of cases. In trial proceedings he records motions, prepares judicial orders, and can make available copies of trial transcripts for a fee. He receives applications, motions, fines, and transacts other court business. Most important of all, procedurally, he carries out the desires of the judge in the manner and method of seating the representatives of the press—for at a major trial in a small courtroom it is not necessarily true that all reporters automatically are given seats at the press table. To avoid this headache, and also the confusion involved in the arrangements for telephones, teletypes, and other communications, many wise clerks tacitly yield their authority to a committee of reporters.

The judge, who presides at trials, is seldom a source of news although it is customary for any new reporter to introduce himself before a trial begins. Under his authority to enforce his orders on penalty of contempt of court findings, the trial judge in effect can regulate the conduct of reporters and their methods of operation. He can bar TV and still photographers and even artists, if he believes it necessary for the proper conduct of the trial, and he can halt too frequent movement of reporters in the aisles even if they are doing their work.

At the time of a jury's verdict, if the courtroom doors are ordered closed by the judge, the result can be a lot of signaling and scrambling by reporters at a major trial to get the news out. Few courts are realistic about this aspect of their proceedings, which means that reporters almost invariably are thrown on their own resources.

The prosecutor, often called a District Attorney or a State Attorney, and defense lawyers are among the primary sources for reporters in a criminal proceeding. In civil trials reporters consult the lawyers for the plaintiff and the defendant as well as others interested in the proceedings. Often, when a case has attracted public interest, reporters are likely to find themselves under the greatest pressure from the rival attorneys for a more favorable description of their respective positions.

Prosecution and Grand Juries   In prosecutors' offices there are frequently several investigators and other officials who develop into excellent news sources. However, because prosecution news sources often are fruitful, a reporter must be on his guard against even an unconscious slant in his material in the state's favor. Moreover, under no circumstances must he ever let himself be put in the position of trading information which he may have received from the defense for the sake of a few tips from the prosecution. This kind of conduct is unethical and also constitutes grounds for immediate discharge. Confidences given to a reporter are inviolate.

Most reporters make a point of knowing as many minor court officials as possible. Such persons as the bailiff, who keeps order in the court, and the court stenographer, who takes a complete record of the proceedings, can be of invaluable assistance on many occasions. Like the clerk of the court, they have such intimate knowledge of court procedure and judicial quirks that they can help a reporter check his facts and avoid many a pitfall.

News organizations keep a date book for all "futures" such as the scheduling of court trials and other legal proceedings. But such "futures" cannot anticipate changes in the calendar. The reporter's only recourse, therefore, is to check the calendar daily, study the docket for new cases, consult the clerk and other court attaches for indications of other news breaks, and maintain contact with the prosecutor's office and the more active lawyers in the area. He can also follow up arrests, hearings in the inferior courts, and grand jury proceedings for later news developments.

Grand jury proceedings are secret, but reporters often have a fairly accurate notion of what is going on through talking with witnesses and the prosecutor who submits evidence. A grand jury, as distinguished from a trial jury, is charged with the duty of hearing evidence in connection with the commission of a crime and deciding whether to return an indictment or presentment on the recommendation of the prosecutor. Frequently news of such actions is withheld, sometimes through the cooperation of the press, until those indicted can be arrested on bench warrants.

It should be remembered that an indictment is an accusation, drafted on the basis of one-sided evidence, and each separate charge or count in it must be proved in court. Everything in a report of an indictment, presentment, or information, therefore, must be heavily qualified. While it is customary to note the penalty attached to the crime specified, reporters should always point out that it will apply only upon conviction.

Criminal Procedures   In a newsworthy case a reporter frequently follows the action from the time an arrest is made. The arraignment of the defendant for pleading quickly follows. If the court has jurisdiction, as in the case of a misdemeanor, the case may be disposed of with a hearing and a verdict, or it may be postponed. If the court does not have jurisdiction, the judge usually binds the defendant over for possible action by the grand jury, the usual course for felony charges. Of course, the judge has the authority to throw the case out of court if, in his opinion, there is not sufficient evidence to warrant further proceedings. This does not happen often. The only other powers the judge of an inferior court may exercise is to admit the defendant to bail or refuse to set bail.

Action by the grand jury depends largely on the decision of the prosecutor to proceed. In cases where the evidence is decisive, the grand jury may return an indictment quickly. Where the prosecution is having its troubles, a considerable time may pass before anything happens. If the grand jury fails to act, the defendant is freed. If an indictment is returned, the defendant then must be arraigned again to plead to the specific charge and to reopen the question of bail. Such hearings are held in the courts of original jurisdiction, which also are the scene of the subsequent trials.

Legal strategy begins with the arraignment in the inferior court. There are so many legal moves that may be open to the prosecutor and the defense that reporters are always well advised to consult with both in advance, wherever the news is of sufficient importance, for an explanation of the possibilities. Where a reporter is known and trusted, it is not unusual for both sides to talk to him. The best a young reporter can do is to seek some impartial legal source, usually a friendly lawyer or court attache, to explain what moves are likely to be made.

The reporter who goes into court cold, without either legal knowledge or some more immediate background, is likely to make mistakes. A thorough advance briefing is often necessary.

Civil Proceedings   Matrimonial suits, actions for damages, and occasional petitions in bankruptcy or receiverships are of primary interest to newspapers in civil proceedings. The field of civil law is so great, and complications within states so numerous, that any general plan of procedure would be riddled with exceptions.

A brief outline of the system of law will show why this is so. Civil law, as distinguished from criminal law, may be divided into actions at law and suits in equity. Actions at law deal primarily with property and with personal matters such as damage suits and enforcement of contracts. Suits in equity are brought to compel or bar action. Foreclosures and receiverships are also covered by equity proceedings. Many states have abolished the distinction between actions at law and suits in equity, which is a complicating factor.

Even lawyers of experience, venturing into branches of civil law with which they are not familiar, cheerfully confess that they have to look up considerable material. It is, therefore, mandatory for a reporter not only to have a law dictionary handy, but also to obtain sufficient technical background whenever he is assigned to a particular civil suit.

Sometimes reporters know of civil actions before they are filed through tips from friendly lawyers or court attaches. In any case, by looking over the clerk's docket they can find any complaint, or petition that has been filed in a civil action. They need only its serial number and a helpful official to look up the original petition and get the story from it.

Civil suits begin with the filing of the complaint, but in some states the mere act of filing does not constitute privilege. Once the petition is brought before a judge, however, it becomes a part of a judicial proceeding and is thereby privileged. The issue cannot come to trial, however, until the defendant files his answer and legal skirmishing in the form of pleadings is concluded. As has been pointed out, all this may take many months. The lapse of time and the legal technicalities thereby conspire to limit the news value of many civil actions. They may, in due course, be settled out of court and noted in the record. In major law suits lawyers announce such settlements, but the "run-of-the-mill" civil actions come and go with few except those directly concerned being the wiser.

Covering civil actions involves mainly covering lawyers. And since the pleadings are usually highly technical and what lawyers say outside court is not privileged, there are probably no more than three news stories in the average civil suit—when it is filed, when it is answered, and when a settlement or verdict is made known.

The exception, of course, is the matrimonial action. Newspapers that specialize in them must also be wary of libel suits, since a lawyer may prepare a sizzling complaint for a wife in a divorce suit without knowing that she is, at that moment, about to be reconciled with her husband. Suits for divorce, annulment, separation, and alienation of affections are, like crime news, popular with the commercial press. However, they are not particularly popular with reporters who cover them because of the very real difficulty in obtaining material that is privileged and fair to both sides. When the law permits still further complications, such as the sealing of papers in a divorce action, then the use of news of such suits becomes impossible until the trial begins.

It is, therefore, a matter of considerable risk to use an item about a divorce suit or separation involving prominent persons; only in Reno or other jurisdictions that cater to matrimonials can a reporter consider that such work is ever as simple as it seems.

The Camera in Court   The enforcement of the American Bar Association's Canon 35, prohibiting picture-taking during trial proceedings in court, has been a source of controversy for many years. Originally adopted in 1935 as a protest against the circuslike atmosphere at the trial of Bruno Richard Hauptmann for the murder of the Lindbergh baby, it has been amended since (in 1962) to take account of modern conditions. The text now reads:

> Proceedings in court should be conducted with fitting dignity and decorum. The taking of photographs in the courtroom, during sessions of the court or recesses between sessions, and the broadcasting or televising of court proceedings are calculated to detract from the essential dignity of the proceedings, distract the witness in giving his testimony,

degrade the court, and create misconceptions with respect thereto in the mind of the public and should not be permitted.

While the canon has not been applied in all 50 States, it has been considered to be effective in more than half of them. The Supreme Court's reversal of the Estes case, on the ground that he had to submit to live television in a Texas State court over his objections, has effectively stopped judges from proceeding with such experiments. Moreover, when cameras were brought into the courtroom in the Jack Ruby murder case, they did not notably stimulate public enlightenment. The fight continues over the presence of still cameras and is not likely to be soon resolved.

TRIAL STORIES

An outline of the coverage of criminal trials, especially those that attract considerable public attention, may be based at least in part on the various stages of the proceedings. These form the framework for the drama and rising tension of the trial.

Criminal Trial Steps   The selection and swearing in of the jury is the first step in a criminal trial.

Then follows the opening address of the prosecutor, in which he details the crime and relates how he intends to prove the defendant guilty. The defense may follow with its opening statement or delay until the end of the prosecution's case, except in such states as New York where the defense must follow the prosecution.

The state puts on its witnesses next, with the prosecutor conducting direct examination and the defense cross-examining. Re-direct and re-cross-examination are permitted, if requested.

When the state's case concludes, the defense always asks for a directed verdict of acquittal on the ground that the charges have not been proved. The court usually denies such requests.

The defense's case follows. Its witnesses go through direct and cross-examination, as have those of the state.

Both sides then may put on rebuttal witnesses.

The summing up follows—invariably a field day for lawyers in a criminal trial. The prosecution generally speaks first, and the defense closes, each seeking to convince the jury with arguments, pleas, and rhetoric. Both sides rest their case after that.

The judge then charges the jury. He sums up the law in the case, tells the jury its possible verdicts, and explains the meaning of each verdict. He emphasizes that the state must have proved its case beyond a reasonable doubt.

When the jury returns to the courtroom, the foreman announces the verdict. If it is a finding of guilt, the judge then may remand the prisoner and set a date for sentencing, or he may pronounce sentence immediately, depending on the law in the state.

Civil Trial Steps   Civil trials generally follow this procedure, except that the state is usually not a party to the case and there may be no jury.

Opening statements are made by the attorneys for the plaintiff and defendant, in that order. The plaintiff's case then is presented, followed by the defendant's case. Following rebuttal, closing statements are made by the plaintiff and defense. Both sides then rest their case.

A judge, sitting without a jury, generally takes the case under advisement. He may announce his decision in a law journal, or he may permit copies of the decision to be distributed to reporters. He has the option, of course, of announcing his decision as soon as the case is concluded but seldom does so in matters that are at all complicated.

Reporters' Preparations   The first step any reporter should take when he is assigned to cover a major trial out of town is to be certain that he has a seat in the courtroom, adequate communications, and a place to sleep. Once he is on the scene, he should make himself known to the judge, court clerk, attorneys, and as many of the principals in the case as he can reach. If he is alone, he should provide himself with some assurance that his copy will be moved—either through a messenger or telephone or teletype service. Next, he should note the full names, addresses, business and home telephone numbers of everybody in the case in a notebook and keep it with him at all times.

A reporter for a morning newspaper has no particular problems about maintaining coverage while he is writing his story, except if his paper has an early deadline. A reporter for an afternoon newspaper or wire service knows that if he leaves the courtroom to write, phone, or dictate a lead, he may miss the biggest break of the day. Consequently, he may write his story in longhand in court, a procedure at which Damon Runyon was past master, or he may enter into an arrangement with a reporter for a noncompeting morning newspaper to cover for him while he writes his story. In no case, however, should he leave such an important matter to chance.

Trial Coverage   The problem in trial coverage is to hold down the file. A reporter needs a sixth sense to tell him when to begin taking notes on a line of testimony, and when a seemingly promising witness really will provide no news at all. Sometimes, through a mistake in judgment, a reporter can miss important testimony but he can always recover during a recess by consulting the court stenographer, if he cannot get a fill-in from a colleague.

Regardless of what else he may file, a reporter at a major criminal or civil trial must learn to take questions and answers on significant points and file them. The Q and A in newspapers makes fascinating reading. Even in a half-column trial story, some Q and A should be included if it is at all possible.

In handling a lead based on the testimony of a witness whose name means nothing to the public at large, a reporter may have recourse to methods of handling that have long been used in trial coverage. He may begin his story by writing that a certain charge was made, or a certain story was told, at so-and-so's trial on a first-degree murder indictment. The person who made the charge or told the story can then be identified in the second or third paragraph. Another variation is to begin by writing that a state's witness or a defense witness testified to a particular point at the trial, with identification of the witness later.

Throughout, the reporter generally knows what is likely to happen next procedurally and he usually can obtain a list of all except the surprise witnesses from the prosecution or defense before the day's hearing begins. If he is persistent, he may even have an outline of what the witness is supposed to establish so that he will not be surprised. This is important only in connection with the reporter's relations with his home office and his arrangements for filing a long story, or a comparatively short one. Planning is part of a reporter's work, too.

As the day of the judge's charge and the jury's deliberations approaches, the reporter should prepare a 500- to 800-word history of the trial for possible use at the time of the verdict. Once the jury retires, he should file such material to his office as B Copy in anticipation of a verdict. Any more current material, such as the jury's return to the courtroom for instructions or any significant actions of the defendant, may be sent later as A Copy to precede the B copy. Dummy leads for the possible verdicts should be held.

Therefore, when the jury does come in, the reporter is ready. As soon as the foreman announces the verdict, he selects the proper dummy lead and sees that it is filed either by teletype or open telephone line. He can then write a "live" new lead, giving the color and drama of what actually happened. Throughout, the emphasis is on anticipating the news rather than lagging behind it, on planning rather than leaving coverage to chance.

It should not be imagined that newsmen for the electronic media are exempt from all the preparatory work that must be done by reporters for newspapers, wire services, and the news magazines. Just because they talk into a microphone, or try to produce key figures before the television cameras after the verdict, the electronic journalists have no special sense that enables them to know what is going to happen. Many a report that is seemingly ad-libbed before the microphone has been prepared with just as much care as a story for a major newspaper. In short, the newsman who serves television must be just as careful as his colleagues. He has all the hazards of those who write for an edition—and none of their built-in safeguards. His words are written on the wind and he cannot recall them, once they are uttered.

Covering the Verdict   Here are three examples of cases that, in effect, take the public into the courtroom to see and to hear exactly what the reporter has experienced. Each story is quite different from the other; each depends, however, on the arts of the journalist for its effect. The first is the celebrated second verdict in the Sheppard case, as reported in the Cleveland *Plain Dealer*:[5]

> Samuel H. Sheppard was found not guilty last night in the 1954 slaying of his first wife, Marilyn.
>
> A jury of seven men and five women deliberated nearly eight hours before returning the verdict at 10:23 last night after a 19-day trial.
>
> Sheppard gleefully slammed his hand down on the trial table after Common Pleas Judge Francis J. Talty read the verdict.
>
> Sheppard had to be restrained in his joy by Defense Counsel F. Lee Bailey and co-Defense Counsel Russell A. Sherman.
>
> "Sit down!" ordered Bailey. Sheppard sat down and burst into tears. A woman in the back row screamed, "Thank God!"
>
> Other women could be heard screaming in the corridor outside the second-floor courtroom in the Cuyahoga County Criminal Courts Building.
>
> When the commotion had subsided, Judge Talty commended the jury for its service.
>
> Sheppard's second wife, Ariane, covered her face and sobbed softly. She was sitting in the second row of the seats in the small courtroom jammed with nearly 60 spectators, 27 of them reporters.
>
> As the jury was dismissed, Sheppard broke for the rear of the courtroom, thrusting a sheriff's deputy aside. "I'm going to see my wife," he said.
>
> He leaned off the bar rail and embraced his wife. She threw her arms around him. "Oh, baby," he sobbed. "Oh, baby."
>
> Leaping and pushing his way through the crowd that had massed in the corridor, the former osteopathic neurosurgeon shouted, "He's my man!" and clasped the stocky Bailey around the neck.
>
> Bailey, who had worked to have Sheppard freed in 1964 on a writ of habeas corpus, looked on and beamed. This was the moment he had waited for—for 1,827 days, he had told the jury, ever since he became interested in the celebrated Sheppard case in 1961 . . .
>
> Marilyn Sheppard, 31, died with more than 25 bone-deep wounds in her head. She was four months pregnant with her second child.
>
> Asleep in the next room was the Sheppards' 7-year-old son, Chip,

---

5 Cleveland *Plain Dealer*, November 17, 1966.

now a 19-year-old freshman at Boston University. He testified in the current trial that he never awakened the night or morning of the murder.

Sheppard told authorities in 1954 that he was attacked and knocked out twice by one or more unknown assailants when he rushed to the rescue of his wife and later when he pursued a shadowy form to the beach behind the Lake Road home.

A jury of seven men and five women convicted Sheppard of second degree murder in 1954 after a 65-day trial, including five days of deliberation. Sheppard served nearly ten years before he was released from prison on $10,000 bail by a U. S. district court in 1964 . . .

The United States Supreme Court's attack on prejudicial publicity, which it gave as the reason for the order to free the defendant and give him a new trial, has had its effect on the coverage of the mass media in most cases since. One of the most depraved, which became the subject of a best-selling book, was that of the "Boston Strangler." Yet, as the following brief account of the verdict shows, the New York *Daily News* told the story with a great deal of restraint:[6]

CAMBRIDGE, Mass., Jan. 18—The self-confessed Boston Strangler, Albert H. DeSalvo, was found legally sane by his jurors today and sentenced to life in prison. His jurors convicted him of ten criminal charges he admitted he committed against women as the "Green Man."

Judge Cornelius J. Moynihan sentenced the 35-year-old former Army sergeant to life for armed robbery and imposed prison sentences of nine to ten years and three to five years on the other charges,

None of the sentences will be started pending an appeal.

With their verdict, the all-male jury agreed with Assistant District Attorney Donald Conn that DeSalvo is not mentally diseased, but is a "cunning" sociopathic thug who robbed out of greed and took sexual liberties with his victims as a sort of fringe benefit.

The jurors refused to acquit DeSalvo on the ground of insanity. The defense had portrayed him as a sick vegetable man capable of murder and rape and as an "uncontrollable" schizophrenic who was a victim of his own diseased mind and sexual perversions. . .

The verdict came shortly after 6 P.M. As each indictment was read aloud by Clerk Howard M. Colpitts, the jury foreman, F. Hunter Rowley, a securities analyst from Concord, answered, "Guilty as charged."

DeSalvo stood as he heard the verdict, flanked by his two guards and his lawyers.

The jurors got the case at 12:35 P.M. after two of the 14 men who had been hearing testimony since last Wednesday were eliminated. In his 35-minute charge, Judge Moynihan told the jurors to consider each of the ten indictments separately, and to return a separate verdict on each. The possible verdicts, he said, were guilty, not guilty, and not guilty by reason of insanity.

---

[6] New York *Daily News*, January 19, 1967, p. 3.

"The defendant," said the judge, "is not on trial for homicide. The defendant is not on trial for rape."

When a jury reports it is "hopelessly deadlocked," the experienced reporter does not conclude at once that he is about to base his story on a hung jury. In the following story, the jury reported three times that it was unable to reach a verdict. Yet, this is what finally happened:[7]

> Donald Jay Davis, 22, was convicted today of the murder of an off-duty policeman, Floyd DeLoach, and received a life sentence.
> Relieved that he had escaped a death sentence, Davis rose and told the ten-man, two-woman jury: "Ladies and gentlemen of the jury, thank you very much."
> The jury foreman, Hugh Granberry, said that the jury had been hung 11-1 for imposing a death penalty before the majority yielded to the dissenting juror and agreed upon a life sentence.
> The dissenter was a woman juror who believed Davis was a "good boy" who had chanced to get into trouble, Granberry said.
> "If we had known that Davis was wanted for robbery in Abilene, he would have got the death penalty by the second vote," Granberry said. The jury did not learn during the trial that Davis was wanted in Abilene.
> DeLoach, 30, was slain at a North Side bowling lanes parking lot where he was working as a uniformed security guard.
> —Houston *Chronicle*

JUVENILE DELINQUENCY

The nation's 3,000 juvenile courts have been put on notice by the United States Supreme Court that they must give children most of the procedural protections guaranteed to adults in the Bill of Rights.[8] This means that when children are brought before juvenile judges in delinquency hearings, they must be given timely notice of the charges against them and they must have adequate warning of their right to remain silent and not incriminate themselves. Moreover, they must be accorded the right to have a lawyer, court-appointed if necessary, and to confront and cross-examine their accusers and other witnesses against them.

"Under our Constitution," wrote Justice Abe Fortas for the court's majority in a key decision, "the condition of being a boy does not justify a kangaroo court."

Since many states do not permit the use of the names of juvenile defendants, and hold juvenile proceedings without a reporter's presence,

---

[7] Houston *Chronicle*, September 25, 1966.
[8] *The New York Times*, May 16, 1967, pp. 1 and 36.

the effect of the Supreme Court's decision is likely to scale down still further the surveillance of the children's courts by the news media. Generally, newspapers do not use the names of juvenile defendants and seldom report on juvenile cases because of the extreme difficulty of learning anything of consequence about the usual run-of-the-mill proceedings.

The press does not seem likely to be able to challenge successfully the legal curtain that is being lowered over the fate of juvenile defendants. Few newspapers, in any case, show disposition to do so.

PART 4

INTERPRETIVE
JOURNALISM

chapter 24

Politics, Government, and the News Media

The story of politics and government in an expanding United States presents the news media with one of their greatest challenges. There are many ways of meeting it. The growth of the metropolitan newspaper in the suburbs is one of them. The expansion of the news magazines in areas where there are poor newspapers is another. Finally, the commitment of leaders in local television to the cause of good government is an added potent force. All these add up to a different kind of journalism and the growth of a different motivation for the news media in the reporting of government at every level.

THE "NEW" JOURNALISM

Basic to these changes in journalism as a profession is the development of the twin functions of interpretation and analysis of the news. The outlines of these forms of reporting—*grand reportage*, in the French press—have been apparent since the years before World War II. They are still evolving, amid trials and tests and some misgivings, out of the sound principles and procedures of the past.

There is nothing particularly revolutionary about this seemingly new journalism. Its roots go as far back into American history as the beginning of the New Deal and the inauguration of new principles in government. The telling of this story revealed the inadequacies of the deadpan news account, but with few exceptions there was no change in professional techniques until the even sterner test of World War II. The greatest of these exceptions was the radio commentator, one of the most potent forces in strengthening interventionist sentiment before Pearl Harbor. It is ironic, indeed, that the rise of television stifled these magnificent, challenging voices.

Since World War II, a majority of the American press has adopted a new concept of journalistic responsibility, more universal in its approach to public service. Television, with its basic fear of controversy and commentary, has lagged behind the press in this respect although there have been occasional programs of brilliance and discernment. As for the news magazines, despite their generally excellent performance, their fault has been—in the words of a cynical professional—that they "tried to put an angle on everything, including the weather."

Yet, under the leadership of the press, the news media as a whole have progressed. The journalism of analysis and comment has been the principal result. Basically, it seeks to explain as well as to inform. It dares to evaluate, to measure, to teach. By and large, its methods are an adaptation of some of the more practical techniques of mass communication. These are intended to produce a broader interpretation of the news of politics and government at all levels and more accurate ways of evaluating public opinion.

Those who champion the more complex approach to the telling of the news seek to improve newspapers first, hoping the other media will emulate them and thereby help to create a better-informed electorate and better government. There are risks, of course. The public has never really understood the fine professional distinction between the work of editorial writers, columnists, and reporters. The "new" journalism is likely to blur the lines between them still more. Consequently, not all newspapers accept their broadened responsibilities for interpretation and research in public attitudes. As for the electronic media, all save the leaders shy away from it. Only the news magazines, as a group, enthusiastically practice the art in their columns even though the result is not always certain of public approval.

In practiced hands, the new techniques are being used in the news media as a whole to report politics and government to a far greater extent than any other field. The trouble is that there are not really very many practiced hands as yet; moreover, editors are rather careful about selecting staff members to do interpretation and analysis. For in the broadest sense, these functions are extensions of the editorial rather than the news-reporting branches of journalism. Those who interpret the news, therefore, are given extraordinary power and must be capable of exercising it wisely.

THE POLITICAL STORY

The first rule of politics is that those who would govern must first get themselves elected to office. Consequently, much of the interest of the news media in politics and government has always been based on the coverage of elections. In the past, most news organizations got along fairly well between elections with a city hall reporter and an all-purpose political analyst. The electronic media and the news magazines, of course, left the day-by-day routine very largely to the newspapers and concentrated either on interesting personalities or key issues. The wire services did the rest.

Why Coverage Broadened   Today, it is not enough to cover city halls, legislatures, and political clubhouses or headquarters for "official" news. The power of most city political machines has waned. The movement of city people to the suburbs has given rise to many new and complex areas of government responsibility.

An expanding city that spills over its political boundaries soon obliterates the traditional pattern of city-suburban organization. Yet, even though the metropolis becomes a single urban community, it has no political unity. It becomes a "formless conglomeration of independent jurisdiction, each going its own way," or it gives rise to intrastate organizations with an independent governmental function such as the Port of New York Authority. With more than 125 million Americans already living in urban areas, and no end in sight to the national expansion, it is apparent that more cities and towns will be grappling each year with the problems of the metropolitan area.

It is scarcely possible, therefore, for any news organization—even a great newspaper with a large staff and generous news space—to cover the story of the expanding metropolis at two or three central points with a base at City Hall. Newspapers that circulate throughout a state or in large metropolitan area have sought to meet the problem by expanding their city desks into metropolitan desks and setting up integrated reporting teams of specialists. The old suburban desk, which specialized in notes about chicken dinners and visits from Aunt Susie, now exists only on newspapers that are still published in the tradition of 1890. Indeed, the old two-man combination of city hall reporter and political analyst simply cannot handle the "Metro" story as it is now developing.

In New York, Chicago, Philadelphia, Detroit, Milwaukee, St. Louis, Los Angeles, and a score or more of other cities, the major newspapers long since have devoted their efforts to covering much more news of government than the political. Some of this has been done by teams, much of it by specialists. The "Metropolitan Section" has become an established part of the newspaper. And in the leading local television stations that pay attention to the needs of their communities, the report in depth and the documentary have helped in the process of informing the public.

Why the Change?   The reasons for this change in emphasis are not difficult to find. A suburban campaign for a school bond issue, for instance, can create greater turmoil in the immediate community than an election for a United States Senator. An extension of zoning can arouse more passion than the election of a governor. And people who do not know their congressman or assemblyman suddenly find out, when a new bridge or road is to be built near them, that they can appeal only to their elected representatives if all other avenues are closed. The pollution of air and of water has become an expensive and tricky issue. In many cities and towns, where the inner core of business has visibly decayed, bond issues for urban renewal have become major matters for voters to decide.

The temper of the voter has changed, as well, and the focus of the story of government has shifted accordingly. In the days of low taxes or no taxes, when the old schools and roads and sewers were good enough for a city population, nobody became very excited about the laggard processes of local government unless a vibrant new political personality appeared or municipal graft became a major annoyance.

But as city voters have shifted to the suburbs, leaving many decaying slum areas to seething minority population groups, problems have multiplied both inside and outside the city boundaries. The agitation for civil rights has been intensified within the ghetto areas. Throughout metropolitan areas, there has also been an enormous increase in voter interest in the provisions for new housing, new streets and highways, new schools, new hospitals, more water, and all the other facilities on which the modern urban areas depend. Necessarily, taxes have climbed steeply. The electorate, well aware of the current parlous state of municipal financing, has not been indifferent to the prospect of still more taxes.

It is no wonder that the news media have been hard pressed to tell this story as it should be told. The old theory of telling the news in bits and pieces, just as it happened in a haphazard pattern or no pattern at all, has been shattered. Nor has it been possible, in a time when the needs of national defense have soared past $70 billion annually, to separate purely local concerns from national and international affairs. All thought of an isolated America, safe between its two oceans, has been banished forever by the presence of American and Soviet satellites circling the earth and strange new vehicles shooting for the moon and outer space. It has been forcefully demonstrated, in these and other ways, that the preservation of the more abundant life is linked to what happens in the far reaches of Asia and Africa as well as Washington, the state capital, and city hall.

The Gray Areas   Yet, while the news media have expanded their efforts to cover the metropolis, there has been no comparable effort—with certain brilliant exceptions—to tell the national and international story. It has not been a case of lack of material. The wire services have increased their national and international files. The news magazines have developed highly profitable international editions. The big newspaper syndicates have merchandized foreign news at a profit. On television, the documentary has been used with excellent effect to bring the world into the American living room; the pity, however, is that the effort has not been either consistent or widespread. More correspondents for American news organizations cover Washington and major foreign capitals than ever before in peacetime. Yet, despite all these advances, it is a sad truth that the news media as a whole have not done very well in presenting national and international news except for crisis coverage.

Lester Markel, founder of the International Press Institute, pointed out this failing when he said:

> Unless there is free, full, and accurate communication among nations, international understanding cannot be achieved. In such communication the press (the word includes newspapers, television, radio, and all the other media) plays a vital role: it must function internationally in a wholly responsible way. But the fact is that the press is not doing the kind of a job in the international area that is needed. Too much of it is devoted to entertainment rather than to information, to sensation rather than to solid reporting. . .
>
> One of the basic problems of journalism is to make international news comprehensible as well as comprehensive, to translate global happenings into the language of Main Street everywhere. There are editors who say that their readers are not really interested in international news. This means to me only that these editors are failing to do the job of presenting and interpreting the significant news. If important news is not read, it is because to a large extent the reading is too difficult. What is certain is this: The average reader must be reached if we are to attain a sound public opinion on which democracy wholly depends.[1]

It will take time for this viewpoint to gain more adherents. The new sewer on North Main Street is still featured over the downfall of an Asian ruler unless it means an American troop landing. In the absence of extraordinary pressures, the American news media generally do not change as rapidly as the communities they serve. The new journalism has been many years in gaining the status it has now achieved. Even at the local and state levels, where it is most accepted, a great deal of improvement can be made in telling the story of politics and government.

---

[1] Markel, Lester, IPI Affairs, *IPI Report*, monthly bulletin of the International Press Institute, February 1967, pp. 15–16.

HOW TO INTERPRET POLITICAL NEWS

Basically, interpretation adds the factor of judgment to what is called straight news—the unvarnished recital of fact which may or may not represent the truth. For example, a distinguished speaker may make news with a startling statement, but that does not necessarily mean his statement is true; accuracy represents something far greater than putting down the quotes in order and getting middle initials right. The interpretive writer is given the responsibility of considering the news in this perspective.

The difference between interpretation and editorialization, broadly, is that the interpreter applies the rule of reason to the news but stops short of recommending what should be done about it. The province of the editorial writer is to urge a course of action upon the reader or the viewer. The following are some of the ways in which interpretation may be legitimately used in the news media:

1. In the print media, interpretation may be written into the main news story or it may be made the subject of an analysis as a separate article. In the electronic media, an interpretive statement may be made during the course of a newscast; more rarely, a separate commentary may follow by an analyst of established reputation.

2. For all media, the invariable rule is to give the news first and then, at an appropriate point, tell what it means. If there are several possible meanings, with no real indication of which may be correct, the fairest procedure is to give the report in precisely that way. In any event, the public must be given the facts on which an interpretation is based so that each individual may determine for himself the soundness of the analysis in the light of the evidence.

3. If an interpretive lead is used on a story to give it meaning, the interpretation must be documented immediately. If the explanation is not complete and convincing, a straight news lead is better with a qualified interpretation interjected later.

4. The interpretive nature of a sidebar should be clearly indicated to the reader at the outset by some such approach as this: "Here is the meaning of the proposed two-cent increase in the state's gasoline tax," or, "This is how the new electric rate will affect your bills." The news, as such, should not be repeated in the sidebar on the assumption that the main story will make the basic facts clear.

5. The writer's byline goes on an interpretive story and serves as the best guarantee that an impartial explanation of events is being given. While it may be necessary at times to use such phrases as "Authorities said," or, "Observers believed" or, "Informed sources said," the reporter must in all cases have discussed the story with these unnamed authorities, observers,

or informed sources. The opposition often can discover, quickly enough, when a reporter's informed sources are imaginary—sometimes with embarrassing consequences.

6. When a story explains itself, it should be told without recourse to interpretive techniques. If a story needs perspective in the form of background dates, or a paragraph about a previous action or decision, it should be given but this usually does not constitute interpretation.

7. While much of the above may be adapted for use by writers for the electronic media, the main problem of presenting interpretation on radio and television is that relatively few newsmen are permitted to do it. Yet, as the pre-World War II radio analysts and Edward R. Murrow proved, interpretation for listeners and viewers can be dynamic and it can be documented on the air with even greater ease than in print.

8. In writing for news magazines or Sunday newspaper roundups, the tendency of the journalist often is to overanalyze and overinterpret. Even if the reader does know the basic facts of a given situation, usually a frail assumption, it is a mistake to ply him with too much opinion when he simply is not interested in it. This is the basic weakness of many an editorial page as well.

EXAMPLES OF INTERPRETATION

These are some of the ways in which interpretation is used to give meaning to the news:

The Interpretive Lead   In the following, the routine news lead would have been based on the White House briefing for labor leaders. Instead, the reasonably obvious conclusion was drawn:

> WASHINGTON—A proposal to merge the Labor and Commerce Departments into one super-Cabinet post appeared doomed today.
>
> Leaders of the AFL-CIO emerged from a White House briefing on the Administration's pet project without enthusiasm. Without labor's support, an Administration source conceded, the plan could not get through Congress.
>
> While the labor leaders reserved comment for the time being, it was learned that they would fight the program if it ever reached the House and Senate. One leader said, "If agriculture is entitled to a separate department, labor is, too." . . .

The Interpretive Paragraph   Particularly in reports of legal actions, it is not enough to say that a witness testified or was cross-examined. The purpose of the testimony or the cross-examination must be indicated as quickly as possible. One way in which it can be done follows:

The State hammered away today at a key defense witness in the murder trial of Theron J. Wildener, who is accused of slaying a bank guard during a $100,000 robbery last year.

In an hour-long attack on the testimony of Wildener's girl friend, Emmaline Lindenhurst, District Attorney Millard Carew sought to shake her story that she and the defendant were riding in a car 40 miles from town at the time the robbery occurred.

Repeatedly, he had Miss Lindenhurst tell her story and tried to trap her into inconsistencies. But the witness, a dark-haired, bespectacled, 29-year-old secretary calmly answered his questions without a trace of nervousness. . .

An Analyst's Conclusions   Often, in reporting an election, it is necessary to give conclusions rather than a cumulative total of elected representatives. Thus, the analyst goes beyond the figures at hand in the following lead:

In a stunning upset, the Republicans appeared today to have wrested control of the Legislature from the Democrats for the first time in 20 years.

While the Democrats still held a nominal advantage in the Senate as of 1 A.M., having elected 36 candidates while the Republicans had 33 seats, they were trailing in all nine remaining contests. Thus, it appeared probable that the new Senate would consist of 42 Republicans and 36 Democrats.

In the House, the Republican margin was even greater, with 61 sure seats to 48 for the Democrats, and an even split likely on the remaining ten undecided contests . . .

A Tabular Summary   In stories about taxes, budgets, social security, and other matters that vitally affect millions of individuals, a tabular summary is often the simplest and the most effective way of explaining a complicated matter. This is one good method:

WASHINGTON—You'll pay more under the new Social Security Law that goes into effect next month but your retirement benefits will be greater.

The changes were voted at the last session of Congress and signed into law by the President. They affect almost every family in the United States.

Here is a summary, calculated by wage brackets, of what you and your employer will pay under the new law and the net increase: . . .

Fact Sheet Method   When a new program of wide public interest is undertaken, one of the easiest ways to present the factual material in a meaningful way is to draw up what amounts to a fact sheet. Thus, if a state undertakes a legalized lottery for the first time, the data could be presented as follows:

Here is how the state's new lottery will operate when it goes into effect:

Tickets will be priced at $1 each and will be available at state and city offices. There will be three drawings for prizes during the year, but separate tickets must be purchased for each.

The winning ticket in each drawing will be worth $100,000, with $75,000 for second place, $50,000 for third place, $20,000 for fourth place, and $5,000 each for the holders of the next 11 tickets.

The lottery will be operated by the State Tax Commission for the benefit of the State Department of Education . . .

Interpretive Sidebar   Many newspapers, and nearly all radio and television stations, go out of their way to label separate interpretive pieces as "News Analysis" because they necessarily involve considerable personal judgment by the writer or commentator. The piece is generally all comment because the news is told separately and in detail. A budget analysis, for example, could begin as follows:

The new Defense Department budget of more than $70 billion undoubtedly means that many of the Administration's domestic programs will have to be cut back.

Congress is not going to like it in an election year, but—as most members of Congress agree—there is very little they can do about it. Limiting funds for the "War on Poverty" is not going to be popular, to point to only one cause that will suffer, but slashing at the heart of the nation's defense in a war situation is going to be even less acceptable.

Few Congressmen are taking seriously the President's contention that the nation can maintain a defense establishment second to none and still carry out all the domestic programs that are vitally needed. "We can't have guns and butter, too, no matter what the President says," one of the President's strongest supporters remarked privately when he first learned of the new Defense Department total. . .

As interpreting the news has become more popular in the news media, and particularly the press, all these methods have become virtually standard in telling the story of politics and government. Certainly, it cannot be done without recourse to analysis and interpretation.

LOCAL AND STATE GOVERNMENT

During an election year the focus of public and press interest in government is the political contest. Most actions taken by elected executives, councils, or legislatures are reported in the light of their effect on the campaign. But in between, when the normal business of government goes on without interruption, a quiet calm descends on the centers of administrative, legislative, and judicial action. Without the drama of election, the work-a-day processes of government are handled all too routinely in the news media and become mere adjuncts to the news. The all-too-familiar tendency of local and even some state officials to conduct their business in executive sessions helps dry up much of the remaining interest so that the story of government at the local and state level tends to suffer.

Reporters Need Help   It takes dedication on the part of editors to give their reporters the sense of drive and incentive that they need to do the job of covering news of government. A reporter who feels there is no interest in his beat, and senses a lack of support, can rarely do an effective job. When a newspaper decides to go after the local government story, the sparks of interest can fly. Oxie Reichler, ex-editor of the Yonkers (N. Y.) *Herald Statesman* and past president of the New York Society of Newspaper Editors, tells this story:

> One Sunday morning our public water supply became contaminated. Fearful of civic alarm, health officials decided to have a brief announcement read at all church services. They were aghast at my suggestion that we planned to print an extra edition and deliver it to every doorstep in town—whether subscribers or not—with the urgent headline, "Boil Your Water."
> People would panic, I was told. I argued that Americans panic only at rumors, never when full facts are provided. Over stout opposition, we printed that paper and distributed it. We later were praised by the officials, and shown appreciation by the community.

Had the reporter who turned in the story been discouraged, and told the paper would print nothing, the story of local government would have suffered accordingly.

Reporting on Government   As in the case of general political coverage, the reporting of government requires primary background knowledge.

Many cities have the mayor-council form of government, but the city manager-commission format is making headway. In counties the traditional method of organization by boards is giving way to a county executive plan. On the state level the governor and the legislature remain the principal sources for the government story. And in metropolitan areas new forms of government that cut across state lines, such as the Port of New York Authority, are developing greater powers.

Reporters must be familiar with these systems and their adjuncts. They must also have a knowledge of the pertinent charters and constitutions, plus the source materials and daily records that are available for inspection, before they can hope to get a maximum of meaning out of public meetings and press conferences with officials.

It is an old reportorial habit to write stories in terms of persons rather than problems, colorful incidents rather than studied analyses of material in which the public should be interested. All journalists know that it is much easier to sell a story if the name of a controversial official is attached to the lead in some way, such as being for or against a particular proposal. The news media like the specific, abhor the abstract.

Sometimes, the government story is abstract. The increasing need for water facilities, the rise in mental hygiene cases that perplexes many states, and the public indifference to civilian defense facilities are all government problems that cannot be made clear in terms of conflict, or whether an alderman points with pride or views with alarm. Such stories have to be told through a reporter's eyes, if they are to be presented in depth. There is no special time element about such accounts, for the problems will be with us for a long time. Magazines for many years have done interesting work in this field, and the other media are following them.

In fact, over and above the day-to-day spot news stories of government, the technique of the "take-out," the delineation of an issue of public importance, is becoming more widely recognized as a useful journalistic tool. It is contributing to a quickening of interest in governmental processes.

What Is Covered   As even the youngest reporters know, the mayor's office usually is the best source of news in a town or city, as is the governor's office in a state. City councils must be covered, and legislatures when they reach the bill-passing stage. Beyond that, the choice of which of the myriad offices of government to cover becomes a matter of individual selection by assignment, tip, or hunch.

Governors and mayors, in all but the smallest towns, have a subordinate official, usually an exnewspaperman, to deal with the press. However, it is still necessary to establish a firm contact with the top official himself and deal with him directly on occasion. The same is true of the city's chief fiscal officer, whether he is called comptroller or city treasurer, and the head of the council or aldermanic board. The police commissioner, city clerk, head of the board of education, and the directors of such bureaus as hospitals, health and the like are all major sources. The rest of the local officials, on city or county level, are dealt with as they become newsworthy.

The coverage of state business is more of a problem because the selection of news sources is greater and the opportunities for coverage fewer on the whole. In a city hall, or in a suburban area handled by a newspaper bureau, a reporter has the advantage of continuity and experience. He is on the job every day, and establishes a familiarity with the business at hand and the officials who are conducting it. At the state level fewer reporters are assigned for year-round coverage. The tendency now is to send political writers to handle the legislature only in its opening and closing stages and to cover the governor when his actions affect the locality, except where state coverage is also a local story. This means there are comparatively slender permanent special staffs, with wire services doing most of the work. Therefore, the reporter who is assigned to the state capital in the closing week of the legislature arrives cold, tries for a frantic fill-in from friendly officials, and is likely to end up duplicating the wire service accounts.

The same is true of the television newsman, sent out with a camera crew at the last minute to pick up an important story at city hall or the state house. He is dropped into a special situation, without background and usually with little comprehension of what is going on, and must compete with wire service, newspaper, and even radio reporters who have been covering the beat for months, sometimes years. Inevitably, the latecomer—regardless of his medium—is at a disadvantage; with its dependence on interesting film sequences, television is particularly vulnerable.

The more enlightened (and wealthier) television stations have long since concluded that it is not only good journalism but good business to station a firstrate political analyst at the state house as well as at the more important city halls within their area. Thus, the newspapers are not always going to have it their own way in maintaining detailed local political coverage. While competition between newspapers is dying out, competition between the media is rapidly growing.

It is one way of guaranteeing that the story of politics and government will continue to be told from the local level up to the White House.

COVERING BUDGETS AND TAXES

Of all the news media, the newspaper alone is able to give full space and mature consideration to budget-making and programming for new taxes at the local level. With very few exceptions, radio and television give such news a fast brush-off and go on to something more exciting. But in fact, nothing is more important to the cause of democratic self-government than a public presentation of the costs of government and the proposals through which elected officials seek to meet them. Without this kind of information, the public is left completely in the dark.

Every budget story must be told with scrupulous regard for detail—what is to be spent, why it is to be spent, why it is an increased or decreased sum over last year, and where economies may be possible. Hand in hand with spending proposals must be an estimate of whether taxes are to be increased and, if so, how much. Necessarily, the tax estimate places an enormous burden on the reporter because public officials, understandably, are usually not very willing to admit that their spending plans are going to cost the public more money. And where there is a tax reduction, the writer had best be careful before he breaks into loud hosannas. Too often, such projections prove on final examination to be less than realistic in an inflationary time.

Here is a county budget story, which blends all these factors into a coherent whole:

A record $127.9 million budget for Mattox County was recommended yesterday by County Executive Fairfield Winston Jr., who also promised a tax cut. The proposal, which is for the year beginning Jan. 1, represents an increase of $14.7 million over this year.

Because the five eastern townships of the county will do their own policing effective Jan. 1, with the transfer of all county police functions to the five western townships, the county tax rate for the eastern townships will be cut from $3.49 to $3.20 for each $100 of assessed property valuation. The five western townships, which are largely suburban, will get only a one-cent reduction from $5.58 to $5.57 for each $100 of assessed property valuation.

The tax cut was made possible by a healthy boost in the total assessed real estate valuation of the county, which will be $1,196,222,871 beginning Jan. 1. This represents an increase of $74,188,266 over the current year.

In his budget message to the County Board of Supervisors, Winston argued that the full value of the property should be considerably higher. He also used $6.1 million in estimated surplus from this year's budget and more than $1 million in economies to arrive at his next year's budget figure.

Winston's Republican opponent, Garfield Sprague, scoffed at the possibility of a tax cut despite the big increase in spending in the proposed new budget. "I'll believe it when I see it," he said.

The proposed budget provides pay increases of up to ten per cent for the county's 4,500 employees over a five-year period.

Estimated revenues for next year include $60.2 million from property taxes, $61.6 million from state and federal aid programs, and the remainder from miscellaneous sources such as departmental fees, reimbursements, and sales of assets.

The biggest expenditure again is for the Welfare Department, which takes 40 per cent of the budget. The police are next with 18 per cent. With the consolidation of the 1,500-man County police force in the western townships, including an additional 100 men requested by Commissioner Boise Nathan, the police spending will rise to $22,593,663, up more than $2,500,000. The rest of the spending is for public works, six per cent; mental health, 8.5 per cent; colleges, 3.5 per cent; judicial, two per cent, and 22 per cent for miscellaneous services.

chapter 25

Public Opinion, Polling, and Elections

Everybody recognizes the existence of something called public opinion in an open society, but few agree on what it is or how it operates. Nor is it easy to define.

In a far smaller and less complicated United States nearly a century and a half ago, Alexis de Tocqueville called it the "predominant authority" that acted by "elections and decrees."[1] In a moment of disillusion with the vagaries of the British public, Sir Robert Peel was less admiring; to him, it was "that great compound of folly, weakness, prejudice, wrong feeling, right feeling, obstinacy, and newspaper paragraphs which is called public opinion."[2] In the early twenties, Walter Lippmann argued that it was "primarily a moralized and codified version of the facts," and that "the pattern of stereotypes at the center of our codes largely determines what group of facts we shall see and in what light we shall see them."[3] In our own time, a sociologist, W. Phillips Davison, has concluded that public opinion should be treated as a "consensus that influences the behavior of individuals who contribute to the consensus . . . a form of organization

---

1 Alexis de Tocqueville, *Democracy in America* (Vintage Press, New York: 1954) Vol. 1, p. 129.
2 Walter Lippmann, *Public Opinion* (Macmillan, New York: 1922) p. 197.
3 Walter Lippmann, *Public Opinion*, p. 125.

(that) is able to coordinate the thought and action of a large number of people. . ."[4]

Of one thing there is no doubt. Whether it is the "predominant authority," a "great compound of folly," a "pattern of stereotypes," or a "consensus," the measurement of what is called public opinion has become of transcendent importance in modern mass communications. It forms the basis of much advertising and merchandising practice, determines what shall and shall not be seen on television, locates new enterprises as varied in character as food markets and newspapers, provides trends (or the illusion of trends) in political campaigns at all levels of government, and dominates the coverage of national elections. The journalist has not been able to escape the implications of this expanding activity. It has placed him squarely in the middle of the computer age.

MEASURING PUBLIC OPINION

While the public opinion poll has been a familiar feature of American journalism for a quarter-century or more, it has assumed greater importance since television has come of age. The television networks in their impatience over the measured pace of election reporting by wire services and newspapers, first formed their own reporting organizations to do a faster job. Then, still not satisfied, they engaged experienced analysts of public opinion to project fragmentary election returns early on an election night into almost immediate declarations of winners.

This practice, adapted from circulation stunts of aggressive newspapers of forty and fifty years ago, naturally ran into a great many risks and some spectacular errors. But unlike the old-time election extra with the flash result, television election reporting has exerted a continuing influence on the whole election process. For all its disadvantages, it has come to fulfill a public need.

Whether or not the intense competition with television has anything to do with it, the average newspaper editor and political reporter still regard poll-taking with far more suspicion than belief. It is true that some individual poll-takers have acceptance on various newspapers and newspaper groups, primarily because their pre-election verdicts are more often right than wrong. But by and large, the various devices for reading the public's mind on popular issues, product acceptance and elections have more prestige in the electronic media, advertising, and sociology than in the day-to-day practice of newspaper work. The trend is changing slowly as

---

[4] W. Phillips Davison, *International Political Communication* (New York: Praeger, for the Council on Foreign Relations, 1966) p. 66.

newspaper editors and publishers learn how to use the tricky computerized versions of public taste and public likes and dislikes. But pollsters and newspapers, with some exceptions, generally operate in an atmosphere of mutual distrust.

An older generation of newspapermen, now gently fading out of print, always delighted to recall the famous wrong guess of the *Literary Digest* in 1936—the selection of the Republican Presidential candidate, Governor Alfred M. Landon of Kansas, over President Franklin D. Roosevelt on the basis of postcard polls of telephone subscribers that missed the mass public. Moreover, as an additional debit against the pollster, the newspaper people of that day liked to point out that it was no scientific analyst, but an old politician, Postmaster General James Aloysius Farley, who called the 1936 election right, 46 States for Roosevelt and two for Landon. Yet, even as the *Literary Digest* later suspended publication, George Gallup was building up his American Institute of Public Opinion and rising to fame and public acceptance.

Nearly all pollsters and newspapers were spectacularly wrong in the last election before the television era, the 1948 Presidential campaign which was narrowly won by President Harry S. Truman over Governor Thomas E. Dewey of New York, the Republican candidate. The picture of a grinning Truman delightedly holding up the Chicago *Tribune*, with a banner headline proclaiming a Dewey victory, is a favorite in every journalistic album of the era. Yet, the poll-takers did not go out of business as a result.

The closeness of the 1960 Presidential race, in which Senator John F. Kennedy so narrowly edged out the Republican nominee, Vice President Richard M. Nixon, was not one that gave much comfort either to the traditional newspaper analyst or the electronic media. It was a time when there was much emphasis on the undoubted truth that most poll-takers claim to be only within 3 percentage points on either side of a particular election result. Yet, in subsequent elections, particularly the runaway victory of President Lyndon Baines Johnson over Senator Barry Goldwater in 1964, this important qualification was all but forgotten by a large section of the public. This was, of course, equally true of Nixon's 1968 Presidential race.

Criticisms   In adapting the Vote Profile Analysis and similar systems to election night use in order to be able to make an early call on who won and who lost, the networks took some long chances and scarcely gave the impression of sober responsibility. In one case, that of the American Broadcasting Company in the 1966 Congressional elections, a number of important races were called wrong. Nor was television alone in its election errors. The respected New York *Daily News* poll, which disregarded the sociological niceties in several particulars, came a cropper for the fourth time in its history in 1966 when it predicted Governor Nelson A Rockefeller of New York would not be re-elected. He won easily from his Democratic opponent, Frank D. O'Connor, president of the New York City Council. In several Presidential preference primary elections in 1968, Senator Eugene J. McCarthy upset most of the media analysts before finally losing the Democratic nomination to Vice President Hubert H. Humphrey.

However, poll-taking and election forecasting have become so deeply imbedded in the American political system—and in American journalism as well—that they have continued to develop despite all setbacks. Their credibility has suffered from time to time, particularly when hired pollsters of some repute issued findings that tended to support the positions of those who paid them. Yet, on the whole, this has not seemed to affect their public acceptance.

There are critics who point out cynically that polls and pollsters often tend to favor Republican candidates, in line with the generally Republican sympathies of most newspaper publishers, television proprietors, and news magazine owners. Certainly, this was not true in the Johnson election of 1964 when the liberal Republican press, frightened by Senator Goldwater's extreme conservatism, largely bolted to the Democratic side. In other years, it has been possible to document such an accusation against irresponsible newspapers. As for the electronic media, both the regulatory powers of the Federal Communications Commission and the watchfulness of the press have prevented so far any massive campaign for one Presidential candidate against another.

Reasons for Forecasts   It may well be asked why the news media go in so heavily for surveys of public opinion in connection with the reporting of politics and government, and elections in particular. One very good reason is that such forecasts, and the basis for them, are a part of the business of the political reporter and his news organization. Long before there were polls and other real or fancied scientific devices for sampling public opinion, it was an important part of a political reporter's job to talk with people of all kinds to determine which candidates were most likely to win. Newspapers prided themselves on the work of their political analysts, many of them famous in the pretelevision days, and advertised their successes as seers.

However, the most compelling reason for the press's continued interest in the drift of political campaigning is that it cannot stand for an "equal time for all candidates" position, such as the one that hobbles television. While reputable newspapers do make an effort to be fair in this respect, an "equal time" commitment would rob them of their independence and quickly reduce them to the level of an official gazette. No newspaper that cherishes its independence can duck a controversy in a political campaign by acting as a mere recording device that plays back speeches and rival claims, but does not undertake to evaluate them.

True, there are risks that a political evaluation may prove to be wrong. It has happened before and it will happen again. But even worse is the failure of an independent newspaper to take a position. It would seem that the area of choice for a responsible news organization lies in the selection of people and methods to perform as honest a job as is humanly possible in recording the swings of public opinion during a political campaign. It is obvious that such probings may produce estimates on Page 1 that run counter to the candidates of the newspaper's choice on the editorial page. (The 1966 New York *Daily News* poll that predicted a Rockefeller loss ran contrary to its editorial position.) It is equally obvious that when a poll shows that the candidates of a newspaper or news magazine are leading, the opposition will quickly charge that the poll is "rigged."

These are the risks that the press must take. The news is not distributed from an ivory tower, but in the midst of the swirling life and struggle of the city or town. Its most useful servants, the journalists, are not permitted to wait in amused aloofness for the dust to settle and then make keen, penetrating, but entirely academic judgments. They do not write for history, but for the edition. Judgments must be made whenever necessary in the course of a political campaign, and by and large they can be justified only if they prove to be accurate.

POLLING TECHNIQUES

The oldest and least sophisticated type of public opinion poll is the man-in-the-street survey. It is still used by many newspaper city editors who cling to the notion that any reporter, unschooled in the simplest statistical procedures, can talk to 20 or 30 persons picked at random and come up with a valid reflection of public opinion in a given area. The reporter generally works hard at his assignment, taking the names, ages, addresses, occupations, and relevant additional background for his respondents. He also will make certain to report accurately what they say. And yet, such exercises come near the truth only by the sheerest accident because the sample seldom is representative of all voters in the region under consideration, known in statistical terms as the "universe."

The Random Sample A reliable public opinion research organization goes at the task by trying, from the outset, to develop a random sample that will come reasonably close to representing the "universe," whether it is a village, a county, a state, or the entire nation. The most difficult, time-consuming and costly technique is the so-called probability method in which the trained interviewer is told he must find certain people, chosen in advance by complicated statistical methods, who are representative of the whole. By contrast, the quota method provides the interviewer with a list of the types of people he must locate but leaves the choice pretty much to his own desire.

Regardless of the method, a sample of a few hundred persons may be found representative of a metropolitan region and a few thousand may be used to develop a national pattern of opinion. In the probability method, the primary sampling units may be drawn at random from a list of all counties and metropolitan areas in the United States. These are then further reduced to urban blocks and rural segments, also picked at random. Next, within each selected block or segment, every dwelling unit is listed and a fixed number is selected at random. Finally, in the selected dwelling units all adults are enumerated; from each, one person is chosen, again at random. The sample that is selected in this way has a high probability of reflecting all the characteristics of the "universe" from which it is drawn. Factors of age, sex, economic status, ethnic and religious grouping, and other relevant factors are all represented in the sample. Thus, the interviewer must track down and speak at length with each person on his list in order to get answers to a list of predetermined questions.[5]

The Quota Method   In the quota method, of course, the interviewer tries to represent, in his sample, all the elements necessary to duplicate the "universe" but, consciously or unconsciously, his own prejudices enter into the selection process. The only advantage of the quota method over the probability method is that it is faster and cheaper; however, in the end, it may not be a great deal more reliable than the ancient man-in-the-street poll when it is conducted by an experienced newspaperman who knows the makeup of his community and conscientiously tries to pick people representative of it.

To the uninitiated, it may seem to be sheer madness to try to determine national trends by polling a handful of citizens in a town, a few hundred in a state, a few thousand nationally. And yet, except for the house-to-house enumeration process every decade, the Bureau of the Census has been using the random sampling technique for years to determine population growth. The popularity of television programs is determined by devices attached to sets in less than 1,500 homes selected at random throughout the nation by one major service organization. A number of well-established research organizations—Gallup, Roper, and Louis

---

[5] S. A. Stauffer, *Communism, Conformity and Civil Liberties* (Doubleday, New York: 1955) pp. 13–18.

Harris among them—have sampled public opinion on everything from sex to Presidential elections with an impressive record of accomplishment.

No one of experience in the field claims absolute accuracy for any public opinion study. Usually, the allowance for error on either side of the final result is put at three per cent, and sometimes it goes as high as five per cent. In a close political fight, or in a television rivalry between great public favorites, it is obvious, therefore, that any poll must be used carefully. However, in just such tense situations, caution is often thrown to the winds and polling organizations find themselves in deep trouble. Whether they like it or not, their findings are put to grotesque uses, particularly during political campaigns, when one side or the other will claim victory on the basis of a lead of as little as one-half of one per cent.

Checking Trends   The use of selected voting units—a ward or election district in a big city or a county in a rural district—is a favorite indicator of political trends but even that is not foolproof. Every major polling organization has a well-guarded list of such units, picked originally because they "voted right" in a number of Presidential, Gubernatorial, and Senatorial elections and were painstakingly researched thereafter. On the theory that Arshamamoque County has been "right" in eight Presidential elections, for example, the trustful pollster proceeds on the assumption that the individuals who reside there constitute a collective Delphi. Before election day, these surveys make interesting reading; however, when a series of such units throughout the country becomes the basis for a sweeping forecast of early victory on election night, an analyst sometimes can be very wrong. He may not have had the good luck to talk with enough "right" people in the "right" county, or underlying political forces may have changed. Therefore, the results he feeds into the computers to provide a television miracle for the whole country may kick back at him.

Just as television has fallen into the practice of making early claims of victory for one candidate or another on election night, newspapers resolutely insist on running their own forecasts on the Sunday or Monday before election day. Both practices have built-in hazards. It is one thing to predict an election in September and quite another the day before the voters, as the time-honored election leads have it, troop to the polls. The press forecasts are based on all available polls, private estimates by respected political leaders, the public claims—or lack of them—by the candidates, and the reporters' own feelings about the matter. When the campaign is one-sided, it is no great trick to call an election. But when all the usual factors are in conflict, then the analyst is well advised to make no forecast. One of the oldest sayings in American newsrooms is: "They can't hang you for what you *don't* write."

PREDICTIONS

Any election forecast should have suitable qualifications throughout, even though the result may seem to duplicate many years of similar pre-election accounts. This is a sample of the usual type of forecast lead:

> Mayor Hammond Garvell appears likely to win re-election on Tuesday if the vote is as large as expected.
> A sampling of typical voter opinion, plus talks with professionals in both parties and the findings of private polls, indicated today that the Mayor was expected to defeat his opponent, Hereford Cates.
> But even Mayor Garvell's closest aides emphasized that, as an independent running for re-election, he must count on a heavy turnout at the polls—always a sign in this city that the independent voter is making his influence felt . . .

"Foregrounding" Politics A considerable segment of political writing in newspapers and news magazines and analytical comment on television is based on the summation and interpretation of coming events. The holding of conventions, listing of known candidates and issues, and analysis of rival claims is one familiar report of this type. Another is the planning for a campaign during a given period and the conclusions that may be drawn from it in terms of objectives.

Best known of all is the pre-election day summations giving the time, places, and candidates involved in the voting, the registration figures, probable vote totals, analysis of issues, weather, and whatever conclusions the writer or analyst wishes to make. On television, this type of information can only be given in sketchy form. It generally takes two solid pages of newspaper type to give the voter all the material he needs to make a decision on numerous candidates, propositions, and referenda. This, certainly, is the place where a good newspaper is priceless and the electronic media are at a complete disadvantage.

Many accounts of future events in a political campaign are loosely termed forecasts and consequently summon up a picture of a reporter or newscaster with a slightly lopsided crystal ball beside his typewriter. By tradition this type of story is called a "think-piece" or a "dope story," both derogatory terms for a frequently useful and informative article that is done by a knowledgeable reporter. A more accurate term would be "foregrounding the news" since such stories must have a factual base. They consider various alternatives—which candidates are stronger, which issues are most likely to dominate an election, which geographical areas are the key to the campaign.

Often it is neither possible nor desirable to guess at what may happen and the wise political correspondent does not try. In preparation for a foreground piece, he may talk with anywhere from ten to twenty persons of all shades of political opinion—leaders and followers—and sometimes more. When he has been on a particular political beat for years, of course, he knows fairly well what he may expect from his sources and sometimes does not have to consult as many of them. When he writes, "The candidate's opponents are convinced," or, "The candidate's managers believe," he has actually talked with them. He does not write anything without considerable thought and inquiry.

Consequently, the stentorian "I predict—!" of the cock-sure columnist is not for the more modest political analyst, whatever his medium. The perpendicular pronoun usually is not for him. He does not say, "I know . . . " when no one can possibly know, but writes that "it appears likely," or, "It seems possible," or, "There is some reason to believe." In terms of analysis, he does not say, "This will happen," when no one knows for certain that anything will happen. Instead, he calmly lists all the major possibilities and discusses them one by one, indicating which are the most likely to occur.

Whereas the bombastic guesser merely gives his prediction based on usually superficial evidence, the career political analyst must document any assumption he makes by giving whatever facts he has to support his conclusions. The difference between a guesser and a reporter in politics, therefore, is that one plays fair with the public and the other does not.

The line between the two is clear. As Bernard M. Baruch once said, "Every man has a right to his opinions, but no man should be wrong about his facts." That is especially true of reporters in politics.

COVERING ELECTIONS

Before the growth of television as a political force—and an enormously expensive one—a national or state election campaign was likely to last three months or longer. Automobiles bore local candidates into every part of their constituencies, and campaign trains transported state and national candidates for tens of thousands of miles. It was a sensation when Franklin Delano Roosevelt actually flew to Chicago to accept the Democratic Presidential nomination in 1932. His frequent "fireside chats" to the nation made radio a magnificent political instrument long before television was born.

It was the golden age for political reporters. They had time to get acquainted with candidates, to wear out shoeleather talking with ordinary people as well as political leaders, to know the public mind reasonably well in an age when public opinion polling was a novel idea, and to form conclusions based on exhaustive—and sometimes exhausting—experiences. Newspapers in those days were stuffed with political news, or what passed for it, for half a year or more during a major campaign. And a political reporter of consequence was much sought after—a public figure in his own right.

The Reporter's Job   Today, the bulk of political campaigning for almost all offices is done in a month, sometimes even less, except for a Presidential or Gubernatorial campaign that may run an additional week in its most intensive stage. The marvelous exposure of television, plus its mounting expense, limits political campaigning in two ways. First of all, the wise candidate must guard against overexposure; to bore people to death is an even greater political crime than to fail to project an attractive and appealing image. But even more important, all except the millionaire politicians of the sixties—Lyndon Baines Johnson, the Kennedy brothers, Nelson Aldrich Rockefeller, and the like—must be careful of television expenditures that can bankrupt a political party.

There are still political caravans in the modern era, but they generally move by air in national and state campaigns. Trains, autos, and buses are usually for the smaller fry. It becomes a national sensation when a candidate for high office actually takes to the sidewalks and walks a few blocks, shaking hands at random, to show he is a fine, down-to-earth fellow who loves the people. Once, during a campaign for the Governorship in New York, Nelson Rockefeller dropped in at an East Side delicatessen store in New York City and bought a salami at cut-rate from an admirer. This caused a disgruntled customer to complain to the proprietor: "To a Rockefeller you have to give bargains." The story went all over the country.

Because of the primacy of television in reporting political speeches as they are delivered, giving the public an intimate glimpse of major candidates, the newspaper function now is a double one—to analyze the news as well as to present it. All the best newspapers still publish full texts of important speeches, when they are available, and give at length the political news that television can only summarize in its news programs. This, plus the importance of the analyses offered by distinguished newspaper correspondents and columnists, makes the press a political power during any campaign. The politician who turns his back on newspapers in the mistaken notion that he need only appear on television very quickly discovers that editorial pages are not to be discounted.

Nevertheless, the political reporter for any major news organization— wire services, newspapers, news magazines, and the electronic media—is up against an almost impossible job today. He soon finds his work is so concentrated that he has little time to talk to the candidates or their managers, let alone the public at large. In a national campaign, if he tries to talk with local politicians or voters at an airport, he usually risks missing the candidate's speech or the aircraft. Moreover, the newspaper practice of using advance texts either in full or as the basis for a news story has been severely restricted by the general uncertainty that advances will hold up. In airplane tours, or modifications of the old whistle-stop train tour, most candidates develop what they call a basic speech which is given over and over again. No political reporter sends such material more than once. In consequence, the business of campaign coverage tends to become a humdrum affair except in the hands of an experienced reporter who knows where to look for news or an analyst of more than ordinary capability.

Team Reporting   Some newspapers have tried to develop new methods of political reporting to maintain the competition with television and, to a far lesser extent, radio. A number of the better ones have formed teams of reporters to cover various aspects of a political campaign—to sound out the sentiment of acknowledged community leaders or political chieftains at the state level, to gather detailed information on the effect of the campaign, even to sound out public opinion by using reasonably sophisticated polling methods. The team report is lengthy, but usually most informative, and it presents material that often cannot be obtained from any other source.

But team reporting is not the whole answer, by any means. In one respect, there is no change in a political reporter's life. For newspapers, the political campaign remains a story primarily for wire services, the electronic media, and the morning papers. Except for luncheon speeches and afternoon auto tours, the main effort for a political reporter is at night because the major political speeches are delivered at a time best suited for television's enormous audiences. For morning newspapermen, therefore, this means much of the day is spent in preparing for the coverage of the big story at night. For afternoon newspapermen, time and effort are required to locate that ever-elusive fresh angle on an old speech or to talk to enough sources to foreground the news. To fall back on a routine beginning is deadly.

A political analysis, a news essay in the form of a reflective summary, even a political profile give a certain freshness to a newspaper that a stale rehash of a televised speech, printed in the morning papers, cannot rival. James M. Perry, in the weekly *National Observer*, turned on a dull Monday to a consideration of Pennsylvania politics as follows:

> HARRISBURG, Pa.—Milton Shapp, until recently an obscure Philadelphia industrialist, will spend $2,000,000 of his own money this year in an effort to win election as governor of Pennsylvania. No one before— not George Earle or Arthur James or John Fine or even William Scranton—ever thought the job was worth that kind of cash.

But Mr. Shapp, in more ways than one, is a phenomenon. He wants desperately to be governor of Pennsylvania. So he's willing to spend all the money that's necessary to fulfill his life's ambition. More importantly for the future of American politics, Mr. Shapp and the people who work for him have learned how to spend money to win elections . . .[3]

The writer went on to analyze the amounts that have been spent in recent years by various candidates to try to win elections and concluded that money, while important, is not everything. His piece required considerable research—far beyond the quick rewrite of the next day's schedule which is now well-nigh useless. But then, it is the willingness to go into research—to dig for something that isn't completely obvious—that distinguishes the successful journalist from the routine hand. Much of the best newspaper work on political campaigns is being done on the basis of such research.

THE POLITICAL ROUTINE

There is, unhappily, a routine about the life of the political reporter as there is about almost everything else in journalism. It has to be done and done well. Consequently, no reporter should attempt to cover politics without adequate preparation. This includes accurate knowledge of the political machinery with which he is dealing, the laws on eligibility, voter registration and campaigning, and the background of past elections. He should know the geographic and ethnic facts about the areas he is covering, the principal elective officials and other officeholders, and the various party leaders. A knowledge of political philosophy, as well as practical politics, is mandatory.

The outline of a political reporter's principal activities, regardless of the medium for which he operates, will show why:

Nominations The coverage of the nominating process is the first in the political progression that leads to public office. Candidates may be nominated by petition, by primary election, or by convention, and the routine of all must be known. Sometimes a combination of two or three of these is necessary, depending on particular laws, customs or practices, which vary, not only by the state, but sometimes even by the county or town.

Preconvention Maneuvers The well-informed political correspondent must resign himself to an enormous amount of travel. Where conventions are decisive in the nomination of candidates, as in national and some state elections, the journalist must keep in touch with the principal leaders, the main

---

[6] *National Observer*, September 26, 1966. Mr. Shapp lost in November.

candidates and, the key members of their entourage. This cannot be done by telephone. There is no way to cover politics other than to be on the spot; mere dependence on polls and a quick skimming of the local papers can lead to treacherous oversimplifications. At a time when the management of political campaigns for ex-movie stars and other newcomers to government is being turned over to hired political publicity firms, who work for anybody who is willing to pay, the political writer must see for himself the unprincipled political maneuverings that are being conducted in various parts of the country. The correspondent must be alert for switches from one candidate to another by community leaders, announcements from the rival camps, signs of excessive expenditures for mysterious purposes, and deals to block one candidate in order to throw the nomination to another.

Conventions   Television has come to dominate the political conventions at national and state levels. This is first of all because of the importance to both major parties of television exposure for their candidates. Almost of equal importance is television's ability to pay for a substantial amount of the convention costs by being assured of exclusive privileges of one kind or another. This does not mean that newspapers, wire services, and news magazines do not cover the conventions and do not, on the whole, do a good job. On the contrary. A capable, hard-hitting and discerning press has never been more necessary in the coverage of political meetings of all kinds. The range of television's roving eye, focused on the sensation of the moment, is limited. Moreover, with so much news to bring into the nation's living rooms, there is often little time for television's capable analysts to give the background and significance of what the public sees and does not see.

The duty of the political analyst for all media, including electronic, is therefore increased. He is responsible for everything going on in front of the cameras, and at the same time must be painfully aware that he must find out somehow whatever is happening outside the range of television.

In the press section, therefore, those who write politics must handle advance texts, do leads, know what is going on behind the scenes, arrange for coverage of set events and unscheduled caucuses outside the convention hall, and keep up with the candidates themselves. It is a man-killing job. Finally, on roll-call votes, the reporter cannot rely merely on the television computers to flash the word of a nomination at the instant it happens. He must maintain the same calculation through modern methods and keep the cumulative totals. If this were a perfect world, then television would always be right and the newspaper reporters could go home. But it has not turned out that way. As soon as the nomination is won, the press must be off— often ahead of the cameras—to interview the candidate, the candidate's wife, his children, his managers, and sometimes even his servants.

Registration   The routine business of reporting on voter registration is more than a recounting of figures. Comparative registration figures, handled by a knowledgeable political analyst, often can tell the story of an election week before it happens. Before a writer attempts such a feat, however, he must be sure that he knows the territory as well as the politicians who operate in it. Guesswork with registration figures, like guesswork in any other area in the news, can be disastrous.

Campaigns   It is difficult enough for a political writer to keep up with campaign tours, speeches, press conferences, and high-level strategy without trying to decide what it all means. Yet, unless there is a continual effort to report politics in depth, the correspondent fails in his primary assignment. The public, more than ever, requires the publication of careful, analytical articles at regular intervals in a swift, shifting campaign. Nobody tells a correspondent, as a rule, when he should write a wrapup, roundup or situationer—as the story is variously known. His instinct must tell him. He must therefore be familiar with the issues, as well as with the candidates; the points of difference, as well as the points of similarity. Samuel Lubell has often made the point that a political analyst's work begins with the day *after* an election. This piece from the *Christian Science Monitor*, the opening of which is given here, is presented as supporting evidence:

> ATLANTA—The most visible lesson from the recent elections in the Deep South is the same one Northern elections indicated. To wit: the Negro voter has become a power at the ballot box.
> But another major trend in Southern politics may prove almost as far-reaching. It is the continued growth of Republican strength.
> The elections generally obscured this second trend. Only Mississippi and Louisiana among Deep South states held a substantial number of elections. (Louisiana's actually were primary elections.)
> And in these two states Republicans fared badly. However, these are the only two Southern states where the GOP is weakening. Elsewhere it is on the rise . . .

Election Day   The proceedings on election day, once so boisterous in the average American city, are reasonably quiet today. In big cities, with few exceptions, there is almost a holiday air instead of the uproar of stolen ballot boxes, chicanery, the running in of floaters as voters and other tricks of the bad old days of political machine dominance. These things still happen on occasion, but not as openly as they once did. If an election is being stolen, the political bosses try not to make a public announcement of it. Trickery at the polls, in consequence, is rather difficult to detect on election day; it comes to light long afterward, if at all.

Because all the action of vote-tabulating, early election claims, statements of victory, and concessions of defeat take place on election night; the news organization staffs on election day itself are generally light. Skeleton crews run the afternoon papers; as for the mornings and the wire services, they are at peak strength because this is, primarily, their story and television's. Whatever news there is on election day has to be summarized, in the absence of violence or irregularities, in a report of a light or heavy vote, the statements of notables at the polls, last-minute action by the candidates and their managers, and a roundup of activity in the area. It is a tribute to the functioning of a democratic society that election day attracts so little fuss in this era and is, on the whole, a relatively honest operation which still lacks a great deal in efficiency, as long lines outside the polling places indicate. Violence may occur, but it is rare.

Election Night   The important thing about election night work is the effort that goes into organizing it. In the press and in the electronic media, the news staff that generally does the best job is the one that prepares for it with the greatest care. Sometimes the preparations for an election night begin as much as six months in advance. During the final weeks, the compilation of background figures, campaign materials, data covering everything from biographies to party platforms, and the outlining of actual assignments are almost as important as the day-to-day coverage of the news. No good news organization goes into election night without complete, pretested planning and batteries of the best calculators and computers available, with trained personnel to run them.

Election coverage is the kind of thing the American news media do best. Once the polls close and the first figures start flowing from the newsrooms, partisanship is nearly always forgotten by the working journalists and all effort is concentrated on reporting who won, how victory was achieved and what it means.

Tabulating the Vote   The public's attention is riveted on the television screens on election night and the electrifying announcements, a few minutes after the polls have closed, that one candidate or another has won. The electronic performance is risky, but it is in the journalistic tradition. Before the days of radio, newspapers like the Kansas City *Star* made it a practice to put out early Presidential extras announcing a victor. The *Star*'s extra was based on the tabulation of a few key national voting units with a history of having been "right" on a number of previous elections; to some extent, this is also the basis of the television announcements. When there is a wide swing between the candidates, or when the result is known even before the polls close, such journalistic flings are harmless and delude nobody. It is when the vote is very close that television can look bad in making a desperate early gamble at announcing a victory. Gradually, the major television news organizations have learned the bitter lesson that newspapers absorbed in the years before the electronic media took primacy in such spot news reporting. They have become far more careful with the announcement of who won—and why—and have generallly adopted a stance of responsibility that befits the journalist far better than a wild-eyed claim of exclusivity.

HANDLING THE FIGURES

The basis of any voting announcement, whether it is given by the wire services, television, or rival media, is the vote total itself, the number of districts it represents and the identities of these districts. No fragmentary vote is worth anything unless the source is identified, so that it can be compared at once with previous records. Thus, any voting result that is important enough to be made known should contain the number of voting districts, the area, and—if possible—the time as follows:

> 442 out of 1,346 election districts in Great Bear County, on the state's northern border, gave these totals at 10:32 P.M.:
> Jones (D)   60,024
> Smith (R)   50,555
> 26 election districts in the 64th Ward, in the heart of Central City's south side, gave these totals at 9:30 P.M.:
> Brown (D)   2,022
> Green (R)   2,366

The names of election units change, of course, from one place to another, but whether they are wards or districts, the practice is the same. On the basis of a sufficient cross-section of the voting, and a knowledge of past performance in the same area, a projection of the figures can be computed and an indicated voting result can be given. Thus, on the basis of a 25 per cent voting return, an experienced political analyst can calculate what will happen and make an announcement that reads something like this:

> On the basis of returns from one-quarter of the city's districts two hours after the polls closed, Smith led by 40,662 to 32,634 for Jones, his Democratic rival. This gave him an actual plurality of 8,028 over Jones and an indicated plurality of more than 30,000 if the same vote ratio continues.

The political analyst knows, of course, if it is possible for the same ratio to continue. He has all the statistics on past performances at his elbow. Therefore, he can quickly tell if the vote yet to come is from districts that are preponderantly Democratic or Republican, and guide himself accordingly in making his projection of the results. Where cities are heavily Democratic and rural districts are heavily Republican, as is true in such states as Illinois, New Jersey, and New York, the initial returns from the cities, being tabulated faster, often show Democratic candidates far in the lead.

But such early trends can be misleading. A check of a candidate's performance in a particular city may show that he is receiving a considerably smaller percentage of the vote than he has in past years, which could mean his eventual defeat. Voting percentages, consequently, tell the election story at a very early time, and the wise political analyst watches them without finally committing himself until he notes a decisive shift.

It is on the basis of such calculations, done with computers by the television networks, wire services, and the larger newspapers, that quite accurate announcements can often be made of the victory of a candidate who is actually trailing in the early voting returns. That, too, is why some candidates concede elections long before the total vote is known (although it has happened, but rarely, that a candidate conceded defeat and was in fact elected by a surge of late returns).

Doing the Story   The writing or telling of the political story, actually, is the simplest part of the election night performance. The coverage of the returns, an unofficial service performed at the national level by a combination of news media working with public officials, is the first business of the journalist and it is an intricate and time-consuming job. Once the wire services were content to wait until the figures were supplied by slow-moving election board machinery; however, the television networks stepped in and hired hordes of temporary reporters—students, housewives, and the like—to go to the precincts and get the returns. It was this kind of competition that finally forced the press to step up its own activity and, eventually, led to the alliance with the electronic media on major elections.

Two decades ago, before television, the great newspapers went into election night with a rather primitive tabulation system. Adding machines were brought in from the advertising and business departments, with operators, to be located near editorial personnel who were compiling the long and detailed voting tables from wire service and telephoned figures. When an edition went to press, the tables were put into a page form; then, they were taken out following the edition and work continued on them until they were complete.

Uses of the Computer   The rise of the computer, plus the faster service of television based on modern methods of statistical analysis, have revolutionized the whole intricate business of tabulating election returns. However, it still takes a lot of manpower and infinite pains, and the possibilities of error are as great as ever. No journalist will ever say that election night duty is easy.

The stories of election results—written and verbal—are based on the tabulated figures, which are shown on television at the familiar panel of everchanging totals. Once, a writer had to calculate his own projections and estimate his own indicated pluralities. Now it is done for him by computers. (A majority is the difference between candidates where only two are running; a plurality between two candidates is the difference where more than two are running. A candidate may have a plurality over the second man in a three-man race and a majority over the combined total of his rivals.)

The key to the successful newspaper story on election night is the organization of the piece. It should be assembled in such a way that it need not be completely rewritten every time a voting total changes. Often, figures are left out of the lead for this reason. The lead is merely based on the fact that one candidate is leading, the actual returns being given immediately afterward in tabular style so that they can be changed quickly by substituting an insert.

Qualifying the Story   Until a vote total is final, or very close to it, it is difficult to put together a detailed analysis. Consequently, it is well in reporting on election night to use such qualifications as, "On the basis of scattered returns," or, "Partial and unofficial returns showed Smith had a narrow lead 30 minutes after the polls closed." In a newspaper or wire service account, the progress of the vote-reporting, if carried chronologically, can make a detailed and interesting running story but there is not space for more than one such account in blanket election coverage as a rule. Such things have to be summarized in print, and on the air as well.

The only time a political correspondent can consider the election to be over is after the final figures are in and uncontested, or when all candidates save the winner have conceded defeat. Until then, a careful writer will phrase his lead to read something like this:

> Robert J. Epperson apparently was elected Mayor last night by an indicated plurality of 40,000 votes.
> Although no concession of defeat came from his rival, Arthur Ahlgrenson, Epperson claimed victory on the basis of returns from half the city's districts which gave him a commanding lead . . .

Sometimes, in a close election, a candidate may be the victor on the basis of final and unofficial returns and his opponent may charge fraud, demand a recount, or both. Circumstances dictate how the story should be presented, but it is only logical to report that one candidate has scored a victory which is being contested. The charges of fraud should be used in a lead only when there appears to be some basis for them. But the closeness of an election in itself is not *prima facie* evidence of fraudulent activity. In a famous case in New York State, a judgeship was decided by only one vote. On a recount, the apparent loser was turned into a victor by only one vote. Subsequent court action failed to justify suspicions of fraud in the outcome.

It is also a fallacy for a reporter to jump to the conclusion that there is something phony about an election because he finds inexplicable contradictions in the figure between votes registered and votes cast. Sometimes, clerical errors in mimeographed handouts prior to election lead to such confused situations. Consequently, while the reporter must use the familiar fraud charges invariably made by losers in a close election, he cannot conclude that there is some basis for them until he is able to check the facts with responsible officials and both candidates. It is seldom that such things can be done on election night. Generally, they must await the official count two to three weeks after election day.

Styles vary in the reporting of election results in newspapers. Some carry the actual figures in a box preceding the story, where the reader can see them before he looks at anything else. Others like to use a lead saying who won, and then immediately summarize the salient figures, even though television has already done the job. Here is a general style in use on many newspapers and wire services, which is also familiar to television audiences who have heard it present-tensed and read by exhausted second-string announcers late at night after the first team has gone home:

Arthur J. Wingate scored a surprise victory last night over his Democratic opponent, George Berling, who was seeking a third term as Governor.

The Republican triumph in the state, which ran counter to a nation-wide Democratic trend, was the result primarily of deep inroads that Mr. Wingate made into normally Democratic pluralities in Central City, largest municipality in the state.

Governor Berling conceded defeat at 11:15 last night. The concession followed a conference with Gunnar Dahlquist, chairman of the Democratic State Committee, and Mayor Franklin Quest of Central City.

At 12:32 A.M., with nearly complete state-wide returns in, 10,132 out of 11,110 districts gave:

Wingate (R)   2,834,263
Berling (D)   2,378,767

Nearly complete returns from Central City at that hour indicated that Mr. Wingate, 54-year-old industrialist from Willow Grove, had cut the usual Democratic plurality there to less than 400,000 votes. Four years ago, Governor Berling was able to carry the city by almost 700,000 votes . . .

The unofficial results, reported on election night by the news media are seldom upset by challenges, charges, or recounts, but the final result must await the official canvass. When there is an election upset, it is major news.

chapter 26

The Big Story:
Washington, the UN, the World

The most important story of our era concerns Washington, the United Nations, and the world. It is the story of an age of political, social, and economic upheaval when man smashed the atom and reached for the stars and the moon. Whether reporters are at work in the halls of Congress, in the councils of the United Nations, or in the shadow of the Kremlin, they record the decisions that will lead eventually to world war or world peace.

Out of the 60,000 working journalists in the United States, a comparatively small number become Washington, United Nations, or foreign correspondents. Nearly every reporter has had such aspirations in his career at one time or another. Some, who are adequately prepared and who serve their apprenticeship in less important posts, may be given outstanding managerial or editorial responsibilities instead. Others, without sufficient background or experience for such an exacting assignment, either apply in vain or are tried and fail. Still others tire of waiting for an opportunity, drift into assignments of various kinds, or seek careers in different fields. For those who have the background, learning, ability, and good fortune to survive the rigorous tests of practical journalism, the privilege of covering the great national and international developments of our time is among the finest rewards the profession has to offer.

With few exceptions, the experienced national affairs correspondent is a person of maturity, culture, discrimination, and resourcefulness. Whether he is a graduate of Harvard or Columbia or no university, an expolice reporter, copy editor, or baseball public relations man, he has proved himself against the most difficult journalistic competition the world has to offer.

THE CORRESPONDENTS

The first characteristic of such a correspondent is expertness in journalism. He also often has a quick, inquiring mind, a profound understanding of national and world affairs, a wide acquaintanceship, an agreeable personality, and a diplomatic manner coupled with an aggressive drive for news. A United Nations or foreign correspondent requires in addition the gift of languages and the ability to soak up the essential history, geography, and culture of any nation to which he is sent.

All such specialists know their communications and costs as a matter of course. They also know that they are expected, above all, to conform to the first requirements of journalism—accuracy, good judgment, and the unfailing ability to meet deadlines.

The correspondent who approaches any national or international story with his mind made up is like the man who is convinced he will never be in a train wreck. Some day he is likely to be surprised. Nor can a correspondent carry his prejudices into the news arena with him. One who annually predicted the end of the League of Nations was finally proved to be correct, but only after nineteen years of mistakes.

With the growth of the United States as a world leader, both national and international coverage have increased in the American news media although considerable improvement is still possible. Moreover, the foreign news media have sent correspondents to Washington in such numbers that the nation's news capital has become the single most important dateline in the world. What is said and done in Washington has global repercussions. The United Nations, too, is an important continuing source of news, particularly when it becomes deeply involved in peace-keeping efforts.

What the Public Wants However, it would be a mistake to assume that the interest of the American people in foreign affairs is constant and widespread or that foreign interest in the United States is steadily maintained. There are peaks and valleys, best illustrated by the assignment of foreign correspondents by American news organizations. After World War II, a crack force of several thousand foreign correspondents for American news organizations was demobilized with even greater rapidity than the armed forces of the United States. The various world crises stimulated temporary buildups of a younger correspondents' corps in trouble sectors, notably the Soviet blockade of West Berlin in 1948–1949, the Korean War of 1950–1953, the abortive Suez War and Hungarian revolt of 1956, the Cuban missile crisis of 1962, the escalation of the Vietnam War beginning in 1965, the six-day mideast war of 1967 and the Russian invasion of Czechoslovakia in 1968.

With the coming of the century's seventh decade, more correspondents were serving abroad for American news organizations than at any time since World War II but the total of full-time, regular-salaried employees in this category was still less than 1,000. At the United Nations, it was reported that 1,000 to 1,500 correspondents covered every crisis, but the actual number of full-time day-to-day correspondents at New York headquarters was probably less than 50. It was only in Washington that the total number of correspondents of all nationalities and media could really be taken at something approaching face value.

WASHINGTON NEWS CENTERS

The Washington press corps, which can mobilize more than 2,000 representatives of domestic and foreign news media at peak periods, is the most prestigious in the world and the most important. It is also the most stable in terms of duration of assignment. While many medium- and small-size American dailies make no secret of their prejudice against printing much foreign or United Nations news, and the local electronic media are even less satisfactory in this respect, it takes a petty type of editor to cut down on essential national coverage. This is the kind of information a democratic nation must have, together with the necessary background, analysis, and interpretation. Any news organization that pretends to be of some importance to its community takes pride in its Washington correspondence. Those that cannot afford their own people in Washington see to it that they subscribe to one of the big newspaper syndicates that make national news available at a relatively modest cost as a supplement to wire service reports.

The Washington correspondent thus is broadly representative of large newspapers and small ones, wire services of all kinds, news magazines and monthly magazines, syndicates, radio, and television. In addition, local media send correspondents to Washington for specific stories, a practice that is now being used with considerable success on major overseas assignments. And foreign news media frequently do the same thing at times of peak interest in American affairs. It becomes important, therefore, to know how to establish a temporary base in Washington and operate effectively.

Those who are assigned to work in the nation's capital as members of bureaus generally are lucky because their associates ease the breaking-in period and provide advice on such problems as housing, commuting, schools for children, and so on. But for those who go to Washington for the first time on their own, it is a bewildering and sometimes traumatic experience. A wise newcomer will make himself known to the chiefs of the wire services and syndicates to which his newspaper subscribes, his Congressional delegation and the key information personnel at such central spots as the White House, State Department, Pentagon, and House and Senate Press Galleries.

Because of the publicity attached to the National Press Club, and the proximity of news teletype machines, the loner in Washington sometimes tries to work there on the basis of a temporary membership. However, as a rule, he is likely to be overwhelmed there by press agents of all kinds. It is a much sounder practice to work out of a place like the Senate Press Gallery, when Congress is in session, or to pick a particular story each day and follow it through, whatever the location. One inflexible rule for newcomers in Washington is to get to all assignments well ahead of time to meet the newsmakers and their staff personnel. Another is to insure that there is quick access to a telephone or wire for filing—sometimes far easier said than done in Washington on a major story.

In a work of this nature, which can be only a survey of overall Washington coverage rather than an in-depth study, all that can be attempted is a brief enumeration of the principal points of news and a few suggestions on what to do and what not to do. These are as follows:

The White House The President of the United States, being the single most important news source in the country, is given intensive daily coverage by every important news organization in the nation and others abroad. The small press room, with its tiny cubicles situated just off the reception room for the Executive Offices, holds only a small number of the correspondents regularly assigned to the White House. The President's press secretary is generally available once or twice a day for news conferences, announcements, or background material. He and his assistants are the gatekeepers who can ease the newcomer's approach to members of the Presidential staff and the various offices directly responsible to the President. The better known correspondents, of course, make their own appointments and often conduct a substantial part of their business by telephone except on breaking stories. On days when the President is having a news conference, it is usual for 200 or more correspondents to attend if there is advance notice. If the conference is hastily called, a frequent practice during the Johnson administration, only the regulars have time to attend. Because television cameras are often set up in the reception room to catch important visitors as they leave the President's office, those who want to avoid publicity for one reason or another enter and leave the White House by other routes, which makes things difficult for both the electronic and pad-and-pencil reporters. A number of news conferences of subordinate officials, many for background, are held in a medium-sized room called the "Fish Room," after the fish pictures on its walls. And when the President is about to

The Defense Department (DOD) has its own information setup under an Assistant Secretary of Defense, which includes representatives of all military services, and a big press room on the second floor of the Pentagon where each service has a desk manned by a number of officers. In addition, the Army, Navy, and Air Force each has its own staff of information personnel (Army and Air Force each has a consolidated external and internal information program). Thus, nearly 1,000 officers in the Pentagon are assigned to some facet of public relations activities. In turn, they direct the information and public relations work of small staffs and individuals at each post and base throughout the world; thus, a small army of public relations officers is assigned specifically to work with press and public and within the armed forces themselves. In the longish and somewhat musty room assigned to Pentagon reporters, opposite the Pentagon press room, there are almost as few places for the working press as there are at the White House. But generally, only a score or so of correspondents turn up daily for the routine chores of coverage. But when the Secretary of Defense holds a news conference, or the Joint Chiefs of Staff figure in the news, the response is very heavy. Otherwise, the Washington press corps does much of its routine business with the various military desks by telephone.

The Supreme Court   The correspondents assigned to the Supreme Court on a regular basis are few in number and highly specialized in their background and training. Not any reporter can be assigned on a minute's notice to go galloping over to the highest court in the land on a decision day to pick up the text of a ruling in a major case and write an understandable account of the proceedings. Some of the regulars who cover the court are lawyers; others have had some legal training. Even those without special backgrounds in the law have to develop their own knowledge in order to function properly.

Treasury   One of the most important innovations developed by the Treasury Department is the "Budget School" which is held for several days prior to the release of the Federal budget. Correspondents, many with special training in economic affairs, have a chance to study this formidable document and talk with the nation's leading authorities on it before presenting their accounts to the public. This kind of preparation is woefully lacking in many other areas of coverage in Washington, where it is needed. The Treasury has shown that it is possible to enter into a workable agreement with the press on matters of importance to the public, such as government expenditures and the prospect of new taxes, to give correspondents time for study and reflection. In affairs of this nature, the few paragraphs scrambled together for a deadline ten minutes away can sometimes be totally misleading. It is better to wait, in agreement with the source and with the competition, and give the whole story in proper perspective.

Agriculture   The correspondents who cover the Department of Agriculture, like those at State Defense and the Treasury, are generally highly specialized in the field and work for news organizations with a particular interest in the subject. The daily routine of agricultural reports is ably carried by the wire services. But for detailed, in-depth reportage on matters of importance to both farmer and consumer, the press must turn once more to the specialist.

Other Areas   All except the largest and richest news organizations necessarily are unable to staff the many other important government departments daily. Consequently, the Justice Department, the Post Office, the Labor Department, the Departments of Commerce, the Interior and Health, Education, and Welfare, to name only a few, are covered by the wire services for the majority of the Washington press corps. Individual correspondents with a special interest in the affairs of Justice or Labor, for example, may spend much more time there than others. Or, the whole group may strain the facilities of a single department, such as Labor, during a national strike emergency. The point is that even the large press corps in the nation's capital has to work on the "firehouse principle" for everything except the top newsmaking sources. And woe betide the unfortunate correspondent who guesses that he can spend a quiet day researching a favorite project at the Department of Health, Education, and Welfare only to find out that the President has sent an emergency message to Congress in his absence from contact with his regular news sources.

HAZARDS IN PRESS RELATIONS

The pressures of public policy and national safety sometimes make for difficulties between the government and the press. Such was the case with missile publicity until the United States began doing as well as the Russians. It also happens, now and then, that efforts to use the press as an instrument of diplomacy backfire with embarrassing and sometimes disastrous consequences.

Starting a Flap   When Dean Acheson as Secretary of State apparently drew a Pacific defense perimeter for the United States in an address which omitted all mention of Korea, his political opponents blamed him for egging on Communist arms in North Korea. Acheson contended the charges were purely political, and obviously no Secretary of State knowingly would have invited the Communists to march south across the 38th parallel in 1950. But the charges hurt him.

Only three years later his successor, the late John Foster Dulles, placed himself in a position that was almost as bad. He was invited to a background dinner by several Washington correspondents and was understood by them to have suggested a Korean war settlement near the 38th parallel and a Formosan UN Trusteeship. In accordance with professional practice, the selected correspondents sent up the trial balloon next day and ascribed the proposal to an unnamed high official. Indignant Congressmen demanded to know who was bartering away a Korean peace. Foreign newsmen and others who were not bound to confidence revealed Dulles as the spokesman, and the Secretary promptly denied he had ever made compromising statements. James Reston commented sardonically in *The New York Times* that the administration had "denied the truth without actually lying."

One of President Eisenhower's experiences was even more discomfiting. He told reporters on his campaign train in 1952, off the record, that he would not yield to Democratic demands for a disclosure of his personal finances and tax records. As Homer Bigart wrote in the New York *Herald Tribune* on October 10, 1952:

> By putting this off the record, the general had the reporters in an awkward position since their previous stories had clearly indicated that the general's financial statement would soon be forthcoming.
>
> Also they were uncomfortable in the knowledge of something that possibly could have an important bearing on the Presidential election and which they could not publish without violating a confidence. They knew the odds were ten to one that the news would not stay under wraps very long. Other reporters who were not at the conference would hear of it and break it and that was what happened.

Bigart, of course, wrote his account after the story was broken by correspondents who were not on the campaign train and after General Eisenhower had finally decided to release his financial records.

The Credibility Gap   The government, on its part, has increased the problems inherent in any attempt to present truthful information to the public during times of crisis. During the Eisenhower administration, the prestige of the White House was invoked in 1960 to deny that a missing U-2 spy plane had invaded Russian air space. Within 24 hours, when the Soviet government publicly displayed evidence that the aircraft had in fact been shot down deep inside its territory, President Eisenhower had to take the responsibility for the diplomatic untruth.

Similarly, during the abortive attempt to help a rag-tag bunch of

Cubans invade Castro's Cuba in 1961, President Kennedy tried and failed to cover up the key role of the CIA in organizing the disaster. In the Cuban missile crisis a year later, both President Kennedy and the press showed how effectively the two could work together in the interests of national security by withholding crucial information about Soviet involvement until the American government was ready for its "eyeball to eyeball" confrontation with Moscow. However, in 1963, the Kennedy administration once more supported the issuance of false information by the Diem regime in South Vietnam regarding the strength of its program for beating the Vietcong. In this instance, the press truthfully disclosed the extent of the Diem disaster.

In the light of this record, the succeeding Johnson administration often was blamed for primary responsibility for the creation of a "credibility gap" between the government and the public. Certainly, the premature claims of victory in South Vietnam that were made by the President's leading advisers and generals damaged the prestige of the administration. But President Johnson, in fact, was drawn along a path that had been traversed by his two predecessors. Arthur Sylvester, the Assistant Secretary of Defense for Public Affairs who served under both Presidents, stated the prevailing governmental philosophy of the time in these words: "I think the inherent right of the government to lie to save itself when faced with nuclear disaster is basic." Despite the furor over the bluntness of his phrasing, there were not many of influence in either the higher echelons of government or the press who disagreed with him. The argument really turned on what constituted an "admissible lie" and what kind of lying was inadmissible regardless of circumstances. Truth, as it turned out, was the first casualty in an atomic crisis, as well as in a war.

FREEDOM AND SECURITY

The government and the news media will always agree to the general proposition that no news should be made public in time of crisis that violates national security. However, no agreement appears to be possible on exactly what constitutes national security in any given set of circumstances. It follows that the responsibility of determining what information should be withheld is exercised primarily by the government. However, when and if the press learns that information is being wrongfully withheld for reasons other than national security, its responsibility is to make prompt disclosures of such material in the public interest.

This posture of basic conflict between a democratic government and the free press has been the subject of continuing discussion between journalists and responsible public officials for many years. The relationship is by no means typical only of the United States. As long ago as the Crimean

War in the middle of the nineteenth century, William Howard Russell's disclosures of tragic mismanagement of the British military brought great prestige to *The Times* of London and caused the downfall of the Aberdeen government. Such instances may be documented in every practicing democracy where there is an effective, competent, and critical free press.

It is the prevailing theory that the public interest is best served by a continuing rivalry between the two forces. However, if the conflict is pushed to excess, and if all restraint is abandoned by both government and press, then the probable result is bound to be anarchy.

"In choosing between freedom and secrecy," wrote James Russell Wiggins, editor of the Washington *Post*, "we must remember that each has its risks. Our free ways sometimes are dangerous; but our secret ways are dangerous, too. One differs from the other, but is not necessarily less risky than the other."[1]

Walter Lippmann, toward the close of a lifetime of illustrious service as a journalist, argued that a government must be given the right of "quiet diplomacy" to try to resolve crises before they lead to a resort to arms. Yet, he also conceded that the public must be informed. "The question," he wrote, "is a perennial one in a democratic society. For true negotiation is impossible if it has to be done publicly and yet a free people cannot be left in the dark . . . The problem can be stated so that it sounds insoluble. But as a matter of fact it is not at all impossible, although it requires the gifts of leadership for a competent government to keep the public well informed without destroying the privacy which is essential to diplomatic negotiations."[2]

In national and international affairs, where so much impinges on national security, the correspondent and his editor are well aware of all the eloquent philosophy on both sides of the question of whether to reveal or suppress. Despite all the pressures upon them, it will be their decision finally as to what material in their possession will be passed on to the public. This is the highest responsibility of the journalist in an open society. To exercise it, he must stand or fall on his own judgment.

THE PRESIDENTIAL NEWS CONFERENCE

It is a peculiarly American custom to have the President of the United States regularly face the questions of newspapermen, wire service, news magazine, and radio-TV correspondents. Until the turn of the century, it

[1] J. R. Wiggins, *Freedom or Secrecy* (New York: 1964, revised) p. xi.
[2] Clinton Rossiter & James Lare, eds., *The Essential Lippmann* (New York: 1963), p. 374.

had occurred to no President to do this, and the newspapers themselves were not particularly interested. Then, President Theodore Roosevelt took to talking with reporters and consigning them to the "Ananias Club" when they published stories he did not like. His successor, President William Howard Taft, had a few favored correspondents in for social evenings at the White House, but that was about all.

It was President Woodrow Wilson, with his stated devotion to "pitiless publicity," who began the Presidential press conference. However, by modern standards, he did not hold many of them, and, like President Harry S Truman, he had a run-in with the press over stories written about his daughter. On one occasion, after a story speculating on Margaret Wilson's romantic inclinations, the furious Wilson threatened to punch the next gossip-writing reporter in the nose. The idealist, who advocated "open covenants openly arrived at," seldom tried out his theory.

The Beginning   President Warren Gamaliel Harding, an Ohio newspaper editor, tried to be chummy with the press and held regular conferences for a time. Then, when he was trapped into publicly contradicting his Secretary of State, Charles Evans Hughes, and found out Hughes was right, the President forced reporters to submit all questions in writing. It was a custom that was continued by Presidents Calvin Coolidge and Herbert Hoover.

The founding of the Presidential news conference as we know it today was the work of President Franklin Delano Roosevelt. As a past master at the art of handling reporters and editors, and a talented politician who enjoyed jousting with the press, he saw to it that news conferences were held on the average of twice a week during his four terms. Under Roosevelt's regime, because of the pressures of World War II, the system of press officers and public information officers spread through the government. This was, truly, the era of the reporter; everything was done to serve him and to satisfy his needs. The written questions were done away with.

Truman and Ike   President Truman continued F.D.R.'s system. Although he did not hold as many news conferences as his predecessor, they were every bit as expert. Truman enjoyed the hostile question, the loaded question, and the persistent reporter quite as much as Roosevelt, and was always in command of the situation. Since TV was born in the latter part of his term as a political force, he never had to make the decision to bring the cameras into the White House. But what he did do, after a reporter spilled a bottle of ink on the carpet of the Oval Room in the White House, was to move the news conference into the old Indian Treaty Room of the adjoining State, War, and Navy Building. It was, therefore, no longer a White House conference.

Under President Eisenhower the final shred of protection for a Chief Executive was ripped away. Historically, Presidents had been given the privilege of having their answers to all questions published in indirect discourse. When Presidents permitted direct quotation of a few words or perhaps a sentence, it was a major event. But, once Eisenhower permitted TV cameras to record the Presidential news conference and go on the air with the film, following review, it was impossible to keep the press from using direct quotations. So, after a brief check, Presidential news conferences in the Eisenhower regime were on the record—a realization of Wilson's pledge of "pitiless publicity."

The Kennedy Era   During President Kennedy's 1,000 days, the televised news conference attained perfection as a dramatic spectacle, whatever may have been said about its usefulness as a device for the public disclosure of news about government. The President generally enjoyed them. He was, in the best sense of the word, a performer. Instead of remaining in the White House and causing the correspondents to line up in an uncomfortable group before his desk, he transferred the whole performance to the capacious auditorium of the State Department. It became a show and he was, in every way, the star. When he appeared on the stage, with cameras focused on him and two sensitive microphones aimed at the audience of newsmen, friends and gate-crashers who often numbered as many as 400 or 500, everybody was assured of a firstrate performance. The President could be authoritative and serious at one moment, gay and disarming at another; he could turn aside a question with a quip, and flatter a critical lady correspondent with a smile. This was the Kennedy style. He did away with the safeguard of reviewing a tape of his televised conference and, with a supreme gesture of self-confidence, let the entire business go out live. It was a pity, having achieved such progress in televised news, that the television industry seldom bothered to make available the full-scale news conference to the public.

All the Way with LBJ   During President Johnson's years in office, the contrast with the Kennedy style was striking. First of all, LBJ did not have the natural photogenic charm of his youthful predecessor and he realized it. He also did not like television as a medium; his discomfort in front of the cameras was usually so transparent that he aroused a certain amount of public sympathy although it seldom was registered in the press. Finally, the somber Texan—during much of his tenure in the White House—engaged in a running feud with the press. While he had his stalwart supporters among the correspondents, most of them were against him and usually admitted as much. This had very little to do with politics, since Democrats are usually in the majority among the Washington press corps. Rather, the feeling between LBJ and those who covered him was based on a mounting mutual mistrust. One casualty was the free-swinging Presidential news conference. Generally, when President Johnson called in reporters, he gave very little advance notice and he also placed the television crews under a considerable handicap. It was his style to crowd people around him and use up a considerable amount of his time with the reading of announcements. He made no secret of his dislike of many of the correspondents. The feeling was mutual. It accounted for a considerable part of the bad press that was characteristic of the Johnson administration, even though LBJ was returned to office in 1964 with the largest plurality in the history of the Presidency.

Admittedly, it is unfair to ask a President of the United States to summarize the State of the Union before the assembled press in no more than 30 minutes each week, to act the part of a popular television idol, and to snap out the answer to every random question put to him. No amount of advance briefing can prepare the President for every eventuality; nor can every President be expected to be a consummate actor and paragon of political wisdom on all occasions. Similarly, it is asking a great deal of several hundred assorted newsmen to sit—or stand—around a President, take notes on what he says, and then run for the wire to file or telephone a complete and accurate account—with background and interpretation—of everything that happened. Yet, this is what the competitive wire service and afternoon newspaper reporters must do whenever there is a Presidential news conference. For all the hoopla that goes with televised news conferences, the networks generally show no more than a few chosen minutes of each one, and sometimes these are not too illuminating. Thus, the public must actually depend for full information and full texts on the morning newspapers for the most part, and not many of these give the full coverage that the event warrants.

It is clear that the Presidential news conference is diminishing in its usefulness. Just how long it will last, no one really knows. But except for such star performers as President Kennedy, the news conference represents a chore and a potential political burden for every President. The risk, for most of them, is not equal to the return in exposure to the public.

But far worse than the political risk in excessive public exposure is the continued threat of physical danger to the leading figures in American government when they go to the public during political campaigns or on other occasions. The assassinations of President Kennedy and his brother, Senator Robert F. Kennedy, and the Rev. Dr. Martin Luther King, Jr. have demonstrated the need for better protection and better supervision of public appearances by leaders in public life. Yet, when tragedy strikes, the news media have no choice. The event must be covered—and covered thoroughly with full awareness for the needs of the public, the rights of whatever prisoners may be taken and the canons of good judgment and good taste.

The two following excerpts from the Los Angeles *Times'* voluminous coverage of the fatal shooting of Senator Kennedy illustrate how the press operates in the television age. It must be borne in mind that both the shooting and the death occurred after midnight, Pacific Coast time, so that most of the country did not see the television footage or hear the radio reports. It was a rare instance in which almost as many people learned from the newspapers what had happened as they did from the faster electronic media.

The Shooting   Here is the beginning of the Los Angeles *Times'* story of the shooting (in an edition of 104 pages that was already on the presses) on June 5, 1968:

> Senator Robert F. Kennedy was shot in the right ear early this morning in a kitchen of the Ambassador only a few moments after he had made a victory statement upon capturing the California Democratic presidential primary.
>
> The New York Senator's condition was listed as critical at the Good Samaritan Hospital, where he was in the intensive care unit.
>
> A suspect in the shooting was arrested minutes after the shots were fired and was taken to the police administration building downtown under heavy guard. The suspect was not identified.
>
> Inspector Robert Rock of the Los Angeles police said that only one suspect was involved. The police also have the gun that fired the shots, Rock said.
>
> Witnesses nearby said Kennedy's head was covered with blood and a woman standing nearby was also splattered with blood. Also shot was Paul Schrade, UAW official. The shooting occurred at 12:20 A.M.
>
> Shouts and screams filled the packed hall as the call went out over the public address system for a doctor. Three came to Kennedy's aid as his campaign assistants pleaded for his supporters to be calm and clear the hall.
>
> The senator appeared to be in great pain but conscious. As he was lifted into the police ambulance, he was heard to say:
>
> "Oh, no! No! Don't!"
>
> Mrs. Kennedy whispered to him, apparently trying to comfort and reassure her husband. Then she entered the ambulance, doors were closed behind them and the vehicle sped away. . .

The Death   Next day, on June 6, 1968, as the last edition of the Los Angeles *Times* was on the press with 158 pages, Senator Kennedy died. Once again, much of the country awoke next morning to hear and read of the tragic story. This was the beginning of the *Times'* report:

> Senator Robert F. Kennedy died at 1:44 A.M. today of bullet wounds inflicted by an assassin at the Ambassador early yesterday.

The announcement was made at 2 A.M. outside Good Samaritan Hospital by the Senator's press secretary, Frank Mankiewicz, after eight hours of silence about the stricken man's condition.

Mankiewicz said: "I have a short announcement, which I will read at this time. Senator Robert Francis Kennedy died at 1:44 A.M. today, June 6, 1968. With Senator Kennedy at the time of his death were his wife, Ethel, his sister, Mrs. Stephen Smith, and his sister-in-law, Mrs. John F. Kennedy. He was 42 years old."

Kennedy was shot down at a moment of triumph.

Police said he was shot by a young Jordanian who was described as a pro-Nasser nationalist seeking revenge over what he felt was the Senator's pro-Israel stand.

Investigators said the gunman mingled with the tumultuous throng celebrating Kennedy's presidential primary victory early yesterday at the Ambassador, then fired point-blank at him as he sought to leave through a hotel kitchen.

Captured and turned over to the police, the man was identified as Sirhan Bishara Sirhan, 24, a native of what was Jordanian Jerusalem prior to the Israeli occupation. . .

THE UNITED NATIONS STORY

The United Nations is not difficult to cover. Most of the larger national delegations have agreeable, if somewhat uncommunicative, press officers but there are other ways of obtaining such news as they have. The United Nations itself has a corps of able and experienced press officers, who are accustomed to briefing the press individually or in groups and who are trained in accurate straight news reporting rather than propaganda techniques. At the UN documents counter and in the UN year books and other source materials, correspondents easily can find the pertinent background on almost any issue that is before the organization. They are showered daily with documents and resolutions when the Council or the Assembly sessions are under way. All Secretaries General in one way or another have demonstrated their willingness to stand up for the principle of news coverage at the UN, rather than propaganda blasts.

The procedures and issues confronting the organization, the rules of its subsidiary bodies, and the interpretations of the Charter are complicated, but no more so than the same attributes of the Congress of the United States and American Constitutional law. Correspondents who have proved able to cope with the intricacies of the news in Washington need not quail over a United Nations assignment.

Yet, year in and year out, the same regulars cover the United Nations with a few other familiar faces added at crisis periods. Visiting correspondents, editors, and publishers invariably argue that the story has become too repetitious, too complicated, too far over the heads of the average American readers. They ask for "down-to-earth" coverage, whatever that may mean, and a simplification of reporting. That is always desirable, but then, how simple is the coverage of the United States Supreme Court? The story is there. It is vital and meaningful. Some stories are told because they must be, others because they should be, and the United Nations is in the latter category. The opportunity is still there, no matter how neglected it may be. Within the profession there are many able and well-qualified correspondents who could do the story of the United Nations if they were given a chance. Tomorrow, because of the detailed UN studies in many of our universities, many more such reporters will be available.

Methods and Sources   These are the four principal sources for the United Nations story:

1. The open meetings, speeches, and resolutions of the various components of the organization. These are chiefly the General Assembly, Security Council, Economic and Social Council, and Trusteeship Council with their subsidiary committees.

2. The foreign delegations which, however reticent they may be about their own business, generally may be relied on in a highly unofficial way to give background information on what is going on elsewhere behind the scenes. Some, of course, do not; but delegations—like lawyers—are prone to try their cases in the newspapers at home and abroad if they see some profit in doing so.

3. The United States Mission to the United Nations. This is an extension of the State Department, but it has its own public affairs and public information officers plus an excellent library. The information staff is highly competent, but it usually does not have too much freedom of action for obvious reasons. Not all negotiations can be carried on with a brass band.

4. The United Nations' own information staff and the resources of the Secretary General. Over the years the UN has developed a system of chronological reporting of all major meetings, with takes of copy available for correspondents an hour or so after delivery. This small, but qualified, news staff clears through a city desk of its own on the second floor of the UN Secretariat Building and may be consulted by correspondents. Thus, it is possible for one correspondent to cover all the principal UN meetings on any given day if he has some leeway in his deadlines and the will to do a lot of reading, questioning and background research.

The Secretary General, being responsible to all UN members, cannot very well be expected to make earth-shaking pronouncements affecting them, but he manages to make news in his own way at periodic news conferences during the year and in his reports to the organization. Some of his principal assistants are as adept in handling the press and quietly putting out background information as anybody in the news department of the

British Foreign Office. The UN press liaison staff, with its excellent veteran personnel, completes the roster of UN sources.

Physically the center of UN press coverage is the third floor of the Secretariat building, where the press liaison, documents counter, briefing room, and some correspondents' offices are located. Wire, cable, telephone, and other communications facilities are available here, too. Accreditation is handled easily, and with a minimum of red tape, the chief requirements being a letter from a managing editor of a newspaper, or other appropriate official, requesting privileges for a correspondent.

What confuses new correspondents most is that they must consult the *Journal*, the daily schedule of UN meetings, for a list of the subjects and documents under discussion at any given session and also obtain tickets for a meeting. The tickets and documents are easily obtained, but the latter are not as simple to digest. A correspondent going to his first meeting is likely to be in a daze unless he knows enough to look for a UN or US or British briefing officer in the corridors and insist on a fill-in.

Veteran correspondents, who know their way around, seldom attend routine meetings but have them piped in by loud speaker to their offices in the Secretariat building. Texts of important speeches are obtainable in advance and so are resolutions. An alert correspondent, covering the delegates' lounges, often can also pick up news of such resolutions in their various drafts but he learns to beware of all except a final draft. In dealings between nations, as between individuals, many proposals are put forward for bargaining purposes and then withdrawn.

The United Nations has more than doubled in size since it was founded in 1945 and the task of the correspondent, accordingly, has become far more complex. When there were a few more than 50 nations in the world organization, it was very much like a pleasant little club. The United States generally did the talking for most of the Americas, although Argentina and Brazil sometimes rudely interrupted. The British were the spokesmen for the Commonwealth, except for Nehru's India. The pre-deGaulle French were tractable people, and most obliging. Similarly, the pre-Nasser Egyptians usually were able to give the Arab line and the Soviet Union was the unquestioned spokesman for the Soviet bloc. After the triumph of the Chinese Communists, everybody was a little embarrassed about calling Formosa the representative of the Chinese people, a member of the Big Five, and a power with a veto in the Security Council. But that was not a serious obstruction. Thus, it was possible with a few well-placed telephone calls to determine what was happening in the UN and what was likely to happen.

Today, with 125 nations in the world organization, nothing is certain. Both the United States and the Soviet Union have lost considerable authority in their respective power blocs and cannot pretend to speak with finality for those associated with them. Britain's fortunes, having declined, no longer make London the unquestioned spokesman for the Commonwealth; Rhodesia and South Africa, to mention only two countries, have had some objections to British policy in the past and are likely to have more. The Arabs are split. The Latin Americans, after Castro, are scarcely in a monolithic mood. The Africans are in open revolt against Western influence. And in Asia, the Vietnam War has completed the process of readjusting the influence of Japan and other powers. The correspondent who tries to cover this kind of organization with a few well-placed telephone calls is likely to have many surprises, all of them unpleasant. Moreover, even when the news of so relatively weak an organization is assembled, it may not always command much attention in the world's media.

It is a commonplace among UN correspondents not to expect great sensations in the usual routine meetings of the General Assembly, the Security Council, or their associated bodies. The average morning of debate may have little to recommend itself in the way of news. A correspondent may also talk with representatives of a score of delegations in the course of a working day without finding anything that is particularly usable. There is much routine at the UN—perhaps too much—but as in any other assignment there may be many days of routine before the correspondent comes across a solid break in the news of major proportions. All he can do is to play for the breaks, and occasionally try to anticipate them.

The Commentary   Straight news aside, many thoughtful journalists believe that the commentary is perhaps the best way of putting UN news before the public. Whether it is written for publication or used by a radio or television commentator, it is far more than an interpretive piece. It has the freedom of expression usually reserved for a columnist or an editorial, although it represents the views primarily of a correspondent. This is the beginning of such a piece:

By Louis B. Fleming

UNITED NATIONS—A large number of diplomats here think the nicest thing about the current session of the General Assembly of the United Nations is that it will be over today.

There are other diplomats, however, who find some hopeful signs beneath the gloss of frustration, repetitious and pretentious resolutions, and general ennui.

For one thing, it is argued, this Assembly operated with remarkable calm and relatively little nastiness despite the existence of one major war in Vietnam and the aftermath of a second in the Mid-East.

For another, the invisible diplomacy of this Assembly may have been more substantive and constructive than for many years and thus may pave the way for some creative action next year or the year after.

Certainly, the Assembly has operated with efficiency under the presidency of Corneliu Manescu, foreign minister of Romania, the first Communist ever to preside over a U. N. Assembly. And it was not easy, because of major dislocations.

The Assembly proceedings were certainly overshadowed by action in the Security Council, first on the Mid-East, finally on the Cyprus crisis. But diplomats point out that the Mid-East solution represented a compromise by the Soviet Union and the United States. Both major powers reacted to the pressure of smaller powers generated not only in the Council but also in the Assembly.

A sign of the times was the willingness of the Assembly membership to accept a record cut in the budget, even though it affected some of the projects sacred to the Afro-Asian-Latin majority. The final figure will be about $6 million under what Secretary General U Thant proposed . . . .

—Los Angeles *Times*

FOREIGN CORRESPONDENCE

The average foreign correspondent is no devil-may-care youngster risking his neck on some foolish but glamorous exploit, but a rather sedate and settled family man of good background and education. He travels a great deal from his established base, which is changed every two or three years. If he has to take risks in his sometimes hazardous routine, he does so because it is a part of the job—not just for the fun of it. In war zones, particularly in a guerrilla war, he is every bit as valid a target as a soldier to an enemy who seldom observes the Geneva Convention.

What He's Like   A profile of the foreign correspondent, compiled in the mid-1960s from questionnaires to which 140 Americans responded, gives his average age as 41, with eight under 30 and four over 60. Nearly all are married or have been at least once, and nearly half have one or two children. They are not very skilled in foreign languages, with many claiming to speak a little French and some admitting that they know no foreign language well. They are nearly all college graduates with an average of 10 years' service abroad, earn an average of $12,000 to $15,000 a year, and are overwhelmingly Democratic or independent in their political affiliations.[3]

In an elite group of foreign correspondents, 28 from *The New York Times* and 13 others who have won Pulitzer Prizes, these characteristics are emphasized to an even greater degree. They average 22 years of experience in journalism, with at least ten years overseas. Of the 41, 33

---

[3] Frederick T. C. Yu and John Luter, "The Foreign Correspondent and His Work," *Columbia Journalism Review*, Spring 1964, pp. 5–7.

have bachelors' degrees and 11 of these have graduate degrees as well. Only two in the group have never been married. As for mastery of foreign languages, they also do not show impressive skills.[4] Finally, in a survey of 91 correspondents for American news organizations in Asia, it develops that their range of estimated annual costs averages about $30,000 a year for top-ranking newspaper correspondents, magazine writers, and television correspondents outside war zones. For wire service people and stringers it is considerably less. The expense of maintaining a correspondent in an important area for a year may run as high as $50,000 a year for major news organizations.[5]

How to Be One   The manner of becoming a foreign correspondent is still as great an uncertainty as ever, despite all the talk about modern personnel methods. Some are chosen for the job and trained rigorously for it with special courses in great universities and hours of practice in a foreign language. Many more happen to be at the right spot at the right time and fall into it. A few adventurers persuade editors to try them, with indifferent results as a rule (although sometimes there are pleasant surprises). The rest of the foreign correspondents work their way up slowly in the news agencies and on newspapers having foreign staffs, and quite often are picked off by the ever-watchful news magazines and electronic media for their own foreign staffs.

While most of the dependable older men and the few women who are established foreign correspondents can count on fairly decent pay, there are youngsters who are willing to work for less than they could earn on a police beat at home. It is only when the action is rough and the risks are very great that the younger people tend to get top preference, particularly in war zones. In television's first war, the Vietnam conflict, the youngsters often dominated the battle coverage.

For the intricacies of foreign reporting, in or out of war zones, veterans are naturally preferred and some of them cannot be held back from the most dangerous assignments. Harrison E. Salisbury of *The New York Times* was 58 years old when he filed his reports from behind enemy lines in Hanoi in late 1966 and early 1967. Peter Kalischer of CBS was past 50 when he led camera crews into action in Vietcong territory in South Vietnam to get battle footage. So was Leland Stowe when he won a Pulitzer Prize for the reporting of the Nazi blitzkrieg that overwhelmed Norway in World War II. And Herbert L. Matthews was older than that when he penetrated the Cuban mountain stronghold for the first American interview with Fidel Castro, then just a Cuban guerrilla leader, in 1957.

---

[4] S. M. Polster, *Editor & Publisher*, March 4, 1967, p. 14.
[5] John Hohenberg, *Between Two Worlds* (New York: 1967), pp. 412–417.

The Status of Foreign Correspondence   Regardless of how well American foreign correspondents do their job—and in most cases the experienced reporter gives a competent performance—few of them are satisfied with the state of the art. Editors are even more restless, despite the slow but demonstrable gains in the public's demand for a better quality of foreign news and in its use by the leading news media.

There is an almost universal feeling in news offices, where such things matter, that the big story overseas is not often told in terms that can be communicated to the average man. The usual surveys, with their findings of minimum use of foreign news in a large section of the American press, are depressing to anybody who has worked in the field and knows how much talent and effort go into foreign news coverage. Admittedly, the crisis story and the war story get through in volume. But the straws in the wind, the first signs of danger, the stories that should put the American public on guard, do not seem to be widely used except in newspapers of great prestige and influence.

Everything has been and is being tried to arouse more general reader and viewer interest—straight news, features, interpretation, backgrounders, situationers, roundups, commentaries, surveys in depth, long interviews, first person accounts by the reporters themselves, filmed narratives, and documentaries. Correspondents send the "official" news—the governmental actions and associated material that must be covered. They go out in the streets and talk to and film plain people, hoping somehow to make a story out of that on the theory that a curbstone interview with an uninformed Frenchman, Filipino, Indonesian, or Pakistani will shed brilliant enlightenment on an uninformed American.

THE FLOW OF FOREIGN NEWS

There is no lack of available foreign news. For all media, both AP and UPI probably average around 200,000 words a week each in inbound foreign news to be edited for distribution to all members of the former and clients of the latter. If the average newspaper uses 10,000 words a week (the electronic media naturally cannot use anywhere near that amount) the wire service editors regard it as something of a triumph. Some of the newspapers that have foreign services and syndicate them to others probably furnish as much or more to their clients.

The Audience   No one really knows how large the audience for foreign news is in the United States, although both wire service and syndicate editors agree that it is slowly increasing from the rock bottom estimates of the readership surveys. This is a part of the evidence:

In a few years, the Los Angeles *Times* has built the second largest newspaper foreign service in the world, with nearly a score of bureaus, and syndicated it through about 200 newspapers. Similarly, the Washington *Post* has expanded what was once a small service into a major source of independent foreign news. *The New York Times*, with the largest and most comprehensive foreign service, has syndicated its material to more than 200 newspapers; moreover, its appeal to nearly one million daily readers is based to a substantial extent on its foreign and national news coverage.

New foreign services are also doing well—Copley and Cowles among them—and older ones like the *Christian Science Monitor*, Chicago *Daily News*, and Baltimore *Sun*, are being revitalized. It is worth mentioning that the *Monitor*, in a survey of its new readers, found that 60 per cent were taking the paper for its foreign news. Papers like the St. Louis *Post-Dispatch* and Miami *Herald* now send out specialists and even teams to do global coverage; papers like the Washington *Star* have established small but mobile foreign staffs on a permanent basis.

In areas where there are poor newspapers with minimal national and international coverage, the news magazines sell much of their six million copies a week with detailed foreign news sections. The overseas editions of both *Time* and *Newsweek* are highly profitable. As for the TV networks, while they still take most of their information from the wire services, they are developing sophisticated staffs of foreign correspondents who work mainly with their cameramen. Business news organizations like the McGraw-Hill and Fairchild publications have comprehensive staff coverage of all major foreign business centers.

Foreign News Space   The better publications run significant foreign news reports and pride themselves on their coverage, regardless of the less enlightened attitudes of the majority of the news media.[6] *The New York Times* publishes an average of 16 to 18 columns a day of foreign dateline news, and considerably more in war-time. The Los Angeles *Times'* foreign file averages around 10 or 11 columns; the Washington *Post*, around 9; the *Christian Science Monitor*, 9 or 10, and perhaps 30 or so other leading papers with an aggregate circulation of about 10 million to 12 million use anywhere from four to six columns a day of such foreign dateline material.

The *Wall Street Journal* runs a major foreign piece from one of its own excellent correspondents at regular intervals, with a considerable impact on its more than one million national readers. And when the *New Yorker* magazine does a foreign story by one of its small but brilliant group of

---

[6] Foreign news estimates based on my own surveys in 1963 and 1964, published in appendices of *Between Two Worlds* (New York: 1967) and subsequently updated.

writers on international affairs, it often has national significance as well. The same is true of the infrequent television documentaries on foreign affairs.

This does not excuse the far from satisfactory performance of the preponderance of American dailies and weeklies in .the publication of foreign news, or the paucity of such material on the air when there is no war. But as has been shown, the pattern, on the whole, is mixed. It could be a great deal better. But it also has been a great deal worse.

THE FOREIGN CORRESPONDENT'S JOB

The duty of the foreign correspondent is to tell the story of the people in the nation to which he is assigned, not merely the official acts of the government and the announcements of the press attachés. It is a difficult and demanding job, requiring long hours of work at periods of the day and night that are often inconvenient to anybody with a family. Facts are the basis of any report, and the facts must be explained and made meaningful through the methods of modern journalism.

Where one man is assigned to cover an entire country, it is perfectly obvious that he must depend on the mass communications facilities of that country to keep himself informed of the broad flow of the news. He cannot merely read papers, listen to the radio, see what the AP or the UPI are sending, be friendly with the government's information people, and let it go at that. He must develop his own sources at every level, and that takes an enormous investment of time—and often money, as well. No editor takes kindly to the steady provision of dinners and drinks for foreign news sources, as charged on an expense account.

In countries such as the Soviet Union a correspondent is more or less tied to the official sources whether or not there is censorship. In the democratic countries of the West, however, there is freedom of action if the correspondent knows what to do and how to do it. At the outset of any assignment he, of course, makes himself known to the Press Wireless and other communications people with whom he will deal, checks in at the American Embassy and the foreign ministry of the country to which he is accredited, and picks himself a story. Just how he works to develop information is largely dependent on individual reporting traits and circumstances, but no correspondent can afford merely to pick up a few facts and file them.

Drew Middleton has observed:

> Some facts are easy to come by: what the minister said, how many votes the Socialists received, the exact text of a diplomatic note. But it takes hours of digging to uncover the related facts, often the most important ones. Why did the minister speak as he did the precise moment

and what were the reactions of his colleagues? Why did the Socialist vote fall or rise? What was the intention of the government in sending the diplomatic note? If the story is to have perspective, the answers must be obtained.

Yet, even after he has the necessary facts, the correspondent's job has only begun. He must relate the facts to the economic, political and social conditions of the moment and explain the material to the reader.

Propaganda It is a great popular delusion that the average American overseas is a ready victim for the wiles of foreign propaganda. The American politician who participates in a foreign conference is usually despaired of in advance. As for the foreign correspondent, even his own editors sometimes refuse to believe him if his story happens to coincide with claims that are being put out by a propaganda agency.

The fundamental difficulty here is to define propaganda and separate it from the journalistic commodity that is called news. Propaganda need not necessarily be based on false or misleading information; the "big lie," in fact, has certainly been less effective in the past than the truth—when the truth happened to serve propaganda ends.

If this assumption is correct, then the test of propaganda and news in one respect may be based on the purpose that motivates the originating source. Thus, if an item of news is circulated for no purpose other than general information, it is likely to serve a propaganda end only by accident. If the same item is deliberately put out by the originating source to sway the mass mind and influence behavior, then it is obviously propaganda. Of course, few propagandists are foolish enough to label their more subtle ventures, but no propagandist is likely to deceive an experienced correspondent for very long.

In working abroad, therefore, a reporter becomes accustomed to sift every story he handles for propaganda values. He knows that the foreign press officer, who seems so selfless and willing to please while in the United States, is likely to do much more of a straight propaganda job on his own home grounds. As a visitor in the United States, he is often somewhat timid of arousing charges that he is a source of self-serving propaganda. At home he must try to present his government in the best possible light. It is his job. No nation, of course, goes to the lengths of the Soviet Union in putting a propaganda twist on everything.

The Information Revolution In the 1920s the following was a typical beginning for a cabled message to an American newspaper sent at press rates:

PARIS 17182 BRIAND LOCARNOWARD SAFTERNOON ET-
CONFERRING STRESEMANN STOP TIS REPORTED FRANCO-
GERMAN PACT NEAR PARA

When this was "unskinned" or decoded and rewritten in the home office, it came out like this:

> PARIS, Sept. 17—French Foreign Minister Aristide Briand went to Locarno this afternoon and began conferring there with German Foreign Minister Gustav Stresemann. It was reported that a Franco-German Pact was near.

The simple code, with its complicated use of prefixes and suffixes, survives here and there in service messages sent by old hands in the foreign service. The time code in its block of five digits (following the dateline in the Paris message above) also may still be seen in some places primarily because it is a handy way to identify messages. (YOUR 17128 GARBLED PLS RPT) In a five-digit code the first two digits are for the day of the month (09 would be the ninth, 17 the seventeenth); the next two digits are for the hour of the day, assuming a 24-hour clock (03 would be 3 A.M., 18 would be 6 P.M. at the message's point of origin), and the fifth digit would be for the appropriate part of the hour (one being 10 minutes past the hour, 2 being 20 past, 3 being 30 past, etc.). If a six-digit code was used, the exact minute could be noted.

The coming of highly sophisticated methods of transmission in the world-wide information revolution has made this kind of work cumbersome and out of date. The coming of communications satellites and high quality cables means high speed transmission at ever-increasing quality for both pictures and Telex messages. The coded message, except for service use, thus actually costs more because it takes a considerable time for it to be prepared for use in the home office. Under current practice by news organizations with large volumes of news to transmit, circuits are contracted for on a time basis. A global wire service, for example, would keep 24-hour circuits going for two-way transmissions across the Atlantic. Under such circumstances, copy is transmitted in much the same way across or under oceans as it is over land lines or in the newsroom of a major organization.

For a foreign service like that of *The New York Times*, transmissions of certain kinds of data at 1,000 to 1,500 words a minute is not unusual. Moreover, the system of telephone dictation into recording devices, which are quickly transcribed, is gaining favor at a number of overseas points as a rival to Telex. For television, the satellite system has been a great advantage; with the increase in satellites and the growth of sophisticated cable channels, enormous improvements already are in sight. Before the 1970s are over, transatlantic satellites alone will provide some 42,000 simultaneous voice-data channels or 24 full-time color television channels. Eventually, the laser beam will be developed in such a way as to provide almost unlimited communication capacity.

Costs   There is, of course, a flaw in the undoubted brilliance of this extension of the computer age—cost. While some charges have come down in line with increased speed and volume of transmissions, the transmission of words and pictures from abroad remains out of reach as a daily operation for all except the largest and wealthiest news organizations. It is true that a few organizations of modest size maintain correspondents overseas, but they must watch their costs.

Press rates are still set by the International Telecommunications Union, mainly through the annual meetings of representatives of participating governments at Geneva and elsewhere. It is a general procedure that carriers must charge government-fixed rates and these can vary widely under transmissions paid for by the word rate, instead of a fixed time period. For example, in the late 1960s, the rate between New York and London was three cents a word, between New York and Moscow six cents, and between New York and Paris seven cents.

Between New York and Leopoldville it was ten cents and between New York and Saigon, during the height of the Vietnam War, a whopping 19 cents. It was even higher between Peking and London and between Djakarta and New York.[7] Even the old penny-a-word "Commonwealth Rate" finally gave way to the inflationary trend.

With this kind of expense, it is no wonder that the humble mailer has come back into its own. The jet plane, which joins New York and Europe or Los Angeles and Tokyo in a few hours, makes air mail practical for news that was once sent at deferred cable or radio press rates. It is still necessary to put a dummy dateline on mailers (LONDON, MARCH 00) so that the day of publication may be inserted as needed, but it is questionable how much longer that will be accepted procedure. The supersonic transport (SST) may do more to make foreign news available to small-sized publications than the satellite, the sophisticated cable, and the still popular but less dependable radio teleprinter circuits.

Since both Japanese and British mass-produced newspapers are using facsimile transmission for regional editions, and the *Wall Street Journal* is pioneering in the same field in the United States, it is obvious that the newspaper-in-the-home is no longer a dream. With a combination of electronic transmission and reproduction devices, the television set may yet become a medium for delivering facsimile print-outs at the touch of a button. If there is any inflexible law in journalism, it is the law of change.[8]

---

[7] *Dateline, 1967: Moving The News*, published by Overseas Press Club. See table, pp. 54–55.
[8] *Dateline, 1967*, pp. 25–34 passim.

CENSORSHIP

An even greater impediment to the flow of news across national borders than transmission costs is the rise of censorship in new and pernicious forms. In one guise or another, censorship exists over more than three-quarters of the earth's surface and it is gradually gaining even in the home of free expression, Western Europe.

The crude total censorship of the early twentieth century, in which dispatches were held up or mutilated in whole or in part, is no longer as widespread as it once was. Instead, particularly in the Communist world, the system has been changed to place the correspondent in the position of censoring himself for fear of being expelled. Thus, the Soviet Union formally abolished censorship in 1961 and permitted Western correspondents to inaugurate two-way teletype communication with their home offices if they wished to do so. A certain amount of liberalization followed. Correspondents, cautiously testing the boiling point of the regime, found they could transmit some criticism in low key and even speculate on the course of events behind the Iron Curtain. But they also found out that the Soviet Union was as quick as it ever had been to expel correspondents it deemed unfriendly and to bar from within its territory news organizations it held to be essentially hostile. In Communist China, too, correspondents found that there was no formal censorship in the accepted sense of the term but they were held on a tight leash in both their movements and what sources they were permitted to contact. The West had to depend for the most part on Japanese correspondents, Reuters, and Agence France Presse to cover the tumultuous events of Chairman Mao Tse-tung's great cultural revolution in the late 1960s, for representatives of United States news organizations entered mainland China only if they were approved by Peking or resorted to claims that they were non-Americans or represented non-United States agencies.

In effect, the system of precensorship was far more effective than the old way of holding up correspondents' copy or cutting it up with shears. Many a correspondent, fearing expulsion, found himself hung up between a desire to give his news organization decent coverage and not to offend the country to which he was accredited. The truth of the correspondents' findings was seldom at issue. The Communist government of Poland, for example, did not question the truth of A. M. Rosenthal's dispatches to *The New York Times* but found he had "probed too deeply" and therefore expelled him. Subsequently, he won the Pulitzer Prize for his dispatches from behind the Iron Curtain.

In Czechoslovakia in 1968, Moscow's extreme sensitivity over press criticism by a liberal Communist regime led directly to a military invasion and takeover. And in Peking, the Chinese served warning on venturesome correspondents by holding Reuters' Anthony Grey under house arrest for more than a year, although he had been guilty of no crime and never received any specification of the charges against him.

By sealing up the sources available to correspondents, military or dictatorial regimes also found it possible to apply a very thorough censorship without accepting the onus of being censors. Thus, in the terrible carnage that followed the failure of the Communists to take over in Indonesia in the Fall of 1965, the policy of admitting correspondents in limited numbers and keeping them away from prime sources actually delayed for months the world's knowledge of what was going on outside the apparent order established in Djakarta. This kind of unadmitted censorship is the most difficult procedure for a correspondent to penetrate and to explain. Yet, it exists to a degree in many countries that boast of a "free" press.

The censor the correspondent never sees and the harsh voice that cuts off a telephone connection in a monitored call are the two figures in a censorship pattern that are the most difficult to bear. These are usually minor officials with set instructions, which they often interpret with unreasonable strictness. All the correspondent can do is to file his protests and carry his case to the authorities of his own embassy as well as those of the country to which he is accredited. He doesn't often win a battle of this kind, but he must always stand his ground for as long as possible.[9]

---

[9] Numerous examples of outstanding Washington and foreign correspondence may be found in Snyder and Morris, *A Treasury of Great Reporting* (New York: Simon & Schuster, Inc., 1949) and in Hohenberg, *The Pulitzer Prize Story* (New York, Columbia University Press, 1959) and *The New Front Page* (New York, Columbia University Press, 1966).

chapter 27

The Specialist

The growth of specialized reporting is one of the most stimulating aspects of modern American journalism. When the newspaper constituted the main reliance of the nation for its news and features, the average editor was content to go with his established departments— business and finance, sports, entertainment, women's news, and weekly columns devoted to religious and cultural activities. Today, under the pressure of changing American patterns of living and increasing competition among the news media for the public's interest, the old ways have been found wanting.

There is a demonstrable need for broadened coverage of such fields as science, education, health, housing, civil rights, urban renewal, social welfare, and many others. Medicine, military affairs, labor and industry, space exploration, and kindred fields are a regular part of the news of the day. The old departments are wearing a new look. And new departments, such as those devoted to the problems of youth, are groping for a deeper meaning. The whole area of service news dealing with home-making, travel, recreation, and self-improvement, to name only a few subjects, is just beginning to be explored.

Somehow, the newspapers and wire services are trying to find the resources—both human and financial—to deal with this age of specialization on a competitive basis with the magazines, radio and television, and the motion pictures. The old notion that any good reporter can cover any story, and do it well, is dying. Slowly, perhaps even reluctantly, American journalism is turning to the specialist.

It should not be imagined that these latest additions to news organization staffs are being taken, green and unripened, from the nation's campuses. A young physician does not at once perform a brain operation. Nor does a young lawyer try his first case before the United States Supreme Court. Even the most promising specialists in journalism, similarly, usually undergo basic training to learn the principles and disciplines of their profession. There, they find that their stiffest competition comes from the journalists in their middle years who, noting the signs of the times, have gone back to the classroom to prepare themselves for greater responsibilities.

The large and prosperous metropolitan newspapers, the news magazines, and the television networks can support specialists in science, medicine, space, and the like, but their smaller competitors necessarily must be more modest. The syndicate and the wire service are the first reliance of the newspaper of small size but large ambitions. The local station usually has to rely on the networks for specialized coverage of major news events.

Yet, for all the media, the new areas of journalism must be explored. Interest is very high. And the trend is all in favor of the specialist, although it is unlikely that he will ever be in the majority in the average news organization. Somebody must still cover the Girl Scouts, the Chamber of Commerce, the two-alarm fire, the death of a respected citizen, the automobile accident, and the missing child.

One of the best indicators of professional interest in advanced training for journalism is the rapid progress that has been made by foundations in offering fellowships for specialized studies. The Nieman Foundation at Harvard, the first in the field, now has competition at Columbia, Stanford, Northwestern, and a number of other universities. The short refresher courses at the American Press Institute are becoming increasingly popular. The future may not belong entirely to the specialist, but no wise editor is likely to disregard him.

SCIENCE WRITING

Man's giant vault into space, almost at the outset of the atomic age, has done more than anything else to stimulate the trend toward specialization. The spectacular live coverage of space shots on television has quickened public interest and led the newspapers and news magazines to turn to broader methods of communicating science news to mass audiences through the printed page. The science-trained newscaster and the science reporter for the print media have a great advantage over their less skilled brethren who can only tell what they see and hear because they do not know enough to explain what is going on.

The reporting of science is being done with considerable competence today and it is bound to improve. It was not always so. During the first half of the twentieth century, the pioneering science writers often had to struggle for time and space to tell their exciting and meaningful stories. The nation owes a debt to them because they managed, despite all obstacles, to lay the basis for the expert reportage of the present day. Among those who did the job were William L. Laurence of *The New York Times*, John J. O'Neill of the New York *Herald Tribune*, Howard Blakeslee and his son, Alton, of the Associated Press; Delos Smith of United Press International, David Dietz of Scripps-Howard Newspapers, and Gobind Behari Lal of International News Service.

Basically their training was as journalists, but they also acquired a scientific background that won them and their colleagues the respect of the nation's scientists. At a time when a meeting of the National Association for the Advancement of Science attracted only a handful of reporters, most of them self-taught, these hard-bitten professionals competed successfully with the run of general news. It was no accident that one of their number, "Atomic Bill" Laurence, was borrowed by the United States government from his newspaper so that he could write the official dispatches announcing the creation of the atomic bomb.

For some twenty years before the beginning of World War II, the relatively few science writers in the country quietly went about their business. They had scant recognition, outside the Pulitzer Prizes that were granted to a few of their number in 1923 and 1937, but they persisted in bringing the news of science to people who were not particularly interested in science.

It was through such pioneering that suspicious and reticent scientists eventually learned to trust the most responsible science reporters with their secrets. The reporters, on their part, developed a technique of turning scientific abstracts into news stories and then submitting them in advance of publication to their scientific authors for checking. Thus, a mutual growth of confidence benefited both the scientists and their colleagues of the press. During World War II, this collaboration increased. Thereafter, in the first years of the atomic age and the opening of space exploration, the science reporters came into their own. Such experts as Jules Bergman of the American Broadcasting Companies and Earl Ubell of the Columbia Broadcasting System gave television the kind of prestige and know-how that it needed to compete with the top science writers of the daily and weekly press. As younger men came along, the distribution of science writers became fairly general among the leaders of the media.

Today, a major meeting of pure scientists, physicians, or engineers is a national event, covered by every news organization of standing in the country. In the international field any session dealing with atomic energy or space flight attracts almost as many reporters as a summit conference. It is not unusual for 500 reporters to go to Geneva for an atomic conference. The leading scientists have willingly turned themselves into briefing officers on such occasions, with generally excellent results. The wire services, never ones to waste words, do not hesitate to send stories of 1,000 words or more on important scientific developments.

What Is Covered   Out of the enormous amount of material that is published in scientific and scholarly journals, it is obvious that only a small part can be translated into popular terms and used widely by the news media commanding a mass audience. Consequently, a considerable volume of science news of a technical nature appears in specialized publications first. Scientific conventions account for almost as much news of science, being prime sources of new developments and new ideas. Entirely on their own, science writers study almost anything bearing on the development of atomic energy and space exploration for the germ of a significant news account. Sometimes they learn of such developments from their own sources in government and industry; on other occasions, they may be able to deduce clues to future developments from their own background and knowledge.

The increasing emphasis on studies of air and water pollution has deepened public interest in such matters and broadened the scope of the writer of popularized science. This is also true of the emphasis on medical reportage and progress in improving conditions in hospitals. But whole areas of mathematics, physics and chemistry, and other natural sciences are still relatively uncovered in the daily and periodical press because the developments are so far above the level of public understanding. As for television reporting of science, it will never be able to compete with the excellence of press coverage except in such areas as space flights if it waits to develop its own public. The way these things usually are done is for the press to educate as it informs.

Here is the essential portion of a report on emphysema, distributed by the Associated Press and widely published in American newspapers, which is a model of its kind:

By Frank Carey

NEW YORK—A young resident doctor at Bellevue Hospital stood at the bedside of a frail little man in his early sixties who was obviously fighting for every breath.

"Look," said the doctor. "Here's the pinnacle of distress—and this poor guy is typical of severe cases of this condition. They act like they just finished the four-minute mile run every minute of their lives."

He referred to respiratory failure; a virtual shut-off of breathing power—which can be brought on by an insidious but potentially devastating and potentially lethal lung disease called emphysema.

Emphysema (pronounced em-fih-see-muh) is rated by the United States Public Health Service as "the fastest growing crippler disease in the United States today"—constituting a public health menace of potentially epidemic proportions unless somehow checked.

The malady, whose basic cause or causes remain unknown, is characterized by a so-far irreversible destruction of lung tissue. This results in abnormal distention of the spongelike lung, a loss of its wondrous elasticity, and an entrapment of life-sustaining air within it.

There's also an obstruction of certain airway tubes—with overall result that many victims can have frequent and extreme difficulty in exhaling and even mild cases can occasionally have such difficulty upon exertion.

While the cause remains to be pinpointed, the Public Health Service, and many private physicians, contend that tobacco smoking—especially cigarette smoking—and air pollution are, at the least, among the aggravating factors. Even spokesmen for the tobacco industry concede smoking may be an aggravant but they challenge any contention it's a proven cause.

The Health Service says:

At least 2,000,000 Americans, and possibly up to 14,000,000, are estimated to have chronic obstructive respiratory diseases, including emphysema; chronic bronchitis, which usually is a fellow-traveler of it; asthma, bronchiectasis, and certain forms of chronic pneumonia . . .

ECONOMIC NEWS

One of the outstanding developments within the last two decades has been the emergence of an informal, popular, and often uninhibited economics story. Whether the subject is business or labor, the stock market or foreign trade, or the innumerable offshoots thereof, the innovators on the *Wall Street Journal* and the nation's leading business pages show their irreverence for the stuffy old forms of traditional financial news handling. This is one of the reasons for the phenomenal growth of the *Wall Street Journal* into the second largest daily newspaper in the land, with more than one million circulation (at 15 cents a copy) serviced by its numerous regional printing plants. It is, of course, not the only reason because the *Journal* is the complete financial newspaper in a nation where financial success is the principal goal of so many young people.

Nor is the *Journal* alone in profiting from the revolution in the presentation of economic news. The McGraw-Hill magazines, headed by *Business Week*, and the Fairchild group, of which the daily *Women's Wear* is the most prominent, both have found a new prosperity in their devotion to the unorthodox and the unusual in their respective fields. The financial pages of the Philadelphia *Bulletin*, presided over by J. A. Livingston, are closely read by many people who would not otherwise worry too much about financial news because he digs for interesting and unusual subjects. The financial columnist, Sylvia F. Porter, has built a nation-wide audience

Or, there is this one which is equally worn:

The strike at the ————— plant entered its —————th day today without any prospect of immediate settlement. ————— —————————, representing the management, blamed labor's excessive demands for the deadlock . . . . .

In the columns of a good newspaper, news of labor affairs is by no means confined to strikes and lockouts or violence on the picket lines. A more sophisticated approach to the reporting of conflicts between industry and labor has developed, so that a good newspaper takes care not to label itself a pro-industry partisan in every dispute but tries to give both sides to the story. If ever newspapers were tempted to slant a story, it was during the series of strikes that closed some papers and helped bring about the death of others during the 1960s; yet, in the leading newspapers, the story was usually told with scrupulous fairness. What happened on the editorial page was something else again, but that is the place where management has the right to express its opinion and to make room for the opinions of others. As for television, its own test came in the 1967 strike of the American Federation of Television and Radio Artists, which pulled nearly all of its distinguished figures off the program schedules. While the coverage was not particularly distinguished, and seldom given in depth, it was fundamentally honest. And that, at least, is progress.

EDUCATION NEWS

With nearly 60 million Americans going to school and about half the nation's population under 25, the coverage of education today is a challenge to all the news media. The day of the "school reporter," the unhappy cub who is tagged on his first day with the unwelcome task of getting a few paragraphs about education into the newspaper, has been over ever since World War II although a lot of editors still don't realize it. The school page on a lot of newspapers is still a collection of uninteresting and dispensable items. And when there is a program devoted to education on television, some of the clichés uttered by the participants make a teacher squirm. There is greater room for progress in the reporting of education news than in many another specialty. But it will take well-trained journalists to do the job—men and women who understand the problems of the schools and know how to write about them.

If it is the responsibility of the news media to entrust the education assignment only to a qualified reporter, then it is equally the responsibility of the community leadership to see that he is given access to the news of education. The cooperation between press and school is no less important than the understanding between teacher and parent, but unhappily these conditions are easier to write about than to create. Where the old mutually critical attitudes between press and school can be cast aside, and a sympathetic examination of joint problem areas can be undertaken, the cause of education is likely to be advanced.

The old journalistic weakness for emphasizing trouble rather than achievement is only a part of the difficulty in achieving a balanced presentation of the news of education. In many cities, the extreme sensitivity of school administrations to criticism handicaps even their defenders when they embark on a purely fact-finding mission. Such sensitivity often is exceeded only by that of the press itself when it is under heavy community criticism. In such situations, there is little possibility for a constructive dialogue and school and press drift into postures of mutual hostility. This is particularly true in some of the struggles over school integration in northern cities.

In recent years a number of newspapers and television stations have tried to pay special attention to the activities of youth in order to lessen tension. These youth sections—"Teen Pages" on newspapers and programs such as "Youth Wants To Know" in the electronic media—have grown in popularity among the younger generation. Where students are given a reasonably free hand to report on the news of their schools and social organizations, a great many dividends often accrue. One of the most significant is the formation of the habit of reading the news, listening to it and watching it—certainly one of the first responsibilities of citizenship.

Here is the theme of one of many articles in the Boston *Herald* in a series entitled, "Report Card on Boston Schools," which sought to focus the attention of the community on ways to help cure the ills of education:

> What the rest of Boston schools lack is being put into the Boardman School in Roxbury.
>
> The Boardman is the focal point of the school department's model substitute system—a little school system within the big city school system.
>
> The subsystem includes four interconnected schools in the Roxbury-North Dorchester area—a preschool, elementary school, the Boardman junior high, and the high school. The system, funded by the Federal government, is a proving ground "in which promising existing programs can be explored and in which new programs can be developed," according to Evans Clinchy, director of the subsystem.
>
> Clinchy, who heads the Office of Program Development in the Boston schools, is the only outsider in the administration. He was formerly associated with the Educational Facilities Laboratory of the Ford Foundation in New York and Educational Services Inc., of Watertown.
>
> Many of the changes envisioned for the subsystem are fundamental educational practices taken for granted in most other school systems. These include requiring teachers to stay after school, selection of teachers on the basis of interviews rather than test scores, and emphasis on learning rather than discipline.

Other features of the subsystem are becoming common practice in many school systems such as in Pittsburgh, Atlanta, and Miami. These features include nongraded organization and an 11- or 12-month school year . . .

NEWS OF RELIGION

The news of religion for many years suffered an extremely low priority in the daily press except on Monday mornings and religious holidays. Even then the reports of church services—dutifully gathered by underpaid part-time reporters such as students and off-duty copy boys and sometimes the clergy themselves—usually were buried in accounts of weekend or holiday traffic either leaving or entering the city. Religion, in a few words, was not generally considered to be news unless a minister happened to get himself murdered—the spectacular case of the Reverend Dr. Edward Wheeler Hall and his choir singer, Mrs. Eleanor Mills, who were found laid out beneath an old apple tree in DeRussey's Lane in New Brunswick, N. J., in 1925. There were exceptions to the generally discouraging performance of the press in the coverage of religion, but they weren't many.

The changed attitude that is so apparent today in a large section of the press, including television, scarcely means that the editors have suddenly "got" religion. Rather, the clergy of all the great religions represented in the United States have made a concerted, if uncoordinated, effort to work outside as well as inside the churches and synagogues to a greater extent than ever before. The ecumenical movement, begun with such a flourish by Pope John XXIII and carried on by his earnest successor, Pope Paul VI, did much to focus the attention of both Catholic and non-Catholic on the new life that is pulsing through the Church of Rome. The frequent participation of clergy of all faiths in the various civil rights causes of the 1960s also stimulated new interest in the work of the churches. Then, a tiny group suddenly began discussing the unthinkable and headlines began flaring throughout the nation: "Is God Dead?" And on television and radio stations there were lively discussions of the "new theology" and its radical beliefs. Naturally, the old evangelists found new popularity in this controversial atmosphere. One of them, the Rev. Dr. Billy Graham, became so well known that he was a frequenter of the White House.

Necessarily, the Monday morning column of sermons (and sometimes on Sundays in communities with large synagogues) is no longer adequate to tell the news of religion. Both the major wire services have editors specializing in religion, as do the weekly news magazines and the better newspapers. And it is not at all unusual to find clergy in the inevitable panel discussions on television, exchanging views with the laity and with each other.

THE CULTURAL STORY

The audience for cultural affairs in the United States today is larger than the sports audience in most major metropolitan centers. In New York City, a season's audience at the available theatres, concert halls, art galleries, and museums would be greater than the combined attendance at professional baseball, football and horse-racing events. In Los Angeles, with its magnificent new art and theatre complexes, the cultural event is often even bigger news. The same thing is true for any city in the nation that has enough cultural attractions to merit widespread attention.

With few exceptions, however, the news media are not able to turn loose a large and competent staff of critics to assess the cultural activities of their communities. Most papers that value their good name try to publish a varied assortment of news and features about cultural subjects devoted to amusements and women's interests. Television condescends to allow a few able critics all of one or two minutes to review a play and occasionally ventures on a documentary; however, when a play like Arthur Miller's *Death of a Salesman* is displayed on the small screen, it becomes a national event. Truly, cultural news has come into its own but critics and commentators knowledgeable enough to give it meaning cannot be created overnight.

Certainly, the America of abundant leisure time is entitled to a better display of critical writing on cultural subjects than it presently enjoys except in leading newspapers and magazines. Just as the growth of classes in dramatic art at our universities provided the stage with appreciative and literate audiences, without necessarily spawning a new crop of playwrights, so the increasing emphasis on cultural news is creating readers with higher critical standards. When the critics are given greater liberties on television, there is no doubt that the mass culture of today will take an even greater battering.

Higher standards among audiences will have to be met in one way or another. If the news media cannot do it by developing critics from younger people on their own staffs with the requisite backgrounds, then they will have to publish more critical material from syndicates or wire services or recruit home-town talent from nearby centers of higher education. But it is nonsense to devote all the energies and wealth of a community to creating a firstrate art center, repertory theatre, or symphony orchestra and then permit the local news media to publish hack criticism or no criticism at all.

Among newspapers, there are generally two ways of handling cultural events. The first method, and unhappily the largest in the United States, is the group that runs either a news story on a new book, play, movie, concert, or art exhibit, or contents itself with a "puff"-type review. The second method, which may be smaller but is by all odds the most influential, endeavors to run both reviews and criticism of cultural events of interest to the community. There are, unfortunately, civic leaders and even advertisers who regard any decent attempt at critical writing to be a dastardly attack on the fair name of a great community project, but no newspaper of integrity can afford to pay serious attention to such people. It is a good newspaper's function to provide honest reviews and criticism of any public performance or showing, and nothing should be permitted to interfere with such necessary journalistic activity.

There is, of course, a profound difference between a review and a critique. The review is done quickly under deadline pressure, as a rule, while criticism is generally written by someone with expert qualifications after due consideration has been given to a performance, book, or exhibit of one kind or another. This is not to say that criticism—in the form known as a critique—cannot be done expertly under pressure. The great New York drama critic, Brooks Atkinson, did his best work by taking only 45 minutes to an hour to do a critique of a play he had just seen and he took a quiet pride in always making his deadline. In answer to furious academics who charged that he should have taken more time to think over a spectacle that had cost hundreds of thousands of dollars to produce, he invariably replied, "Either I like it or I don't like it, and that isn't going to change even if I wait a week to write my review."

Thus, a review and a critique may be done by the same person, one for a daily newspaper and the other for a Sunday paper. Or, a daily reviewer may well write at greater length and depth for a monthly magazine or express his views on television if he is fortunate enough to find a culture-minded station. At any rate, it is one of the oddities of cultural journalism that the critique generally reinforces the conclusions of the deadline review, unless they are done by different persons. A critic seldom changes his mind; moreover, if perchance one publicly admits he is wrong, it is worth mentioning in the news columns.

The review, far more than the critique or the news story, is the dominant form in serious cultural journalism at the daily level and in the news magazines. The monthlies and specialized publications such as the *Saturday Review* and the *New Yorker* go in for critiques because they have the contributors and the time to do them well. Although the style of reviewers varies widely, the exigencies of deadline journalism are bound to influence its structure. In general, therefore, most reviews begin with a general statement of the subject and the writer's reaction to it. If a plot is involved, it is stated briefly—usually in no more than two or three paragraphs. Nothing is worse than a spirited retelling of a plot at second hand. The work of the author, composer, or players is then summed up, with appropriate comparisons to other attractions or past performances. A paragraph or two is given to other detail, if any. And in the concluding paragraph the opening statement is generally amplified and strengthened so that the reader may be in no doubt over the reviewer's position.

In structure, then, the review follows the news story format rather closely, but it is compact and tightly knit. It strives not to say blankly that something is just good or bad, wonderful or terrible, but to define a more precise reaction and give the reasons for it. Moreover, a review should be sportsmanlike. It should not belabor an innocent little high school performance of *Dear Brutus*, pummel a hapless young first novelist, or destroy the nice girl soprano who had the bad judgment to try the Bell Song from Lakme at a church social. The premise of a professional reviewer is that, in such cases, the less said the better. However, if a novelist of stature writes a trashy book or a renowned playwright gives the public a dull and meaningless drama, then it is obviously the duty of an honest reviewer to say so, and it is the obligation of an honest newspaper to permit him to do it. Sometimes, of course, critics make mistakes, but it is better to have mistaken critics than no critics at all.

The better magazines have always had an admirable record in this sensitive area of journalism and they have sought diligently for critics with a fresh viewpoint. At the turn of the century and for some years thereafter, when newspaper criticism was at a very low ebb, such magazines as *Harper's* and the *Atlantic Monthly* kept the critical function alive. Consequently, the current effort of television to find a place for both reviews and criticism and a mass public willing to watch, listen, and learn should be regarded with sympathy and not with derision. A communications form with such a short and spectacular history must be given time to develop its own critical approach. It is all to the good that a few new critics already have been found who can speak to millions, not thousands, even if their time is too short by the familiar standards of print.

Books   The book boom is one of the cultural phenomena in the United States. Sales have increased from $700 million in 1954 to more than $2.5 billion currently. New titles have gone from 10,000 to more than 30,000 in less than 20 years. More people are reading than ever before, more authors are being published than ever before—and yet there are only a handful of daily book reviewers. In fact, only about 20 per cent of the daily newspapers in the United States publish book reviews of any kind. The papers argue that book publishers advertise very little. The bookmen reply tartly that books are news and should not be dependent on the amount of advertising that is done for them. The basis of the argument is that more than 50 per cent of total sales and about 90 per cent of publishing profits are accounted for by text and reference books for students, which generally require little advertising in the daily press and also are seldom reviewed.

we shall pay for using this most powerful instrument of communication to insulate the citizenry from the hard and demanding realities which must be faced if we are to survive."

Nor has Murrow been alone in his critical view of television. A year after his celebrated speech, Eric Sevareid of CBS and Martin Agronsky of NBC argued over WGBH-TV in Boston that television had yet to meet the test of handling news courageously in all critical cases. And in 1966, when CBS ran an installment of "I Love Lucy" for the fifth time instead of televising a Senate hearing on the Vietnam War live, Fred Friendly quit as the president of CBS News and later wrote a book about it in protest.

Just as Murrow and Friendly have headed the critics of television, with occasional assists from some of their distinguished colleagues, the most effective criticism of newspapers in this era has come from such newspapermen as Walter Lippmann and James Reston plus a few outspoken editors like Norman Isaacs of the Louisville *Times* and *Courier-Journal* and Turner Catledge of *The New York Times*. They know more about the weaknesses of the press than lesser lights and have never been afraid to discuss them. Many a critic could emulate their candor.

SERVICE NEWS

Women's pages of newspapers, neglected for many years, are trying to make themselves over into worthwhile media of information and comment on women's special interests—homes, fashions, domestic attitudes, arts, and crafts. The magazines have had a long lead over the daily press in this area. It is also one area in which television has a built-in superiority to almost anything the press can do. The very fact that few young women have sought what seemed to them to be a dead-end newspaper job shows the fundamental weakness of most women's pages and women's sections in the daily press today. As the most crushing blow of all, male editors have been put in charge of some women's pages to try to pump new life into them.

The first task in this much-needed reform has been to sweep out the odds and ends of stale publicity that has cluttered women's pages for years. Also, sensible editors have put a limit on junketing, realizing full well that most junkets call for publicity payoffs in one form or another. It is, of course, difficult to eliminate the evil of "puffery" in a part of the press that is a prime target for hordes of press agents. But where controls have been applied, improvement has been noted almost at once.

A serious effort also is being made now by many once-dead women's pages to present service news—news of homemaking and decorating, of craftsmanship in the world of fashion, of the uses of modern furniture and antiques, of food and drink, of travel, of medicine and health, of family interests, of the manifold uses of leisure time. There has been a revival of pictorial journalism on women's pages—unusual and interesting pictures rather than the eternal "mugg" shots of engaged girls and brides, most of them homely.

In point of reader interest, some of the leading women's pages in the daily newspapers are now on a par with the better women's magazines. But neither can appeal to women in the same intimate manner as television. Consequently, the reform movement in the press has a long way to go.

SPORTS WRITING

The sports pages have produced some of the best writing in American journalism; also, some of the worst. The superior sports reporters have always been on good terms with the English language, as well as sports, and have handled both with loving care. They have taken advantage of the freedom of expression that is the birthright of every sports writer and used it to communicate with a mass public in more or less original terms. The youth of America, therefore, has learned something more than merely who won and who lost by reading Damon Runyon and Grantland Rice, Ring Lardner and Bill McGeehan, Red Smith and Bob Harron and Bob Considine.

Television's superior attraction—the presentation of the game itself in all its fascinating detail—has not solved the problem of bad sports writing, as some had hoped. There are few sports commentators who have the good sense of a Red Barber and let the viewer watch the game, giving him only the most necessary information and explanation. For the most part, between the nonstop talk of the commentators, much of it graceless, and the deluge of advertising, the viewer must cope with mangled and sometimes incomprehensible English.

What it comes down to is this:

The amateur sports reporters have never quite grasped either the disciplines of sports or the English language. They have written and spoken in overexpert terms of simple games and loaded their reportage with faded clichés, a frequent source of annoyance. Instead of using their freedom of expression with grace and meaning, they have cluttered it with nonessentials. They have fawned on the great names of sports, whether the great names deserved it or not, and trafficked with the gristle, the shabby hangers-on. They have, on occasion, shrilly rebuked the boy who dropped a fly ball in the last of the ninth inning and lost the game. And that is the heart of the matter. The amateurs have never learned to play the game— the most important facet of a sports reporter's work. And this is the difference between them and the relatively small group of professionals who dominate sports on and off the field.

The Techniques   Heywood Broun, a distinguished if somewhat academic sports writer before he turned to belles lettres and causes, once used himself and his bitter enemy, Westbrook Pegler, as an illustration of the techniques of sports reporting.

"There are two kinds of sports writers," said Broun, quite soberly. "There is the first, the 'Ah, wonderful!' school, of which I hope I am an exponent. And then there is the second, the 'Ah, nuts!' school, of which Pegler is the leader. You may, if you wish, choose between them."

Allowing for a certain amount of Brounian exaggeration, the fundamental thesis is sound. The romantic school of sports reporting—more prevalent today on television than in print—sees everything in terms of heroic combat, of great deeds achieved by superbeings. The more realistic, and somewhat more reasonable, school accepts sports for what they are— a game played either by amateurs or professionals for the entertainment of the multitudes.

The basic approach is something ingrained in the reporter, whether he ad-libs for a minute or two hours on radio or television, or writes two paragraphs or three columns. He must have a point of view. Somehow, the bitter battle over interpretation that has been fought in the news columns never had a great deal of application to sports. As far as sports are concerned, there has always been interpretation and even editorialization in the tales of athletic skill. Here, the deadpan reporter and the cautious "down-the-middle" rewrite man have been hooted out of the sports office and carefully dumped on makeup in a particularly dark part of the composing room. They never have gained a foothold in radio and television, both being comparatively modern communications arts.

Once the sports fan had to wait until the paper came out to get the sports results. But for nearly a half-century there has been no way of competing with the swiftness of radio. And for nearly a quarter-century, television has brought the game or the race or the spectacle into the barroom, the living room, and even, on occasion, the auditorium. Thus, the fan who once hung around the news stand, waiting for the first edition to come up, now often knows as much as the sports writer about the game and has even stronger opinions. In fact, because the sports writer has to turn his attention to his notes and his story, he may miss some of the very things that the stay-at-home fans see on television and hear the sports commentators discuss. Yet, there is no sign that sports pages are in less demand, which can only mean that the fan still reads his favorite sports author to agree or disagree with the commentary in the newspaper.

For contests in sports, therefore, the game is still the thing. But since a very large part of the sports public knows the final score from radio or television before the paper comes out, what becomes important in the written story is to relate how and why the result was achieved. It means that the techniques of the feature writer have now become all-important on the sports pages, although some editors still insist on the fast summary straightaway lead (just as if television didn't exist). It is also almost pathetic to pick up even a great newspaper and note that a sports writer has described the first-quarter of a night football game, which ended long before the paper was purchased. The newspapers have taken many years to adjust to the electronic realities and some have not quite made it yet. But the sensible ones have adapted the methods that make general news writing more effective and readable and applied them to the sports page.

One of the signs of the times is the insistence of UPI on giving editors an alternative to the straightaway sports lead, which may be dummied as follows for baseball (with appropriate variations for any other kind of game or race):

> Pete Smith's home run in the ——— inning with ——— men on base gave the ——— an ——— to ——— victory today over the ——— and put them in ——— place in the ——— league.

"Certainly this packs a lot of information into a minimum amount of space," says Roger Tatarian, editor of UPI. "Certainly, it prevents any wear and tear on the imagination, which means stories can be written faster this way—and speech does have advantages: minutes saved in hitting a newspaper sports desk and in getting to the composing room."

But, as Tatarian points out, the net effect of such glazed and frozen sports writing is to bore the fan who already knows what has happened. Thus, the realistic sports writer proceeds on the assumption that his electronic rivals already have done a good job of covering the news in words and pictures. Moreover. even if the sports page reader doesn't happen to know that the Tigers slaughtered the Yankees, the headline will tell him and the lead need not belabor the tragic event. For example, a writer can do this with a rather ordinary and lackluster baseball game:

> WASHINGTON (UPI)—It was this kind of an opening day game—the President went home after five innings.
> He didn't miss much. As a contest, the Washington Senators–New York Yankees game that inaugurated the baseball season was over even before then. It ended for all practical purposes when Bill Robinson hit a single . . .

There is one other thing editors could do to compete with radio and television for the attention of the sports-minded public—quit printing partial results and wait until a contest is over before publishing the story. Nobody will ever miss the dummy accounts that read something like this:

> The Pirates and the Giants clashed today in Candlestick Park for a crucial series that will determine second place in the National League pennant race.
> At the end of two and one-half innings, the score was 0-0.

This kind of sports writing went out in 1900. It lingers on today because nobody has quite gotten around to burying it.

The Patterns   Neither the radio and television talkers nor the writers, of course, can take on a sports assignment without an intimate knowledge of the events they are describing. In both fields of reporting, the two greatest necessities are accuracy and restraint. Sports followers invariably pride themselves on being experts. They like to hear and read about "inside" strategy, just as the literati gossip endlessly about the famous people on whom characters in a sensational new novel are supposedly patterned. However, some games are more easy to describe than others—and that depends on the patterns of the sport.

An essentially simple game like baseball is easily reported. The game's play-by-play, the result and the reasons for it can be quickly summarized, then documented with a description of the key plays. A few other details, and the account is complete enough for a post-game electronic roundup or a sports story. Not every baseball game, after all, is handled as if it were a World Series drama.

Boxing and horse-racing, too, have essentially simple patterns and need not be told in too complicated a fashion. What matters here, particularly in television, is the detail that makes the tiny images on the small screen come alive—the blow by blow in a fight and the enormously intricate "call" in a horse race. By comparison, accounts of competitions in crew, swimming, tennis, polo, and golf are handled with relative ease.

In football, however, the pattern of the game becomes increasingly complicated and difficult to follow. The effort of a play-by-play commentator here must be to simplify, wherever possible, and to explain to the viewer what happened and why it happened instead of prattling excitedly about the confusing technicalities. In a summary, oral as well as written, it becomes necessary to analyze the result, to select the principal plays, and to give the public a sense of participation in the reporting.

The many events in track and field, each with special complications, also require a good deal of guidance from professionals who are intimately acquainted with the sport. This is particularly true during the great spectacle of the Olympic Games every four years; unhappily, such reportage usually turns out to be the worst, rather than the best, of the year because the American commentators and reporters know only their own competitors as a rule and habitually tend to give the results of each race as a triumph of American righteousness or a blow to the Stars and Stripes. Actually, in any track meet, the reporting can be done very nicely—and interestingly— if the expert-for-the-day will bother to acquaint himself with the teams in advance, look up the necessary background and records, and come to the field an hour before the meet begins to do a final checkup. To wait until the first event begins is to bog down completely in detail. But if it is known in advance that the pole vault, the mile run and the hurdles are likely to develop the most interesting contests, then the meet becomes a relatively easy matter to cover.

As for basketball, with its seven-footers and its statistical labyrinths, this is less a job for a sports reporter than for a certified public accountant. It may be fun to play, but it is a bore to follow on television and even worse to describe in print.

It is clear, therefore, that the patterns of sport have much to do with the pattern of sports journalism. The big money sports, such as horse racing, boxing, baseball, and football, are the ones with the most public appeal; in general, professional sports have the widest following. The amateur sports frequently are interesting only to alumni of schools and friends of participants except for the football colleges that compete for national championships annually and reap profit and fame from their television contracts.

However, the newest development in sports, the vast interest in such audience participation events as stock car racing, motor boating and sailing, hunting and fishing, skating and skiing, and the like have opened new vistas on the sports pages. Such events are not easy for television to cover with any degree of consistency. Moreover, the cult of the automobile has become so widespread among teen-agers that the ordinary newspaper simply can't represent their interests. Tom Wolfe once argued, with typical exaggeration, that nothing in the news media today comes even close to representing the real desires of the "in" group of sports-minded youth. However, it is essentially true that a very large proportion of the younger people in the sports audience has climbed down out of the grandstand and taken possession of the playing field. The day of the expert player is far from being over, as Wolfe suggests, but the amateurs are developing new interests that will eventually strain the resources of the news media.

Handling the Sports Story   The incomparable Red Smith, viewing an Army-Navy football game at Philadelphia, began his account as follows:

> As some churlish historian of America's great undergraduate pastime wrote years ago, "It was an ideal day for football—too cold for the spec-

tators and too cold for the players." For 100,000 citizens of assorted nations, including Russia and Monaco, whose chattering teeth rattled like castanets upon the necks of bottles in Municipal Stadium yesterday, that just about sums up the fifty-ninth match of Army and Navy.

Eventually, Smith got around to mentioning the size of the Army's victory, 22-6, which wasn't particularly important to him because everybody who read him knew it anyway. What was more important to his readers was his point of view:

> The entertainment seemed flat by comparison with Army–Navy contests of the past. It was just too perishing cold. Reluctant to quit a slugging match which they had traveled many miles to watch, the customers nevertheless started making their numbed way toward the exits when the first half ended, longing for a warm hotel room with the guy across the courtyard beating his wife . . . .

What Smith has done for the newspaper, David Brinkley frequently can do for television in reporting news other than sports. But the basic difficulty with the average sports writer and commentator is that they immerse themselves in technicalities to such an extent that they often forget entirely about the game itself and the people who contest it and who watch it. The electronic reporters become slaves to the mound of equipment with which they are obliged to travel and the technicians who operate it. The newspaper reporters worry about writing three separate accounts of a single event in order to cover all editions of a newspaper—a time-consuming and expensive procedure that provides no advantage in these times of instant communication.

Because the technique of doing multiple stories of one sports event is still practiced in a large section of the daily press, the essentials are recorded here without assurance that they will survive many more years:

1. *The advance story.* The advance begins with a situation lead, relating that two teams are facing each other or that a field of seven horses is ready for the big race of the day. The remainder of the story merely discusses the background of the event, gives whatever detail there is on the participants and the crowd, and winds up in such a way that the running account of the early part of the game can be added on. If the contest is under way before the edition closes, a brief high insert can give the early scoring. Necessarily, even in an early edition, the advance is bound to look foolish. It assumes that the public is entirely dependent on the newspaper to find out what happened and will buy a later edition to get the full details. This used to happen, but it hasn't been true for many years.

2. *The running story.* Depending on the style of the paper, the chronological story of the game is told as B copy or B matter or merely

slugged "Running" or "Play by Play." As an edition approaches, a two paragraph lead is written by the reporter at the scene or an editor in the office and put on top of the opening of the chronological account. Once the event is over, a final wrap-up lead is written and the details of the end of the game are put at the bottom of the piece.

3. If the running story is well done within reasonable space, it should stand. But frequently, sports writers have the urge to do the whole exercise over again on the dubious theory that they will produce magnificent prose the second time around. Unfortunately, it rarely turns out that way.

Nobody can do his best under these wretched circumstances. If the objective is to keep pace with radio and television, it is impossible to attain. If it is to "save space" for the final story, the theory is lacking in practicality. Such "saved space" is always wasted space. The news magazines manage to do pretty well with their weekly summaries of sports and do not arouse great feeling among the sports-minded public that it is being cheated. Sooner or later, the newspapers will come around to the obvious—that the best way to do a sports story is to wait until the event is over and then give it the well-considered treatment it deserves. Few sports events are big enough to call for edition-by-edition coverage against electronic competition.

A generation that was thrilled by the "Ah, wonderful!" sports writing of an expert Heywood Broun has been suceeded by a generation that prefers the inexpert sports commentaries of his son Heywood Hale Broun on television. And that is the measure of the generation gap in sports.

chapter 28

Public Service Journalism

Public service journalism is based on the assumption that the journalist is the watchdog of the public interest. It is most effective at the community level, where a serious newspaper or a station with a good staff of radio or television newsmen often can provide the basis for effective leadership. At the state, regional, and national levels, it becomes increasingly difficult for a journalist to operate because of the complexities of the issues that are involved in the protection of the public interest. Yet, the more courageous leaders among the newspapers, the magazines, and the electronic media have established a tradition of public service in the United States that has come to be a hallmark of American journalism. If the newspapers are the first and most numerous in the field, that is because they have been at it longer and have had greater experience. But the magazines, too, have a proud record going back to the glorious "muckrakers" at the turn of the century. And television need only recall Edward R. Murrow's single-handed crusade against McCarthyism to validate its own credentials in public service, although the electronic media must always face the specter of government licensing and regulation in anything they do.

Whatever the difficulties that are involved, it has become accepted in the United States that a demonstrable interest in public service is one of the keys to the successful practice of journalism today.

THE CHALLENGE

There is no conceivable way in which a newspaper can bid for the respect and favor of its community and avoid risk, controversy, and sometimes a bitter struggle for survival. Realistic publishers know it. So do their editors. Yet, day after day, in this dark era of perpetual crisis, newspapers of all sizes and political faiths accept the challenge of public service in America.

Press Crusaders Many American editors, with the support of courageous and public-spirited publishers, have taken an unpopular position in a crisis as a matter of principle. The critics of the press may observe, with some justification, that the bravery of newspapers sometimes has varied in direct proportion with their distance from the scene of danger. Yet, over more than five decades, the records of the Pulitzer Prizes have been studded with instances of newspapers both large and small that took unpopular positions based on principle even though they were right on the firing line.

When a rioting mob blocked the attendance of the first Negro student at the University of Alabama and virtually forced the administration to bar her from classes, Buford Boone of the Tuscaloosa, Ala., *News* wrote a scathing rebuke of rule by violence. By his example and his forthrightness he brought calm and order to an overwrought community.

When the Ku Klux Klan revived its night-riding violence in North Carolina, two small weeklies—the Whiteville *News Reporter* and the Tabor City *Tribune*—fought both fear and indifference to end an era of floggings with numerous convictions and jail sentences for the ruffians of the Klan.

A woman reporter and a small Texas daily—Caro Brown and the Alice *Echo*—combined to lead a campaign that ended the rule of a political gang in neighboring Duval County where gunplay, and even violent death, had replaced the peaceful right of free suffrage, free assembly, and a free press. In Oregon Editor Robert W. Ruhl and the Medford *Mail Tribune* performed a similar service in a political situation no less dangerous for the community. In New York Alicia Patterson and her paper, *Newsday*, fought a powerful labor racketeer and broke his hold in Nassau County by getting the evidence that sent him to jail.

Those who serve and read newspapers may well ponder the warning written by Harry Ashmore in the *Arkansas Gazette* at a time when the paper was pleading for moderation in the crisis over the integration of white and Negro students at Little Rock's Central High School. He wrote:

> Somehow, some time every Arkansan is going to have to be counted. We are going to have to decide what kind of people we are—whether we obey the law only when we approve of it, or whether we obey it no matter how distasteful we may find it. And this, finally, is the only issue before the people of Arkansas. . . .

In a sense, also, it is the only issue that frequently confronts the newspaper that must decide whether to attack an unpleasant and risky problem, or merely walk around it and pretend it is not there.

The Electronic Crusade The intercession of a few powerful radio commentators headed by Elmer Davis in the campaign to provide American aid to the Allies in World War II showed how influential the electronic media can be. A score or more of leading local television stations in the 1960s, acting in the spirit of Elmer Davis and Edward R. Murrow, have gone on to establish an enviable record for public service. The bulk of the electronic media may remain inert for long periods of time (and this is also true of newspapers and magazines) but there can be no disputing the power of radio and television to act in the public interest when their proprietors choose to do so.

The small-minded and the fearful have always cautioned, "Beware of television. A demagogue could use the medium to sway the public and turn the nation into a dictatorship. To permit television to crusade and to editorialize is a dangerous thing." But to Senator Joseph R. McCarthy, television was not his pathway to power but to his downfall. Of course, it is true that the free press can be twisted in the wrong hands to bring out the worst in a democratic society rather than the best, and this applies to television as well as to the other news media, but that is a risk that must be faced. The alternative is a supine, commercial, cowardly press for which the public would have only the most deserved contempt.

As an example of what television can do, the staff of WTVJ-TV in Miami, Florida, conducted an anticrime crusade in the latter part of the 1960s that sent racketeers scurrying to cover and shook up Dade County's law enforcement machinery. In the Minneapolis-St. Paul area, WCCO Radio played a leading part in alerting the area to flood danger. One of the great electronic pioneers, KDKA Radio in Pittsburgh, campaigned against unjust government condemnation procedures in setting up a highway right of way. And in New York, WABC-TV delved into the difficulties and complications in dealing with the problems of mental retardation. In New Orleans, Seattle, San Francisco, Chicago, Jacksonville, and other communities, radio and television came to life with hard-hitting and sometimes distinguished efforts in many fields of public service that were not calculated to improve their audience ratings. And in this respect, radio and television have emulated some of the best recent work of crusading newspapers and magazines.

New Areas of Public Service While the role of the news media as watchdogs in the governmental processes is the most familiar and the most celebrated, the thrust of public service journalism today is in the direction of such new areas as civil rights, the war on poverty, and other modern causes. Both the press and the electronic media have done far more than to report the civil rights crisis in all its confusing and sometimes tragic elements. At the local level, many newspapers and stations have done exhaustive studies of the role of the Negro in the community and what can be done to improve his lot. The same is true of the war on poverty. At the national level, a great deal of excellent work has been done by some of the magazines, *Look* and *Life* in particular. One of the most interesting experiments was conducted over a period of years by the Gannett Newspaper Group, which painstakingly sought out stories of civil-rights successes to try to counteract the mass of headlines and news commentaries about the clashes and the failures. Another was an attack on the courts by a small newspaper, the Riverside (California) *Press-Enterprise*, to obtain justice for an Indian tribe.

In the struggle for legislative reapportionment following the United States Supreme Court's ruling that districts should be of approximately equal size—the "one man, one vote" decision—several newspapers took decisive action to bring about vote reforms in their states. One of the great successes was in Kansas, where the Hutchinson *News* went to court in order to help achieve true legislative reapportionment. In New York, WMCA Radio played a key role in the reapportionment battle. In the crusade for the conservation of natural resources, the Louisville *Courier-Journal* fought Kentucky mining interests in order to push a stiff law to control strip mining through the Legislature. And in Wisconsin, the Milwaukee *Journal* refused to be restrained by the protests of manufacturers in its campaign against water pollution—an effort that was climaxed by the strongest laws in the country to safeguard the State's water supply.

There have been other major efforts in new areas of public interest. The St. Louis *Post-Dispatch* led a drive to obtain a bond issue to renew the decaying center of the city and succeeded, but only after an initial failure. In two score or more communities, newspapers also were the main reliance of civic improvement groups for similar crusades for urban renewal. The Chicago *Daily News* originated one of the most unusual campaigns—a drive to popularize birth control among underprivileged families in Illinois and provide them with information at State expense. And the Detroit *Free Press* did much to spread both news and understanding of the ecumenical movement originated by the Vatican Council.

Much more can and will be done by the news media in these and other new areas of public service.

What Public Service Is Not   There are, of course, many ways to counterfeit journalistic public service. But it is to the credit of American journalism that only a few newspapers, magazines, and radio-television stations are cynical enough to attempt to gain public favor through such questionable tactics.

Here and there, a news organization may be found that makes feeble gestures for traffic safety, control of drug addicts, harsh treatment for sex deviates, and the like while prudently keeping at a safe distance from a fight with an unscrupulous political machine. Sometimes, a newspaper maintains a façade of righteous opposition to gambling in any form while publishing lottery numbers results for the policy racketeers. Now and then, a station, magazine, or newspaper will whip up a ten-minute crusade against sin and, having exposed the fact that sin exists, drop the matter to go on to something else to capture public curiosity.

Such phony crusades fool nobody, least of all the public. Whatever circulation or listener or viewer interest is aroused during the brief spurt of activity drops off sharply when it ends. And very real damage is done to the news staff, which recognizes at once that its leadership has an integrity quotient of zero. Good people will not stay with such a shabby organization for very long.

A Tradition of Conscience   Contrast such parodies of public service journalism with the concern voiced by Ashmore at the twentieth anniversary of the Nieman Fellowships at Harvard over whether serious newspapers were really informing the American people.

> Perhaps what we need most of all is simply the courage of our own convictions—to recognize that news is not merely a record of ascertainable facts and attributable opinions, but a chronicle of the world we live in cast in terms of moral values. We will err, certainly, and we will be abused—but we will at least be in position in the watchtowers, trying to tell the story in all its dimensions.

This is the kind of editorial conviction that has brought Pulitzer Prizes for public service in journalism to editors and newspapers that have served the public interest. For every prize winner there have been many in the ranks of journalism who have labored without awards and with precious little recognition on the smaller but no less important aspect of the news of the day.

That is the highest tradition of journalism—the tradition of conscience, as Joseph Pulitzer, Jr. has aptly phrased it. Without it an editor becomes a rubber stamp for the prejudices of the mob, and a newspaper is nothing more than a wad of paper for shelving or a wrapping for fish instead of a respected chronicler of life itself.

A Publisher's View   Paul Miller had this to say to the newspapers of the Gannett group, of which he is president:

> We must make our newspapers stand for something. If you do, your readers and advertisers may not always love you. Still, few of us can

> enjoy both love and respect. . . . As between the two, love and respect;
> I for one will settle for respect. . . .

Such is the realistic approach of a publisher who wants his papers read by the communities they serve, and who feels it is worthwhile to brave both controversy and disapproval to do it.

EDITORIALS

The editorial page is undergoing a much-needed revival and the editorial voice of radio and television is growing stronger. Even the news magazines are coming around to the need for a separate section for editorial comment—*Time*'s weekly essay being an example—but they still scatter their editorial views through the news columns. The new stress on editorial opinion is due in large part to the expansion of public service journalism; for, without the strongest kind of editorial support and the total mobilization of the resources of the entire news organization, many a crusade would wither and die in a few days.

It is true that almost 200 American daily newspapers still are so fearful of expressing an editorial opinion that they do not have an editorial page, thus making their product nothing more than a glorified shopping throwaway. Among the electronic media, there are stations so craven that they do not even have a news program, let alone an editorial opinion. But these are not representative of the news media as a whole. Nor is it valid to assume that only a large and powerful news organization dares to assert its editorial leadership in its community and region, and sometimes the nation as well. Some very small newspapers, dailies and weeklies, and some local radio and television stations of modest resources have taken strong editorial positions, sometimes in defiance of both community and advertiser sentiment.

There are many definitions of what editorial opinion should be, and how a properly conducted editorial page or editorial program should operate. Certainly, it must be something more than the voice of the proprietor, the vehicle for promoting his own interests and prejudices and those of his leading editors. Properly conducted, an editorial section should represent a community or region of the country; many, of course, contend that they speak for the nation but not very many could prove it if challenged. Moreover, such a section should be a marketplace of ideas, and not a grab-bag of columns and reprints intended to please all segments of the audience. No matter what parties are represented in a debate on any given issue, the point of view of the news organization itself must be made unmistakably clear. It must, as Paul Miller has said, stand for something. It cannot put out pious editorials about the safety of the American home, the beauties of American motherhood, and an annual plea for a safe and sane Fourth of July without arousing the contempt of any who bother to read, look, or listen. If that is all an editorial section has to say to the community, naturally it amounts to nothing.

What Editors Believe   By 1980, forecasts indicate that about 85 per cent of Americans between 18 and 21 will be going to college and by 1985 there will be 88 million college graduates in this country as against 47 million in 1960. Consequently, the recruits in our news organizations today who aim to be the leaders of American journalism tomorrow cannot be ignorant, narrow, prejudiced stand-patters. They must be prepared to move with the times, which means—in one word—leadership. And the one place where leadership can best be exerted in journalism is in the editorial section, page, or program.

It is customary, in any discussion of the editorial function, to note that editorial pages rank comparatively low in any survey of readership of newspapers and programs devoted to editorial opinion are close to the bottom in radio and television audience measurements. What these surveys do not show, of course, is the quality of those who read the editorial page and listen to editorial programs. In most communities and regions, it is primarily the leaders who pay the closest attention to editorial content and who are the most likely to be influenced by it. Thus, despite low total diffusion, the editorial section can have an enormous impact on the decision-making process and community leaders are well aware of it.

"There are those who contend that the editorial page is as dead as a dodo bird," says Mark Ethridge. "It is dead where the editor is dead from the neck up and afraid from the neck down. It is dead where the editor doesn't know what is happening in the way of profound sociological changes in the United States and still writes to the 12-year-old."

Much has been made of the tendency of some radio and television stations to editorialize, but actually the function as yet does not have the importance of press comment and is not likely to equal the press in impact in the forseeable future. There are too many limitations on the electronic media, for one thing. For another, the electronic editorialist is still in the process of trying to establish a place for himself in a section of the mass media that is devoted primarily to entertainment. And finally, there just aren't very many talented editorial writers who are willing to devote their services entirely to television.

This is not to say that television and radio both have not made a good beginning on the use of the editorial function. In some instances, the electronic editorializing has been both courageous and brilliant; without doubt, there will be more to come. But it is a fact that of the television stations owned completely or in large part by some 130 newspapers in the nation,

opposes the interests of most of the proprietors. In his most important manifestation, he is an editorial columnist with a signed article that appears at regular intervals on the editorial page of a major newspaper and is widely syndicated. Walter Lippmann was the most important of these in the United States until his retirement at the age of 77, which gives some notion of the durability of the breed. Among the leaders who remain are James Reston, Joseph Alsop, Drew Pearson, and their many competitors. Curiously, with the rise of the influence of the serious columnist, the gossip columnist who came to public prominence in the 1930s has all but disappeared. Vendors of banalities such as Walter Winchell no longer are important in the American press.

In the field of radio and television, the principal power and authority reside in those who comment on the news, in addition to reading it. These are led by Walter Cronkite and the team of Chet Huntley and David Brinkley. The old-fashioned commentators such as Eric Sevareid, who was still taking two or three minutes to do an electronic column on network CBS news programs in the latter 1960s, have not as yet been replaced. There is, in fact, an uneasy feeling among television news people that a commentator who merely sits and stares at the audience while voicing his views cannot be very effective. Just how television intends to develop a new breed of commentator, in consequence, remains to be determined. But there can be no doubt that the function will be carried on in one way or another. Popularity has nothing to do with it because a commentator cannot expect to be as attractive to the public as a movie star. But he can attain a great deal more respect.

The Age of Blandness   For the present, therefore, the columnist exercises his influence primarily through the newspaper and in many places actually exceeds the unsigned editorials in importance and readability. It used to be taken for granted that a columnist would be carried in a newspaper even if he occasionally differed with the management's views, but would be dropped if he proved to be consistently antagonistic. On some newspapers, this is still true, particularly those who take with great seriousness their advocacy of distinctive policies and political positions. But with the growth of a great editorial blandness in the American press, it has become fashionable to load up the editorial page and the "op ed" page with a selection of columnists of all conceivable points of view except the outright Communists. This is what is known as a "mix" and is intended to please everybody. Thus, when the liberal-minded New York *Post* became the only surviving paper in the city's afternoon field, one of its first moves was to sign up the conservative columnist, William Buckley. Such marriages of convenience are, of course, invariably uneasy and not generally inclined to last. But the tendency is one that is widely apparent in American journalism, particularly where so many cities have only one newspaper or one owner of two newspapers.

It is an amiable pretension of many columnists that they are reporters. Some of them actually do go out to the scene of a news story and then with the slightly condescending air of royalty on a slumming tour. Few of them have ever worked as reporters and even fewer have had to sweat through an investigation. It should also be remembered, in this connection, that no reporter—even one who may interpret the news—has the privilege of stating his personal views on any subject with the extravagance of the owner of a signed column. Nor is a reporter's reward, in the slightest, commensurate with that of a columnist.

Some columnists are sensibly modest; others are almost unbearably arrogant in their pretensions toward shaping public opinion. But whether they are nationally syndicated or used locally by a single newspaper, they must be assured of a certain faithful minimal readership if they are to stay in business. As a result, all except the top columnists tend to deal in controversy that pulls in mail—one of the principal pieces of evidence that they are indeed read.

Letters to the Editor   A glance at the morning mail, addressed to the editor of any newspaper, usually determines very quickly the seriousness with which the public accepts a paper's efforts to advance the interest of the community. The published letters, judged by their sources and content, are an equally good measurement. For if the letters column is not given serious treatment, or if it is filled with the semiprofessional writers who like to see their names in the paper, then it may be a reflection on the degree of acceptance the paper has in the community.

A few papers, including some with substantial circulations, still run fake letters on the editorial page daily because the ones they get are either too illiterate or too dull. But in general, such papers are not any more serious about their letters than about much else. As a rule, they have no pretensions in the public service field.

INVESTIGATIVE REPORTING

The mouth-filling title, investigative reporting, is given to news originated by reporters with, or sometimes without, editorial direction. It simply means that one or more reporters go out on a story, usually after receiving a tip from their desk, a reader or some other source, and come up with significant information that would not ordinarily have been developed through regular or official sources. By its very nature, investigative reporting has come to be considered gumshoe work in the field of crime, but it actually covers a considerably larger area. Reporters who have had to investigate hospitals or state mental institutions, private charities, or the high cost of education, the queer ways of some budget-makers and the intricacies of Congressional expense accounts have had just as difficult a time as any amateur Sherlock Holmes who set out to catch a murderer.

The "Diggers"   Next to the publisher who provides the means and the editor who furnishes the will and the full extent of a newspaper's editorial resources, the investigative reporter is the key to any successful inquiry. And, while the newspaper is primarily associated with the investigatory process, some magazines have done very well at it and the electronic media are beginning to develop formidable sleuths and "diggers" of their own.

Methods   Some reporters have done brilliant work in unearthing wrong-doing by acting as detectives or accountants, and sometimes both, but the standard way to handle any investigatory assignment concerned with government is to deal with a public official or a committee that has the right of subpoena. While public office-holders are not supposed to deal exclusively with one reporter, or one news organization, it frequently happens that a cooperative investigative reporter who knows his way around can get some official help.

Most editors agree that the three most important steps in any investigation are to give proper evaluation to the tips that come in, pick the right reporter to conduct the inquiry, and assure him strong direction and plenty of help when he needs it. When Arthur R. Bertelson was managing editor of the St. Louis *Post-Dispatch*, he had this to say about the whole process:

> Once a tip is investigated and shown to have some merit, we spread out. If necessary, we will detach other members of the local staff to look into areas of their specialization.
> If somebody who knows how to read tax records is needed, we have one available. If it becomes necessary to have a part of the team in Washington, we have people in our Washington bureau who have the necessary savvy to go into the angles there. That is, they know the right doors to knock on and the right people to see.
> If it becomes apparent that we are onto something really big, we will detach a task force of whatever numbers we need and take the penalty of losing them from the staff for X number of days. In most cases we will keep the regular staff intact until our first two editions are out of the way, then send everybody out, if possible, to work on the investigative story.

Some Advice   Wallace Turner, whose investigative work helped expose labor racketeering in Oregon while he was a member of the staff on the Portland *Oregonian*, gives this advice on method:

The most important official to the investigative reporter is the prosecutor. You have to rely on him. A newspaper which tolerates an ineffective prosecutor is short-sighted in both its own and in the public's interest. Get him out of the box!

The vast powers of a Congressional committee can help or hurt your exposé efforts, depending on what the staff and the committee want to do. Your decision on whether to cooperate must be made on the basis of the facts that present themselves at the time.

Fred Olmstead, city editor of the Detroit *Free Press*, argues that no investigation can be successful unless reporters are given the time to do a decent job. He gives these suggestions:

> Don't overlook a tip from any source. Some of the best leads may come from the tips that don't look promising. Many—perhaps most—won't pan out. But don't overlook any possibilities.
>
> Stay within the law. Don't attempt to open safes or burglarize offices for 'evidence.' Don't be a policeman.
>
> Make plans before you start. Don't leap into it. Check the evidence and keep checking as you go along. Keep up your lines of communication with those working in the field.
>
> Keep going. The investigative way is hard, but don't stop if you think you have something. If your curiosity is burning you as it should, you won't.

Some Leaders   Clark Mollenhoff of the Des Moines *Register-Tribune*, one of the nation's leading investigative reporters, has based his career on an almost constant inquiry into the acts of public figures in Washington. He played a leading part in the cases involving two Presidential favorites, Sherman Adams in the Eisenhower administration and Robert G. (Bobby) Baker in the Johnson administration, and in such inquiries as the TFX aircraft involving the Defense Department and the Dixon-Yates power investigation.

"It is doubtful," he says, "if we will ever eliminate corruption in the Federal government but it must be kept under closer control or it can spread with devastating impact. Nothing speeds the growth of corruption more than policies that foster arbitrary secrecy. Secrecy allows little scandals to become major scandals, costly to the taxpayers, devastating to our foreign-aid programs, to our position of defense readiness, and to our national morale."

A newspaper like the St. Petersburg (Fla.) *Times* proceeds with investigations as a matter of public policy and sometimes accomplishes results out of proportion to its size. In one instance, a staff of *Times* reporters headed by Martin Waldron demonstrated that the Florida highway system was being extended through costly and questionable administrative practices. As a result, the highway administration was shaken up from top to bottom; in the reforms that followed, Florida taxpayers were assured savings of millions of dollars and better roads as well.

"We get tips from everywhere," says Donald K. Baldwin, the St. Petersburg newspaper's executive editor. "Some come from disgruntled public employees, unhappy politicians, publicity seekers, persons looking for money . . . We carry on several low-pressure inquiries all the time. Then, if we get a break, we pull out all the stops and take off."

The investigative art is by no means confined to male reporters. Two of the most active and accomplished are Miriam Ottenberg of the Washington *Star*, who has broken many an exclusive story about crime and racketeering, and Lois Wille of the Chicago *Daily News*, whose work ranges from inquiries into juvenile gangs to the propagation of birth control methods. They operate alone or as part of an investigative staff with equal facility.

One of the newest developments in the spreading popularity of investigative reporting is the growth of what is known as the "Action Line" column. This is a specialty originated by the Houston *Chronicle*, and quickly picked up by several scores of other newspapers and radio-television stations, that try to help citizens who have complaints. It is a highly personalized service. Someone may write in or telephone to an "Action Line" reporter about a tax matter, a piece of condemned property, a case of official neglect, or even a missing pet such as a talking crow. The "Action Line" (it has many different names, depending on the whim of the editor) then is supposed to get action on the complaint. Surprisingly many are handled, the results being publicized daily in the column or on the air. Some newspapers and stations let young reporters or even journalism students handle these matters. Others, like the Washington *Star*, believe them to be of such importance that reporters of prestige like Miriam Ottenberg are assigned to the job for specific periods.

Writing   Investigative stories may be done in a variety of ways. When the subject matter is familiar and little explanation is needed, straight news style usually applies. But when the investigation deals with a complicated matter, particularly in the field of government, it is essential to weave interpretive material into the account wherever necessary. However, an investigative story should not resemble an editorial or a signed column unless a considered decision is made by top management to present the case in this manner. Generally, an investigative piece gains in effect if it is written in a calm, restrained, and detached style which depends on reason rather than a heavy-handed emotional appeal. If there is a crime in investigative writing, it is compounded of inaccuracy and dullness.

Here is the beginning of an investigatory piece in the Washington *Star* on the progress of the war against poverty in the Kentucky back country:

By Haynes Johnson

LITTLE CREEK, Ky.—Back in the hollow the wind was coming up and the heavy clouds were threatening snow, but inside the wooden cabin it was warm, comfortable, and somewhat drowsy. The young father of three threw another piece of coal into the stove, watched it flare up and went on talking about his own small battle in the national war on poverty.

"If I give you a quarter to buy a hamburger, you're still going to be hungry again tomorrow," he said. "But that's what they are doing. They're trying to solve it with money and money alone won't solve it. They jumped in too quick and threw in the money and said, 'Here is your check.' "

He knows all about those checks as do more than 2,700 other men, women and children in this county whose sole support is Federal poverty money from Washington. They are benefiting from what is called officially the Work Experience and Training Program, financed here in Breathitt County and in 12 other counties of the area by $1,123,713 in Federal money a month.

The hill men have another name for the program. They are members, they say, of the "Happy Pappy" program. As unemployed fathers, they get up to $250 a month, which makes them very happy pappies indeed.

To hear the men talk, most of them have no intention of getting off the program. It means, particularly in the bleak winter months, less hunger, more warmth, a glimmer of hope for the young, some comfort for the old. But it brings no great upsurge of hope, no sense of change. The "way things are" in Breathitt County, from the firmly entrenched power structure, to the litter of stripped automobiles in the creeks, is, one feels, the way things will continue to be . . .

Lois Wille began one of her stories about Chicago's juvenile gangs in this manner for the Chicago *Daily News*:

By Lois Wille

Few people know the terrible pressures of being chief of a gang.

"Sometimes I just get weary, real weary," sighed a slight, handsome, 18-year-old. He took off his narrow, dark sunglasses, rubbed his eyes, and continued:

"I been thinking of giving it all up. Getting a steel company job. But then I worry. If I quit, what happens to my boys? They'll try to quit. And that means another group might attack."

He shook his head and put his glasses back on. "No, I got to see it through—for them."

The boy means it. In his world, he is a man of awesome responsibilities. They may seem strange, absurd, even criminal to the rest of mankind—but that doesn't make them any the less real to him.

He is president of one of the dozens of subgangs that make up the South Side's supergang, the Mighty Blackstone Rangers. He doesn't want his name used because he says there is too much danger of retaliation. From police, from his employer, from his Blackstone superiors. And, of all people, from his mother.

"She worries about me sometimes," he said. "She reads the newspapers and she thinks all we do is fight. But I tell her she doesn't understand. This group is based on protecting the neighborhood and our loved ones."

He doesn't look particularly strong, and his voice and manner are soft, not commanding. So how did he get to be a gang president?

"I have always been the chief," he says. "I was born to lead. . ."

This is one of the rare straight editorial pieces that lead off a newspaper's investigatory series. It was done by Gene Miller with the consent of his superiors at the Miami *Herald* because both wanted to arouse public sentiment to right what they thought had been a great injustice.

By Gene Miller

This is a personal account of a two and one-half year failure. It is about a girl imprisoned for two murders in Louisiana. Her name is Mary Katherin Hampton. I believe she can be proved innocent.

I want to label this newspaper story clearly. It is opinion.

Let me try to make something else clear at the beginning. Most newspapers, this one included, try hard to be fair. I sometimes think that if the twentieth century press could report the crucifixion of Christ, the second paragraph would be an explanation from Pontius Pilate.

The point I am trying to make is this: In the case of Mary Hampton, I am personally far beyond a position of so-called journalistic fairness.

The State of Louisiana, I believe, is inflicting a terrible wrong upon Mary Hampton; a wrong judicial and moral. Somehow, by incompetency, by ignorance, by stupidity, by ineptitude, perhaps by sheer carelessness, or possibly by deliberate design, the State of Louisiana erred judicially.

Mary Hampton, in my opinion, no more committed the crimes for which she is incarcerated than did Grandma Moses or Mamie Eisenhower. Yet, perhaps worse than her imprisonment is the attitude of the State of Louisiana. It refuses to examine the possibility of error, let alone acknowledge or rectify the error. . . ."

The climax of the story was told in matter-of-fact straight news style by the uninvolved UPI as follows:

ST. GABRIEL, La. (UPI)—Mary Katherin Hampton, a frail, blinking shell of a woman, left the Women's State Penitentiary Wednesday for what she hoped was peace and oblivion.

Miss Hampton had been imprisoned since April 24, 1961 after being sentenced to dual life sentences for two murders she said she never once admitted.

Her case was taken up by Miami *Herald* reporter Gene Miller and Lie Detector expert Warren Holmes, also of Miami, when they became convinced she was innocent. They enlisted the help of F. Lee Bailey, the Boston defense lawyer who helped free Dr. Sam Sheppard.

Miss Hampton was arrested at 17 and sent to prison at 18.

She was accused of the murder of a barmaid, Hermine Fiedler, in Boutte, La., on Dec. 31, 1959. She was then at Crestview, La., 332 miles away, as proved by a ticket for auto violation of Emmitt Monroe Spencer, with whom she was driving. She also was accused of murdering Benjamin Yount, a customer at a bar, when she was 470 miles away. . .

THE CRUSADE

Crusade is a story-book term. To the somewhat less than demonstrative professionals who are assigned to them, crusades are called almost anything else—campaigns, investigations, series, reports, or (depending on who is doing the work) a "hatchet job." Newspaper people simply feel uncomfortably like do-gooders if they are called crusaders, although it was a term in which the fiercely combative Joseph Pulitzers, father and son, gloried.

What Is a Crusade? There have been many kinds of crusades, some of them conducted with the aplomb of a brass band marching between the halves of a football game and others handled so quietly that they blended into the regular flow of the news. Generally, a crusade has been defined as an attempt by a newspaper, using the best talents of its editors, writers, and reporters, to serve the public interest. In this way it differs from the type of investigatory story that attempts to attain no particular end short of presenting all the facts in a given situation. However, many a series of articles that began as an investigatory job has turned into a crusade by involving all parts of the newspaper. The unique feature of a crusade is that it attempts to accomplish some public good.

There have been crusades as long as there have been newspapers, but, of course, that name was not given to them until comparatively modern times.

One of the earliest campaigns was the successful effort of British journalists to win the right to write reports based on the proceedings of the House of Commons. Another was John Peter Zenger's fight to print the truth about colonial government in America without being thrown in jail for criminal libel—a crusade won for him by a colonial jury. There have been many others—William Lloyd Garrison's campaign against slavery in *The Liberator*, George Jones's *New York Times* attack on the Tweed ring in 1870, Henry M. Stanley's successful effort to find David Livingstone in darkest Africa, a New York *Herald* stunt. Many more such exploits brighten the history of journalism.

The Pulitzer Prizes It was Joseph Pulitzer I who established the crusade as a way of life for American newspapers and embedded the idea firmly in the prizes for distinguished journalism that bear his name. His brilliant campaign to raise the money to bring the Statue of Liberty from France and place it on a pedestal in New York harbor established him as a leader in journalism in the mid-eighties. His New York *World* fought Tammany Hall, predatory financial interests, bad housing, the white slave traffic, bribe-taking politicians, and many another journalistic battle. By precept and example he kindled the torch of public service for American journalism so that light could be cast in dark places—a torch that has been held proudly aloft by all who have followed in his footsteps.

The New Crusades   In 1961, *CBS Reports* put out the sensational documentary, "Biography of a Bookie Joint," which immediately touched off an uproar in Boston. It was television's version of the newspaper-inspired crusade and it was done by Fred W. Friendly and his staff with all the care, vision, and imagination of a superior press investigation. The difference was that the film was in itself the best evidence of the connection between the bookmakers and the police. Here, it was not necessary to make charges supported by statements of eyewitnesses and, on occasion, still pictures. The television cameras, trained on the bookie joint, faithfully recorded the things that happened in front of them. However, despite that, the results of the exposé were mixed. While a police shakeup followed and while some bookmakers were convicted, no police officer was either dismissed or convicted for being connected with the bookie joint. Television thus learned the hard lesson that newspapers and magazines have learned over the years—that even the best-documented campaign can fail to achieve a major result unless the news organization keeps the pressure on even after public interest has lapsed. A newspaper can do this with greater ease than a television station because of the difference in philosophy between the two organizations.

Thus, while newspapers are likely to continue their leadership in the field of crusading, the participation of television and of the weekly and monthly magazines in the growth of public service journalism is bound to have an effect on public opinion. It is clear that, despite the demonstrable rivalry of the news media in this as well as in other areas of journalism, the public has come to look upon them as an interlocking communications system. When the system operates well, the principal news organizations share in public approval; however, when it operates poorly or disastrously, then the whiplash of public disapproval is bound to be felt by all those involved. There is no longer such a thing as a print news system or an electronic news system; a few minutes spent on the front pages or network news programs will show that they depend on each other in varying degree. And that is as true in the field of the crusade as it is in straight news coverage. A story broken by a newspaper will become common property within a matter of minutes if it is worth anything. The same is true of the electronic media or the magazines.

How Crusades Begin A crusade may begin by design or entirely by accident, depending on circumstances.

A photographer in Buffalo happened to take a picture of a city truck unloading supplies at a private contracting job, thus revealing a major municipal scandal that rocked the City Hall. A penciled notation on a card, found by a reporter for the Seattle *Times*, resulted in clearing a University of Washington professor of charges of Communist activity. A wrinkled newspaper clipping about an Air Force lieutenant who was losing his commission because some of his relatives were left-wing sympathizers led to a great television exposé by Edward R. Murrow.

There are also crusades that originate because of strong convictions or journalistic policies. Among them are the many in support of bond issues for schools and urban renewal, the attacks on manufacturers and advertisers who deface the countryside with sooty factories, billboards, and other litter of the commercial age; the campaigns against pollution of air and water, and the crusades for the modernization of archaic governmental units. These things take a determination of policy at the highest level of the news organization by its proprietors and its managers. Once they have made their decision in favor of action in the public interest, it becomes the work of the editors and the reporters to dig out the facts in each case in an effort to win public support. On the basis of the information that is developed, editorial positions stand or fall; consequently, it has happened that even the worthiest crusades have failed because the news organization acted before it was in possession of the evidence it needed. People are not convinced by flaring headlines or by solemn pronouncements over television as much as they are by solidly documented analyses.

Once an issue is raised in which the public interest is involved, it is too late to turn back. The newspaper, magazine or station that starts the uproar has no choice but to see it through, come what may. True, there have been venal crusades, silly crusades, phony crusades—but generally the public has not been taken in by them for very long. As Robert J. Blakely pointed out in his Don R. Mellett Memorial lecture:

> In itself a "crusading" newspaper is neither good nor bad. That depends in large part upon its motivations. There are newspapers that "crusade" for ulterior reasons—to build up circulation or to grind an axe rather than to sharpen the sword of justice. These are contemptible. They injure the innocent. They rarely accomplish beneficial results that endure, always stopping short when the cream of sensationalism has been skimmed and never pressing to where they touch the really powerful and dangerous elements of the community. . . .

But to me the free press reaches its zenith in a good newspaper looking for a fight in a good cause in its own avenues and alleys. Few personal satisfactions can match the knowledge that one is making one's community a better place in which to live. . . .

Development of Crusades   Sometimes a crusade turns entirely on the results of a one-man investigation. At other times its effectiveness depends on the amount of pressure that can be developed on the editorial page. Other crusades call on the whole symphony of journalism that is represented in the various departments of a newspaper—the investigatory reporter, the editorialist, the columnist, the photographer, the cartoonist, and the editor and publisher working together as a team. Regardless of method, the secret of the success of every crusade is the determination of top management to persevere and to support to the hilt every staff member who is out on the job. No reporter, no editor, can make a crusade achieve its end unaided. Nor can they work effectively if they have the slightest doubt that their newspaper will support them if they become too deeply involved. When crusades have failed, lack of support rather than lack of effort has been the primary reason.

This is as true of the magazines and television as it is of newspapers. A single newsman or a team of correspondents can accomplish little, no matter how worthy the crusade, unless all the resources of the news organization are mobilized to assist them.

Examples   Many a crusade is won simply by hard and consistent work, backed by a determined editor and publisher. This was the case in the Louisville *Courier-Journal*'s drive to tighten Kentucky's laws against strip mining. The campaign opened with editorial demands for reform as early as 1962, followed by news stories and, in 1964, a dramatic portrayal in the newspaper's rotogravure section entitled, "Ravaged Land." In the following year, more than 200 columns of news space were devoted to the subject together with editorials and still another supplement highlighting the consequences of unchecked strip mining and pollution on the Kentucky countryside. Finally, in 1966, in large part because of the *Courier-Journal*'s unremitting pressure, the Kentucky Legislature passed what was then called the "toughest strip mining legislation in America" and the Governor signed it. The following is how the executive editor of the *Courier-Journal* wrote about the campaign:

By Norman E. Isaacs

It is late spring and there is no lovelier part of America at this season than Kentucky's Bluegrass region. Famous old horses like Citation trot over the lush, rolling fields. The frisky young colts nip at each other playfully. The white fences stretch for miles. Around Lexington and Versailles, the new industrial plants are antiseptically modern and busy.

But every Kentuckian knows how deceptive this can be as a picture of his state. For only seventy air miles away begins the contamination of both land and water. There is erosion. There is vast waste, not only of the land but of human beings. Here begins the poverty belt of Appalachia.

In the western part of Kentucky is another blighted zone, a once handsome land now pocked by vast dunes of mud and whitish rock, where the streams are as poisoned as the ground.

The stinking mess that exists in parts of eastern and western Kentucky is the direct heritage of politically excused commercial plunder. It is the result of strip-mining turned loose, of loggers free to overcut the great forests at will, of oil and gas speculators permitted to let the runoffs pollute the watersheds.

Gone are the natural protections of the mountain towns; each year water gushing down the slopes of the strip mine spoilbanks tears through these towns with mounting violence. Once all of it was beautiful and unspoiled, the "great meadow" and the "happy hunting ground" of Indian lore. Now thousands of acres are taken out of production yearly by the giant mining machines . . .

Contrasted with the deliberate campaign that is undertaken as a matter of public policy, the Detroit *Free Press* began a crusade for Half-Way Houses—a place where juvenile delinquents have a decent chance of rehabilitation—after a vicious outbreak of juvenile crime. In this campaign, a stabbing of a high school boy who refused to give two 16-year-old youths a dime was the immediate cause of the newspaper's decision to intervene. As a result of the series of articles, Michigan and Detroit political and civic leaders backed the proposal for Half-Way Houses and the Legislature approved the necessary enabling legislation and the funds. Here is how the *Free Press* explained its purpose:

By Van G. Sauter

Michigan taxpayers save $5 a day on every juvenile delinquent transferred from the Boys Training School to a Half-Way House.

It costs $10.34 a day to maintain a teen-age delinquent at a training school in Lansing. It costs $5.50 a day to maintain the same youth in a Half-Way House operated by the State.

These figures substantiate Wayne County Juvenile Judge James H. Lincoln's contention that Half-Way Houses not only provide good rehabilitation but real financial savings. Lincoln wants a Statewide program of Half-Way Houses because they will:

*Provide a good home and counseling for delinquents being returned to society.

*Free space in the training schools for hoodlums still on the streets.

*Save money.

As envisioned by Lincoln, the teen-ager, after serving some time at the training center, would be transferred to the care of the Half-Way House.

"This would be his home," the judge said. "He would leave during the day for school or work, and then return at night. He would have free time, too, but it would be supervised."

What is needed in a Half-Way House?

"You don't need the Taj Mahal," the judge said, "but any clean and manageable building that will accommodate 15 to 25 boys plus some offices."

A Federal project in Detroit has nine paid employees. A couple who serve as housekeepers staff the Half-Way House operated in Lansing by the training school. The counseling and job placement services for the Lansing operation are performed by the regular staff of the training school . . .

The intervention of a newspaper through legal action is still another form of crusading. This was the course taken by the Hutchinson *News*, with more than 50,000 circulation in Kansas although it is published in a city of 38,000, in order to bring about a more equitable apportionment of the Kansas Legislature. Despite violent criticism from some readers and threats from some advertisers, the *News* persisted for three years in its crusade. It pointed out that in 1961, a majority of the members of the State Senate were elected by only 27 per cent of the people, while a majority of the members of the State House of Representatives were elected by only 18 per cent of the people. The most glaring example of unequal districting, as it so happened, was in the *News* home county, Reno, with one House district of 49,398 people and another of only 9,718 people.

While the *News* won its battle in court, the fight was carried on briskly in its own news columns in a variety of ways. This was a column of analysis prominently published while the battle was on:

By John McCormally

What, exactly, do the foes of reapportionment of the State Legislature fear?

The Supreme Court has ruled that seats in both houses of Legislatures should be based on population—that each representative should represent as nearly as practical the same number of people so that each citizen's vote will count for as much as any other citizen's.

You'd think, from the outcries, that the court had ordered everyone to join the Democratic Party, or had banned prayer in church as well as in school.

What are they afraid of—those who now frantically are crying states' rights, imploring the Founding Fathers and castigating the courts?

Why, the people, that's what they're afraid of. Ever since the first kings started toppling and the first revolutionary thoughts began to find their way into print, they've been afraid that if the people ever really got control of their own governments, all hell would break loose.

The Communists are afraid of this, just as the American colonial merchants and landlords were, and just as today's defenders of the status quo in Kansas are. We play a little game about it. We talk about democracy. We quote Lincoln about government of, by and for the people. We talk about the will of the people. The will of the majority.

But we don't mean it . . . .

One of the newest forms of crusading is based on the work of specialists. The San Francisco *Chronicle*, featuring the work of an architectural critic, Allan Temko, has successfully campaigned against the design of ugly buildings and even an impractical bridge design. This is an example of Temko's work—a discussion of what a new Cathedral should look like long before it was built:

By Allan Temko

It is not often in the twentieth century that the chance to build a great church comes to a city as wealthy and vigorous as San Francisco, and the prospect of a new St. Mary's Cathedral, crowning an equally new cityscape in the Western Addition, is stirring indeed.

The Cathedral should, and can, be a great building in every sense of greatness, if only the Church and the City together make the best of this opportunity. But will they? San Francisco, never one to hide its candle under a bushel basket, has rarely put into practice the high cultural doctrine it so persuasively preaches.

Now that the City has a chance to create religious architecture on a grand scale, it should marshal its full creative capacities if it is to meet the challenges a cathedral presents.

What kind of a Cathedral is needed in so enlightened a community as San Francisco? What innovations of design have been made possible by liturgical reform? Should the services be conducted in a circular space, as in Oscar Niemeyer's magnificent, flaring crown of concrete and glass at Brasilia, or in a long nave, as in Sir Basil Spence's Anglican Cathedral at Coventry, which one critic has described as an "Establishment" church?

Surely, a San Francisco cathedral should reflect the most progressive thought in the Church today. It should be the architectural equivalent of the late Pope John's great encyclical on world peace. Consequently, before the Archbishop engages any architects permanently and invests heavily in designs that may be obsolete, he could do worse than discuss the problem with theologians of the stature, say, of Jacques Maritain.

Then, with a strong liturgical program established, the Church could follow the same procedure so thoughtfully adopted across the Bay when architects were chosen for the new Oakland Museum. No less than ten architectural firms of the highest distinction were interviewed for this carefully considered project . . .

In all these diverse crusades, as in the investigatory reports of which crusading is the upshot, the emphasis in the writing is on originality. The old bam-socko blueprint for opening a crusading series has undergone a significant change, although there are times when it is still worth using. Moreover, the old litany of raising rhetorical questions in the first article that are never really answered is seldom seen any more. If there is a flaw in the writing method, it is in a tendency to lean far too heavily on the newspaper's support through profuse editorialization instead of digging hard for factual documentation to support the newspaper's position. It is still a hard truth that the facts should dictate the direction of a crusade, instead of treasured opinions, no matter how high-minded, that do not at the outset have sufficient factual support.

TOWARD THE FUTURE

The great change in journalism during the last quarter-century or more is in the beliefs of those who are intimately concerned with the identification, gathering, distribution, and presentation of the news. Because, whatever definition may be offered, news actually tends to be what the journalist says it is. With the coming of a different kind of journalist, now largely college-trained and tending toward multiple degrees, news symbols have shifted in importance. Moreover, the aggressive drive of television in the development of illustrated news of the highest importance, such as space travel and war scenes, has added a new factor to the dimensions of journalism. Whether the newspapers and magazines like it or not, they must try harder to present the news in depth, background it, and explain it as long as they cannot normally be the first with the latest developments. The slow but significant expansion in the kind of public that demands such journalistic improvement fully justifies all the effort that is being put into it.

This does not mean, of course, that commercial television is about to solve overnight the very considerable problems it must overcome in the creation of news programs of far greater substance than is possible today. Nor can public television accomplish in a year or two what the networks have been trying to do, when the spirit moves them, for more than two decades. As far as the newspapers are concerned, the sensational press is not about to go out of business. And a mere glance at a newsstand in passing will confirm the impression that there are more cheap, flashy magazines than there are good ones.

Nevertheless, the idea is gaining headway, at least in the more thoughtful echelons, that journalism can achieve only temporary gains by approaching the news for whatever circulation or viewer interest can be wrung out of shock and sensation. There is a point at which even the least sophisticated people no longer are shocked, but merely rendered numb. Journalism must stand for something if it is to be respected. No less than the holding of public office, the difficult business of informing the public is an act that must be based on good faith. It is therefore inevitable that the concept of journalism as a public service is bound to increase in strength. Today, it is a trend. Tomorrow, it will be a necessity.

APPENDIXES

A Glossary For
Journalists

1. Print Journalism

A copy Also known as *A matter*. Part of a news story, based mainly on advance material, that is later completed by placing a lead on top of it. Used by newspapers mainly.

Ad An advertisement.

Add Additions of any kind to a news story.

Advance News story based on factual material about a forthcoming event, such as the advance text of a speech, parade line of march, etc.

Agate 5½ point type; as a unit of advertising, 14 agate lines equal one column inch.

AMs Morning newspapers.

Angle An approach to a story; also, various parts of a story.

ANPA American Newspaper Publishers Association.

AP Associated Press.

APME Associated Press Managing Editors.

Art Any newspaper illustration.

Assignment Duty given to a journalist.

Automatic typesetting System of setting type in which a punched tape is fed into a machine, activating the keyboard.

Bank Also called a *deck*; the part of a headline that usually follows the top or the cross line, often both.

Banner A headline across Page 1, of four columns or more; sometimes known as a *streamer*. It is often confused with a *binder*, a headline across the top of an inside page.

B copy Also known as *B matter*. Part of a news story, based mainly on advance material, which may be completed by topping it first with A copy and then with a lead. Many newspapers omit the A copy and top B copy with a lead directly.

Beat   An exclusive story; also, a series of places regularly visited by a reporter to gather news.

Ben Day   Process named for Editor Ben Day of the New York *Sun*. It is a shading pattern of dots or lines used in photoengraving as background for photos, type, or line drawings.

BF   Bold-face type. It is heavier and darker than regular type.

Body   Part of a story that follows the lead. Also, the name of type in which regular newspaper reading matter is set.

Book   Sandwich of copy paper and carbons on which news material is written.

Box   Brief story enclosed by a border; many modern boxes have only top and bottom borders. Those put in the middle of a related story are called *drop-ins*.

Bulldog   Early newspaper edition.

Bulletin   Brief dispatch containing major news. Usually no more than 40-50 words.

Byline   Signature on a story.

Caps   Capital letters. Also called *upper case*.

C & LC   Caps and lower case (small letters).

Caption   Descriptive material accompanying illustrations, cartoons, etc.

Center spread   Also called a *double truck* on tabloids. The two pages in the center fold of a newspaper.

Chase   Metal page form into which type is locked.

City editor   Boss of the local news staff in the United States. In Britain, he is the financial editor (the City is the financial section of London).

City room   Properly, the news room. Seat of the editorial operation of a newspaper.

Clip   A newspaper clipping. Called a *cutting* by the British.

Copy   Universally known as the name of material written by a journalist.

Copy desk   Where copy is edited, cut, and headlined. Not to be confused with the proof room, where typographical errors are caught in proof.

Copy editors   Also called *copyreaders*. They edit and headline the copy. Not to be confused with *proofreaders*, a function of the mechanical staff, whose duty is to catch errors in proof.

Correspondent   When a reporter goes out of town, he sometimes calls himself a correspondent. In broadcast media, a correspondent is a job classification of more importance than the basic *newsman*.

Cover   To obtain news.

Credit line   To credit a picture, cartoon, etc., to the source.

Crop   Reducing the size of an illustration before it is put into printed form.

Crusade   Also known as a *campaign*, a *series*, a *long reporting job*. It is an effort by all parts of an editorial staff to persuade the public to act, or to refuse to act, in some matter involving the public interest.

Cub   An untrained newspaperman, usually a reporter. A term used more by the public than by newspaper people, who generally call a beginner a first-year reporter.

Cut An engraving, but also applied to all kinds of newspaper illustrations.

Cutlines The part of a caption that describes an illustration; usually set in bold-face type.

Dateline The place from which a news story is sent. Many newspapers now omit the date from the dateline.

Deadline Closing time for all copy for an edition. There are different deadlines for the city desk, news desk, copy desk, lockup of pages in the composing room, etc.

Deskman An editor in the newsroom.

Dingbat Decorations in type.

Dope story Also called a *think piece*; soft news, supposedly based on reliable opinion, which seeks to develop trends.

Dummy A drawing, usually freehand, outlining the position of news stories and cuts on a page by designating slugs and kinds of headlines.

Dupe Also called a *blacksheet*. Carbon copy of a story.

Ears Boxes on either side of the nameplate on Page 1 of a newspaper—one usually encloses the weather, the other the name of the edition.

Edition Remake, or revision of some of the pages of a newspaper, including Page 1. The only complete edition on which every page goes to press is the first one.

Editorial Comment on the news in the name of the news organization itself; opinion intended to shape or otherwise influence public thinking.

Em Through usage this term has become interchangeable with a pica, the name applied to a lineal measurement of 12 points (one-sixth of an inch) or to a square of 12-point type. Originally an em was the square of any size of type.

En Half an em. Also called a *nut* to avoid phonetic confusion.

File The act of dispatching copy to or from a news center, except when it is sent by a messenger.

Filler Small items used to fill out columns where needed; in larger stories, used to plug up columns. A filler is known by a number of names: (*AOT*, any old time; *CGO*, can go out, and a lot of purely local terms).

Flag Newspaper nameplate on Page 1.

Flash In general news, a rarely used message of a few words describing a momentous event. It consists only of the place of filing, less than a half-dozen words of text, the signature of the sender, and the time sent. In sports, flashes are used for results and are quite common.

Folio Page number and name of the paper.

Folo Also called *follow, follow-up, follow story*. Sequence of news events after a news break.

Fudge   So-called stop-press or last-minute news. By setting the fudges in a fudge box, a segment of a cylinder that holds lines of type one or two columns wide, stopping the main presses to make last-minute news can be avoided. The fudge runs separately; while it is being changed, blank white space runs in a boxed-off segment of Page 1.

Future book   Date book of future events. Items that go into it are called *futures*.

Gang coverage   Unrestricted mass coverage of a major event, as contrasted with pool coverage.

Handout   Generic term for written publicity.

Head   Name for all headlines.

Hellbox   Repository for dead or discarded type.

Hold for release   Also known as *W.O.*, or *Wait Order*. Instruction placed on news that must not be used until receipt of a release, either automatic or by message.

HTK   Abbreviation of *Head To Kum* (printers' spelling). Written on copy when the headline is to be written after the copy is cleared.

Human interest   News or features with emotional appeal.

Insert   Addition to a story written in such a way that it can be placed anywhere between the end of the first paragraph and the beginning of the last paragraph.

Italics   Type face with characters slanted to the right, as contrasted with Roman, or upright, characters.

Jim-dash   A 3-em dash.

Jump   Continuation of a story to another page.

Jump line   The continuation line giving the succeeding, or preceding, page numbers.

Justify   To fill out a line of type, a column of type, or a page of type.

Kill   Elimination of news material at any stage in the processing. Because the word has such a mandatory character, the word *eliminate* is used on minor corrections. This is to emphasize the instruction, *kill*, when it is given.

Layout   Arrangement of illustrations.

Lead   Beginning of a story, which may be a sentence, a paragraph, or several paragraphs, depending on the complications involved.

Legman   A reporter; usually, those who gather but do not write news.

Libel   Any defamatory statement expressed in writing, printing, or other visible form.

Ligature   Two or more united characters of type, such as æ, fi.

Lobster   The working shift on newspapers and wire services that usually begins with midnight and runs through to about 10 or 11 A.M. Such hours as midnight to 8, 1 to 9, 2 to 10 in the morning are usually called the lobster shift, or lobster trick.

Lockup   Deadline in the composing room for getting all page forms off the floor and into the stereotype department.

Logotype   Also called a *logo*, usually by printers. A single matrix containing two or more letters used together, such as AP, or UPI. It is also another name for the flag, or nameplate.

Lower case   Small letters.

Makeup   Assembling the newspaper or magazine in the composing room.

Markup   A proof or clipping, pasted on paper and marked to show where changes are to be made and what new material is to be used.

Masthead   Statement, usually on the editorial page, of the newspaper's ownership, place of publication, and other offices. Sometimes confused with the flag or nameplate.

Matrix   Mold from which type is cast, ranging in size from individual letter molds on a Linotype machine to the matrices, or mats, used in the stereotype process.

Metropolitan edition   Combined city and suburban edition.

Morgue   News library.

Must   When this word is put on copy, it means the story must be used. Only editors in authority can designate musts. A *B.O. Must* is a business office must, usually dictated by policy considerations.

New lead   Also called a *New top, Nulead,* or *NL.* It is a fresh beginning on a story already sent or in the paper and is so written that it joins with the old story smoothly at a paragraph that can be designated at the end of the new lead. A *lead all* is a short top that fits on a new lead.

Obit   An obituary; announcement of a death, including a biography appropriate in length to the news importance of the subject.

Overnight   Also called *overnite* or *overniter.* It is a story filed by a reporter or turned out by a rewrite man for the first edition of an afternoon newspaper of the following day; also, for the overnight cycle of a wire service. In morning newspaper terminology an overnight refers to an assignment to be covered the next day.

Overset   Type left over from an edition. Usually wasted.

Pi   To upset or otherwise mix up type.

Pica   12-point type, and also a lineal measurement of 12 points. Also called an *em* (although technically this is incorrect).

Pick up   Also written *pikup* in printers' shorthand. This is the name for that portion of a story in type that should be placed at the end of a new lead, or other new news material.

Pickup line   Line at top of wire service copy that includes the word "add," the point of origin of the story and the last few words of the preceding page. It is used to assemble the whole story in order.

Pix   Editors' shorthand for pictures.

Play   The display given to a story or picture. Most editors talk of playing a story, rather than playing it up or down; these latter expressions are more frequently used by the public.

Point   Basic printing measurement, roughly equivalent to one-seventy-second of an inch.

PMs   Afternoon newspapers.

Pool   Selection of one journalist or a small group of them to cover for a large group or gang.

Precede   Brief dispatch, such as a bulletin or editorial note, that introduces a story but is separated from it by a dash.

Printer   Also called a *Teletype* or *TWX*. It produces copy by electrical impulses actuated by a perforated tape, or some other means.

Proof   Inked impressions of type, usually in galley form, for the purpose of making corrections.

Query   Brief message from correspondent or stringer offering a story for publication.

Replate   Also called a *makeover*. Redoing a page, and sometimes several pages, between editions. This is what is known as an "Extra."

Rewrite man   A writer for a newspaper or wire service, whose work consists in part of redoing stories and in part of writing original copy for the reporters who turn in notes by telephone or wire.

Rim   Outer edge of copy desk.

Rocket   Critical inquiry message from desk to correspondent.

Run   A reporter's beat. Seldom heard in metropolitan areas.

Running story   Another name for the B Copy–A copy–lead process. Usually it means a chronological story of an event topped by successive leads as the news changes.

Runover   Another name for a *jump*, or continuation from one page to another.

Schedule   List of assignments or of headlines.

Scoop   An exclusive story. The name has fallen into disrepute among newspaper people because of its misuse in movie, radio, and TV soap operas.

Shirttail   Additional material, related to a longer story, and separated from it by a dash.

Short   A brief story for a newspaper or wire service.

Sidebar   A separate piece, related to a main story on the same subject.

Situationer   An interpretive story describing a particular news situation. It differs from a *backgrounder*, which may or may not include interpretation in a factual summation of news backgrounds.

Slot   Seat of the head of the copy desk, also known as the slot man.

Slug   Each story has a name, which is called a slug. The slug must be included with each page of copy and goes after the page number.

Split page   First page second section in a paper of two sections.

Spread   Any story that takes a headline big enough to be used at the top of an inside page.

Stereotype   Plate cast from a mold of a page form of type. The plate, a curved surface, is locked on the press that prints the paper.

Stet   Copy editors' and printers' instruction, "Let it stand." Generally used to restore parts of a story, sentence, or word that have been eliminated by mistake.

Stick   About two inches of type.

Stringer   Occasional correspondent, or tipster, paid by the piece or by the amount of space his material occupies.

Swing shift   A shift operated by workers for a period, who then move to another shift, swinging one shift to another on different days.

Take   A page of copy, which may contain as little as a paragraph.

Thirty   Telegraphers' Morse code symbol for "The End," seldom used now to indicate the end of a story. Usually, this is designated by such symbols as xxx or # # # or by the initials of the writer and the time he finished writing.

Tight   Used in the sense of a tight paper, meaning there is not much available news space.

Trim   To cut a story.

Turn rule   Sometimes written only as *rule* or *T.R.* When this is given as an instruction on copy, it means the printer is to look for changes in the story. Thus, "T.R. for 2d ADD STORM" means that a second addition to a story about a storm is expected. Or "T.R. for Nulead Storm," means that a new lead on a story about a storm is expected. These turn rule instructions are set in type and should be thrown aside by the printer when they are fulfilled.

UPI   United Press International.

Wire service   A press association, a wholesaler of news.

Wrapup   Also called a roundup. Summary of events in a broadly developed news situation.

2. Broadcast Journalism

ABC   American Broadcasting Companies.

Academy leader   Film marked off in seconds, spliced to newsfilm, as a lead-in.
Anchor man   Chief newscaster in a team.
Arbitron   Audience measuring device used by American Research Bureau.
Atmospherics   Electrical disturbances in atmosphere.
Audio   Sound transmission, or reception.
Audio frequency   Vibrations normally audible to human ear.
Audimeter   Audience measuring device used by A. C. Nielsen Co.

BBC   British Broadcasting Corporation.
Back timing   Exact length of closing segment of newscast, timed in advance, to determine moment when segment should begin for program to end on schedule.
Balop   Card, picture or similar object flashed electronically on a viewing screen. (The term is derived from Balopticon, an opaque projector trade-marked by Bausch and Lomb, used for such work.)
Blooper   Embarrassing error.
Blow up   Enlargement of portion of picture, chart or map.
Bridge   Written segment joining film clips of a differing nature.
Bring it up   Order for increase in volume.

CATV   See cable television.
CBC   Canadian Broadcasting Company.
CBS   Columbia Broadcasting System.
CU   Close up.
Cable television, or CATV   A system of wired television in which programs are received by a central source and redistributed to subscribers for a monthly fee plus original installation fee. Central reception is based on efficient high antenna that intercepts signals, which then are channeled by wire to subscribers.
Cathode ray tube   Tube that produces picture on its large fluorescent end surface by means of electron beam emanating from its cathode, or negative, electrode.
Call letters   Station's signature.
Communications satellite   Space vehicle placed in orbit about earth to facilitate global transmission of data by radio, TV and radio-telephone signals. Echo I, launched in 1960, was the first. Other early examples Telstar, Relay, Syncom.
Coaxial cable   Long copper tubing containing large number of wire conductors held in place by insulating discs, making possible transmission of television signals, telephone, and telegraph messages simultaneously.
Compatibility   System in which color broadcasts may be received in black and white on sets not specially equipped to receive color.
Cue   Signal in script or by hand or word to start or stop speech, movement, film, tape, sound effects, music, or other parts of program.
Cut   To eliminate, to halt.
Cutaway   Subsidiary scenes that can be fitted by film editor into main action.

Dead area Also called "blind spot." It refers to areas where reception is difficult.

Diode Two-element electron tube or semiconductor that changes (rectifies) alternating current into pulsating direct current.

Double projection A system in which two projectors are used, one for sound and the other for visual material, in producing a segment of integrated newsfilm and sound.

ECU Extreme close up.

ET Electrical transcription.

ETV Educational television.

Easel shot also called limbo; an object such as a still photo or a chart or map that can be picked up by a studio camera.

Electron Particle of matter, a constituent of the atom, that carries an elementary charge of negative electricity.

Ether Upper region of space, or the rarified element that is supposed to fill it.

FCC Federal Communications Commission.

FM Frequency modulation, a virtually static-free system of broadcasting by radio. It adjusts the frequency of the transmitting wave in accordance with the sound being sent, as contrasted with AM, or amplitude modulation, which adjusts the wave in accordance with its maximum departure from normal.

Fading Fluctuation of sound or image in broadcasting.

Feedback Sharp noise or hum, such as may be caused by a microphone placed too close to a speaker.

Fidelity Degree of accuracy with which sound or visual material is reproduced in radio or television.

Flip card Card containing material (charts, pictures, credits, etc.) that may be flipped before camera in studio.

Fluff An error in speaking or reading from a script.

Frame One of a series of pictures on film; there may be 24 to 28 frames of film shown in a second.

From the top Begin all over.

Facsimile System of electronic transmission of written, printed or photographed material. It is done regularly over 800 miles in Japan in reproducing the newspaper Asahi in editions in Tokyo, Sapporo on the northern island of Hokkaido, and elsewhere. Process is put to numerous uses in Britain and the U. S., as well.

Geiger Counter Device for detecting radioactivity.

Generator A machine that converts mechanical into electrical power.

Ground Connection from broadcast receiver to the earth.

Heaviside Layer Also called Kennelly-Heaviside Layer. It is the ionosphere, region of electrically charged air that begins about 25 miles above the earth's surface and makes possible the transmission of radio waves over great distances.

High frequency   A frequency is the number of complete cycles of alternating current that occur in one second; high frequencies are between 6,000 and 30,000 kilocycles.

Iconoscope   A trademarked electron pickup or camera tube that uses an electron scanning beam to convert photo-emissions into television signals.

Image Orthicon Tube   A trademarked electron pickup or camera tube, a refinement of the Iconoscope.

Interlock   Separate projection of sound and film, locked together in synchronization. Expression describes a type of film, for example, as "16 mm color interlock."

Interference   The effect of two electrical waves on each other.

Intro   Introduction of a filmed or taped portion of a program in script or spoken form.

Jamming   Interference from an undesired source, effectively blocking the reception of signals.

Jump cut   Undesirable element of television, in which there is an irregular or unnatural continuation of movement.

Kenotron   An electron rectifying tube.

Kinescope   Trademarked picture receiving tube, either by direct view or projection. It also refers to the film, sometimes called a "kinnie," that is made from the monitor kinescope as the program is in progress.

Kilowatt   A unit of electric power. A watt is the work done by one ampere electric current under a pressure of one volt. A kilowatt is one thousand watts.

LS   Long shot.

Laser   Concentrated light beam. Acronym for "light amplification by stimulated emission of radiation."

Level   Volume of transmitted sound.

Live   On the spot broadcast or telecast.

Live mike   An open microphone.

Limbo   Objects such as still pictures, charts, and maps that can be picked up by a studio camera. Also known as easel shots.

Long wave   Radio waves with a length of 600 meters or more and frequencies under 500 kilocycles.

Low frequency   A frequency below radio frequencies, usually between 10 and 100 kilocycles, one that can be heard by the human ear; an audio frequency.

MCU Medium close up.

MS Medium shot.

Microwave Very short electromagnetic waves, usually between one and 100 centimeters in length; basis for microelectronic circuits in line of sight transmissions and in space technology.

Monochrome image Black and white.

Monitor To view or hear a program.

NAB National Association of Broadcasters.

NBC National Broadcasting Company.

Newsfilm Film of current events designed for use on television, usually developed in the negative, after which a positive print is made for use on the air.

Night effect Attenuation of transmitted or received signals, usually after sunset, often attributed to changes in the ionized upper atmosphere.

On Camera Script notation of what is to be shown.

Out Cue Last few words of a strip of sound on film or sound on tape, indicating that next section of newscast must be started.

PBL Public Broadcast Laboratory—experimental educational television.

Pan Moving the camera horizontally to include several objects or scenes in its sweep.

Photoelectric cell Cell containing a substance sensitive to light that controls emissions of electrons, either from a Cathode Ray tube or similar source.

Prop Various devices—so-called stage properties—used in a televised news program or documentary.

RP Rear screen projection, requiring the use of a positive transparency that projects a picture in back of the television newscaster on a full screen.

RPM Refers to revolutions per minute of a recording—commonly 33, 45, and 78 RPMs.

Radiation Transmission of radio waves through space in every direction; in its widest sense, the term refers to all forms of ionized radiation, including electromagnetic, particle, and acoustic.

Radio channel The band or bands of frequencies within which a transmitter is permitted to operate by law.

Radio frequency Incapable of being heard by the human ear, as contrasted with audio frequency, referring to radio waves that can be heard.

Radio wire The wire service teletypes that are hooked up specifically to a central source that provides news written for radio and television use at periodic intervals.

Roll cue Three to four seconds' signal before newsfilm segment must be shown on a news program.

SIL   Silent film.

SOF   Sound on film.

SOT   Sound on tape.

Scan   Causing a beam of electrons to sweep rapidly across a surface in a succession of narrow lines, varying in brightness, so that a transmitted image is faithfully reproduced. In the U. S., the standard is 525 lines every one-thirtieth of a second.

Segue   Overlapping of dialogue, sound effects or music, one fading in as the other fades out. Prounced "seg-way."

Signal   Electric energy that conveys coherent messages.

Split page   Method by which television news script is written, with audio directions in one column on one side of the page, and video directions on the other side of the page in a second and separate column.

Static   Disturbing electrical effects, caused by atmospheric electrical phenomena, that disrupt sound in electronic receivers.

Still   Single photograph used in television, usually an 8 × 10 inch glossy. Less satisfactory copy, of course, is also used at times.

Standby   Written account of an event, held for use in case filmed version fails for any reason. Standby copy is then read.

Slug   Title for each piece of film considered for use in a news program; also used as a title for each piece of radio copy.

Straight up   When the second hand reaches 12, "straight up."

Switch   Shifting from one locale to another, introducing the change in scene with a call in throw cue and signaling the switch back to headquarters with a return cue.

Switcher   One who does the actual switching of the program at an order from the news director.

TCU   Tight close up.

Telop   Like a Balop, this is a card or picture flashed electronically on a viewing screen from an opaque projector.

Telenews   Newsfilm syndicate, formally titled News of the Day.

Telstar   A pioneering communications satellite.

Transistor   Arrangement of semiconductor materials, usually germanium and silicon, separated by a vacuum, that takes the place of a vacuum tube; used as a voltage and current amplifier and for other functions of a vacuum tube.

UHF   Ultra high frequency band, consisting of Channels 14 through 83, as con- contrasted with VHF, very high frequency, the commercial broadcast band consisting of Channels 2 through 13.

UPI Newsfilm   Newsfilm, formerly Movietone News, distributed by United Press International.

VCU   Very extreme close up.

VHF   Very high frequency, Channels 2 through 13, the commercial broadcasting band.

VO   Voice over, meaning dialogue or live narration over silent film or studio action.

VTR   Videotape recording.

Video   Pertaining to or used in the reception or transmission of an image on television, as contrasted with audio, which refers to sound only.

Videotape   A band of magnetic tape that records image and sound simultaneously and can be played back and rewound in seconds. It can be stored indefinitely, erased, used many times over a period of years.

Vidicon   Type of television camera often used for closed circuit, industrial, and military work.

Vizmo   A 5 × 7 transparency used in rear screen projection.

Viznews   British Commonwealth newsfilm group, titled Brzina Viznews, to indicate the countries involved—Britain, Australia, New Zealand, India, and some others.

Vizs   Plural of Vizmo.

Voice of America   U. S. government broadcasting service overseas, a part of the U. S. Information Agency.

Wave   Moving electronic disturbance in a medium, such as space, having a regularly recurring time period.

Wavelength   Distance between any point in a wave and the corresponding point in the wave immediately preceding and following it.

Wave trap   A circuit that can be tuned to cut out any undesired signal.

Wired radio   Form of radio transmission in which current carrying the signals is sent over established wire systems, such as telephone or telegraph lines. The equivalent for television is the system known as CATV, which generally provides its own wire system hooked to telephone poles already in place.

Wrapup   Rounded narration and/or filmed news program that summarizes a single major event or the day's news.

A Model Style Book

Note: Material on capitalization, abbreviation, punctuation, and the use of numerals is adapted from the AP-UPI Style Book, *which is most generally used by the news media.*

News Writing Instructions

1. The purpose of all news writing is to communicate information, opinions, and ideas in an interesting and timely manner. It must be accurate, terse, clear, and easily understood.
2. Writers should use relatively short, simple sentences, and paragraph liberally. A sentence, or two, or three to a paragraph should be sufficient. Unity and coherence should be maintained.
3. Wherever possible, one idea to a sentence should be used. To attain this end separate sentences may be made out of qualifying or descriptive phrases or clauses when desirable.
4. Short, familiar words should be used in preference to long, strange words. Unfamiliar words should be defined for the reader. Geographical points should be located.
5. Try to use vigorous verbs. Wherever possible, use the active rather than the passive voice. Use adjectives sparsely and make each one count.
6. Writers must be specific. Instead of reporting that a girl is tall, she should be described as being six feet four. Instead of writing that a speaker is disturbed, say he shouted and banged on the table.
7. Writers should try to relate an event to the particular community or public. The death of five in a fire in Atlanta is of relatively little interest to people in Chicago, unless there is something about the victims that particularly interests Chicago.
8. Try to relate statistics to something the public can quickly grasp. Instead of writing that India is a needy nation, say that the average Indian earns

less than $100 a year. Instead of describing Lebanon as a tiny country, write that its coastline is 120 miles long, or about the same size as Long Island's.

9. The simplest form of news story is divided into two parts—the lead and body. The lead tells what happened, simply, briefly, and effectively. Do not crowd in everything that happened—just the main news. The body of the story documents the lead with facts in a diminishing order of importance.

10. In a hard, or spot, news story everything should be attributed to an identifiable source. If that cannot be done, the public should be told why.

11. In a speech or interview or public statement, all statements made by a speaker must be attributed directly to him. In reporting an arrest it must be specified that the police version of the alleged crime is being given.

12. News must be explained. To that end, experienced writers are given the privilege of interpretation. In this process the news should be told first. Then the public should be told what it means, if the writer is in a position to know. But no reporter has any right to urge a course of action on the basis of the news. That is editorialization.

13. Use meaningful quotations whenever possible but use partial quotations sparingly. They are misleading, at times. Whenever a quotation is used, it should begin a new paragraph.

14. *Don'ts:*

Do not write tortured, unnatural, or excitable prose.

Do not write topsy-turvy sentences.

Do not overwrite, either in length or in meaning. The uses of restraint are of great importance in journalism.

Do not inject a personal point of view in a news story, unless you are given permission to do so. Do not use the pronouns "I" or "we" except when you are writing a first-person story. News is generally told in the third person.

Do not switch tenses continually in writing news. Most news is best told in the past tense for newspapers, and in the present tense for the electronic media. The rule for sequence of tenses should be observed.

Do not neglect to feature the time element in a news lead. Today is the key word for the electronic media and in most afternoon newspaper leads, while yesterday is used in most local stories written for a morning newspaper.

15. When in doubt about anything in a story, leave it out until it can be checked. Never take anything for granted in journalism.

16. Always meet deadlines. Go with what you've got.

Copy Preparation for Newspapers

[Note: To prepare copy for wire services, radio and television, follow directions in the chapters that refer specifically to their special requirements.]

1. All copy must be typewritten on one side of a sheet of newsprint, or similar paper, 8½ × 11 inches.

2. Write your name in the upper left-hand corner. On the same line, following your name, give the source of the story. If it is rewritten from clips or wire

services, identify the paper or the agency. If it is from a reporter, name him. If you have covered the story yourself, use the word "assigned" as the source.

3. Begin the story one-third of the way down from the top of the first sheet, but leave only a one-inch top margin for other sheets. Indent paragraphs at least one-third of the width of the sheet. Leave at least a one-inch margin on the sides and at the bottom. Do not crowd too many sentences or paragraphs on a page.

4. All copy should be triple-spaced to allow for editing.

5. If the story ends on one page, indicate the end with a mark such as xxx, # # #, 30, or your initials and the time you finished writing. You may also simply write (end it).

6. If the story continues, write (more) at the lower right-hand corner of the page. Some papers use merely a diagonal pencil stroke and arrowhead pointing toward that corner.

7. Every story written for newspaper and wire services use must have a name. This is called a slug. Generally it is one word, usually the key word that describes the story. Thus, a snowstorm could be slugged *snow*, a heat wave *heat*, an automobile accident *auto*. Where there are many stories in one category, such as obits, two words should be used: *Smith—obit*. Where there are several stories, all related, two words also are generally needed: *Smith—politics*, or *Jones—politics*.

8. There are two principal ways of numbering news stories.
   a. Most newspapers use the consecutive method. Thus, the slug is written on the first page, about two inches under your name. If the story is continued, the slug goes at the top left of the second page and the figure 2 is written after it. The third page would be identified similarly.
   b. Wire service copy generally is written with a slug on the first page, just as newspaper copy is prepared. But the second page begins with a pickup line—the slug, the word ADD, the point of origin of the story, and the last words of the previous page. Thus, the second page of a UPI story about a rocket shot would carry the top line: "1st ADD ROCKET CAPE KENNEDY . . . SUCCESSFULLY FIRED."

9. All paragraphs should end on a page. No sentences should be run over from one page to another. Words should not be split at the end of a line.

10. Write no more than one item on one sheet of paper.

11. Use a soft black pencil, but never a ball-point pen, in making corrections. Write legibly. Printing is even better. Underscore all *u*'s and *w*'s, overscore all *n*'s and *m*'s.

12. If you must eliminate material, use the character xxxxxx on the typewriter. If you are reading copy after you have finished typing, draw a line through the words to be eliminated and write in any material that is to replace it.

13. If material is eliminated, but you want it restored, write the word *stet* in the margin and indicate the part to be restored. Paragraphs are designated with a right angle mark thus, ⌐.

14. Check the spelling of any unfamiliar word and all proper nouns and put a light check mark above each one to show the desk that you have done so.

15. Read your own copy carefully before handing it in. Nothing is more annoying to an editor than bad spelling and grammatical errors. Make certain that your copy is clean in all respects.

Capitalization

1. Titles preceding a name are capitalized, but are used in lower case when they stand alone or follow a name.
2. Titles of foreign religious leaders are capitalized when they precede a name, but are used in lower case when they stand alone or follow a name. Exceptions are Pope and Dalai Lama, which are always capitalized. However, the term, pontiff, referring to the Pope, is lower cased.
3. Titles of authority are capitalized when they precede a name, but are used in lower case when they stand alone or follow a name.
4. When titles are long and cumbersome, they should follow a name. They are then lower cased.
5. As a general rule, false titles should not be used. However, when it becomes necessary to use a false title such as defense attorney before a name, it is lower cased.
6. When such terms as Republic, Union, or Colonies refer to the United States, they are capitalized. Similarly, capitalize the French Fifth Republic or the Republic of Korea.
7. Capitalize the Capitol, meaning the building. Lower case capital, meaning the city. The U. S. Congress, Senate, House, and Cabinet are capitalized. So is Legislature when preceded by the name of the state, City Council, and Security Council.
8. Committees such as House Ways and Means Committee are capitalized, but not the word committee when used by itself. Similarly, such titles as International Atomic Energy Authority and Interstate Commerce Commission are capitalized, but not authority and commission when used alone.
9. Courts are capitalized—Supreme Court, Court of Appeals and the like.
10. When referring to the U. S. system, Social Security is capitalized but it is lower cased when used in a general sense.
11. Titles of U. S. armed forces are capitalized, but foreign armed forces are lower cased with the exception of Royal Air Force, Royal Canadian Air Force and French Foreign Legion.
12. The title, Joint Chiefs of Staff, is capitalized but not chiefs of staff.
13. Historic events, holidays, ecclesiastical feasts, special events, fast days, and names of hurricanes and typhoons are capitalized.
14. Arctic Circle and Antarctica are capitalized but not arctic or antarctic.
15. Specific regions are capitalized—New York's West Side, the Far East, and Michigan's Upper Peninsula, for example.
16. Political or ideological areas are capitalized (East-West) but not just a direction.
17. Names of fraternal organizations are capitalized.
18. The Deity, He, His, and Him—when denoting God—are capitalized but

not who, whose, and whom. Satan and Hades are capitalized, but not hell or devil.

19. Names of wars are capitalized.

20. Indian, Negro, Chinese, Caucasian, and other names of races are capitalized but red, black, yellow, and white are not. While it is correct to use "colored" in African usage, it is not so used in the United States except in the title of an organization: National Association for the Advancement of Colored People.

21. Capitalize common nouns when they are part of a formal name (Columbia River, Aswan Dam) but not river and dam standing alone.

22. Species of animals, flowers, and so on, are capitalized (Afghan, hound; Peace, rose;) but not the common nouns standing alone.

23. Trade names and trademark names are capitalized. Coke and Thermos, for example, are registered trademarks, the former for a soft drink and the latter for a vacuum jug. Instead of trademark names, it is preferable to use a broad term.

24. Books, plays, musical compositions in general, and formal dance titles are capitalized and used in quotation marks.

25. Names of formal organizations are capitalized (World's Fair, Boy Scouts) but not common nouns (fair, scouts).

26. Capitalize nicknames of states or of well-known organizations (Evergreen State, Leathernecks).

27. Capitalize awards and decorations.

28. Where proper names have acquired a common meaning, they are lower cased (dutch oven, brussels sprouts).

29. Capitalization of names in all cases should follow the preference of the individual.

Abbreviations

1. Spell out the names of organizations, firms, agencies, groups, and committees when they are first mentioned, then abbreviate when they are referred to again in the same story. AFL-CIO is an exception.

2. Military terms, time zones, airplane designations, ships, and distress calls are abbreviated. Periods are dropped in such abbreviations as EST, MP, USS New Jersey, SS Lurline, SOS and B70.

3. Names of business firms are abbreviated. (Lehman Bros., Jones & Co.)

4. In addresses, abbreviate Ave., St., Blvd., Ter., but not Lane, Road, Oval, Drive, Place, Plaza, Circle, or Port. Ordinal numbers are used in addresses, such as 22 W. 38th St. In a Washington address, such as 2525 16th Ave. NW, there are no periods in NW. When no addresses are given, it is Fifth Avenue, Sunset Boulevard, Main Street.

5. Use periods with most lower case abbreviations. At the first mention of speed, it should be miles per hour, thereafter m.p.h. Exceptions to the period rule are film sizes (16 mm) or armament (155 mm rifle).

6. For versus use vs. (with period).

7. Names of states are abbreviated when they follow cities, towns, air bases, Indian agencies, national parks, and so on, but not when they are used alone. Alaska, Hawaii, Idaho, Iowa, Ohio, Maine, and Utah are never abbreviated. Reasonably well known areas, such as Canadian provinces or Caribbean islands, are also abbreviated if they are preceded by a city or town but obscure places must be spelled out.

8. To avoid confusion, B. C. the era must be preceded by a date and B. C., the Canadian province, must be preceded by a city or town.

9. United States and United Nations may be abbreviated in titles, but periods must be used with both: U. N. Educational, Scientific, and Cultural Organization; U. S. Atomic Energy Commission. Standing by themselves, U. S. A. and U. N. may be used in direct quotations or in texts. But United States and United Nations must be spelled out when used as nouns.

10. Religious, academic, fraternal, or honorary degrees may be abbreviated, capitalized and used with periods (M.A.) but lower cased when spelled out (master of arts).

11. Titles may be abbreviated and capitalized: Mr., Mrs., M., Mlle., Dr., Prof., Sen., Rep., Asst., Lt. Gov., Gov. Gen., Dist. Atty. If used after a name, these are lower cased.

12. The title Mr. is never used with the full name of a man except on the society page. Once the full name is used, Mr. may be put before the last name the next time it is mentioned (John Johnson the first time, then Mr. Johnson).

13. Do not abbreviate Christmas. Do not abbreviate San Francisco (Frisco). Do not abbreviate guaranteed annual wage (GAW).

14. Do not abbreviate such nouns as association, port, point, detective, department, commandant, commodore, field marshal, general manager, secretary-general, secretary, treasurer, fleet admiral, or general of the armies. (Use Gen. Eisenhower and Adm. Nimitz, both correct).

15. Months are abbreviated when used with dates, except for March, April, May, June, or July. Days of the week are abbreviated only in tabular matter or financial routine.

16. St. and Ste. are abbreviated (as in St. Louis or Sault Ste. Marie) but not Saint John, N. B. The mountain is abbreviated (Mt. Rainier) but not the city, Mount Vernon. An army post is abbreviated (Ft. Monmouth) but not the city, Fort Lauderdale.

17. Unless the individual himself does it, do not abbreviate names such as Alexander, Benjamin, Frederick, William.

Punctuation

Punctuation is used to clarify meaning. When it does not do so, it should be omitted. These are some common rules:

The Period

1. Use a period after a declarative sentence.

2. Use a period after an imperative sentence that is not exclamatory.
3. Use a period after a letter or number in a group, series or list of items.
4. Omit periods after most headings, captions, subheads, figures, roman numerals and chemical symbols.
5. Omit periods after nicknames, after per cent and after tabulated matter.
6. Use a series of periods to indicate that quoted matter has been omitted. Usually it is a series of three.
7. Use a period with abbreviations and as a decimal point.
8. Use a period before the closing parenthesis mark when an entire sentence is enclosed. If the final words of the sentence are parenthetical, the period goes outside the closing parenthesis.
9. Use a period after Mr. and Mrs.

The Comma
1. Use a comma to clarify meaning by separating words and figures when necessary: Whatever is, is right. Jan. 12, 1984.
2. Use commas to separate a series of qualifying words, except before "and" and "or" as follows: He was stocky, bald, short and talkative. It is either red, white or brown.
3. Use commas to separate parenthetical matter.
4. Use commas between name, title and organization, in scores of games, to set off appositives.
5. Omit the comma between the name and abbreviation of persons, before the dash or ampersand, in telephone numbers, street addresses, years and serial numbers. Omit comma before "of": Jones of Columbia.

The Semicolon
1. The semicolon is used principally to separate phrases containing commas in order to avoid confusion, to separate statements of contrast and statements too closely related.
2. The semicolon is used in sports scores and balloting: Giants, 6; Dodgers, 5. Yeas, 52; Nays, 52.
3. Use a semicolon in a series of names and addresses: John Jones, Massapequa; Doris Smith, Amityville; David Johnson, Riverhead.

The Colon
1. The colon's principal use is to introduce listings. It also introduces statements and marks discontinuity.
2. It is used in reporting time. He ran the mile in 3:59.
3. It is used in introducing a resolution. Resolved:
4. It separates chapter and verse in scriptural references.

Quotation Marks
1. Quotation marks enclose direct quotations, complete or partial.

2. They are put about words or phrases in political argument, ironical use, accepted phrases or nicknames, coined words or words of unusual meaning. Use sparingly in such cases.
3. When there are several paragraphs of continuous quotations, each paragraph should be started with a quotation mark, but it should be omitted from the end of all paragraphs except the final one.
4. Commas and final periods go inside quotation marks. Other punctuation marks go inside quotation marks only when they are part of the quoted matter.
5. Semicolons and colons always follow quotation marks.
6. Interior quotes take single quotation marks.
7. Titles of books, plays, movies, operas, statuary, paintings, TV, and radio programs and songs all take quotation marks.
8. Fire engines, ships, aircraft, horses, cattle, sleeping cars, homes, characters in fiction, or on the stage and common nicknames do not take quotation marks.
9. Do not quote the names of newspapers or magazines.
10. Do not quote trial testimony. Simply list it as Q. and A.

The Apostrophe

1. The apostrophe is used for possessives and in some abbreviations.
2. In possessives, the apostrophe generally is used between a singular noun and the added "s" (except when the noun ends in "s"). For plural nouns ending with "s" or "ce" the apostrophe only is added.
3. Use the apostrophe to mark the omission of such word contractions as it's, I've, etc. (Do not use with pronoun its.)
4. Omit the apostrophe where it is not a part of a proper name (as Governors Island).
5. One apostrophe only is used to indicate common possession, as The Army, Navy and Air Force's ideals. Use in Court of St. James's.

Parenthesis

1. Parentheses set off material that is not a part of the main statement.
2. They also set off an identification or grammatical element of a sentence that is closely related to the main statement.
3. They set off figures or letters in a tabular series in a sentence.
4. Unless the parenthetical matter is a complete sentence, it is placed before the period. Do not use around such designations as Sen. Smith, R-Maine.
5. Parentheses, like quotes, are used only at the beginning of a series of parenthetical paragraphs except for the final paragraph, where a closing parenthesis is placed after the final period.

The Dash

1. The dash marks an abrupt change of thought.
2. The dash is used to separate.

3. It is used after the logotype in a dateline and before the first word of the story.

The Hyphen

1. Just as the dash separates, the hyphen joins. It is used to form compound words. It is also used in abbreviations and in scores. As a rule, "like" characters take the hyphen, "unlike" characters do not.
2. Two or more words that form a compound adjective are hyphenated unless one of them is an adverb ending in "ly." The combined adjective elements that follow a noun do not take a hyphen, however.
3. Do not hyphenate commander in chief, vice president, today.
4. Use a hyphen for like characters in abbreviations (A-bomb, U-boat) but not for unlike characters (B52, W7ERD, MIG15, IC4A).
5. Do not use a hyphen for upstate, downstate, homecoming, cheerleader, textbook, makeup, cannot, bookcase.
6. Use the hyphen in prefixes to proper names, in writing figures, in various types of measures if used as adjectives.

Exclamation Point   It is used to indicate surprise, appeal, incredulity, or other strong emotions. Use sparingly.

Question Mark   It follows a direct question, marks a gap or uncertainty. In the use of question and answer material, paragraph both Q. and A. when they run to some length.

Ampersand   It is used in abbreviations and firm names: AT&T, Smith, Barney & Co.

Numerals

1. The general rule is spell below 10, use numerals for 10 and above.
2. Use numerals exclusively in all tabular and statistical records, latitude and longitude, election returns, times, speeds, temperatures, highways, distances, dimensions, heights, ages, ratios, proportions, military units, political divisions, orchestra instruments, court divisions or districts, handicaps, dates, and betting odds.
3. Use July Fourth or Fourth of July.
4. Figures should be used for all man or animal ages. For inanimates, spell out under 10. Spell out casual numbers such as Gay Nineties.
5. Use Roman numerals for personal sequence—World War II, Pope Pius VI, Act I, Shamrock X.
6. Designate highways U. S. 17, Interstate 40, New York 58.
7. In amounts of more than a million, round numbers take the dollar sign and million, billion, and so on, are spelled. Carry decimals to two places: $4.75 million. For exact amounts: $4,756,342.
8. For less than a million, use $500, $1,000, $440,000.
9. Use same decimal style for figures other than money, such as population, automobile registration, etc.

10. In amounts of less than a dollar spell out "cents."
11. Use figures in stories dealing with percentages and time sequences.
12. Use bracketed letter (M) after a figure in the millions, bracketed letter (B) after figure in the billions.
13. Confine fractions to 8ths—⅛, ¼, ⅜, ½. Others require a hyphen— 3-16, 7-20, 9-10. Used alone, fractions are spelled out: three-eighths of a mile.

Copy Editing Terms
And Symbols

SYMBOL	MEANING
. . . worry. ⌐She said . . .	Begin a new paragraph. Use right angle symbol.
No ℗ There was . . .	No paragraph. Use indicated symbol.
(MORE) ⟶	Story is continued. Circle word "more" or use arrow.
(30) xxx ###	End of story. Use one of the three symbols.
John Smith	Set in capitals. Use double line under letter or word.
Is it really true?	Set in italics. Use single line under word.
BF	Set in bold face. Use symbol as indicated.
⊙ ⊗	Period. Circle a period or a cross.
,/	Comma. Use comma and diagonal mark for emphasis.
„ Hamlet ⌒	Quotes. Use carets as indicated.
The was unclear.	Insert a letter or word. Use caret and write it in.
Ding-dong	Insert a hyphen. Use caret and hyphen above.
⑥ (Gov.)	Spell out figure or word. Use circles.
(Mister) (twelve)	Abbreviate word or use numeral. Use circles.
would	Underscore U's and W's. Draw lines under them.
nevermore	Overscore N's and M's. Draw lines over them.
STET Then he said,	Restore text, eliminated by mistake. Use word STET.
thunderous	Transpose letter or word. Draw indicated symbol.
⌐	Indent from left. Use indicated symbol.

⊏	Indent from right. Use indicated symbol.
⊐ ⊏	Center: indent on both sides. Use indicated symbol.
gentle͡man	Close up. Draw marks as indicated.
Boy/Scout	Separate. Use slash as indicated.
Here is the M̸odel.	Make it a small letter. Use diagonal mark.
The ~~beautiful~~ girl . . .	Eliminate. Cross it out and close it up.
(set 2 col 10 pt)	Printer: Do not set this in type. Circle it.

Standards for Journalists

1. Code of Ethics

or

Canons of Journalism

*

American Society
of Newspaper Editors

*

The primary function of newspapers is to communicate to the human race what its members do, feel, and think. Journalism, therefore, demands of its practitioners the widest range of intelligence, or knowledge, and of experience, as well as natural and trained powers of observation and reasoning. To its opportunities as a chronicle are indissolubly linked its obligations as teacher and interpreter.

To the end of finding some means of codifying sound practice and just aspirations of American journalism, these canons are set forth:

I

Responsibility—The right of a newspaper to attract and hold readers is restricted by nothing but considerations of public welfare. The use a newspaper makes of the share of public attention it gains serves to determine its sense of responsibility, which it shares with every member of its staff. A journalist who uses his power for any selfish or otherwise unworthy purpose is faithless to a high trust.

II

Freedom of the Press—Freedom of the press is to be guarded as a vital right of mankind. It is the unquestionable right to discuss whatever is not explicitly forbidden by law, including the wisdom of any restrictive statute.

III

Independence—Freedom from all obligations except that of fidelity to the public interest is vital.

1. Promotion of any private interest contrary to the general welfare, for whatever reason, is not compatible with honest journalism. So-called news communications from private sources should not be published without public notice of their source or else substantiation of their claims to value as news, both in form and substance.

2. Partisanship, in editorial comment which knowingly departs from the truth, does violence to the best spirit of American journalism; in the news columns, it is subversive of a fundamental principle of the profession.

IV

Sincerity, Truthfulness, Accuracy—Good faith with the reader is the foundation of all journalism worthy of the name.

1. By every consideration of good faith a newspaper is constrained to be truthful. It is not to be excused for lack of thoroughness or accuracy within its control, or failure to obtain command of these essential qualities.

2. Headlines should be fully warranted by the contents of the articles which they surmount.

V

Impartiality—Sound practice makes clear distinction between news reports and expressions of opinion. News reports should be free from opinion or bias of any kind.

1. This rule does not apply to so-called special articles unmistakably devoted to advocacy or characterized by a signature authorizing the writer's own conclusions and interpretation.

VI

Fair Play—A newspaper should not publish unofficial charges affecting reputation or moral character without opportunity given to the accused to be heard; right practice demands the giving of such opportunity in all cases of serious accusation outside judicial proceedings.

1. A newspaper should not invade private rights or feeling without sure warrant of public right as distinguished from public curiosity.

2. It is the privilege, as it is the duty, of a newspaper to make prompt and complete correction of its own serious mistakes of fact or opinion, whatever their origin.

Decency—A newspaper cannot escape conviction of insincerity if while professing high moral purpose it supplies incentives to base conduct, such as are to be found in details of crime and vice, publication of which is not demonstrably for the general good. Lacking authority to enforce its canons the journalism here represented can but express the hope that deliberate pandering to vicious instincts will encounter effective public disapproval or yield to the influence of a preponderant professional condemnation.

2. The Television Code

of the National Association of Broadcasters (excerpt)

V. Treatment of News and Public Events

NEWS

1. A television station's news schedule should be adequate and well-balanced.

2. News reporting should be factual, fair, and without bias.

3. A television broadcaster should exercise particular discrimination in the acceptance, placement, and presentation of advertising in news programs so that such advertising should be clearly distinguishable from the news content.

4. At all times, pictorial and verbal material for both news and comment should conform to other sections of these standards, wherever such sections are reasonably applicable.

5. Good taste should prevail in the selection and handling of news:

Morbid, sensational, or alarming details not essential to the factual report, especially in connection with stories of crime or sex, should be avoided. News should be telecast in such a manner as to avoid panic and unnecessary alarm.

6. Commentary and analysis should be clearly identified as such.

7. Pictorial material should be chosen with care and not presented in a misleading manner.

8. All news interview programs should be governed by accepted standards of ethical journalism, under which the interviewer selects the questions to be asked. Where there is advance agreement materially restricting an important or newsworthy area of questioning, the interviewer will state on the program that such limitation has been agreed upon. Such disclosure should be made if the person being interviewed requires that questions be submitted in advance or if he participates in editing a recording of the interview prior to its use on the air.

9. A television broadcaster should exercise due care in his supervision of content, format, and presentation of newscasts originated by his station, and in his selection of newscasters, commentators, and analysts.

PUBLIC EVENTS

1. A television broadcaster has an affirmative responsibility at all times to be informed of public events, and to provide coverage consonant with the ends of an informed and enlightened citizenry.

2. The treatment of such events by a television broadcaster should provide adequate and informed coverage.

VI. Controversial Public Issues

1. Television provides a valuable forum for the expression of responsible views on public issues of a controversial nature. The television broadcaster should seek out and develop with accountable individuals, groups and organizations, programs relating to controversial public issues of import to his fellow citizens; and to give fair representation to opposing sides of issues which materially affect the life or welfare of a substantial segment of the public.

2. Requests by individuals, groups, or organizations for time to discuss their views on controversial public issues should be considered on the basis of their individual merits, and in the light of the contribution which the use requested would make to the public interest and to a well-balanced program structure.

3. Programs devoted to the discussion of controversial public issues should be identified as such. They should not be presented in a manner which would mislead listeners or viewers to believe that the program is purely of an entertainment, news, or other character.

4. Broadcasts in which stations express their own opinions about issues of general public interest should be clearly identified as editorials. They should be unmistakably identified as statements of station opinion and should be appropriately distinguished from news and other program material.

VII. Political telecasts

1. Political telecasts should be clearly identified as such. They should not be presented by a television broadcaster in a manner which would mislead listeners or viewers to believe that the program is of any other character.

(Ref. Communications Act of 1934, as amended, Secs. 315 and 317, and FCC Rules and Regulations, Secs. 3, 654, 3, 657, 3, 663, as discussed in NAB's "A Political Catechism.")

3. NAB Radio Code of Good Practices (excerpt)

I. PROGRAM STANDARDS

A. NEWS

Radio is unique in its capacity to reach the largest number of people first with reports on current events. This competitive advantage bespeaks caution—being first is not always as important as being right. The following standards are predicated upon that viewpoint.

1. News Sources Those responsible for news on radio should exercise constant professional care in the selection of sources—for the integrity of the news and the consequent good reputation of radio as a dominant news medium depend largely upon the reliability of such sources.

2. News Reporting News reporting shall be factual and objective. Good taste shall prevail in the selection and handling of news. Morbid, sensational, or alarming details not essential to factual reporting should be avoided. News should be broadcast in such a manner as to avoid creation of panic and unnecessary alarm. Broadcasters shall be diligent in their supervision of content, format, and presentation of news broadcasts. Equal diligence should be exercised in selection of editors and reporters who direct news gathering and dissemination, since the station's performance in this vital informational field depends largely upon them.

3. Commentaries and Analyses Special obligations devolve upon those who analyze and/or comment upon news developments, and management should be satisfied completely that the task is to be performed in the best interest of the listening public. Programs of news analysis and commentary shall be clearly identified as such, distinguishing them from straight news reporting.

4. Editorializing Broadcasts in which stations express their own opinions about issues of general public interest should be clearly identified as editorials and should be clearly distinguished from news and other program material.

5. Coverage of News and Public Events In the coverage of news and public events the broadcaster has the right to exercise his judgment consonant with the accepted standards of ethical journalism and especially the requirements for decency and decorum in the broadcast of public and court proceedings.

6. Placement of Advertising A broadcaster should exercise particular discrimination in the acceptance, placement, and presentation of advertising in news programs so that such advertising should be clearly distinguishable from the news content.

B. Controversial Public Issues

1. Radio provides a valuable forum for the expression of responsible views on public issues of a controversial nature. The broadcaster should develop programs relating to controversial public issues of importance to his fellow citizens, and give fair representation to opposing sides of issues which materially affect the life or welfare of a substantial segment of the public.

2. Requests by individuals, groups, or organizations for time to discuss their views on controversial public issues should be considered on the basis of their individual merits, and in the light of the contributions which the use requested would make to the public interest.

3. Programs devoted to the discussion of controversial public issues should be identified as such. They should not be presented in a manner which would create the impression that the program is other than one dealing with a public issue.

C. Community Responsibility

1. A broadcaster and his staff occupy a position of responsibility in the community and should conscientiously endeavor to be acquainted with its needs and characteristics in order to serve the welfare of its citizens.

2. Requests for time for the placement of public service announcements or programs should be carefully reviewed with respect to the character and reputation of the group, campaign or organization involved, the public interest content of the message, and the manner of its presentation.

4. Free Press and Fair Trial

The following guidelines have been mutually agreed upon by the News Media, Bench and Bar in the State of Washington for the reporting of criminal proceedings and constitute a model of voluntary cooperation to protect the rights of free press and fair trial:

The proper administration of justice is the responsibility of the judiciary, bar, the prosecution, law enforcement personnel, news media, and the public. None should relinquish its share in that responsibility or attempt to override or regulate the judgment of the other. None should condone injustices on the ground that they are infrequent.

The greatest news interest is usually engendered during the pretrial stage of a criminal case. It is then that the maximum attention is received and the greatest impact is made upon the public mind. It is then that the greatest danger to a fair trial occurs. The bench, the bar, and the news media must exercise good judgment to balance the possible release of prejudicial information with the real public interest. However, these considerations are not necessarily applicable once a jury has been empaneled in a case. It is inherent in the concept of freedom of the press that the news media must be free to report what occurs in public proceedings, such as criminal trials. In the course of the trial it is the responsibility of the bench to take appropriate measures to insure that the deliberations of the jury are based upon what is presented to them in court.

These guidelines are proposed as a means of balancing the public's right to be informed with the accused's right to a fair trial before an impartial jury.

1. It is appropriate to make public the following information concerning the defendant:

(a) The defendant's name, age, residence, employment, marital status, and similar background information. There should be no restraint on biographical facts other than accuracy, good taste, and judgment.

(b) The substance or text of the charge, such as complaint, indictment, information or, where appropriate, the identity of the complaining party.

(c) The identity of the investigating and arresting agency and the length of the investigation.

(d) The circumstances immediately surrounding an arrest, including the time and place of arrest, resistance, pursuit, possession and use of weapons, and a description of items seized at the time of arrest.

2. The release of certain types of information by law enforcement personnel, the bench and bar, and the publication thereof by news media generally tends to create dangers of prejudice without serving a significant law enforcement or public interest function. Therefore, all concerned should be aware of the dangers of prejudice in making pretrial public disclosures of the following:

(a) Opinions about a defendant's character, his guilt, or his innocence.

(b) Admissions, confessions, or the contents of a statement or alibis attributable to a defendant.

(c) References to the results of investigative procedures, such as fingerprints, polygraph examinations, ballistic tests, or laboratory tests.

(d) Statements concerning the credibility or anticipated testimony of prospective witnesses.

(e) Opinions concerning evidence or argument in the case, whether or not it is anticipated that such evidence or argument will be used at trial.

Exceptions may be in order if information to the public is essential to the apprehension of a suspect, or where other public interests will be served.

3. Prior criminal charges and convictions are matters of public record and are available to the news media through police agencies or court clerks. Law enforcement agencies should make such information available to the news media after a legitimate inquiry. The public disclosure of this information by the news media may be highly prejudicial without any significant addition to the public's need to be informed. The publication of such information should be carefully reviewed.

4. Law enforcement and court personnel should not prevent the photographing of defendants when they are in public places outside the courtroom. They should not encourage pictures or televising nor should they pose the defendant.

5. Photographs of a suspect may be released by law enforcement personnel provided a valid law enforcement function is served thereby. It is proper to disclose such information as may be necessary to enlist public assistance in apprehending fugitives from justice. Such disclosure may include photographs as well as records of prior arrests and convictions.

6. The news media are free to report what occurs in the course of the judicial proceeding itself. The bench should utilize available measures, such as cautionary instructions, sequestration of the jury, and the holding of hearings on evidence after the empaneling of the jury, to insure that the jury's deliberations are based upon evidence presented to them in court.

7. It is improper for members of the bench-bar-media or law enforcement agencies to make available to the public any statement of information for the purpose of influencing the outcome of a criminal trial.

8. Sensationalism should be avoided by all persons and agencies connected with the trial or reporting of a criminal case.